KAUA'I

THE GARDEN ISLAND

Making the Most of Your Family Vacation

7th Edition

John Penisten

Prima Publishing
Published in affiliation with
Paradise Publications

KAUA'I, The Garden Island: A Paradise Family Guide

© 2001 Paradise Publications, Portland, Oregon

First Edition:	May 1988	Second Edition:	May 1989
Third Edition:	January 1991	Fourth Edition:	October 1995
Fifth Edition:	September 1997	Sixth Edition:	March 2000
Seventh Edition:	November 2001		

Published by Prima Publishing, Roseville, California. Member of the Crown Publishing Group, a division of Random House, Inc.

Random House Inc. New York, Toronto, London, Sydney, Auckland

PRIMA PUBLISHING and colophon are trademarks of Random House, Inc., registered with the United States Patent and Trademark Office.

WARNING -- DISCLAIMER

Illustrations by Janora Bayot
Maps by John Stenersen
Layout and Typesetting by Paradise Publications
Consultant: Kim Morris

Library of Congress ISSN data on file

01 02 03 04 HH 10 9 8 7 6 5 4 3 2 1
Printed in the United States of America

Seventh edition

Visit us online at www.primapublishing.com

CONTENTS

I. INTRODUCTION

Introduction 10

II. GENERAL INFORMATION

a. Kaua'i Best Bets 13
b. History of Kaua'i 22
c. Kaua'i Names and Places 35
d. Island Facts and Figures 37
e. Hawaiian Words and Their Meanings 40
f. What to Pack 41
g. Traveling with Children 41
h. Especially for Seniors 48
i. Travel Tips for the Physically Impaired 49
j. Weddings/Honeymoons 52
k. Parties and Receptions 59
l. Helpful Information 60
    Including: Websites, Television,
       Periodicals, Free Information
m. Getting There 70
n. Getting Around (Including Rental Cars) 80
o. Grocery Shopping 84
p. Annual Kaua'i Events 86
q. Weather 91
r. Map Index 95

III. WHERE TO STAY - WHAT TO SEE

a. Introduction 97
b. CONDOMINIUMS & HOTELS - INDEX 102
c. Central/Eastside (Kapa'a/Lihu'e/Nawiliwili/Wailua/Waipouli) 106
d. South Shore to West Shore 148
    (Koloa/Po'ipu/Lawa'i/Port Allen/Hanapepe/Waimea/Kekaha/Koke'e)
e. North Shore (Anahola/Kilauea/Princeville/Hanalei/Ha'ena) 192
f. Private Vacation Homes & Cottages/Rental Agents 210
g. Retreats/Large Groups/Reunions 230
h. Cruise Lines 233
i. RENTAL AGENTS 235

IV. RESTAURANTS

a.   Introduction 245
b.   Ethnic Foods 248
c.   A Few Words About Island Fish 250
d.   Dining Best Bets 252
e.   Catering Services 254
f.   RESTAURANT - ALPHABETICAL INDEX 255
g.   RESTAURANT - FOOD TYPE INDEX 259
h.   Restaurants - Central/Eastside 265
i.   Restaurants - South Shore 301
j.   Restaurants - North Shore 321
k.   Luaus 337
l.   Nightlife 340

V. BEACHES

a.   Introduction 343
b.   Best Bets 350
c.   BEACH INDEX 351
d.   Western Shore 353
e.   Southern Shore 356
f.   Eastern Shore 360
g.   Northern Shore 364

VI. RECREATION AND TOURS

a.   Introduction 375
b.   "Best Bets" 375
b.   Activity Booking Services 378
c.   Airplane Tours 378
d.   All Terrain Vehicle Adventures 379
e.   Bicycling/Motor Bike Adventures 379
f.   Billiards 380
g.   Boat Trips (Refer to Sea Excursions and Snorkeling)
h.   Bowling 381
i.   Bridge 381
j.   Camping 381
      State Parks 381
      County Parks 386
k.   Canoes 387,423
l.   Cultural Tours (See Museums)
m.   Dancing 387
n.   Fishing (Fresh Water & Ocean) 388
o.   Garden Tours (see Museums) 412
p.   Golf 391
q.   Hang Gliding 394
r.   Helicopters 394
s.   Hiking 397
t.   Horseback Riding 402
u.   Hunting/Shooting Ranges 404

VI. RECREATION AND TOURS (Continued)

v.   Jet Skiing 405
w.   Kayaking 405
x.   Land Tours 408
y.   Luaus (Refer to Restaurants)
z.   Movies/Movie Rentals/Movie Tours 410
aa. Museums/Garden and Cultural/Historical Tours 412
bb. Polo 420
cc. Rental Equipment 420
dd. River Excursions (Also See Kayaking) 420
ee. Running 421
ff. Scuba Diving 421
gg. Sea Excursions, Sailing, Cruises 424
hh. Snorkeling 428
ii. Snuba 431
jj. Spa/Fitness Center 431
kk. Surfing 432
ll. Tennis 433
mm. Theater 433
nn. Waterskiing 434
oo. Whale Watching 434
pp. Wildlife Refuges 434
qq. Windsurfing 436

VII. RECOMMENDED READING 436

VIII. INDEX 440

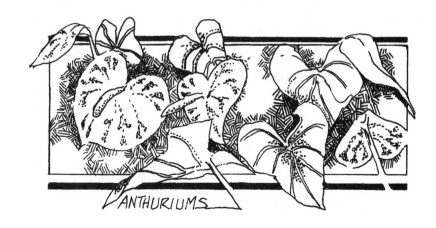

ANTHURIUMS

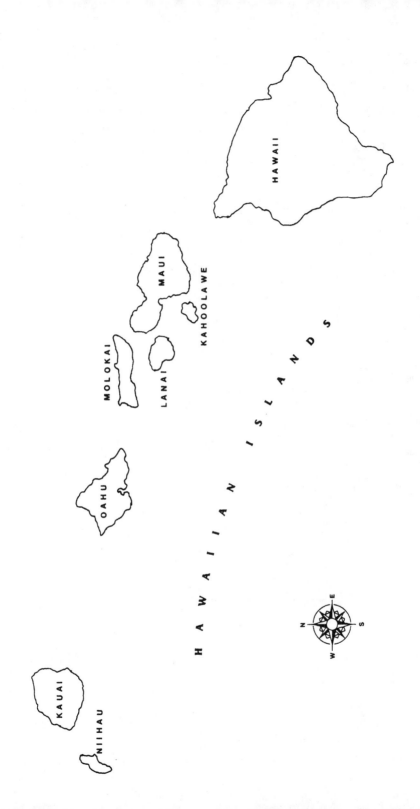

HAWAIIAN ISLANDS

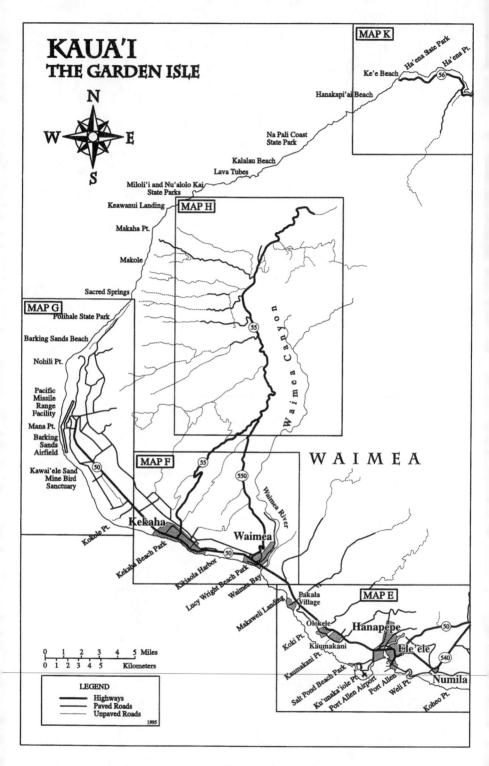

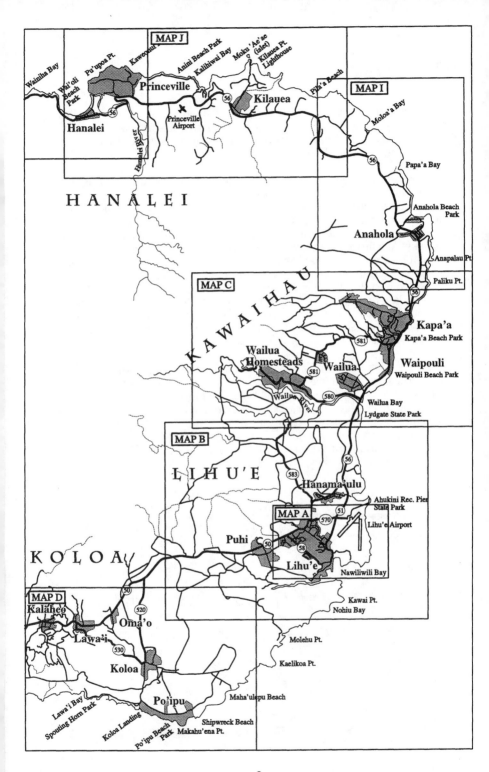

INTRODUCTION

Congratulations! You've selected Kaua'i, The Garden Island, in the Hawaiian Islands as a vacation destination. Or you are seriously thinking about it anyway. You've made the right decision because Kaua'i is simply a great place to visit, vacation on and get away from it all.

The Hawaiian Islands are an archipelago of diverse and unique natural beauty composed of equally diverse and unique tropical ecosystems. There are mountains, of course, old volcanoes reaching from the sea, some extinct, some dormant, some still active. There are jagged rain forest-clad peaks, some stark and steep, others gracefully sloping, reaching through puffy clouds to the blue Pacific sky. And there is the Pacific Ocean surrounding these islands, influencing and controlling the life on land. And where land meets ocean, there is a melding of nature's palette, bright blues and greens from water, reef and sky, mixed with the white, golden, black and even green sands of the beaches, accented by the stark black lava rock and sheer cliffs that plunge into the sea. Nature has blessed the islands of Hawai'i with similar yet distinct characteristics. Each somewhat like the others, yet each with its own attributes and special features. Kaua'i has all of this and more.

Kaua'i has long been known as "The Garden Island." It's an apt name. For this island, perhaps more than the others, has the visual features and characteristics so often associated with the stereotypical "Garden of Eden." Invariably, when the subject turns to tropical islands, the word "paradise" works its way into the discussion. It's an overused, perhaps unfair even, term to describe any place really. Like artwork, beauty is in the eye of the beholder. So too is a descriptive term like "paradise." But to many, that term describes Kaua'i. To them it is a paradise. You'll get no argument from me on that point.

HELICONIA, BIRD OF PARADISE   JANORA BAYOT

10

Kaua'i has lush tropical valleys, high cascading waterfalls tumbling into jungle pools, upland rain forests dense with tropical vegetation and a high tree canopy alive with rare birdlife. There are arid desert canyons populated with specially adapted plant life, mountain ridge trails with panoramic lookouts, rivers and streams winding down from remote interior valleys, and isolated tranquil beaches where only the rolling surf on the shore breaks the silence. Coral reefs teem with tropical fish and diverse forms of marine life, coastal and mountain hiking trails lead to scenic vistas that can be reached on other way.

Kaua'i is not a sedentary sort of place. With its lush tropical beauty and embracing mild climate, you'd almost think Kaua'i is the place to slip into a state of blissful idleness. Well, you can do that if you wish. You can choose to lay around the pool or beach, *mai tai* in hand, and just soak up the ambiance of the place. But, to the contrary, Kaua'i is loaded with adventure and activity. From Waimea to Hanalei, you'll find a variety of exciting, educational and heart-pumping activities and experiences. You can ride a bike down a canyon, hike a mountain ridge trail through the rain forest, scuba or snorkel a reef or underwater cave, take a horseback trail ride along a scenic coastline, paddle your own canoe up a jungle stream, hike to a waterfall for a picnic lunch, cruise by boat or helicopter by the famed Napali Coast, follow a historic heritage trail, take in a Hawaiian luau, visit a wildlife refuge, shop for island-style Aloha-wear clothing and coral or shell jewelry, enjoy a real local-style gourmet plate lunch or a five-star fine dining experience, and...well, you get the picture. On Kaua'i, there are so many things to see, do and experience, you'll probably not have enough time to do them all. So, you'll have to come back again!

This is the seventh edition of this book, having first been published in 1988. Much has changed on Kaua'i since the first edition, but at the same time much of Kaua'i remains the same. While the man-made structures and influences have changed (mostly thanks to Nature's intervention, i.e. hurricanes), the physical attributes and features of Kaua'i mostly remain the same. And another thing that remains unchanged is the genuine warmth and friendliness of Kaua'i's people. For it is the people of Kaua'i that make it such a special place. Kaua'i's multi-cultural community has been able to grow and develop together because of something called the "Aloha Spirit." Some may argue against it, but there is little doubt that the "Aloha Spirit" is alive and well on Kaua'i. How else to explain how Kaua'i "weathered" a major hurricane ten years ago that left it severely crippled and damaged? How else to explain how one small island, lacking in the way of major resources, survived a decade and more of a devastating economic decline? How else to explain how communities have come together in the face of the disaster of having their major industries, sugar mills and plantations, go out of business? These challenges and difficulties may not yet be entirely resolved on Kaua'i, but its people are working together for future solutions and embracing the "Aloha Spirit" in doing so. In that sense, "The Garden Island" is experiencing a rebirth, regrowth and revitalization that will hopefully make it an even better community than before.

That's what makes Kaua'i such a great place to visit. It's not only the physical beauty of the land and environment, the exciting adventures and experiences that await visitors, its wealth of culture, heritage and history, but it is the wonderful folks who call Kaua'i home. They welcome guests with the "Aloha Spirit" and are happy to share their island home with them.

As a journalist and resident of the Big Island of Hawai'i for many years, it has been my pleasure to spend a good deal of time on Kaua'i, our neighbor island to the north end of the chain. I have been impressed by the variety and diversity to be found on such a small island. There is much to see, do and experience on Kaua'i and I won't claim to have seen and done it all. Far from it. This book is a revision and update of the previous edition done by Dona Early and Christie Stilson. As I worked on this book gathering update material and doing research, I was continually impressed with the volume and scope of work and attention to detail the previous authors provided. A tip of the "coconut papale" (hat) to Dona and Christie! I've tried to enhance and provide additional details and updated information plus new listings and information on all the related sections of this book, to build on what was already provided. I hope in that I have succeeded.

"Kaua'i-The Garden Island: Making the Most of Your Family Vacation," is all about helping you and your *ohana* (family) to see, experience and enjoy your vacation on Kaua'i to the greatest extent possible. And whether you consider Kaua'i a "Paradise" or not, it is hoped that this book will help you to discover, or for returning visitors, to rediscover this beautiful island. Kaua'i is one of the most scenically beautiful islands in Hawai'i. But it goes beyond that. There's almost something magical about Kaua'i, the grandeur of the Waimea Canyon, the splendor of Hanalei and the North Shore, the gorgeous beaches of Po'ipu, Ke'e and Lumahai to name a few, the peacefulness of early morning at Koke'e, the cathedral-like forest canopy of the Awa'awapuhi Trail. And there are so many other features worthy of note. The magic of Kaua'i is there waiting for each individual to discover and savor for him or herself. If this book helps you do that, to experience the essence of Kaua'i, get the most from your precious vacation time and expense, to enjoy yourself and the time with your *ohana*, and to learn something about this special island of Kaua'i, then this book will have achieved its goal.

You are also invited to share your viewpoints and vacation experiences about Kaua'i. Send any information or inquiries to the author at: Paradise Publications, 8110 SW Wareham Circle, Portland, OR 97223 or Email: Paradyse@worldnet.att.net

Aloha!

John Penisten

GENERAL INFORMATION
KAUA'I'S BEST BETS

BEST FOOD SPLURGE: Sunday Brunch at the Kaua'i Marriott (with or without champagne) and the champagne Sunday Brunch or Friday evening seafood buffet at the Princeville Hotel.

BEST SUNSET AND COCKTAILS: South Shore: The Beach House, Brennecke's, or The Point at Sheraton Kaua'i in Po'ipu. North Shore: the lounge off the lobby at the Princeville Hotel with the sunset over Bali Hai. In Lihu'e, Whalers Brewpub at the Kaua'i Lagoons offers microbrewed beers with a spectacular view of the ocean and lighthouse as a backdrop.

BEST SUNSET DINING VIEW: North Shore: The Bali Hai Restaurant with views of Hanalei Bay and the Hamolokama mountains and waterfalls. The Hanalei Cafe at the Princeville Resort. South Shore: The Beach House restaurant in Po'ipu.

BEST BEACH SUNSET: From Ke'e Beach with the Napali for a backdrop or at the other end of the Napali coast at Polihale Beach, or anywhere along the west shore around Kekaha.

BEST PHOTO OPP SPOT: The Kalalau Valley Lookout at Koke'e State Park (if it's a clear day, the valley is often shrouded by misty swirling clouds covering the magnificent view, but if you're patient, it might clear up)

BEST PHOTO EXCURSION: By helicopter into the Waimea Canyon or along the Napali Coast

BEST DAILY BREAKFAST BUFFET: Hyatt Regency Kaua'i.

BEST DINNERS IN PARADISE: A Pacific Cafe and Roy's Po'ipu Bar & Grill

BEST STEAK DINNER ON THE ISLAND BAR NONE: King's Steakhouse & Tropical Bar in Hanapepe--they feature prime Black Angus kiawe-broiled steaks, a sheer indulgence for beefeaters.

BEST LUAU VALUE: Check the local Kaua'i newspapers for advertisements listing local luaus that might be held by churches or other organizations as fund raisers-usually a great value and you're sure to enjoy some great food and entertainment!

BEST ROMANTIC DINING: Tidepools at the Hyatt, Hanalei Cafe at the Princeville Hotel, or Gaylord's at Kilohana

BEST TRADITIONAL ITALIAN FARE: Cafe Cara in Koloa

BEST FAMILY DINING: Barbecue Inn in Lihu'e and Hanama'ulu Restaurant & Tea House in Hanama'ulu

BEST FAMILY DINING ATMOSPHERE: Keoki's Paradise for the great tropical atmosphere, the homey feel of Ono Family Restaurant, and the fun of an old-fashioned ice cream parlor at Beezers.

BEST PIZZA: Brick Oven Pizza in Kalaheo. Pau Hana wins for unusual toppings and best pizza on the North Shore. Aloha Kaua'i Pizza at the Coconut MarketPlace is great for to-go pizza. Pizzetta in Koloa also turns out a good product.

BEST BURGERS: Duane's Ono Burgers at Anahola

BEST FRESH BAGELS AND BAKED GOODS: Kilauea Bakery

BEST COOL TREATS: Lappert's Ice Cream at one of their many locations. A shave ice at Halo Halo Shave Ice, in Hamura Saimin, Lihu'e, or anything from Beezers.

BEST SALAD BAR: Duke's Canoe Club

BEST TAKE-HOME FOOD PRODUCTS: Fresh papaya salsa, Hanapepe-made taro chips, or fresh produce from People's Market in Puhi. "Nuts-o-wot" roasted peanuts from Waimea. Fresh produce and Made in Kaua'i products located roadside in Hanalei. (Note: some produce must be pre-inspected to go through airport agricultural checks, including pineapple and papaya!) And, if you can keep it chilled long enough (try a foam cooler with ice), or you can opt to freeze it too, a container or two of fresh made "Hanalei Poi" from Hanalei Poi Company. Once you eat this poi, you'll never go back to the stuff in plastic bags. It is truly fresh, mild and tasty and not sour or strong like the bagged varieties.

And it's good to report that Kaua'i Coffee is establishing its own sought-after reputation as a quality product. Bags of fresh ground or whole beans are available at retail stores or you can buy direct from Kaua'i Coffee Company at their visitor center in Kalaheo or by calling 1-800-545-8605.

BEST (AND MOST AFFORDABLE) SEAFOOD RESTAURANT: Keoki's Paradise; Emerson's Seafood Restaurant is a close second.

MOST CONVENIENT SHOPPING HOURS: Walmart in Lihu'e which opens at 6 am (Sundays at 8 am) and stays open nightly until 10 pm!

BEST ALOHA WEAR: Hilo Hattie! The "aloha wear" at Aloha Wear also comes highly recommended (as shown by the van of seniors we saw shopping for their Lei Day muumuus!)

BEST CHEAP ALOHA WEAR: While not for every traveler, the Salvation Army can be a great place to pick up some Hawaiian clothes to wear on your vacation. A muu muu for less than $5 is great for a beach cover-up or for wearing to a luau. There are two Salvation Army thrift store outlets. Hanapepe (4465 Puolo) is open Tuesday-Friday 9 am-noon and Saturday 9 am-3 pm. Hours for the Lihu'e location (4028 Rice St. by Mid-Pac Auto) are Tuesday-Saturday 10 am-4 pm. The Kaua'i Humane Society Thrift Shop (3100 Kuhio Hwy.) is open Tuesday-Friday 9:30-5:30; from 10 am-2 pm on Saturday.

BEST LEIS: People's Market in Puhi, the Blue Orchid in Koloa, Flowers Forever in Lihu'e, JC's Flowers & Mini Mart in Kapa'a; for last minute leis in a hurry, try any of the Kaua'i supermarkets.

MOST SPECTACULAR RESORT GROUNDS: Hyatt Regency Kaua'i.

BEST ROMANTIC ADVENTURE: A trip up the Wailua River to Fern Grotto in a kayak for two, then wait and join a boat tour group to walk to the Fern Grotto to listen to the "Hawaiian Wedding Song." The 6 ½ mile hike on Awa'awapuhi Trail at Koke'e State Park to the gorgeous overlook on the Napali Coast, a close second.

BEST EXCURSIONS:
Most spectacular: a circle-island helicopter tour.
Most unusual: a kayaking trip around the Napali Coast.
Most serene: any of the hiking trails into the superb Waimea Canyon.
Best adventure on foot: the first two miles of the Kalalau trail on the Napali coast.
Most exciting cruise: a catamaran snorkel cruise along the Napali Coast.
A world away: a helicopter tour of the isolated island of Ni'ihau.
Unusual land tour: Hawai'i Movie Tour: see the island and some special island sights!

BEST CHANCE OF GETTING RAINED ON: The Wai'ale'ale Crater, the wettest spot on earth!

BEST CHANCE OF GETTING SUNNED ON: Any beach along the South or West Shores.

BEST BEACHES:
Most scenic: Lumaha'i Beach or Ke'e on Kaua'i's North Shore.
Unspoiled: Maha'ulepu, Honopu and Lawa'i Kai.
Best for kids: Salt Ponds, Lydgate Beach Park, or Po'ipu Beach for protected kiddie wading area.
Best dolphin spotting: Kauapea (Secret) Beach has fresh springs and dolphins can sometimes be spotted!

BEST KAUA'I SPARE-NO-EXPENSE-GET-AWAY-FROM-IT-ALL RESORT: Princeville Resort or Hyatt Regency Kaua'i.

BEST KAUA'I BARE-BONES, ON-THE-CHEAP ADVENTURE LODGING: Koke'e Lodge at Waimea Canyon (About the only thing more economical is a tent.)

BEST LOCATION AND GET-AWAY-FROM-IT-ALL-ON-THE-NORTH-SHORE CONDO: Hanalei Colony Resort.

BEST HOTEL VALUE: Holiday Inn Kaua'i.

BEST BUDGET INN: Garden Island Inn.

BEST BOOKING AGENT: We were impressed with Suite Paradise, they offer particularly good rates for week long stays if you are looking for a Po'ipu destination. And they are open Saturday and Sunday for taking your reservations!

BEST DISCOUNTS: There really are not any great island discount or coupon books for Kaua'i like other destinations seem to have. Many of the free visitor magazines and publications available widely do offer various shopping, tours and activities, or dining coupons. These are worth checking out. Most of the rental car drive guides have coupon pages and some coupons may be provided when you rent a car. Some hotel and condo properties give guests a complimentary coupon book and you might inquire with your front desk upon checking in.

The beach activities are subject to weather and ocean conditions!

BEST BEACH "PERIOD": Po'ipu Beach was named the #1 beach in the country for 2001 by the annual "Dr. Beach Top Beaches of the USA Survey" as conducted by Dr. Stephen Leatherman, Florida International University.

BEST SNORKELING:
Beginners -- Po'ipu Beach and Lydgate.
Intermediate/Advanced -- Tunnels (only for strong swimmers).

BEST BODY SURFING: Shipwreck Beach.

BEST SURFING: In front of the old Waiohai called "Acid Drop," Beach House, or Hanalei Bay.

BEST WINDSURFING: Beginners -- 'Anini.
Intermediate -- Tunnels or Maha'ulepu.

BEST SWIMMING: Po'ipu Beach, Hanalei Bay, Salt Ponds.

BEST FLOWERS: Sunshine Markets around the islands; People's Market in Puhi.

BEST NIGHT SPOTS: Lizard Lounge Bar & Grill and Rob's Good Times Grill; many restaurant bars and resort lounges offer live music and entertainment on various evenings each week.

UNUSUAL GIFT IDEAS: Hawaiian motif needlepoint canvases and fabrics or an original Oriental doll quilt from Kapai'a Stitchery in Lihu'e. Mouse pads with Hawaiian designs may be the perfect gift for all your internet friends (available at Big Kmart and probably elsewhere) or be an angel and bring home one of Uncle Eddie's Aloha Angels dressed in a variety of muu muus, hula skirts, sea shells, or tapa cloth. These collectible ornaments have their own shop at the Hanapepe Cafe and are also sold at the Sheraton, Marriott, and Princeville hotels or by catalog. Movie buffs will enjoy The *Kaua'i Movie Book*, a full-color account of films, TV shows and documentaries all shot on Kaua'i. Available at bookstores or support the non-profit Wilcox Foundation at (808) 245-1198. The Kaua'i Products Store at Kukui Grove not only has a nice selection of locally-made products, they also have homemade fudge! Made fresh daily on the premises, it comes in tropical flavors like chocolate or vanilla macadamia, Kona coffee, and pina colada. Roy's has a do-it-yourself chocolate souffle kit for making his signature dessert at home. Or purchase some tropical scented lotions, soaps, or candles from Island Soap & Candle Works. Scented with island fragrances like plumeria, torch ginger, or pikake, they are all hand-made using natural ingredients and even more fun -- you can watch them being made at their factory and gift shop in the Kong Lung Center in Kilauea or Koloa Town!

REALLY UNUSUAL GIFT IDEAS: "Uncle" Bill Ford makes custom Hawaiian coconut golf clubs -- a souvenir novelty gift that actually works! Contact him at PO Box 1403 Koloa, Kaua'i, HI 96756, call (808) 742-9250 or Email: unclebillford@webtv.net. And here's a really "novel" idea: Po'ipu-based Paradise Works will create a custom, personalized romantic adventure novel as a remembrance of your visit to Kaua'i. You just need to fill out a questionnaire with information about your trip to Kaua'i. Cost is $29.95. They are located at Accents at the Hyatt Regency Kaua'i. Call (808) 742-2457, FAX 742-9146 or visit their website < www.ParadiseWorks-Inc.com >.

BEST T-SHIRTS: The Red Dirt shirts are a way to take a little bit of Kaua'i home with you, but Crazy Shirts are still the more popular and somewhat more expensive than the run-of-the-mill variety, but better quality. And now they come in flavors! Coffee, chocolate, beer, *Li Hing Mui* (local preserved Chinese plum), and chile pepper colored tee's look - and smell - yummy! They come in clever packages (the coffee shirt comes in a coffee bag); they're preshrunk - and colorfast!

BEST FREE STUFF:

Kaua'i maps from The Hawai'i Visitors Bureau or the Chamber of Commerce.

Hiking trail maps, guides, brochures from State Division of Forestry and Wildlife.

A tour of the Guava Kai Plantation in Kilauea.

The Kamalani playground for the kids at Lydgate Park.

Free bi-monthly lectures and field tips on a variety of Kaua'i history topics through the Kaua'i Historical Society. (808) 245-3373

Free movies at the Princeville Hotel for resort guests and dining guests.

Free camping permits at state parks on Kaua'i.

Na Pali Eco Adventures sponsors whale slide shows during the winter season. This presentation is complimentary at various locations around the island. Check with (808) 826-6804 for days, times, and location.

Every Friday, the local galleries in Hanapepe host "Art Night" with at least one of them providing refreshments and an art demonstration. Decorative lighting adds to the mood for visitors to enjoy a festive stroll, watch artists doing portraits, and enjoy the hula show and local Hawaiian music.

A scenic drive along Kaua'i's North Shore.

Free admission to the Fayé Museum -- exhibits and photos of a pioneer sugar family at Waimea Plantation Cottages. Open 9-9 daily.

The Royal Coconut Grove Lounge (at the Kaua'i Coconut Beach Resort) has free pupus every afternoon from 4:30-5:30 pm.

Radisson Kaua'i Beach Hotel offers daily arts & crafts demonstrations (quilting, seed leis, nut ornaments) in their lobby.

Sunset torchlighting ceremony at the Hyatt Regency.

Free coffee tasting at the Kaua'i Coffee Company Visitor Center & Museum

A free Dune Walk Tour guided by the Kaua'i Historical Society is offered every other Monday 9-10 am at the Hyatt Regency. The tour's focus is on prehistoric native Hawaiian sites and sand dunes of Makawehi.

Many free produce and flea-market swap meets pop up around the island on various days; Saturday community Farmers' Markets in Hanalei, Kilauea, and Kapa'a

Free introductory scuba lessons at resort pools.

Waimea Town Celebration in February; Koloa Plantation Days in July.

Free Yoga class offered 10 am-noon on the second Saturday of each month at the Institute for Yoga Science at Kaua'i Village in Kapa'a. Call (808) 828-0999.

The public is invited to special Hawaiian Exhibits offered each morning in the Aupaka Terrace at the Kaua'i Marriott. The exhibits and times vary daily but include Coconut Frond Weaving, Hula Dance Class, Hawaiian crafts, and displays of Hawaiian quilts, featherwork, and Ni'ihau leis.

Free self-guided tour of Moir Cactus Gardens and Hawaiian Gardens at the Kiahuna Plantation in Po'ipu. (Plants are marked.) Call (808) 742-6411.

Not quite free, but for a small donation, even this counts: Enjoy a hike with an interpretive guide along the many trails of the Koke'e area. Offered during summer months only by the Koke'e Natural History Museum. You can also opt to do the hikes on your own for free. Pick up a trail guide/map at the museum.

The Koke'e Natural History Museum also offers free guided and trail clearing hikes (through the Research Conservation Program) from June through mid-September. The museum sponsors a number of environmental and cultural festivals throughout the year. For further information contact them at PO Box 100, Kekaha, HI 96752 or call (808) 335-9975.

The Exhibition Hall at Kukui Grove Shopping Center is a cooperative effort between the Garden Islands Arts Council, and Kaua'i Society of Artists. The Exhibition Hall regularly features the most creative and energetic efforts of the art community.

Watch jewelry being designed and created at The Goldsmith's Gallery in the Kinipopo Shopping Village in Wailua.

Free hula and Tahitian Dance at Po'ipu Shopping Village, 5 pm Mon & Thurs.

Free daily hula and Polynesian shows (5 pm) at the Coconut MarketPlace. The center is located 15 minutes north of Lihu'e between the Wailua River and Kapa'a. To check their current schedule call (808) 822-3641.

Free shuttle between Kukui Grove Shopping Center and Po'ipu Resort area. Call the shopping center office at (808) 245-7784 for pick-up points and time schedule. (Some pickup points as far as Wailua.)

A two-hour guided Crater Hill hike is offered daily at the Kilauea Point National Wildlife Refuge. It'll cost you $2 admission to the Refuge, but the guided hikes are free. Early reservations are recommended. Call (808) 828-0168 or sign up at the visitor center.

Special events and children's activities at Borders Books at the Kukui Grove Shopping Center.

Take a self-guided tour of the Hawaiian artifacts, museum-quality art and handcrafted items at the Kaua'i Heritage Center of Hawaiian Culture & the Arts at Kaua'i Village in Waipouli (Kapa'a). They also offer a varied number of video presentations, lectures and workshops. Many of them are free.

Ma's in Lihu'e gives you a free cup of coffee when you order a meal!

Free hula show Friday at 6pm at Kukui Grove Center.

A Sunday service in Hawaiian at the Waioli Hui Church in Hanalei or the Waimea Foreign (Foreign, in this case, means English speaking!) Hawaiian Church to enjoy the exceptional choir and appreciate the great acoustics! Lihu'e Lutheran is a quaint 150-year-old church that also features Hawaiian music. 6 pm at the Kukui Grove Center.

On the first Saturday of the month, admission is free at the Kaua'i Museum. This monthly event features special family activities. You can obtain a calendar of events by writing 4428 Rice St., Lihu'e, HI 96766 (808) 245-6931.

Lae Nani condominiums in Kapa'a offers a cultural tour of the *heiau* located mauka of the property and has a map available.

Visits to Kaua'i's wilderness areas are free: Waimea Canyon; Koke'e State Park; Alakai Wilderness Preserve; Napali Coast State Park.

The public is invited to *E Kanikapila Kakou*, a free, 12-week Hawaiian music program that features local composers each week. Held every Monday (Feb-May) at 7pm at St. Michael's and All Angels Parish Hall. Call 246-3994 for schedule and more information.

Watching the sunset from Ke'e Beach on the North Shore, from Polihale Beach or anywhere along the western coastline.

Following the *Koloa Heritage Trail* which highlights the various cultural, historical and geographical important sites of the Koloa and Po'ipu areas. Get a free trail guide/map from Po'ipu Beach Resort Association, 742-7444.

The annual Kaua'i Aloha Festival events throughout the month of October, part of the statewide Aloha Festivals, are mostly free, but special Aloha Festival ribbons are sold for $5 each as a fund-raiser and the ribbons get you into any of the events. Call the Kaua'i Visitors Bureau Office for details, 245-3971.

The many and varied annual events that are offered at no charge. (See monthly calendar listing).

Free copy of *Kaua'i Update* newsletter! Send a self-addressed stamped envelope to us at Paradise Publications and indicate you'd like the latest copy of our Kaua'i newsletter.

BEST GIFT FOR FRIENDS TRAVELING TO KAUA'I: Send a self-addressed, stamped envelope for a complimentary copy of the *Kaua'i Update* newsletter. (Subscriptions also available.) Or purchase a copy of *Kaua'i-The Garden Island: Making the Most of Your Family Vacation* for them.

THE SEVEN WONDERS OF KAUA'I

Kaua'i is a scenic tropical wonderland with varied terrain, geography and natural features. It's a lush, green garden of Eden for the most part, little wonder it's nickname is "The Garden Island." And there are generally seven features or attractions visitors shouldn't miss while on Kaua'i.

1. The Napali Coast-here majestic sea clffs rise to 4,000 ft. above the uninhabited North Shore. Sea caves, lush hidden valleys, deserted white sand beaches and some of Kaua'i's most awe inspiring views. It's accessible by air, boat or a strenuous 11-mile hike on the Kalalau Trail.

2. Kalalau Trail-it's a full day 11-mile hike traversing five spectacular valleys, over splashing mountain streams and tumbling waterfalls and cascades, and past the ruins of several ancient Hawaiian settlements. The trail begins at the end of the road in Ha'ena State Park on the North Shore and ends at Kalalau Beach.

3. Kilauea Point National Wildlife Refuge-one of the most visited wildlife refuges in the country, a historic lighthouse sits atop the rocky peninsula on Kaua'i's northern most point and is home to nesting seabirds in the surrounding cliffs and whales, dolphins, seals and turtles in the ocean depths below.

4. Waimea Canyon and Koke'e State Park-this is the "Grand Canyon of the Pacific," a geological wonder stretching 10-miles long, 3,600 ft. deep, and a mile wide. There are numerous hiking trails, picnic areas, lodge cabins and camping grounds, and scenic overlooks. There's also a small natural history museum to visit.

5. Wailua River and Falls-take a half-mile hike to the lookout above the point where Hawaiian chiefs once jumped to prove their courage. A boat trip up Kaua'i's biggest river takes you to the beautiful Fern Grotto, a massive lava tube adorned with lush tropical flora.

6. Mt. Wai'ale'ale-this is the highest point on Kaua'i at 5,208 ft. and the acknowledged wettest place on Earth with over 400-inches of annual rainfall. The spectacular lush beauty of this mountain watershed area can only be seen from the air via helicopter or plane.

7. Hanalei Valley, Bay and River-this valley on the North Shore is rich in history and heritage and was once home to a thriving native Hawaiian community. The valley produces the bulk of the state's taro root used for the staple food, poi. In the 1800's, the bay was an important harbor for whaling and trading ships.

HISTORY OF KAUA'I

This brief history focuses on the island of Kaua'i. Please refer to our recommended reading section for information which will augment the history of the Hawaiian Islands in general.

Although it is not the usual way to begin an historic narrative, this history of Kaua'i begins with a jump to September, 1992. The reason is that the natural disaster that visited Kaua'i then, Hurrican Iniki, had a significant impact on the island and even yet there are still a few lingering effects. On September 11, 1992, life was forever altered on Kaua'i when hurricane force winds swept across the island. Few structures were left undamaged and although some hotels, condominiums and other island businesses were able to quickly rebuild, others took years to recover. Still other business closed their doors forever. But, inevitably, from the destruction sprang new growth and rebirth. In spite of insurance nightmares, hotels were renovated and remodeled, new restaurants opened and old ones were refurbished and improved. And sadly, a few hotels never did rebuild and reopen.

Hurricane Iniki left a heavy footprint throughout the island in the way it altered physical attributes and geography; the way it impacted important commercial industries like tourism, fishing, and agriculture; and the way it affected the attitudes, philosophies, lifestyles and even lives of its people. Many residents left after the second hurricane to hit the island within only ten years. A hurricane had also struck Kaua'i in 1982. Many others felt that with two hurricanes behind them they could probably face anything and be stronger for it. The facts about Hurricane Iniki were rapidly sent out to the world via the news media. Every devastating detail was reported, and we eagerly watched the good and bad news as it unfolded. But now that the day-to-day effects have diminished faded into the past, and the facts have become historical statistics, they can be neatly and benignly tucked into the section on Weather and its sub-category: Hurricanes.

That done, let's go back a few million years to the creation of Kaua'i, The Garden Island. Far beneath the warm waters of the Pacific Ocean is the Pacific Plate, which moves constantly in a northwest direction. Each Hawaiian island was formed as it passed over a hot vent in this plate. Kaua'i, the oldest of the major islands in the Hawai'i chain, was formed first and has since moved away from the plume, (the source of the lava) so it is no longer growing. But the ocean that created these islands millions of years ago has all but swallowed them back, leaving only atolls of coral reef. The archipelago known as Hawai'i spans 1,523 miles with 132 islands, shoals and reefs that reach as far west as the Aleutian Islands of Alaska. The Big Island is now the youngest in the chain and is continuing to grow. A new island called Lo'ihi (which means "prolonged in time"), southeast of the Big Island, is growing beneath the surface of the Pacific and is expected to emerge from the oceanic depths in a few thousand years. The State of Hawai'i is comprised of eight major islands: Hawai'i, Maui, Kaho'olawe, Lana'i, Moloka'i, O'ahu, Ni'ihau and Kaua'i. The islands are organized into self-governing counties: the County of Hawai'i (often called the Big Island), the County of Maui (including Maui, Kaho'olawe, Lana'i and Moloka'i), the City and County of Honolulu (O'ahu), and the County of Kaua'i (including Kaua'i and Ni'ihau). The major islands lie in a curving arc stretching southeast to northwest from about 18-23 degrees north latitude and 155-159 degrees west longitude in the North Pacific Ocean. Of the eight major islands, all are populated except for barren and desolate Kaho'olawe. Ni'ihau is only sparsely populated but is also privately-owned and closed to outsiders. Few are allowed to visit, except on arranged hunting and fishing excursions.

The Northwest Hawaiian Islands are unpopulated (except for Midway Atoll) and are mostly low-lying coral atolls that are protected wildlife preserves. These islands, which stretch all the way out to near the 180th. meridian International Dateline, include Nihoa, Necker, La Perouse, Gardner, Laysan, Lisianski, Pearl and Hermes, Midway, and Kure.

The northernmost islands of the "eight" major islands, Kaua'i and Ni'ihau, were created together, emerging from the surface of the sea at the same time. They are actually dissected domes separated by the shallow 17-mile wide Kau'lakahi Channel. Lehua to the north and Ka'ula to the south are two tiny uninhabited islets that are also part of Ni'ihau and the County of Kaua'i.

Midway Atoll in the Northwest Hawaiian Islands, previously under the control of the U.S. Navy as a base, is now a part of the National Wildlife Refuge and tours are now available there, departing from Honolulu

The interpretations of the name Kaua'i prove to be varied. Harry Franck, in his 1937 publication entitled *Roaming in Hawai'i*, noted that the translation was "to light upon" or "to dry in the sun." The reason might possibly be because driftwood landed on the shores of Kaua'i more often than on other islands.

It lies very much in the path of the trade winds and of ocean currents. He continues: "The more commonly accepted meaning of the name is 'fruitful season or time of plenty,' because in olden times Kaua'i was the only island of the group which never suffered from famine on account of drought. In very ancient times, it was known as Kaua'i-a-mano-ka-lani-po, which freely translated means 'The fountain-head of many waters from on high and bubbling from below.'"

Kaua'i is young in geological terms, but its birth probably began about 6 million years ago and continued for about 3 million years. It lay dormant for another 1.5 million years before having a resurgence of volcanic activity which created the eastern portions of Kaua'i over the course of more than 1.5 million years. The most recent volcanic activity occurred on the southern shore more than 40,000 years ago. Compared with Maui's most recent volcanic activity which occurred only 200 years ago, Kaua'i is the grandfather in the chain of major Hawaiian islands. Kaua'i is much smaller today than when it was first formed. Over eons of time the crashing waves and storms eroded the North Shore, reducing the island's diameter from over 30 miles to 25, a small price to pay in return for the dramatic result of the erosion: the splendor and majesty of the incomparable Napali Coast.

Kaua'i's other phenomenon of nature, Waimea Canyon, was formed when a huge fault broke open and was further eroded by the Waimea River. Kawakini and Wai'ale'ale are the twin peaks of the single shield volcano that formed the island. Mt. Wai'ale'ale is considered the wettest place on earth. Harry Franck's book, *Roaming in Hawai'i*, tells that "in very ancient days the topmost peak was called Ka-wai-kini, 'waters in multitudes' and survey maps still record that appropriate old name. But today it is more familiarly known as Wai'ale'ale (which means 'rippling waters' or 'sparkling waters'), for the surface of the little lake at the summit is never still."

Due to the years of erosion, Kaua'i has many land characteristics unique in the Hawaiian islands. With a total of 136 miles of coastline, Kaua'i has more sandy beaches per square mile than any other of the major islands. The Napali coast on the North Shore is another of mother nature's wondrous creations, rising as much as 3,000 feet from the sea.

Kaua'i is also home to Hawai'i's only navigable rivers, seven of them, although official reports vary, citing as few as five and as many as nine. Kaua'i today is a blend of 555 square miles of desert, mountains, beaches and rain forests, making it Hawai'i's fourth largest island.

Life began in the waters surrounding the island in the form of marine creatures. Fish, mammals and microscopic animals found homes under the sea while generations of coral polyps attached themselves to the barren volcanic rock and ultimately created a coral reef. Kaua'i remains on the fringe of the coral reef system. Thus, many of its beaches lack a protective reef and require more caution.

On land, life began slowly, sporadically and quite by accident. Spores of ferns and moss, as well as tiny seeds, were carried by the winds. The few that survived altered the composition of the barren rock by breaking it down into bits of debris and fertile soil. Insects were tossed about by storms and washed ashore on floating debris.

Birds blown off course began to colonize, not only populating the island with their own species, but with larger seeds and grasses that they inadvertently carried on their feet, feathers, or in their intestinal tracts. The introduction of each species of flora or fauna was a rare event, taking thousands of years. With no predators, birds flourished. The only mammals to arrive without the help of man were the seal and the bat, and neither provided any threat to the birdlife of the islands. Since the mongoose was never introduced to Kaua'i, the birds continue to flourish here.

Just as the creation of life is explained in two equally valid interpretations -- the scientific and biblical -- the population of the Hawaiian Islands must be explained both by legend and science in equal measures of credibility. Kaua'i was the first home of the Hawaiian volcano goddess, Madame Pele (until her sister drove her out) as well as being the first Hawaiian island populated by the Polynesians.

Although the dates vary greatly, sometime between 200 A.D. to 700 A.D., it is thought that the first Polynesian explorers came to Kaua'i from the Marquesas Islands to the far south. Findings suggest that their ancestors came from the western Pacific, perhaps as far as Madagascar. Centuries later, they were followed by the Tahitians, who came via the Big Island of Hawai'i, and from their word manahune (or outcast) came the reality-based legend of the menehune, the Hawaiian leprechaun. Driven out by her sister, Madame Pele moved to the Big Island taking her fire with her. She now makes her home in the volcano of Mauna Loa and is no longer associated with Kaua'i.

The Polynesians and Tahitians, however, settled on the island between the 11th and 14th centuries and began much of what we know as Hawaiian culture on the island of Kaua'i. The Polynesians brought their double-hulled canoes, laden with the food staples of taro and breadfruit as well as pigs, chickens and dogs (presumably the required quarantine time was more lenient back then), which

supplemented their diet of fish. They also introduced a number of plants, including ginger and sugar cane (to name just a few). It was fortunate they arrived so well prepared, as Kaua'i offered them little in the way of edible plants. It is estimated that by the 1700's, the Hawaiian population may have risen as high as 300,000 persons, spread throughout the main eight-island chain.

Taro is the root from which poi is made, and it was used not only as a food by early Hawaiians, but as a dye for their tapa cloth and also to seal the lengths of the cloth together. It was used medicinally: rubbing a raw root stock on a wound was said to stop bleeding; the raw leaf stem rubbed on an insect bite was reported to reduce swelling and alleviate pain, and undiluted poi was used as a poultice for skin infections. The root would last for months without spoiling and, at one time, more than 300 varieties of taro were found in the islands. Today, fewer than 90 varieties are cultivated.

The Tahitians initiated a class system and the concept of *kapu* or *taboo*, which was composed of rigid sanctions and religious laws. However, they also introduced the pleasures of surfing, kite flying, the beauty of the floral lei and the idea and spirit of *aloha*.

Four principal gods, Kanaloa (the god of the land of departed spirits), Kane (the god of war), Ku (the god who oversaw sacrifices) and Lono (the god of harvest and peace), formed the basis of the Hawaiian religion until the missionaries arrived. The stone foundations of *heiau*, the ancient religious temples, can still be found throughout the islands. The governing chief was called the *Ali'i*, and it was he who kept order by establishing various *"kapus."* It was *kapu*, for example, for men and women to dine together. It was not until the death of King Kamehameha about 1819 that the appointed regent of Hawai'i, Ka'ahumanu, broke the kapu system when she persuaded Liholiho, heir of Kamehameha, to eat with her and his mother, Keopulani, in public. Thus began the breakdown of the old *kapu* system, the old beliefs and religion. Soon after, the influence of the western world began to spread throughout the islands with the arrival of the first missionaries from America.

The lower portion of the Wailua River was the sight selected as sacred by the high chiefs and kahunas on Kaua'i. This location, along with another at Waialua on O'ahu, were deemed two of the most sacred places in all the islands. Here you will find remains of seven *heiaus* where the early Hawaiians worshipped their gods. Future members of the *ali'i* were born at the sacred birthing stone located here. Rituals were an important part of their life, both in birth and in death. Human sacrifices were sometimes a part of the rituals performed.

Another goddess, Kapo, queen of the lei, is still honored each year on Lei Day. While most leis are made of island flowers, feather leis made with the exotic yellow plumage of the *o'o* were once reserved for Polynesian royalty.

The all-purpose Hawaiian word *"aloha"* means both hello and goodbye and encompasses all the principles, subtleties, variations and essence of the word "love."

Where science and legend exist side by side, you will discover some distinct differences about the islands. A business would not consider construction without first receiving a blessing of the land and often several more blessings during the construction. When a business prepares for a grand opening, *ti* leaves stretched across the threshold are gently untied (never cut), and the *kapuna* (minister/priest) will enter the building with holy water, words of reverence and gratitude to the creator. This is followed by a welcome to the family and friends. Perhaps this explains the power and strength of the people to rebuild and why these islanders have such hospitable and nurturing spirits. It has a base in reality in the *aina* -- the land -- and comes out as the spirit of *aloha*.

The islands were left undisturbed by western influence until the 1778 arrival of Captain James Cook. In search of the Northwest Passage, he first spotted and visited Kaua'i on January 19, 1778. His arrival was heralded by the local people, as his ship was believed to be a *heiau* for the god Lono. Cook stopped briefly at Ni'ihau and continued on to O'ahu and Maui. He brought with him to the island of Ni'ihau, melon, pumpkin, and onion seeds. On a later voyage, Cook was killed in a dispute and confrontation with Hawaiians at Kealakekua Bay on the Kona Coast of the Big Island of Hawai'i.

The arrival of Europeans brought not only tremendous changes for the Hawaiian culture, but also the introduction of diseases which killed the Hawaiian people in huge numbers.

One scholarly speculation is rarely spoken of in the history of the Hawaiian Islands, but it is at least interesting enough to bear mentioning. The sketches of early Hawaiians show them adorned with their ceremonial cloaks and unusual helmet-shaped headgear. It has been theorized (although rejected by historians) that perhaps Gaetan, a Spanish explorer enroute from the Philippines to Mexico in 1542, may have accidently stumbled across the Hawaiian Islands. The headdress of the royal regalia does bear a striking resemblance to helmets worn by the early Spanish conquistadors, and the colors chosen by the Hawaiians for this garb are the royal Spanish colors. Another interesting question involves the apparent knowledge and use of metal by the early Hawaiians. There are no ore deposits in the Hawaiian islands, yet when Cook arrived on Kaua'i and natives came aboard, they began clamoring for and seizing metal items. In *Kaua'i The Separate Kingdom*, Edward Joesting writes, "The Hawaiians had a knowledge of the importance of metal and eagerly sought these objects (from Cook) in trade for provisions." How did these 18th century Hawaiians know the importance of metal? How had they become introduced to the usefulness of it? Could there be some truth to this theory? Then again, it is perhaps merely coincidence.

King Kamehameha I

Kamehameha the First was born on the Big Island of Hawai'i about 1758. Kamehameha became known as a fearsome warrior with great ambition for power and control. He was the nephew of Kalaiopi, who ruled the Big Island. When Kalaiopi died, his son came to power, only to be subsequently defeated by Kamehameha in 1794. Kamehameha began his quest to conquer all the islands and unite them under one kingdom. The great chieftain, Kahekili, was Kamehameha's greatest rival. He ruled not only Maui, but Lana'i and Moloka'i, and also had kinship with the governing royalty of O'ahu and Kaua'i. King Kahekili died in 1794, leaving control of the island to his sons, Kalanikupule. A bloody battle (more like a massacre since Kamehameha used western technology, strategy, and two English advisors) in the Iao Valley resulted in the defeat of Kalanikupule in 1795.

In the early 1790s, when Kamehameha was attempting to gain control of all the islands, The King of Kaua'i, Kaumuali'i, realized he had the advantage of having an island more removed from the rest of the Hawaiian chain. He had no interest in relinquishing his power to Kamehameha. The first attempt to overtake Kaua'i was made by Kamehameha in the spring of 1796. Encountering a storm, many of his soldiers never reached the island, being forced to turn back. Others who reached the island were killed at Maha'ulepu Beach. A later attempt by Kamehameha was thwarted when typhoid struck his soldiers. In 1810, realizing the inevitable, Kaumuali'i agreed to turn over control of his island to Kamehameha. Thus, King Kamehameha the Great, as he came to be known, achieved his destiny by uniting all the islands of Hawai'i under one kingdom. Later, after Kamehameha's death, his widow Ka'ahumanu, wishing to further establish the loyalty of Kaumuali'i, forced the last King of Kaua'i into marrying her. Still doubtful of his allegiance, Ka'ahumanu went a step further. Kealiiahonui, the son of Kaumuali'i, still lived on Kaua'i and his potential power as an opposing force prompted her to take him as her second husband. When the missionaries arrived and found this polygamous practice abhorrent, Ka'ahumanu released Kealiiahonui from his marriage vows.

The last King of Kaua'i, Kaumuali'i, died on May 28, 1824, on the island of O'ahu, never returning to his home island of Kaua'i. Some histories report that he died on Maui. This information, however, is incorrect. He fell ill, quickly worsened, and died on O'ahu. Following the funeral services, his body was taken to Maui for burial. Kapiolani, royal wife of King Kamehameha, had become close friends with Kaumuali'i. Prior to the death of Kapiolani, an arrangement had been reached that at his death Kaumuali'i would be laid to rest next to her. Thus his burial is in Lahaina on the island of Maui.

Kaua'i was briefly inhabited by the Russians during the reign of Kaumuali'i. The Russian traders erected several forts. The remains of one, Fort Elizabeth, can still be found at the mouth of the Waimea River. Little remains but a few mounds of dirt at Fort Alexander, located on the bluff at Princeville. Another earthen fort in the Hanalei area called Fort Barclay, after a Russian general, has eroded completely away. Georg (with no "e") Scheffer was a German who worked for the Russian American Company. This trading company sent Scheffer to recover goods from one of their vessels that had gone aground off the coast of Kaua'i.

29

When the ship was beached, King Kaumuali'i had seized the shipload of pelts, as well as everything else on board, stating that it now belonged to him.

Georg, a botanist and a physician, arrived first on O'ahu. After aiding the royal family when they were ill, he soon had endeared himself to the King. Scheffer reached Kaua'i in the spring of 1816 and expected that he might need force to regain the merchandise held by Kaua'i's King. He was surprised when Kaumuali'i warmly offered to return it. For a number of reasons, Kaumuali'i was eager to be on good terms with the Russians. Gifts were exchanged and Scheffer was later given the entire valley of Hanalei and subsequently bestowed Russian names on the Hanalei Valley, calling it Schefferthal and renaming the Hanapepe River the Don. King Kaumuali'i figured he could better protect his island from Kamehameha with the Russians as allies. Scheffer promised the King Russian protection. In *Kaua'i: A Separate Kingdom*, Edward Joesting writes, "The co-monarchs of Kaua'i (Kaumuali'i and Scheffer) now plotted the conquering of these islands. On July 1, 1816, they entered into a secret agreement.

When Kamehameha learned of this plan in 1817, Scheffer was ordered out of the islands. Interestingly, Georg Scheffer spent his last years in Brazil, having purchased a title for himself. He died Count von Frankenthal in 1836.

Kamehameha united all the islands and made Lahaina (on Maui) the capital of Hawai'i. It remained the capital until the 1840's when Honolulu (on O'ahu) became the center for government affairs.

Liholiho, the heir to Kamehameha I (also known as Kamehameha the Great), ruled as Kamehameha II from 1819 to 1824. Liholiho was not a strong ruler so Ka'ahumanu, the widow of Kamehameha I, proclaimed herself prime minister during his reign. (While Ka'ahumanu is said to have been the most favored wife of Kamehameha I, she did not have the bloodline of the *ali'i* royalty and therefore could not be his royal wife.) Ka'ahumanu ended many of the *kapus* of the old religion, thus creating a fortuitous vacuum which the soon to arrive missionaries would fill. The first missionaries arrived with their families from New England in 1820. On Kaua'i they were welcomed in 1821 and established mission houses around the island.

The missionaries caused drastic changes to the island with the exposure and education of the natives both spiritually and intellectually. It was the missionaries who set up guidelines that forbade the native women to visit the ships in the harbor. Also, horrified by the bare-breasted Hawaiian women, the missionary women quickly set about to more thoroughly clothe the native ladies. The missionary women realized that their dresses would not be appropriate for these more robust women and, using their nightwear as a guideline, fashioned garments from these by cutting the sleeves off and enlarging the armholes. The muumuu was the result, and translated means "to amputate or to cut short."

Over time, many of the missionary descendants eventually turned to business and commerce and became successful sugar planters. The island was soon blanketed with fields of green sugar cane. Sugar was to prove vital to the economic future of Kaua'i. The Polynesians who migrated from the Central Pacific brought with them the first varieties of *Ko*, or sugar cane. The early Hawaiians had many varieties of this grass which was used as a sweetener, as medicine for childbirth, and reportedly, as an aphrodisiac. The first successful sugar plantation in Hawai'i was established in Koloa (which means the place of long cane) in 1835 by Ladd & Company. William Hooper, a junior partner in Ladd & Company, established the plantation for that company by leasing 980 acres for $300 a year from King Kamehameha III. During the Civil War, Louisiana's shipping of sugar had been cut off which created a void that Hawai'i would step into and help fill. This was also the first sugar to be exported from the islands.

While the first workers in the sugar cane industry were Hawaiians, the increasing development brought workers from the four corners of the globe, which has helped shape much of Kaua'i's history and cultural diversity. During the next few decades, immigrants began arriving from both Asia and Europe to work in the fields and mills. In 1838, a few Chinese laborers were working for Hooper, but it was not until 1852 that the first contract laborers from China arrived in Hawaii. In 1868, more than 150 Japanese laborers left their homeland to work in the islands.

The first Portuguese contract laborers were recruited in the Azores and arrived in 1877. By that year, in the height of the sugar industry on Kaua'i, eight plantations had been established. They included Ele'ele, Grove Farm, Hanalei, Kapa'a, Kawaihau, Kilauea, Koloa, and Lihu'e. Castle and Cooke recruited a group of 629 Norwegian men, women and children who arrived in 1880. Larger groups of Chinese and Japanese immigrants continued to arrive in the 1880's. In 1902, the first Korean laborers arrived and they were followed by laborers from the Philippines in 1906.

A number of various crops have been attempted in Kaua'i, but for a variety of reasons, some of them proved successful, others failed. The financial adviser to King Kamehameha I, a Spaniard named Don Francisco De Paula Marin, introduced to the islands produce which would soon thrive in the warm tropical climate: limes, guavas, pineapples, and mango. Guava quickly flourished in the islands and today it grows wild around Kaua'i in addition to being commercially grown.

In the 1860's, rice cultivation was attempted in Hanalei, Wailua, and Kapa'a. Labor proved too expensive and production ceased after only a few years.

Silk production was tried experimentally in Koloa and Hanalei between 1836 and 1845. Exports of raw silk by 1844 were small and the problems of droughts and insect pests caused heavy losses. Another factor was the difficulty in finding skilled labor -- "but G.W. Bates blamed the destruction of the industry, upon the religious zeal of the natives, who refused to feed the silkworms on Sunday." (Source: *Hawai'i and Its People* by A. Grove Day.)

A try at tobacco in Hanalei was a failure due to heavy rains. While it proved more successful on the south shore, it was never harvested commercially. One of the other more unusual crops was tapioca, which was attempted in Koloa.

Today, tourism is Kaua'i's major industry, while sugar continues to be the island's largest agricultural crop. Papaya, guava and coffee are also becoming increasingly important as the island diversifies its agricultural economy. In fact, Kaua'i now has the largest producing coffee plantations in the state. White shrimp, raised in state-of-the-art aquaculture ponds in Kekaha, has recently become a successful export.

Kaua'i has also become well-known on the big screen. The beauty of the island with its spectacular scenery has allowed Kaua'i to play a role in more than 50 movies and full-length television features. *Jurassic Park, Uncommon Valor, Flight of the Intruder, Raiders of the Lost Ark, Blue Hawaii, Outbreak, King Kong* and *South Pacific* are only a few. More recently, Disney's *George of The Jungle* and the sequel to *Jurassic Park, The Lost World,* were partially filmed on Kaua'i. You may have noticed in the original *Jurassic Park* that when they showed an island map it was even shaped like the island.

The selection of Kaua'i for the location may be more than coincidence as the author of *Jurassic Park*, Michael Crichton, resides at least part of the year on the North Shore of the island! For more information on Kaua'i in the movies check the RECREATION & TOURS section. We have a complete list of films shot on the island and information on a Movie Tour.

While visiting the Hawaiian islands, you may never see some of the native species of birds and plant life. Most of the remaining endangered native species can now only be found in protected areas. The more aggressive species that have been introduced over the past centuries have encroached on these fragile native ones and many endemic varieties have become extinct. Several refuges and botanical gardens on Kaua'i offer the visitor the rare opportunity to see these species at close proximity. See *Garden Tours* in the Recreation Chapter.

The Hawaiian State Flag was designed for King Kamehameha I in the first part of the nineteenth century. The British Union Jack in the corner acknowledges the early ties the islands had with England. The eight horizontal stripes of red, white and blue signify the eight major islands in the Hawaiian chain. King Kalakaua composed the state's national anthem, "Hawai'i Pono i".

A history of Kaua'i cannot be complete without a discussion of the *Menehune*, which were alluded to previously. An early account in the logs of Captain Cook tells of a people he found in Hawai'i that were smaller in stature and lighter skintoned than most other Hawaiians. He described them as being a servant class. But are the menehune the stuff of myth or fact? The folklore says that the Menehune would work at night, creating vast projects such as the Menehune (or Alekoko) Fishpond, (still seen today, located off Nawiliwili Road) and the Menehune Ditches. Among the speculated theories, perhaps the most probable is that the

Menehune were people from Tahiti who called themselves Manahune. In earlier times, while still in Tahiti, they had been conquered by warriors from the nearby island of Raiatea. It was theorized that the term Manahune might mean "conquered people" and thus could be construed to mean that they were lower in the social order rather than smaller in size. A census conducted in the early part of the nineteenth century showed that there were 65 Menehune living in the Wainiha Valley. Archaeologically, there have never been any bones that indicate a dwarf population was ever present on Kaua'i. While the Menehune are a part of island storytelling throughout the Hawaiian chain, they seem to have their roots on Kaua'i. If something goes wrong, you can blame it on the Menehune! So, if you lay down your sunglasses for just a minute, and discover them in the next room a little later, you can figure that the *Menehune* must have been up to their mischief. If something is unexplainable, then it probably was the Menehune. Whatever the facts, the legends of the Menehune are colorful and add to the richness of the island's folklore.

There are a number of good books that will cover the history of the island and its people. The bibliography lists a number of resources still in print. Other books with good general historical background on all the islands are *Hawaii, the Islands of Life* and *Shoal of Time* by Gavan Daws, *Hawaiians: An Island People,* by Helen Pratt, and *Modern Hawaiian History,* by Ann Rayson.

HISTORY OF NI'IHAU

Ni'ihau, located 17 miles west of Kaua'i, continues to be Hawai'i's only privately owned island and visitation is allowed only by arranged hunting and fishing excursions via Ni'ihau Safaris and Helicopters (see Tours & Activities and Ni'ihau section). The island of Ni'ihau is slightly more than 47,000 acres with dimensions of 18 miles by 6 miles. The highest elevation is 1,281 feet at Paniau. Lake Halali'i is 841 acres and although the largest inland lake in Hawai'i, it is more a salt flat that only becomes a lake (with a depth of five or six feet) during heavy rains. Mullet are raised in the lake until the waters recede, then they are caught and sent to market.

The contemporary human history of the island of Ni'ihau began when Mrs. Eliza McHutchenson Sinclair, a widow, relocated from New Zealand. Although she considered the purchase of a piece of beachfront property on O'ahu (which we now know as Waikiki) in 1863, she visited the island of Ni'ihau following a brief rainy spell and found it quite to her liking. She purchased the 46,000 acre parcel from King Kamehameha IV for the price of $10,000 on January 20, 1864. It was not until later that she discovered Ni'ihau suffers from a serious shortage of water, which continues to this day. Eliza Sinclair enjoyed only three long and hot summers on her new island before purchasing land on the western side of Kaua'i in Makaweli. Additional acreage was purchased in Hanapepe and this formed the bulk of the land used by the Gay & Robinson sugar plantation. Abrey Robinson inherited control of the family estate when Eliza died in 1893 at the age of 92. Abrey, born in 1853 in New Zealand, studied law at Boston University before returning to Kaua'i. He implemented some plans to improve the island by undertaking reforestation, initiating irrigation systems, and introduced to the island Arabian horses, cotton and honey.

In 1898 Hawai'i became a territory of the United States and Abrey began limiting outside influences and also began raising cattle and sheep. While crops proved difficult due to the arid climate, they have found that kiawe charcoal is a product they can produce.

It was not only O'ahu that got involved in the opening of World War II. Ni'ihau played a role in the drama as well. Following the attack on Pearl Harbor, a lone Japanese pilot encountering engine failure was forced to ditch at Ni'ihau (nearly landing on an outhouse). The pilot was captured by the Ni'ihauans and resident Howard Hawila Kaleohano seized the documents he was carrying. Later these papers would assist in the breaking of the Japanese communication code. While five men made the trip across the channel to Kaua'i for help, the prisoner apparently managed an escape, taking his machine guns with him. The spunky Ni'ihau residents, however, had become fed up with this intruder's poor manners and overpowered him. One island resident, Benjamin Kanahele, was shot three as times as he tried to convince the pilot to act more civilized. Following the hit by a third bullet, Benjamin became so angry that he promptly grabbed the pilot and threw him against the wall with such force that the pilot was killed.

At the time of Cook's visit, the population may have numbered as many as 10,000 individuals. By the time of the Sinclair purchase, the island had a population of 1,008. Dogs were raised by the Ni'ihauans for food and the Sinclairs ordered the destruction of all the canines to safeguard the new herds of sheep and cattle. More than 700 *kanakas* (people) left the island rather than destroy their dogs. The island population currently numbers in the neighborhood of 230 persons, 95% of whom are descendants of the Robinson Family (whose matriarch was Eliza Sinclair), speaking Hawaiian and maintaining the customs of old Hawaii. The island offers one paved road, no telephones and power is limited to that supplied by a generator. There are a few cars and transportation is mostly provided by donkeys and horses. The town of Pu'uwai is where the local residents live.

Today the island continues to be a working cattle and sheep ranch and has become famous for its beautiful shell necklaces. Made from very small shells collected on the island's beaches, the colored strands range in speckled hues from yellow to blue or white. The necklaces are very intricate and it may take hundreds of shells to find one or two that are in perfect condition. The price of these necklaces range from hundreds to thousands of dollars. Look for them on display at gift and jewelry stores and appreciate the craftsmanship of these fine pieces of Hawaiian art.

For more information on this remote island, an excellent resource is *Ni'ihau: The Traditions of an Hawaiian Island* by Reriorterai Tava and Moses K. Keale, Sr. Published in 1989, it is an outstanding account of the history of the island and its people from ancient to modern times.

KAUA'I NAMES AND PLACES

AHUKINI - altar (for) many (blessings)

ALAKA'I - to lead

'ELE'ELE - black

HA'ENA - red hot

HANAKAPI'AI - bay sprinkling food

HANALEI - crescent bay

HANAPEPE - crushed bay (due to landslides)

HA'UPU - recollection

KAHANA - cutting

KA-HOLUA MANU - the sled course (of) Manu

KA-LA-HEO - the proud day

KA-LALAU - the straying

KA-LAMA - the torch

KA-LIHI KAI - seaward Kalihi (the edge)

KA'LIHI WAI - water Kalihi

KANAKA-NUNUI-MOE - sleeping giant

KA-ULA-KAHI - the single flame (streak of color)

KA-UMU-ALI'I - the royal oven

KA-WAI-KINI - multitudinous water

KA-WAI-HAU - literally this translates to ice water. (Apparently the name denotes a reference to an American missionary lady who drank only ice water.)

KE-KAHA - the place

KIKI A OLA - container (acquired) by Ola

KI-LAU-EA - spewing, much spreading (referring to volcanic eruptions)

KILOHANA - lookout point or best, superior

KOKE'E - to bend or to wind

KOLOA - place of long cane, the word "ko" means sweet sugar cane grass. Another source says it was named for the steep rock formation called "Pali-o-koloa."

KO'OLAU - windward

LIHU'E - cold child

MANA - arid

MILO-LI'I - fine twist (as sennit cord)

NA-MOLO-KAMA - the interweaving bound fast

NA'PALI - the cliffs (This is one word, not two!)

NA-WILIWILI - the wiliwili trees

NIU-MALU - shade (of) coconut trees

NOUNOU - throwing

PO'IPU - completely overcast or crashing (as waves)

POLI-'AHU - garment (for the) bosom (referring to snow)

POLI-HALE - house bosom

PRINCEVILLE - no Hawaiian translation, this area was named for the young Prince of King Kamehameha IV and his wife, Queen Emma. They visited the North Shore of Kaua'i in 1860 with their son Prince Ka Haku o Hawai'i. Plantation owner Robert Wyllie selected this name in honor of the young prince.

PUHI - blow

PU'U KA PELE - the volcano hill

WAI'ALE'ALE - rippling water or overflowing water

WAI-LUA - two waters

WAI-PAHE'E - slippery water

For more information on Hawaiian place names consult *Place Names of Hawai'i* by Mary Kawena Pukui, Samuel H. Elbert and Esther T. Mookini.

ISLAND FACTS AND FIGURES

Collectively, the islands are known as Hawai'i, the name coming from the largest island in the chain, also Hawai'i, or Hawai'i Island, and known locally as the "Big Island" due to its size (larger than all the other islands combined). The name Hawai'i was also given to the entire group after King Kamehameha the Great, of Hawai'i Island, unified the islands under one kingdom. Thus, the islands came to be known simply as "Hawai'i." It does make for a bit of confusion, especially for first-time visitors. The islands as an entity have a nickname, state flower, bird, mammal, tree, and fish. However, each individual island also has its own unique identity. Here is a little background on each.

HAWAI'I OR THE HAWAIIAN ISLANDS

Nickname: The Aloha State
State Flower: Hibiscus
State Tree: Kukui
State Bird: Nene Goose
State Fish: Humuhumunukunukuapua'a
State Mammal: The Humpback Whale
State Capital: Honolulu

KAUA'I

Nickname: The Garden Island
Island color: Purple
Flower: Mokihana (fragrant berry)
County Seat: Lihu'e
Area: 550 sq. miles
Length: 33 miles; Width: 25 miles
Coastline: 90 miles
Highest point: 5,243 ft. Kawaikiki

O'AHU

Nickname: The Gathering Place
Island color: yellow/gold
Flower: Ilima
County Seat: Honolulu
Area: 595 sq. miles
Length: 44 miles; Width: 30 miles
Coastline: 112 miles
Highest point: 4,003 feet at the top of Ka'ala Peak

NI'IHAU

Nickmane: The Forbidden Island
Island color: white or brown
"Flower:" Pupu Shell
Main Town: Pu'uwai
Area 73 sq. miles
Lenght 14 miles; Width 16 miles
Coastline: 40 miles
Population: 250
Highest point: 1,281 feet at Paniau

MAUI

Nickname: The Valley Isle
Island Color: Pink
Flower: Lokelani (cottage rose)
County Seat: Wailuku
Area: 729 sq. miles
Length: 48 miles
Width: 26 miles
Coastline: 40 miles
Highest point: 10,023 ft. Haleakala

KAHO'OLAWE

Nickname: Lonely Island
Island Color: Gray
Flower: Hinahina
Area: 45 sq. miles
Length: 6 miles
Width: 10 miles
Coastline: 20 miles
Population: currently only goats
Highest point: 1,477 ft. Moa'ulanui

MOLOKA'I

Nickname: Friendly Island
Island Color: Green
Flower: White Kukui Blossom
Main Town: Kaunakakai
Area: 260 sq. miles
Length: 38 miles
Width: 10 miles
Coastline: 88 miles
Highest point: 4,961 ft. Kamakou

LANA'I

Island Color: Orange/gold
Flower: Kaunaoa
Main Town: Lana'i City
Area: 140 sq. miles
Length: 18 miles
Width: 13 miles
Coastline: 47 miles
Highest point: 3,366 ft. Lana'ihale

HAWAI'I

Nickname: The Big Island, also the Volcano Isle and the Orchid Isle
Island color: Red
Flower: Red Lehua
(flower of the Goddess Pele)
County Seat: Hilo
Area: 4,038 sq. miles
Length: 93 miles
Width: 76 miles
Coastline: 266 miles
Highest point: 13,796 ft. at the peak of Mauna Kea

LOIH'I

This is the site of the most recent underwater lava building in the islands.
Located over the "hot spot" off the east coast of the Big Island of Hawai'i. It
is continuing to grow and not expected to emerge for several thousand of
years.

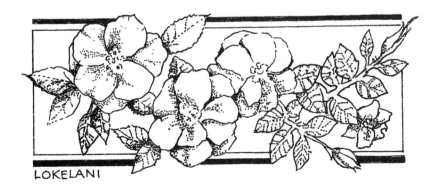

LOKELANI

The Hawaiian language was first written down by American missionaries. Using the written language they created an alphabet with only twelve letters, five of which are vowels. The key to the language is to remember to pronounce each letter, except for some vowels which run together as one. In some cases, substitute the "v" sound when "w" appears. The - ' - symbol you see is a glottal stop and instructs you to say each letter separately (such as *ali'i*). Also, pick up a copy of *Instant Hawaiian*, this small handy guide will have you speaking like a *kama'aina* in no time!

Following are some of the more commonly used Hawaiian words that you may hear:

HAWAIIAN WORDS AND THEIR MEANINGS

ali'i (ah-lee-ee) chief
aloha (ah-loh-hah) greetings
hale (Hah-lay) house
hana (HA-nah) work
hana hou (ha-nah HO) to do it again
Heiau (heh-ee-ah-oo) temple
haole (how-lee) a caucasian
kai (kye) ocean
kahuna (kah-HOO-nah) teacher, priest
Kama'aina (Kah-mah-ai-nuh) native born
kane (kah-nay) man
kapu (kah-poo) keep out
keiki (kayee-kee) child
lanai (lah-nah-ee) porch or patio
lomi lomi (loh-mee-LOH-mee) to rub or massage
luau (loo-ah-oo) feast
makai (mah-kah-ee) toward the ocean
malihini (mah-lee-hee-nee) a newcomer or visitor
mauka (mah-oo-kah) toward the mountain
mauna (MAU-nah) mountain
mele (MAY-leh) Hawaiian song or chant
menehune (may-nay-hoo-nee) Hawaiian dwarf or elf
moana (moh-ah-nah) ocean
nani (NAH-nee) beautiful
ono (oh-no) delicious
pali (PAH-lee) cliff, precipice
paniolo (pah-nee-ou-loh) Hawaiian cowboy
pau (pow) finished
poi (poy) a paste made from the taro root
pua (POO-ah) flower
puka (POO-ka) a hole
pupus (poo-poos) appetizers
wahine (wah-hee-nay) woman
wiki wiki (wee-kee wee-kee) hurry

WHAT TO PACK

When traveling to paradise, you won't need too much. Comfortable shoes are important for all the sightseeing. Sandals are the norm for footwear, although with periods of heavy rains, some close toed shoes might be recommended. Dress is casual for dining, although a few restaurants require men to wear sport shirts with collars. Clothes should be lightweight and easy care. Cotton and cotton blends are more comfortable for the tropical climate than polyesters. Shorts and bathing suits are the dress code here! A lightweight jacket with a hood or sweater is advisable for evenings and the occasional rain showers, especially on the North Shore! If you are headed for a stay on the North Shore (particularly in the winter months) we've found it advantageous to throw in a pair of slacks and a sweater or sweatshirt. The only need for warmer clothes is if your plans should include hiking at higher elevations or visiting the Koke'e area. Tennis shoes or hiking shoes are a good idea for longer hikes.

Sunscreens are a must and we recommend you toss in a bottle of insect repellent. A camera, of course, needs to be tucked in and perhaps your video camera. A hat with a brim is a good idea for protecting the head and neck from the sun while touring or just sitting on a beach. Binoculars are an option and may be well used if you are traveling between December and May when the whales arrive for their winter vacation, or used to enjoy the incredible sea and land birds found on the Garden Isle. Special needs for traveling with children are discussed in the next section. Anything that you need can probably be purchased once you arrive. Don't forget to leave room in those suitcases for goodies that you will want to take home!

TRAVELING WITH CHILDREN

Traveling with children can be an exhausting experience for parents and children alike, especially when the trip is as long as the one to Kaua'i. Unfortunately, there are currently no direct flights from the mainland to Kaua'i. Your trip to the island includes a stop on O'ahu and a transfer to one of the outer island airlines.

Packing a child's goody bag for the long flight is a must. A few new activity books or toys that can be pulled out enroute can be sanity-saving. Snacks (boxes of juice are a favorite with younger children) can tide over the little ones at the airport or on the plane while awaiting your food/drink service. The new squeeze-it juice drinks are also very portable and can be frozen in their plastic bottle, providing a cool drink when the need arises. A thermos with a drinking spout works well and is handy for use during vacations. A change of clothes and a swim suit for the little ones can be tucked into your carry-on bag. (Suitcases have been known to be lost or delayed.) Another handy addition is a small night light, as unfamiliar accommodations can be somewhat confusing for little ones during the bedtime hours. Disposable diapers are a real travel convenience, but are very expensive in the islands. You might wish to fill up any extra space in that suitcase with these! And don't forget a strong sunscreen!

Children may have difficulty clearing their ears when landing. Many don't realize that cabins are pressurized to approximately the 6,000 foot level during flight. To help relieve the pressure of descent, have infants nurse or drink from a bottle, and older children may benefit from chewing gum. If this is a concern of yours, consult with your pediatrician about the use of a decongestant prior to descent.

CAR SEATS: By law, children 3-4 years of age must have seat belts unless they are in a federally approved car seat. Federally approved car seats are required for all children from birth up to three years.

While some rental agencies do have car seats for rent, you need to request them well in advance as they have a limited number. Many rental car seats have probably seen better days, and sometimes they are not the most up-to-date design and maybe only marginal for child safety. Prices run about $5-15 per day. You might be better off to bring your own. Several styles are permitted by the airlines for use in flight, or it may be checked as a piece of baggage.

BABYSITTING: There are no full-time childcare services on Kaua'i. Arrangements for childcare can be made through your hotel concierge and the front desk at most condominiums will be able to assist you. Service is expensive and will run you about $10 per hour. As you can easily figure from the rates, spending much time away from your children can be costly. Consider the feasibility of bringing your own sitter, it may actually be less expensive, and certainly much more convenient. It could be an option that could work well for you. Grandmothers work well too!

CRIBS: Many condominiums and most hotels will be able to provide you with a rental crib. Prices run about $5 per day, $30 per week. There are many portable, cribs that can be packed into a large duffle bag. They weigh under 20 pounds and can be purchased for about the same price as a 10-day rental.

Ready Rentals, PO Box 508, Koloa, HI 96756, (808) 823-8008 or toll free 1-800-599-8008 has cribs, car seats, high chairs, strollers and more for rent on a daily or weekly basis. They offer Jerri Zoomer strollers and even twin baby strollers. They can also be reached on email: readyrentals@aloha.net; Web: <www.readyrentals.com>

FOR EMERGENCIES: See listing under HELPFUL INFORMATION in this chapter.

DINING: You'll soon discover, if you have not already, in the restaurant /dining out section of this book that a children's menu is often referred to as a "Keiki Menu." A few restaurants that offer menus (or child-size portions) for the young traveler include: Barbecue Inn, Whalers Brewpub, Buzz's Steak & Lobster, Duke's Canoe Club, Gaylord's, Bali Hai, JR's Plantation, Oki Diner, Kountry Kitchen, Chuck's Steak House, Keoki's Paradise, Wailua Family Restaurant, Waipouli Deli, and The Bull Shed. You can get a "Kitten's Menu" at TomKat's; feed the "Little Cowboys" at JR's Plantation; or ask for the "Menehune Menu" at any of the Camp House Grill locations. A Pacific Cafe and The Beach House will serve any item on their menu at half size for half price. And kids (under 12) eat free at the Kuhio Dining Court at the Holiday Inn SunSpree Resort! Be sure to ask for children's menus or prices wherever you dine.

BEACHES - POOLS: A precaution on the beach that is often neglected is the application of a good sunscreen -- always reapply after swimming! It is easy to forget that in the cool pool or ocean, you are still getting those strong rays of sun.

There is a natural kiddie wading pool at Po'ipu Beach Park that is ideal for toddlers and very young swimmers. The handy nearby access to bathrooms can be a plus for the traveling family, too! To the west of Po'ipu Beach is a small protected cove known as Baby Beach. This can be accessed from Spouting Horn Road to Ho'ome Road. Good swimming locations for the younger set might also be found at Lydgate Beach Park and at Salt Pond Beach Park. At both locations you'll find an ocean pool made from boulders. Kids will love exploring a variety of sea creatures found in the tidepools here and at 'Anini Beach. Several beaches do have lifeguards on duty. Unfortunately, many people underestimate the power of the ocean and drownings occur far too often on Kaua'i. Beaches are generally not posted with flags (as on some other islands) if the surf is creating conditions which are unsafe. Most beaches only have a generic warning sign posted. If the surf is up, choose a different activity that day, or just enjoy a picnic on the beach. Some beaches are fine for children in the summer, but are definitely NOT an option during the higher surf of winter.

The Kamalani playground at Lydgate Beach Park will give your lively young ones a chance to expend some of their energy. The park's volcano slide, tree-house, spider web rope ladder, tire swings, and caves were designed especially with active 6-10 year olds in mind! Another wonderful new playground is the park at the entrance to the Princeville Resort on the North Shore.

Few resorts have pools with the very young traveler in mind. The Point, a south shore condominium, has a toddler pool. The Radisson Kaua'i Beach has a keiki pool along with a new pool and artifical beach area. The Kaua'i Coast Resort at the Beachboy also has a keiki pool. We recommend taking a life jacket or water wings (floaties). Packing a small inflatable pool for use on your lanai or court-yard may provide a cool and safe retreat for your little one. Typically resorts and hotels DO NOT offer lifeguard services.

CHILDCARE PROGRAMS: Some hotels and resorts offer season children's and youth programs. Most are offered only during spring, summer, and Christmas-New Year's holidays. A few are available year round. Generally, only resort guests can partake of these childcare programs, however, sometimes they are open to non-hotel guests.

Holiday Inn Sunspree Resort Kaua'i has various activities offered when the hotel is full (free) in their Children's Activity Center. (808) 823-6000.

Aston Hotels & Resorts on Kaua'i offer various children's activities seasonally. For details, inquire when making reservations at any Aston property or call 1-800-321-2558.

The Hyatt Regency Kaua'i Resort & Spa's daily Camp Hyatt program offers children 3 through 12 the opportunity to have fun while learning about island life. The Camp's learning adventures -- covering such topics as archaeology, Hawaiian crafts, local history and ecological preservation -- are part of the resort's overall commitment to responsible tourism development for Kaua'i. In addition to its learning adventure program, the regular Camp Hyatt schedule includes a variety of activities including cruising down the 150-foot waterslide, face painting, tennis and Hawaiian arts and crafts like seashell sculpture, sand crafts, shell bracelets, Hawaiian leaf stencil painting, and more. Camp Hyatt is available seven days a week to resort guests ages 3-12. Children under three may attend when accompanied by a babysitter. Camp hours are from 9am to 4pm. The cost of $45 per child includes lunch and a Camp Hyatt t-shirt, in addition to all the supervised activities. (Half day sessions are also available.) There is a ratio of one counselor for every four children, or one for every two children between the ages of 3 and 5. Exclusive Camp Hyatt programs can be arranged for groups staying at the resort. (Kinda makes you want to be a kid again, huh?) Night Camp is available from 4-10pm daily, providing children 3-12 years with a variety of supervised activities including games, Hawaiian crafts and computer and video games. The cost for Night Camp is $10 per child.

There are also special Holiday Activities for children during the Christmas season, Easter and Halloween. Easter Sunday is the only day of the year that Camp Hyatt is closed. Instead, children are invited to take part in the annual Easter Egg Parade which winds its way through the resort groups and ends with an Easter Egg Hunt and Festival. For Halloween, Camp Hyatt kids are assisted in making their own special costumes then taken on a trick-or-treat excursion through the various hotel departments. During the summer season, the resort hosts complimentary Family Fun Theater Nights on Wednesdays in the Alii Gardens. The event offers popular movies that were filmed on Kaua'i along with popcorn and soft drinks. Rock Club Just for Teens is held during the summer season. It offers a "cool" activity room where teens can gather to socialize. Offered daily from 11:30am until 7 pm, Rock Club offers a variety of unsupervised teen-oriented activities such as music videos, ping-pong, darts, as well as popcorn and other munchies. The Rock Club is complimentary to teens 13 to 17 years. (808) 742-1234.

The Kiahuna Keiki Klub at the **Kiahuna Plantation** is for registered resort guests and is offered Monday through Friday 9 am until 3 pm. It is offered during the summer as well as during spring and winter breaks. Kids are exposed to the Hawaiian culture through activities like lei making, 'ukulele lessons, hula dancing, and story telling. Other activities include beach walks, lagoon fishing and arts & crafts. Activities are based on the age level of the children participating. Cost is $15 per child for half day session, $30 for full day. (808) 742-5411.

Kaua'i Marriott Resort and Beach Club features a program for 5-12 year olds called Kalapaki Kids. Provided for hotel guests only, activities include boogie boarding, hula, traditional Hawaiian games, crafts or making ice cream sundaes! The program is available year round. Rates run $25 (9-11:30am) $30 (11:30am-3pm) or $45 for the full day. Pass per child runs: Three day $120, five day $190, seven day $252. (808) 245-5050.

Radisson Kaua'i Beach Resort's Keiki Klub is summer fun for children 5-12 years of age. Activities include beach combing, ukulele lessons, movie, pool play, Hawaiian face painting, swan/duck feeding, fishing derbies. Also included are excursions to Smith's Tropical Paradise and Fern Grotto! Full day program 8:30am-3:30pm is $30. Also available are 8:30am-11:30am (without lunch) $15, 8:30am-12:30pm with lunch $20.00, 12:30pm-3:30pm without lunch $15, 12:30pm-3:30pm with lunch $20. (808) 245-1955.

The **Princeville Hotel's** Keiki Aloha program is available for children ages 5-12 years of age and is designed with play in mind. Qualified youth counselors plan a full schedule of activities including snorkeling/beach play, sandcastle creations, Hawaiian arts & crafs, shell collecting and more. The program runs year round, but is closed Sundays. Charges other than summer are $50 for full day for the first child, $40 each additional child. Does not include lunch. $10 per hour for one child and $1 for each additional child from the same family for childcare. Call for latest rates. (808) 826-9644.

Sheraton Kaua'i Resort entertains young guests with their Keiki Aloha Children's Program. Activities range from lei making and other Hawaiian arts & crafts to kite flying and ukulele lessons. The program is available year round. Price is $45 for a full day of play, $25 for half day. (808) 742-4016.

SHOPPING: The Coconut MarketPlace is one of the best all around family malls on Kaua'i. Lots of small shops ensure that there will be something for every member of the family. While mom visits the art galleries, fashion and jewelry stores, the younger members will enjoy the Gecko Store or the Islander Trading Co. to see the parrots. You'll find mother-daughter outfits at Made for Mom & Me -- or match with your pets at Sweet Blossoms & Gypsy's Pet Corner! If everyone wants something different for lunch, it shouldn't be a problem. There's Kaua'i Aloha Pizza, Taco Dude, the Fish Hut, or Eggbert's, just to name a few. MarketPlace phone (808) 822-3641. On the North Shore, pull off the road at Kilauea and stop in at the Little Grass Hut next to Mango Mama's. Unique gifts and whimsical toys along with "Baskets of Aloha" are sold to benefit the Na Kamalei School. At Princeville Center, there's the Kaua'i Kite and Hobby Company, and in Hanalei visit Rainbow Ducks, Toys, and Clothing.

MOVIE THEATERS: The twin Coconut MarketPlace Cinemas adjoin the shopping center and offer bargain matinees before 6 pm. Recording (808) 822-2324. For information (808) 821-2402.

Kukui Grove Cinemas has four screens in their theater which is across the street from the Kukui Grove Shopping Center. Phone (808) 245-5055 to hear a recording.

Waimea Theater has first-run films. For showtimes and information call (808) 338-0282.

OTHER ACTIVITIES WITH KIDS: The Kaua'i Children's Discovery Museum offers island-wide exhibitions, events, and programs in science, culture, arts, and nature. Science on the Move (November-February); StarNight Planetarium (June-August); Coral Reef Kids Camp (July-August) For more information on what and where call them at (808) 823-8222.

Storybook Theatre of Hawai'i involves children in good storytelling activities and invites them to watch the filming of Cablevision's *Russell the Rooster Show,* weekdays at 6 am and 3 pm, weekends at 8am. Call or FAX (808) 335-0712. A multi-media center is being developed in Hanalei. A long way from being finished, they are the producers of this cablevision kids show. Their long-term goal is to have a center where youth will do all aspects of the television production, from script writing to behind the camera stuff. Awesome goals!

Older children will enjoy a luau. The Kaua'i Coconut Beach has a program which offers a free luau for each child with a full-paying accompanying adult on several evenings each week. Call (808) 822-3455 for current schedule.

The free hula show at the Coconut MarketPlace (currently Mon, Thurs & Sat at 5 pm) often features child performers. The younger children in your traveling family might enjoy this casual, outdoor performance.

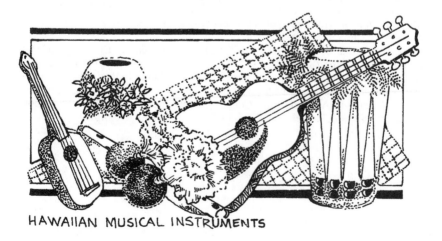

HAWAIIAN MUSICAL INSTRUMENTS

You'll find a Fun Factory game arcade at the Waipouli Town Center next to Foodland. They are open Monday-Thursday, 10 am-10 pm, Friday & Saturday till midnight.

Visiting Waimea? Take time to stop at Darri's Delites for shave ice, pastries, popcorn, and even better is their full service crackseed. (This Asian treat is actually a form of flavored and dried fruit with the pit still in it.) Located at 4492 Moana Rd. along Kaumuali'i Highway. (808) 338-0113.

Paradise Fun is an air-conditioned, indoor play facility for children ages 6 months and up. Now located in their new larger facilities at the Kukui Grove Shopping Center, they offer a snack bar, video arcade, big screen tv, and soft playground. All children must be accompanied by an adult 18 or older unless you take advantage of their drop-off while you shop childcare! Hours of operation: 9:30am-6 pm, till 9 on weekends. Admission from $2.50-6.95 depending on age. A great place to go on a rainy day! Phone (808) 241-7050.

Joe-Jo's Clubhouse at 9734 Kaumaulii Hwy. in Waimea is a small store, but fun and festive. A good place to take the kids after the scenic wonders of Waimea Canyon. Joe-Jo's has balloons plus nachos, hot dogs, pizza pockets, saimin, cookies, and shaved ice with over 60 flavors. Open 10 am-6 pm daily. (808) 338-0056.

Borders Bookstore in the Kukui Grove Shopping Center has thoughtfully created a play corner. They also have a children's book section and a large Hawaiian book section. They schedule events, from storytelling to clown visits. And it's all free!

Keiki Adventures Kaua'i specializes in guided Eco Tours for kids! Hiking, swimming, snorkel tours, exploring dry caves and ancient Hawaiian ruins are just a few of the activities that include healthy lunch and snacks, footwear, rain gear, day packs and hiking sticks. 1191 Kuhio Hwy., Kapa'a, HI 96746. Phone or FAX them at (808) 822-7823, or call toll-free 1-800-232-6699.

Lihu'e Lanes is now a completely smoke-free bowling alley. They currently offer daytime specials: $6 Mon-Fri, between noon and 2:30 pm; $10 on Saturdays 3-5 pm. A great idea on a rainy afternoon. They also have a snack bar with a kid friendly menu which includes pizza, burgers and even cinnamon toast! Located in Lihu'e at the Rice Shopping Center. (808) 245-5263.

EXCURSIONS: Hiking, mountain biking, bass fishing at one of the reservoirs, or a horseback tour of the beach and sand dunes, a trip to the Kilauea Lighthouse to view the seabirds, a visit to Spouting Horn or the North Shore's unusual wet and dry caves! Kaua'i abounds with natural beauty that will be enjoyed by the traveler of any age.

Kayaking the Wailua River is a soft-adventure suitable for families. And there is a fairly easy hike to a secluded waterfalls as well. Take a picnic lunch along and explore. Kayaks are available for two, so pair up with one of the kids and enjoy the scenic wonders on one of Kaua'i's navigable rivers. The Wailua River trip is picturesque and affords a chance to hear the "Hawaiian Wedding Song" performed when the tour boats arrive at Fern Grotto. Park your kayak and follow the visitor group to the Ferm Grotto where entertainment is provided. Stay around after the tour boat leaves and enjoy the silent beauty of this unique location. Check *KAYAKING* in the RECREATION & TOURS section of this guide. Older children will also enjoy horseback riding, or trying their skills at boogie boarding at Po'ipu Beach Park next to the kiddie pool.

ESPECIALLY FOR SENIORS

More and more businesses are beginning to offer special savings to seniors. RSVP booking agency offers special rates for seniors who book their accommodations through them. They are listed in the Rental Agents section of our accommodations chapter. Remember that AARP members get many travel discounts for rooms, cars and tours. Whether it is a boating activity, an airline ticket or a condominium, be sure to ask about special senior rates. And be sure to travel with identification showing your birthdate. Check the yellow pages when you arrive on Kaua'i for the senior discount program logo. Look for a black circle with white star in the ads.

The County of Kaua'i, Office of Elderly Affairs at 4444 Rice St. #105, Lihu'e, HI 96766 (808) 241-6400 provides advocacy to elderly persons and their families.

The Lihu'e Chapter of AARP has monthly membership meetings at 1 pm on the second Monday of each month at Lihu'e Neighborhod Center. Call the AARP office at (808) 246-4500 or stop by 4212A Rice St. (look for the sign in back) to pick up brochure information or just to visit and "talk story."

Kaua'i Senior Centers, 4491 Kou Street, Kapa'a, HI 96746. (808) 822-9675. They sponsor centers in Kilauea, Kapa'a (main office), Lihu'e, Koloa, Kalaheo, Kaumakani, Kekaha, Hanapepe, and Waimea. They provide programs including dancing lessons, quilt making and health classes, 8 am-noon.

Many restaurants and hotel dining rooms like Kukui's at the Kaua'i Marriott provide AARP discounts. Just ask about any "senior discounts." And Chuck's Steak House at Princeville offers a senior dinner menu. Jolly Roger has a great $7.95 lunch and dinner menu for seniors while Wailua Family Restaurant offers almost a dozen all-day $9.99 senior dinners (including salad bar!) from 10 am. Kaua'i Coconut Beach has early bird dinner specials in their Flying Lobster restaurant; Holiday Inn SunSpree Resort offers them at The Palms Restaurant in the Kuhio Dining Court. Buzz's Steak & Lobster has a nightly early bird for $8.95 with salad bar and Al & Don's (at the Kaua'i Sands Hotel) offers senior dinners from $5.95.

Love's Bakery at 4100 Rice St. offers senior specials Tuesdays and Fridays. Gaylord's, Kaua'i Coconut Beach, and Princeville all offer senior discounts on their luaus. Just remember to ask about any applicable "senior discount." As they say locally, "No ask, no get!"

Kukui Grove Shopping Center has a gathering place for seniors to enjoy coffee and refreshments, exercise, talk story, do crafts -- they are even putting in computers so you can email the grandkids back home! Call (808) 245-7784 for hours and more information.

The Salvation Army can be a real treasure trove for the adventurous shopper. A muumuu for a couple of dollars is perfect for that luau. Locations in Lihu'e and Hanapepe.

Kaua'i has some interesting annual events for seniors: The Annual Seniors Extravaganza showcases talented seniors (January/Kaua'i War Memorial Convention Hall); rubber ducks race down the Waimea River at the Kaua'i Senior Center's Quacker Race (September/Lucy Wright Park); and First Hawaiian Bank's "Prime Time Health Fair" offers displays, information, and exhibits along with entertainment and bingo (October/Kukui Grove Shopping Center.)

A number of airlines have special discounts for seniors. Some also have a wonderful feature which provides a discount for the traveling companion that is accompanying the senior. Coupon books for senior discounts are also available from a number of airline carriers.

The local Kaua'i Bus also offers discounts for senior citizens.

TRAVEL TIPS FOR THE PHYSICALLY IMPAIRED

Make your travel plans well in advance and inform hotels and airlines when making your reservations that you are a person with a disability. Most facilities will be happy to accommodate. Bring along your medical records in the event of an emergency. It is recommended that you bring your own wheelchair and notify the airlines in advance that you will be transporting it. Other medical equipment rental information is listed below.

Additional information can be obtained from the State Commission on Persons with Disabilities on Kaua'i at 3060 Eiwa St. Room 207, Lihu'e, HI 96766 (808) 274-3308 which can provide general information on accessibility for private and public facilities on Kaua'i. For information on accessibility features and technical assistance regarding access standards contact the Commission on Persons with Disabilities, 919 Ala Moana Blvd. #101, Honolulu, HI 96814. (808) 586-8121 or inter-island toll free 1-800-468-4644. On Kaua'i call the toll free local number, 1-800-274-3141 for a directory of individual extensions.

Travel Tips for the Physically Impaired

Contact Parents with Special Keikis c/o Easter Seal Society of Hawaii, Kauaʻi Service Center 3115 Akahi, Lihuʻe, HI 96766. (808)245-7141. They provide support and education for parents of children with disabilities. Although primarily for community services for residents, another good resource is the Kauaʻi Center for Independent Living. Contact them at 4340 Nawiliwili Road, Lihuʻe at (808) 245-4034.

ARRIVAL AND DEPARTURE: On arrival at the Lihuʻe airport you will find the building easily accessible for mobility impaired persons. Parking areas are located in front of the main terminal for disabled persons. Restrooms with handicapped stalls (male and female) are also found in the main terminal.

TRANSPORTATION: The only public transportation is The Kauaʻi Bus which charges riders $1 per ride. Seniors, students, or disabled with ID are 50¢. A monthly pass for persons with disabilities runs $12.50. Caregivers traveling with eligible individuals will not be charged a fee. All buses are lift equipped. Carry-on baggage is limited to 9" x 14" x 22". Food and drinks are prohibited. As part of their ADA paratransit service, door to door pickups are available for qualified individuals. Reservations must be made 24 hours in advance; ID may be required. Each bus has a destination sign on the front and curb-side of each bus which displays a route number. Schedules are available which show the route the bus travels and the times along that route. Route 100: Kekaha-Koloa-Lihuʻe. Route 200: Lihuʻe-Koloa-Kekaha. (Both have limited service to Koloa; only one stop pre day.) Route 300: Discontinued. Route 400: Hanalei to Lihuʻe. Route 500: Lihuʻe to Hanalei. Route 600: Lihuʻe-Kapahi-Lihʻue. Route 700 circles the Lihuʻe area.

For additional information phone the County Transportation Office at (808) 241-6410 between the hours of 7 am and 5 pm on Monday-Saturday.

ACCOMMODATIONS: Each of the major island hotels offer one or more handicapped rooms including bathroom entries of at least 29" to allow for wheelchairs. Due to the limited number of rooms, reservations should be made well in advance. Information on condominium accessibility is available by calling State Commission on Persons with Disability on Kauaʻi at (808) 274-3308. They publish the "Aloha Guide to Accessibility" available for $3-5 per category section. Gaylord's Restaurant at Kilohana has handicapped access and Victoria Place B&B and Poʻipu B&B Inn are a few of the Bed and Breakfasts that have a handicapped accessible room.

ACTIVITIES: Espirit de Corp Riding Academy has horses trained to handle physically-challenged riders. (808) 822-4688. Ocean Quest Watersports Co. offers diving tours and classes for the "Differently Abled." They advise you to call before you arrive as some paperwork is required for this program. Toll free: 888-401-3483. County of Kauaʻi Parks & Recreation sponsors integrated programs for youngsters with developmental disabilities. (808) 241-6668. ARC of Kauaʻi provides recreational programs for persons with disabilities, transportation provided. (808) 245-4132. Call Easter Seals of Hawaiʻi on Kauaʻi regarding other activities (808) 245-7141.

BEACHES: Lydgate State Park, Hanalei Pavilion Beach Park and Salt Pond Beach Park are the only beach parks which currently are considered to have disabled access, but their facilities may not meet the ADA guidelines for disabled access.

MEDICAL SERVICES AND EQUIPMENT: *American Cancer Society* (808) 245-2942. They provide equipment including walkers, wheelchairs, etc. on loan without charge for home use, with priority to persons with cancer. *Garden Island Oxygen Supplies* (808) 245-1931. They rent, sell and service oxygen tanks and ancillary equipment. *Home Infusion Associates* (808) 245-3787. Rents and sells medical equipment including wheelchairs. *Ready Rentals* (808) 823-8008 or 1-800-599-8008 also offers wheelchair rentals. *Kaua'i Hospice* (808) 245-7277 has hospital beds. *Gammie Home Care* has an outlet in Lihu'e at 3215 Kuhio Hwy, (808) 632-2333. <www.gammie.com> They can provide medical equipment rentals, from walking aides to bathroom accessories or wheelchairs as well as oxygen services. It is again recommended that you contact any of these services well in advance of your arrival.

Accessible Vans of Hawai'i has been renting vans to travelers with disabilities visiting Hawai'i since 1979 and has units available on Kaua'i. These special vans feature lower floors, electric sliding ramps for wheelchair users plus a 4-point safety securement wheelchair tie-down system. The front passenger seat is removable to allow for excellent sightseeing and viewing from the van. Accessible Vans rent by the day, week, month or long term. Deliveries and pickups may be arranged for the Lihu'e Airport or Nawiliwili Harbor as well as hotels, island tours, or even private homes. Accessible Vans of Hawai'i works with the Kaua'i Center for Independent Living to have a local contact and delivery person for their special-needs clients. Rentals of one or two days are $109 per day, 3-4 days is $99 and it drops for longer rentals. Collision damage insurance waiver is $12 daily. Email: avavans@maui.net or their website at <www.accessiblevans.com>. Reservations 1-800-303-3750 or FAX (808) 879-0649.

WEDDINGS & HONEYMOONS

With tropical waterfalls, lush gardens and idyllic beachfront settings, a wedding ceremony on Kaua'i can fulfill all your dreams.

While the requirements are simple, here are a few tips (based on current requirements at time of publication) for making your wedding plans run more smoothly. We advise you to double check the requirements as things change!

Both bride and groom must be over 18 years of age. (16-17 years old with written consent from parents or legal guardians.) Blood tests and birth certificates are not required, but you do need a photo ID to show proof of age such as a driver's license or passport. You do not need proof of citizenship or residence. If either partner has been divorced, the date, county and state of finalization for each divorce must be verbally provided to the licensing agent. If a divorce was finalized within the last 30 days, then a decree must be provided to the licensing agent.

A license must be purchased in person in the state of Hawai'i. The Department of Health can give you names of the licensing agents on the island. You need to make appointments with these licensing agents. Both bride and groom must appear in person before the agent. If you are working with a wedding coordinator service, they will make all the necessary arrangments.

If you have questions, the local registrar on Kaua'i can be contacted at (808) 241-3495. Recording with information (808) 241-3498. The marriage license fee is currently $50 cash, no checks. There is no waiting period once you have the license, but the license is valid for only 30 days and only in the State of Hawai'i.

One wedding agency indicated that your personal vows for a Catholic wedding require special arrangements between your home priest and the Kaua'i priest. If both bride and groom are practicing Catholics, the Church requires that you marry within the church building, unless you are granted special permission from the Bishop in Honolulu.

Check with the Chamber of Commerce on Kaua'i for information regarding a pastor. Many island pastors are very flexible in meeting your needs, such as an outdoor location, etc. For $7 ($8 on a credit card charge) they will mail you a wedding packet the includes a Kaua'i Vacation Planner, list of wedding coordinators, photographers, florists, churches, and a marriage license application. Kaua'i Chamber of Commerce, 4272-B Rice St. or PO Box 1969, Lihu'e, HI 96766. Phone (808) 245-7363, Website: < www.kauaichamber.org >

Appointments must be made with the marriage license agents on Kaua'i. The current list (subject to change):

Kawaihau District: Lynn Kubota (808) 822-5122; Grace Apana or Walter Smith, Jr. (808) 821-6887.

Lihu'e District: Theresa Koki or Annabelle Pacleb (808) 274-3100.

Hanalei District: Dayna Santos (808) 826-7742.

Koloa District: Val Coyaso (808) 332-7076.

For copies of current requirements and to receive necessary forms, write in advance to the State of Hawaii, Department of Health, Marriage License Section, PO Box 3378, Honolulu, HI 96801. (808) 586-4544.

"A Wedding in Paradise" can be found at < www.aweddinginparadise.com > The site offers information on wedding related services and information on unusual and adventurous options. They also have an "estimator" which allows the viewer to calculate expenses.

The Kaua'i Wedding Professionals Association Directory & Bridal Guide is a great source of information. In addition to comprehensive listings and information on all their members, they offer helpful tips on wedding requirements, planning, and photography. For a copy of the booklet, send $3 to KWPA, PO Box 761, Kapa'a, HI 96746. Website: < www.kauaiwedpro.com >

WEDDING BASICS:

The Hyatt Regency Kaua'i, Princeville Resort and other island hotel resorts frequently offer "honeymoon" or "romance" packages. Since these may vary seasonally, inquire directly with the property when making your reservations.

Wedding Chapels:
Aloha Church, Assembly of God, (808) 241-7717

Chapel By the Sea at Kaua'i Lagoons, Lihu'e. Extraordinarily beautiful site, albeit very expensive!! Call (808) 632-0505 and see listing under Wedding Coordinators below.

Koloa Church, founded in 1835, is located at 3269 Po'ipu Rd. Outdoor weddings also available. Write them at PO Box 668, Koloa, HI 96756. (808) 742-9956

Butterflies!!
Butterflies Over Hawaii, 644 Kamalu Rd., Kapa'a, HI 96746. This Kaua'i-based company does the helicopter flower drop one better by releasing from 10 to 100 Hawaiian Monarch butterflies at your wedding or special event. (Released at the moment of pronouncement at your wedding, it symbolizes both your - and their - transformation and new beginnings!) The butterflies are raised in greenhouses

with protective care and their graceful release is a humane and environmental alternative to throwing rice or releasing balloons. The butterflies' survival rate upon release is close to 100%. Prices range from $74.95 to $499.99 for release of 100 butterflies. (808) 823-9408, or call 1-888-BUTRFLI toll free. Email: butrfly@aloha.net Website: <www.butterfly-hawaii.com>

Formal wear rentals:
A Formal Affair, Kapa'a offers tuxedo rentals and wedding formal wear (808) 822-0748. Also for formal wear needs, try Robert's in Lihu'e (808) 246-4653 and in Hanapape 335-5332.

Limousines: Custom Limousine (808) 246-6318; Kaua'i Limousine (808) 245-4855, 1-800-764-7213; Kaua'i North Shore Limousine (808) 826-6189; Town & Country Limousine throughout Hawai'i 1-888-563-2888.

Catering:

Some caterers specialize in wedding catering and arrangements. Check the below and also the CATERING SERVICES in the RESTAURANTS chapter.

Heavenly Creations, custom catering and a personal chef. Special wedding and honeymoon services include a romantic dinner on the beach or a personalized treasure hunt leading to a secluded beach and a champagne picnic or buried treasure of goodies. Phone or FAX (808) 828-1700 or call toll-free 1-877-828-1700. <www.aubergines.com/heaven/>

Contemporary Flavors, (808) 245-2522 at Puhi are wedding specialists, preparing custom catering for all occasions, cake and ice carving, pupus, etc. Web: <gtesupersite.com/contemflavor>

Terrace Restaurant at Kaua'i Lagoons, (808) 241-6010, specializes in weddings and has a variety of set menus available.

Gaylord's at Kilohana, (808) 246-9333, are wedding specialists who can create all the essentials for a perfect wedding experience.

Video tape services:

Hawaiian Creative Video	(808) 822-5784
I DO Video Productions	(808) 823-6130
Video Lynx	(808) 821-1379 or toll free 1-888-310-3038.

Photographers:

Linc Rydell Photography	(808) 822-2520
Rainbow Photography	(808) 828-0555 or toll free 1-888-828-0555.
The Wedding Photographer	(808) 245-2866
Kilohana Studio	(808) 332-9637

WEDDING COORDINATORS:

A professional wedding coordinator can help make your wedding day a memorable event and save you much time and effort in the process. They can handle all the details. A basic wedding package costs anywhere from $250-750. Add a few extras and the price will increase to anywhere from $500-2,000 and up. Although each coordinator varies the package slightly, a basic package will probably include assistance in choosing a location (public or private), getting your marriage license, selecting a minister and a varying assortment of amenities such as champagne, a small cake, or leis. Video taping, witnesses, or music are available for an extra charge. There are a variety of beautiful public facilities at which you may be married. However, wedding companies do have a variety of private locations which may be rented for an additional fee and this can range anywhere from $50-$300. Smith's Tropical Paradise has one of the most affordable. In addition, many hotels and resorts offer comprehensive wedding coordination services.

"Beautiful Seas" wedding packages are available for couples who choose marriage aboard ship in Hawai'i on *American Hawai'i Cruises*. It includes the services of an official to perform the ceremony, a small wedding cake, live Hawaiian music, a flower lei and floral headpiece for the bride and a lei or boutonniere for the groom, champagne and keepsake flutes, photography service and a 24 5X7 photos in a souvenir album. The wedding package price is $750 plus cruise fares. See Weddings & Honeymoons in this chapter for information on tests and licenses. For honeymooners that marry on the Mainland on a Saturday, they don't have to "miss the boat" to enjoy a Hawaiian Islands honeymoon cruise. While the normal departures are on Saturday from Honolulu, the "Sea and Shore" honeymoon enables couples to board the ship in Nawiliwili, Kaua'i. After six days on board ship, the honeymooners will enjoy a seventh night at a Waikiki Hotel. Call 1-800-765-7000.

Aloha Kauai Fantasy Weddings, 3225 Akahi Street, Lihu'e, HI 96766. (808) 245-6500, Fax 823-8488. This coordinator has several different packages with various amenities available. Plumeria is $575; Lotus is $675; Orchid Deluxe is $1900, or $2400 with 7 nights guest house accommodations. Video packages are available. Email: mokihana@hawaiian.net; Web: < www.kauaiweddings.com >

Bali Hai Weddings, PO Box 1723, Kapa'a, HI 96746. (808) 821-2269, fax 822-7379. Toll free 1-800-776-4813. Email: balihai@hawaiian.net; Web: < www.kauai-wedding.com > Contact Marcia Kay Cannon. Add to the Essentials Package ($350) a variety of options including a sunset cruise, photographer, flower arch way, horse and carriage, conch shell ceremony, or limousine from $35-300. Assistance with travel and honeymoon accommodations.

Barefoot Kauai Weddings, PO Box 3185, Princeville, HI 96722.(808) 826-9737, Fax 826-1233; Basic Wedding package $300; Aloha Barefoot $650; Deluxe Barefoot $1140; video packages are extra. Email: clairevk@gte.net; Web: < www.barefootkauaiweddings.com >

Chapel by the Sea at Kaua'i Lagoons, 3351-A Hoolaulea Way, Lihu'e, HI 96766. (808) 632-0505. FAX (808) 632-0303. Toll free 1-800-724-1686; Web: <www.GardenIslandWedding.com> Weddings are scheduled 5 times daily. The use of the chapel, floral arrangements, lei or bouquet, minister and solo musician runs $1,200. Photography packages start at $300, edited video $425. Add a ride in a private white wedding carriage $400 or white limousine $250. Cake and champagne options up to $300.

Coconut Coast Weddings and Photography, PO Box 385, Hanalei, HI 96714. (808) 826-5557. Toll Free 1-800-585-5595. FAX (808) 826-7177. Complete packages with special emphasis on scenic North Shore locations and photography. Barefoot & Basic package $300; Coconut Coast package $825; Hanalei Bay Wedding $1125; Orchid Wedding $1850; Extra add-on amenities and services available at cost. They also offer travel services for wedding & honeymoon packages. E-mail: <cocowed@aloha.net> Website: <www.kauaiwedding.com>

Gaylord's at Kilohana, 3-2087 Kaumuali'i Hwy (mailing address: PO Box 1725, Lihu'e, HI 96766.) (808) 245-1087, FAX (808) 245-7818. A basic wedding package begins at $550 and includes your choice of setting, a non-denominational minister and a one hour use of a wedding carriage. They can arrange for intimate or large receptions. You can also arrange to hold your wedding at their luau, the food and entertainment are already there and so are the "instant" family and friends! Email: gylords@aloha.net or Website: <www.gaylordskauai.com>

Hanalei Colony Resort, PO Box 206, Hanalei, HI 96714. (808) 826-6235, Fax 826-9893, toll free 1-800-628-3004; Email: weddings-events@hcr.com; Web: <www.wedding-in-kauai.com> Various wedding packages available at the beautiful setting on the North Shore. Simple Kauai Wedding $375; Tropical Isle Wedding $750; Wedding in Paradise $1200; Ultimate Wedding in Paradise $1600; various other options and amenities available.

Hyatt Regency Kaua'i, (808) 742-1234, toll free 1-800-633-7313. The Hyatt's wedding department offers extensive wedding services. The wedding coordinator can provide you with a list of "10 Helpful Tips for Getting Married on Kaua'i" to help you plan your wedding before you leave home. They have various wedding and vow renewal packages available. Check with the resort for the latest details.

Island Weddings & Blessings, PO Box 603, Kilauea, HI 96754, (808) 828-1548, FAX (808) 828-1569. Toll free 1-800-998-1548; Email: wedding@aloha.net; Web: <www.travel-kauai.com/islandweddings> A "Simply Special" wedding package begins at $250. Their "Island Romance Package" includes a wedding ceremony, private location, officiant, witness, tropical outdoor location, two leis, and 26 photos or a video for $885. The "Island Memories Package" adds a bouquet, boutonniere, and champagne toast for $985. They offer non-denominational as well as religious ceremonies. Videos and other options available.

Kaua'i Aloha Weddings, 356 Likeke Place, Kapa'a, HI 96746. (808) 822-1477, FAX (808) 822-7067. This Hawaiian owned and operated company offers couples the opportunity of having their marriage performed by ordained ministers in the Hawaiian language. Each ceremony begins with the blowing of the conch shell followed by a special Hawaiian language blessing and lei exchange for the couple. Packages range from $295 to $1,795 for ceremonies which include Hawaiian songs sung to the accompaniment of a slack key guitar and hula dancer. There are basic ceremony packages, plus Fern Grotto, Historic Church, Hawaiian Wedding, and Royal Blue Hawaiian Wedding packages. Check with them for details. Email: haunani@aloha.net; Web: < www.kauaialohawed.com >

Kaua'i Coconut Beach Resort, PO Box 830, Kapa'a, HI 96746. (808) 822-6664, toll free 1-800-760-8555; Email: joniy@hawaiihotels.com; Web: < www.kcb.com >. They offer a variety of wedding packages and have an on-site wedding coordinator, Joni Youn.

Kaua'i Fantasy Weddings, PO Box 3671, Lihu'e, HI 96766. (808) 245-6500. Photo packages or wedding packages available from $375-1,600. Hans Hellriegel has been a photographer for thirty years. He says each wedding is unique and he always falls a little in love with each bride. He has taken wedding couples to the beach, up into the mountains, to a church, with ceremonies held at sunrise, at sunset or during the day.

Kaua'i Marriott Resort & Beach Club, Kalapaki Beach, Lihu'e, HI 96766. (808) 246-5091, Fax 245-2993, toll free 1-800-246-5620; Email: kamika.smith@marriott.com; Web: < www.marriott.com > The Marriott has a variety of wedding packages and services plus on-site wedding coordinators.

Mohala Wedding Services, PO Box 1737, Koloa, HI 96756. (808) 742-8777, 1-800-800-8489, FAX (808) 742-8777. Jona and Jim Clark work as a team to put together your wedding package. Jim is an ordained minister who performs the ceremonies, Jona and her musical partner sing the "Hawaiian Wedding Song." A Japanese garden setting, a beachside wedding, a sunset ceremony on a Kilauea estate on the North Shore with Bali Hai as a back drop or choose a garden *heiau* or gazebo with a waterfall. Packages run $300-1,450. Private locations run slightly more. Other options include cake, flowers, limo or carriage, musicians, tuxedo rental and video as well as a Hawaiian dove-releasing ceremony from $50-365. E-mail: mohala@hawaiian.net or Website: < www.mohala.com >

Princeville Hotel, PO Box 3069, Princeville, HI 96722-3069. (808) 826-2282, 826-2297, Fax 826-2288, toll free 1-800-826-1260. The Wedding & Catering Service handles the various wedding services and packages.

Radisson Kaua'i Beach Resort, 4331 Kaua'i Beach Drive, Lihu'e, HI 96766. (808) 246-5515, Fax 245-3956, toll free 1-888-245-7717; Web: < www.radissonkauai.com > The Radisson has an on-site wedding coordinator and a variety of packages and services available. Check for latest rates and details.

Rainbow Weddings & Celebrations, 6057 Lokomaikai Place, Kapa'a, HI 96746. Tel/fax (808) 822-0944. This coordination service has two wedding packages available. The standard Bali Hai Package is $325. The Paradise Package has additional amenities and services, $725. Email: vows@RainbowWeddings.com; Web: < www.rainbowweddings.com >

Sheraton Kaua'i Resort, 2440 Ho'onani Road, Po'ipu Beach, Koloa, HI 96756. (808) 742-4037, Fax 742-4041. The on-site wedding coordinator, Lynn Sagucio, can assist with a variety of weddings services and packages. The Romance Wedding package is $1225; Premier Wedding package is $1650; the Nature Wedding package is $795. Extra add-ons available. Check with the coordinator for details. Email: lynn_sagucio@sheraton.com; Web: < www.sheraton-kauai.com >

Smith's Tropical Paradise Weddings offers wedding packages in the Fern Grotto and in the Smith's own gardens. Wedding times for the Grotto are currently only 8:30 am, 11:30 am, 4 pm and 5 or 6 pm. As for ceremonies in their gardens, the hours are more flexible. They do not do ceremonies on major holidays. Fern Grotto packages run $575-$925 (with optional video $235-295). They include your own private boat with entertainers, minister, photography, leis, and assorted extras. Wedding packages in the Smith's Tropical Paradise Gardens run $185-$465. They also offer a special candle and torchlight wedding ceremony at 6 pm for $1,075. 174 Wailua Rd., Kapa'a, HI 96746. (808) 821-6887, 821-6888 or FAX (808) 822-4520. Email: smthwedd@aloha.net; Web: < www.hawaiian.net/ ~ zx/smith >

The Vow Exchange, PO Box 1255, Kilauea, HI 96754. Tel/fax (808) 828-0336, toll free 1-800-460-3434; This coordinator has various amenity packages available from $395, $775, $1,100 and up including all arrangements, place of your choice, etc. Check with them for details. Email: vowex@gte.net; Web: < www.vowexchange.com >

Tropical Dream Wedding, PO Box 422, Lawa'i, HI 96765. (808) 322-5664, 1-888-615-5655. FAX (808) 332-0811. They specialize in custom wedding planning and also offer island concierge services, vacation activity planning, and travel arrangements. Wedding packages range from $450-2845 inclusive. There are basic starter packages, and Private, Chruch, Specialty, and Resort packages available. Email: kkkauai@aloha.net or Website: < www.hi50.com/tdw >

Wedding in Paradise, PO Box 1728, Lihu'e, HI 96766. (808) 246-2779, 1-800-733-7431, Fax (808) 246-2676. A basic package with a non-denominational minister and a choice of locations begins at $295. Their average packages run about $680 and include photography, leis, musician, and bouquet. They provide a set of photographs with their brochure which gives a good feeling for their location selections. Wedding sites include Terrace Garden in the Limahuli Valley, Fern Grotto Wedding (basic package $900), Japanese Garden in Kukuiolono or a private white sand beach estate on Pakala Beach. Hosted weddings are $880 and include a wedding coordinator, table with linens, chairs, champagne, beverage and cake. Other options include photography, leis, videography, music and flowers dropped from a helicopter. Email: psi@hawaiian.net; Web: <www.paradiseservices.com>

Weddings on the Beach, PO Box 1377, Koloa HI 96756. Tel/fax (808) 742-7099, 1-800-625-2824. Fern Grotto wedding packages start at $575 or get married at an oceanfront estate for $435. Wedding coordinator Judy Neale offers ocean view or ocean front weddings from $285 and an "Everything" wedding package for $1,100. Or how about an ocean adventure where your wedding site is aboard a 56 ft. sailing trimaran? The two-hour sunset cruise wedding runs $1,400 with flowers, video, photos, toast, and buffet all included on board. Limousine service, video, food and beverages, musicians, flowers, and photography services are available as options. And if you'd like to receive a complimentary 8x10 color print or an extra copy of your original video, just mention this book! Email: judyn@hawaiian.net or Website: <www.weddingsonthebeach.com>

PARTIES & RECEPTIONS

Kilohana offers an assortment of "theme parties" available for business or personal celebrations. A Paniolo Hoedown, a Garden Party, a Murder Mystery, a Kilohana Luau, South Pacific, Polo, Rock Around the Clock, Mad Maxx, or Casino Party are among the possibilities available. For information contact Kilohana, PO Box 3121, Lihu'e, HI 96766. Call (808) 245-5608.

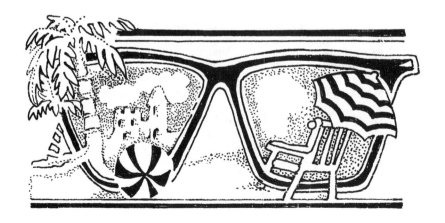

HELPFUL INFORMATION

FREE INFORMATION: Racks located at the shopping areas can provide helpful information and lots of brochures! Some of them have coupons, which (if it was something you were planning on doing anyway) may save you a few dollars.

The Kaua'i Visitors Bureau and the County of Kaua'i have compiled a free *Illustrated Pocket Map* which you can pick up at their Lihu'e office or order by calling their toll-free number (see below.) It is a nicely done island map that gives a lot of in-depth information.

The Chamber of Commerce also has a helpful free map (with "real" streets!) which you can pick up at any Big Save or McDonald's. Or call the Chamber office at (808) 245-7363. The Kaua'i Visitor Information Hotline, begun after Hurricane Iniki to keep visitors apprised of the recovery process, continues its services. This hotline offers live tourism industry updates, directly from Kaua'i. The phones are staffed by local volunteers and the number is good for all the U.S. and in Canada. Phone 1-800-262-1400, 5 am-4 pm daily Hawaiian standard time. (A recording on the weekends.) Or send them your toll free FAX 1-800-637-5762.

COUNTY OF KAUA'I TOURISM SUPPORT: Office of Economic Development, 4444 Rice Street, Lihu'e, HI 96766.
Toll free Visitor Info Hotline 1-800-262-1400, (808) 241-6390, Fax 241-6399; Email: hotline@kauai-hawaii.com; Web: <www.kauai-hawaii.com>

KAUA'I VISITORS BUREAU: 4334 Rice St., Room 101, Lihu'e, Kaua'i, HI 96766 (808) 245-3971, FAX (808) 246-9235. Web: <www.kauaivisitorsbureau.com>

PO'IPU BEACH RESORT ASSOCIATION: PO Box 730, Koloa, HI 96756. (808) 742-7444. FAX (808) 742-7887. They also have a toll-free number 1-888-744-0888. E-mail: <info@poipu-beach.org> or look up their electronic brochure on the internet at <www.poipu-beach.org> The Po'ipu Beach Resort Association provides up to date information on accommodations, activities, dining, shopping, transportation and service in the Po'ipu, Koloa and Kalaheo areas of Kaua'i. Contact them to request a free 36-page guide.

WEST KAUA'I VISITOR & TECHNOLOGY CENTER: 9565 Kaumualii Hwy., Waimea (808) 338-1332. HOURS: Open daily 9am-5pm. Pictorials, graphics, and displays with touch-sensitive screens provide information on all of Kaua'i's activities, not just Waimea.

TELEVISION: We anticipate that you'll be much too busy enjoying the island to do much television viewing. The KVIC station on either channel 3 or channel 18 (depending on your area of the island) will have on-going programs aimed at you, the visitor. It's a guided tour from your room that might offer you a little more insight at something you might not have planned on doing! NOTE: the island's two cable services have combined and are in the process of merging all the stations so they be reached at the same channel throughout the island. In the meantime, the following are channels on basic cable service. Channel numbers may vary according to area on the island and/or changes in cable service. Check the local newspaper TV program listings as well.

2	KHON (FOX)
3	KFVE or KVIC (Visitor Information Channel)
4	KITV (ABC)
5	KFVE (or HBO)
6	Local programs
7	Local Origination (part-time) or QVC
8	KHNL (NBC)
9	KGMB (CBS)
10	PEG (Educational Access)
11	KHET (PBS)
12	PEG (Public Access)
13	Government Access
14	TBS (Turner Broadcasting Systems) or Headline News
15	L/O (Local Origin) or CNN
18	KVIC (Visitor Information Channel) or ESPN
19	Program Guide
20	QVC or The Learning Channel
21	PPV- L/O or The Discovery Channel
22	CSPN or TBS
23	ESPN or E! Entertainment Network
24	TDC (The Discovery Channel)
25	TLC (The Learning Channel)
26	USA
27	CNN
28	CNN-HN (Headline News)
29	AMC (American Movie Classics)
30	MTV (Music Television)
31	VH-1 (Video Hits One)
32	TNN (The Nashville Network) or Nickelodeon
33	COM (Comedy Central) or Lifetime
34	Lifetime or Nashvile Network
35	TNT or MTV
36	NICK (Nickelodeon) or VH-1
37	America's Health or CNBC
38	CNBC or CSPAN
39	Weather Channel or A&E (Arts & Entertainment)
41	E! Entertainment Network or Home & Garden
42	ESPN 2 or AMC

RADIO: KONG at 570AM/93.5FM has the largest signal on the island. They play 80's and 90's adult contemporary as well as Hawaiian and offer local news, surf, weather, and what's happening on Kaua'i. KFMN-97FM also has adult contemporary, but KUAI at 720AM is a bit more eclectic: they play mostly Hawaiian along with adult contemporary, hits from the past, young country and also offer news features, local news and sports. KKCR at 91.9FM is Kaua'i's non-profit community radio. Weekday mornings offer Hawaiian and Slack Key music. Other weekly programs include Vintage Hawaiian Music, Monday evening Sunset Jazz, Saturday "Rocks!" and Sunday morning classic music. Email: kkcr@Hawaiian.net or visit their website at < www.kkcr.org >

EMERGENCIES: The main hospital in Kaua'i is found in Lihu'e. G.N. Wilcox Memorial Hospital is located at 3420 Kuhio Hwy., Lihu'e. Phone (808) 245-1100.

The following provide general out-patient health services to persons requiring health care:

> Kaua'i Medical Clinic (Main Clinic) 3420-B Kuhio Highway, Lihu'e (808) 245-1500
>
> Kaua'i Medical Clinic (Koloa) 5371 Koloa Rd. (808) 742-1621
>
> Kaua'i Medical Clinic (Kilauea) Kilauea & Ola Sts. (808) 828-1418
>
> Kaua'i Medical Clinic (Kapa'a) 4-1105 Kuhio Hwy. (808) 822-3431
>
> Kaua'i Medical Clinic (Ele'ele) 4392 Waialo Road (808) 335-0499

Wilcox Hospital and the above clinics are Kaiser Permanente affiliated providers and now serve Kaiser members. Call 1-800-966-5955 for benefit information.

See the section on Helpful Information for additional numbers. Calling 911 will put you in contact with local fire, police and ambulances.

PERIODICALS: *The Garden Island* newspaper is published six days a week. They can be reached at 3137 Kuhio Hwy., PO Box 231, Lihu'e, HI 96766 (808) 245-3681. Subscriptions are available by mail. The other island newspaper, the *Kaua'i Times*, was purchased in 1995 by *The Garden Island* newspaper. The publication, sort of a two for one arrangement, now includes the *Kaua'i Times* which comes out on Saturday. Subscription runs $15 per month.

The Honolulu Advertiser, PO Box 3110, Honolulu, HI 96802, (808) 525-8000; the Kaua'i Bureau contact is (808) 245-3074. Web: < www.The Honolulu Advertiser.com >

Honolulu Star-Bulletin, 7 Waterfront Plaza, Suite 210, 500 Ala Moana, Honolulu, HI 96813, (808) 529-4700; the Kaua'i Bureau contact is (808) 245-7575. Website: < www.Starbulletin.com >

If you are relocating to the islands, a copy of the Kaua'i *phone book* is a handy resource. Call GTE on Kaua'i at 1-800-888-8448 and they'll drop it in the mail free of charge. (If you have no plans to move, there is a $15 fee for the volume.)

The Chamber of Commerce offers an extensive Relocation Packet which includes the *Kaua'i Data Book* (demographics & statistics), detailed map, and information on businesses, schools, rental management companies, accommodations, auto shipping, and the local newspaper. Send $15 to Kaua'i Chamber of Commerce, Box 1969, Lihu'e, HI 96766 or call (808) 245-7363 to charge to your credit card ($16). Email: kcofc@aloha.net or Website: < www.kauaichamber.org >

101 Things to Do On Kaua'i is available free at stands around the island, or it can be ordered by sending $5 to 101 THINGS, PO Box 388, Lihu'e, HI 96766. Many of the ideas are suggestions for free activities, such as a walking tour of Koloa town or a visit to local *heiau* sites.

Kaua'i Magazine is available at bookstores or magazine stands for a cover price of $5 per copy. This quarterly full-color magazine contains a calendar of events, local columnists, and in-depth articles on Kaua'i's people and places. "Business, Community, and Lifestyle" is the focus of *Inside Kaua'i*, a bi-monthly magazine available for $4 an issue.

As mentioned previously, there are a number of free publications, small magazines or booklets that are available at racks around most visitor areas. Most of these free publications offer lots of advertising. However, they do have coupons which will give you discounts on everything from meals to sporting activities to clothing. It may save you a bit to search through these before making your purchases. We found the *Beach & Activity Guide Kaua'i* to be particularly helpful and informative with a lot of detail and cross referencing! *This Week Kaua'i* and *Kaua'i Gold* are a couple of others worth looking through. *Menu* magazine is a great resource for restaurants that shows actual menus and enticing color photos.

WEBSITES: As the Internet continues to expand, so to do various sources of information on everything Kaua'i. Website addresses are listed where possible throughout the text for those visitor industry businesses having them. But it was impossible to determine whether every related business had an Internet presence or not or to actually locate it if they had one listed. There may be some instances where the code < WWW > is used to indicate that a website exists but that the address was unavailable for a given listing. Either searching the net or calling the business for their website address are two options if you are interested in viewing it. E-mail addresses are also difficult to find. E-mail addresses are included where possible in listings throughout the text. Following are some general websites that might be of interest or provide relevant information. These will have other links to additional sources of information. Please note that the " < " is not part of the URL address, it simply indicates where the address begins and " > " indicates where it ends.

Kaua'i Vacation Planner < www.hshawaii.com/kvp/ > is a good site with activities, feature stories, maps, calendar of events, weddings, shopping, dining and transportation information. The website is part of the larger *Hawai'i State*

Vacation Planner <*www.hshawaii.com*> site. This comprehensive site on the Hawaiian Islands has separate pages highlighting each island. The site is part of <www.BestPlacesHawaii.com> The general information about what to see around Kaua'i is well laid out. Put out by the Kaua'i Visitors Bureau, it's not a complete listing of dining, recreation, and other options but it provides quite a lot of information. While there are a few exceptions, most of the listings are folks that are members of the Kaua'i Visitors Bureau. You can get a free printed version by calling 1-800-262-1400.

Any individual or organization can add to the calendar website of the Hawai'i Visitor and Convention Bureau regardless of whether or not they are a Kaua'i Visitors Bureau or HVCB member. Check out the Hawai'i Visitor and Convention Bureau sites: <www.gohawaii.com> and also at <www.visit.hawaii.org> You can also find general information at the Kauai Visitors Bureau site: <www.kauaivisitorsbureau.com> plus the County of Kaua'i site, "Kaua'i: Hawaii's Island of Discovery" at <www.kauai-hawaii.com>

A very comprehensive and detailed site is Hawaii.com: <www.hawaii.com or www.hawaii.net> Either of these gateways provide much information and many links on general information on living in Hawai'i, visiting Hawai'i, moving to Hawai'i and/or just dreaming about Hawai'i. The visiting Hawai'i section is very detailed. The Alternative-Hawai'i site is also a general information guide covering accommodations, restaurants, things to see and do, and much more: <www.alternative-hawaii.com/index.html>

The Travel Information Network Hawai'i has available the "Kaua'i Travel and Vacation Guide" which provides lots of additional information on visiting Kaua'i, things to do, etc. Check it at: <www.travel-kauai.com>

For information to bed & breakfast lodging try: Ohananet at their website <www.ohananet.com>, as well as Kauai Bed & Breakfast <www.virtual.hawaiian.net/bnb> and Hawaii-Inns <www.hawaii-inns.com>

Some regional destination areas on Kaua'i also have general information websites. For the South Shore and Po'ipu Resort area, try: <www.poipu-beach.org>. For the East Side and Coconut Coast area, try: <www.kauai-hawaii.com/coconut>.

The *Garden Island* newspaper has a new website with abbreviated information of the daily paper. <www.kauaiworld.com> *101 Things to Do on Kaua'i* is a local free publication that can also be accessed at website <www.kauai101.com> The *Hawai'i State Vacation Planner* offers accommodation, restaurant, activity and other listings for the state with individual sections for Kaua'i and the other Hawaiian islands. <www.hshawaii.com> Discover current statistics for Kaua'i at the *Hawai'i State Data Book* at <www.state.hi.us> *Kaua'i Chamber of Commerce* is at <www.kauaichamber.org> *Hawai'i State Government* has a comprehensive website listing with all sorts of information available on the islands. See the site at: <www.hawaii.gov>. For more specific information and data on the visitor industry or business in general, check the Hawai'i State Department of Business, Economic Development and Tourism site at: <www.hawaii.gov/dbedt>

These websites also have Hawai'i information: < www.mele.com > is a site for Hawaiian music. The *Kaua'i Film Commmission* sponsors a site at < www.filmkauai.com > which includes Quicktime Virtual Reality 360 degree shots of some scenic spots on Kaua'i. If you're a displaced former Hawai'i resident, or someone who just needs a fix of something Hawaiian, you may find the site < www.sunjose.com > of interest. This electronic store has a wide product line of Hawaiiana and Hawai'i-related items. They carry everything from jewelry to hats, clothing, Hawaiian print fabrics, books, artwork and even Hawaiian food products to give that special "taste of the islands" in cooking sauces, flavorings, spices, condiments, jams, jellies, macadamia nuts, and even Portuguese sweet bread!

Kaua'i made products and crafts are available on the World Wide Web. *The Kaua'i Products Council* has its site at: < www.kauaiproducts.org > All items featured are from Kaua'i and are handcrafted and produced by local artisans and craftsmen. You can also check on the Calendar of Events page to see what local craft shows, expos, and festivals might be happening.

There are various websites covering Hawai'i and Kaua'i tour operators. *HawaiiVisitor.com* at < www.hawaiivisitor.com > has lots of general information on tours, packages, activities, weddings, and related information. *Globus Tours/Atlas Travel Web* also has general information available at: < www.atlastravelweb.com >. *Haddon Holidays* is one of many companies that offer packages to Hawaii. You can visit their website at < www.haddon.com > *Pleasant Hawaiian Holidays* has a site at < www.2hawaii.com >.

Even if you book through a travel agent, you might be interested in checking airline flight schedules and prices on the internet. With the spread of internet service, you can even book your reservation online directly with the airlines or various booking services:

Air Canada: < www.aircanada.ca >
Aloha Airlines: < www.alohaairlines.com >
American Airlines: < www.aa.com >
America West Airlines: < www.americawest.com >
Canada 3000 Airlines: < www.canada3000.com >
Continental Airlines: < www.continental.com >
Delta Airlines: < www.delta.com >
Hawaiian Airlines: < www.hawaiianair.com >
Northwest Airlines: < www.nwa.com >
United Airlines: < www.ual.com >
TransWorld Airlines: < www.twa.com >

America On-Line has an "Aloha Chat." It happens the second and fourth Wednesday of each month between 9-11pm EST at keyword: Travel Cafe. No commercialism, just people asking questions about and sharing their experiences in Hawaii. It has proven to be a very popular chat site and might be an interesting resource for people to "tap" in and find out answers to questions they have from real people and not companies trying to sell stuff. The catch is you have to be an AOL customer!

SUN SAFETY: The sunshine is stronger in Hawai'i than on the mainland, so a few basic guidelines will ensure that you return home with a tan, not a burn. Usea good lotion (one with a high sunblock number rating) with a sunscreen, reapply after swimming and don't forget the lips! Be sure to moisturize after a day in the sun and wear a hat to protect your face. Exercise self-control and stay out a limited time the first few days, remembering that a gradual tan will last longer. It is best to avoid being out between the hours of noon and three when it is the hottest. Be cautious of overcast days when it is very easy to become burned unknowingly. Don't forget that the ocean acts as a reflector and time spent in it equals time spent on the beach.

FOR YOUR PROTECTION: Do not leave valuables in your car, even in your trunk. Many rental car companies urge you to not lock your car as vandals cause extensive and expensive damage breaking the locks.

ISLAND FAUNA: There are few dangerous land and sea creatures in Hawai'i. And not to be alarmists, it makes common sense to use good judgment. Mosquitos were the gift of a ship called the *Wellington*, which arrived on Maui in 1826. They soon spread to the other islands and can be most irritating in the wetter, forested areas. It is worth packing a bottle of repellent. The only other creepy crawler that is to be avoided is the centipede. Chances are you won't ever encounter one, but should one come out of anywhere, try to avoid it. They spend most of their time undercover. Generally they show up only when the landscape crews are trimming the palm trees or raking yard rubbish and they are disturbed. One groundskeeper noted that if you step on one end they can swing up the other end around your sandal and inflict a sting. If you see one; avoid it, the sting is extremely painful.

LAYSAN ALBATROSS

Hawai'i has no snakes and it is with very serious concern that a snake or two has been seen, caught and destroyed in the islands over the past decade. Great care is taken to ensure that none come to the islands unintentionally as part of ship or airplane cargo and dogs are even trained to sniff them out. The brown tree snake is among the most feared, for on Guam it has virtually destroyed their wild bird population. There is an on-going program to prevent the arrival and introduction of the brown tree snake into Hawai'i.

One of the big problems is the illegal importation--smuggling--of exotic species like snakes, frogs, fish, lizards, birds, etc. into the islands. Over the last several years, under the amnesty program, many species have been surrended voluntarily. Some have been captured in the wild. Such species have included 3-foot long iguanas, a cobra snake, several types of pythons, and even several South American piranha fish. What I'm wondering is, how did the people get these critters into Hawai'i in the first place?

The bufo toad is a very friendly fellow that can be found all around the islands, but generally is more noticed after a heavy rain, or unfortunately flattened on a road. In 1932 this frog was brought from Puerto Rico to assist with insect control. They don't mind being held, and can be turned over and seem to love having their stomachs rubbed. However, on the bufo toad you will notice a lump behind their head which carries a poison. The poison awaits a sharp blow or puncture to cause it to squirt out. A handy defense for this amphibian and dogs or cats quickly learn not to bother them. The poison can cause them to become seriously ill or can be fatal. Their body secretions can be irritating to the skin, especially eyes, and it is suggested that you just enjoy watching them instead.

There are also a few areas on the Big Island and other islands that have recently had a couple of species of Caribbean tree frogs established. The small, but noisy, critters got into the islands by hitchhiking aboard imported plants, so the theory goes. The tiny frogs are a bit of a nuisance because they make a quite loud and very noticeable chirping sound, mostly at night when people are trying to sleep. It's hoped the infestation will avoid Kaua'i. But these things have a way of eventually migrating to other areas.

On Kaua'i you'll see no mongoose, the only major Hawaiian island without these animals which prey on birds and their eggs. Consequently, Kaua'i is blessed with more birdlife than other islands.

The other Hawaiian creature that cannot go without mention is the gecko. They are finding their way into the suitcases of many an island visitor in the form of tee-shirts, sunvisors and jewelry. This small lizard is a relative of the chameleon and grows to a length of three or four inches. They dine on roaches, termites, mosquitos, ants, moths and other pesky insects. While there are nearly 800 species of geckos found in warm climates around the world, there are only five known varieties found in Hawaii. They are the only lizards which can vocalize, and different species make different sounds. The house gecko is the most commonly found, with tiny rows of spines that circle its tail, while the mourning gecko has a smooth, satiny skin and along the middle of its back it sports pale stripes and pairs of dark spots. The mourning gecko species is parthenogenic.

This means that there are only females which produce fertile eggs -- no need for a mate! Smaller species have a life expectancy of five to seven years and larger geckos in captivity have reached 20 years of age.

The stump-toed variety is distinguished by its thick flattened tail. The tree gecko enjoys the solitude of the forests, and the fox gecko, with a long snout and spines along its tail, prefers to hide around rocks or tree trunks. Females make sure their eggs are well hidden before leaving them for ever more. The little ones will hatch in one to three months, breaking out of their eggshell with a specially designed "egg tooth" attached to their nose.

The first geckos may have reached Hawai'i with early voyagers from Polynesia, but the house gecko may have arrived as recently as the 1940s, along with military shipments to Hawaii. Geckos are most easily spotted at night when they seem to enjoy the warm lights outside your door. They each establish little territories where they live and breed so you will no doubt see them around the same area each night. They are very shy and will scurry off quickly. Sometimes you may find one living in your hotel or condo. They're friendly and beneficial animals and are said to bring good luck, so make them welcome.

Birdlife abounds on Kaua'i, and no doubt the first you will note are the chickens! Wild chickens? Yes! The wild chickens that you may see in the area of Koke'e and the lodge are descendants from the ones brought by the Polynesians, but you will find chickens just about everywhere you turn on Kaua'i these days. Hurricane Iwa, and to a greater extend Hurricane Iniki, caused a number of domesticated chickens to escape and they are obviously proliferating in paradise. Those descendants of the Polynesians have now inter-mixed with the domestic varieties that you will see many diverse colorations, particularly on the roosters. The roosters can be a bit of a nuisance in rural areas where their alarm wake-up calls are not always appreciated!

The songbirds of Hawai'i owe a great deal of credit to Mrs. Dora Isenberg. The *New York Herald Tribune* (September, 1938 edition) carried the following historical background:

"Thanks to the efforts of one woman, the Hawaiian Islands are now the home of thousands of gaily colored songbirds from all parts of the world. Mrs. Dora Isenberg began her hobby of importing songsters forty years ago in celebration of Hawaii's joining the United States [as a territory]. After permitting them to get acclimated in her garden on Kaua'i Island, Mrs. Isenberg gave the birds their freedom. Her first attempts were unsuccessful when fourteen larks from the Orient were released and never heard of again. But, undismayed, Mrs. Isenberg continued her efforts, and many other people took up the hobby, with the result that today the islands boast thousands of such imported birds as the Peko thrush, African ringneck dove, Mongolian thrush, Chinese thrush, Bleeding Heart dove, meadow-lark, tomtit, and cardinal."

The goats found in the Koke'e area are descendants of those brought to the islands by Captain Cook. They have done significant damage to the vegetation and hunting for them is allowed. A pair of binoculars, or even a sharp lookout at one of the Waimea Canyon viewing areas and you might spot one or more. They blend in so well with the bare rocky terrain that you may almost fail to spot one even if it's standing within a few feet of you.

AQUATIC SAFETY: DO NOT DRINK WATER FROM STREAMS, WATER-FALLS, OR PONDS!!! Drinking of fresh water from streams, waterfalls and/or pools is not safe at any location. While there are many micro-organisms and parasites that can wreak havoc with your system, one of the most dangerous is Leptospirosis. This finds its way into rivers and streams in the urine of rodents and cattle and can be fatal. The symptoms are flu-like and because they do not result until 1 - 4 weeks after contamination, people who are infected may not connect their illness with a possible contamination weeks earlier. It can also be contracted through the skin if there are open sores or cuts. Be sure to pack your own drinking water should you do any hiking. Or, if you do choose to drink stream water, be sure to boil it thoroughly and/or treat it with water purification tablets. As for cautions you should use in and around the ocean, we cannot emphasize enough the importance of ocean safety. More folks drown off the shores of Kaua'i than any of the other islands. With the dangerous currents take heed of the signs and markers indicating beach safety, never swim alone, and please refer to the section on Beaches for additional guidelines.

HELPFUL PHONE NUMBERS:

EMERGENCY: Police - Ambulance - Fire 911

NON-EMERGENCY POLICE:
Non-emergency requests 241-6711
Crime Stoppers 241-6787
Weather 245-6001
Poison Control 1-800-362-3585
Sexual Assault Crisis (YWCA) 245-4144
YWCA Shelter 245-6362
Consumer Protection 274-3200
Kaua'i County Office of Elderly Affairs 241-6400
Transportation for Elderly or Handicapped 241-6400
Transportation: Airports Division 246-1401
Transportation: Highway Division 274-3111
Kaua'i Chamber of Commerce 245-7363
Po'ipu Beach Resort Association 742-7444
Kaua'i Visitors Bureau 245-3971
The Kaua'i Bus 241-6410
Time of Day 245-0212
DIRECTORY ASSISTANCE:
    Local . . . . 1+411
    Inter-island (charge) 1-808-555-1212
    Long distance outside area code (charge) . . . . 1+ area code+555-1212

HELPFUL PHONE NUMBERS (CONTINUED)

HOSPITALS:
Wilcox Memorial in Lihu'e: 245-1100
West Kaua'i Medical Center-Waimea 338-9431

LAND AND NATURAL RESOURCES:
Division of State Parks
State Parks Camping Permits 274-3444
Main Office 274-3446
Koke'e 335-5871
Wailua Marina 822-5065
Division of Aquatic Resources 274-3344
Forestry & Wildlife 274-3077

The *Aloha Pages* in the front of the *Kaua'i* phone book has various hotline numbers to call for community events, entertainment, etc. on Kaua'i. While the call is free, the companies pay to be included, so information is biased. The front section of the telephone book also has some great street maps.

GETTING THERE

-- AIRLINES AND MORE

CRUISING THE ISLANDS: One pleasant way to see the Hawaiian islands is aboard the ***American Hawai'i Cruises*** ship, the *S.S. Independence*. This 1,021 passenger, 682-foot ship provides comfortable accommodations and friendly service during its seven-day sail around the islands. In 1993, American Hawai'i Cruises was acquired by The Delta Queen Steamboat Co. public company, now American Classic Voyages, Co. American Hawai'i Cruises acquired the *Nieuw Amsterdam* from Holland America Line not long ago. This new U.S. flag ship has been renamed *MS Patriot* and joined the *Independence* in service in Hawai'i in 2000. The 704-foot *MS Patriot* was completely refurbished and offers nine passenger decks, five lounges, two restaurants, a fully equipped spa and fitness center, two outdoor pools and a 230-seat theater. (Note: Two new U.S. flag 1,900 passenger, state-of-the-art cruise ships being built for American Hawai'i Cruises will enter service in Hawaiian waters in early 2003 and 2004.)

On board either *The Independence* or the *MS Patriot* you'll enjoy some outstanding Hawaiiana programs. Hawaiian costumes, hands-on Hawaiian museum exhibits, cabins with Hawaiian names, traditional Hawaiian church services, menus filled with Hawaiian specialties, and tropical flowers in every room are among the changes which bring the essence of Hawai'i on board. American Hawai'i Cruises has Kumu (Hawaiian teachers) on board to instruct passengers about the culture and history of Hawaii. Both ships offer fully handicap-accessible suites.

Currently the **MS Patriot** departs Honolulu on Saturdays. It travels a seven day route from Honolulu to Nawiliwili, Kaua'i; Kahului, Maui; Hilo, Hawai'i and Kona, Hawai'i. Also available are a number of "Theme Cruises" which range from Big Band cruises to one which combines with Hawai'i's Aloha Festivals. The ship comes into port at each of the major islands for a day (or in some cases two) for touring. The SS Independence sails a similar around-the-islands-route from Kahului, Maui, its homeport.

"Beautiful Seas" wedding packages are available for couples who choose marriage aboard ship in Hawai'i on **American Hawai'i Cruises**. It includes the services of an official to perform the ceremony, a small wedding cake, live Hawaiian music, a flower lei and floral headpiece for the bride and a lei or boutonniere for the groom, champagne and keepsake flutes, photography service and a 24 5X7 photos in a souvenir album. The wedding package price is $695 plus cruise fares. See Weddings & Honeymoons in this chapter for information on tests and licenses. For honeymooners that marry on the Mainland on a Saturday, they don't have to "miss the boat" to enjoy a Hawaiian Islands honeymoon cruise. While the normal departures are on Saturday from Honolulu, the "Sea and Shore" honeymoon enables couples to board the ship in Nawiliwili, Kaua'i. After six days on board ship, the honeymooners will enjoy a seventh night at a Waikiki Hotel. See Weddings & Honeymoons in this chapter for information on tests and licenses.

American Hawai'i Cruises offers shore excursions which include opportunities for passengers to discover the "hidden" Hawaii. Trips include the opportunity to hike through a rain forest to discover a hidden waterfall. The idea of a cruise is to give you a taste of each of the islands without the time and inconvenience of traveling by plane in-between islands. In fact, it would be impossible to see all the islands in a week in any other fashion. For additional information contact American Hawai'i Cruises 1-800-765-7000 or FAX (504) 585-0630.

AIRLINE/TRAVEL PACKAGES INFORMATION: The best prices on major air carriers can often be arranged through a reputable travel agent who can often secure air or air with car packages at good prices by volume purchasing. Prices can vary considerably so comparison shopping is a wise idea. Be sure to ask about senior citizen and companion fare discounts.

Another alternative is to book a package trip through one of several agencies which specializes in Hawai'i travel. While Creative Leisure uses major airlines (we were quoted on United), others use charter services.

"Airfare Only" is available through Sunquest on their Sun Country Charters and Pleasant Hawaiian Holidays who use commercial carriers including Delta Airlines, Hawaiian Airlines, United Airlines and American TransAir.

Avalon Travel offers "theme" tours to Kaua'i that range from Culinary (with an emphasis on dining and exploring Hawaiian Regional and Pacific Rim cuisine) to Art & Garden (visit artists' homes and explore the "Garden Isle") to Wellness and Rejuvenation Retreats (created for those interested in personal growth, natural healing and spiritual enrichment). Their annual KauaiQuest is a "Festival of Spirit & Discovery" offered every October to coincide with Kaua'i's Aloha

Festival Events. They promise their "insider" tours/retreats to be educational, cultural, and inspirational with "programs designed for those who wish to experience the local culture and environment on a deeper and more authentic level." These "land only" tours run seven days/six nights and are priced from $1,599. (Price includes lodging, meal plan, presentations, professional guide, and land excursions.) Call Karol Avalon at 1-888-552-7375; Email: karol@avalontravel.com or visit their website at < www.avalontravel.com >

Classic Aloha Vacations PO Box 627, Hanalei, HI 96714. 1-800-200-3576 or toll free FAX 1-888-826-7155. Website: www.classic-aloha.com or Email: cav@aloha.net Classic Aloha offers a nice selection of properties on all the islands, with photos of each. Their staff of five agents on three islands are happy to answer any questions you may have! As a Hawai'i wholesaler who sells to agencies all over the mainland and Canada, the website allows them to offer excellent rates on hotels, condos, car and airfare.

Creative Leisure 1-800-426-6367, (808) 778-1800. While you may not find the most inexpensive packages, Creative Leisure utilizes moderate to expensive, higher end condominiums and hotels (which include Whaler's Cove, Hyatt Regency, Po'ipu Kai, Embassy Vacation Resort, Princeville Hotel, Kaua'i Beach Villas, The Cliffs, Pali Ke Kua, Lae nani, Lanikai, Kiahuna Plantation, Waimea Plantation Cottages and Kaua'i Marriott). They offer the advantage of traveling any day you choose and the option of staying as long as you want. Rates are for the entire unit, not per person. Year-round discount airfares are available on United and you will receive full Mileage Plus credit for all United Airlines and Aloha Airlines travel booked through them. TravelGuard insurance is also available. You can combine and include other islands as a part of your package, or even a stopover in San Francisco. Customer service is a high priority with them, and it shows! PO Box 750189, Petaluma, CA 94975.

Pleasant Hawaiian Holidays ★ 1-800-242-9244. This is one of the oldest established travel wholesalers and operators of package tours to Hawai'i. They provide a wide range of air/room packages, fly/drive/room packages, air only packages, and land only options. They work in conjunction with American Trans Air direct to Maui and Honolulu from L.A. and San Francisco. They also utilize Hawaiian Airlines, United, and Delta, as well as numerous hotels and resorts, and rental car companies on all islands. Web: < www.pleasantholidays.com >.

Kaua'i properties include the Hyatt Regency Kaua'i, Princeville Hotel, Whaler's Cove, Aston Po'ipu Point, Kaua'i Marriott Resort, Hanalei Bay Resorts & Suites, Outrigger's Kiahuna Plantation, Aston Kaua'i Beach Villas, Radisson Kaua'i Beach Hotel, Kaua'i Coconut Beach Resort, Islander on the Beach, and Plantation Hale. A $45 fee will waive any cancellation or penalties should you have to adjust your travel plans. Their "Last Minute Desk" is for those of you trying to find space on short notice -- right up to the day of departure!

Suite Paradise ★ is a condominium rental agency which specializes in the "Best of Po'ipu." In addition to accommodations they offer very attractive rates on car/condo packages. They can arrange ticketing on regularly scheduled airlines (United, Delta, Northwest, TWA, Continental and Hawaiian) at discounts with their air ticketing affiliate. Call Suite Paradise at 1-800-367-8020 to request information on all their vacation options. They have a wonderful, helpful staff. Contact Suite Paradise to receive information on these airline contacts. See their URL at <www.suite-paradise.com> or e-mail: <mail@suite-paradise.com>

Sunquest Holidays 1-800-357-2400 - isn't the new kid on the block, but they are new to serving Hawai'i bound vacationers. If you are from the midwest, you might be familiar with Sun Country which books trips to exotic Caribbean destinations. Not long ago, they added Hawai'i, utilizing Los Angeles as their gateway to the Pacific. This means that if you live in the Southern California area you might get a great deal, but the rest of us have to make our own travel arrangements to the LAX airport. They do, however, fly (DC-10's) every day of the week which allows you to customize the length of your vacation stay. Land only, air only and combination packages including rental cars are available for O'ahu, Maui, Kaua'i and The Big Island. They offer some unique and intriguing incentives! By booking early you can take an extra $20 off the published airfares. Sunquest Holidays also offers FREE children's holidays for youngster up to 19 years of age. You get one free child per two full-paying passengers, when sharing a room and using existing bedding. A minimum seven night stay is required. Other children qualify for package discounts, which are still a good deal! Travel protection insurance, in the event you have to cancel at the last minute, is available as is travel insurance. Dollar Rent a Car handles the ground transportation (Hawai'i Rental Vehicle Surcharge of $2 per day not included in prices) and Aloha Airlines is the carrier used for inter-island flights. Single or multiple island packages are available. For airfare only, rates are staggered based on the day of the week you depart and the time of the year. Some very outstanding week long package rates. Worth calling to request a catalog.

Remember! Be sure to check all the air carriers. Experience has taught us that a little leg work pays off! Sometimes the best deal may be through one of these agencies, but if you have the time, it may be worth a thorough investigation (and you may be pleasantly surprised). During one trip we discovered that United Airlines had a promotional special that far and away beat these packages and even the charters!! Always make sure you let the airline know if you are flexible on your arrival and departure days. You may be able to squeeze into some price cut promotion that offers an even better value on your flight dollar.

The main airport is in central Kaua'i, at Lihu'e. There has long been talk regarding a runway extension of the Lihu'e Airport. Extending the runway would allow for direct international flights and larger planes from the U.S. Mainland. The state legislature has appropriated funds for review of this project.

In Princeville, on the North Shore, there is a small airstrip. It is used for small planes and helicopters and some inter-island commuter flights.

FLIGHTS TO THE ISLANDS

Most of the airlines have their own websites. These are especially handy for getting checking flight schedules, flight availability, doing a tentative itinerary, fare checking and comparing, or even booking your own tickets online. Often the airline websites have better price deals than can be had from a travel agent or even from the airline's own reservation system agents. So, checking into online booking can be worth your time to compare. The major American and Canadian carriers that fly from the mainland to the Honolulu International Airport on Oʻahu follow below. Only two of these carriers, United Airlines and Canada 3000, have direct flights to Lihuʻe Airport on Kauaʻi.

AIR CANADA - Reservations in the U.S. and Canada 1-888-247-2262; Web: <www.aircanada.ca>. They've taken over Canadian Airlines as a subsidiary operation and both airlines schedules can be accessed via the same website.

ALOHA AIRLINES ★ - They have expanded to the US mainland using all new Boeing 737-700s. Destinations now include Oakland (San Francisco Bay Area), Orange County (Los Angeles) and Las Vegas. These points are served from Honolulu, Maui and Kona with various daily services and connecting services from Kauaʻi. For reservations and information, call toll free 1-800-367-5250 U.S. & Canada. Their Honolulu number is (808) 484-1111, on Kauaʻi (808) 245-3691; Web: <www.alohaairlines.com>.

AMERICAN AIRLINES - Toll free from the mainland and all island 1-800-433-5436; Web: <www.aa.com>. Five flights per day to Honolulu with connections to inter-island carriers.

AMERICA WEST AIRLINES - Reservations in Hawaiʻi, 1-800-235-9292; Web: <www.americawest.com>

CANADA 3000 AIRLINES - Reservations in Hawaiʻi, 1-877-658-3000; Web: <www.canada3000.com>; providing seasonal flights to Lihuʻe Airport, Kauaʻi via Honolulu from Vancouver.

CONTINENTAL AIRLINES - 1-800-523-3273 toll free from mainland; Web: <www.continental.com>. Flights to Honolulu with connecting inter-island carriers to Kauaʻi.

DELTA AIR LINES - Reservations 1-800-221-1212; Web: <www.delta.com>. They fly non-stop out of Atlanta, Dallas, Fort Worth, San Francisco and Los Angeles into Honolulu. Inter-island carriers will connect you to Kauaʻi from there.

HAWAIIAN AIRLINES - Toll free from the mainland 1-800-367-5320; in Honolulu (808) 838-1555; on Kauaʻi or from the neighbor islands, call 1-800-882-8811; Web: <www.hawaiianair.com> Hawaiian offers both scheduled and charter flights from San Francisco, Los Angeles, Portland, Seattle, Las Vegas and San Diego direct to Honolulu with service connecting hourly to Kauaʻi.

Hawaiian Airlines also fly trans-Pacific routes to Papeete, Tahiti and Pago Pago, American Samoa in the South Pacific. They use DC-10's on the mainland and South Pacific services. In early 2001, they began replacing the inter-island fleet of older DC9's with the first of 13 new 100-passenger twin-jet Boeing 717-200s. News reports also have it that they are looking at replacing the DC-10s used on the trans-Pacific flights with new Boeing 767s. If you plan to do a lot of island hopping, Hawaiian's "Island Pass" offers unlimited travel on all islands for 5, 7, 10, or 14 days. (Approximately $229-409). Check with Hawaiian or your travel agent. for coupon books which can bring the cost down to about $55 for a one-way ticket.

NORTHWEST AIRLINES - 1-800-225-2525; Web: < www.nwa.com >. They are partners with Hawaiian Air for flights from Honolulu to Kaua'i.

PLEASANT HAWAIIAN HOLIDAYS ★ - 1-800-242-9244, (818) 991-3390, Fax: (805) 495-4972; Web: < www.pleasantholidays.com >. They use L-1011's on their American Trans Air flights from San Francisco and Los Angeles. (With a seat configuration of 3-4-3, we were told by a tall individual to stay away from the middle 4 seats, which seem to have less leg room.) They use Hawaiian, Delta, and United in their packages which offer different planes. Many of their United flights offer direct service from Los Angeles to Lihu'e. From Honolulu they work with Hawaiian Airlines connecting with their convenient hourly shuttle to Kaua'i.

TRANS WORLD AIRWAYS - Reservations from mainland and Hawai'i, 1-800-221-2000; Web: < www.twa.com > Daily flights to Honolulu from their hub city, St. Louis.

UNITED AIRLINES ★ - United Reservations & Flight information: 1-800-241-6522; Web: < www.ual.com > United has more flights to Hawai'i from more U.S. cities than any other airline. Currently they fly direct from Los Angeles to Lihu'e offering one flight daily that leaves around 5 p.m. in the evening and arrives at approximately 8 p.m. They also provide seasonal flights from San Francisco to Lihu'e during the summer. Check with your travel agent, the airline directly, or their website for the most current information on flight schedules. If you choose to go through Honolulu, you can book in conjunction with their Aloha Airlines partner to Kaua'i which will usually give you a better fare. You can always book the inter-island air travel via Hawaiian or Aloha on your own separately if you can get a better price elsewhere.

INTER-ISLAND FLIGHTS

Hawai'i is unique in that its intrastate roads are actually water or sky. For your travel by sky, there are two major inter-island air carriers that operate between Honolulu and Kaua'i. And, unless you are traveling from the mainland or Canada on United Airlines or Canada 3000 direct to Lihu'e Airport on Kaua'i, you will have to pass through Honolulu International Airport to connect to one of the local carriers for the flight to Kaua'i. If you plan on doing some inter-island excursions, you may want to check into the multi-day flight passes with either Hawaiian or Aloha. Also, you might want to check with any local travel agency on purchasing a book of inter-island flight coupon tickets for either Hawaiian or Aloha. These coupons are discounted over the cost of regular inter-island tickets and the savings can be considerable.

Travel agents schedule at least an hour and a half between arrival on O'ahu and departure for Kaua'i to account for any delays, baggage transfers, and the time required to reach the inter-island terminal. The flight time from O'ahu to Lihu'e on Kaua'i is just 25 minutes. Currently there are no inter-island carriers using the Princeville airport. When returning from Kaua'i to Honolulu, make sure you have plenty of time before your connecting flight to the mainland. Otherwise you might make your flight, but your baggage won't!

Traveling from the main carrier to the inter-island terminal can be rather exhausting and confusing. You will probably need to take one Wiki-Wiki shuttle bus to the baggage claim or another drop-off point and then pick up another to take you to the nearby inter-island terminal. The inter-island terminal is next-door to the main international terminal, but the walking distances from your arrival gate or baggage claim area may be a bit far. There are rental baggage carts in the terminals to help you transport baggage to the next terminal. Of course, if your baggage is tagged through to Kaua'i, you don't have to worry about it until you reach Lihu'e Airport.

If you do arrive early, check with the inter-island carrier. Very often you can get an earlier flight which will arrive on Kaua'i in time to get your car before returning to pick up your luggage when it arrives on your scheduled flight.

If you are traveling "light" and have brought with you carry-on luggage only, be advised that what is carry-on for the major airlines may not be carry-on for the inter-island carriers. For example, those new small suitcases with wheels and long handles that extend out to pull along behind you MUST be checked by many of the inter-island carriers. Knowing this in advance, you may be able to pack those items that are more fragile in a smaller tote bag.

ALOHA AIRLINES ★ - For reservations and information, call 1-800-367-5250 U.S. & Canada. Their Honolulu number is (808) 484-1111, on Kaua'i (808) 245-3691. The website is: <www.alohaairlines.com> Aloha operates over 180 flights daily throughout the islands using an all-jet fleet of nineteen Boeing 737-200s and new 737-700s which they use on their trans-Pacific flights. They serve the five largest island airports including Honolulu, Kaua'i, Maui, plus Hilo and Kona on the Big Island. They offer e-ticketing, first class service, Drive-Thru Check-In at Honolulu and porter-assisted Curb-Side Check-in at both Honolulu and Lihu'e. Aloha has frequent service between Honolulu and Kaua'i daily, roughly on the half-hour from early morning to night. They also have two daily non-stop flights between Kaua'i and Maui.

In 2000, Aloha began service to the U.S. West Coast, and now provides twice-daily service between Honolulu and the San Francisco Bay Area via the Oakland International Airport, with a continuing leg to Las Vegas. Aloha expanded this service and also has daily non-stop service between Oakland and Maui. In 2001, the airline expanded these mainland flights by including direct service between Kona on the Big Island and Oakland. And Aloha's newest daily non-stop trans-Pacific flight links both Honolulu and Maui with Orange County, California, at John Wayne Airport. At the same time, the airline also launched daily service between John Wayne Airport-Orange County and Las Vegas' McCarran International Airport. Vacation travelers to these popular destinations of Hawai'i, Disneyland/Orange County, and Las Vegas can now travel conveniently to each destination on Aloha Airlines.

Aloha also operates weekly scheduled trans-Pacific services from Honolulu to the Central Pacific destinations of Midway, Johnston, and Christmas Islands, as well as the Marshall Islands plus long-range and inter-island charter flights upon request. All trans-Pacific flights to the mainland or Central Pacific feature Aloha's signature service of Hawaiian Regional Cuisine in the First-Class cabin by noted island chef Alan Wong and other special amenities. In Coach Class, Aloha offers an enhanced package of amenities including free movies and headsets, a complimentary mai tai cocktail, "oshibori" towel service, and freshly-baked cookies and milk.

The airline has one of the best "on time" records and is able to keep on schedule. It recently won recognition for its top-ranked on time performance according to the Air Travel Consumer Report (2001), released by the U.S. Department of Transportation. The report noted that 87.5 percent of Aloha's domestic flights operated on time. It has long had one of the lowest passenger complaint records of all U.S. Airlines. In fact, Consumer Reports magazine gave Aloha their highest rating for "Superior Value" in both customer satisfaction and low rates (the same reason they have always earned our "star" rating) which the airline backs up with a service guarantee!

When making reservations on Aloha Airlines, you should inquire about any special promotions, AAA membership discounts, passes, or coupon books that are currently available. The website has information on current promo specials. But remember that airfares are a continuously changing phenomena. Prior to press time, Aloha was offering a special "Flex Fare" of $49.99 per one-way ticket anywhere within Hawai'i. But it's available only on selected flights. Also, at present, for a flat rate (approximately $320 depending on the season) you can buy a 7-day pass which allows unlimited travel on Aloha Airlines to all islands. Sort of Hawai'i's version of a Eurail Pass! If you have a family or plan lots of inter-island excursions, you might also want to consider buying a book of coupon tickets from a local travel agency. Coupon tickets can significantly reduce the standard one-way fare to around $65-70, a considerable savings over the regular one-way fare. Be sure to check into their Fly/Drive packages for rental cars - they offer some really great deals, especially during slow season. For 5,000 United Mileage Plus miles, you can receive a free round trip ticket! Current flight schedule is available on the world wide web at < www.alohaairlines.com >

HAWAIIAN AIRLINES, toll free from the mainland 1-800-367-5320; on Kaua'i or from the neighbor islands, call 1-800- 882-8811. Hawaiian offers both scheduled and charter flights from San Francisco, Los Angeles, Portland, Seattle, Las Vegas and San Diego direct to Honolulu with service connecting hourly to Kaua'i. They also fly trans-Pacific routes to Papeete, Tahiti and Pago Pago, American Samoa in the South Pacific. They use DC-10's on the mainland and South Pacific services. In early 2001, they began replacing the inter-island fleet of older DC9's with the first of 13 new 100-passenger twin-jet Boeing 717-200s. News reports also have it that they are looking at replacing the DC-10s used on the trans-Pacific flights with new Boeing 767s. Web: <www.hawaiianair.com>

If you plan to do a lot of island hopping, Hawaiian's "Island Pass" offers unlimited travel on all islands for 5, 7, 10, or 14 days (5 day-$324, 7-day $345, 10-day $409, 14-day $469, with children's and senior discounts). Flight coupon books are also available which can bring the cost down to about $65-70 for a one way ticket. Check with Hawaiian or your travel agent for any relevant special promo programs when you are planning your trip.

LIHU'E AIRPORT: Congratulations! It has been a long day of travel, but now you're here! Most visitors to Kaua'i will arrive at the island's major air terminal. The Lihu'e Airport covers 804 acres and is located on the southeast coast of the island of Kaua'i, about 1 1/2 miles from the town of Lihu'e. It is a blissfully simple airport with only a handful of gates and one baggage claim area. In addition to the chairs at the individual gates, there is a small centralized seating area surrounded by convenient pay phones and a gift shop. The airport operates two runways and offers passenger and cargo transportation. Currently the runway length does not allow direct international or overseas domestic air service by large aircraft, but there has long been talk regarding a runway extension of the Lihu'e Airport. Extending the runway would allow for direct international flights and larger plans from the U.S. Mainland. The state legislature has appropriated funds for review of this project.

When you arrive (mid-day only), you'll find an unexpected greeting of Kaua'i aloha: live music at the Lihu'e airport every Monday, Wednesday and Friday from 9am until noon. And at baggage claim, there is a self-service counter with guava juice (from Guava Kai Plantation) plus flavored and regular coffee from Kaua'i Coffee - all complimentary! There is also a closed captioned video that is shown in the baggage claim area which provides safety information on roads, beach and ocean usage, and hiking trails as well as crime prevention. (And have your baggage claim check handy -- this airport actually checks!!)

IMPORTANT!!! ARRIVAL AND DEPARTURE TIPS! During your flight to Honolulu, the airline staff will provide you with a visitor information sheet. This is used by the Hawai'i Visitors and Convention Bureau to track the number of visitors and their island destinations. This is also the opportunity to report any animals, fruits, vegetables or plants that will need to be inspected upon arrival in Honolulu.

AGRICULTURAL INSPECTION: On your return, you will have to take your checked as well as carry-on baggage through agricultural inspection. Where your luggage will be inspected will depend upon your travel plans. If you are checking baggage at the Lihu'e airport which will be transferred directly to your connecting flight in Honolulu, then you will need to go through the agricultural inspection at the main entrance of the Lihu'e airport before proceeding to the airline ticketing counter to check in. Don't bother checking your carry-on baggage at this point, as you will just have to do it again in Honolulu. If you have a connection on O'ahu, you will arrive in Honolulu and begin trekking from your inter-island flight to your mainland carrier. Almost mystically an agricultural inspection center will appear. Don't bother looking, they seem to just find you! (In case this is your first trip, they look just like a "regular" airport baggage security center.) At this point you will need to have your carry-on baggage inspected. You'll be amazed to see the apples, oranges and other fruits stacked up on the agricultural inspection centers. Even though they may have originally come from the mainland US, they will not pass inspection to get back there! Any fruits which you wish to take home, i.e. papaya and pineapple, can be specially boxed, inspected and sealed from reputable island retailers. Generally, you will not have trouble with flowers and/or leis. If you are unsure what is transportable, contact the U.S. Department of Agriculture at (808) 245-2831.

DISTANCES FROM THE LIHU'E AIRPORT TO OTHER AREAS

Car rental agency counters are located directly across from the baggage claim areas of the Lihu'e Airport. From the Lihu'e Airport it is a 20 minute drive to Kapa'a, 30 minutes to Po'ipu, 60 minutes to Hanalei, 75 minutes to Ha'ena, and 90 minutes to the Waimea Canyon, barring traffic tie ups.

KAUA'I'S TRAFFIC WOES

This book would be doing the visitor a disservice if we failed to mention Kaua'i's traffic woes. The fact is that Kaua'i's roadways are very busy and the town centers can be quite congested with traffic. It is a fact of life and must be understood by visitors. Some visitors arrive here thinking there will be few cars on the roads, but that's just not the case. Kaua'i is no different than any other growing community. The numbers of vehicles clogging the roadways continues to increase each year. There is essentially one highway that goes around the island (it doesn't quite encircle it due to the disruption of the rugged Napali Coast on the North Shore). Numerous roads branch off from this main highway in the various population centers. And because large trucks and busses use the same roads as the rest of us, expect to get caught up in slow moving traffic at times. And use extreme caution when making left-hand turns against oncoming traffic. Better yet, avoid left-hand turns if you can. But visitors should expect to drive in high traffic areas around Kaua'i. It may not be quite as bad as the rush-hour freeway traffic in your city or area, but it will be heavy nonetheless. Being prepared for it will help you handle it. Just remember to take your time, look around, and enjoy your time amidst the special beauty and appeal of Kaua'i. One other thing you may notice and pick up on is that many drivers around the islands "drive with Aloha." They'll wave you across an intersection, let you make a turn in front of them, and generally give the other driver a break. Hopefully you'll take the hint too and learn to "drive with Aloha."

GETTING AROUND

Here's an insider tidbit for you. If you find yourself without an essential map of Kaua'i, check out the nearest phone book. It has a couple of pages of very good color maps that will get you by in a pinch. Since every condo and hotel will have a copy, you might find this a handy and helpful reference! Uh, no, I didn't say to tear the pages out of the phone book... And because Kaua'i has its own peculiar ideosyncrasies like other places, we'll pause here with a brief aside. It seems most appropriate in the category of "getting around" the island, in general, to make note of this interesting fact. The street addresses may easily confuse you as you are trying to locate a particular establishment. You may see a number such as 3-5920 next to 5924, as an example. The number in front of the dash stands for the area of the island. 0-1 is Waimea, 2 is Koloa, 3 is Lihu'e, 4 is Kapa'a and 5 is Hanalei. That seems fairly clear, but it can get a little confusing as to where the cut off point is for each of those areas. Another problem is some people use the first number and the dash and some do not. So, all we can say is, good luck!

The only public transportation is The Kaua'i Bus which charges riders $1 per ride. Seniors, students, or disabled with ID are 50¢. Monthly bus passes are available for $25 which provide unlimited rides. A monthly pass for senior citizens, students, and persons with disabilities runs $12.50. Caregivers traveling with eligible individuals will not be charged a fee. Carry-on baggage is limited to 9" x 14" x 22". Food and drinks are prohibited. Each bus has a destination sign on the front and curb-side of each bus which displays a route number. Schedules are available which show the route the bus travels and the times along that route. Route 100: Kekaha-Koloa-Lihu'e. Route 200: Lihu'e-Koloa-Kekaha. (Both have limited service to Koloa; only one stop pre day.) Route 300: Discontinued. Route 400: Hanalei to Lihu'e. Route 500: Lihu'e to Hanalei. Route 600: Lihu'e-Kapahi-Lih'ue. Route 700 circles the Lihu'e area. For additional information phone the County Transportation Office at (808) 241-6410 between the hours of 7 am and 5 pm Monday-Saturday. Trans Hawaiian Kaua'i sponsors the Coconut Coast Trolley which operates between 10am and 10 pm daily. The Trolley runs north between the Kaua'i Marriott and the Coconut Marketplace; south between Kapa'a Town and the Wailua Marina. A feeder shuttle provides transfer (by reservation) from Po'ipu, Lihu'e, and Nawiliwili Harbor. One-way service is $2; a one-day pass is $5. Call (808) 245-5108 for schedules and more information. There is a free shuttle between Kukui Grove Shopping Center and the Po'ipu Resort area sponsored by Kukui Grove and Grove Farm Land Corporation. (Daily from 8:45-4:30 pm). Call the shopping center office at (808) 245-7784 for pick-up points and schedule. A free shopping shuttle, with two routes, is also sponsored by Hilo Hattie. One offers pick up four times daily at the Kaua'i Sands, Aston Kaua'i Coast Resort, Kaua'i Coconut Beach Hotel, Holiday Inn Sunspree and Radisson Kaua'i Beach Hotel. The second route has pick ups and drop offs twice daily to and from the Hyatt Regency Kaua'i, Embassy Vacation Resort Po'ipu Point, Kiahuna Plantation, Sheraton Kaua'i Hotel and Lawa'i Beach Resort. Other hotel or condominium pickups are available, but space is limited and reservations are required. The shuttle drops off at the Hilo Hattie store in Lihu'e. Call Hilo Hattie at 245-3404.

FROM THE AIRPORT: After arriving, there are several options. Taxi cabs, because of the distances between areas, can be very costly, i.e., $35 from Lihu'e to Po'ipu ($65 Lihu'e to Princeville). That would pay for your economy rental car for the first day or two!

LIMOUSINE SERVICE: Custom Limousine (808) 246-6318; Kaua'i Limousine (808) 245-4855, 1-800-764-7213; Kaua'i North Shore Limousine (808) 826-6189; Town & Country Limousine throughout Hawai'i 1-888-563-2888.

LOCAL TRANSPORTATION: If you don't choose a rental car, you will find The Kaua'i Bus does service island-wide and taxi companies are available.

Ace Kaua'i Taxi 639-4310
Akiko's Taxi (808) 822-7588, 639-8545
Bran's Taxi (808) 245-6533, 639-3609
City Cab (808) 245-3227 (Cell phone 639-7932)
Kaua'i Taxi Company (808) 246-9554
North Shore Cab & Tours (808) 826-6189
Scotty Taxi (808) 245-7888 (Cell phone 639-9807)
South Shore Cab (808) 742-1525 (24-hour and emergency service)
Taxi Guy 1-800-829-4489
Taxi Hanalei 639-1188

RENTAL CARS AND TRUCKS: Given the status of public transportation on Kaua'i, a rental car is still the best bet to get around the island and, for your dollar, a good buy. The rates vary, not only between high and low season, but from week to weekend and even day to day! (One rate quoted on a Wednesday had gone up $8 by Saturday!) The best values are during price wars, or super summer discount specials. Prices vary as much within the same company as they do between companies and are approximated as follows: Vans $63-120, small Jeep $48-100 (popular and in limited supply, so make reservations well in advance), Mid-size $35-57, Compacts $25-45. Add to the rental price a 4% sales tax, a $2 per day highway road tax, and at some companies, a new "vehicle license fee" that tags on another 15-36¢ per day. Some rental car agencies have also been discussing the reinstitution of mileage charges of 25¢ a mile or more. Be sure to inquire!

A trend that poses good news for travelers is that the inter-island airlines, as well as many condos and hotels, are offering rental cars at discounts greater than if you were to book directly. Aloha Airlines offers some very competitive rates with your inter-island tickets. Some resort hotels and condominiums are offering a free rental car as a part of their package. Be sure to ask about these!

On Kaua'i there are currently no companies which rent motorhomes or campervans. Vans are available from a number of agencies, but camping in them is not encouraged.

The policies of all the rental car agencies are basically the same. Most require a minimum age of 21 to 25 and a maximum age of 70. A few require a deposit or major credit card to hold your reservation. All feature unlimited mileage with you buying the gas (from $2.05 and up per gallon in mid-2001--expect that price to go up by the time you read this in fall, 2001 or later). Several service stations around the island have gotten involved lately in something of a mini-gas war and they now take 5¢ off a gallon on certain days of the week. It might be a Tuesday, or it might be a Saturday. There seems to be no set pattern. And how long it will last is anybody's guess. You just have to be on the lookout as you are driving around and jump at the opportunity. You definitely should fill up the tank before you return your car as the rental companies charge a lot more per gallon of gas to do it for you. In fact, all the car rental agencies will offer you a "gas deal" at rental time but decline it as it will cost you more. Unless of course that you don't know how to pump your own gas or don't want to. Please note that there are limited gas stations located on the North Shore and in far western Kaua'i.

Insurance is an option you may wish to purchase, which can run an additional $15-20 a day. A few agencies will require insurance for those under age 25. Most of the car rental agencies strongly encourage you to purchase the optional collision damage waiver (CDW) which provides coverage for most cars in case of loss or damage. We suggest you check with your own insurance company before you leave to verify exactly what your policy covers. Some credit cards now provide CDW (Collision Damage Waiver) for rental cars if you use that credit card to charge your rental fees (usually a practice with Gold Cards). This does not include liability insurance, so you need to check to see if your own policy will cover you for liability in a rental car. NOTE: Rental companies prohibit cars on any unpaved roads, like the one to Polihale Beach in west Kaua'i. The rental agencies will provide you with a map showing restrictions. Should you travel on these roads they will hold you responsible for any damage.

Discounts are few and far between. You might be able to use some airline award coupons or entertainment book coupons, but they are often very restrictive. If you are a member of AAA you can receive a discount on rental cars. (Then there is buyer beware ... we sampled one online company "Hawai'i on Sale." We encountered multiple problems and found them completely unorganized, irresponsible and unreliable. We had a similar report back from the person who originally recommended them!) In our research, it was found that Thrifty had the best rates of the car rental companies. But as with anything, it's always best to check around and compare rates. Also check car rental company websites for the latest online specials. Check with Aloha Airlines for some great rates with their inter-island fly and drive packages. And remember that weekly rates are always a better value, even if you're only there for six days. Most of the major car rental company booths are at the Lihu'e airport and pick-up and return areas are conveniently located right behind the agency counters and across the street from the airline terminal and easy to find. Preferred customers get only a slight advantage by picking their cars up at the airport. The rest of the companies offer a convenient shuttle bus to travel the short distance to their rental office.

In Princeville at the airport there is only an Avis outlet.

RENTAL CAR LISTING:

AA ALOHA CARS-R-US, 1-800-655-7989

ALAMO RENT A CAR, 1-800-327-9633
Lihu'e: (808) 246-0646

AVIS, 1-800-321-3712
Lihu'e: (808) 245-3512
Hyatt Regency: (808) 742-1627
Princeville: (808) 826-9773

BUDGET. 1-800-527-0700
Lihu'e: (808) 245-1901

DOLLAR, 1-800-800-4000
Inter-island: 1-800-342-7398
Lihu'e: (808) 245-3651

HAWAIIAN RIDERS Exotic Cars
Kapa'a: (808) 822-5409
Po'ipu: (808) 742-9888

HERTZ,1-800-654-3011
Lihu'e: (808) 245-3356
Kaua'i Marriott: (808) 246-0027

NATIONAL, 1-800-227-7368
Lihu'e: (808) 245-5636

SEARS RENT A CAR 1-877-283-2468

TOOLMASTER HAWAII
Pickup & Truck rentals
(808) 246-1000

THRIFTY,1-800-367-2277
Neighbor Islands: 1-800-367-5238
Lihu'e: (808) 246-6252

WESTSIDE U-DRIVE
(808) 332-8644

MOTORCYCLES, MOPEDS, BICYCLE RENTALS

Gary's Motorcycles of Kaua'i, 4558 Kukui, Kapa'a, HI 96746, (808) 822-4644. They rent a full line of Harley Davidson motorcycles, all models; inquire with them for the latest daily/weekly rates.

Hawaiian Riders, 4-776 Kuhio Highway, Kapa'a, HI 96746; (808) 822-5409; also 2320 Po'ipu Road, Po'ipu, (808) 742-9888. They rent mountain bikes ($10-16 day, $7-10 half day). They also rent mopeds ($50 day, hourly rates available), many Harley Davidsons available (begin at $69 day). Located in Kapa'a across from McDonald's.

Kaua'i Cycle and Tour, 1379 Kuhio Highway, Kapa'a, HI 96746; (808) 821-2115; Web: <www.bikehawaii.com/kauaicycle> They rent Cannondale and specialized mountain bikes. Rates: $15-35 day; $40-85 for 3-days; $75-150 for week. Open Mon-Fri 9 a.m.-6 p.m., Sat 9a.m.-4 p.m., closed Sun.

Kealia Outfitters, 4-1345 Kuhio Highway, Kapa'a, HI 96746; (808) 821-2107. They rent a variety of mountain bikes, recreational and beach equipment, etc. Call for latest rates.

Outfitters Kaua'i, 2827A Po'ipu Rd., PO Box 1149, Po'ipu Beach, HI 96756. (808) 742-9667, 1-888-742-9887. FAX (808) 742-9667. Email: info@outfitterskauai.com; Web: <www.outfitterskauai.com> This outfitter offers mountain bike rentals for your own exploration along with car racks, kid's seats, helmets, and plenty of directions. They have a number of biking tours and biking combined with other adventures including hiking and kayaking. Their Bicycle Downhill Canyon to Coast is a guided trip available for sunrise or sunset tours daily; includes light breakfast, snacks, beverages. Downhill Bike Ride rates: Adults $72, children 10-14 years old, $60.

Ray's Motorcycle Rentals, Kapa'a, (808) 822-HOGG, has only Harley Davidsons for rent; various models and rates.

Tropical Trike Rentals, Kapa'a, (808) 822-5700, has three-wheeled special motorcycles and other cycles for rent.

GROCERY SHOPPING

Grocery store prices may be one of the biggest surprises of your trip. Just expect things to be more expensive, on the average, than at your hometown supermarket and then you won't be too surprised!. Things will probably be anywhere from 25-35 % or more expensive. While there are many locally grown and produced foods from Kaua'i farms and dairies, most food products must be flown-in or shipped to the islands from the mainland or elsewhere. The local folks can shop the advertisements and use the coupons, but that's not easy to do when traveling.

The following is a comparable grocery-basket list of products at Kaua'i supermarkets. This list was compiled in mid-2001 to meet publishing deadlines, so expect these prices to change after the fall, 2001, publication of this book:

FRUITS & VEGETABLES:
Bananas $0.79-0.99 lb; Delicious apples $0.89-1.69 lb; Head lettuce $1.09-1.49; lb; Russett potatoes $0.79 -1.19 lb

MEATS:
Lean ground beef$2.39-3.19 lb; Extra-lean ground beef $2.69-3.79 lb; Top sirloin steak-boneless $4.99 lb; 7-bone chuck steak $1.99-4.49 lb; 7-bone chuck roast $1.69-3.99 lb; Cross rib boneless roast $2.49-4.19 lb; Beef ribeye steak $8.99 lb; New York strip steak $8.99 lb; Mainland pork chops $3.49-4.49 lb; Foster Farms whole chicken $0.79-1.79 lb; Chicken thighs $1.69-2.49 lb; Cut-up chicken fryers $1.19 lb.; Oscar Mayer bacon $5.45-5.99 lb; Oscar Mayer weiners/franks $3.75/3.99 lb.

PAPER PRODUCTS:
Soft & Gentle toilet tissue $0.99-1.99
Kleenex tissue $1.99-3.19

BEVERAGES:
Half gallon. Whole milk $3.19; Half gallon Orange juice $3.49-4.99; Pepsi-Diet Pepsi-7Up/12 pak $3.75; Coca Cola-Sprite/12 pak $3.50-4.99; 12 pak Bud Light beer $7.99-8.69; 6 pak Bud Light beer $5.29; 12 pak Coors Light beer $8.99-9.89; 6 pak Coors Light beer $4.97; Folger's Instant Coffee 8oz $6.55-6.89

BASICS:
1 dozen island fresh eggs $2.27-2.53; White bread-1 lb loaf $2.75-2.99; Wheat bread-1 lb loaf $2.75-2.99; Cheerios 15 oz box $5.39-5.55; Frosted Flakes 15 oz box $5.59-5.75; Kelloggs Corn Flakes 18 oz $4.95-4.99; Ritz crackers 15 oz. $4.09-4.39; Soft Imperial margarine $2.29; Kraft American cheese-24oz $4.19-5.49; Skippy Peanut Butter 18 oz $2.99-3.79; Welch's Grape Jelly 18 oz $2.59; Nabisco Premium Saltines $2.79-2.89

SNACKS AND GOODIES:
Lay's potato chips-12 oz $2.97-3.99; Frozen Tombstone Pizza $6.39-6.89; Frozen DiGiorno Pizza $5.00-7.49; Eggo Frozen Waffles $3.29; Half gallon Breyer's Ice Cream $4.29; Half gallon Meadow Gold ice cream $5.49; Oreo Cookies 1 lb $3.89-3.99.

The various local farmers' markets can save you some money on fresh local fruit and veggies. And be on the lookout for fruit and veggie stands and booths as you drive around the island. Look for the *Sunshine Market*, an outdoor farmer's market held at different locations around the island. It's advised to call the Office of Economic Development (808) 241-6390 to check on their schedule, but currently they run: Monday-Koloa Ball Park at noon; Tuesday-Kalaheo Neighborhood Center at 3:30 pm; Wednesday-Kapa'a New Town Park in Kahau at 3 pm;

Thursday-Hanapepe Park at 3:30 pm and Kilauea Neighborhood Center at 4:30 pm; Friday-Vidinha Stadium parking lot in Lihu'e at Hoolako Street 3 pm; Saturday-Kekaha Neighborhood Center on Elepaio Road at 9 am. Private farmers' markets are also held Saturday AM/Kilauea Lighthouse Road; Tuesday AM/Hawaiian Farmers of Hanalei (Waipia); Monday 3 PM/Kukui Grove Shopping Center; West Kaua'i Agriculture Assoc. several times a day at Po'ipu Road at Cane Haul Road; and Haupu Growers, L.L.C. daily on Koloa Bypass Road.

The Hanalei Town Farmers Market operates Saturday mornings until about noon at the Hanalei Community Center, Malolo Street and Kuhio Highway, next to the soccer playing field next to Wai'oli Church. This open market specializes in farm fresh organic fruits and vegetables, plants, etc. grown in the area by local farmers and gardeners.

If you are a devoted ad shopper (even on vacation), check the Wednesday paper for grocery specials. On the South Shore you can shop at Big Save in Koloa. On the East shore there is a Big Save in Kapa'a and a 24-hour Safeway at Kaua'i Village. In Lihu'e you'll find a Big Save across from the state and county government buildings, and in the Kukui Grove Shopping Center there is a Star Market. In Waipouli, the Foodland is open 24 hours a day and has a full service Bank of America in the store, not just an ATM! On the West Side there is a Big Save in Waimea and in Ele'ele. On the North Shore, choose between the Big Save in Hanalei or Foodland in Princeville. All major stores accept Visa or Mastercard. These larger stores offer the same variety as your hometown store and the prices are better than at the small grocery outlets. The best part of shopping for food in Hawai'i is discovering the interesting specialty markets. You'll find wonderful fresh fish, and fruit and vegetable markets in all the towns. "Health" foods can be tracked down at Papaya's in Kapa'a or Vim 'N Vigor in Lihu'e.

ANNUAL KAUA'I EVENTS

There are numerous annual community social, cultural and historic celebratory events held throughout the year on Kaua'i which are of interest to residents and visitors alike. The following is not a complete list but notes some of the more popular and widely known events that have been announced. Dates/times, contact numbers/person change frequently, so, for the latest detailed information, specific dates, times, etc. it is suggested to access online events calendars for the latest. Try: <www.alternative-hawaii.com> and/or <www.gohawaii.com>. You might also check with the Kaua'i Visitors Bureau: 4334 Rice Street, Lihu'e, HI 96766, (808) 245-3971, Fax (808) 246-9235. For the current dates of these events, contact the Hawai'i Visitors and Convention Bureau, 2270 Kalakaua Avenue #801, Honolulu, HI 96815, toll free 1-800-GOHAWAII; Web: <www.gohawaii.com> Request the Hawai'i Special Events Calendar. The calendar also gives other event information and the current contact person/phone for each event. Also check the local papers for dates of additional events. The *Kaua'i Update* newsletter will also advise you on current events!

JANUARY
- New Year's Day Mochi Rice Pounding, various island locations
- New Year's Day Bowl Bash with big screen tv at Kukui Grove Shopping Center, 245-7784
- Annual E Pili Kakou E Ho'okahi Lahui Hula Retreat, Kaua'i Marriott, 262-7656
- Rainbow Arts Festival. Family fair with visual and performing arts, Hanapepe Town Park, 335-0712
- Annual Keike Fun Run, Kilohana Plantation, Lihu'e, 246-9090

FEBRUARY
- Annual Hula Ho'iki Celebration of Hawaiian Tradition, Kaua'i War Memorial Hall, 823-0501
- Chinese New Year. Celebrations around the island.
- Annual Waimea Town Celebration, entertainment, food, crafts, games, etc., third weekend in February, 335-2824
- Annual First Hawaiian Bank Hat Lei Contest, Waimea Town Celebration, 338-1332
- Annual Captain Cook Caper Fun Run, 2-5-10K Fun Runs, Waimea Town Celebration, 338-1475
- Annual Ukulele Contest, Waimea Town Celebration, 335-2824
- Annual Lappert's Ice Cream Eating Contest, Waimea Town Celebration, 335-2824
- Annual Kaua'i Community College Used Book Sale, 245-8239
- Kilohana Long Distance Canoe Race, kicks off Kaua'i canoe racing season, 335-2824

MARCH
- Annual Intermediate Band Festival, War Memorial Convention Hall, Lihu'e
- Annual School Art Festival, Kaua'i Museum Mezzanine Gallery, Lihu'e, 245-6931
- Garden Island Spring Fantasy Orchid Show, Hanapepe, 742-6600
- March 26 is Prince Kuhio Day, a State Holiday.
- Prince Kuhio Festival Celebration, 822-5521 or 826-9272
- Prince Kuhio Outrigger Canoe Race, Hanamaulu to Wailua Beach, 822-1944
- Spring Po'ipu Community Craft Fair, Po'ipu Beach, 823-8714

APRIL
- Slack Key Guitar Concert series, Hanalei Community Center, 826-1469
- Annual Business Canoe Race, Hanamaulu Beach, Kaiola Canoe Club, 651-8355
- April through August is Polo season at Anini Beach Polo Field, 822-3740
- Aloha Aina Festival, hula, music, Hawaiian cultural fest, Po'ipu Beach, 823-8714
- Annual Kaua'i Student Film Festival, Kaua'i Community College Performing Arts Center, 632-0272
- Annual Bonsai Exhibition, Border's Bookstore, Kukui Grove, Lihu'e, 246-0862

MAY

- Kaua'i Museum Lei Day Celebration, Lihu'e, 245-6931
- May 1st, Lei Day, is celebrated around the island with various other programs and events
- Kaua'i Annual Garden Fair, Kukui Grove Pavilion, 828-2120
- Annual Royal Pa'ina, celebration of Hawai'i's multi-ethnic heritage, food and entertainment, 245-3373
- Kaua'i Community College Orchestra Spring Concert, KCC Performing Arts Center, 245-8270
- Annual Traditional Hawaiian Music Competition at War Memorial Convention Hall (808) 245-8508
- Annual "Visitor Industry Charity Walk," entertainment, food, Kukui Grove Pavilion, 332-5235
- Kaua'i Community College Band Spring Concert, KCC Performing Arts Center, 245-8270
- Annual Mother's Day Orchid Show, Kapa'a, 823-6921
- Kaua'i Seniors Extravaganza, Kaua'i War Memorial Convention Hall, Lihu'e, 632-0122
- Annual Kaua'i Chorale Concert, KCC Performing Arts Center, 822-5633
- Kaua'i Polynesian Spring Festival, Kukui Grove Park & Pavilion, 335-6466

JUNE

- Annual Taste of Hawai'i Culinary Fair, Smith's Tropical Paradise, sponsored by Kapa'a Rotary Club , 245-2903
- Annual Prince Albert Music Festival, Princeville Resort musical celebration, 826-7546
- King Kamehameha Day Celebration and Festival, Lihu'e, 586-0333
- Annual Kaua'i Cowboy Kanikapila, entertainment and dinner fundraiser for Waimea Boys & Girls Club, 338-1418
- Annual Ha'ena to Hanalei 8-mile run. Sponsored by Hanalei Civic Canoe Club
- Summer O Bon Festival Season beings (June-August), Buddhist tradition of welcoming spirits of ancestors with prayers, services, and bon dances plus food, games & crafts booths, Fri. & Sat. nights at Buddhist temples island-wide
- "Made on Kaua'i Trade Show," homemade & homegrown Kaua'i products exhibition at Kukui Grove Center.
- Kaua'i Ocean Festival, water events, food booths, entertainment, benefit for the Kaua'i Food Bank, 246-3809
- Annual Banana Poka Festival and Forest Education Fair, Koke'e Natural History Museum, 335-9975
- Kaua'i Cowboy Round-Up Celebration, various events celebrate Waimea's cowboy heritage, 338-1332
- The Hawai'i Guitar Festival-Neighbor Island All Star Concert, KCC Performing Arts Center, 245-8270
- Pacific Missile Range Facility Independence Day Celebration, Barking Sands, fireworks, etc. 335-4195

JULY
- July 4th. Concert in the Sky fireworks show, food, music, family fun, Vidinha Stadium, Lihu'e, 634-9100
- Koloa Plantation Days, week-long celebration of old Koloa Town's history & heritage, 822-0734
- Annual Chili Cook-Off to benefit Kaua'i Humane Society, Kaua'i Village in Kapa'a, 822-4904
- Kukui Grove Shopping Center Anniversary celebration with music, food, and prizes, 245-7784

AUGUST
- August 21 - Admission Day, a state holiday.
- Trout fishing season in Koke'e State Park streams and reservoir, Land & Natural Resources Dept. 274-3344
- Garden Island Orchid Show, Lihu'e Convention Center, Lihu'e, (808) 247-3345
- Aloha Festivals - Kaua'i, statewide Aloha Festivals events kick-off, toll free 1-800-852-7690
- Napali Challenge Canoe Race, Hanalei Bay to Kekeha, 241-0079
- Kaua'i County Farm Bureau Fair, Vidinha Stadium, Lihu'e, 828-2120

SEPTEMBER
- Na Wahine Hula, women's hula competition at Hyatt Regency, Po'ipu, 742-1234
- Mokihana Festival, annual music and dance competition, crafts, lectures, workshops, etc., 822-2166

OCTOBER
- Biennial North Shore Taro Festival, Princeville Hotel, cultural-culinary shows and more, 826-6202
- Annual Matsuri Kaua'i Japanese Culture Festival, Lihu'e, Japanese cultural activities fair, 332-8452
- Aloha Festivals, various parade, cultural, Hawaiian heritage events island-wide, toll free 1-800-852-7690
- Annual "Eo E Emalani I Alakai Festival" commemorates Queen Emma's journey to Koke'e and the Alakai Swamp with hula and music outdoors at the Koke'e Lodge, 335-9975
- Kaua'i Community Oktoberfest, Kaua'i Veteran's Center, 332-7376
- Coconut Festival highlights importance of the coconut; food, crafts, entertainment, Kapa'a Beach Park, 246-0089
- Hanapepe Coffee Festival, parade, music, art -- and coffee! 335-0046

NOVEMBER
- Hawai'i International Film Festival, shows island-wide, toll free 1-800-752-8193 or (808) 528-FILM.
- PGA Grand Slam - Po'ipu Bay Resort Golf Course, 742-8711
- Kapa'a Town Veteran's Day Parade
- Hawaiian Christmas Fair, Princeville Golf Club House
- Malama Pono Holiday Fundraiser, Kaua'i Marriott, entertainment, pupus, silent auction, 822-0878

DECEMBER
- Kilohana Craft Fair at Kilohana, Lihu'e, 245-5608
- Kaua'i Museum Christmas Craft Fair, Lihu'e, 245-6931
- Kaua'i Chorale Christmas Concert, KCC Performing Arts Center, 245-8270
- Christmas Fantasy Faire, crafts, food, refreshments, entertainment, 828-0014
- Annual Waimea Lighted Christmas Parade and caroling in Waimea, 335-2824
- Santa's Village, Christmas parade, craft fairs, and holiday entertainment, Kukui Grove Shopping Center, 245-7784
- Audubon Christmas Bird Count, Koke'e State Park & Natural History Museum, volunteers count birds, 335-9975

THESE ON-GOING EVENTS ARE HELD DAILY, WEEKLY AND/OR MONTHLY (DATES WILL VARY) Call the respective group/organization for details and current dates/times of these on-going events. Keep in mind that contact numbers/persons may change from year to year.

CJM Country Stables Rodeo and Roping Series, year around, 822-0811

"Wonder Walks" Guided hikes at Koke'e State Park and other sites, Natural History Museum (June-Sept), 335-9975

Kaua'i Museum Free Tour, every Tuesday, 10 a.m.,245-6931

Hanapepe Art Night, hosted art gallery shows every Friday in Hanapepe, 335-0343

Kaua'i History Program Series: lectures and field trips by Kaua'i Historical Society, 245-3373

Coconut Marketplace Entertainment, daily free show at 5 p.m. often includes hula and Hawaiian music, 822-3641

Crater Hill Hikes, Kilauea Point National Wildlife Refuge,Kilauea, daily guided nature hikes, 828-0383

Tiare Tahiti Dance Show, Po'ipu Shopping Village, every Monday and Thursday, 5 p.m., free

Walking Tour-Old Waimea Sugar Plantation, every Tuesday-Thursday-Saturday, 9 a.m., 335-2824, 337-1005

WEATHER

When thinking of Hawai'i in general, and Kaua'i in particular, one visualizes bright sunny days cooled by refreshing trade winds, and this is the weather at least 300 days a year. What about the other 65 days? Most aren't really bad - just not perfect. Although there are only two seasons, summer and winter, temperatures remain quite constant for Kaua'i. The North Shore, however, tends to be slightly cooler and rainier. Following are the average daily highs and lows for each month and the general weather conditions.

January	80/64
February	79/64
March	80/64
April	82/66
May	84/67
June	86/69
July	86/70
August	87/71
September	87/70
October	86/69
November	83/68
December	80/66

Winter: Mid-October through April, 70 - 80 degree days, 60 - 70 degree nights. Tradewinds are more erratic, vigorous to none. Kona winds are more frequent causing wide-spread cloudiness, rain showers, mugginess and even an occasional thunderstorm. 11 hours of daylight.

Summer: May through mid-October, 80 degree days, 70 - 80 degree nights. Tradewinds are more consistent keeping the temperatures tolerable, however, when the trades stop, the weather becomes hot and sticky. Kona winds are less frequent. 13 hours of daylight. Summer type wear is suitable all year round. However, a warm sweater or light-weight jacket is a good idea for evenings and trips such as to Koke'e. If you are interested in the types of weather you may encounter, or are confused by some of the terms you hear, read on.

Average water temperature ranges between 74 degrees in February to a warm 80 degrees by October. For additional information on surf conditions on Kaua'i call the Weather Information Recording at (808) 245-6001 or Marine Forecast / Hawaiian Waters for their recording at (808) 245-3564.

TRADE WINDS: Hawai'i's weather is greatly affected by the prevailing northeast trade winds which are an almost constant wind from the northeast through the east and are caused by the Pacific anti-cyclone, a high pressure area. This high pressure area is well developed and remains semi-stationary in the summer causing the trades to remain steady over 90% of the time. Interruptions are much more frequent in the winter when they blow only 40 to 60% of the time.

KONA WINDS: The Kona Wind is a stormy, rain-bearing wind blowing from the southwest, or basically from the opposite direction of the trades. It brings high, rough surf to the resort side of the island - great for surfing and boogie-boarding, bad for snorkeling. These conditions are caused by low pressure areas northwest of the islands. Kona winds strong enough to cause property damage have occurred only twice since 1970. Lighter non-damaging Kona winds are much more common, occurring 2 - 5 times almost every winter (Nov-April).

KONA WEATHER: Windless, hot and humid weather is referred to as Kona weather. The interruption of the normal trade wind pattern brings this on. The trades are replaced by light and variable winds and, although this may occur any time of the year, it is most noticeable during the summer when the weather is generally hotter and more humid, with fewer localized breezes.

KONA LOW: A Kona low is a slow-moving, meandering, extensive low pressure area which forms near the islands. This causes continuous rain with thunderstorms over an extensive area and lasts for several days. November through May is the most usual time for these to occur.

RAIN: Paradise would not be paradise without it and parts of Kaua'i do tend to receive more than the other islands. With the Northeast trade winds reaching the North Shore of Kaua'i first, they deposit a greater share on this coastline. The Hanalei/Princeville area receives up to 45 inches per year. The East side fares better, receiving only 30 inches per year. The south and western coastlines receive between 5 and 20 inches per year. And then there is Mt. Wai'ale'ale in Kaua'i's interior, officially the wettest place on earth with a record 665.5 inches of rain falling in 1982. The general annual average rainfall tends to be in the 450-475 inches range for Kaua'i's second highest peak.

HURRICANES: Hurricanes (called typhoons when they are west of the 180 degree longitude) have done damage to the Hawaiian islands on several occasions. The storms which affect Hawai'i usually originate off Central America or Mexico and most of the threatening tropical cyclones have weakened before reaching the islands, or have passed harmlessly to the west. Their effects are usually minimal, causing only high surf on the eastern and southern shores of some of the islands. At least 21 hurricanes or tropical storms have passed within 300 miles of the islands in the last several years, but most did little or no damage. Hurricane season is considered to be July-November. Hurricanes are given Hawaiian names when they pass within 1,000 miles of the Hawaiian islands.

In August of 1950, Hurricane Hiki went to the north of Kaua'i, but still brought 70 mile per hour winds to the island. In 1957, Kaua'i felt the force of two hurricanes which also passed nearby. Both Hurricane Della in September and Hurricane Nina in December skirted a mere 100 miles from the southwestern shore of Kaua'i, bringing high winds and high surf. Hurricane Dot struck the island in August, 1959, with winds nearing 100 miles per hour. In this decade before much development, major damage was restricted to crops. Hurricane Iwa in November, 1982, passed between Ni'ihau and Kaua'i with gusts up to 100 mph causing extensive damage to crops and property.

Hurricane Iniki (which means piercing wind) struck Kaua'i with incredible force in September, 1992. It was a direct hit. By coincidence, Iniki struck Kaua'i within the same time period that Hurricane Andrew struck Florida so hard. As Iniki crossed the Pacific, it had time to develop winds that blew at 165 miles per hour with one gust at Napali on the Makaha Ridge which recorded a speed of 227 miles per hour. Iniki was considered a Category Four hurricane. Category Five is the highest. Trees were uprooted, homes were destroyed, property damage was extensive and island wide. Power and phone lines were down for weeks. Due to the remoteness of the island, help was slower to arrive to Kaua'i than to Florida. While the news media continued to focus on Florida for weeks following Hurricane Andrew, after a few days of coverage, Kaua'i was almost forgotten. Residents refer to Iniki (and Iniki Day) as 911. A little pun since it occurred on September 11th, 9-11!

Kaua'i has been much slower to recover from this latest natural disaster. Only two major resorts, the Hyatt Regency and Princeville had reopened within two years following the hurricane. The former Westin Kaua'i reopened in 1995 as the Kaua'i Marriott Resort. The Sheraton Kaua'i didn't open again until the end of 1997.

Even good things can result from tragedies. Within hours of Hurricane Iniki, Kaua'i residents were pulling together to begin to normalize their lives. They began with neighbors helping neighbors. No one was untouched, but those with dwellings suffering only minor damage were welcoming neighbors into their homes. Kaua'i continues to rebuild and grow stronger because of Iniki. Government agencies have begun to work in closer harmony, to make plans for the safety of the population of Kaua'i should any other disaster strike the island and its people.

TSUNAMI: A tsunami is an ocean wave produced by an undersea earthquake, volcanic eruption, or landslide. Tsunamis are usually generated along the coasts of South America, the Aleutian Islands, the Kamchatka Peninsula, or Japan and travel through the ocean at 400 to 500 miles an hour. It takes at least 4 1/2 hours for a tsunami to reach the Hawaiian Islands. A 24-hour Tsunami Warning System has been established in Hawai'i since 1946. When the possibility exists of a tsunami reaching Hawaiian waters, the public will be informed by the sound of the attention alert signal sirens. This particular signal is a steady one minute siren, followed by one minute of silence, repeating as long as necessary.

Immediately turn on a TV or radio; all stations will carry CIV-Alert emergency information and instructions with the arrival time of the first waves. Do not take chances, false alarms are not issued!! Move quickly out of low lying coastal areas that are subject to possible inundation.

The warning sirens are tested throughout the state on the first working Monday of every month at 11 am, so don't be alarmed when you hear the siren blare! The test lasts only a few minutes and CIV-Alert announces on all stations that the test is underway. Since 1813, there have been 112 tsunamis observed in Hawai'i with only 16 causing significant damage.

Tsunamis may also be generated by local volcanic earthquakes. In the last 100 years there have been only six, with the last one November 29, 1975, affecting the southeast coast of the island of Hawai'i. The Hawaiian Civil Defense has placed earthquake sensors on all the islands and, if a violent local earthquake occurs, an urgent tsunami warning will be broadcast and the tsunami sirens will sound. A locally generated tsunami will reach the other islands very quickly. Therefore, there may not be time for an attention alert signal to sound. Any violent earthquake that causes you to fall or hold onto something to prevent falling is an urgent warning, and you should immediately evacuate beaches and coastal low-lying areas.

There have been two tsunamis in recent history which struck Kaua'i doing serious damage to property and taking human life. In 1946 and in 1957, a tsunami did the most destruction to the North Shore of Kaua'i. A tsunami alert is always taken seriously, but fortunately the most recent (1995) tsunami generated a wave of only two inches.

For additional information on warnings and procedures in the event of a hurricane, tsunami, earthquake or flash flood, read the civil defense section located in the forward section of the Kaua'i phone book.

TIDES: The average tidal range is about two feet.

SUNRISE AND SUNSET: In Hawai'i, day length and the altitude of the noon sun above the horizon do not vary as much throughout the year. This is because the temperate regions of the island's low latitude lie within the sub-tropics. The longest day is 13 hours 26 minutes (sunrise 5:53 am, sunset 7:18 pm) at the end of June, and the shortest day is 10 hours 50 minutes (sunrise 7:09 am and sunset 6:01 pm at the end of December). Daylight for outdoor activities without artificial lighting lasts about 45 minutes past sunset.

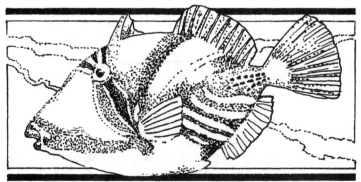

HUMUHUMUNUKUNUKUAPUAA

MAP INDEX

HAWAIIAN ISLANDS MAP 7

KAUA'I ISLAND 8, 9

MAP A CENTRAL AND EASTSIDE KAUA'I: Lihu'e and Airport 107

MAP B CENTRAL AND EASTSIDE KAUA'I: Lihu'e-Hanama'ulu-Puhi   113

MAP C CENTRAL AND EASTSIDE KAUA'I: Wailua-Waipouli-Kapa'a . 121

MAP D SOUTH SHORE KAUA'I: Po'ipu-Koloa-Lawa'i-
Kalaheo 147

MAP E SOUTH SHORE KAUA'I: Ele'ele-Hanapepe 159

MAP F SOUTH SHORE KAUA'I: Waimea-Kekaha 163

MAP G WESTERN KAUA'I: Pacific Missile Range 165

MAP H UPCOUNTRY KAUA'I: Waimea Canyon-Koke'e 167

MAP I EASTSIDE AND NORTH SHORE KAUA'I: Anahola 193

MAP J NORTH SHORE KAUA'I:
Kilauea-Princeville-Hanalei 197

MAP K NORTH SHORE KAUA'I: Hanalei-Ha'ena 205

ALL ISLAND BEACH MAP 344, 345

HANALEI IN THE MOONLIGHT

Hanalei in the moonlight
Silver shadows on the sea
Hanalei in the moonlight
A kiss, sweet memories

Hanalei in the moonlight
Lovers hand in hand
Hanalei in the moonlight
Strolling barefoot in the sand

Chorus:
E ho'i mai 'oe, e ku'u ipo
E ho'i mai 'oe, e ku'u ipo
I ka nani o Hanalei

Return to me my love
Return to me my love
To the beauty of Hanalei

E ku'u ipo, eia ho'i au
Ka u'i mālama a o Hanalei
'O ka pā kōnane a ka mahina
'Ōlinolino mai i ka 'ili o ke kai

Here I am my love
The glowing beauty of Hanalei
The brilliance of the moon
Glitters on the surface of the sea

By Kawaikapuokalani K. Hewett

WHERE TO STAY
WHAT TO SEE

INTRODUCTION

Kaua'i has considerable variety in lodging and accommodations for visitors of every budget category. According to the Hawaii State Department of Business, Economic Development and Tourism data, Kaua'i has 198 hotels, apartment hotels, Bed & Breakfast operations, bungalows, cottages, hostels and lodges. There are also 40 condominium properties having vacation rental units. There are some 6,872 vacation rental unit accommodations on Kaua'i. The island inventory includes 3,871 hotel rooms, apartment hotel units, B&Bs, bungalows, cottages, hostel and lodge rooms. In addition, there are 3,001 condominium units in vacation rental programs. And there are a number of various accommodations, B&Bs, lodges, rental homes, cottages and the like that were probably not included in the count for one reason or another. That may well boost the number of available accommodations to something over 7,000.

The island can easily be divided into three main areas, with perhaps some sub-areas: Princeville and Hanalei -- North Shore; The East/Central region; and the third which we have grouped into one area that includes the South and West shores. This last area covers Po'ipu Beach and the Koloa areas, and continues to the west side to include the accommodations in the Waimea and Koke'e areas. This chapter contains a list of essentially all of the condominiums that are in rental programs as well as the island's hotels.

Bed & Breakfasts are a booming business and an alternative that has become increasingly popular over the years. Kaua'i has a variety of economy to luxury class B & B units around the island. The last few years have seen a rapidly expanding B & B segment of Kaua'i's hospitality industry. Whereas previously there were only a handful of such operations scattered around the island, now B & B lodgings can actually be found in just about every area. Visitors seek out B & B lodging because of the more personalized service and experience to be had. B & Bs often put visitors more in-touch with local residents who can provide unique and special insight into Kaua'i's local culture, activities, experiences, etc. thus making a vacation experience that much more meaningful.

Traditionally B & B means a room in a private home, usually with a shared entrance and bath. Such rooms generally range from $55 a night. Other B & Bs, cottages, inns, condos and studios with private entrances and/or baths range from $60 to $200 a night depending on quality, features and amenities provided. Bed & Breakfast operations are sprinkled around the island in the East Side/Central (Lihu'e), North Shore, and South Shore/West Side. They are listed within each respective area as a separate group.

97

Also included at the conclusion of this chapter are several of the Bed & Breakfast agencies which handle many more homes than it was possible to include in this volume. Related websites have been listed where available. Refer to RENTAL AGENTS at the conclusion of this chapter. Note that very few Bed & Breakfast facilities accept any type of charge cards. Some also do not allow children for various reasons.

Remember when calling Hawai'i to adjust for the time difference. Most offices are open during business hours Hawai'i standard time and some only weekdays. Bed & Breakfast homes would no doubt really appreciate calls during the day or evening (Hawai'i time).

HOW TO USE THIS CHAPTER: For ease in locating information, the properties are first indexed alphabetically following this introduction. In each of the three distinctly different geographical areas, we have divided the condominiums and listed them in order of price and then alphabetized them for quick reference.

Keep in mind that in providing directions, we may refer to the Hawaiian terms of *mauka*, which means towards the mountains and *makai*, which means towards the ocean. On these islands it is much less cumbersome to utilize this form of indicating direction than the standard north, east, south, and west!

Often the management at the property takes reservations, but some do not. In some cases there are several rental agents handling units in addition to the on-site management and we have listed an assortment of these. We suggest that when you determine which condo you are interested in that you call all of the agents. Be aware that while one agent may have no vacancy, another will have several. The prices we have listed are generally the lowest available (although some agents may offer lower rates with the reduction of certain services such as maid service on check in only - that means your room is clean when you arrive - rather than daily maid service). You may find that one of the package air/condo/car options will be an all-around better value than booking each of these separately.

Prices are listed to aid your selection and, while these were the most current available at press time, they are subject to change without notice. As island vacationers ourselves, we found it important to include this feature rather than just giving you broad categories such as budget or expensive. After all, one person's "expensive" may be "budget" to someone else!

For the sake of space, we have made use of several abbreviations. The size of the condominiums are identified as studio (S BR), one bedroom (1 BR), two bedroom (2 BR), and three bedroom (3 BR). The number in parentheses refers to the number of people that can occupy the unit for the price listed and that there are enough beds for a maximum number of people to occupy this unit, i.e. 2 BR (max 4). The description will tell you how much it will be for additional persons over two, i.e. $10/night. Some facilities consider an infant as an extra person, others will allow children free up to a specified age. The abbreviations o.f., g.v., and o.v. refer to oceanfront, gardenview, and oceanview units.

Some of the prices may be listed with a slash dividing them. The first price listed is the high season rate, the second price is the low season rate. More and more properties are going to a flat all-season rate. A few include the summer months as high season, and a few others have complicated matters by having a three season fee schedule. The abbreviation <WWW> means that there is a website available. Websites for rental agencies, hotel/resorts, and individual properties have been provided where available. It is recommended that websites be checked for the latest rates and specials as well.

All listings are condominiums unless specified as a (Hotel). Condos are abundant, and the prices and facilities they offer can be quite varied. We have tried to indicate our own personal preferences by the use of a ★. We felt these were the best buys or special in some way. However, it is impossible for us to view all the units within a complex, and since condominiums are privately owned, each unit can vary in its furnishings and its condition.

WHERE TO STAY: As for choosing the area of the island in which to stay, we offer these suggestions:

SOUTH SHORE/WEST SIDE: Along the south and west shores you'll find it generally sunny and warm; the Po'ipu area generally has the best beach conditions but the Hanapepe, Waimea and Kekaha areas are also warm and sunny. During the winter months the south shore beaches are generally safer. The region has varied attractions like the Grand Canyon of the Pacific, Port Allen cruise boats to Napali Coast, activities, accommodations, dining, etc.

NORTH SHORE: If you want incredible scenery, lots of lush green vegetation and are eager to get just a little further away from civilization, then the North Shore may be for you. With varied accommodations you can choose between luxury and moderate. The Anahola, Kilauea, Princeville and Hanalei areas have varied attractions, activities and accommodations available. During the winter months, high surf can make the North Shore ocean conditions very dangerous.

EAST SHORE/CENTRAL: Affectionately known as the Coconut Coast, you'll find the best selection of affordable accommodations in this area. Centrally located, you can easily drive to either the South Shore/West Side or North Shore for the many varied activities they offer. Lots of options available in activities, attractions, dining, shopping, accommodations, and more.

HOW TO SAVE MONEY: Kaua'i has two price seasons. High or "in" season and low or "off" season. Low season is generally considered to be April 15 to about December 15, and the rates are discounted at some places as much as 30%. Different resorts and condominiums may vary these dates by as much as two weeks and a few resorts are going to a flat, year-round rate. Ironically, some of the best weather is during the fall when temperatures are cooler than summer and there is less rain than the winter and spring months. (See GENERAL INFORMATION - *Weather* for year-round temperatures).

For longer than one week, a condo unit with a kitchen can result in significant savings on your food bill. While this will give you more space than a hotel room at a lower price, you may give up some resort amenities (shops, restaurants, maid service, etc.). There are several large grocery stores around the island with fairly competitive prices, although most things at the store will run about 30% higher than on the mainland. (See GENERAL INFORMATION - *Grocery Shopping*.)

Most condominiums offer maid service only on check-out. A few might offer it twice a week or weekly. Additional maid service may be available for an extra charge. A few condos still do not provide in-room phones and a few have no pool.

(A few words of caution: condominium units within one complex can differ greatly so, if a phone or other amenity is important to you, ask!) Some may offer free local calls while others will tack on an extra $1 per local call. Many have added microwaves to their kitchens. Some units have washers and dryers in the rooms, while others do not. If there are no in-room laundry facilities, you will generally find that most have coin-operated laundry facilities on the premises. Travel agents will be able to book you at any of the Kaua'i hotels and in most island condominiums.

If you prefer to make your own reservation, we have listed the various contacts for each condominium and endeavored to quote the best price generally available. A little phone work can be very cost effective! Rates vary between rental agents, so check all those listed for a particular condominium. We have indicated toll free 800, 877 or 888 numbers for the U.S. when available. Some toll free numbers are not valid from Canada or inter-island. For additional Canadian toll free numbers, check the rental agent list at the end of this chapter. Look for an (808) area code preceding the non-toll free numbers.

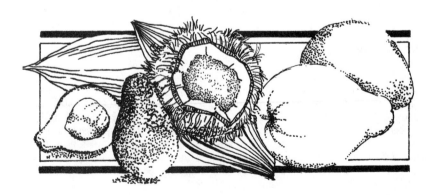

You might also check the classified ads in your local newspaper for owners offering their units for rent, which may be even a better bargain. Although prices can jump, most go up only 5-10% per year. To the prices listed, you will need to add sales tax of 4% plus a transient accommodations tax which is currently 7.25% Also check the individual rental agency or hotel/condo websites for the most current room rates and discount or seasonal specials, room/car packages, senior discounts, etc.

GENERAL POLICIES: Condominium complexes require a deposit (usually equivalent to one or two nights stay) to secure your reservation and insure your room rate against price increases. Some charge higher deposits during winter or over Christmas holidays. Generally a 30 day notice of cancellation is needed to receive a full refund. Most require payment in full either 30 days prior to arrival or upon arrival, and some do not accept credit cards. Night owls beware! Many condos have initiated early check-out times of 11 am or even 10 am, although some are compensating by providing an earlier check-in of 2 pm (instead of 3 pm). The usual minimum condo stay is three nights with some requiring one week in winter.

Christmas holidays may have steeper restrictions with minimum stays as long as two weeks, payments 90 days in advance and heavy cancellation penalties. It is not uncommon to book as much as two years in advance for the Christmas season.

PLEASE NOTE: ALL CONDOMINIUMS HAVE KITCHENS, TELEVISIONS, AND SWIMMING POOLS UNLESS OTHERWISE SPECIFIED.

Most condominiums have ceiling fans, but many have no air conditioning. After arriving from a long flight with a car full of luggage, one of the most unpleasant surprises may be to discover that you are on the third floor of a condominium complex that does NOT have an elevator. A surprising number of multi-level complexes are equipped only with stairs.

Monthly and oftentimes weekly discounts are available. Room rates quoted are generally for two. Additional persons run $10 and up per night per person with the exception of the high class resorts and hotels where it may run as much as $25 to $35 extra. Many complexes can arrange for crib rentals. (See GENERAL INFORMATION - *Traveling with Children.*) We have tried to give the lowest rates generally available, which might not be through the hotel or condo office, so check with the offices as well as the rental agents. Variations in prices may be due to the amenities of a particular unit or the general condition of the condo. When contacting condominium complexes by mail, be sure to address your correspondence to the attention of the manager. The managers of several complexes do not handle any reservations, however, so we have indicated to whom you should address reservation requests. If two addresses are given, use the P.O. Box rather than street address for your correspondence.

CONDOMINIUM AND HOTEL INDEX

A Bed of Roses B&B 129
Alihi Lani Condos 181
Alii Kai I 222
Alii Kai II 223
Aloha Aina B & B 218
Aloha Breeze B & B 174
Aloha Condos 211
Aloha Country B & B 129
Aloha Mana Garden Cottage 125
Aloha Plantation B & B 218
Aloha Sunrise Inn 211
Alohilani B & B 130
Anahola Alohaloha 125
Anahola Cottage 126
An Angel Abode 211
Anchorage Point 211
Anderson's Hale Nalu 170
Anini Beach Cottages 211
Anini Beach Hale 212
Anne's Condos & Studios at Princeville Resort 212
Anuenue Platantion Cottage 126
Aston Kaha Lani 137
Aston Kaua'i Beach Villas 138
Aston Kaua'i Coast Resort at the Beachboy 138
Aston Po'ipu Kai 181
Bamboo Jungle B & B 174
Banyan Harbor Condominiums 135
Best Western Plantation Hale 139
Boulay Inn 170
Brennecke's Beach Cottage 170
Candy's Cabin 130
Classic Vacation Cottage 170
(The) Cliffs at Princeville 223
Coastline Cottages 171
Coco's Vacation Rental 171
Condos Kauai 212
Coral by the Sea B & B 174
Devaki's Vacation Rental 213
Embassy Vacation Resort - Po'ipu Point 186
Emmalani Court 223
Garden Island Inn 136
Garden Island Sunset Vacation Rentals 181
Garden Isle Cottages-Oceanfront 174
Glo Manor House 213

Gloria's Spouting Horn 175
Hale 'Aha 218
Hale Awapuhi 145
Hale Hoku 182
Hale Honu Townhouses 213
Hale Ho'o Maha 218
Hale Hyette B & B 175
Hale Ikena Nui 175
Hale Kaulana 126
Hale Kua B & B 175
Hale Lihu'e Motel 134
Hale Lii B & B 219
Haleluia by the River 219
Hale Makani 126
Hale Manu B & B 220
Hale Moi Cottages 221
Hale O Wailele 126
Hale Pau Hana 127
Hale Steward 213
Hale Tutu 130
Hall's Plantation Estate 171
Hamaguchi Hale 214
Hanalei Bay Resort 225
Hanalei Bay Villas 223
Hanalei Colony Resort 224
Hanalei Inn 221
Hanalei Plantation Cottages and Kauikeolani Estate 215
Hanalei Properties 214
Hardy's Happy Hula Hut 214
Hempey's Garden Island B&B 131
Historic B&B 220
Holiday Inn Sunspree Resort 139
Honu Kai Vacation Villas (and B&B) 171
Hotel Coral Reef 136
House of Aleva B & B 131
Hyatt Regency Resort & Spa 186
Island Enchantment 230
Island Home B & B 176
Islander on the Beach 137
Jan's Kauai Kondo Kompany 172
Jungle Cabana and Jungle Bungalow 214
Kaha Lani (Aston) 137
Kahili Mountain Park Cabins 230
Kai Mana Cottage 215
Kakalina's B & B 131
Kalahea Hale 176

Kalaheo Inn 176
Kalaheo Plantation Vacation Rental 172
Kalama Dreams Cottage 127
Kaleialoha Oceanfront Accomodations 127
Kamahana 224
Kapa'a Sands 140
Kapa'a Shore 140
Kaua'i Beach Villas (Aston) 138
Kaua'i Coast Resort at the Beachboy (Aston) 138
Kaua'i Coconut Beach 141
Kaua'i Condo's at Poipu Kai Resort 172
Kaua'i Cove Cottages 176
Kaua'i Hideaways Guest Cottages 173
Kaua'i International Hostel 134
Kaua'i Kondo 215
Kaua'i Marriott Resort & Beach Club 145
Kaua'i Sands 142
Kauikeolani Estate and Hanalei Plantation Cottages 215, 231
Keapana Center 231
Keapana Secluded Garden Cottage 128
Kekaha Oceanfront Vacation Rentals 173
Kiahuna Plantation 188
KK Bed & Bath 135
Koloa Landing Cottages 180
Koke'e Lodge 180
Kuhio Shores 182
Lae Nani 142
Lampy's B & B 134
Lani Aina Beach Hale 216
Lanikai 146
Lani Keha B & B 132
Lawa'i Beach Resort 182
Love Nest Cottage 216
Mahina's Women's Guest House 137
Makahuena Resort 182
Makaleha Mountain Retreat 128
Makana Crest 128
Marjorie's Kaua'i Inn (and B & B) 177
Maukalani at Lawa'i 173
Mohala Ke Ola 132
Motel Lani 135
Nihi Kai Villas 183
Noho Kai at Anini 216
North Country Farms B & B 220
Old Koloa House B & B 177
Ole Kamaole's Beach Houses 177
OM Orchard Retreat 217
Opaekaa Falls Hale B & B 133
Pali Kai Cottages 143

Pali Ke Kua 225
Pali Uli 225
Paniolo 222
Paradise Found 128
Pavilions at Seacliff 220
Plantation Managers Home 217
Plantation Retreat 129
Po'ipu B & B 178
Po'ipu Crater Resort 183
Po'ipu Kai 172
Po'ipu Kapili 183
Po'ipu Makai 184
Po'ipu Palms 184
Po'ipu Plantation Resort 178
Po'ipu Point (See Embassy Vacation Resort)
Po'ipu Shores Condominiums 189
Pono Kai 143
Prince Kuhio 180
Princeville Resort (Sheraton) 226
PRIVATE HOMES & COTTAGES 125, 170, 210, 228
Pu'u Po'a 228
Pua Hale at Po'ipu Beach 173
Puamana 225
Radisson Kaua'i Beach 143
RETREATS 230
River Estate 217
Rosewood B & B and private homes 129, 133
Sandpiper Village 222
Sealodge 222
Secret Beach Estate Cottages 217
Sheraton Kaua'i Resort 190
South Shore Vista B & B 178
Strawberry Guava B & B 179
Sugar Mill Cottages 179
Sunset Kahili Condos 173
Tip Top Motel 135
Victoria Place 179
Waikomo Stream Villas 184
Wailua Bay View 144
Waimea Plantation Cottages 195
Waioli Vacation Rental 218
Waonahele at Kupono Farms B & B 134
Whaler's Cove 191
YMCA 231
YWCA 232

CENTRAL AND EASTSIDE

Kapa'a - Lihu'e - Nawiliwili - Wailua - Waipouli

In this section we will begin at Lihu'e and travel up the west coast in a northerly direction to Hanama'ulu, Wailua, Waipouli, and Kapa'a.

INTRODUCTION

Kaua'i's main airport is located in Lihu'e, so this is probably the first place you'll see. It's not exactly the garden spot of the Garden Isle, but it is the least touristy area of the island. Lihu'e is a busy county seat town where all the government and many "big" business offices are located and the place to find everyday necessities like the post office, discount shopping, banks, churches, and a library. It also offers the best selection of inexpensive local restaurants.

Hotels, motels, and condos in Lihu'e are generally less expensive than other parts of the island and several provide convenient access to the airport. But with the exception of two resort areas, accommodations are generally very basic. Even if you stay at another property for the duration of your stay, Lihu'e area lodgings are worth considering for a night if you have a late evening arrival or an early morning departure.

And don't worry about being too far away from the "good stuff." The Anchor Cove and Harbor Mall shopping centers are very close, as is the Kaua'i Museum, and there are plenty of restaurants in the area - from funky local dining and ethnic places to fine dining selections. The Radisson Kaua'i Beach Hotel and adjacent Aston Kaua'i Beach Villas along with the Kaua'i Marriott Resort & Beach Club are the only real visitor quality resorts in the area. The Kaua'i Marriott is located next to Nawiliwili Harbor at Lihu'e with the Radisson and Aston Beach Villas a couple of miles north of the general Lihu'e area. Further north along the Coconut Coast area are an abundance of affordably priced hotels and condominiums and there is plenty of wonderful natural beauty and activities to be enjoyed as well.

As you exit from Lihu'e Airport, the first stoplight intersection is Kapule Highway #52 and Ahukini Road. This intersection has undergone major recon-struction in recent months with extensive beautification work, plantings of tropical plants, flowers and trees, building of lavarock walls, all to make the area more visually appealing to arriving visitors. If you're heading north toward Kapa'a and the North Shore area, turn right at this intersection. If you're heading into Lihu'e or to Po'ipu or the westside, continue straight ahead on Ahukini Road into Lihu'e. If you're heading to the Kaua'i Marriott, turn left at this intersection for a shortcut to the resort in lower Lihu'e town.

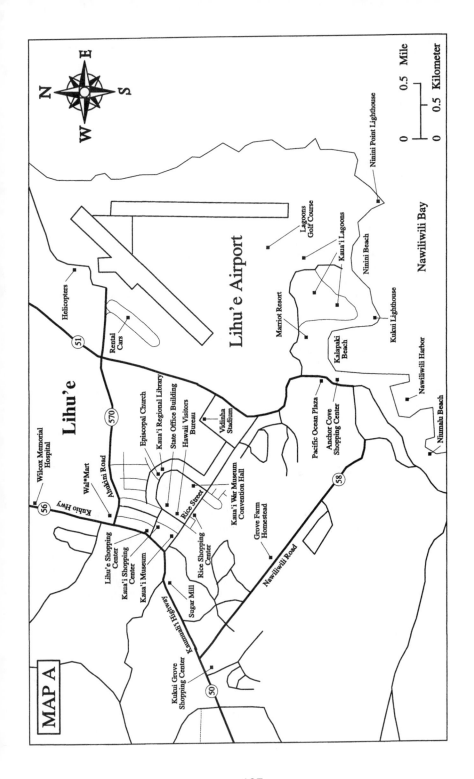

MAP A

N E S W

0   0.5   Mile
0   0.5   Kilometer

Lihu'e

Lihu'e Airport

Nawiliwili Bay

Helicopters

Rental Cars

51

570

Wilcox Memorial Hospital

56
Kuhio Hwy

Wal*Mart

Ahukini Road

Episcopal Church

Kaua'i Regional Library

State Office Building

Hawaii Visitors Bureau

Vidinha Stadium

Kaua'i War Museum
Convention Hall

Rice Street

Lihu'e Shopping Center

Kaua'i Shopping Center

Kaua'i Museum

Sugar Mill

Rice Shopping Center

Grove Farm Homestead

Kaumali'i Highway

Nawiliwili Road

58

50

Kukui Grove Shopping Center

Marriot Resort

Pacific Ocean Plaza

Anchor Cove Shopping Center

Lagoons Golf Course

Kaua'i Lagoons

Ninini Beach

Kalapaki Beach

Kukui Lighthouse

Nawiliwili Harbor

Niumalu Beach

Ninini Point Lighthouse

WHAT TO SEE

LIHU'E

The word Lihu'e means "open to chill" and according to the *Kaua'i Talking Guidebook*, the town was named in 1837 by the Governor who relocated from the Big Island. His home town there (also called Lihu'e) had a cooler climate and was a more appropriate name than here on Kaua'i.

Because of our unusual island-state, mayors in Hawai'i govern counties which consist of one or more islands rather than areas of land. The island of Kaua'i (along with Ni'ihau) is a county of the state of Hawai'i and Lihu'e is the county seat. The historic county building was built in 1913 and, with its sprawling lawn and tall palm trees, it is a focal point of Lihu'e. Although government agencies are not usually high on one's list of visitor attractions, you may find the need to visit one or more while you're here on Kaua'i.

The *Kaua'i Visitors Bureau* is always a good place to start to pick up some brochures and ask for information. It is located at 4334 Rice Street, Room #101; tel (808) 245-3971, fax (808) 246-9235.

The *State Parks and Recreation Department* - a place you will need to go to if you plan on doing any camping, hiking, or generally any nature-oriented trips -is located in the State Building at 3060 Eiwa. This is where you will be able to pick up your permits. Phone (808) 274-3444 Division of State Parks - Camping permits.

The *County Parks and Recreation Department* is at 4444 Rice, Suite 150. Phone (808) 241-6670 or for permits and reservations phone (808) 241-6660.

If you spend any time at all in Lihu'e you'll become quite familiar with Rice Street. It seems this single road can get you anywhere you want to go! From the Kaua'i Visitors Bureau, you can turn from Rice onto Hardy to reach the *Kaua'i War Memorial Convention Hall* and the Regional Library. The library has an excellent selection of Hawaiian titles, many of which are now out-of-print. If you are a Hawaiiana buff, you might like to include this on your itinerary! The Kaua'i Community College, 3-1902 Kaumuali'i Highway on the west edge of Lihu'e also has a good Hawaiiana section in their library.

If you are hot after a day of sightseeing and shopping, take a short detour to Halo Halo Shave Ice. It is part of *Hamura Saimin* and it, too, is just off Rice Street. Just around the corner from *Hamura Saimin* is *Ma's* a good local-style eatery and just down the street is also *Barbecue Inn*, a great family-style restaurant.

Further along Rice Street is the *Rice Shopping Center*. It houses the island's only bowling alley, a Filipino bakery, and a couple of local style eateries. But before that, you'll find the main post office and, just across the street, the Kaua'i Museum.

The *Kaua'i Museum* ★ is a great place to get acquainted with the island's history. It is located at 4428 Rice Street in the Wilcox Building that was originally constructed in the 1920's as the first public library. Mrs. Emma Mahelona Wilcox offered $74,000 in February of 1922 for the construction of a permanent library in memory of her husband, Albert Spencer Wilcox. The building, designed by Hart Wood, was dedicated on May 24, 1924. In 1954 work began to create a Kaua'i Museum and it officially opened on December 3, 1960. In 1969 the adjacent Albert Spencer Wilcox Library building became the central building of the Kaua'i Museum Complex. The original museum building was named after William Hyde Rice. The museum offers a combination of permanent and changing exhibits. Some tell the story of the island's volcanic creation while other displays explain the role immigrants have played in creating the multicultural community that exists here today. The ancient people and their culture, the discovery by Captain Cook, missionary occupation, royal families, and agricultural history are all explored. Their 30 minute aerial film tour of Kaua'i provides a great base for planning your island excursions. Art, music, dance, religion, language, farming, surfing, healing, and the transition from royalty to statehood are all covered. The Kaua'i Museum gift store has quite possibly the best selection of Hawaiian titles as well as some wonderful handcrafted gift items. There is no admission charge if you wish to visit only the gift store, just advise them at the front counter. The museum is free to all on the first Saturday of each month. They have periodic special presentations and family activities. Open weekdays 9 am-4 pm, Sat. 10 am-4 pm, closed Sunday. (808) 245-6931.

The *Kaua'i Historical Society,* 4396 Rice Street, (808) 245-3373, is involved in various historical and educational activities on the island, including an informative historical "dune walk" that is offered in conjunction with the Hyatt Regency. They also work in partnership with the Kaua'i Museum and Grove Farm Homestead and sponsor Elderhostel programs. They do maintain an office in Lihu'e, but they are not open to the general public. Their 3,000 volume collection, however, is available to the public for research and education, Monday through Friday, by appointment only. Donations and contributions are welcomed. Family membership is $25 per year. Call for information.

Rice Street ends at the Lihu'e Shopping Center where it meets the Kuhio Highway. If you turn right and travel north for a half mile, you will find *Hilo Hattie*, a mainstay for traditional aloha wear. They also sell an assortment of packaged Hawaiian food products and giftware items. Just up the street is a branch of the national chain, *Walmart*. This drug and sundry store has most things you might have forgotten to pack. Although we still like the comfortable feeling of a *Longs Drug Store*, Walmart does have clothes and a larger selection of most items and you can't beat their long hours of operation! They open at 6 am (Sundays at 8) and stay open nightly until 10 pm! If you choose to head south on the highway, it becomes the Kaumualii Highway (Route 50) and a short drive will take you to the *Kukui Grove Shopping Center*. The new 10-hole Grove Farm Golf Course at Puakea is nearby, so those golf lovers could partake of a short game while the shop-aholics in your group shop!

Kukui Grove is the island's largest shopping center and is the location Macy's, the major department store. (The former Liberty House was sold in 2001.) The

Kaua'i Products Store has a lovely selection of locally made quilts, muumuus, jewelry, lotions, keiki clothing -- even homemade fudge! Nature's of Hawai'i offers unusual Hawaiian curios and aloha wear. The Soul Garden Bath & Body Shop features organic soaps, lotions, bath & shower gels, oils, and blend-your-own Hawaiian fragrance products. And you don't want to miss a stop at Dollar Plus, where all items are priced at $1.25. There are a few restaurants and eateries to be found in the mall, but better and more reasonable dining will be found back in the town of Lihu'e.

Turning left (south) onto the Kaumualii Highway from the Kukui Grove Shopping Center and along the road a short distance, you'll find a turnout viewing area. This is a good location to take a glance at the Hoary Head Mountain Range which rises south beyond and behind the Kukui Center. Look closely (real close!) and you will see the *profile of Queen Victoria*. Her head is slightly tipped back and she has a crown perched on the top of her head. A finger is pointing up as if she is reprimanding someone in the distance beyond. In fact, this natural feature is becoming more obscured with time as natural vegetation changes the distant profile line. Just beyond is Puhi, an old plantation town. The old town boasts a farmers' market, various shops, a couple of restaurants and is home to Kaua'i Community College. Just before you reach Puhi, you'll pass by the legendary plantation estate of Kilohana. *Kilohana* ★ is reminiscent of the grandeur and elegance of an earlier age. At the time when sugar was king on the island and prosperity reigned, plantation owners would build luxurious homes. One of the grandest on Kaua'i was the home of Gaylord Parke Wilcox and is known as Kilohana. Built in 1935, this 16,000 square foot Tudor mansion was designed by a British architect named Mark Potter. The property was named for the large cinder cone which is located above and behind the property. The grounds are carefully landscaped and inside furniture came from the exclusive and expensive Gump's in San Francisco. The Kilohana Shops and Galleries are well deserving of a bit of wandering, before or after you enjoy your meal at Gaylord's Courtyard Restaurant. You'll find several tour options for exploring this 35-acre estate. The Canefield Tour is a step back into the history of sugar cane on Kaua'i. A wagon ride takes you back in time to 1835 with historical background on the property. Our guide was interesting and informative and nonplussed by the rain showers as our wagon, drawn by two Clydesdales, navigated through the fields. In 1865 the second sugar plantation, the Lihu'e Plantation, was established along the Wailua River. It was the first to bring immigrant workers and to use stone grinders in the processing of the cane. George Norton Wilcox, the son of island missionaries returned to the island in 1864 following his studies at Scheffield (Yale) in engineering. He purchased 900 acres of wasteland for $10,000. When he broached the subject of irrigation, others thought he was crazy. He proceeded to dig a ditch 11.2 miles in length to bring water from Mt. Wai'ale'ale. The ditch, dug by hand, took two years to complete. His introduction of foreign immigrants from the Philippines, Germany, Australia, Japan, and elsewhere was the start of the cultural diversity that is evident in the islands today. George was concerned that most of the workers would chose to return to their homelands following their contract. He approached them inquiring what would entice them to remain. Their answer resulted in Grove Farm providing single-family, 300 sq. ft. homes for the workers. These camp houses were designed after those used in logging camps in Oregon and Washington and were sent to Hawai'i in ready-to-assemble units. The only differences between these cabins and those in the Pacific Northwest logging camps were the lanais which were added to the front and the use of tin for the roofs. (Because of the cane burning and risk of flying cinders, a wooden roof would have been a fire hazard.) He also introduced chemical fertilization, developed hybrid strains of cane, and when the depression struck the country, George diversified. He died in 1933 at the age of 89 leaving everything to his nephew Gaylord. Gaylord built the 16,000 sq. ft. Kilohana home for his wife Ethel. Gaylord continued management of the company and ensured its continued success to this day. This sugar cane tour takes about an hour, but may not be a lively enough experience to keep the interest of youth. Those interested in a deeper background on the Wilcox family might enjoy the more lengthy tour at the Grove Farm Homestead.

The carriage ride is a shorter, more romantic excursion around the grounds. Carriage rides are available daily 11 am-6:30 pm. Horse dawn Sugar Cane Tours are set up by advance reservations, (808) 246-9529. Admission to Kilohana and its grounds is free, carriage rides are $8 adults/$4 children. Sugar Cane Tours are $21 adults/$10 children. Kilohana and the shops open daily at 9:30 am. Gaylord's serves Sunday brunch 9:30 am-3 pm, lunch Monday to Saturday 11 am-3 pm, and dinner nightly from 5 pm. Located just outside Lihu'e, travel east along Kaumualii Highway, Route 50. Kilohana is on your left just before the town of Lihu'e. If you are arriving from the north or east, travel Kuhio Hwy., Route 56 south and west through Lihu'e. Bear right at the traffic light at the end of Kuhio Hwy. Kilohana will be 1.4 miles down Kaumualii Highway on your right. Kilohana (808) 245-5608.

Returning to the Kukui Grove Shopping Center, but at the opposite (Nawiliwili) end, is *Big Kmart*. Adjacent is *Borders Books and Music* which is worth a stop. This is a bookstore chain, but in addition to books it there is also a terrific selection of music and videos as well as the drifting scent of espresso from their in-store cafe! They offer special events (free!) and their children's corner is a nice touch for the traveling family. 4303 Nawiliwili Rd., Lihu'e, HI 96766. (808) 246-0862.

Also on Nawiliwili Road about 1/4 mile south of the shopping center is the *Grove Farm Homestead* ★ which provides visitors with a fascinating look into the island's past. Kaua'i's history can be traced to the beginnings and growth of the sugar plantations. Grove Farm, one of the earliest sugar plantations, was founded in 1864 by George Wilcox, Gaylord's uncle. Today, this historic museum showcases the old sugar days and Hawai'i's politics from the monarchy to statehood. A two-and-one-half hour tour takes visitors through the original home, which was enlarged in later years to accommodate a growing family. The property, which includes the gracious old Wilcox home and the cottage of the plantation laundress, is situated amidst tropical gardens, orchards, and rolling lawns. The tours are small and intimate and the guides knowledgeable about the island's sugar industry and its history. Minted ice tea (with homegrown mint) and Grove Farm icebox cookies baked in an old wood stove in the farm house (Miss Mabel's favorite!) are served for refreshments. This living legacy was left by Miss Mabel Wilcox, the last surviving niece of George Wilcox, who wanted her family home to be preserved. She lived here until the time of her death in 1978.

TA PUA ELAMA

Ta pua a 'o Ni'ihau
Onaona me ta ho'ohihi,
I ta nui lehulehu,
Ta pua Ēlama.

Ta pua a 'o Ni'ihau
Onaona me ta ho'ohihi,
I ta nui lehulehu,
Ta pua Ēlama.

Ta pua o tou lei,
E mohala mau loa ana,
I pulama ia e ta lehulehu,
Ta pua Ēlama.

Mahalo a nui loa,
Mai to'u pu'u wai,
He mele teia nou,
E ta pua Ēlama.

Used with the permission of Chucky Boy Chock. This is dedicated to
Elama Kanahele, who did all the Hawaiian translation. Her patience
time and expertise will always be treasured. Mahalo to her 'Ohana
and the beautiful people of Ni'ihau.

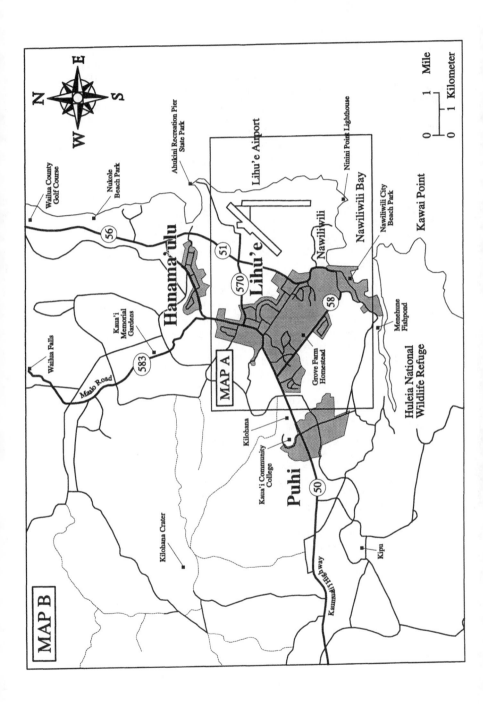

MAP B

MAP A

N
W   E
S

Wailua County Golf Course

Nukole Beach Park

56

Hanama'ulu

Ahukini Recreation Pier State Park

Lihu'e Airport

Kaua'i Memorial Gardens

Waihua Falls

583

Maalo Road

51

570

Lihu'e

Nawiliwili

Nawiliwili Bay

Ninini Point Lighthouse

Nawiliwili City Beach Park

Kilohana

58

Grove Farm Homestead

Menehune Fishpond

Kawai Point

Huleia National Wildlife Refuge

Kilohana Crater

Kaua'i Community College

Puhi

50

Kaumuali'i Highway

Kipu

0   1   Mile
0   1   Kilometer

113

The property opened to the public in 1980. Most visitors miss touring the Grove Farm Homestead because reservations need to be booked well in advance. This is quite possibly Kaua'i's best cultural experience and well worth the phone call three months or more in advance of your island arrival. Cost is currently $5 per person with tours available Mondays, Wednesdays and Thursdays. (808) 245-3202, PO Box 1631, Lihu'e HI 96766. As an anecdote, it's interesting to note that Steve Case, who grew up and went to school in Honolulu, going on to found America Online (AOL), recently purchased Grove Farm. With Grove Farm's large land holdings and developments on Kaua'i, there may be some interesting changes coming under the new owner.

NAWILIWILI

Following Nawiliwili Road past Kukui Grove and the Grove Farm Homestead will take you toward the harbor. The route you travel is through scenic Lihu'e, again following Rice Street but in the opposite direction from before. Here, Rice Street becomes Hwy. 51 and will take you down past the Kaua'i Marriott Resort and on toward the harbor.

The **Kaua'i Marriott Resort & Beach Club** is located above the Nawiliwili Harbor at Kalapaki Bay. After being closed to hurricane damage in the early '90s, the hotel sat vacant for a few years before Marriott took over the property and converted it into a combination timeshare and hotel. Major renovations converted the once European-style of this lavish resort to one with a Hawaiiana atmosphere. The much-improved property now has a more pleasing island-style ambiance. This hotel is the tallest building on Kaua'i. After its original construction in the '70s, local zoning laws changed so that no building on Kaua'i could be taller than a palm tree. Next door at Kaua'i Lagoons is the Terrace Restaurant and further along, the Whalers Brewpub. Wedding services are available in the romantic gazebo. Continuing on toward Nawiliwili Harbor, you will pass the **Anchor Cove Shopping Center** and the **Harbor Mall**, visitor-oriented shopping areas located across the street from each other on Rice Street. Nawiliwili was named for the abundant wiliwili trees that once thrived in this area. Nawiliwili Harbor became Kaua'i's main deep water harbor upon its completion in 1930. Following the completion of the harbor, Lihu'e became the island's major city. **Nawiliwili Park** was refurbished in 1995. The area has been improved with the addition of playground areas, barbecues, and picnic tables. Since then the park has also added professional volley ball courts. If you have some recreational time consider stopping by the kayak rental at Nawiliwili's small boat harbor which offers half day trips up the river past the Menehune Fish Pond. (Refer to RECREATION chapter for specifics.)

The **Menehune Fish Pond** is a spot you may easily miss. Follow Hwy. 51 toward the Nawiliwili Harbor and look for the Wilcox Road sign. Follow it left onto Niumalu Road. Then turn right onto Hulemalu Road where a visitors bureau sign indicates the Menehune Fish Pond. From this turn-off it is another 6/10 of a mile to the lookout which will be on your left. The fish pond appears to be just a small pond adjacent to the Huleia River (or Huleia Stream, depending on the map you follow). Portions of *Raiders of the Lost Ark* were filmed along this waterway. Again, no historical background exists about the building of this pond, but legend tells that it was done by the menehune who were interrupted during their nighttime work and quit, leaving the pond unfinished with *pukas* (holes) in it! Some years ago a family tried to rebuild the gates to make the fish pond once again a working proposition, but plans or events changed and it was never made operational. The only way to see this up close is to do it by kayak along the Huleia River. Tours up the river - which begin near the Nawiliwili boat harbor - are available from operators such as Island Adventures, Aloha Canoes & Kayaks, and others. The access road to the pond is posted as "No Trespassing" and while that doesn't stop some people from venturing beyond, we prefer to let the property owners maintain their legal rights.

Located along the Huleia River is the *Huleia National Wildlife Refuge*, which is home to the endangered koloa duck. In 1973, 241 acres were purchased to provide a habitat for water birds. The lands, once taro and rice fields, are now breeding and feeding grounds for a variety of waterfowl. The refuge is located in a relatively flat valley along the Huleia River which is bordered by a steep wooded hillside. There are 31 species of migratory birds which inhabit the area, 18 of which were introduced. A special permit is issued annually to a commercial kayaking business for access through an upland portion of the refuge. The refuge, adjacent to the Menehune Fish Pond, is not open to the public. If you continue exploring the roads beyond the Menehune Pond you'll find some nice vistas of the Huleia Wildlife Refuge. We also found a little fruit stand that had piles of papaya and operated on the "honor system". The papayas were each labeled with a black marker indicating the price. We picked out the one we liked, dropped the money in the can, and were on our way. Oh, wondrous Kaua'i!

WHERE TO SHOP

Harbor Mall and Anchor Cove are located across the street from each other on Rice Street as you head towards Nawiliwili. The *Harbor Mall* has several boutiques along with Cafe Portofino, Kaua'i Chop Suey, and Tokyo Lobby restaurants. At *Anchor Cove* you will find a Crazy Shirts outlet, a Wyland Gallery, and J.J.'s Broiler. If you plan to be on Kaua'i for a while, especially if you are staying in a condo and plan to make some of your own meals, check out the *Holsum/Orowheat Thrift Store* at 4252 Rice Street (at the corner of Rice and Hardy) for great bargains on bread and packaged baked goods. (Visitors always ask how people can afford to live in Hawai'i when groceries are so expensive. This is one of the ways!) They are open Mon-Fri from 8 am-4 pm, Sat. until 3. Sunday 9 am-2 pm. Try to go on a Wednesday when their day-old products (or those nearing their expiration date) are further discounted for mo' bettah bread bargains. Call (808) 245-6113. There is also a *Loves Bakery* at 4100 Rice St. with discounted bread items and specials for seniors on Tuesday and Friday. Open 9 am-4:30 pm and just south on Hwy. 50 is the *Kukui Grove Shopping Center*. Located at 3-2600 Kaumualii Highway, it is the largest shopping center on Kaua'i, but small by mainland standards. This mall has been impacted by the economic downturn around the islands and many shop fronts are empty. You will find Longs Drug Store, Big Kmart, convenient ATM's, a Star Market and a Borders Bookstore along with specialty shops and restaurants. For those movie devotees, there is a nearby four-screen cinema. Kukui Grove has a complimentary shuttle service to the shopping center with pick-up points from Po'ipu to Wailua.

For shuttle service information call (808) 245-7784. As noted earlier, America Online founder, Steve Case, recently purchased Grove Farm which owns the Kukui Grove Shopping Center. There may be changes and improvements coming in the near future for the shopping center development to revitalize the entire complex. It all depends on what the new owner has in mind for his new property. Stay tuned.

In Lihu'e town, Highways 50 and 56 meet and merge with the Kaumuali'i Highway #50 heading south and west while the Kuhio Highway #56 heads north through the Coconut Coast to the North Shore. You no doubt noticed passing under the old conveyor belt system of the now closed Lihu'e Sugar Mill very near to where Highways 50 & 56 meet (intersection with Rice Street). The mill closed in fall, 2000, harvesting its last loads of cane, much to the lament of many saddened to see the end of an era on Kaua'i. It follows the trend of the last few years all over Hawai'i with the once thriving sugar industry dying off. Gay & Robinson operates the last sugar mill at Makaweli in west Kaua'i.

Kaua'i Fruit and Flower Co. is on the *makai* (ocean) side of the road as you travel north on the Kuhio Highway toward Kapa'a. Stop by and visit Chucky Boy Chock (and Whitney, the dog) and sample the pineapple juice! This is the real stuff, straight from the pineapple. Or try the Dole Whip, a pineapple soft serve ice cream. In the 1960's the building was an old wood mill where Mrs. Chock's grandfather used to work and do wood carvings. They still sell wood carvings as well as other art work and gift items, plus there is a flower shop with protea and orchids. The main part of the operation is produce and you can purchase pre-packaged and pre-inspected pineapples, papayas, onions, and tropical flowers to take home. Mail orders, too! 1-800-943-3108 from the mainland. (808) 245-1814.

On the Kuhio Highway, just past the Kaua'i Medical Center on Lihu'e's north-side, you'll come to the intersection of Ma'alo Road (Hwy. 583). Near this intersection is a longtime shopping landmark, the ***Kapai'a Stitchery,*** 3-3551 Kuhio Highway. This shop will be of interest to anyone who enjoys sewing, especially quilters. They have a large selection of brightly colored fabrics, Hawaiian quilt squares, and supplies, plus a variety of craft items. Needlepoint fanciers will appreciate the beautiful hand-painted canvasses of local settings. The store is open 9 am to 5 pm Monday through Saturday. There are a couple of other shops nearby, including a cigar humidor and tobacco shop.

Just beyond Kapai'a Stitchery at the fork in the road, turn left onto Ma'alo Road, Hwy. 583. This is a rather narrow winding road that passes through former cane fields of Lihu'e Sugar Mill. At slightly more than three miles from the turn-off onto Ma'alo Road you will arrive at ***Wailua Falls.*** (You'll recognize it from the opening of *Fantasy Island*!) There is parking where the road dead ends. A picturesque camera shot can be taken at this vista. There is a path which leads down to the base of the falls. However, the trail is dangerous, steep, and slippery and not recommended. Many have been seriously or fatally injured and we suggest you enjoy the falls from the lookout above. Wailua, whose name means "two waters," was once actually two rivers which have merged into one. The river below is the largest navigable river on the island of Kaua'i and should definitely be explored during your Kaua'i stay.

Retrace your route back down to Hwy. 56 and continue northward. At mile marker #2 along Hwy. 56 you will be in **Hanama'ulu** where you'll find the Hanama'ulu Restaurant & Tea House, J.R.'s Plantation restaurant and a Shell Gas Station. Back in 1875, Hanama'ulu was a plantation camp. Cane was transported by oxen to Lihu'e until a mill was built in town. It continued to operate until 1918.

The **Radisson Kaua'i Beach Hotel**, a few miles beyond, has various popular evening activities. The **Aston Kaua'i Beach Villas** are located next door. Near mile marker #4 is the **Wailua Golf Course**. Green fees on this municipal course are $20-25 weekdays and $30-35 weekends for eighteen holes of play. The golf course runs into the **Lydgate Park** area , with the **Holiday Inn SunSpree Resort** located adjacent. Lydgate Park has one of the island's safest beaches with two pools made of lava rock. One is very shallow, the other slightly deeper. There is also a lifeguard on duty. The fish are able to swim into the pools and are very tame. You might like to pick up a bag of fish food at one of the dive shops or check Safeway. This is a great place to give those wanna-be snorkelers a chance to try out this sport. The adjacent **Kamalani Playground** is a terrific spot to let the kids burn off all that extra energy!

WAILUA

This area is a three-mile length along the Kuhio Highway. The region was of special religious importance to the *kahuna* and *ali'i* of ancient times. In fact, it is considered to be one of the two most sacred spots in all of the Hawaiian Islands. The **Wailua River** cuts back into a verdant valley with many splendors to be shared. The name Wailua means "two waters" as the Wailua River was originally two rivers.

A recent addition to transportation alternatives on Kaua'i is the **Coconut Coast Trolley** operated by Trans Hawaiian Kaua'i from 10am to 10pm daily. Fares are $2 for a one way ticket or $5 for an all-day pass. (Phone 245-5108.) Northbound stops include Maui Marriott, Hilo Hattie, Radisson, Holiday Inn Sunspree, and the Coconut MarketPlace. Southbound stops include Kapa'a Town--ABC Store, Kaua'i Village, and Smith's/Waialealae Boats. A feeder shuttle provides transfer from Po'ipu, Lihu'e and Nawiliwili Harbor. This is a demand type of service and they reserve the right to not stop or pick up at locations based upon lack of demand. They suggest you call for reservations 245-5108 to insure stops at Hyatt Regency, Embassy Vacation Resort, Kiahuna Plantation, or Sheraton Kaua'i.

A river cruise up to **Fern Grotto** is an excellent way to learn how Hawaiian royalty lived. The river and its surrounding land were once part of the royal grounds. Boat cruises run upriver daily to this natural rock cavern filled with maidenhair ferns. Boats depart every half hour from 9 am to 3:30 pm. (There is no departure at 12 noon.) Smith's boats have musical entertainment on board. With a $15 charge for adults, $7.50 for children, it is certainly a pleasant way to spend an hour and a half. The Fern Grotto gift shop was one of the few places we found that had authentic Hawaiian plant starts packaged to pass through customs. You may wish to rent a one or two person kayak at the mouth of the Wailua to enjoy this lovely river at your own pace.

The 30-acre *Smith's Tropical Paradise and Botanical Gardens* is situated alongside the Wailua River and provides a wonderful opportunity to learn the names of the island's flowering trees and plants. Peacocks, ducks, colorful bantam roosters, and other birds inhabit the gardens, too. Bird food is available and carrying a sackful is almost certain to attract an entourage.

Smith's meandering pathways will take you onto a Japanese island, through a sweet-smelling hibiscus garden, into a bamboo forest, and past a variety of fruit and nut trees. Along the way you'll see a replica of an Easter Island statue and grass huts representing several island cultures. The gardens are fairly empty in the mornings; they open at 8:30 am and close at 4 pm. A luau is held here on Monday, Wednesday, and Friday evenings.

Turn *mauka* (toward the mountains) at the Coco Palms (closed for renovations) onto Kaumo'o Road for a short, but interesting, detour. Where the *Wailua River* meets the sea was, in ancient times, the place where Kings were born. Located along the Wailua River and winding upward toward Mount Wai'ale'ale are a series of seven *heiaus*. This area was an important population center in early Hawaiian times.

Located on a part of Lydgate State Park and just above the mouth of the Wailua River, is the *Hauola O'Hanaunau or Place of Refuge*. It's noted often as a "City of Refuge," a misnomer, as there never was a "city" here in the strict sense of the word. The refuge, actually more of a temple, and the adjacent ruins of *Hikina a Ka La Heiau* are distinguished by a low wall which encircles them. It was at *Hauola* that *kapu* breakers, criminals, or defeated warriors sought refuge from punishment and even death, provided they could reach the enclosure before their pursuers could catch them. After spending a time in the refuge, as determined by the resident *kahuna* (priest), they could return to the outside world cleansed and forgiven. Six of these religious sites are located within a mile of the mouth of the Wailua River. Most are easily spotted, while the *Malae Heiau* is located directly across the highway from the *Holiday Inn Sun Spree* on a knoll just above the road leading down to the Wailua Marina and *Smith's Tropical Paradise*. Long overgrown by heavy brush and trees, the *heiau* has recently been undergoing clearing and restoration by local Hawaiian civic groups. It's still obscured from view by a row of bushes and trees, but you can walk up to the *heiau* and marvel at its size. This is the largest *heiau* on the island, measuring 273 feet x 324 feet with rock walls several feet high. Don't enter the *heiau* or climb the rock walls which are loose and could cause injury. Respect and admire these Hawaiian cultural ruins. They are sacred to the Hawaiian people.

Turning up Kuamo'o Drive, Highway 580, between the Wailua River and the Coco Palms, go .2 of a mile on the left side to the site of *Holoholoku Heiau*. This site is actually mislabeled and information in publications has continued the erroneous details. Don and Bea Donohugh, authors of the first three editions of this Paradise Family Guide, enlisted an archeologist to visit the site to confirm their suspicions. The archeologist verified that the site marked as the *Holoholoku Heiau* was actually the location of an old pig pen. The *heiau* itself no longer exists, but its location would have been at the cemetery located on the top of the hill. Some books on Kaua'i say that the *heiau* was converted to a pig pen, but this would seem inaccurate given the archeological investigation. If a *kapu* (a rule or law) was broken, the penalties were stiff. Often death was the penalty for just having your shadow cast on an *ali'i*. However if you could reach a special *heiau*, like the Holoholoku, it would be a place of refuge and you could return forgiven. Behind the pig pen is the Royal Birthing Stone, the spot where royalty were born. Pregnant women of the *ali'i*, ruling class, would give birth in huts next to the birthstone to ensure the royal status of the newborn infant. The early Hawaiians tried to "improve" their royal line and one way they felt this was possible was to inter-marry. It was not uncommon for a brother to marry a sister. As the years progressed, due to diseases and other causes, the numbers of *ali'i* diminished. A common woman could be chosen to give birth at this special and sacred site and her child would then become an *ali'i*. The **Wailua River State Park** is another 2.7 miles on the left and here you will also find the **Poli'ahu Heiau**. This interpretive center along the scenic bluff explains the importance of the Wailua River Valley to the Hawaiians in earlier times. Wailua was a center for the Hawaiian *ali'i* (royalty) and *kahuna* (priests).

The fertile valley soil and plentiful supply of fresh water were ideal for supporting the large Hawaiian population which once inhabited this region. Adjoining the overlook is the **Poli'ahu Heiau**. The stones were brought from the bluffs to build this religious site which was used for ceremonies until the traditional ways were abolished in 1819. This is named after Poliahu, the goddess of snow and a sister to Pele. This is also believed to be a *luakini heiau*, which means a place of human sacrifice. An undesirable person was preferable: a prisoner of war, a person who had broken a *kapu* or sometimes a slave, but never a woman. They were generally killed in their sleep and then placed as an offering upon the altar. A large enclosure of black lava rock was once the personal temple of Kaua'i's last king, Kaumuali'i. This temple was reportedly built by the menehune.

You will see a dirt road just before the interpretive center. While very unimproved and rutted, the road is marked by a sign indicating the way to the **Bell Stone**. You will find two large rocks which appear to be a gateway. By following the path to the end you will be treated to another lovely view of the Wailua Valley. You will have to experiment to discover which of these stones made a resonant sound when struck. At the birth of a royal child, the stone was pounded to signal the arrival of a new member of the *ali'i*.

Just beyond, at 2.8 miles, is the **Opaeka'a Falls** lookout on the right side of the road and the Wailua River lookout on the left. Both are easily accessible and there is a paved parking lot with restrooms. The Opaeka'a Falls lookout affords a wonderful opportunity to see this 40 foot waterfall. This lovely waterfall has multiple cascades and flows year round. After walking the viewpoint trail, you can cross the highway for a view of the Wailua River and the Kamokila Hawaiian Village.

The family-owned and operated business, **Kamokila Hawaiian Village**, is a re-creation of a Hawaiian village with huts, canoes, refurbished taro fields and demonstrations of lei making, poi making, and other native arts & crafts.

Located opposite Opaeka'a Falls, the Kaumo'o Road entrance is just past the Wailua Bridge. Visitors can take a narrated cultural tour, a canoeing adventure on the nearby Wailua River, or kayak to Fern Grotto to discover a secret waterfall and pool. Village Tour $5, Village and Kayak Adventure $25. Open Monday-Saturday 8 am-5 pm. For kayak reservations or information on tour packages call 823-0559. Email: kamokila@hawaiian.net

WAIPOULI

The Waipouli area of Kaua'i offers some excellent hiking opportunities. A section on hiking from Craig Chisholm's *Kaua'i Hiking Trails* is included under hiking in the RECREATION chapter of this guide.

The lush tropical region of this area is synonymous with Kaua'i. *Sleeping Giant Mountain* offers a majestic backdrop for this region. In her book, *Legends of Old Hawai'i*, Betty Allen retells the legend of the Sleeping Giant.

To summarize it, this tale began long ago in Kapa'a where a fisherman and his wife lived. This fisherman always caught the largest of fish and one day when he pulled in his net he found the biggest fish he had ever caught. When the fish began to cry he realized it was no ordinary fish, but an *akua* (good or evil spirit) and took it home to his wife. The only thing that kept the fish from crying was when they fed him poi. His appetite was enormous, so people from all around came to feed him. The fish then transformed into a young giant that grew larger and larger as they continued to feed him poi and sweet potatoes. He grew so large that he could no longer walk and he lay down. They sent for a *kahuna* who told them that they needed to sing to the giant, but he would not reveal which song should be sung. The villagers began to sing to the giant, but to no avail. A small girl named Pua-nai was nearby looking at the rocks on the ground. Suddenly she began to sing a song she had never heard before and the giant miraculously changed to stone. They say that the giant sleeps yet today. (As long as he still sleeps, hikers can walk on his "forehead" and stand on his "face.")

Continuing up Kamao'o Road 4.8 miles, you will pass an Agricultural Research Station. Continue on to the Wailua Reservoir which is one of several fresh water fishing areas on Kaua'i. Several hiking trails have their trail heads in this area.

At 5.45 miles, you will enter the Hawai'i State Forest Reserve. If you plan a day of hiking, the location of the **Kuilau Ridge Trail** head is at 5.5 miles and just beyond is the **Keahua Arboretum**. The Arboretum has suffered from hurricanes and neglect, but still offers a quiet retreat for a picnic. Several streams cross the road from here on in and, depending on the waterflow and your rental car, you may choose not to proceed further. As you retrace your path down the road, look off to the left side just beyond the Agricultural Research Station, for a small pull out. A view of the reservoir with Sleeping Giant Mountain behind is a fine reward.

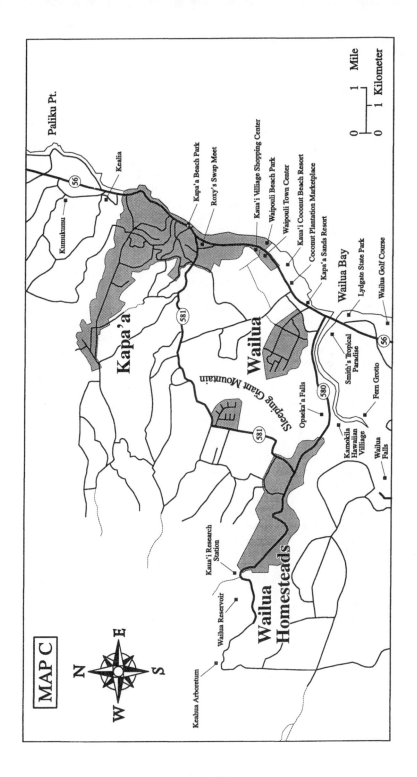

MAP C

Keahua Arboretum

Wailua Reservoir

Kaua'i Research Station

Wailua Homesteads

Wailua Falls

Kamokila Hawaiian Villiage

Fern Grotto

Smith's Tropical Paradise

Opaeka'a Falls

Sleeping Giant Mountain

Wailua

Wailua Golf Course

Lydgate State Park

Wailua Bay

Kapa'a Sands Resort

Coconut Plantation Marketplace

Kaua'i Coconut Beach Resort

Waipouli Town Center

Waipouli Beach Park

Kaua'i Villiage Shopping Center

Kapa'a

Roxy's Swap Meet

Kapa'a Beach Park

Kealia

Kumukumu

Paliku Pt.

0   1   Mile
0   1   Kilometer

Back down to the Kuhio Highway #56, reset your odometer at zero and turn northward and continue towards Kapaʻa. On your left you'll see the once famed *Coco Palms Resort*. This area of palms was once the dream of a German plantation owner who, in the early 1800's, hoped to raise coconuts and sell copra, or dried coconut meat, to the mainland. From the copra, coconut oil can be made. His dreams were dashed, but the tall and elegant trees remain. The *Coco Palms* was one of Kauaʻiʻs more elegant hotels for a long time. But the '92 hurricane, which struck Kauaʻi hard, did considerable damage to the property and it has remained closed since. In mid-2001, it was announced that the property had finally been sold and plans were being made for a full renovation to reopen the property. Stay tuned.

Miss Sadie Thompson was filmed here and the scene where Tatoo on *Fantasy Island* goes flying by in the jeep was also filmed in this coconut grove. Should you see the ghost of Elvis around, it is because he was also here during a portion of his filming of the movie *Blue Hawaiʻi*. You, too, can have a Blue Hawaiʻi wedding. Entertainer Larry Riviera (who used to perform with Elvis) still serenades wedding parties and includes an Elvis-style barge ride as part of the ceremony. You won't have to wear hard-hats, but we understand weddings held on the grounds must include one security guard with each three guests as protection against those falling coconuts!

At a brief .6 of a mile past the intersection of Kuamoʻo Road you will pass the largest shopping center on the east coast of Kauaʻi. The *Coconut MarketPlace* has something for everyone. Located between the Wailua River and Kapaʻa, it is open daily from 9 am-9 pm. Phone (808) 822-3641. This is one shopping center the kids may enjoy more than most with shops such as *The Gecko Store, Crazy Shirts,* and plenty of inexpensive eateries. A selection of jewelry and art galleries as well as a two-screen movie theater are also found here. Two of the more interesting shops are operated by Patrick and Mary Dunn. Their *Islander Trading Company* specializes in Hawaiian articles from decades ago. Old ukuleles, Aloha shirts, Hawaiian ceramics and prints make interesting perusing. New items include Hawaiian rubber stamps, seashells, and other gift items. It also has a bird store and you can pay for a handful of feed to share with some of the colorful parrots and macaws. *Island Accents* looks like an abundant flower shop, but everything is artificial! *Nutcracker Sweet* is an eclectic book and gift shop. Other unusual shops include *Bodacious* which features Petite thru Plus clothes, *Ye Olde Ship Store* (with scrimshaw ships in a bottle and ships' models), *Y Knot a Tie,* and *Russian Treasures.* You'll find Hawaiʻi keepsakes, quilts, handmade dolls, and other gift items at *Made for Mom & Me* or bring home a souvenir for your pets at *Sweet Blossoms & Gypsy's Pet Corner!* There is Polynesian and Hawaiian entertainment daily (at 5 pm) and it is free! The restaurants (Aloha Kauaʻi Pizza, the Fish Hut, Eggbert's, Palm Tree Terrace and Buzz's Steak & Lobster to name a few) remain open even after the shops close. Check the restaurant section of this book for dining details.

The relatively new Kapa'a bypass is an old cane road that was converted to a narrow two-lane alternate route to alleviate the traffic congestion through Kapa'a Town. The bypass road runs alongside the Kuhio Highway (56) and can be accessed from Wailua near the Coconut MarketPlace to the traffic light in Kapa'a Town. But unless you're in a hurry, we suggest continuing along Kuhio Highway.

At 1.3 miles past the Coco Palms begins the row of strip malls that line the highway between Wailua and Kapa'a. The first is the *Waipouli Town Center*, not to be confused with the other two "Waipouli" malls. A *Foodland* grocery store, *Fun Factory* (video arcade), *Blockbuster* (video rentals), *Lizard Lounge & Deli* and the popular *Waipouli Restaurant* are here. The neighboring McDonald's and a small stream divides this center from the next.

Kaua'i Village in Kapa'a, is an eight-acre shopping center featuring over 30 stores and restaurants. Tenants include *Longs Drug Store, Waldenbooks, Crazy Shirts*, and a variety of gift shops. The restaurants at Kaua'i Village range from fine dining at *A Pacific Cafe and Emerson's Seafood Restaurant*, to more casual eateries like *Papaya's, La Playita Azul* and *Camp House Grill*. There is also a new *Chocolats, Mon Amour* shop specializing in exquisite Leonidas Belgian chocolates. The *Kaua'i International Theatre* is also here. The 62-seat playhouse offers six shows per season with guest performers and other entertainment in between productions.

The shopping village is distinguished by its turn-of-the century plantation architectural design, landmark three-story clock tower, garden courtyard, and two Whaling Wall murals by internationally-known environmental artist Wyland. There is plenty of room in the open air courtyard graced with a ten-foot waterfall and a series of landscaped ponds and streams to relax while other members of your group are off shopping. Or take a self-guided tour of the Hawaiian artifacts, art, and handcrafted items at the *Kaua'i Heritage Center of Hawaiian Culture & the Art*. The Village also has a Hawaiian Garden with indigenous (without human aid) and endemic (found only in Hawaii) plants growing with plaques which label them and provide some historical information.

Only 1/10 mile ahead is the next in a string of malls and mini-malls. *Waipouli Plaza* is the location of *King & I Thai Cuisine. Waipouli Complex* is another 2/10 of a mile and the last mall before Kapa'a. Here you'll find the *Aloha Diner* and the *K.C.L. Barbecue Drive Inn*. It is also the home of *Popo's Cookies*. The bakery makes coconut, chocolate chip, macadamia, and their new "granola great" cookies for all retail outlets. But you can buy them fresh and cheaper here! They also have "hard ice," thirst-quenching ice cakes in strawberry-cream, grape, orange, and lemon-lime. Open Monday-Friday, 8:30 am-3 pm, Saturday 9 am-2 pm, closed Sunday.

KAPA'A

Kapa'a was a center for rice cultivation until sugar cane replaced it as the major agricultural industry in the 1920's. Life went along peacefully for this quiet town on Kaua'i's western shore until tourism discovered Kapa'a in the 1970's.

The **Hongwanji Temple** is located across the street from the **Big Save Market**. A little further, turning onto Waikomo Road, is the **Jodo Mission**.

There are several roads which travel into the island to follow and/or cross the Kapa'a Stream and lead to **Ho'opi'i Falls**. Along Hwy. 56, Kawaihau Road is the first option. Follow this road which then intersects with Hauaala Rd. Just outside of Kapa'a, turn onto Mailihuna Road, which also connects with Hauaala Road. Hauaala Road meets Kealia Road, and if you follow it northeast, you will reach the Kaneha Reservoir.

WHERE TO SHOP

At Wailua Village, in a historic sugarcane shack, you'll find *Bambulei*. They have collectibles, antique Hawaiian memorabilia, jewelry, silk and linen Aloha shirts, one-of-a-kind lamps, tacky treasures and things that are both funky and elegant. Caffe Coco is located next door.

Across the street at the **Kinipopo Shopping Village** (356 Kuhio Hwy.), *The Tin Can Mailman* specializes in used and rare books with an emphasis on Hawaiiana and South Pacific subjects. Owner Will Mauck also stocks art prints such as Matson menus and botanical prints. There are plenty of new books, too. Open Tuesday, Wednesday & Friday, 10:30 am-5:30 pm, Thursday from 2 pm, and Saturday 11 am-5 pm.

The town of Kapa'a is a small town gone tourist, but it is still a very pleasant place to dine or shop. The Sunnyside Market (open 8 am-7 pm) at **Roxy Square** still sells fresh produce, tables full of papaya, bananas and more, and take home food products. They've also expanded to include crafts, gifts, snacks, beverages, coffees, candy, and tee-shirts -- even shrunken heads! Check out the small non-descript eatery, *Dori's Garden Cafe,* serving up sandwiches, salads, smoothies and beverages, located at the back of the building. *William & Zimmer* specializes in gifts and furniture made from koa wood.

Across the street is a new store operated by the Kaua'i Historical Society. The *Kaua'i History Shop* (245-3373) is located in the historic Kawamura building. Staffed by volunteers from 10am-4pm weekdays, they offer local gifts, books and a map of the island *heiau* (temples). Also check out *Kia Gallery* for an eclectic assortment of crafts, jewelry, artwork, clothing, mats, vases, and household items. Near the center of Kapa'a town in the historic Hee Fat Marketplace Building on the Kuhio Highway here, there is *Pancho & Lefty's Cantina & Restaurante* upstairs.

At the intersection of Kuhio Highway and Kukui is *Beezers,* an old-fashioned ice cream parlor that offers some cool treats and upstairs of that is *Da Kine Dogs* for a great variety of hot dogs, sausages and sandwich fare. *Mermaids Cafe, Thai-Thai,* and *Wasabi's* are just around the corner on Kuhio Highway. And further down, is the Pono Market filled with lots of island favorites in their deli!

North of Kapaʻa Town, you'll find the *Kountry Kitchen* family restaurant and next to that you'll see *Two Frogs Hugging.* This whimsical little shop offers hundreds of unique and unusual gift items from banana & coconut leaf baskets and notebooks to wooden flowers and candlesticks as well as pottery items, treasure boxes, teak and mahogany furniture -- and yes, carved statues of "Two Frogs Hugging!" The *Black Pearl Gallery* is a jewelry store located in the same building.

BEST BETS

Banyan Harbor and *Garden Island Inn* - convenient and inexpensive. *Radisson Kauaʻi Beach Hotel* and *Aston Kauaʻi Beach Villas* - resort surroundings and amenities in a separate coastal area, yet close to the airport and downtown Lihuʻe. *Kauaʻi Coconut Beach* - this may be the best travel bargain with the use of an Entertainment discount card. *Kauaʻi Marriott Resort & Beach Club* - a little more expensive, but a lovely and luxurious atmosphere. *Bed & Breakfast* - Try Rosewood B&B - it is simply wonderful!

PRIVATE VACATION HOMES & COTTAGES

ALOHA MANA GARDEN
PO Box 550, Anahola, HI 96703. Toll free 1-888-833-4485 or (808) 822-4485; Email: ramcrab@aloha.net; Web: < www.alohamana.com > This oceanview and gardenview vacation rental has three fully-furnished units available. The Hibiscus Suite, Coconut Suite and Alii Suite are on a seven-acre fruit and flower estate and just a short stroll from Aliomanu Bay. *Rates: Alii Suite oceanview $225 nightly; Hibiscus Suite oceanview $140 nightly; Coconut Suite gardenview $95 nightly.*

ANAHOLA ALOHALOHA
4194 Anahola Road, Anahola, HI 96703, mailing address 1191 Kuhio Highway, Suite 293, Kapaʻa, HI 96746. Fax (808) 821-9032; Email: dboulton@implicity.com; Web: < www.alohavacationrentals.com/alohaloha > The Alohaloha Beach House is located on beautiful Anahola Bay with its miles of sandy beaches providing one of Kauaʻi's longest stretches of coastal walking beach. The bay is partially sheltered by offshore reefs, making for great swimming, snorkeling, fishing, boogie-boarding and surfing conditions. The Beach House has great views of the bay, special features include surround sound theatre, hot tub, computer controlled lighting and stereo in every room. House is fully furnished for luxurious vacation living. There are 2 bedrooms, sleeper sofa in living room, spacious kitchen, hot tub, patio deck and all the amenities. The Beach House is a modified A-frame. The only thing between the house and the beach is the front lawn.
Rates: $320 nightly (4 people) extra person $40; $2000 weekly, extra person $200

ANAHOLA COTTAGE
4488 Aliomanu Road, PO Box 493, Anahola, HI 96703. (808) 822-4691 or 639-0389, Fax (808) 822-3591; < www.vrbo.com/vrbo/2425.htm > Email: flo@aloha.net This is a separate studio cottage surrounded by tropical greenery and under the shade of monkeypod trees in quiet and tranquil Anahola village. The unit is simply but comfortably furnished with island-style decor, has a full kitchen, queen bed, ceiling fan, TV/VCR, living room, and lanai with meadow view. It's just 10 minutes to Kapa'a town activities, shopping, dining, etc. and just a 5 minute walk down a quiet country lane to a white sand beach. The host is a licensed massage therapist.
Rates: $75 nightly; $475 weekly

ANUENUE PLANTATION COTTAGE
PO Box 226, Kapa'a, HI 96746-0226. Toll free 1-888-371-7716 or (808) 823-8335, Fax (808) 821-0390; Email: cottage@anuenue.com; Web: < www.anuenue.com/cottage > This is a comfortable, smoke-free one bedroom cottage with full kitchen, living and dining areas, laundry, and full bath. The bedroom opens to a lanai and has queen bed. TV/VCR, telephone available. Enjoy the panoramic tropical mountain and ocean views, waterfalls, rainbows, birds, sunsets and star-filled skies from this modern and private ridgetop cottage.
Rates: $95 nightly; discount on weekly rates

HALE KAULANA
PO Box 131, Lihu'e, HI 96766. (808) 822-7023 or 634-6490; Email: jitmura@aloha.net; Web: < www.vrbo.com/vrbo/517.htm > This is a two-acre agriculture estate in the Puu PiloValley in the Wailua area. It's just minutes from the beach. The 2-bedroom, 1-bath cottage sleeps four; full kitchen, a/c, TV/VCR, laundry and there are two kayaks available for guest use. Enjoy watching the horses and goats graze the surrounding pastures.
Rates: $80 nightly (3 night minimum)

HALE MAKANI
872 Kamalu Rd., Kapa'a, HI 96746. (808) 822-5216, FAX (808) 822-5478. E-mail: rosewood@aloha.net; Web: < www.rosewoodkauai.com > The home offers a 180-degree ocean view backed by spectacular views of the Sleeping Giant and Anahola Mountain ranges. There are three guestrooms, sleeping up to 7 people. The master bedroom has a King bed and private bath plus jacuzzi hot tub on private deck. One bedroom has one twin bed and two folding mattresses. The other bedroom has a Queen bed, large front deck with wide ocean views. Shared bath is down the hall. The fully equipped kitchen, dining and living area is one large room. BBQ on the deck and all the comforts of home. Near to shopping, dining, beaches, activities, easy access to other areas of the island.
Rates: $125 per night

HALE O WAILELE
Mailing address, 41-648 Kalanianaole Highway, Waimanalo, HI 96795. Toll free 1-800-775-2824, Fax (808) 259-6397; Email: kahuna@aloha.net; Web: < www.planet-hawaii.com/kahuna > The "House of Leaping Waterfalls" is a luxurious home located on a tropical flower plantation.

It's an appropriate name as the home is located at the foot of the Makaleha Mountains with great views of the waterfalls that drop off the cliffsides of the tropical mountains. It's an ideal family getaway or romantic honeymoon retreat. There are three well-appointed guest suites. Ka Lumi Wa'a-the Canoe Suite; Ka Lumi Kahiko-the Ancient Suite; and Ka Lumi Manu-the Bird Suite. Each has special features, furnishings, and decor but all are very comfortable. It's only minutes away from Kapa'a town and nearby beaches, shopping, restaurants, and area activities. Suites have all amenities for relaxing vacation stay. House sleeps 6 adults.
Rates: $200 nightly for Ka Lumi Wa'a master suite; $300 for the entire house

HALE PAU HANA

PO Box 1, Anahola, HI 96703. Toll free 1-866-822-2525; Email: hph@aloha.net; Web: < www.halepauhana.net > This country accommodation has three non-smoking guest rooms available. Located amidst tropical flower gardens and fruit orchards, the property borders Anahola Stream and guests can kayak down to Anahola Beach. The Nui Room has a queen bed, private bath and lanai. Waena Room has queen bed, private lanai and shared bath. Lii Room has twin beds and shared bath. There is a common fully-equipped kitchen, living-dining area, TV/VCR plus coolers and beach equipment to borrow for beach and picnic outings.
Rates: Lii Room $60 nightly; Waena Room $85 nightly; Nui Room $95 nightly (3 night minimum stay required)

KALAMA DREAMS COTTAGE ★

6528 Kalama Road, Kalama, HI 96746. Toll free 1-866-218-9250 or (808) 822-5977; Email: dubey@aloha.net; Web: < www.lauhala.wm/kalama > This secluded one bedroom cottage borders great expanses of horse ranch and state forest reserve lands backed by the Waialeale and Makalehu mountains. It's located four miles from the beach in the heart of the verdant Wailua Valley and perfectly situated for hiking, biking, horseback riding, river kayaking, etc. Beachside water sports are nearby including swimming, snorkeling, diving, fishing, surfing, shelling or just sunning and beachcombing. The unit has a full kitchen with breakfast bar and dining nook and all appliances plus outdoor BBQ. Bedroom has queen bed, full bath; sleeper sofa in living room, TV/VCR, telephone, original artwork decor and bamboo furnishings. The cottage is near the owner/residence of Dr. & Mrs. Steve Dubey, naturopathic physician and registered nurse.
Rates: $95 nightly (3 night minimum); $595 weekly; monthly rates by arrangement

KALEIALOHA OCEANFRONT ACCOMMODATIONS

4936 Aliomanu Road, PO Box 687, Anahola, HI 96703. Toll free 1-888-311-5252 or (808) 822-3000, Fax (808) 823-6363; Email: essie@hawaiian.net This oceanfront accommodation has varied units available and is on Kaua'i's beautiful and secluded northeast coast. There is a cozy Hawaiian bungalow "Da Fish Shack," a two bedroom/two bath upstairs unit "Kahalekai Iluna," a one bed-room/one bath upstairs unit "Hibiscus Hale Lani," and a downstairs studio "Hibiscus Hale Honua." Email inquiries to Esther Medeiros, owner.
Rates: $70-160 nightly

KEAPANA SECLUDED GARDEN COTTAGE
5620 Keapana Road, Kapaʻa, HI 96746. Toll free 1-800-822-7968, (808) 822-7968; Email: keapana@aloha.net; Web: <www.planet-hawaii.com/keapana> There is a simple elegance about this one bedroom island-style cottage surrounded by lush tropical gardens. It's a nature lover's dream come true. The home is simply but very comfortably furnished with all the necessary amenities. Enjoy strolling the grounds and taking in all the tropical greenery and various plants. It's a thriving botanical garden. Home is conveniently located halfway between Hanalei on the North Shore and Poʻipu on the South Shore, just five minutes from Kealia Beach and a couple more to Kapaʻa town for shopping, dining, and activities. Five night minimum stay.
Rates: $85 nightly; $540 weekly.

MAKALEHA MOUNTAIN RETREAT
7124A Kahuna Road, Kapaʻa, HI 96746. (808) 822-5131; Email: charlottehoward@webtv.net; Web: <www.makaleha.com> This is a secluded 2-bedroom/1-bath cedar home at the base of the Makaleha Mountains and provides some spectacular waterfall views and sweeping landscape views. They also have a separate garden studio located in a citrus grove. It's just minutes from Kapaʻa town shopping, dining, area activities and beaches. 3 night minimum stay.
Rates: Cedar Home $135 nightly; Garden Studio $60 nightly; extra person $15

MAKANA CREST
PO Box 3671, Lihuʻe, HI 96766, (808) 245-6500 and in Seattle, WA at (206) 242-4866; Email: mokihana@hawaiian.net; Web: <www.hshawaii.com/kvp/hans/index.html> Located behind Sleeping Giant mountain in a quiet country setting just eight minutes from beaches, town areas, etc. This cottage is 750 square feet with two furnished bedrooms and a bathroom with a shower, sleeps four. One bedroom has a queen bed, the other twins. A microwave, dishwasher, basic utensils included in the kitchen and cable TV provided. The guest cottage is on the acreage of the owners home. The property is landscaped with citrus and macadamia trees, and a fish pond. The view features 5,000 foot Mt. Waiʻaleʻalae Crater. Easy access to all area activities, beaches, shopping, dining, etc. And they can even arrange a wedding.
Rates: $100 per day (three day minimum) or $600 per week.

PARADISE FOUND
c/o Marissa Henderson, General Delivery, Anahola, HI 96703. (808) 821-1567, Fax (808) 821-1560; Email: paradise@rfreedom.com; Web: <www.rfreedom.com/paradise/paradise.htm> This secluded honeymoon studio is located at the end of the valley road, at the beach, on Moloaʻa Bay. It's in the center of a beautufil crescent bay and next to the river flowing into the bay. There's a white sand beach around the bay and lots of marinelife to spot like whales, dolphins, turtles and monk seals on occasion. The unit has a private entry and lanai, king bed, full kitchen and bath. Quiet, except for the surf on the shoreline, and away from it all.
Rates: $135 nightly; $900 weekly

PLANTATION RETREAT
6538 Kahuna Road, Kapa'a, HI 96746. (808) 822-7832; Email: bananas@aloha.net; Web: < www.plantationretreat.com > This secluded accommodation is in a lush tropical jungle setting. The "Riverview Cottage" hangs on a cliff overlooking a rushing river. There are swimming holes, rope swings, bananas, coconut trees, and the famous 50-ft. tall tree growing out of the bathroom--the only one of its kind on the island! This environmentally-friendly cottage also has a jacuzzi. Other units include the main "Plantation House" and the "Rainforest Cottage." Guests have use of mountain bikes for exploration. *Rates: Riverview Cottage $85 nightly, $570 weekly; Rainforest Cottage $85 nightly, $570 weekly; Plantation House $95 nightly, $640 weekly;*

ROSEWOOD ★
Rosemary and Norbert Smith have expanded their vacation rental accommodation pool. In addition to their Rosewood Bed & Breakfast accommodations they also handle a number of homes, cottages and villas in the Coconut Coast area and southern Kaua'i coast. Contact (808) 822-5216, or FAX (808) 822-5478 or E-mail: < rosewd@aloha.net > NO CREDIT CARDS. Their home properties include Victorian Cottage (two bedroom/one bath) $115, Thatched Cottage (one bedroom one bath $85), Bunkhouse accommodations which are small rooms with shared baths $40-50, Traditional B&B in the main plantation home with king bed, private bath and breakfast included. Other properties include a one time cleaning fee $65-75 and the rates are: Hale Lani 2BR 2 BTH $125; Hale Pilialoha in Po'ipu with 2BR 2BTH near Baby Beach $150; Sleeping Giant Cottage 1BR $75; Plantation Hale Condo 1 BR $95; and others. Prices are double occupancy. Minimum stay three nights. All properties are non-smoking.

BED & BREAKFASTS

A BED OF ROSES BED & BREAKFAST
6581 B Pu'upilo Road, Kapa'a, HI 96746. (808) 822-0853, Email: rosebedkauai@yahoo.com; Web: < www.geocities.com/rosebedkauai > This secluded and well-hidden B&B has lots of privacy for those wanting to escape the hustle and bustle. It's just four miles from beach activities and convenient to shopping, dining and more. You can enjoy a Kaua'i sunrise from your own private lanai deck surrounded by a peaceful garden environment. King bed, cable TV, BBQ, fridge, kitchenette. In season, guests can pick their own oranges, limes, bananas or macadamia nuts.
Rates: $65 per night; $455 per week; $1950 per month

ALOHA COUNTRY BED & BREAKFAST ★
505 Kamalu Road, Kapa'a, HI 96746. (808) 822-0166, 947-6019, FAX (808) 822-2708, 946-6168; Email: wery@aloha.net; Web: < www.aloha.net/ ~ wery/index-acb.htm > Located on the east coast of Kaua'i behind Sleeping Giant Mountain. From the outside, the main house (5,000 sq. ft. on a 2-acre estate) looks like a Spanish villa. On the inside, there is a choice of lounge areas: a comfy, Victorian sitting room with plush flower-patterned cushions

and plump pillows. Or the central living room remodeled with black and green marble, black leather couches, high ceilings, and an enormous fireplace. Upstairs, the three private luxury suites are decorated in beautiful woods, with antique furniture, canopy beds, and large walk-in closets. The primary residence suite offers a king-size bed, TV, refrigerator, microwave, sitting and dining area, and private bath with jacuzzi. Separate detached units in the backyard include a luxury apartment with queen bed, day bed, TV, full kitchen, sitting and dining area, and large open deck. A studio apartment includes queen bed, sitting and dining area, kitchenette, private bath, TV. The two-bedroom cottage includes queen beds, living room with kitchenette, dining area, one bath, TV and private front yard. Fresh flowers in all rooms and all have ceiling fans; shared laundry facilities. Non-smokers only.
Rates including breakfast in Main Residence: Suite I, $75, Suite II with jacuzzi $85, 2 BR Presidential Suite $150 nightly. Private detached units: Apartment 1 $90, Studio Apartment $80, 2BR Cottage $120 nightly.

ALOHILANI BED & BREAKFAST INN
1470 Wana'ao Rd., Kapa'a, HI 96746. Tel/fax (808) 823-0128, or toll free 1-800-533-9316; Email: alohila@hawaiian.net; Web: <www.hawaiian.net/~alohila>. Hosts Sharon Mitchell and William Whitney offer their home which takes its name from the Hawaiian words meaning "Bright Sky." Located above Kapa'a town, their rates include breakfast of fresh squeezed juices, tropical fruits, and home baked breakfast breads and muffins. They offer the Malulani Guest Cottage at $109 per night, $695 weekly for two. The Kumulani guest cottage has a fully equipped kitchen and is set apart among the trees. It features ocean and mountain views, a king-size bed, and a living room area with sleeper sofa at $99 per night, $650 per week. Pa'ana a ka la "Sunshine" Atrium features wide French doors which open onto a lanai with a valley view. It has a queen size bed, sleeper sofa, and small refrigerator and microwave at $109 per night, $695 per week; ceiling fans, lanai, hot tub, BBQ, gazebo. In addition they have a two bedroom condominium across from Kalapaki Beach which rents for $109 per night, $650 per week or $1995 per month.

CANDY'S CABIN
5940 Ohe St., Kapa'a, HI 96746. (808) 822-5451. Located in the Wailua Home-steads, your hostess is Candace Kepley. A studio apartment with a king-size bed, living area, private bath, lanai, and refrigerator. Very roomy and adequate for a family. If you choose breakfast, you'll find some home baked goodies. Stroll around the grounds and see the family of mallard ducks that visit from the nearby stream. Located 15 minutes from the Lihu'e airport. *Rates for two run $65 per night, No minimum stay.*

HALE TUTU
7230 Aino Pono Street, Kapa'a, HI 96746. Toll free 1-888-HALETU2 (425-3882), (808) 821-0697, Fax (808) 822-9091; Email: tutu@haletutu.com; Web: <www.haletutu.com> This is "Grandma's House," (Hale Tutu) a modern private residence located in the cooler uplands above and overlooking the Wailua and Kapa'a areas of the eastside Coconut Coast. There are three guestrooms. The Nokekula (Swan) Room has Hawaiian style furniture, large closet, and private whirlpool spa, fridge, TV/VCR. The Hawaiian Room is full of antiques and has

large walk-in closet, fridge, TV/VCR, pool and garden views. The lower level Nai'a Room has a small kitchenette, TV, and garden views. All guests have use of an outdoor spa and pool for lap swimming plus use of fully equipped kitchen. 3 night minimum stay. *Rates: Nokekula (Swan) Room $105 nightly; Hawaiian Room $95 nightly; Nai'a Room $85 nightly*

HEMPEY'S GARDEN ISLAND BED & BREAKFAST

6087 Kolopua Street, Kapa'a, HI 96746. (808) 822-0478, Email: hempey@hawaiian.net; Web: < www.hawaiianbedandbreakfast.com > This comfy B&B is nestled behind the Sleeping Giant Mountain on a half-acre of beautifully landscaped tropical grounds just minutes away from Wailua Bay, shopping, dining and area activities. There are five guest rooms and a private studio with various bed arrangements (king, queen, twins), some share a bath, some have private baths; also shared kitchenette, TV, computer with internet access. A generous Hawaiian breakfast is included in each night's stay. Hosts speak French, Portuguese, Italian and Spanish. *Rates: $60-70 nightly (no breakfast); $75-85 nightly (with breakfast)*

HOUSE OF ALEVA

5509 Kuamo'o Rd., Kapa'a, HI 96746. (808) 822-4606. Hosts Ernest and Anita Perry offer two upstairs rooms with a bath to share. A single room downstairs has a private bath. Breakfast tailored to your particular health needs and tastes. Located two miles inland up Highway 580 along the Wailua River and directly across from Opaekaa Waterfall. *Rates: $55 per night per couple, $40 sngle.*

KAKALINA'S B & B

6781 Kawaihau Rd., Kapa'a, HI 96746. Toll free 1-800-662-4330, (808) 822-2328, Fax (808) 823-6833. E-mail: klinas@aloha.net < www.kakalina.com > Located on a three-acre working tropical flower farm in the foothills of Mt. Wai'ale'ale your hosts are Bob and Kathy Offley. Their Hale 'Akahi unit is two rooms on the ground floor with a private entrance featuring king-size beds, shower, deep bath for soaking, and kitchenette. The Hale 'Elua unit is a ground floor studio with queen size bed, ceiling fan and private bathroom with shower and full-size kitchen. Each unit has color TV, microwave oven, refrigerator and laundry facilities. Hale Kolu is a 1-BR located above Hale Elua with an ocean-view. A mile away is their other vacation rental, The Ginger Room. This one-bedroom home does not include the breakfast feature, but it offers a queen size bed, living room, dining room, full kitchen and private bath. *Rental rates run $75-90 with 10% discount for weekly stays.*

LAMPY'S BED & BREAKFAST

6078 Kolopua Street, Kapa'a, HI 96746. Phone or FAX (808) 822-0478 or 639-4779. Located five minutes from Wailua Bay. Each of the three bedrooms is furnished with country decor and offers a private entrance and private bath; choice of King, Queen or twin beds. Sitting room has TV/VCR and fully equipped breakfast bar. Breakfast is served each morning in the garden Gazebo. Bright cheery accommodations in a quiet rural area. Convenient to all area beaches, shopping, dining, activities. *Rates: Single, $50 nightly; Double, $55 nightly; Studio $65 nightly. Extra persons $10 additional. Weekly rates. Cash, Money Orders, Travelers Checks only.*

LANI KEHA B & B

848 Kamalu Road, Kapa'a, HI 96746. Toll free 1-800-821-4898, (808) 822-1605, Fax (808) 822-2429; Email: lanikeha@hawaiian.net; Web: <www.lanikeha.com> This spacious island home is situated in the Kapa'a area of east Kaua'i nestled on three-acres at the foot of the Sleeping Giant Mountain. There are beautiful mountain panoramas from all the windows. Just 10 minutes from area beaches, activities, attractions, shopping, dining of the Kapa'a town area. There are three guest rooms, private baths and for guest use there is a full kitchen, laundry, large lanai, TV, etc. There is a 2 night minimum stay.
Rates: 1 BR king or twin beds, $55-65 night; 1 BR Suite king bed, $80 night

MOHALA KE OLA

5663 Ohelo Rd., Kapa'a, HI 96746. Toll free 1-888-GO-KAUAI. Phone or FAX (808) 823-6398. Email: Kauaibb@aloha.net; Web: <www.waterfallbnb.com> Host Ed Stumpf invites you to "Rejuvenate in Paradise" at Mohala Ke Ola, their Bed & Breakfast retreat. Located above the Wailua River Valley near Opaeka'a Falls on the eastern shore of Kaua'i, they have mountain and waterfall views. Breakfast of fresh island fruit on a private terrace, enjoy the pool, and relax in the jacuzzi. You can enjoy a Hawaiian Lomi Lomi massage or rejuvenate with other body treatments included shiatsu, acupuncture, and Reiki. Quiet and peaceful surroundings along with a congenial and friendly atmosphere. Ed will greet you at the airport or assist if you need some shopping help. He also speaks fluent Japanese and is very knowledgeable about sightseeing and activities. They offer four guest rooms, each with a private bath, and all non-smoking. The entire property was recently renovated with all new furniture. They have also added a new pond and more tropical landscaping. Three night minimum requested. *Rates: King's View $105 nightly; Pool View $100 nightly; Garden View $85 nightly; Kamaaina Room $75 nightly.*

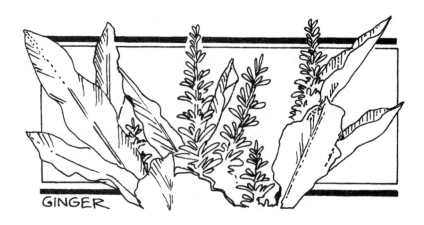

GINGER

OPAEKAA FALLS HALE BED & BREAKFAST
120 Lihau Street, Kapa'a, HI 96746. Toll free 1-888-822-9956 or (808) 822-9956, Fax (808) 822-3911; Web: <www.opaekaafallskauai.ws> Email: custland@pixi.com; This nicely maintained private home has spacious self-contained guest units with all the comforts expected. Guests enjoy over 1000 sq.ft. of living space, private entrance, large lanai deck overlooking the swimming pool, views of the Wailua Plains and Wailua River, beautifully landscaped gardens surrounding the home. Featured are king and queen beds, fully equipped kitchens and dining rooms, cable TV, private bath, etc. Conveniently near to the noted and historic Wailua River Complex, area activities, attractions, shopping, dining, and more. Hawaiian-style continental breakfast included. Wir spechen Deutsch.*Rates: Royal Palm Unit (upstairs) $110 per night; Queen Emma Room (lower level) $90 per night*

ROSEWOOD BED & BREAKFAST ★
872 Kamalu Rd., Kapa'a, HI 96746. (808) 822-5216, FAX (808) 822-5478. E-mail: rosewood@aloha.net; Web: <www.rosewoodkauai.com> This home, located in Wailua Homesteads, was formerly an old Macadamia Nut Plantation Home. The area is rural with rolling pastures and grazing cattle framed by a wide mountain range with Mt. Wai'ale'ale in the center. After a nighttime shower, many waterfalls are visible with vivid rainbows. Since they moved to the islands 17 years ago, Rosemary and Norbert Smith have been restoring their home. A second cottage with two bedrooms, designed after the main house is called the "Victorian Cottage."

A smaller one designed with a Hawaiian look, is called the "Thatched Roof Cottage." There are also "Rainbow's End Cottage" and "Sleeping Giant Cottage." Additional options are their "Bunkhouse" rooms which has proven popular with European visitors and hikers. The one-acre grounds include two ponds with small waterfalls plus lots of fruit and flowering trees and bushes. "Thatched Roof Cottage" is a one bedroom cottage with a king-size bed, screened lanai, kitchenette with hot plate, microwave and small refrigerator. The toilet and sink are indoors, but the hot/cold shower sits outside enclosed in the garden surrounded by native plants.

The "Victorian Cottage" offers two bedrooms and one bath, also an outdoor hot/cold shower. The master bedroom is downstairs with a queen bed, upstairs is a loft bedroom with two twin beds. A sofa opens into a sleeper bed. The kitchen is full sized and includes a dishwasher, and a washer/dryer. The unit has a television and telephone with fax. The two "traditional" units in the main house each have a private bath. They have a king bed, which can be converted to two twins. Breakfast is left in the cottages, and, for main house guests, is served in the kitchen. "Rainbow's End" and "Sleeping Giant Cottage" have varied sleeping arrangements, but are self-contained units with full amenities.

The bunkhouse has three separate rooms and a shared outside shower. Each room has its own sink, toaster, coffee maker, and small refrigerator. The larger room offers a microwave. Bunkhouse #1 has twin bunk beds, Bunkhouse #2 has a sofa bed that opens to a queen plus a queen bed in the loft. Bunkhouse #3 consists of a Queen bed in the loft. None of the bunkhouse units include breakfast or maidservice. Breakfast may be provided for an additional $5 per day per person. All units are non-smoking. Conveniently located just four miles from beaches, shopping, and restaurants. Also available for rent is a one bedroom condo at Kapa'a Shores and several area homes and cottages. (See Private Homes for rental homes.)

Rates: Victorian Cottage $125; Thatched Roof Cottage $105; Rainbow's End Cottage $115; Sleeping Giant Cottage $85; Traditional $85; Bunkhouse #1 and #3 $40 per night; Bunkhouse #2 $50 per night.

WAONAHELE AT KUPONO FARMS
7084 Kahuna Road, Kapa'a, HI 96746. Toll free 1-877-822-1515, (808) 822-7911, Fax (808) 821-0999; Email: kupono@aloha.net; Web: < www.planet-hawaii.com/kupono > This is a lovely modern ranch-style home surrounded by the rain forest, thus its Hawaiian name, "The Rain Forest." There are six very spacious, comfortably furnished guest rooms each with king beds, TV, phone, private lanais, whirlpool bath, and lovely rain forest views. Includes full Hawaiian style breakfast.
Rates: Mountain view $120 nightly; Ocean view $140; Waterfall view $175-450

BUDGET

HALE LIHU'E MOTEL
2931 Kalena St., Lihu'e, HI 96766. (808) 245-2751. Twenty two one-bedroom units, some with kitchenettes. No air conditioning, but rooms have table fans. Inexpensive and spartan two-story, frame building located near the main business area of downtown Lihu'e. Walking distance to local restaurants, government offices, churches, and banks. Rates including tax are the cheapest in an already inexpensive area. A little unkempt and rundown; not really what you'd envision paradise to be. *Single, double or triple occupancy $22/$25/$30; with kitchenette single $30, double $40, triple $50. Weekly discounts available.*

KAUA'I INTERNATIONAL HOSTEL ★
4532 Lehua Street, Kapa'a, HI 96746; (808) 823-6142; Web: < www.hostels.com/kauaihostel > This hostel is located 10 miles north of Lihu'e Airport in the heart of old Kapa'a Town across from the beach park on Lehua Street which leads off from the main road, Kuhio Highway. This is the place on Kaua'i to meet budget travelers from around the world. Clean, friendly atmosphere, secure safe for valuables. Oceanview dorm rooms, full kitchen and laundry facilities available plus TV, BBQ, pool table, etc. Close to town shops, restaurants, and area activities. Good starting point for adventure seeking hikers, surfers, snorkelers, or those who just want to explore beautiful Kaua'i beaches and its colorful culture heritage and history.
Rates: Dorm bunk beds $20 per night; Private rooms, double bed $50

KK BED & BATH ★
4486 Kauwila Street, Kapa'a, HI 96746. Toll free 1-800-615-6211, (808) 822-7348; Email: kkbedbath@aloha.net; Web: < www.aloha.net/ ~ sugi/b&b.html > The two guestrooms are in the old Kawamura family store warehouse next door to the building that was an old Mom & Pop store for years. Conveniently located in the center of Kapa'a town, close to area attractions, restaurants, etc. The two guest rooms are simply furnished with queen beds, fridge, private bath/shower, clean, non-smoking. These are excellent budget traveler rooms. 3 night minimum stay. *Rates: $35 per person per night; $50 for two; $60 for three*

MOTEL LANI
4240 Rice St. (PO Box 1836) Lihu'e, HI 96766. (808) 245-2965. Email: tkn@hawaiian.net At the corner of Rice and Hardy, the center of the Lihu'e business district. They have ten units, each with shower and one double or two twin beds. Some rooms have air conditioning and no TV, others have a TV and a ceiling fan. There is also a tv in the lobby for guest use. Like Hale Lihu'e, inexpensive and very basic: "A place to sleep." *Rates are $32-50 per night two people, two night minimum. Rates for one night slightly higher.*

TIP TOP MOTEL ★
Located in downtown Lihu'e. PO Box 1231, Lihu'e, HI 96766. (808) 245-2333; Email: tiptop@aloha.net. The 34 rooms are spartan and basic, nothing fancy but clean and decent. This is a family-run operation, combining the Tip Top Motel & Cafe with a bakery and has been going since 1916. They moved to their present location in the early '60's where it is being run by the fourth generation of the Ota family. The coffee shop/cafe and cocktail lounge are still here along with a Sushi Katsu Japanese Restaurant (for dinner only), and smaller version of their famous bakery. The cafe/bakery is noted for its local-style oxtail soup, banana pancakes and macadamia nut cookies. If you're looking for no frills budget accommodations with a great central location on Kaua'i, this is the place. All units are air conditioned. *Single/double $45 (includes tax) $10 key deposit.*

INEXPENSIVE

BANYAN HARBOR CONDOMINIUM RESORT ★
3411 Wilcox Road, Lihu'e, HI 96766. 1-800-4-BANYAN or (808) 245-7333, FAX (808) 246-3687. RESERVATIONS: The management company, Outrigger Lodging Services (OLS), also operates the front desk and runs the property's on-site rental program. 1-800-4BANYAN (422-6926) US & Canada. Email: banyan@aloha.net and Web: < www.vacation-kauai.com > RENTAL AGENTS: Maui & All 1-800-663-6962. Prosser Realty 1-800-767-4707.

There are 148 units on a hilltop near Kalapaki Bay, some have a view of the Nawiliwili Harbor. The rates have always been a good value and have actually gone down recently. Complex has a tennis court, refurbished pool and decking area, plus a separate recreation area with wet bar, shuffle board, etc. Public volleyball courts across the street. The room renovations have created crisp, clean rooms with television, and air conditioning now in all units.

Bathroom lighting is still a bit dim in some of the units, but additional renovation is planned to replace the older fixtures. Washer/dryers, full kitchens (with microwave, coffee maker & starter coffee packet, and dishwasher) and dining area. Townhouses have harbor views. Very convenient to the airport and an easy walk to shops and restaurants of Anchor Cove and Harbor Mall or a short walk to the Marriott. The large front office is comfortable with an amiable, friendly staff and there is plenty of parking. Adjoining the property is a large tree orchard with the second largest banyan tree in Hawaii. Like many others, they have also gone to partial timeshare. *OLS operates the management and front desk. Their rates: 1 BR $85-110; 2 BR $95-140; Room and car packages $99-119. (And be sure to take advantage of their latest offer: mention this book and they'll give you a free upgrade (from a one to a two-bedroom) with any room or package rate!)*

GARDEN ISLAND INN ★
Located in Nawiliwili. 3445 Wilcox Rd., Lihu'e, HI 96766. 1-800-648-0154, FAX (808) 245-7603, (808) 245-7227; Email: info@gardenislandinn.com; Web: < www.gardenislandinn.com >. Renovated 21-room hotel with tropical decor and a cheery cottage-feel to each of the rooms. Clean, comfortable spacious rooms in a quiet location but convenient to activities, shopping, dining, etc. Wilcox Road has been closed to through-traffic so the property is now on a quieter cul-de-sac (though there is still a lot of activity during the day). They'll also provide golf clubs, camping and beach equipment, and you can help yourself to bananas and tangelos from the trees on the property. It's just a short walk to the Kaua'i Marriott, Nawiliwili Beach Park and Kalapaki Beach just across the road. Anchor Cove Shopping Center with J.J.'s Broiler Restaurant is just steps away, and the newly renovated Harbor Mall is just up the road and has eateries like Cafe Portofino, Kauai Chop Suey, and Tokyo Lobby. All rooms have refrigerators, wet bars, TV, microwaves, and coffeemakers. Studios and one-bedroom suites on the third floor. All units are non-smoking and most now have A/C. Comfortable, friendly and reasonably priced too! They also have a condo unit at the Banyan Harbor which they rent.
Rates: g.v. $65-80; o.v. $85-95; 1 BR suites $95-125; condo unit $145.

HOTEL CORAL REEF ★
1516 Kuhio Hwy., Kapa'a, HI 96746. 1-800-843-4659, (808) 822-4481, Fax 822-7705. This was one of the first tourist hotels on Kaua'i's Coconut Coast. The newly remodeled landmark hotel offers clean, quiet, affordable accommodations and has a prime oceanfront setting on a wide white sandy beach in the heart of a popular vacation area. Ground floor rooms are tiled, upstairs rooms are carpeted. The main building provide clean economical rooms with limited views. The oceanfront building offers spacious rooms with beach views and are equipped with refrigerators and a choice of single or double beds. However, the beachfront is not suitable for swimming but great for sunning, strolling, and beachcombing. Pay telephone and television in lobby. Daily maid service. Grocery store and restaurants nearby. Located within walking distance of a public swimming pool and many other area activities, golf, tennis, etc. Room and car packages available.
Rates; O.f. and o.v. rooms range from $59-89; two-room m.v. suites $79. Extra person $10; senior discounts.

MAHINA'S WOMEN'S GUEST HOUSE

Email: mahinas@hawaiian.net; Web: < www.mahinas.com >
This beach house has shared or private rooms for women only. Kitchen, bath and laundry facilties all on shared basis. Clean, quiet and comfortable plus easy access to all area activities, beaches, shopping, dining, etc.
Rates: Shared twin room, $30 per person/ night; Enclosed lanai, Single $30 per night; Private double room $40 per night; Large ocean view king room, Single $50/Double $60; weekly rates available

MODERATE

ASTON ISLANDER ON THE BEACH ★

484 Kuhio Hwy., Kapa'a, HI 96746. (808) 822-7417, 1-800-847-7417, FAX (808) 822-1947; Email: islander@aloha.net; Web: < www.islander-kauai.com > RENTAL AGENTS: Managed by Aston Properties 1-800-922-7866, Email: res.iob@aston-hotels.com; Web: < www.aston-hotels.com >. Pleasant Hawaiian Holidays 1-800-242-9244. Total of 198 units in three story buildings. A small understated lobby is tasteful and reminiscent of a simple, old fashioned Hawaiian plantation. Very pleasing grounds and rooms and an excellent value for your vacation dollar. The hotel features an outdoor pool and spa, restaurant and lounge on the property. All rooms offer king or two double beds, air conditioning, wet bar, refrigerator, microwaves in oceanfront units and suites, color TV and in-room coffee makers. Laundry facilities. Rooms are on the small side. Third and fourth persons are charged $20 per person per night. No charge for children 17 and under when sharing parents room. Room and car packages available. Located on 6.5 oceanfront acres, next to the Jolly Roger Restaurant, and across from the Coconut MarketPlace. This is one of the best beaches on the eastern shore. Check with Aston regarding any seasonal specials that might include rental car, complimentary breakfast or the 5th night free. Complimentary crib on request at time of booking.
Rates: Garden view $110; partial o.v. $120; o.v. $135; d.o.f. $150; Junior Suite $195; extra person $20.

ASTON KAHA LANI ★

4460 Nehe Rd & Leho., Lihu'e, HI 96766 (808) 822-9331. Managed by Aston Resorts 1-800-922-7866, Email: res.khl@aston-hotels.com; Web: < www.aston-hotels.com >. Rental Agent: Maui & All 1-800-663-6962. Two and three story buildings with a total of 74 units. More an attractive, homey apt. building than a resort. Pool, BBQ area, laundry facilities, putting green, and tennis court. Full kitchens with complimentary coffee starter kit. High ceilings, private phones plus lanais, ceiling fans, and daily maid service. One bedroom units have two bathrooms. Located next door to the golf course on the beachfront at Lydgate Park, one of the islands better beaches. Kaha Lani is difficult to find unless you know to turn on Leho from the highway, but when you do, you'll be glad for the quiet seclusion. You're surrounded by a "choice" of landscaping: the soothing ocean front with small stretches of sandy beach, tropical gardens, or the dramatic craggy rock and a red dirt road that borders the property and leads to other beach areas.

The Kamalani playground at Lydgate Park will amuse the children in your party for hours! Ask Aston reservations about special package or promotional options such as Island Hopper Rates if you plan on visiting other islands.
Rates: 1 BR o.v. $220/185, o.f. $260/205; 2 BR o.v. $310/245, o.f. $340/275

ASTON KAUA'I BEACH VILLAS ★
4330 Kaua'i Beach Drive, Lihu'e, HI 96766. (808) 245-7711. RENTAL AGENT: Managed by Aston Properties 1-800-922-7866, or (808) 931-1400; Email: res.kbv@aston-hotels.com; Web: <www.aston-hotels.com>. OTHER RENTAL AGENTS: Maui & All Islands 1-800-663-6962. Pleasant Hawaiian Holidays 1-800-242-9244. Premier Resorts 1-800-367-7052. Three floors (no elevator) 150 units located on 13 acres. These condominiums are part of the complex that includes the Radisson Kaua'i Beach Hotel next door. It is a short, pleasant walk along a pathway leading to the Radisson grounds and to the resort pools, restaurant, shops, etc. The Aston pool (and whirlpool) are centralized, on an attractive raised deck reminiscent of a ship's pool deck. There are plenty of lounge chairs with BBQ grills nearby and elsewhere around the property. Rooms have a safe, washer/dryer, TV/VCR, and pay movies. Clever room decorating matches the shower curtain with the bed quilt. The beds were particularly comfortable with velvety soft blankets and sheets. Lanais, maid service in all units. Air conditioning in bedroom suites only. Inquire about Aston's promotional rates, special packages or Island Hopper Discounts. The complex is on the beachfront but the beach is suitable for strolling, exploring and sunning. Swimming is not advised due to strong currents, surf, etc.
Rates: 1 BR standard $225/190; 1 BR g.v. $245/200; 2 BR g.v. $315/250; 2 BR o.v. $375/310

ASTON KAUA'I COAST RESORT AT THE BEACHBOY ★
4484 Kuhio Hwy., Kapa'a, HI 96746. (808) 822-3441, Fax (808) 822-0843. Aston Hotels & Resorts 1-800-922-7866, Email: info@aston-hotels.com; Web: <www.aston-hotels.com>. Rental Agent: Maui & All 1-800-663-6962.

The resort recently had an extensive renovation and reconstruction program that saw the former guest hotel units converted into 108 vacation ownership units with 69 one-bedroom, 33 two-bedroom units and a few standard hotel rooms. Rooms have air conditioning, television, and lanais. No kitchens, but they do have a bar size refrigerator. Daily maid service is provided. Currently guests receive a complimentary continental breakfast. There is a new resort swimming pool, a children's pool and a jacuzzi along with extensive new landscaping plus a new Activity and Fitness Center building. Tennis courts also available. Located next door to the Coconut Plantation MarketPlace.
Rates: 1 BR Suite g.v. $185; 1BR Suite o.v. $205; 1BR Suite o.f. $220; 2BR Suite w/kitchen g.v. $245; 2BR Suite w/kitchen o.v. $275; 2BR Suite w/kitchen o.f. $295 (Be sure to inquire into Aston's special package rates such as Island Hopper Plans, Senior Discounts, etc.)

BEST WESTERN PLANTATION HALE ★
484 Kuhio Highway, Kapa'a, HI 96746. (808) 822-4941 or Fax (808) 822-5599, and toll free 1-800-775-4253 or Best Western Worldwide 1-800-528-1234. RENTAL AGENT: Best Western on the Web: < www.plantation-hale.com >; Email: ph@aloha.net; OTHER AGENTS: Maui & All 1-800-663-6962. Pleasant Hawaiian Holidays 1-800-242-9244.

A total of 151 rooms in ten two-story buildings, located in the Coconut Market-Place, across the street from the beach. A good spot to stay if you don't plan on getting a rental car. The convenience of the mall provides multiple choices for restaurants and shopping. All units are one bedroom with kitchenettes and refrigerators. No dishwashers. New spas and a pool deck were recently installed. Three pools, BBQ area, and laundry facilities. Air conditioning and daily maid service. Non-smoking rooms available. Second floor units have balconies, first floor have patios.

A one block walk to the beach. The location of this property is between the road leading to the Coconut Beach Hotel and the highway. The last time we stayed here, the street noise was a bit loud, but we understand they have made improvements which seem to have alleviated the problem. We'd recommend requesting one of the oceanview rooms. Rooms now have pay per view movies. There are televisions in both the living room and bedroom to help ease any program disputes!
Rates: 1 BR suite w/kitchen $155-165; 1 BR gv suite $165-175; 1 BR scenicview suite $175-185

HOLIDAY INN SUNSPREE RESORT ★
3-5920 Kuhio Hwy., Kapa'a, HI 96746. 1-888-823-5111. (808) 823-6000, FAX (808) 823-6666; Email < info@holidayinn-kauai.com > Web < www.holidayinn-kauai.com >. RENTAL AGENT: Management is Holiday Inn. OTHER RENTAL AGENTS: Hawaiian Pacific Resorts 1-800-367-5004. Maui & All Islands 1-800-663-6962.

The 216-room oceanfront resort had extensive renovations within the last 2-3 years. This is an affordable full-service, activity oriented property in the middle of Kaua'i's eastern Coconut Coast leisure destination region. This property is a good choice for couples, families and seniors as well as groups. The open lobby has a nice old Hawaiian feel and look about it. The Maile Wing and Pikake Wing feature Garden View and Deluxe Ocean View rooms and one bedroom suites with various bedding available. There are also 13 separate private duplex 1 bedroom suite cottages. Each cottage has a master bedroom plus queen and sofa sleeper in the living area, fully equipped kitchenette, etc. All rooms feature full amenities such as mini-fridge, coffee maker, TV, a/c, clocks, phones/data ports, etc. Smoking/non-smoking rooms available also. Recreational facilities include spa, fitness room, tennis courts, shuffleboard, volleyball and two swimming pools, one geared for families. Hotel grounds feature nicely landscaped Japanese and Hawaiian gardens and koi (carp) pool. The hotel is adjacent to Kamalani Childrens' Playground and Lydgate State Park which has good beach swimming and and enclosed swim/snorkel cove.

Also next to the hotel grounds near the mouth of the Wailua River are the historic ruins of *Hauola Place of Refuge* and *Hikina a Ka La Heiau*. These temples date from very early days when this area was a Hawaiian population center. Directly across the highway is another old temple site, *Malae Heiau*, which has recently been undergoing clearing and restoration. Few hotels on Kaua'i have such important historic sites so nearby. Just below the knoll where the heiau sits, is the famous Smith's Tropical Paradise featuring the botanical gardens and an evening luau program as well as the Wailua Marina where the riverboat tours to the Wailua River Fern Grotto begin. Outfitters offer various other activities like kayaking, water skiing, etc. and the Wailua Golf Course is just a mile away. - Daily maid service, laundry facilities. Restaurants and lounges include the Kahanu Snack Bar at poolside and the Kuhio Dining Court features a lounge, sundries shop and The Palms Restaurant. There are meeting facilities available. Holiday Inn Sunspree Resort Kaua'i provides various free activities for kids in their seasonal Kid Spree Vacation Club. Hawaiiana activities include hula, Hawaiian language lessons, lei making and Hawaiian games. Inquire into kids' activities availability when making reservations. The Coconut Coast Trolley stops here and goes to the local shopping centers.
Rates: Garden view $180, Ocean view $210, Junior Suite $235; 1 BR Cottage Suite $330.

KAPA'A SANDS RESORT
380 Papaloa Rd., Kapa'a, HI 96746. (808) 822-4901, 1-800-222-4901, FAX (808) 822-1556; Email: ksresort@gte.net; Web: < www.kapaasands.com > The postal address is Kapa'a, but they are actually located in Wailua. Minimum maid service daily with full linen change for stays of 7 nights or longer. Twenty-four individually owned studio and two bedroom condominiums. Units all have telephone, color TV, microwaves, and ceiling fans. Conveniently located behind Kinipopo Shopping Village and a short walk from additional shops and restaurants at the Coconut Plantation MarketPlace. Swimming pool, laundry facilities, and attractive lana'is and grounds. Located on a pleasant beachfront. If you are up early in the morning (and sometimes in the afternoon) you can watch sea turtles feeding off the reef just in front of the property.
Rates: Studio o.v. $85; studio o.f. $99 (max 2); 2 BR o.v. $114 (max 4); 2 BR o.f. $129 (max 4). Extra charge of $10 per night for the 5th person in 2 BR unit.

KAPA'A SHORE
4-0900 Kuhio Hwy., Kapa'a, HI 96746. 1-800-827-3922, FAX (808) 822-1457. RENTAL AGENT: Kaua'i Vacation Rentals 1-800-367-5025. Eighty-one units, one and two bedroom condos in a three story buildings. Three night minimum stay, seven night minimum over Christmas holidays. Weekly and monthly discounts. Laundry facilities, some rooms have ceiling fans. Pool, tennis courts, and jacuzzi. *Kauai Vacation Rates: Only 1 BR available for rental $550 per week*

KAUA'I COCONUT BEACH RESORT

PO Box 830, Kapa'a, HI 96746. (808) 822-3455, FAX (808) 822-1830, toll free 1-800-760-8555; Email: wesm@hawaiihotels.com; Web: < www.kcb.com > This is a Hawaiian Hotels & Resorts property (aka Pleasant Hawaiian Holidays). The hotel is located on 10.5 acres at Waipouli Beach on the Coconut Coast and features a swimming pool/jacuzzi, three tennis courts, coin laundry, and a restaurant on the property. Contemporary room decor in pastel colors and matching furnishings. Rooms provide lanai, refrigerator, coffeemakers with free coffee, air conditioning. A handicapped room is also available.

Summer program available for children accompanied by a parent. Offered free to guests June 1-August 31, the activities include hula, lei making and other Hawaiian arts and crafts each morning. They also offer a "Kids Eat Free" policy for families dining on-property. Demonstrations of Hawaiian crafts are given daily year-round as is their traditional torch-lighting ceremony each evening. There is a complimentary summer children's program. Children under age 17 may stay free in rooms with their parents when using existing bedding.

The proximity to nearby Kaua'i Shopping Village (with a Safeway) and just a few blocks to the Coconut MarketPlace make it ideally situated. On the down side, the parking area, while large, can be very crowded and finding a spot can be a little difficult at times. The hallways have poor lighting, making them very dark. But the hotel can be a good value, provided they continue to maintain the quality of their rooms and grounds. Be sure to check the Entertainment book for half price coupons on your stay. The discount makes this a recommended accommodation! (A note: we have had a complaint or two from guests who felt that the rooms were in need of some significant renovations. Hopefully some upgrading will take place soon!)

PATIO DINING

A buffet breakfast is served at their Voyage Room Restaurant and is included with some of their room packages. The restaurant also serves a la carte and buffet lunches. Dinner is served at the Flying Lobster Restaurant. Nightly entertainment is at Cook's Landing Lounge. Their luau and Hawaiian revue received the Hawai'i Visitors Bureau Kahili Award. The resort offers wedding service, and their on-property coordinator can assist you with all your wedding arrangements, from a marriage license to flowers and musicians.

Rates: Standard Room $89; Oceanview Room $109; Oceanfront Room $149; "Coconet" special package includes room and breakfast for two, Standard $95, Part Oceanview $120, Oceanview $135, Oceanfront $159; "Kauai Comback" special package includes room plus breakfast and dinner for two, $125; "Ohana" family rates provide a second room free when the first room is purchased at the rack rate; check with reservations on other available specials at bookting time

KAUA'I SANDS ★
420 Papaloa Rd., Kapa'a, HI 96746. (808) 822-4951, Fax (808) 822-0998. RENTAL AGENT: Sand & Seaside Hotels, toll free 1-800-560-5553 or (808) 922-5737; Email: sandsea@aloha.net; Web: < www.kauaisandshotel.com > This Americanized Japanese complex has Hawaiian/Japanese decor. The black and white exterior could be painted more attractively. The rooms don't get much sun, but this keeps them cool and keeps the dark-colored spreads and carpets from fading - they look brand new. Self-service laundry. They are on a beachfront, but it is better for sitting and ocean watching than for swimming and sunbathing. Rooms are air conditioned. Al & Don's Restaurant overlooks the ocean. Located in Wailua, it is located between Papaloa Road and the Coconut Plantation MarketPlace. Discounts for AAA members and seniors. Free room upgrade for 50+ seniors, free welcome breakfast for two, daily free breakfast for AAA members.

Rates: Standard $98-108; Superior $100-110; Deluxe Poolview $125-135; Deluxe w/Kitchenette $135-145; also check on room and car packages and other specials

LAE NANI ★
410 Papaloa Rd., Kapa'a, HI 96746. (808) 822-4938, Fax (808) 822-1022. Located adjacent to the Coconut MarketPlace in Kapa'a. RENTAL AGENTS: Outrigger Resorts 1-800-OUTRIGGER, toll free fax 1-800-622--4852 or tel (808) 921-6600; Email: reservations@outrigger.com; Web: < www.outrigger.com >. Kaua'i Vacation Rentals 1-800-367-5025. Maui & All Islands 1-800-663-6962. Premier Resorts 1-800367-7052.

They offer 84 units in three story buildings. 1 BR units are 800 sq. ft., 2 BR 2 BTH units are 1,072 sq. ft. These apartments are spacious with nice island-style decor and furnishings; light colors with cane and bamboo accents. Amenities include oceanfront swimming pool, tennis courts, daily maid service if booked with Outrigger, barbecue, and picnic area. All units have ceiling fans, private lanais, and full kitchens with microwaves. Laundry facilities are available on the property, but not in most units.

The central office has a particularly friendly and helpful staff -- meet them when you check in, stop by for your complimentary newspaper, or to mail (postage-free) the set of complimentary postcards that Outrigger provides for you on your arrival! This property has some outstanding oceanfront vistas. While the units are a little older and perhaps not as contemporary in style, they are very roomy, and comfortable.

Lae Nani is situated on seven acres of lovely grounds. A small man-made rock pool along the bay has been created. The rocky promontory along the beach is a remnant of an early *heiau*. A free historical brochure describes *A Self-Guided Tour of Wailua* for you to explore this and other ancient Hawaiian sites in the area. Check with Outrigger for a variety of packages and programs including senior discounts, first night free, room & car, and family plans. Note that Outrigger price includes daily maid service.
Kauai Vacation Rental Rates: 1 BR o.v. $800 week; 2 BR $950 week.
Outrigger Resorts Rates: 1 BR o.v. $220; 1 BR o.f. $270; 2 BR g.v. $240; 2BR o.v. $280; 2 BR o.f. $330

PALI KAI COTTAGES
Five units on a bluff at Kukui'i Point that overlooks Nawiliwili Harbor and Kalapaki Bay. RENTAL AGENT: Kaua'i Vacation Rentals 1-800-367-5025. Surrounded by the Marriott complex and lagoons and on a bluff overlooking Kalapaki Bay. 1 & 2 bedrooms, all have two baths and sleep four.
Kauai Vacation Rentals has 1 BR $800 weekly, 2 BR $1,000 weekly.

PONO KAI RESORT
1250 Kuhio Hwy., Kapa'a, HI 96746. Toll free 1-800-438-6493, (808) 822-9831; Web: <www.extraholidays.com>. RENTAL AGENT: Marc Resorts Hawai'i 1-800-535-0085, toll free FAX 1-800-633-5085, local (808) 922-9700. Maui & All 1-800-663-6962. Kaua'i Vacation Rentals 1-800-367-5025. Amenities include pool, jacuzzi, sauna, BBQ's. Units have ceiling fans, telephones, lanais, full kitchens including microwaves. Lighted tennis courts, shuffleboard, covered recreation area with kitchen facilities, tables and chairs, concierge/activity desk, video rentals. There is an attractive lagoon and bridge leading into the property from the front office and further along, a small Hawaiian garden with pathways for a short, but pleasant stroll. The exterior has recently been repainted to lighter shades over the existing brown. Very central location on the edge of Kapa'a town. (An interesting aside is that this used to be a pineapple cannery!)
Marc Resorts offers:
1 BR $129 (max 4); 2BR $159 (max 6); 2BR w/loft $179 (max 8)

RADISSON KAUA'I BEACH HOTEL ★
4331 Kaua'i Beach Drive, Lihu'e, HI 96766. (808) 245-1955. Radisson Hotels 1-888-805-3843, Web: <www.radissonkauai.com> OTHER RENTAL AGENTS: Maui & All Islands 1-800-663-6962. Pleasant Hawaiian Holidays 1-800-242-9244. There are 347 units in a U-shaped complex of connected buildings surrounding a central courtyard and pool/activity complex on 25 landscaped oceanfront acres. This is the former Outrigger and had a full renovation program completed in mid-2001. All guest rooms and public areas got new furnishings and a new look.

The Radisson is located three miles north of Lihu'e on Nukoli'i Beach (which means the beach of the kole fish). There are three miles of beach for strolling, exploring and discovering, the longest stretch of beachfront of any resort on Kaua'i. While the beach is not really suitable for swimming, there are quiet coves and areas where swimming and snorkeling can be enjoyed. The resort has free scuba lessons available. But be aware that the beach can be unsafe for water activities at times.

Three swimming pools (2 adult, 1 keiki) and a spa amid lush tropical gardens and rockscaped waterfalls. There is also a new sand-bottom pool at the front of the property closer to the actual beach and next to the Driftwood Sand Bar & Grill. Four tennis courts (two lighted), lobby shops, activity desk, and fitness club. Wailua Golf Course nearby. Meeting and banquet space. No laundry facilities. The rooms have daily maid service, air conditioning, refrigerator, television, direct dial phones, and private lanais. Guest rooms and hallways are bright and clean, furnishings are very tasteful with subdued tropical colors and accents.

Naupaka Terrace Steak House is open for breakfast and dinner daily. Shutters Lounge and the Driftwood Sand Bar & Grill at poolside also provide cocktails, beverages, snacks and light meals daily along with nightly Hawaiian entertainment.

A Keiki Klub Summer Program is available for children 5-12 who are guests at the resort. The program is available Thursday through Monday from 8:30 am-3:30 pm. Children are exposed to Hawaiian culture through activities such as lei-making, Hawaiian language games, Hawaiian legends and storytelling, hula lessons, and Hawaiian arts and crafts. Other activities include movies, fishing derbies, beach combing, and shell collecting as well as excursions to Smith's Tropical Paradise and Fern Grotto tours. Half day sessions are $15 per child. Full day program is $30 per child. Cost includes activities, excursions and refreshments. Lunch is provided only in the full-day program.

Check with Radisson for a variety of special discount packages and seasonal programs including first night free, room & car, bed & breakfast, and family plans. Also discounts for seniors, AARP, corporate, etc.
Standard rooms begin at $119; Senior-Business rates $139-149; mountain/garden view super saver $169; mountain/garden $199; ocean view super saver $209; lagoon $219; pool view $239; ocean view $259; 1BR suites from $299

WAILUA BAY VIEW
320 Papaloa Rd., Kapa'a, HI 96746. (808) 823-0960. Located overlooking Wailua Bay. RENTAL AGENT: Linda Owen 1-800-882-9007 or Email: lro@ix.netcom.com; Web: < www.wailuabay.com >, Prosser Realty 1-800-767-4707, (808) 245-4711; Web: < www.prosser-realty.com >. Kaua'i Vacation Rentals 1-800-367-5025. Maui & All 1-800-663-6962.

The apartments are lengthwise, so the living room is at the end facing the ocean and as the name implies, provides a beautiful bay view. Full kitchens, microwaves (in some units), dishwasher, washer/dryers. All units are air conditioned.

King or queen beds, sleeper sofa in living room. Swimming pool and BBQ's. Walking distance to shops and restaurants. Daily maid service. Located on the beachfront with tennis courts across the street.
Rates: Oceanfront 1 BR $85-140; Deluxe oceanfront $99 and up (1-4, max. 4)

EXPENSIVE

HALE AWAPUHI
366 Papaloa Road, Kapa'a, HI 96746. (808) 245-8841. RENTAL AGENT: Kaua'i Vacation Rentals 1-800-367-5025, Email: aloha@kvrre.com; Web: <www.KauaiVacationRentals.com>. Prosser 1-800-767-4707. Maui & All Islands 1-800-663-6962. Just nine units in this property with oceanfront pool. Convenient to shops, restaurants and The Coconut Marketplace.
Beachfront units $170-400; Dlx groundfloor corner unit o.v. 2 BR 2 BTH (1-4) $250/210; 2 BR w/loft (1-4) $320/280; First floor 2 BR 2 BTH (1-4) non-smoking $190/170; 2 BR 2 BTH second floor non-smoking (1-4) $210/190.

KAUA'I MARRIOTT RESORT & BEACH CLUB ★
3610 Rice Street., Lihu'e, HI 96766. (808) 245-5050. MARRIOTT RESERVATIONS: 1-800-220-2925; Web: <www.marriott.com>. OTHER RENTAL AGENTS: Pleasant Hawaiian Holidays 1-800-242-9244. Located on 51 acres overlooking Kalapaki Bay, the Kaua'i Marriott Resort & Beach Club consists of 345 hotel rooms (the Kaua'i Marriott) and a community of 232 one and two bedroom Vacation Ownership villas named Marriott's Kaua'i Beach Club. The villas overlook Kalapaki Beach and Nawiliwili Bay. This hotel/resort in its present incarnation, dates from the 1970's-80's when it was at various times the Kaua'i Surf and Westin Kaua'i. A 1980's makeover left it a pretty gaudy hotel with an overly elaborate out-of-place design motif. In redeveloping the property in the 1990's, Marriott chose a new approach, combining time share with a hotel property.

The $30 million renovation incorporated Hawaiian history and culture into the new interior design, while keeping within the existing architectural elements and scale of the buildings. The result is a much improved image for the Kaua'i Marriott - not nearly as ostentatious or garish, and more reflective of the tropical elegance of Kaua'i. The most significant change was the replacement of the Roman pool in front with a much more subtle lagoon and more natural landscaping. This single element has made a big difference. The pink and beige color scheme is warmer and less showy, but the property is still luxurious just in a more appropriate way. Of course much of the elaborate structures remain, the marble columns and such, but they have made an effort to make them less focal. The elevator down to the lobby is still attractive and fun, kind of like Pirates of the Caribbean at Disneyland. The rooms are attractively furnished and spacious - - not too much excess furniture. Convenient in-room amenities include a mini-fridge, free HBO, and hair dryers.

The villas feature a total of three restaurants and one lounge. Casual poolside dining is available at the Kalapaki Grill, and Kukui's as well as lunches and dinners at Duke's Canoe Club. Aupaka Terrace offers daytime refreshments or evening specialty cocktails, featuring an espresso and ice cream bar. The resort amenities include Hawaii's largest swimming pool and a 20,400 square foot retail shopping center.

The resort offers the Kalapaki Kids Club which focuses on the uniqueness of the Hawaiian Islands and Kaua'i in particular. For example, during the hula classes, the songs that are taught are all from Kaua'i, such as "Aloha Kaua'i." Kids are exposed to the ukulele and various Hawaiian crafts like lei making and lauhala weaving. Reservations need to be made one day in advance. The full day program is available Tuesday through Saturday from 9 am until 3 pm for youthages 5 to 12 years. The program costs $45 and includes lunch, a snack, and a Kalapaki Kids T-shirt.

As for adult activities, there are plenty of those! Special activities and Hawaiian exhibits are scheduled daily including sunrise walk, introduction to snorkeling or windsurfing, or you can even have your portrait done! Exhibits include Hawaiian Woodworking, Ni'ihau shell lei display, Hawaiian quilting, or featherwork. There are eight tennis courts and nearby are the two fine Kaua'i Lagoons golf courses designed by Jack Nicklaus. The hotel still offers complimentary airport shuttle service. Ask about current package options.
Rates: Garden $299; ocean/pool view $354; ocean view $414; suites $649-$2,600

LANIKAI
390 Papaloa Rd., Kapa'a, HI 96746. RENTAL AGENTS: Castle Resorts 1-800-367-5004. Maui & All Islands 1-800-663-6962. Kaua'i Vacation Rentals 1-800-367-5025. Two, three story buildings offer eighteen units, half of these are in the rental program. These ocean-front condominiums provide large lanais as well as full kitchens. Property amenities include pool, BBQ area. Located near Wailua State Park Beach and Kapa'a.
Castle: 1 BR o.v. $250/230; 1 BR o.f. $270/250; 2 BR o.v. $295/270; 2 BR o.f. $315/290

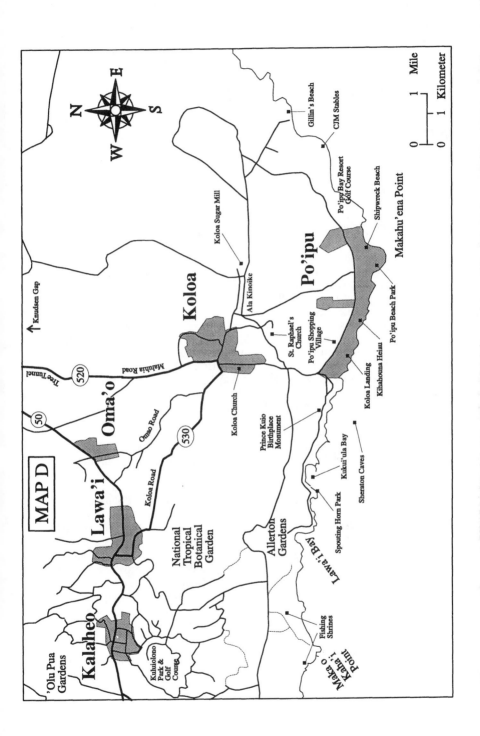

MAP D

Knudsen Gap

The Tunnel

Kalaheo

Lawa'i

Oma'o

Koloa

Po'ipu

'Olu Pua Gardens

Kukuiolono Park & Golf Course

National Tropical Botanical Garden

Allerton Gardens

Koloa Road

Omao Road

Maluhia Road

Koloa Church

Prince Kuio Birthplace Monument

Koloa Sugar Mill

Ala Kinoike

St. Raphael's Church

Po'ipu Shopping Village

Po'ipu Beach Park

Koloa Landing

Kihabouna Heiau

Shipwreck Beach

Makahu'ena Point

Po'ipu Bay Resort Golf Course

Gillin's Beach

CJM Stables

Sheraton Caves

Kukui'ula Bay

Spouting Horn Park

Lawa'i Bay

Fishing Shrines

Makahu'ena Point

Kapa'a Point

N
E
W
S

Mile

Kilometer

0   1

0   1

SOUTH SHORE TO WEST SHORE

INTRODUCTION

Koloa-Po'ipu-Lawa'i-Port Allen-
Hanapepe-Waimea-Kekaha-Koke'e

WHERE TO STAY/WHAT TO SEE/WHERE TO SHOP

This section begins as we head down Hwy. 50 from Lihu'e through Puhi then Hwy. 520 (the tree tunnel) to Koloa, continuing down to Po'ipu and Lawa'i, then following back up to Hwy. 50 (via 530, Lawa'i) eastward to Port Allen, Hanapepe, Waimea, Kekaha, and finally finding the way to Waimea Canyon State Park and Koke'e State Park, the west side's main attractions. As you follow Hwy. 50 toward Koloa, you will turn left onto Hwy. 520. You will not be able to miss the stunning stand of trees which line the road on either side. Walter Duncan McBryde was landscaping his homestead at the turn of the century when he discovered he had an excess of eucalyptus trees. He donated five hundred eucalyptus (also known as swamp mahogany) to the county and they were planted along Hwy. 520. This famed Eucalyptus Grove, known as the *Tunnel of Trees,* has recovered substantially since the '92 hurricane, but a little more time will be required for mother nature to rebuild the canopy effect. In the days before the construction of the Kaumualii Hwy., the tree tunnel was three times longer than its current size. Construction of the highway resulted in the removal of some of the trees, but others remain on their original site along the dirt road through the canefields on the left side as you head to Lihu'e.

A recent addition to transportation alternatives on Kaua'i is the *Coconut Coast Trolley* operated by Trans Hawaiian Kaua'i from 10am to 10pm daily. Fares are $2 for a one way ticket or $5 for an all-day pass. Phone 245-5108. Northbound stops include Maui Marriott, Hilo Hattie, Radisson, Holiday Inn Sunspree, and the Coconut MarketPlace. Southbound stops include Kapa'a Town--ABC Store, Kaua'i Village, and Smith's/Waialealae Boats. A feeder shuttle provides transfer from Po'ipu, Lihu'e and Nawiliwili Harbor. This is a demand type of service and they reserve the right to not stop or pick up at locations based upon lack of demand. They suggest you call and make reservations 245-5108 to insure stops at Hyatt Regency, Embassy Vacation Resort, Kiahuna Plantation, or Sheraton Kaua'i.

If you are staying at the Hyatt end of Po'ipu (Pe'e Road or beyond), the Koloa By-pass at Weli Weli Road now allows you to bypass Po'ipu and go straight into Koloa (and points East or North from there.)

KOLOA

The last volcanic eruptions occurred on Kaua'i in the Koloa area some one million years ago. Traveling around the area you will see cinder cones still dotting the landscape. The word Koloa has several meanings, but the most common translation is "place of long cane." The town of *Koloa* developed along the Waikomo Stream which provided not only fresh water, but power for the first sugar mills. In 1835, Ladd and Company established the first successful sugar plantation in Hawai'i here. King Kamehameha III leased 980 acres to a Bostonian, William Hooper, for $300 a year. The first mill was built in 1836 in an area known as Green Pond. The mill used large koa logs to grind the cane juice. The second mill was built in 1838 in the same location, but used much-improved iron rollers. Ladd and Company built the third mill in 1841 near the confluence of the Omao and Waikomo Streams. The mill was powered by water and firewood fueled the boilers. The chimney stack at the park across the street from the monkey pod tree in Koloa is all that remains of this third mill which was used until 1913. The monument represents the many varied ethnic groups which contributed their labors to the sugar cane industry. The "new" mill was built in 1913 and continued in production for the Koloa Sugar Company until it ceased operations in 1996. McBryde - Koloa's last incarnation once owned by Alexander & Baldwin -has shifted to coffee production as Island Coffee Company. The Waita Reservoir to the east side of Koloa is the largest reservoir in Hawaii. This man-made body of water was built on marshlands between 1903 and 1906 and covers 370 acres.

From its inception in 1835 and then for 21 years, this was the only sugar cane plantation in the Hawaiian islands. The quaint plantation feel of this town continues to this day. A strip of shops occupying the old wooden storefronts line the town of Koloa. *Tomkats* and *Pizzetta* restaurants are adjacent to various art galleries and shops carrying everything from interesting old Hawaiiana prints and reprints to jewelry and souvenirs. Island Soap and Candle Works also has an outlet here in Old Koloa Town in addition to the one up north at Kilauea.

KOLOA

149

The large monkey pod tree was planted in 1925 and lends its shade to the Crazy Shirts store. This building was originally built by Mr. Yamaka who ran a hotel in the back until the mid 1920's when the Yamamoto family began their store at this sight. Behind this is a small mall area with the Koloa Museum. This small, free, museum depicts the development of the sugar industry in this area. The hours it is open seem to be sporadic.

The best deal in town is behind *Sueoka's* grocery. The small "snack shop" is reminiscent of the old Azeka's snack shop on Maui. Walk up to the window and order your grinds. Open just for lunch, it is worth the drive back from Po'ipu Beach to pick up a meal!

The *Koloa Church*, located on Po'ipu Road, was established in 1835. However, this pristine white church was not built until 1859. The design reflects a traditional New England style, typical of the missionary influence in early Hawai'i.

Another of Kaua'i's notable historic religious landmarks is found at Koloa. More than 150 years ago, in 1841, *St. Raphael Catholic Church* opened its doors on Kaua'i. The island's first Catholic church suffered severe damage in the '92 hurricane, but was repaired. The original church had walls that were thickly built. A mortar was made by burning sand into lime and it was then mixed with pounded coral. This was used to hold together the rocks that constituted the walls. A reporting of the church's construction was published in a centennial celebration held in 1941: "The gathering of coral was a saga itself. The men and women swam out to the reef from Koloa beach where they dived under water to break off huge slabs of coral. They would then swim with the slab back to the beach, tie it onto their shoulders and trudge the three miles across the plain to the church." Changes to the original church over the years included the addition of more arched windows and a steeple was added in 1933. St. Raphael was originally a parish school and offered instruction for many years. While the main church seats only 150 persons, you may find three times that many in attendance on Sundays. So, in addition to the rebuilding efforts, the church also has plans for expansion. You might also visit the Lady of Lourdes shrine, built of lava rocks in a secluded spot at the back of the property.

Koloa Landing, about a mile-and-a-half south of town on the coast, was the state's third largest whaling port in the 1800's and was also used for the exporting of raw sugar and sweet potatoes. An inter-island ferry would traverse between the islands, bringing passengers to this port on Kaua'i. The landing as a port sight was abandoned in 1928. Today you can still see the remains of the old mill, and nearby is a sculpture that depicts the history of the area and the various ethnic groups that made their mark on Kaua'i's sugar industry.

PO'IPU

While Po'ipu has no definitive town center, it is none-the-less a wonderful Kaua'i vacation destination. Located on the south shore, there are several excellent accommodations. Po'ipu Beach is located in front of the Kiahuna Plantation. This is one of the island's best all-around beaches for family activities, except during high seas. The Hyatt Regency is located on Keoneloa Beach, fondly referred to as Shipwreck Beach for a long-since-gone wreck that once was beached on this stretch of coastline.

The *Po'ipu Shopping Village* is the largest and only real shopping center in this area. You will find eateries ranging from fine dining to very casual including *Roy's Po'ipu Bar & Grill, Keoki's Paradise, Pattaya Asian Cafe*, and *Shipwreck Subs*. There is also a *Crazy Shirts* and some other fashion shops, jewelry stores, and touristy shops with fine arts and gifts. They have free Hawaiian entertainment and Tahitian Dancers Monday and Thursday at 5 pm.

Prince Kuhio Park is located on Lawa'i Beach Road. Prince Kuhio was the youngest son of Kaua'i's Chief David Kahalepouli Piikoli and the grandson of Kaumuali'i, the last King of Kaua'i. His aunt was Queen Kapiolani and Prince Kuhio was adopted by her and grew up in the royal household in Honolulu. The monument at this park marks the birth site of Prince Jonah Kuhio Kalanianaole. Prince Jonah was known as the "People's Prince" because of his achievements for his Hawaiian people. You can see the foundation of Kuhio's parents' home, royal fishpond, shrine, *Hoai Heiau* where the *kahuna* (priests) meditated and lived, and a sitting bench that faced the grounds. He was born in 1871, and elected in 1902 as a delegate to Congress, where he served until his death on January 7, 1922.

Located just to the east of Po'ipu Beach there is a lava rock outcropping known as *Spouting Horn*. It is named for the shooting geyser of sea water that appears during high tide. The spouting results from the surf washing into the lava tube and being sucked up through a hole in the coastal rock. The geyser reaches heights of as much as 60 feet. This is located at Spouting Horn County Park and is a popular visitor attraction, open to the public at no charge. It is easy to find, follow Hwy. 520 to Lawa'i Rd. (also known as Spouting Horn Rd.). Heed the posted signs which caution about the dangerous rocks. There are a number of local arts & crafts vendors with tents and booths set up next to the parking lot. Take some time to browse the fine bargains in local handmade coral jewelry, the rare and coveted Ni'ihau shell necklaces, bracelets, earrings, various artworks, etc. You're sure to find some nice mementos of your Kaua'i visit here.

If you'd like to experience a little of the pleasures of Robinson Crusoe or Swiss Family Robinson, plan an excursion to *Maha'ulepu Beach*. This is located at the eastern end of the Po'ipu Resort area past the Hyatt Resort. It was here that King Kamehameha I made his attempt to conquer the island of Kaua'i in 1796. Unfortunately, a storm forced a retreat, but the advance forces of Kamehameha's troops arrived on the island unaware of the order to retreat and were quickly killed.

This is also the beach site where George C. Scott portrayed Ernest Hemingway in the movie *Islands in the Stream*. Maha'ulepu Beach is actually a collection of smaller beaches. Bones of ancient and now extinct flightless birds have been found in caves in this area. The beaches offer a diverse assortment of aquatic activities including fishing, surfing, bodyboarding, body surfing, kayaking, windsurfing, snorkeling, and swimming. The three areas along this beachfront are Gillin's Beach, Kawailoa Bay, and Ha'ula Beach.

Gillin's was named for the supervisor of Grove Farm Company, Elbert Gillin, who arrived in the islands in 1912 and relocated to Kaua'i in 1925 where he built his home. He was the supervisor of the Ha'upu Range Tunnel. Following two hurricanes, all that remained was Gillin's chimney, but the home has now been rebuilt. Several feet below this beach are the Rainbow Petroglyphs which were discovered in 1980 after a severe storm took out as much as six feet of beachfront exposing the petrogylphs. Working in reverse, the sea soon chose to cover them up once again. Currents at Kawailoa Bay make it unsafe for swimming or snorkeling. To reach Ha'ula Beach you may park on the east side of Pa'o'o Point and travel to the shore by trail. This area is the south shore's most dangerous beach.

The first beach, Gillin's, on occasion may be good for the experienced snorkeler during calm surf. Ha'ula Beach is often less crowded. Access to these beaches is over private land which is open during daylight hours only, 7 am to 6 pm. The gate is locked at night and no overnight camping is permitted. This private property is owned by the Grove Farm Company. Since access could be denied at any time, please be respectful and take your litter out with you so everyone can enjoy these gorgeous Kaua'i beaches.

Public access is found at the end of Po'ipu Road. Take the dirt road and then turn right onto the cane road. There are no facilities here, so remember to bring your own water. Parking is along side the road.

This area of **Maha'ulepu** is important geologically as well as archaeologically. Many of the early Hawaiian archeological sites were destroyed when the land was cleared for sugar cane. However, scientists have enough information to speculate that this area was heavily populated in pre-contact times. (Referring to the period prior to the arrival of Captain Cook.) The area offered the early Hawaiians excellent fishing grounds and a fertile valley making it a very suitable living environment. It was noted by Captain George Vancouver that from this area the glow of numerous campfires could be seen as he sailed past. Further confirmation was found by the many burial sites located in the sand dunes here. Geologically the area lies below Mt. Ha'upu, which is now only an eroded caldera. The sand dunes have born other rich geological treasures including the fossils of extinct birds. They have identified a flightless bird called a rail, several species of geese, and a long-legged owl. John Clark's *Beaches of Kaua'i* notes that, "Several caves in the vicinity contain two extremely rare insects, one a blind wolf spider and the other a blind terrestrial amphipod."

The ***Po'ipu Beach Resort Association*** provides up to date information on accommodations, activities, dining, shopping, transportation, and service in the Po'ipu, Koloa, and Kalaheo areas of Kaua'i. To request a free 36 page brochure. Contact: Po'ipu Beach Resort Association, PO Box 730, Koloa, HI 96756. (808) 742-7444. FAX (808) 742-7887. Toll free 1-888-744-0888. E-mail: info@poipu-beach.org or look up their electronic brochure at < www://poipu-beach.org >

LAWA'I

Leaving Koloa and heading eastward on Hwy. 530, you'll travel to Lawa'i. Little is known of early Lawa'i. According to an account by David Forbes in his book, *Queen Emma and Lawa'i*, the early maps and photographs show that the valley was cultivated in taro and later in rice. Queen Emma, the wife of Kamehameha IV, probably first saw Lawa'i during her visit in 1856, but returned for a more lengthy stay during the winter and spring in 1871. On arrival she found the area rather desolate, and compared with the busy life in Honolulu, it must have seemed so. In her correspondence with her family on O'ahu she requested many items to be sent, including plant slips. With these plant starts she began to develop one of the finest gardens in the islands.

Queen Emma leased the Lawa'i land to Duncan McBryde for a span of fifteen years in 1876, however, she reserved her house lot and several acres of taro patch land. According to Forbes, "In 1886, after the Queen's death, Mrs. Elizabeth McBryde bought the entire Ahupuaa for $50,000. The upper lands were planted to sugar cane, and the valley was apparently leased to Chinese rice growers and taro planters."

In 1899, Alexander McBryde obtained the land and with a love of plants, he continued to enlarge and cultivate the gardens which were begun by the queen. Alexander McBryde died in 1935 and the land was sold to Robert Allerton and his son John in 1938. They continued to enlarge the gardens, searching out plants from around South East Asia. Today Lawa'i is a horticulturist's dream, with an outstanding collection of tropical plants. The ***National Tropical Botanical Garden*** is a nationally-chartered non-profit organization that is actually made up of five separate gardens. Three are on Kaua'i, one is on Maui, and another is located in Florida. Each of the gardens has an individual name, but they are sometimes incorrectly referred to individually as the "National Tropical Botanical Garden."

The Lawa'i Garden (National Tropical Botanical Garden Headquarters) is located on Kaua'i's southern shore in the lush Lawa'i Valley, and was the first garden site to be acquired by the National Tropical Botanical Garden. The NTBG headquarter facilities are located adjacent to the Lawa'i Garden. The headquarters complex includes a scientific laboratory, an herbarium housing nearly 30,000 specimens of tropical plants, an 8,000 volume research library, a computer records center, an educational center, and offices for staff and visiting scientists. ***Lawa'i Garden*** is a research and educational garden comprising 186 acres. The garden's extensive collections include tropical plants of the world that are of particular significance for research, conservation, or cultural purposes. Special emphasis is given to rare and endangered Hawaiian species and to economic plants of the tropical world.

Of particular interest is the endangered *kanaloa kahoolawensis* (one of only four in the world). This small, woody plant is known only to exist on Kahoolawe. In 1992 two specimens of this plant were discovered on Kahoolawe. This is the first new genus discovered in Hawai'i since 1913 and two have since been grown from seeds at the NTBG. There is also a collection of familiar household products - sugar, vanilla, cinnamon - all seen here in their natural plant state. Palm oil, sandalwood (for scent), koa (for wood items including canoes and furniture), and cuari (used to make sodium pentathol) can also be seen in their original form. *Three Springs* is at the interior of the Lawa'i Garden (toward the mountains). This 120-acre area was acquired as a bequest to the Garden. As yet undeveloped, it will eventually be designed as an additional garden section, emphasizing the beautiful natural land and water features.

The nearby *Allerton Garden* is located oceanfront at Lawa'i-Kai, adjacent to the Lawa'i Garden. The entrance, located across from Spouting Horn, is a 14,000 square foot renovated plantation home that was transplanted from West Kaua'i to become the visitor center for the Garden. This was formerly a private 100-acre estate. The beautifully designed garden is managed by the National Tropical Botanical Garden pursuant to an agreement with the Allerton Estate Trust. The gardens, started by Queen Emma, were lovingly developed and expanded over a period of 30 years by Robert Allerton and his son John. The sculpted gardens contain numerous plants of interest, outstanding examples of garden design and water features, as well as Queen Emma's original summer cottage. The cottage was severely damaged by Hurricane Iniki and plans for restoration are underway. The Moreton Bay fig trees here have giant buttress roots and helped create a prehistoric scene for the filming of *Jurassic Park*. While these trees appear ancient, they were actually planted in 1940. Reservations are required for tours of the Lawa'i and Allerton Gardens. Tour fee for the Allerton Garden or Lawa'i Garden is $25 adults, $15 teens (13-18), $10 children (6-12) for each tour. For information on scheduled tours and reservations for either call (808) 742-2623. PO Box 340 Lawa'i, HI 96765.

HIBISCUS & PALM

KALAHEO

The town of Kalaheo was home to many immigrants at the turn of the century. There was homestead land auctioned by the government beginning in about 1910 and was originally used for growing pineapple with Walter McBryde spearheading the pineapple industry. The population was predominantly Portuguese, Hawaiian and Japanese. The name translates to "the proud day." As you enter into the town of Kalaheo you will pass *Brick Oven Pizza,* considered by many to serve the best pizzas on the island, so stop if you're in the mood for a pizza pie! Just across the highway is *Pomodoro Ristorante Italiano* for some good Italian fare as well. A block further up the hill to the stoplight at Papalina Road in the center of Kalaheo, you'll find *Camp House Grill* on the right, and south on Papalina Road a couple of blocks is the well-known *Kalaheo Steak House.* So, even though Kalaheo is a small town, it has some good eateries.

To take a short and worthwhile detour you need to turn left onto Papalina Road and head south for Kukuiolono Park. Many of the street names are Hawaiian words for parts of the body. For example, *Papalina* means cheek, *Lae* means forehead, *Maka* is eye, and *Opu* is stomach. Glimpse off to your left as you climb the winding road and, if you are fortunate, you'll see a rainbow hanging over Po'ipu. The three huge satellite dishes on the right will warn you that your turn is just ahead. A small white sign on the right is too small and too near the turn off to prepare you for the U turn onto Puu Rd. Enter Kukuiolono Park through the huge rock archway with iron gates. *Kukuiolono Park* is a series of gardens with sweeping Pacific and Lawa'i Valley views. This park was built by Walter McBryde, a founding father of the island's pineapple industry. This beautiful, scenic public park is a popular location for wedding ceremonies. There is also a Hawaiian garden which displays some interesting ancient stone artifacts. There are huge rock bowls and a stone with a shape resembling the island called "Kaua'i iki" or Little Kaua'i. It is said by some that if you haven't seen Little Kaua'i, then you haven't seen Kaua'i. The public golf course located here is open 6:30 am-6:30 pm. No tee-offs allowed after 4:30. This is the best golf value on the island with nine picturesque holes costing only $7! Because of the value it may be crowded, but if you tee-off late in the day and don't have time to finish, it may be well worth the green fees. You might like to stop at the *Kalaheo Coffee Co. & Cafe,* just past the Papalina Rd. intersection and pick up some of their huge sandwiches to enjoy as a picnic up at the park.

ELE'ELE and PORT ALLEN

Just beyond mile marker 14 on the right is a scenic overlook of the Hanapepe Valley. It is a strikingly beautiful vista with the sheer canyon walls in hues of amber, ocher, and red. You will first travel through Ele'ele and Port Allen before reaching the town of Hanapepe, so we'll describe it later. As you continue toward Waimea, you will note a series of substantial looking electrical poles bordering the road on both sides. These were put in following the devastation caused by the '92 hurricane. The poles are supposed to be able to withstand wind forces up to 120 miles per hour. As the road curves downhill you will reach the area of Ele'ele. The most notable landmark is the Ele'ele Shopping Center.

A *Big Save* and *Toi's Thai Kitchen* are here. Turn down toward Port Allen to see one of Kaua'i's two seaports. The Coast Guard has boats here and some are "drones" or target ships. They warn "Target Drone, Stay Clear" in large bold letters. Obviously these in the harbor have either not had a turn at being bombed, or they just got lucky with some misses! You can purchase bags of Kaua'i grown coffee and other coffee-related items at the *Kauai Coffee Company and Visitor Center* located between Kalaheo and Ele'ele on a turn off just past the old McBryde Mill. Enjoy free samples of java while you browse their store. Call (808) 335-5497 or 1-800-545-8605.

You may have noticed that the dirt has become redder as you proceed around the southern coastline. The soil contains a good deal of iron. A very clever entrepreneur has taken advantage of this red clay which has a natural property for staining anything that it comes in contact with. You are sure to have seen the "Red Dirt Shirts" at various shops around the island. If you can't wait to visit, you can order by mail. Paradise Sportswear, PO Box 1027, Kalaheo, HI 96741. Send for a copy of their catalog which depicts their many varied styles.

Port Allen has reemerged as an important commercial boat harbor for visitor activities. With the recent banning of commercial cruise boat operations at Hanalei Bay on the North Shore, many of the cruise boat excursions to The Napali Coast now depart from this location.

HANAPEPE

Hanapepe, which means "crushed bay," was Kaua'i's largest town back in the 1920's and remained so until about 1947 when it experienced a post-war decline. Two decades later, however, the population had dwindled significantly. The area was rediscovered by the Chinese immigrants who began to grow rice here. Hanapepe was once again one of Kaua'i's busiest towns from World War I through the early 1950's.

During the second World War, this coastal village was alive with thousands of GIs and sailors who were sent from the mainland and the rest of Hawai'i to train for Pacific Theater duty and to shore up Kaua'i's defenses. At this time Hanapepe reached its largest population and boasted restaurants, two theaters, two roller rinks, a dance hall -- and a brothel!

Hanapepe boasts that it is the biggest little town on Kaua'i. Fortunately, Hanapepe feels like a step back in time with its plantation era buildings and slow pace. When the highway was widened it was decided to by-pass the town of Hanapepe and it was probably at that time that Hanapepe began to fade into disrepair. The opening of the Kukui Grove Shopping Center in Lihu'e was another blow to shopkeepers who just could not compete. It is a quaint town that has potential for being a wonderful locale for artisans galleries or such. You may recognize this town for scenes from the made-for-television mini-series *Thornbirds*. Many of the buildings were damaged by '92 hurricane will probably not be fully repaired. The *Taro Ko Chips* factory is on the edge of town, and you might catch them when they are open. Mr. and Mrs. Nagamine started this business following their retirement and they cook up chips made from taro grown in fields nearby.

The Green Garden Restaurant has been hopping since the 1940's when the GI's would stop by for a meal and a piece of their wonderful pie. *Yoshiura's General Store* operated as Mikado until World War II and is a classic. The *Hanapepe Cafe & Espresso* is worth a visit. By 4 pm most days, the town is pretty well closed up. Except for Friday night! A number of new art galleries have been springing up in the last year or two, optimistic that perhaps this artisan community will soon be discovered by visitors exploring Kaua'i's western shore. And now these local galleries host "Art Night" every Friday (6-9pm) with at least one of them providing refreshments and an art demonstration. Decorative lighting adds to the mood for visitors to enjoy a festive stroll along the old main street shop buildings, watch artists doing portraits, and enjoy the hula show and local Hawaiian music. The art galleries lining Hanapepe's main street include Kaua'i Fine Arts, Hawaiian Kountry Art Studio, The Art Gallery, Hale Rasta, Kim Starr Gallery, Lele Aka Studio & Gallery, Hanapepe Art Center, Kamaaina Cabinets and Koa Wood Gallery, Aloha Angels Shop, Arius Hopman Studio Gallery and Dawn Traina Gallery. They all have varied open hours and days.

In the middle of town on the north side, is a short walkway to the Hanepape swinging bridge over the Hanapepe River. Take a short break and walk across the river. If you have youngsters, they will enjoy the short walk on the "swinging bridge." The bridge is a short-cut for residents living across the river to reach the town.

One of the most fascinating natural sites in Hanapepe is the salt ponds at Salt Pond Beach. The natural flats along this beach have been used by Hawaiians for generations. Today, this site continues to be used for traditional salt making. The resulting product is used for medicinal and cultural purposes. In late spring the wells, or *puna*, are cleaned and the salt making process runs through the summer months. Mother nature has been kind enough to create a ridge of rock between the two rocky points at Salt Pond Beach, resulting in a large lagoon. The area is fairly well protected, allowing for swimming and snorkeling (except during times of high surf) and is popular for surfing and windsurfing as well. This park is well used, because of its protected swimming area, for families and children. This part of the island is often sunny and warmer, even when there is rain on the south and east shore, Salt Pond Beach can be a great day-long excursion. There are picnic areas, restrooms, a rinse off shower, and generally a lifeguard on duty. Camping is permitted with a county permit. To reach the park, turn *mauka* off Kaumualii Hwy. on Lele Rd. then go past the Veterans Cemetery on Lokokai to parking area.

WAIMEA - KAUMAKANI - MAKAWELI

West Kaua'i continues to grow and evolve into a viable visitor destination. Exploring the area (dubbed the West Kaua'i Sugar Heritage Corridor), begins just outside of Hanapepe. Up until just a few years ago, sugar was king here and the story can be viewed along the highway and from connecting roads, passing through Kaumakani Village, Waimea and Kekaha Town. When the sugar mill closed here just last year, it caused considerable economic hardship. But, as in other communities across the islands, people are retooling and not necessarily retreating. New ideas are being tried and new attempts to revitalize the community are in progress. It's a matter of time to see what works and what doesn't.

Waimea is perhaps the best known, and that is a direct result of the one early adventurer. Captain James Cook first landed in the Hawaiian islands in January 1778 at this site. A monument stands in his honor. In later times, rice was grown in the valleys and swamp, and sugar in the dryer areas that required irrigation. The region also grew taro and raised cattle. As we enter a new millennium, Waimea and the West Kaua'i Sugar Corridor are experiencing an incredible rebirth! Tourists and locals alike are discovering what opportunities can be afforded here!

It is a wonderfully quaint town and with its location on the western coastline, often provides better weather conditions than in other areas of the island. You can pick up a very helpful self-guided map of the Waimea area. It is available at the West Kaua'i Techonology and Visitor Center. It highlights all the places to eat, picnic spots, and beaches, as well as historic sites in or near Waimea including the Russian Fort and Menehune Ditch. Activities in the area include plantation tours at Gay & Robinson Plantation. Annual events include Christmas in Waimea with its Annual Lighted Christmas Parade, the annual Falsetto Competition and Concert, and the Waimea Town Celebration.

Plantation Lifestyles Walking Tour provides insight into plantation life in 1900. In the future, a museum may be built near the ruins of the old Waimea Sugar Mill. The tour, led by volunteers, includes a visit to the Waimea Plantation Cottages with a collection of relocated camphouses that now serve as visitor accommodations.

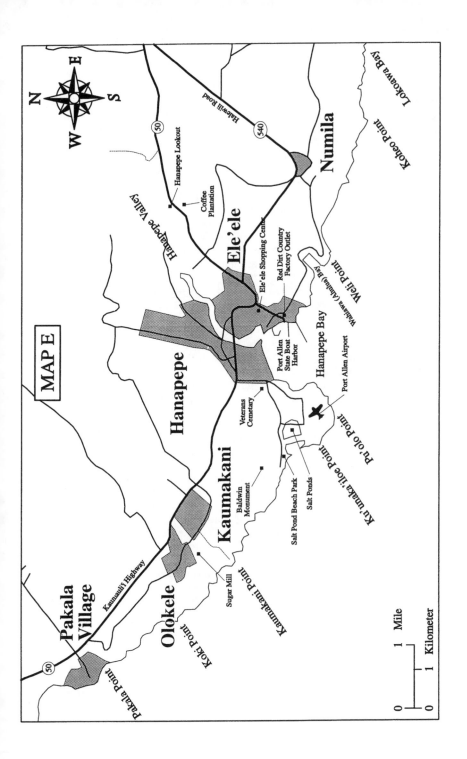

MAP E

Reservations are required for the **Waimea Sugar Mill Camp Museum and Plantation Lifestyles Walking Tour**, a 1 1/2 hour cultural tour in an original sugar plantation village. Limited to 12 people, the tour is currently offered Tuesdays, Thursdays, and Saturdays at 9 am. Cost is $6 adults, $5 seniors 65 and older, and children 12 and under are $3. Waimea Plantation Cottages, PO Box 1178, Waimea, HI 96796. (808) 335-2824

Hawaii's cultural history can be intimately explored through the heart of the sugar plantation. Hawaii's multi-cultural history is due to the need for laborers in the labor-intensive sugar fields of yesterday year. Now you have the opportunity to view field to factory operations at Gay & Robinson. The two-hour bus tour, conducted by Gay & Robinson Tours LLC, is available weekdays and includes the history of the plantation, its operation, processing, the plantation's miles of irrigation systems and views of the private plantation lands. Harvesting operations are seasonal with the months of April through October the best times to visit Gay & Robinson. Tour routes depend on the day-to-day operations. If you don't have time for the full tour, stop by their office on Kaumakani Avenue and view the historic displays. The office is located in the historic Field Office (circa 1900) on Kaumakani Avenue. From Lihu'e, travel Hwy. 50. Just past mile marker 19, turn left on Kaumakani Avenue with its monkeypod trees and old-fashioned streetlights. It is open 8am-4pm Monday through Friday, with the exception of plantation holidays. Tours are at 9am and 1 pm. All visitors on the tour are required to wear safety equipment to enter the factory. They must also wear pants (shorts are okay), low-heeled, closed shoes and they will be provided with safety glasses and hard hats. Cost of the tour is $30. In the not-to-distant future they will be adding other tours of their ditch systems. For tour information call (808) 335-2824. If you want more information on Waimea, pick up a copy of *Touring Waimea* by Christine Fayé. Available at local bookstores.

Just before you reach Waimea, before crossing the river, is **Fort Elizabeth** (also known as the Russian Fort). Built on the mouth of the Waimea River in 1817 by a German doctor, Georg (that's right, no "e") Anton Scheffer, who was employed by the Russian/American Fur Company of Alaska. When he began to fortify his fort the native chiefs grew concerned and notified the king who in turn ordered the Russians out of Kaua'i. There are restroom facilities located here.

Across the river on the other side near the mouth is the **Lucy Wright State Park**. This beach sight was named for a school teacher who taught in Waimea for more than thirty-five years, Lucy Kapahu Aukai Wright. She was born August 20, 1873 in Anahola. Just opposite the parking area at the beachfront is a large boulder with a bronze plaque commemorating the landing spot of Captain James Cook in 1778.

A couple of blocks past the Waimea River, at the Big Save Supermarket on the right, turn right onto Menehune Road. Follow the road up 1.3 miles to the cliff on the left. You will note the cactus which drapes down over the cliff face. Caverns in the cliff are said to be sacred burial sites of the early Hawaiians.

The *Menehune Ditches* extend 25 miles up the Waimea River. The construction of it is of unknown origin, and there is some question that the early Hawaiians had the talents to build in this "dressed lava" stone fashion. A much simpler explanation is the legend that it was built in one night by the menehune to irrigate taro patches for the people in Waimea. Today, you can still see a two-foot-high portion of one of the walls that is marked by a plaque. Frankly, the ditches are not as interesting as one might expect. A picturesque sight formed by the lovely stream and the swinging foot bridge is more pleasant. If you are in luck you will see the local people fording the stream to the other side, or perhaps meet the enormous long-haired boar that goes for a walk and a bath in the stream with her owner. If you're traveling with youngsters, this is a good place to stretch their legs, and yours, and walk across the "swinging bridge." It's a short walk over and back across the stream, but the bridge does "swing" some and the kids will enjoy the experience. There are also good views of the surrounding canyon walls up and down stream. Find a parking space alongside the road.

To get the most of your Waimea visit and exploration of this historic old town, pick up a copy of the "Historic Waimea Main Street Walking Tour" brochure which details the historic sites of the town and provides a good reference and location map. Look for the brochure/map at the baggage claim area literature racks at the Lihu'e Airport upon arrival. Or, check with any businesses in Waimea to see if they have some on hand, or contact: West Kaua'i Business & Professional Association, PO Box 903, Waimea, HI 96796; also try West Kaua'i Main Street, 9691 Kaumualii Highway, Waimea, HI 96796, (808) 338-9957.

The historic and recently restored (1999) *Waimea Theatre* building is Kaua'i's newest venue for movies, live performances, and conferences. This old-fashioned movie theatre (it seats 250!) is located in the heart of town in a 1938 art deco building -- complete with a glass ticket booth in front -- and is worth a visit just to enjoy the architecture and history.

In the center of town on the south side of the highway is *Wrangler's Steakhouse and Pacific Pizza & Deli,* both in the same building. On the west edge of town, Makeke Street and Kaumualii Highway, is *Pualani's Farmer's Market,* which is a snack and deli counter combined with a fruit and veggie stand.

A block further west is the new *West Kaua'i Visitor & Technology Center*, 9565 Kaumualii Hwy., Waimea (808) 338-1332. HOURS: Open daily 9am-5pm. This is a good place to begin your Waimea exploration. Pictorials, graphics, and displays with touch-sensitive screens provide information on all of Kaua'i's activities, not just Waimea. This high-tech, state-of-the-art 7500 square foot center facility opened in 1999 with land leased from the Kikia'ola Land Co. for $1 a year for 30 years. They anticipate more than 500,000 visitors to cross through the doors each year. Utilizing the theme, "Enduring Engineering," visitors follow cultural and historic photographs showing the development of engineering on Kaua'i from ancient days to modern times. From the Polynesian voyagers to NASA's most sophisticated techology. Enjoy old photographs of Waimea, back to the days of grass shacks! There is even a photo of the first movie filmed on Kaua'i, *White Heat* by director Louis Weber. (The film has long since been lost or destroyed.) One unusual model is the Pathfinder which is a pilotless aircraft that was flown at an altitude of 80,000 feet over Barking Sands beach. The museum blends the history of the area with information on the nearby Pacific Missile Range Facility. Not an easy task to undertake, but one that seems to work here. They are looking forward to Phase II! In addition to the displays there are several tenants in the facility. Currently they include Oceanit Laboratories, Inc., Solipsys Corpration, Textron Systems and Trex Enterprises. The center is located at the intersection of Highway 50 and 550, which is the Waimea Canyon Drive.

The monument to **Captain Cook** is found in the center of town. It was placed there in 1928 in celebration of the 150th anniversary of Captain Cook's discovery of the islands and his first landing in the islands at Waimea. The statue was placed in Waimea by the state in 1978 commemorating the 200th anniversary of Cook's discovery at Hofgaard Park and in 1987 was moved to its present location.

The **Waimea Hawaiian Church** was built around 1865 by Reverend Rowell when he had a falling out with the Waimea Foreign Church. It was damaged by the '92 hurricane and totally rebuilt. You might wish to visit a Sunday morning church service which is conducted in Hawaiian.

The **Waimea Foreign Church** was built about 1859 by Reverend George Rowell. According to John Lydgate in a speech given in the early 1900s, the church was built of sandstone blocks cut from a mile or so away near the beach. They were soft when cut, but hardened when exposed to the air. They were transported by bullock-carts and secured with lime mortar. Pieces of the reef were broken off by divers and a 20-foot lime kiln pit was dug. Workers dragged lehua wood down from the mountains with teams of oxen for the woodwork used in the structure. (By the way, "foreign" in this case means English speaking!)

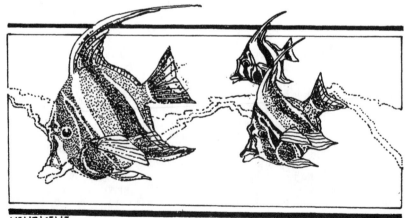

KIHIKIHI   JBayot

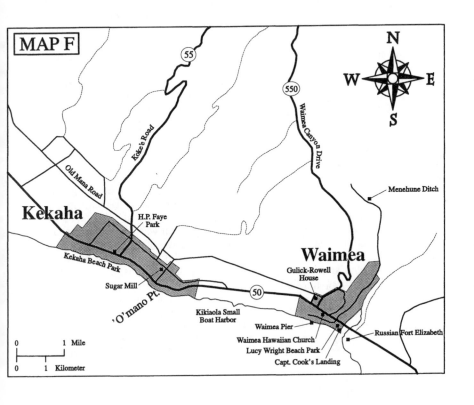

MAP F

Kekaha

Waimea

55

550

Waimea Canyon Drive

Koke'e Road

Old Mana Road

Menehune Ditch

H.P. Faye Park

Kekaha Beach Park

Sugar Mill

'O'mano Pt.

Gulick-Rowell House

50

Kikiaola Small Boat Harbor

Waimea Pier

Waimea Hawaiian Church

Lucy Wright Beach Park

Capt. Cook's Landing

Russian Fort Elizabeth

N
W E
S

| 0 | 1 Mile |
| 0 | 1 Kilometer |

The *Gulick Rowell House* is located near the corner of Huakai and Old Mission-ary Row behind the West Kaua'i Technology & Visitors Center. The old home is just that. Construction of the home began in 1829 by the Reverend Peter Gulick, but was not finished until 17 years later by missionary George Rowell. This is one of the oldest surviving examples of early missionary structures in Hawaii. The 24-inch thick walls provided natural cooling. Unfortnately, it is privately-owned and not a real visitor attraction. However, you can at least drive by and admire the old house and the huge spreading monkeypod tree in the yard, reputed to be the oldest such tree on Kaua'i. The house grounds are nothing special and are in fact overgrown with brush, weeds, etc. and generally unkempt.

At Waimea, Highway 550 turns north and heads up to Koke'e and the Waimea Canyon. A description of this area follows. For now, we will proceed northwest along the Kaumualii Hwy, Highway 50, to Kekaha and you can travel up to Waimea Canyon by that route and then return down via Hwy. 550.

KEKAHA AND POLIHALE

On a clear day from the coast near Kekaha, you can enjoy a clear view of Ni'ihau. There is another small island farther to the north called Lehua which is uninhabited. There appears to be a lower island just beyond Ni'ihau. This, however, is part of the island of Ni'ihau. Kekaha Town was built by sugar and was a typical and thriving company town for more than 100 years. Many of the plantation era buildings still remain in and around the mill. Kekaha Sugar celebrated its 100th anniversary in 1998. The Kekaha Sugar Mill processed its last sugar cane harvest in 2000.

Kekaha Beach Park is a 30-acre stretch of beach with plenty of parking along the highway and restroom facilities. The weather on this part of the island is generally drier, so if you are looking for some sun, visit the western coast. Refer to the beaches chapter for more information on safety conditions for shorelines in this area.

The nearby *Kikia'ola Harbor* has become increasingly popular with the new regulations which have eliminated Hanalei Bay on the North Shore as a tour/cruise boat departure spot. The Corp of Engineers has $4.6 million set aside for renovations over the next few years. If you continue northward you will reach the area of the Barking Sands Airfield and the *Pacific Missile Range*. This is a naval base with testing facilities which runs along the Mana shore.

A huge monkeypod tree in the road with a very unofficial sign will advise you that you are almost to Polihale. You may see some cars parked here. If you choose to stop, be careful your wheels don't become mired in the sand! Then proceed by foot over the dunes to a unique natural formation. Known as *Queen's Pond,* this is a lagoon protected within the reef. It can be safe for a cool dip, but only when the surf is calm. It is said in ancient times a king of Kaua'i was killed

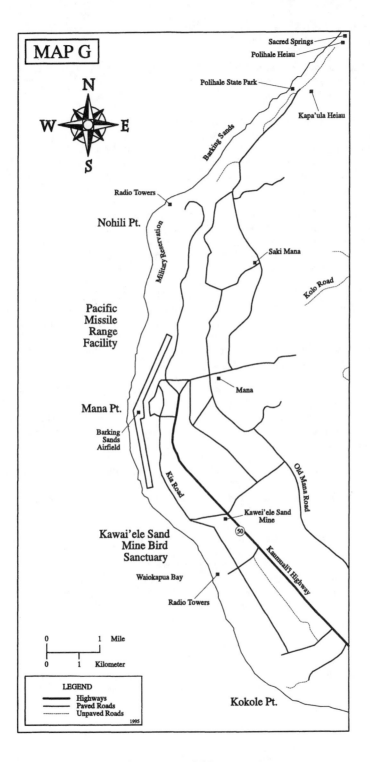

MAP G

Sacred Springs
Polihale Heiau
Polihale State Park
Kapa'ula Heiau

Barking Sands

Radio Towers

Nohili Pt.

Military Reservation

Saki Mana

Kolo Road

Pacific
Missile
Range
Facility

Mana

Mana Pt.

Barking
Sands
Airfield

Old Mana Road

Kia Road

Kawei'ele Sand
Mine

50

Kawai'ele Sand
Mine Bird
Sanctuary

Waiokapua Bay

Kaumuali'i Highway

Radio Towers

0   1   Mile
0   1   Kilometer

LEGEND
Highways
Paved Roads
Unpaved Roads
1995

Kokole Pt.

at Barking Sands, and that today the sand still groans when you rub the pieces between your hands. We tried it, maybe you will have better luck! Some say that merely walking on the dry sand will cause the same effect.

It is another few bumpy and dusty miles along the dirt road before it ends at *Polihale State Park*. (See the beaches chapter for recreational opportunities afforded along the Mana coastline of West Kaua'i.) This beach is unsafe for any water activity, but strolling along the shoreline you should look closely to be fortunate enough to find some of the tiny shells like those that scatter the coastline of Ni'ihau.

If you plan on a visit to Koke'e, it might be a good idea to bring along that sweater, sweatshirt, or lightweight jacket you packed in your bag. The slightly higher elevation can drop the temperature down a few pleasantly cool degrees. While the weather topside may appear overcast from below the mountain, it can also blow through quickly.

Choosing either Hwy. 550 from Waimea or Hwy. 55 from Kekaha you can follow the road as it slowly winds up to *Waimea Canyon*. It is recommended you go to Kekaha and follow Hwy. 55 from Kekaha up to Waimea Canyon and take the other, Hwy. 550, down from the canyon, or vice versa. This offers an opportunity to enjoy some dramatically different scenery. You might want to take this opportunity to check your gas gauge.

The Koke'e Road from Kekaha, Hwy. 55, was built in 1911, but is in fact a better road than the newer road from Waimea. It is the one used by the tour bus drivers. The Waimea Canyon Road, while newer, is much steeper. After about seven miles you will reach the sign for Waimea Canyon State Park. Another 1/2 mile and the Koke'e Rd intersects with the Waimea Canyon Rd. Just before the road mile marker 9 is the Kukui Trailhead. This is one of many trails which riddle the area and offer outstanding day hiking opportunities. Many are reached by main roads, some are accessible by smaller dirt roads. Another 2 1/2 miles and the road fork will advise you of the turn-off to either Koke'e Park or Waimea Canyon.

Waimea Canyon State Park provides unsurpassed opportunities for exploration. Follow Waimea Canyon Drive as it winds its way up 12 miles into the interior of the island, hugging the rim of the canyon for a dramatic panorama. The view of the 3,000-foot deep canyon is staggering. Hues of orange and red are splashed against the tropical green of 1,866 acres of parkland. Mark Twain aptly described this as the *"Grand Canyon of the Pacific."* Contiguous with Waimea Canyon is the Koke'e State Park.

Waimea Canyon Lookout is the first of several lookouts. At an elevation of 3,120 feet, this is a stunning canyon vista. *Pu'u Ka Pele Lookout* is the next stop as you continue to climb. It offers picnic tables and another, slightly different, view of the canyon. *Puu Hinahina* is another vista, viewing out toward Ni'ihau.

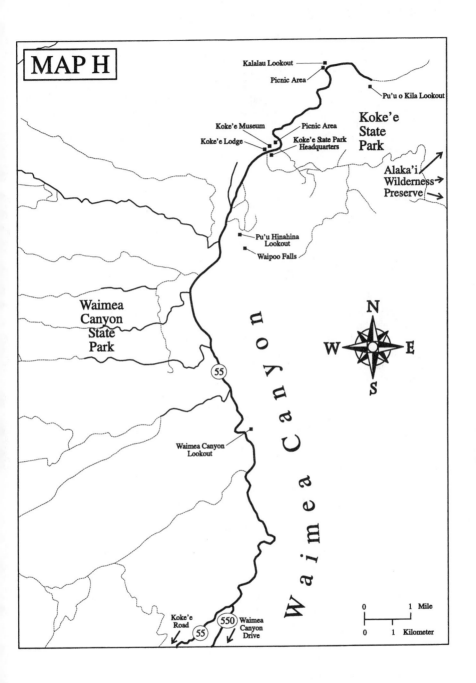

MAP H

Kalalau Lookout
Picnic Area
Pu'u o Kila Lookout

Koke'e State Park

Koke'e Museum
Picnic Area
Koke'e Lodge
Koke'e State Park Headquarters

Alaka'i Wilderness Preserve

Pu'u Hinahina Lookout
Waipoo Falls

Waimea Canyon State Park

Waimea Canyon

55

Waimea Canyon Lookout

N
W E
S

0   1 Mile
0   1 Kilometer

Koke'e Road
55
550 Waimea Canyon Drive

Near the entrance to Waimea Canyon Park is the trailhead to the *Iliau Nature Trail* at the Kukui Trail head. This is a good family hike which follows a short .3 mile trail with an overview of the canyon and the waterfall on the far side of the crater. A relative of the silversword plants found on Maui at Haleakala National Park and the Big Island of Hawai'i grows only here on Kaua'i. The *iliau* is an unusual plant which, like the silversword, blooms with a profusion of blossoms which marks the end of its life.

KOKE'E

The *Koke'e Museum* is nestled amid one of Kaua'i's most scenic wonders. This museum, the oldest on the island, creates more than 100,000 visitors each year and is the only museum in Hawai'i open every day of the year at no charge. The Museum sponsors two annual festivals. In June, they celebrate "The Banana Poka Festival" and the *"Eo E Emalani I Alaka'i Festival"* attracts numerous visitors each October. The museum sponsors the annual December Audubon Christmas Bird Count as well as an assortment of workshops and year-round interpretive programs and exhibits. You might be interested in becoming a *Hui O Laka* member. Contact the Koke'e Museum at PO Box 100, Kekaha, HI 96752. Phone (808) 335-9975, fax (808) 335-6131. And check out the Koke'e Museum's Internet homepage with hiking maps, weather report links, and more to assist in your travel planning. <www.aloha.net/~kokee/> The museum store has a good selection of books about Hawai'i's wildlife, natural history and outdoors. The nearby Koke'e Lodge has a dozen housekeeping cabins available for rent to campers, hikers, etc. See following section for details.

Adjacent to the museum is the Koke'e Lodge Cafe and Gift Shop which provides light breakfast, lunch and snack meals. *Koke'e State Park* offers 45 miles of named hiking trails. The Canyon Trail leads to the east rim of Waimea Canyon and offers a breathtaking view into its depth. The main canyon stretches for 12 miles and drops 3,000 feet. This is an easy trail for even the novice hiker, traversing 1.4 miles. Poomau Canyon Lookout Trail heads through a native rainforest and a series of Japanese plum trees. The 3.25-mile Awa'awapuhi Trail leads through the forest to a 2,500-foot high vista which overlooks the Napali coast and ocean. Halemanu-Koke'e Trail offers stunning views of the Napali Coast including Honopu Valley and the Valley of the Lost Tribe.

A short Nature Trail begins at Koke'e Museum and passes through a koa forest. The Alakai Wilderness Preserve encompasses the Alakai Swamp and is adjacent to Koke'e State Park. The swamp is 10 miles long and two miles wide and spans the basin of the caldera. There are pristine nature trails and a boardwalk over the boggy terrain for viewing some of Hawai'i's rarest flora and fauna. The Alakai Swamp Trail passes through bogs and rain forests to the Kilohana Lookout above Hanalei Bay. Koke'e Museum phone is (808) 335-9975.

Besides hiking, camping, and bird-watching for native Hawaiian bird species, Koke'e Park is noted for its wild plum season in late spring-early summer. The Methley plum thrives in Koke'e and when it's plum season, locals head to the park with bags and baskets to pick the popular fruit. However, the last few years have not been the best as the trees recover from extensive hurricane-wind damage.

Trout fishing is another interest at Koke'e. The state of Hawai'i used to stock the streams at Koke'e annually with yearling rainbow trout raised in hatcheries. However, the program was suspended a few years ago due to what some thought was endangering a species of Hawaiian damsel fly. It was felt the trout were feasting too much on the fly and thus severely reducing the fly's population. The trout stocking program was halted until research studies determine the extent of the problem. Meanwhile, the annual trout fishing season continues during the months of August and September. The streams and reservoir at Koke'e still hold some resident rainbow trout. A fishing license is required. Contact the State Division of Forestry and Wildlife for information, (808) 274-3077.

Continue up Koke'e Road another couple of miles and you will reach the Kalalau and Pu'u o' Kila lookouts. Kalalau Beach, which lies below along the coast, is that part of the Napali which requires an eleven mile hike to reach. On a clear day, this is perhaps the most picturesque location on Kaua'i.

The valley falls below for 4,000 feet and is splashed by waterfalls. *Kaua'i, A Separate Kingdom,* as well as a tale by Jack London, portrays the saga of Ko'olau, his wife, and young son. During the days when leprosy was scourged by forcing the infected victims to be confined to Moloka'i without their family, Ko'olau fled to this valley area. Several others fled as well, but they were eventually tracked down. Ko'olau's son, Kalei, succumbed first to the disease, and later Ko'olau also died from the affliction. His wife, Piilani, buried him in the wilderness. Never infected with this tragic disease, Piilani, returned to Waimea after the death of her husband and son and remarried.

BEST BETS

Po'ipu Kai - several buildings on a large property with nice condo accommodations that are value priced. *Hyatt Regency Kaua'i* - a lovely, tropical resort. *Whalers Cove* - a more expensive but very first-class condominium, an ideal location. *Embassy Vacation Resort at Po'ipu Point* - spacious and elegant with all the amenities of a resort and a condominium combined. *Kiahuna Plantation* - Well located, this is a beautiful upscale property with plenty of amenities. *Koloa Landing Cottages* - Conveniently located near the beach in Po'ipu, very clean, comfortable and economical accommodations. Recommended B&B's: *Po'ipu Plantation Resort* - conveniently located in heart of Po'ipu Resort area, close to beach and activities, cottage units a great value too. Also *Marjorie's Kaua'i Inn* - a great value.

PRIVATE VACATION HOMES & COTTAGES

ANDERSON'S HALE NALU
8691 Kaumualii Highway, Kekaha, HI 96752. (808) 337-9234, Fax (808) 337-0462; Email: pamshale@hawaiian.net; Web: <www.lauhala.com/halenalu> There are two one bedroom/one bath homes with full kitchen, dining area and living room. Kitchens are fully equipped, living rooms have TV/VCR, daybed, and sofa sleepers. Located on the Kekaha beachside on Kaua'i's westside and away from it all. Swimming, surfing, windsurfing, snorkeling, sunbathing, fishing, whale watching, etc. are all just steps away. Public tennis courts are nearby. Some water sports and beach equipment available plus BBQ; laundry facilities available for guests.
Rates: $85 nightly

BOULAY INN
4175 Omao Road, PO Box 522, Koloa, HI 96756. (808) 742-1120; Email: boulayinn@hawaiian.net; Web: <www.hawaiian.net/~boulayinn> This is a completely private one-bedroom upper level apartment unit with wrap around lanai and expansive panoramic views of ocean and surrounding mountains. It has island-style decor, queen bed, living room sofa bed, full kitchen, TV/VCR, ceiling fans and laundry in unit. It's just minutes away from the famed Poipu Beach resort area, three golf courses, beaches, shopping, dining, and related activities.
Rates: $65 nightly; inquire for weekly and monthly rates.

BRENNECKE'S BEACH COTTAGE
3285 Waapa Road, Lihu'e, HI 96766 (mailing address); Toll free 1-888-386-8786, (808) 245-7575, Fax (808) 245-2434; Email: RBWHITE@aloha.net; Web: <www.mmv.com/bbc > This is a two-bedroom, two-bath plantation-style cottage located right next to Brennecke's Beach in the heart of the Po'ipu resort and beach area. You can walk across the street and jump in the water, stroll the beach, or just watch the surf and enjoy the sun. A Master Bedroom sleeps two (king bed) and a second bedroom sleeps two in twin beds. Cottage is complete and comfortable for island-style living and relaxation.
Rates: $1650 weekly (1 week minimum stay)

CLASSIC VACATION COTTAGES ★
2687 Onu Place, PO Box 901, Kalaheo, HI 96741. (808) 332-9201, Fax (808) 332-7645; Email: clascot@hawaiian.net; Web: <www.classiccottages.com> These country-style cottages are off-the-beaten-track and away from the tourist crowds. Situated a bit upcountry from the south shore in the delightful Kalaheo area and just minutes from resort activities at Po'ipu, beaches, golf, etc. but easy access to the rest of Kaua'i's attractions. Choose from the Basic Studio, Garden Studio, Garden View Cottages #1 & #2, or the Executive House. All are fully equipped with all amenities for a relaxing vacation stay.
Rates: Basic Studio $50-65 nightly; Garden Studio $65-80 nightly; Garden Cottage #1 $80-95 nightly; Garden Cottage #2 $75-90 nightly; Executive House $175-250 nightly

COASTLINE COTTAGES ★

4730 Lawai Beach Road, Koloa, HI 96756. (808) 742-9688, Fax (808) 742-7620; Email: jds@aloha.net; Web: <www.coastlinecottages.com> There are four separate fully-equipped cottages right on the water's edge in the Po'ipu Beach resort area. The Studio, 1BR, 2BR and 3BR units all have private oceanfront lanais, full kitchens, living room areas, queen beds, and an extra guest Murphey bed. The Studio unit has mini-kitchen facilities with fridge, microwave and coffee maker. Convenient to Po'ipu Resort attractions, activities, beaches, shopping and dining.
Rates: Studio/1BR $285; 2BR $405; 3BR $650

COCO'S VACATION RENTAL

PO Box 690169, Makaweli, HI 96769. (808) 338-0722; Email: ian@hawaiian.net; Web: <www.hawaiian.net/~ian/index.html> This unit is a 565 sq.ft. guest room with private entrance in a new home on a 12-acre estate located on the Robinson Family Ranch (the family owns Ni'ihau Island). The guest room has a king bed and queen sofa sleeper and accommodates 4 people. There is a full kitchen, living room and bath plus patio, BBQ and laundry. The house is surrounded by expansive ranch lands and orchards of tropical fruit trees. It's within easy walking distance of a secluded beach on Kaua'i's quiet west side, great for surfers and near some premiere breakers. Call collect for reservations.
Rates: $99 with breakfast; $90 without breakfast

HALL'S PLANTATION ESTATE

3527 Papalina Road, PO Box 548, Kalaheo, HI 96741. (808) 332-9111, Fax (808) 332-5408; Email: shelley@hallsofhawaii.com; Web: <www.hallsofhawaii.com> This very modern and stylish country estate home sits on three-acres of well-cared for and maintained grounds overlooking the prestigious national Tropical Botanical Gardens and Lawai Kai Valley behind Allerton Beach. It's near the sunny Poipu Resort area. The valley boasts many acres of coffee orchards plus farms growing bananas, papaya, and tropical floral crops. The country home has two fully-furnished guest suites, the Kahili Mountain Suite and Ficus Guest Suite. There is also the separate Kalaheo Cottage. Each guest suite has living room with entertainment center, fully-equipped mini-kitchen, private bath and lanai, and master bedroom with king bed. The guest cottage has living room and entertainment center, full bath, mini-kitchen, and bedroom with king bed. All guests share a hot tub, BBQ, and laundry facility. Ceiling fans throughout the units and tasteful contemporary Hawaiian decor. Surrounded by tropical flowers, plants and fruit trees with great ocean and mountain views.
Rates: Kahili Mountain Suite or Ficus Guest Suite, $98 nightly; Kalaheo Guest Cottage, $120 nightly

HONU KAI VACATION VILLAS

1871 Pe'e Rd., Koloa, HI 96756. (808) 742-9155. FAX (808) 742-7940. 1-800-854-8363. Email: RJR@Houkai.com Hosts Robert and Patty Rolland offer private oceanfront villas. The property includes a swimming pool and jacuzzi surrounded by a lava rock wall. Brennecke's Beach is 100 yards away. They accept Visa and Master card with a 4% processing fee. All units are non-smoking. A great south shore location! *Rates: $175-500 nightly*

JAN'S KAUAI KONDO KOMPANY
Mailing address, 221 Chapel Lane, Canfield, OH 44406. Toll free 1-800-726-7412; Email: Kondos@aloha.com; Web: < www.cris.com/ ~ equities > This 2-bedroom/2-bath condo unit is located in Po'ipu Sands part of the Po'ipu Kai Resort. It has great oceanviews and is just 350-yards from the beach at Keoneloa Bay. Adjacent to the Hyatt Resort and Po'ipu Bay Golf Course. The unit has all the comforts and amenities for a pleasant vacation, TV/VCR, laundry, full kitchen, two lanais, living room, plus tennis courts and pool. Sleeps up to 6 people. *Rates: $155-225 nightly*

KALAHEO PLANTATION VACATION RENTAL
4579 Pu'u Wai Road, PO Box 872, Kalaheo, HI 96741. Toll free 1-888-332-7812, Tel/Fax (808) 332-7872; Email: kalaheo1@gte.net; Web: < www.kalaheo-plantation.com > This is a finely restored and refurbished 1926-era plantation home with six available guest suites. The home is bright, newly painted, carefully restored. Guest rooms have various bed arrangements, king, queen or twins, and all have kitchens or kitchenettes, private bath and entry. Home is within walking distance of five restaurants in Kalaheo and the public golf course is just around the corner. Easy access to area activities, attractions and just five miles from Po'ipu beaches. Guest rooms can be rented separately or together for larger groups. *Rates: Blue Ginger Room $55; Torch Ginger Room/Gardenia Room $65; Magnolia Suite/Hibiscus Suite $69; Orchid Suite $75; all four main floor units $199 night/$1399 week, (max 8); entire house, six units $350 night/$1950 week (max 16)*

KAUAI CONDO'S AT PO'IPU KAI RESORT
1941 Po'ipu Road, Koloa, HI 96756. Toll free 1-800-203-1192, Fax (414) 427-5325; Email: dickolson@hikauai.com; Web: < www.hikauai.com > There are various nicely furnished one-bedroom condo vacation units offering full amenities, garden or ocean views, easy access to area activities, attractions, shopping, dining, etc. Rent directly from the owner for reasonable rates.
Rates: $100 and up nightly

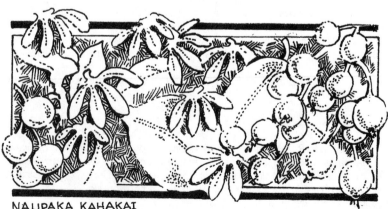

NAUPAKA KAHAKAI

KAUAI HIDEAWAYS GUEST COTTAGES ★

3198A Wawae Road, PO Box 1082, Kalaheo, HI 96741. (808) 332-6421; Email: ani@aloha.net; Web: <www.kauaihideaways.com> These are unique and private modern plantation cottages. They are situated high atop a hill in a quiet neighborhood that has expansive scenery of rolling pastures and ocean views. There are four separate units available. Units have kitchen/kitchenette, laundry, TV/VCR, jacuzzi bath, etc.
Rates: Hale Ani Studio $65 nightly; Hale Keoki Treehouse $75 nightly; Hale Guava Hillside Cabin $95 nightly; Hale Kolea Cottage $125 nightly

KEKAHA OCEANFRONT VACATION RENTALS

7961 Kaumualii Highway, Kekaha, HI 96752. Toll free 1-800-677-5959, (949) 645-7658; Email: rgeraldjones@earthlink.net; Web: <www.iauak.com> This sunny oceanfront lodging is away from the resort crowds and just a short distance from scenic Waimea Canyon on Kaua'i's westside. It's across the road from secluded Kekaha's golden sand beaches. Three accommodations available: one or two bedroom upper or lower duplex at the Hui Aloha or Kekaha La sleeps up to 6 people; a three-bedroom/two-bath home, Hale Moana, sleeps 6 people; a one-bedroom/one-bath cottage, Hale Aloha, sleeps four. The separate guest accommodations are perfect for family reunions, groups or retreats. *Rates: $110-160*

MAUKALANI AT LAWA'I

2381 Kipuka Street, Koloa, HI 96756. Toll free 1-800-745-7414, (808) 742-1700, FAX (808) 742-7392. Web: <wwte.com/hawaii/kauai/poipu2.htm> Email: poh@aloha.net; Po'ipu Beach is a 10 minute drive from this rental home. This one bedroom home is on the second floor of a two story building. A kitchen, laundry facilities and a queen sized bed in the bedroom and queen size sofa bed in the living room. 3 night minimum stay. *Rates: $69 nightly*

PUA HALE AT PO'IPU BEACH

2381 Kipuka Street, Koloa, HI 96756. Toll free 1-800-745-7414, (808) 742-1700, FAX (808) 742-7392. Web: <wwte.com/hawaii/kauai/poipu2.htm> Email: poh@aloha.net;A convenient South Shore location, Po'ipu and Shipwreck beach are less than a 5 minute walk away. "Flower House" features a Japanese waterfall in a tropical garden. Eastern influence is again found in the bathroom where you can enjoy a furo (Japanese style soaking tub). The home features a queen size bed which can be isolated by sliding shoji doors. The unit is within an enclosed walled tropical garden setting which allows for privacy. Four night minimum. No smoking. No children under 8 years. *Rates: $120 per night. Weekly rate $735 with additional nights $105. Price is for double occupancy, additional persons $10 per day, maximum 4 persons. $40 cleaning fee.*

SUNSET KAHILI

1763 Pe'e Road, Koloa, HI 96756. Toll free 1-800-827-6478, (808) 742-7434; Email: info@sunsetkahili.com; Web: <www.sunsetkahili.com> There are one and two-bedroom fully equipped condo units with great ocean views. Units are within walking distance of Po'ipu Beach. There is a pool, BBQ and nearby tennis courts. All amenities provided, laundry, full kitchen, TV/VCR, ceiling fans, etc. Easy access to resort dining, shopping, attractions and activities.
Rates: $99-191 nightly

BED & BREAKFAST

ALOHA BREEZE
4122 Koloa Road, Koloa, HI 96756. (808) 332-9164, Fax (808) 332-9251. Email: Alohabreeze@alohabreeze.com; Web: <www.alohabreeze.com> Aloha Breeze is a delightful inn-style accommodation near the charming old sugar plantation town of Koloa and just minutes from the exclusive Po'ipu Beach resort area, beaches, etc. There are surrounding views of mountains and ocean. Guests can choose from three very nicely maintained accommodations, each with its own special tropical magic to make a stay in Paradise memorable. *Rates: Garden Suite $95 nightly; Balcony House $95 nightly; Lanai Room $65 nightly*

BAMBOO JUNGLE HOUSE B & B
PO Box 1301, Kalaheo, HI 96741. Toll-free 1-888-332-5115, (808) 332-5515. E-mail: serene2@aloha.net or Web: <www.aloha.net/~serene2/> There are three guest suites available, each with private entrance and bath plus full amenities. Discounts extended for multi-day stays.
Rates: Jungle Room $95 nightly; Safari Master Suite $115 nightly; Waterfall Suite $125 nightly.

CORAL BY THE SEA B & B
PO Box 820, Waimea, HI 96796. Toll free 1-888-326-1084, (808) 337-1084, Fax (888) 326-1084. E-mail: Coralsea@Hawaiian.net; Web: <www.hawaiian.net/~coralsea> Hosts Fred and Sharon offer guests a fully equipped non-smoking studio in a residential area within one block of sandy beaches and a short drive to Waimea Canyon. Queen-sized bed, sitting room, private bath with shower. A comfy couch is also a sleeper sofa. B&B, in this case, goes back to the original British meaning of "Bed & Bath" (in fact a number of B&B are discontinuing breakfast, or adding it as an option for an extra fee). Bright coral on the outside, a bit dark on the inside (but it keeps it cool) *Rates: Three night minimum runs $71.50 nightly; $85 for one-two night stays; $429 weekly.*

GARDEN ISLE COTTAGES
2666 Puuholo Rd., Koloa, HI 96756. Toll free 1-800-742-6711. (808) 742-6717, Fax (808) 742-1933; Email: vacation@oceancottages.com; Web: <www.oceancottages.com> These sea cliff cottages are located on a small ocean inlet where the Waikomo Stream meets the ocean overlooking historic Koloa Landing. These are ocean view units. The Hale Waipahu cottages feature open beamed ceilings. A queen bed on the upper main floor and twins on the lower. Four nights deposit required. Also Bed & Breakfast units are available. Two night minimum stay.
Rates: Studio o.f. $98-105; Deluxe 1BR o.f. $118-164; Deluxe 2BR o.f. $193-199; extra person $10

GLORIA'S SPOUTING HORN B & B ★
4464 Lawa'i Rd., Koloa, HI 96756. Tel/fax (808) 742-6995; Email: glorbb@hotmail.com; Web: <www.best.com/~travel/gloria> Completely renovated following Hurricane Iniki in 1992, this custom-designed beachhouse features spacious oceanfront guest rooms and Hawaiian rock baths. Each of the five units includes a telephone, TV/VCR, wet bar with sink, refrigerator and microwave, along with a coffee and popcorn maker. One room offers a unique twig canopy bed. There are complimentary snacks and beverages, beach towels, and mats. The buffet breakfast offers fresh fruits, breads and cereal. Bob Merkle (Mr. Gloria) is a retired minister and can officiate at your wedding on the beach!

The rooms are beautifully appointed, but this lovely property is on the high end of the price spectrum for B&B accommodations. Since children are allowed only ages 14 and above, it is restrictive for families with young children. While it rates quality, we can't give it a star for value. But if you can splurge, look into this one! No charge cards. They also offer condos and apartments at other locations. Three night minimum.
Rates are based on single or double occupancy $225 ($250 during Christmas) plus tax. Weekly discount of $150 except over Christmas.

HALE HYETTE B & B
1663 Keleka, Koloa, HI 96756. (808) 742-2877, Fax (808) 742-2977. Email: bamboo@aloha.net; Web: <www.aalohakauai.com> This unit is one spacious and nicely furnished guest room with private entrance and bath; non-smoking facility. It features nice ocean and mountain views and the amenities of Poipu Kai Resort. Located near the 2nd. hole of the Poipu Bay Golf Course and a short walk to Po'ipu area beaches. Convenient to all resort activities, dining, shopping.
Rates: $110 nightly with breakfast; $100 nightly without breakfast

HALE IKENA NUI
Mailing address: PO Box 171, Kalaheo, HI 96741. Located at 3957 Ulualii Street in Kalaheo. (808) 332-9005. FAX (808) 332-0911. Toll free 1-800-550-0778. Email: pantone@hawaiian.net. Web: <www.kauaivacationhome.com> Hosts Dan and Patti Pantone offer a private 1000 sq. ft. suite featuring a full kitchen, queen bed, full size sleeper couch, private phone, washer/dryer. They also have an extra B&B suite with private bath in the family residence. No charge for children 3 and under. Three day minimum. Convenient to Po'ipu resort activities, beaches, golf, attractions, dining, etc.
Rates: Private Suite $85 nightly, $15 per additional guests; B&B Suite $70 nightly; weekly/monthly rates available.

HALE KUA ★
4896-E Kua Rd., PO Box 649, Lawa'i, HI 96765. (808) 332-8570. 1-800-440-4353. E-mail: halekua@aloha.net; Web: <www.hoohana.aloha.net/halekua/halekua.html> They have a one-bedroom cottage, three one-bedroom apartments (Banana Patch, Taro Patch, and Coral Tree) and a spacious three-bedroom home available for guests. Each unit features a queen-size bed, full bath, kitchen, queen sleeper sofa in living room. Television, telephone, and washer/dryer. Views of the ocean, Lawa'i Valley, and the

mountains, including Mount Kahili. The 8-acre property is planted in tropical fruit and flowering timber trees and is used as a seed propagation arboretum. Owners are planting some 200-acres of old sugarcane land in tropical forest, aimed to eventually be selectively harvested to provide sustainable lumber for a forest products industry on Kaua'i.
Rates: $90 and up nightly

ISLAND HOME B & B

1707 Kelaukia St., Koloa, HI 96756. Toll free 1-800-555-3881, Tel/fax (808) 742-2839; Email: info@kauaibedandbreakfast.com; Web: <www.islandhomebandb.com>. Three units, Master Suite, King Room, Queen Room, all with private entrances, microwaves, compact refrigerators and all the comforts. No children. Swimming privileges at nearby resort pool. Your hosts are Debra van de Taeye and Larry Widhelm.
Rates: Master Suite $90; King Room $80; Queen Room $70; extra person $20; discount without breakfast

KALAHEA HALE

2777 Wawae Road, Kalaheo, HI 96741. Toll free 1-888-332-8144, (808) 332-8100; Email: kalahea@aloha.net; Web: <www.planet-hawaii.com/kalahea> This is a charming and elegant country-style B&B that offers a modern suite which sleeps up to five and has a fully-equipped kitchen. All the amenities included plus a hot tub for guest use. Quiet and peaceful country setting.
Rates: $80 nightly

KALAHEO INN ★

4444 Papalina Road, Kalaheo HI 96741. Toll free 1-888-332-6023, (808) 332-6023, FAX (808) 332-5242. Email: chet@aloha.net or website <www.kalaheoinn.com> Units are very clean and in a good location, right behind Kalaheo Steak House. Each unit has a bath/shower, ceilign fans, kitchenette or full kitchen, TV, VCR, twin or queen beds. There is an on site laundromat. Located in downtown Kalaheo between Po'ipu and the Waimea Canyon. Several restaurants are within a few blocks walk and the Kukuiolono Golf Course is very nearby. This is an excellent lodging choice for the budget minded vacationer. Some 1BR units are on upstairs level, most units are ground level. These clean, comfortable units will appeal to backpackers, hikers, outdoor enthusiasts and others who don't need the glitz of fancy beach resorts and hotels.
Rates: 1BR Units $55-65-75; 2BR Units $95

KAUA'I COVE COTTAGES

2672 Pu'uholo Road, #A, Po'ipu, HI 96756. Toll free 1-800-624-9945, (808) 742-2562. Email: info@kauaicove.com; Web: <www.kauaicove.com> This operator offers romantic and completely private cottages on Kauai's sunny south shore. It's located near Koloa Landing and surrounded by distant majestic mountain views and just steps from Po'ipu Beach. This is one of Kauai's most popular places for scuba diving, snorkeling, ocean kayaking and other activities. Stroll to nearby beaches, beachcomb, watch the turtles swim into Waikomo stream in the evening. You're close to everything the Po'ipu resort area offers, dining, shopping, activities, etc., but in a totally relaxed stress-free environment. The cottages are non-smoking and each features vaulted ceilings, complete kitchen plus private lanai and full amenities for a comfortable and memorable stay. Choose from The Plumeria, The Wild Orchid or The Hibiscus. *Rates: $85-105 nightly*

MARJORIE'S KAUA'I INN ★

3307D Hailima Road, PO Box 866, Lawa'i, HI 96765. 1-800-717-8838, (808) 332-8838; Email: ketcher@aloha.net; Web: <www.planet-hawaii.com/marjorie> This classifies as an "inn" or "Bed & Bath" rather than a Bed & Breakfast since it does not include daily breakfast. The units have a mini-kitchen and on the first night you'll receive a basket with fruits, homemade banana bread, and juice in the refrigerator and coffee with coffeemakers. Each room is a mini studio apartment with a private entrance. There have been some pleasant changes. The "Sunset View" (formerly the Puka Room) has been expanded which allows for additional length plus a new lanai. The interior space allows for a queen bed plus the existing double size futon sofa bed, microwave, coffee pot, toaster, mini-refrigerator, bar sink, kitchen cabinets, cable TV, telephone, dining tables and chairs, private entrance, private bath. The new area has an open beam ceiling providing an even larger and more spacious feel. A sliding glass door and four more windows offer a fabulous view of Lawa'i Valley and the mountains. The unbelievable breathtaking panoramic view of the Lawa'i Valley is truly spectacular. There is a hot tub in a gazebo at the end of the property and that, too, overlooks the valley. Marjorie Ketcher has travel agency experience and is very knowledgeable about activities. She can assist in choosing and booking the activity that best suits the interests of her guests. Her in-room guide lists markets, area hiking opportunities, eateries and beaches. A good value with a superb view. The view along with Marjorie's personal service makes guests return year after year.
Rates: Marjorie's Valley View $93 nightly; Tradewind $88 nightly; Sunset View Room $93 nightly; extra person $15.

OLD KOLOA HOUSE ★

3327 Waikomo Road, Koloa, HI 96756. (808) 742-2099. Email: oldkoloahouse@webtv.net; Web: <www.aloha.net/~keane> This 75-year-old plantation bungalow, once owned by McBryde Sugar Plantation, has been lovingly restored. The one unit B&B is located two miles from Po'ipu Beach and a short walk to old Koloa town. It's a piece of old Hawaii and is surrounded by a small stream and tropical landscaping. It features a queen bed, microwave, compact refrigerator, private entrance, and bath. Continental breakfast the first morning in your room. *Rates: $78 nightly, (two night minimum).*

OLE KAMAOLE'S BEACH HOUSES ★

8663 Kaumualii Highway, PO Box 389, Kekaha, HI 96752-0389. Toll free 1-800-528-2465, (808) 573-2865; Web: <www.virtualcities.com> These units are just eighty feet from the beach and surrounded by groves of bananas and papaya trees. The two units are 2-bedroom/1 bath cottages with full kitchens. Each cottage sleeps up to 6 people. Recreation deck has extra toilet, outdoor shower and BBQ grill. Units are on 12-ft. pilings with 17-step stairs (due to heavy surf flood zone). There are miles of black and white sand beaches to explore adjacent to the location on this sunny westside coast of Kaua'i. Convenient to Waimea Canyon and Kokee State Park with over forty miles of rain forest hiking trails.

Just 15-minutes from Polihale Beach at the end of the road, the beach few know about or visit. The area abounds with activities and attractions. Host provides bagels, bacon, eggs, waffles, fresh island fruit, juice and coffee stocked in your kitchen. *Rates: $99-125 nightly, $15 extra person; (Four night minimum stay)*

PO'IPU PLANTATION RESORT ★

1792 Pee Road, Koloa, HI 96756. Toll free 1-800-634-0263, (808) 742-6757, Fax (808) 742-8681; Email: plantation@poipubeach.com; Web: <www.poipubeach.com> This vacation resort has two types of rental units available. There are nine cottage-style condo units, spacious one and two bedrooms with living/dining room, kitchens, and large lanai area. Units have hardwood floors, tasteful tropical decor, queen beds, a/c and ceiling fans, TV/VCR and free local calls. There is a separate B&B House with three large rooms having king or queen beds, private baths, a/c and ceiling fans, TV plus use of an ocean view lanai room. A new Ocean View Honeymoon Suite is located in the main building housing the office. Daily breakfast provided for B&B rooms. All guests have use of BBQ, hot tub and laundry facilities. Swim towels, beach mats, chairs, etc. also provided. The one-acre grounds are nicely landscaped with flowers, fruit trees and lawns. This comfortable, centrally located resort is near to beaches, tennis, golf, ocean sports, restaurants, shopping, and Po'ipu resort area activities. Great swimming, snorkeling, sunning etc. nearby at Brennecke Beach. 3 night minimum stay at cottages; 2 night minimus stay in B&B rooms. *Rates: Cottage/Condo Units, 1BR g.v. $105 ; 1BR s.v. $115; 1BR o.v. $130; 2BR s.v. $145 (max 4); 2BR o.v. $160 (max 4); Bed & Breakfast rooms: Queen or King Room $90; Master Room $95; Ocean View Honeymoon Suite $150; extra person $20*

PO'IPU BED & BREAKFAST INN ★

2720 Hoonani Rd., Koloa, HI 96756. (808) 742-0100, FAX (808) 742-6843, 1-800-808-2330; Email: info@poipu-inn.com; Web: < www.poipu-inn.com> This B&B includes four bed and breakfast units located in this 1933-era plantation doctor's home. All units have private baths, most with whirlpool tub and separate shower, king bed, refrige, cable TV and VCR, wicker and pine antiques. A honeymoon suite features an ocean view, private lanai and whirlpool tub for two plus air conditioning. Handicapped accessible room available. Carosel horses are used as decor in various rooms and lobby area. There is also a separate private condo unit on adjoining sunny Poipu property. Easy access to all Po'ipu Beach Resort area activities, shopping, dining, golf, beach, etc. *Rates: $125-165*

SOUTH SHORE VISTA B & B

4400 Kai Ikena Drive, Kalaheo, HI 96741 (808) 332-9339 or (808) 332-9201, FAX (808) 332-7771 or E-mail: vista@aloha.net; Web: <www.planet-hawaii.com/~vista> This is a fully equipped 1 bedroom apartment with queen bed, living area with foldout couch bed, kitchenette with microwave, oven and utensils, a private deck and separate entrance, TV/VCR and all amenities. Coffee, tea, and oatmeal provided in the unit. Breakfast provisions stocked in the kitchen for an extra $7.50. It has an oceanview from its hillside location in Kalaheo, just minutes from numerous beaches and two blocks from Kukuiolono Golf Course and an interesting Japanese garden to explore. Minimum stay 3 nights. *Rates: $59-69 nightly*

STRAWBERRY GUAVA B & B

PO Box 271, Lawai, HI 96765. (808) 332-7790; Email: lauria@hawaiian.net; Web: <www.hawaiian.net/ ~ lauria> This private home is located on the edge of the Lihu'e-Koloa Forest Reserve and at the foot of Mt. Kahili in a very quiet country setting. This is for those who appreciate nature's beauty and value solitude and privacy. B&B suites are in a separate wing, all with private entry, bath, sitting room, fridge, queen beds and marvelous country views. Close to area activities. *Rates: $65-75 nightly*

SUGAR MILL COTTAGES

2391 Ho'ohu Road, Koloa, HI 96756. Toll free 1-877-742-9369, (808) 742-9369, Fax (808) 742-6432; Email: chet@aloha.net; Web: <www.travelguides.com/inns> This non-smoking bed and breakfast inn features a dozen luxury studio apartments all with private bath and entry. Inn is within walking distance to Po'ipu Beach in the popular Po'ipu Beach resort area. It has a large pool and 8 tennis courts and easy access to area attractions and activities including a white sand beach, snorkeling, swimming, scuba, golf, tennis, horseback riding and a hiking trail. Amenities include jacuzzis, pool, cable TV. *Rates: $75 nightly*

VICTORIA PLACE

3459 Lawailoa Lane, PO Box 930, Lawa'i, HI 96765. (808) 332-9300. FAX (808) 332-9465. Web: <www.hshawaii.com/kvp/victoria> Email: edeev@aloha.net;Three guest rooms and a studio apartment offer a choice of B & B options. The three main rooms are all charming and look out onto the pool deck. The single room is a little smaller. The sitting area is pleasant with plenty of books and lots of helpful information on touring and dining on Kaua'i. Hostess Edee Seymour is very knowledgeable and eager to share information about the island. No children under age 15.

Raindrop Room, double bed, single occupancy only $60; Calla Lily Room with queen bed $80; Shell Room with twin beds or king-size is handicapped accessible $80. "Victoria's Other Secret" is a studio apartment with private entrance, king bed and day bed, kitchen $100. Add $10 per room during holiday season (mid-December to mid-January). Additional $15 for one night only.

REEF DWELLERS   J. BAYOT

INEXPENSIVE

KOKE'E LODGE CABINS   ★
3600 Koke'e Road, PO Box 819, Waimea, HI 96796 (808) 335-6061. Located at an elevation of 3,600 feet the lodge is located in the 4,345 acre Koke'e State Park. A dozen housekeeping cabins furnished with refrigerators, stoves, hot showers, cooking and eating utensils, linens, towels, blankets, and pillows. Wood-burning fireplaces are also available; logs can be purchased from the lodge shop. Size of units vary from one large room which sleeps three, to two-bedroom cabins that sleep seven. These cabins are VERY RUSTIC and provide the bare essentials and are in no-way luxurious or first-class. They are wilderness cabins in a remote forest setting. But for hikers, backpackers, outdoor enthusiasts and others, they are perfect. Maximum stay is five days and pets are not permitted. Full payment is required for confirmation. *$35-$45 per cabin, per night.*

KOLOA LANDING COTTAGES   ★
2704-B Ho'onani Rd., Koloa, HI 96756. 1-800-779-8773, (808) 742-1470 or (808) 332-6326. Email: info@koloa-landing.com; Web: < www.koloa-landing.com > The cottages are located in the heart of the Po'ipu resort area and in a tropical garden setting across the street from the beachfront. Ho'onani Road runs parallel to the beachfront. This is a quiet resort area, convenient and easy access to area beaches, parks, golf, tennis, activities, attractions, shopping, dining, etc. in Koloa, Kalaheo, Hanapepe, etc. Right across the street from Koloa Landing, a popular spot for diving, snorkeling, fishing and canoeing. All cottages and studios include microwave, telephone, color cable TV, and full kitchens. There are coin operated laundry facilities and gas BBQ are on premises. Two bedroom cottages have large decks. Studios have a queen bed. Cottages include one queen bed and one set of twins. The studios can accommodate two persons, and the cottages sleep four people with room for two extra persons on futon mattresses. The main house sleeps up to six people; families welcome. Clean, comfortable accommodations in quiet relaxing surroundings. This is a great getaway.
Rates: Studio $85 nightly; 1-bedroom $95; 2-bedroom/2 bath cottage $125; 2-bedroom/2 bath main house $140; extra person $10.

PRINCE KUHIO
Mailing address: PO Box 3284, Lihu'e, HI 96766. Property located at: 5061 Lawa'i Rd. RENTAL AGENTS: Po'ipu Connection Realty 1-800-742-2260. R&R 1-800-367-8022. Grantham Resorts 1-800-325-5701. Prosser Realty 1-800-767-4707; Email: holiday@aloha.net; Web: < www.prosser-realty.com >. Kaua'i Vacation Rentals 1-800-367-5025, Maui & All Islands 1-800-663-6962. Studio, one and two bedroom units. All have microwave ovens, full-size refrigerators, cable TV, and telephones. Guest laundry facility on the ground floor. BBQ, pool. Located next to Prince Kuhio Park in Lawa'i area of Po'ipu.
Rates: Studio $70-90; 1 BR $80-120 nightly/$500-770 weekly; Two BR penthouse $135/115.

MODERATE

ALIHI LANI ★

2564 Hoonani Rd., Po'ipu, HI 96756. Located at Po'ipu Beach. RENTAL AGENT: Po'ipu Connection 1-800-742-2260, (808) 742-2233. This property has a total of six units. These condos are spacious with full kitchen plus full-size washers and dryers. Outside is a private swimming pool and sunning deck. This attractive property is located on a rocky oceanfront, but it is a short and pleasant walk down to Po'ipu Beach. With only six units in this property, you won't find crowds at the pool!
Rates: $185-250 nightly/$1600 weekly

ASTON AT PO'IPU KAI ★

1941 Po'ipu Rd., Koloa, HI 96756 (808) 742-6464. RENTAL AGENTS: Managed by Aston Resorts 1-800-922-7866; Email: res.ppk@aston-hotels.com; Web: <www.aston-hotels.com>. Suite Paradise 1-800-367-8020. Maui & All Islands 1-800-663-6962. R&R 1-800-367-8022. Prosser 1-800-767-4707. Garden Island Rentals 1-80-247-5599. Suite Paradise 1-800-367-8020. Po'ipu Connection Realty 1-800-742-2260. Grantham Resorts 1-800-325-5701. Maui & All 1-800-663-6962. Pleasant Hawaiian Holidays 1-800-242-9244. Three hundred and fifty condominium units. Seven resorts within a master resort, like a sprawling apartment complex made up of individual buildings -- each with its own Hawaiian name. The privately owned condominiums include Po'ipu Sands, Manualoha, Makanui, Kahala, and The Regency. Lanai Villas and Bayview offer private homes. The buildings and units are all different, but equal in stature and category of accommodations. Two-story townhouses are stylish and modern with a two bedrooms and two bathrooms on the lower (entry level) floor. Roomy bathrooms with luxury shower and tub. Living room, full kitchen and 1/2 bath upstairs. High ceilings, ceiling fans, wet bar, good assortment of small appliances and kitchen utensils. W/D with handy starter supply of detergent, complimentary HBO, private phone. Interior decoration varies with each owner, but island-style furniture is generally very attractive and comfortable. Po'ipu Kai shares Shipwreck Beach with the Hyatt and fronts Po'ipu Beach Park at the other end of the property. A great location for beach aficionados! Shop around, prices vary greatly depending on rental agent (as can quality of the unit.) Prices may reflect location in resort or amenities such as maid service.
While Aston is the general property manager, other agents have several units in rental programs. Check for best rates. Rates: Studio g.v. $195/150; 1 BR g.v. $270/205; 1 BR o.v. $350/285; 2 BR g.v. $350/285; 2 BR o.v. $435/355; 3 BR/4 BR g.v. $465/305. Inquire with Aston about special packages, promotionals, senior or Island Hopper discounts.

GARDEN ISLAND SUNSET VACATION RENTALS

RENTAL AGENT: Kaua'i Vacation Rentals, 1-800-367-5025. Oceanfront, this 4-plex offers wonderful sunsets and views of Ni'ihau. A short walk to Waimea Town. All units are 2 BR, 1 BTH, and sleep 4.
Kaua'i Vacation Rental Rates: $650 weekly

WHERE TO STAY-WHAT TO SEE

South Shore to West Shore/Koke'e

HALE HOKU
4534 Lawa'i Rd., Koloa, HI 96756. Tel/fax (808) 742-1509; Email: halekoku@hawaiian.net; Web: <www.hshawaii.com/kvp/hoku>. This two bedroom, two bathroom unit provides a full kitchen, washer/dryer, cable TV. Outdoor pool, outdoor shower, and BBQ. Minimum 10 day stay during high season. Four person occupancy; additional $15 for fifth guest.
Rates: 2 BR deluxe o.f. $225/200.

KUHIO SHORES
5050 Lawa'i Beach Rd., Koloa, HI 96756. Located near Prince Kuhio Park. RENTAL AGENTS: Poipu Connection 1-800-742-2260; R&R (800) 367-8022. Prosser Realty 1-800-767-4707 rents a 1 BR oceanfront condominium. Garden Island Rentals 1-800-247-5599.
Rates: 1 BR and 2 BR oceanfronts $100-115 nightly/$850 weekly, plus cleaning fee.

LAWA'I BEACH RESORT
5017 Lawa'i Rd., Koloa, HI 96756. (808) 742-9581. FAX (808) 742-7981. RENTAL AGENTS: Grantham 1-800-325-5701. Maui & All Islands 1-800-663-6962. Suite Paradise 1-800-367-8020. This property has turned into timeshare, but a few units are still in the vacation rental program. Cable TV with HBO, private phone, washer/dryer. Pool, jacuzzi, BBQ grill, limited maid service. Coin-op laundry. Telephones.
Rates: 1 BR/2BR o.f. $179-300

MAKAHUENA ★
Located in Po'ipu. Mailing address: 1661 Pe'e Rd., Koloa, HI 96756. (808) 742-2482. RENTAL AGENTS: Castle Resorts 1-800-367-5004. Grantham Resorts 1-800-325-5701. R&R 1-800-367-8022. Maui & All Islands 1-800-663-6962. Po'ipu Connection Realty 1-800-742-2260. Seventy-nine condominiums. Resort includes pool, tennis court, jacuzzi, and BBQ area. We stayed in a deluxe 2 BR 2 BTH operated by Po'ipu Connection. It was really oceanfront, with a blowhole right outside our lanai! It was a pleasure to open the double doors into the entranceway and be greeted by such a spacious, luxurious unit. The size was enhanced by wall mirrors and high cathedral ceilings and it seemed "huge" but once we settled in, found it to be comfortable and intimate. The furniture was attractive with warm shades made tropical with lots of cane and bamboo. The bedrooms had shoji (Japanese screen) doors, there were ceiling fans throughout, programmed lighting and A/C controls, wet bar, dishwasher, washer/dryer, microwave, and plenty of dishes and utensils. The unit was clean and fresh with new furniture and nice soft carpet. All units have ceiling fans, full kitchens, and washer/dryer.
Po'ipu Connection Rates: 2 BR 2BTH deluxe oceanfront $1600 weekly
Grantham Rates: 2 BR o.f. $205/185; 2 BR premium o.f. $300; 3 BR o.v. $195/175
Castle Resorts: 1 BR g.v. $180/160; 1 BR o.v. $195/175; 1 BR o.f. $235/200; 2 BR g.v. $185/165; 2 BR o.v. $220/190; 2 BR o.f. $250/225; 2 BR deluxe o.f. $365/340; 3 BR g.v. $295/275; 3 BR o.v. $335/310

NIHI KAI VILLAS

1870 Ho'one Road, Koloa, HI 96756, located up the hill from Brennecke's Beach. Grantham Resorts toll free 1-800-325-5701. (808) 742-2000, Fax (808) 742-9093; Email: info@grantham-resorts.com; Web: <www.grantham-resorts.com> RENTAL AGENTS: Prosser 1-800-767-4707. Maui & All Islands 1-800-663-6962. R&R 1-800-367-8022. Suite Paradise 1-800-367-8020. Po'ipu Connection Realty 1-800-742-2260. Garden Island Rentals 1-800-247-5599. Seventy units with one, two and three bedroom. Phones, TV, microwave, kitchens, washer/dryer. Many oceanview. Ocean front swimming pool and tennis courts. Nearby beach is popular for body surfing.

Garden Island Rates: 1 BR $125 / 2 BR 2 BTH $135 plus cleaning fees
Suite Paradise Rates: For minimum 7 day stay, 2BR 2 BTH unit $250-305
Rates quoted are from Grantham:
1 BR deluxe g.v. $149/129
2 BR deluxe o.v. $169/149
2 BR deluxe o. f. $250/230
3 BR luxury o.f. $275/250

PO'IPU CRATER

2330 Ho'ohu Rd., Koloa, HI 96756 (808) 742-7260. RENTAL AGENTS: R&R 1-800-367-8022. Po'ipu Connection Realty 1-800-742-2260. Maui & All Islands 1-800-663-6962. Suite Paradise 1-800-367-8020. Grantham Resorts 1-800-325-5701. Thirty condominiums in a garden setting. Each two bedroom, two bath bungalow is furnished with telephone, cable TV, VCR, microwave, washer and dryer, plus full kitchen. Located near Brennecke's Beach. Resort features tennis, swimming pool, sauna, BBQ.

Grantham: 2 BR 2 BTH garden $139/119
Poipu Connection: 2BR 2 BTH $750-850 weekly
Suite Paradise: 2 BR 2 BTH garden $195 with minimum of 7 day stay

PO'IPU KAPILI ★

2221 Kapili Rd., Koloa, HI 96756. (808) 742-6449, Fax (808) 742-9162. ON SITE RENTAL AGENT: Po'ipu Ocean View Resorts (same address) toll free 1-800-443-7714; Email: aloha@poipukapili.com; Web: <www. poipukapili.com> Sixty 1 and 2 bedroom condominiums in seven low-rise oceanfront buildings. The property features a traditional Hawaiian plantation architecture located in the Po'ipu Beach resort community. Kitchens fully equipped including microwave ovens. One bedroom units are 1,200 sq. ft., two bedroom units are 1,800 sq. ft. These are very spacious units with lots of room to move around and relax, which is what you want on a vacation. Units are well-appointed, very nice clean furnishings and equipped with all the conveniences needed for a great stay. Laundry facilities are available on the property, but two bedroom units have their own washer and dryer. Oceanview pool, and complimentary tennis courts lighted for night play. The property is very private and the attractive and well cared for grounds add to the appeal. As nice as some other units costing much more. Room and car packages are available. (Christmas holiday rates are higher than the high season rates which follow.)

1 BR o.v. $260/200; 1 BR o.v. dlx $300/225; 2 BR o.v. $350/260;
2 BR o.v. dlx $400/300; 2 BR superior $425/325; Penthouse $550/450

PO'IPU MAKAI

1677 Pe'e, Po'ipu, HI 96756. Small swimming pool. Located overlooking ocean. RENTAL AGENTS: Prosser 1-800-767-4707. Grantham Resorts 1-800-325-5701. Maui & All 1-800-663-6962. Kaua'i Vacation Rentals 1-800-367-5025; Email: aloha@kvrre.com; Web: <www.KauaiVacationRentals.com>. Po'ipu Connection Realty 1-800-742-2260. 15 units. Each unit fronts the ocean. *Depending on the rental agent and unit, prices vary greatly!*
Po'ipu Connection Rates: 2 BR 2 BTH $110-155, 3 BR 2 BTH $1150 weekly
Kaua'i Vacation Rental Rates: 1 BR ocean $150/130; 2 BR ocean $160/140; 3 BR ocean $195/170

PO'IPU PALMS

1697 Pe'e Rd., at Po'ipu Beach. (808) 245-4711. RENTAL AGENTS: R&R 1-800-367-8022. Prosser Realty 1-800-767-4707. Po'ipu Connection 1-800-742-2260. Maui & All 1-800-663-6962. There are 12 units in this complex which are located oceanfront. Attractive, homey apartments with two small bedrooms and two baths. The pool and pool deck have been refurbished and the exterior has been recently painted. *Rates: 2 BR 2 BTH $950-1150 weekly*

WAIKOMO STREAM VILLAS

Located in Po'ipu. RENTAL AGENTS: Grantham Resorts 1-800-325-5701. Maui & All Islands 1-800-663-6962. Prosser 1-800-767-4707. Sixty 1 and 2 bedroom units in tropical setting. Units have private lanais and are equipped with kitchen telephone, cable TV, VCR, microwave, washer and dryer. Free tennis, BBQ area and an adult and children's swimming pool are amenities.
1 BR 1 BTH g.v. $115/85 (1-4); 2 BR 2 BTH g.v. $149/119 (1-6)

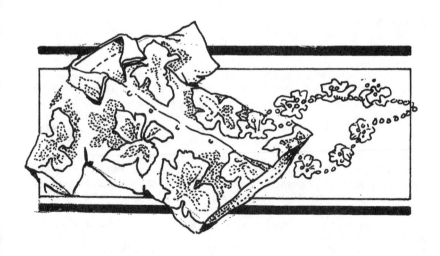

WAIMEA PLANTATION COTTAGES ★

PO Box 367, Waimea, HI 96796. (808) 338-1625. 1-800-9-WAIMEA.
RENTAL AGENTS: Managed by Aston Properties 1-800-922-7866; Email:
res.wpc@aston-hotels.com; Web: <www.aston-hotels.com>. Maui & All
Islands 1-800-663-69692. Visa and Mastercard accepted. Each of their cottages,
originally built between 1880 and 1950 to house plantation employees, has been
fully restored and updated. Located in a lovely grove of palms, these individual
houses are just what you'd expect a Hawaiian home to be. There are forty-seven
cottages spread among 27 acres.

Their property information sheet includes the following history: "In 1884, Hans
Peter Fayé, a Norwegian engineer and farmer, secured a lease from Kalakaua,
King of Hawai'i, for about 200 acres of Mana swamp land, where he successfully
grew sugar cane. He and nearby planters combined their lands to form the
Kekaha Sugar Company in 1898, one of Hawai'i's most profitable cane produc-
ers. By 1910, W.P. Fayé, Limited had privately purchased the neighboring
Waimea Sugar Mill Company. Today, Fayé's descendants manage Waimea Sugar
Mill lands as Kiki'aola Land Company, Ltd."

The Alan E. Fayé Manager's Estate is a two story house circa 1900. This five
bedroom home is 4,000 sq. ft. H.P. Fayé's first home, originally in Mana, 20
miles away, was relocated to the entryway where it now serves as the front desk.
The property is divided into several areas: Seaside, Historic Mill Camp, Hanawai
Courtyard, and Coconut Grove. They also have a 1916 two story beach house
and cottage located on the shore of Hanalei Bay available for rent. They now
have a Waimea Sugar Mill Camp Museum and Plantation Lifestyles Walking
Tour. Reservations are required for this tour which is limited to 12 people.
Offered Tuesdays and Saturdays at 9 am. Cost is $6 adults, $5 seniors 65 and
older, and children 12 and under are $3. Weekly maid service, color cable TV,
telephones, laundry facilities, complimentary tennis, swimming pool. New
amenities include a recreation room featuring a large screen television, lounge
area, video games, and a gift shop which includes a small museum with Hawaiian
arts and crafts and Kaua'i made items.

These units are full of history -- looking at the tiny doors, old fashioned dressers
and end tables, and rattan furniture, you can actually imagine what it would have
been like to be a plantation worker coming in the back door and putting your
"lunch tin" on the oil cloth on top of the tiny table in the quaint kitchen. But the
plumbing has been modernized and though the bathrooms are a bit small, they
have a great walk-in tiled shower with plenty of room. The lighting fixtures are
new, but have an old look. A/C, ceiling fans, tv, stereo, coffee maker and starter
packet of coffee. Pool area is spacious and completely open and overlooks the
ocean. (It can be noisy what with the gravel driveways, crowing roosters, and
squeaky floor boards, but you expect that in an older building and it just adds to
the ambiance!)
*Rates: Studio w/kitchenette $140/130; 1 BR/1 bath Grove View $200/175; 1BR/1
bath Superior Grove View $215/185; 1BR/1bath Superior Oceanfront $240/215;
2 BR/1 bath Grove View $260/220; 2 BR/2 bath Superior Grove View $270/230;
2BR/1 bath Superior Oceanfront $260/300; 3 BR/2 bath Superior Grove View
$300/255; 3BR Superior Oceanfront $335/295; 4 BR/3 bath Oceanfront $375/350*

EXPENSIVE

EMBASSY VACATION RESORT - PO'IPU POINT ★

1613 Pe'e Rd., Koloa, HI 96756. (808) 742-1888. Managed by Marc Resorts. Reservations: Marc Resorts Hawai'i 1-800-535-0085, toll free FAX 1-800-633-5085, local (808) 922-9700. OTHER AGENTS: Maui & All Islands 1-800-663-6962. Pleasant Hawaiian Holidays 1-800-242-9244. They have 218 units. Some units are timeshare. This is another very pleasant luxury property with architectural style like that of the Moana Hotel on O'ahu. The decor is reminiscent of an English country estate with dark greens accented by antique floral patterns. The bathrooms are spacious with big showers and deep tubs. The units have a full kitchen with washer/dryer, microwave and dishwasher. Rooms have stereos, TVs, VCRs and there is enough game software to keep the kids happy!

Nightly two-hour manager's cocktail party includes beverages and pupus. Coffee in rooms with complimentary breakfast in the Club Room by the pool. Breakfast includes assorted juices, fresh fruit, and breads, but be prepared for the activity talk!! The landscaped pool area and whirlpool are surrounded by sand (that is similar to aquarium gravel) with lawn chairs around the border. One bedroom suites have a king bed and sleeper sofa. The two-bedroom suites have a king bed and two twin beds plus a sleeper sofa in the living room. Health Club features workout equipment, steam and sauna baths. Toddler pool and a nice touch are the many sand toys available for the use of those little guests. Check out the volcanic lava flow out on the beachfront and see the family of green turtles that frolic in the surf. Great amenities that are sure to enhance your vacation! Also Pleasant Holidays and Maui & All Islands all offer some special package rates and free night discounts.
Marc Resort Year Round Rates: 1 BR g.v. (max 4) $299; 1 BR partial o.v. $340; 1 BR o.v. $385; 1 BR o.f. $450. 2 BR g.v. (max.6) $350; 2 BR partial o.v. $425; 2 BR o.v. $490; 2 BR o.f. $565. Presidential 3 BR 3 1/2 BTH w/ kitchen $1,000.

HYATT REGENCY KAUA'I RESORT & SPA ★

1571 Po'ipu Rd., Koloa, HI 96756. (808) 742-1234, FAX (808) 742-1557. Reservations 1-800-633-7313; Web: <www.kauai-hyatt.com>. OTHER RENTAL AGENTS: Pleasant Hawaiian Holidays 1-800-242-9244. This Hyatt, while not on as grand a scale as some other Hawai'i Hyatt properties, still has a grand feeling. This property is located on fifty oceanfront acres in the Po'ipu Beach District. The classic traditional Hawaiian architecture is reminiscent of the 1920s and 1930s. It is very open and elegant, with a regal, Hawaiiana look. Even during high occupancy, this resort doesn't feel crowded. A pleasant surprise are the pools, which are heated. With two swimming pools, three jacuzzis, and another "action" pool with waterfalls, slides, water volleyball, a children's area, and five acres of meandering saltwater swimming lagoons featuring islands, each with its own landscaping. There are also four tennis courts with pro shop and tennis professional on the property as well. The Dock offers poolside coffee, beverages, snacks, and light meals. The Seaview Terrace has a comfortable, living room feel, very open and airy with a beautiful view.

The Stevenson's Library is a cruise ship-type bar area, a combination gaming room (complete with pool, backgammon, chess, and more), library, and bar, although very un bar-like. The Ilima Terrace embraces the true Hawaiiana feeling, serving breakfast, lunch, Sunday brunch, and dinner in an open-air arrangement with plenty of foliage and koi filled lagoons. Tidepools restaurant is housed under a thatched roof surrounded by a lagoon island. Dondero's is the fine dining Italian restaurant. The Po'ipu Bay Bar & Grill (in the golf course clubhouse) is now part of the Hyatt.

While the beachfront is pleasant, the winds and surf can come up and make it unsafe for swimming. The Hyatt does post flags advising people of the ocean safety. The guest rooms are light and bright with plantation-style furnishings. As with many Hyatt properties, they offer the Regency Club which are special floors offering special guest amenities such as complimentary breakfast, beverage service, and late afternoon hors d'oeuvres. The resort also features the ANARA Spa to hotel and non-hotel guests. Salon facilities, exercise room, aerobic and yoga classes, as well as an array of wonderful facial and body treatments can certainly be a memorable part of your Kaua'i vacation holiday! See Spas/Fitness Centers in the recreation chapter for more information.

The Hyatt's Wedding department offers extensive wedding services. The wedding coordinator can provide you with an informative list of "10 Helpful Tips for Getting Married on Kaua'i" to help you plan your wedding before you leave home. Unusual and romantic, the resort will even arrange to order a replica of an award-winning Hawaiian bridal gown (*holoku*) for the bride-to-be. The Victorian-styled Hawaiian holoku wedding dress was designed by Maile Jean Amorin, a replica of her grandmother's wedding gown. Wedding packages range from $980 - $1,750. Vow renewal packages start at $730.

HYATT REGENCY KAUAI

187

The Hyatt Regency Kaua'i has developed an innovative Hawaiian program that is free to the general public. Activities conducted by the Kaua'i Historical Society include the Archaeology and Dune Walk along the 500 yard white sand beach fronting the resort and "Talk Story" sessions which focus on the lore and legends of Kaua'i. Leilani Bond, the Hyatt's *kumu* (respected teacher) oversees the Hawaiiana program. She and the 250 students of her hula halau share their knowledge of Hawaiian culture. Traditional arts and crafts are offered Monday through Friday and include poi pounding demonstrations, modern hula instruction, quilting demonstrations, flower lei-making, and even ukulele lessons. Traditional Hawaiian music is featured each evening in the Seaview Terrace from 6-8 pm. A torch lighting ceremony (accompanied by chanting and traditional hula) is a part of the evening guest entertainment four nights each week. A weekly schedule of the resort's Hawaiian program activities is available at the concierge desk.

Room rates are single/double occupancy. No charge for children 18 and under when sharing their parents room using existing bed space. For additional persons 19 and older, $30 charge per night; $50 per night for the Regency Club. Maxi mum four adults or two adults and two children per room.

Hyatt Guest Accommodations: Garden $300; Mountain $375; Lagoon $420; Partial Ocean $470; Deluxe Ocean $560; Regency Club $630

Hyatt Suites: Ocean $785; Regency Club Ocean $885; Deluxe $1,250; Regency Club Deluxe $1,350; Presidential $2950.

KIAHUNA PLANTATION ★
Located in Po'ipu. Mailing address: 2253 Po'ipu Rd., Koloa, HI 96756. (808) 742-6411, FAX (808) 742-1698. RENTAL AGENT: Outrigger Hotels & Resorts manages part of the property and Castle Resorts the other part which makes it all a bit confusing! And there are other property manager agents who handle bookings as well. The reservation number for Outrigger is 1-800-OUTRIGGER, toll free fax 1-800-622-4852, or tel (808) 921-6600; Email: reservations@outrigger.com; Web: <www.outrigger.com>. Castle Resorts 1-800-367-5004; Email: reservations@castleresorts.com; Web: <www.castleresorts.com>. OTHER RENTAL AGENTS: Grantham Resorts 1-800-325-5701. Maui & All 1-800-663-6962. Suite Paradise 1-800-367-8020. Pleasant Hawaiian Holidays 1-800-242-9244. Kiahuna is the largest resort condominium on Kaua'i with 333 units in two and three story buildings and situated on 35-acres of lush gardens and expansive lawns which were once part of Hawai'is first sugar cane plantation. The historic manor house was originally the home of the plantation manager and now is home to the very nice Plantation Gardens Restaurant.

This is what might be called "Classy Hawaiian." The rooms are very attractively decorated and have the feel of a comfortable beach home. They have high ceilings and are nicely furnished with wicker and wood with the bedroom set off in a cozy nook of its own. The kitchens have coffee makings and a microwave with complimentary microwave popcorn. The property has plenty of amenities as well, the Kiahuna Keiki Club, crafts and Hawaiian activities, and free tours of the grounds. The comforts of a condo and the amenities and convenience of a hotel earn this property a star. One and two bedroom units have various garden view, ocean view, and oceanfront categories. All units include living room and dining room, private lanai, fully equipped kitchen, color TV, video tape player, and ceiling fans. Daily maid service, laundry facilities, complimentary beach chairs and towels, gas BBQs. Pool and ten tennis courts. Free tours available of the incredible cactus in their Moir Gardens and the newer Hawaiian Gardens that are located on this resort property. Excellent location on Po'ipu Beach and even more family-friendly with their Keiki Klub Summer Program! Offered seasonally during busier travel periods at Christmas, Easter, and all summer long, the program is open to children ages 5-12 years. Kids are kept busy learning about Hawaiian culture through lei-making, 'ukulele lessons, hula dancing, and story telling. Other activities include arts & crafts, beach walks, and lagoon fishing. The program is $30 per child for a full day session and $15 for a half-day session. Lunch and afternoon snack are included in the full-day session charge.

Castle Resorts:
1 BR g.v. $215/180; o.v. $313/225; o.f. $440
2 BR g.v. $395/330; o.v. $495/405; o.f. $660
Grantham:
1 BR o.f. $25/205
Outrigger:
1 BR suite g.v. $199; royal g.v. $215; partial o.v. $240; o.v. $315; o.f. $425 (1, max 4)
2 BR suite g.v. $340; royal g.v. $370; partial o.v. $400; o.v. $480 (1, max 6)
Suite Paradise: 1BR 1 BTH $265

PO'IPU SHORES
1775 Pe'e Road, Koloa, HI 96756. (808) 742-7700. Managed by Castle Resorts. RENTAL AGENTS: Castle Resorts (808) 524-0900, Fax (808) 596-0158, toll free 1-800-367-5004; Web: <www.castleresorts.com>. Suite Paradise 1-800-367-8020. Maui & All Islands 1-800-663-6962. Thirty-three oceanfront condominiums one, two, and three bedrooms. All suites feature fully-equipped kitchens, color TV, washer/dryer and private lanai. Both the living room and bedroom have oceanviews. The units are more appealing inside than out, with light furniture and walls and attractive lighting. Wood and marble kitchens are fully equipped with microwaves and plenty of counter space. Many of the privately owned units are equipped with VCR's, paperbacks, and even CDs. There is a raised deck area surrounding the pool and a club room complete with kitchen plus magazines and games. The older elevators tended to make a bit of noise, but happily, it was drowned out by the crashing of the waves. While most of the accessible parking area fills up quickly, it is a nice enough property, centrally located and a good value in this price range.

Castle Resorts rates:
1 BR o.f. $250/215; 2 BR o.f. or dlx o.f. $290/225, $310/275; 3 BR o.f. $340/305; Penthouse 2 BR o.f. $400/375
Suite Paradise: 2 BR 2 BTH $335

SHERATON KAUA'I RESORT

2440 Ho'onani Road, Koloa, HI 96756. (808) 742-1661. FAX (808) 742-4041. Sheraton Reservations: 1-800-782-9488. Web: < www.sheraton-hawaii.com >

The resort is situated on 20 acres of oceanfront gardens adjacent to Kaua'i's popular Po'ipu Beach. The resort comprises 413 air-conditioned rooms (including 14 suites). Three wings, each no higher than four stories, provide guests with ocean vistas and tropical gardens with koi-filled ponds. The Garden Wing is located across the street. The resort's artwork and interiors showcase the traditions of Hawaiian culture and diversity of the island. Guest rooms are decorated in natural earth tones and the rooms' furnishings and fabrics use Hawaiian kapa (bark cloth), lei and floral motifs. The property features guest services and facilities including two swimming pools, massage and fitness center, tennis courts, beach activities booth with rental equipment and instruction, and the Keiki Aloha Club children's center. Two swimming pools are available for guest use, one oceanside with pool slide and two children's pools and a whirlpool. The oceanfront pool and surrounding area feature tropical landscaping and they have done a particularly nice job restoring the surroundings to their natural, simple state of ocean and sand rather than trying to improve on nature and add a lot of complicated, man-made landscaping. The koi ponds, tropical gardens, and waterfalls enhance, rather than detract from the natural landscape. In-room amenities include coffee and coffee maker, mini-refrigerator, complimentary safe, hair dryer, color TV with cable, in-room movies, Sony Play Station and video checkout. They have a daily selection of activities including a massage & skincare center plus full service salon at "Stylists," fitness center and beach activities center at the beachfront pool. Tryout scuba with a free lesson offered twice daily. Hawaiian Arts Classes can be attended in the Garden Lobby (reservations required) and include lei making or hula dancing lessons. Their Hawaiian Cultural Court features displays and demonstrations daily in the Garden Lobby.

The Sheraton Kaua'i Resort entertains young guests with their Keiki Aloha Children's Program. Activities range from lei making and other Hawaiian arts & crafts to kite flying and ukulele lessons. The program is available year round. Price is $45 for a full day of play, $25 for half day. (808) 742-4016.

Guests can enjoy Shells, the resort's signature dining room which hugs Po'ipu Beach and serves breakfast,lunch and dinner. Lighter fare and a panoramic ocean vista (with live local entertainment evenings) are offered at The Point, which has both indoor and outdoor seating. A dramatic tile mural of a canoe paddler carving a path across a cresting wave welcomes guests to this casual dining spot. (Great for sunsets and one of the "happening" nightlife locations) Overlooking tropical gardens and carp-filled pools is Naniwa, a Japanese dinner restaurant which is designed to resemble a traditional Japanese Inn. They serve dinner daily. The Oasis Bar & Grill and The Garden Terrace (the resort's poolside restaurants) serve sandwiches and salads. You'll often find live Hawaiian music as a backdrop here.

Sheraton has followed the lead of other resorts and charges a hotel fee. While this one includes some nice amenities, it is unclear why the extra charge is made. Since everyone is required to pay them, why don't they just raise the rates $10? The $10 automatic hotel charge includes free local phone calls, continental breakfast, tennis, fitness center, internet, and more.

Check with Pleasant Hawaiian and other "package" retailers regarding air/room packages that include a stay at this lovely resort property.

Rates: Garden $250; Lagoon $300; Deluxe Ocean Front $360; Ocean Luxury $450; Garden Suite $480; Ocean Front Suite $750

WHALERS COVE ★
Located in Po'ipu. Mailing address Koloa Landing at Po'ipu, 2640 Puuholo Rd., Koloa, HI 96756. (808) 742-7571, direct 1-800-225-2683, Fax (808) 742-1185. Premier Resorts 1-800-367-7052. RENTAL AGENTS: Suite Paradise 1-800-367-8020. Maui & All Islands 1-800-663-6962. Pleasant Hawaiian Holidays 1-800-242-9244. Thirty-eight very luxurious and roomy units. Oceanside pool and BBQ. Located on a promontory overlooking the ocean. Years ago whaling ships anchored at this cove to unload passengers and cargo. Swimming beach one mile away. The cove fronting the property offers very good snorkeling. The units are very spacious and comfortable with very nice furnishings, art decor, fully equipped kitchens, dining area and large patio/lanais. Third floor units have jacuzzi tubs overlooking the ocean. Discounts for longer stays. Great location, convenient to Po'ipu Resort attractions, activities, shopping, dining, golf, tennis, etc. Two night minimum stay.
Premier Resort Rates: 1 BR o.v. $310-445 (max 2); 2 BR $380-545 o.v. (max 0)
Suite Paradise: 2 BR 2 BTH $455

NORTH SHORE

Anahola/Kilauea/Princeville/Hanalei/Ha'ena

INTRODUCTION

The picturesque beauty of the North Shore is unsurpassed in the Hawaiian Islands. Most of the attractions on this side of Kaua'i revolve around the sights provided by Mother Nature. From botanical gardens to postcard perfect sunsets on the beach, here you can ignore the hustle and bustle and simply relax! As you take in the famed North Shore area around the small town of Hanalei, you'll see why this region was chosen as background for the many movies and TV programs filmed here over the years. It has the soaring tropical mountain peaks, jungles, beautiful beaches, plunging waterfalls and spectacular coastal panoramas so typical of Pacific islands. It's that appealing look of the mythical Paradise.

KEALIA

Following the Kuhio Highway #56 north, at mile marker 10 you'll see a long stretch of beach that looks pleasant enough, but the water conditions are not safe. The rip currents along this beachfront are very strong. Kealia was another old plantation town and you may still see some of the old plantation buildings that remain. The word Kealia means "salt encrusted" and it was to this beach that the early Hawaiians gathered salt that had evaporated along the beachfront. From Kealia, the road moves inland slightly as you continue around toward Kaua'i's North Shore.

ANAHOLA

Five miles from Kapa'a and just prior to mile marker 14 is what most visitors see of Anahola: *Duane's Ono Burgers!* (The best place to get a burger on Kaua'i -- in our opinion.) Duane's Ono Burgers are REALLY onolicious! Across the highway is the expanded *Polynesian Hide-a-way & Haw'n Bar-B-Q Chicken*, a roadside stand that now offers plate lunches and sandwiches along with fresh roasted macadamia nuts (in an attempt to compete with the popular *Duane's*).. A few steps away is *Kamaka's* for shave ice and smoothies. Shave ice starts at $1.50, but splurge and get the big one for $2 (it's great shave ice - soft as cotton candy with no crunchy ice pieces!) For uninitiated mainlanders, a "shave ice" is a "snow cone," a popular taste treat cooler throughout the islands. They come in a variety of flavors from strawberry to banana, mango and even more exotic local flavors! Ask for coconut or even li hing mui (ask the shave ice shop to explain!)

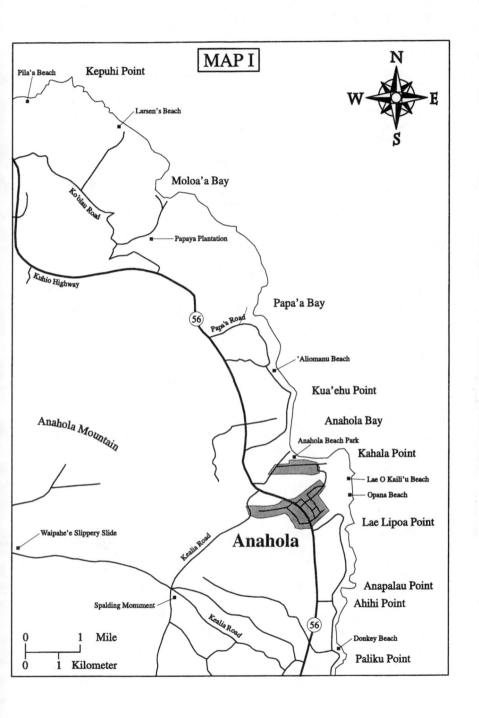

MAP I

N
W E
S

Pila'a Beach

Kepuhi Point

Larsen's Beach

Moloa'a Bay

Koʻolau Road

Papaya Plantation

Kuhio Highway

56

Papaʻa Road

Papaʻa Bay

'Aliomanu Beach

Kuaʻehu Point

Anahola Bay

Anahola Mountain

Anahola Beach Park

Kahala Point

Lae O Kaili'u Beach

Opana Beach

Lae Lipoa Point

Waipahe'e Slippery Slide

Kealia Road

Anahola

Anapalau Point

Ahihi Point

Spalding Monument

Kealia Road

56

Donkey Beach

Paliku Point

0   1   Mile

0   1   Kilometer

Historically, the hole in the mountain (now partially collapsed) above Anahola on the seaward side carries a legend. It tells that the hole was made by the spear of an early Hawaiian giant. The giant threw it at the King of Kaua'i and missed him, piercing the mountain and leaving the hole. And, of course, another version says it was another chieftain who opposed the king and that Kamehameha threw the spear, which went entirely through the rock behind him.

In more recent history, Anahola suffered the effects of a severe flood in late 1991. The heavy rainfall during the night caused the stream to swell and the subsequent flooding came as a surprise to the residents. Not only property, but lives were lost as well.

MOLOA'A

This now sleepy community was once thriving. Prior to the turn of the 20th century, sugar cane and pineapple were booming in this region and so was the population. Just past mile marker 16 on Kuhio Highway you'll want to turn right onto Ko'olau Road. Then right again onto Moloa'a Road and at the fork in the road keep to the left and continue on past private homes. There is public access to the trail, but parking is limited in front of these homes, so please respect their privacy and "no trespassing."

This is as pristine a bay as you may find on Kaua'i. If you happened to catch the lone airing of the pilot episode of Gilligan's Island a few years back on Fox television, you might recognize this bay. While this bay can be especially dangerous during winter and spring surf, anytime there is high surf, dangerous ocean conditions and powerful rip currents can occur. During periods of calm, you can enjoy swimming, snorkeling, and diving here.

CHRIST MEMORIAL CHURCH, KILAUEA

To reach the beaches enroute to Kilauea, Ka'aka'aniu Beach (Larsen's), and Wa'iakalua, will require parking and a short walk to reach. Neither is safe for water activities. Kuhio Highway #56 continues its trek north through agriculture and country estates nestled along the foothills of the surrounding interior mountain ranges. Signs warn that the roads may flood in various low places if there are heavy rains.

As you drive along, looking at the nearby mountains, can you find the profile of King Kong's face or, for those desiring to advance to the expert level of sleuthing, can you spot the transmitting pole disguised as a tree?

KILAUEA

The next stop on the map is Kilauea. The big attraction in Kilauea is the *Kilauea Point National Wildlife Refuge* with its handsome old lighthouse and soaring seabirds over the majestic cliffs and pounding surf below. We'll get to that shortly, but there are a few things worth taking in at Kilauea town. From the highway on the south edge of town, you can turn right onto Kolo into town or go a little farther and turn right on Kilauea Road at the Shell Gas Station. A short distance past Kolo Road on your left you will also find the entrance to *Guava Kai Plantation and Visitors Center*.

If you take this first turn to Kilauea onto Ho'okui, you'll find the *Little Grass Hut* gift shop and *Mango Mama's Cafe*, a former juice and smoothie stand that has expanded to also offer sandwiches, salads, and bagels. Take another left onto Kolo Road and you will pass the *Christ Memorial Episcopal Church*. This small church built of lava rock has beautiful stained glass windows which were sent from England and a hand-carved altar designed by Mrs. William Hyde Rice. While the church had its origins many years ago, the current structure only dates to 1941. Just opposite the church is the next major street, Kilauea Road which heads east to the coast.

Following Kilauea Road about a ½ mile, turn right onto Oka Street, and then its a couple of blocks to the *Roadrunner Cafe & Bakery*. If you're hungry for some good Mexican fare, this is a good place to try. They are open for breakfast, lunch, and dinner. The high-ceiling interior is designed to resemble a Mexican courtyard. They have a bakery next door where you can purchase some taro bread and other baked goodies (808) 828-8226.

The *Historic Kilauea Theater & Community Event Center* is located in the Kong Lung Center at intersection of Kilauea Road and Keneke Street. The historic theater serves as a community events center hosting various local events and productions. The original theater was built in 1930 and was located across the street from the current theater which was built in 1967. The community facility has undergone a recent restoration program.

The historic *Kong Lung Center* in Kilauea is a good place for a stop to browse the shop or for a refreshment stop at *Pau Hana Pizza and Kilauea Bakery* or the *Lighthouse Bistro*. The *Kong Lung Company* is an emporium housed in a restored historic building. Products include a selection of unique, "essential luxury" items.

195

They offer Kong Lung's own T-shirts and backpack-style tote bags, swimwear, tableware, and lamps. The Kong Lung Co.'s structure dates back to 1860 when it was a two-story wooden building housing the Kilauea Plantation General store. In about 1918, the Kilauea Sugar Company's plantation manager tore down the old wooden structure. In the early 1940's the plantation rebuilt the structure using a fieldstone construction method which is unique to Hawai'i and the Chew "Chow" Lung store reopened as the new Kong Lung Store. In the early 1970's, the Kilauea Sugar Company closed and the Kong Lung Center was purchased by local businessmen. The Kong Lung Company was restored to the authentic, plantation-style architecture and design that makes the building historically significant. In 1993, it was placed on the National Register of Historic Places. During the year-long remodel, an old floor-safe was discovered in what is now used as a dressing room. The original butcher's freezer, dating to 1943, is now a large private dressing room. Open 10 am-10 pm daily. Phone (808) 828-1822, FAX (808) 828-1227. *Reinventions*, located up the spiral staircase, is an assortment of new and gently used clothing with a good selection of inexpensive Aloha shirts. (808) 828-1125.

The Lighthouse Bistro recently opened at the Kong Lung Center and offers a full lunch and dinner menu. The adjacent *Kilauea Bakery* and *Pau Hana Pizza* are popular with visitors and local residents alike. Their signature bakery items include Napali brown bread, guava fermented Hawaiian sourdough bread, and tropical fruit layer cakes with whipped cream icing. It began as a bakery only but became very popular with the addition of a pizza, sandwich and light fare menu. Great sandwiches, bagels, pizza, and pastries. They recently expanded and now offer cafe seating inside and a courtyard with a few tables outdoors. Open 6:30 am-9 pm, Monday-Saturday (808) 828-2020.

At the back of the center is the *Island Soap & Candle Works*, a factory and gift shop that makes and sells tropical scented lotions, soaps, and candles. They also have an outlet in Koloa on the South Shore. Scented with island fragrances like plumeria, torch ginger, or pikake, they are all hand-made using natural ingredients. The "factory" looks like an old-fashioned alchemist or apothecary shop where you can watch their soap and candle products being made on the premises. 1-888-528-SOAP < www.handmade-soap.com > Email: soap@aloha.net

On Saturdays, local farmers gather at the nearby **Kilauea Plantation Center** to sell their fresh produce. Fresh vegetables, herbs, flowers, and fruits are available, and most are organically grown. Look for the red flags! Look for expansions of the **Kilauea Fruit Stand** which will be increasing in size and offering more varied locally grown produce along with longer hours.

Continuing onto the lighthouse, we will begin with a bit of history concerning the area geographically, the lighthouse, and the wildlife refuge. **Kilauea Point** is a remnant of the former Kilauea volcanic vent that last erupted 15,000 years ago. Today, there is only a small "U" shaped portion of the vent that remains, which allows for a spectacular view from the 570 foot ocean bluff. The history of the *lighthouse* began in 1909 when the property was purchased for a one dollar token fee from the Kilauea Sugar Plantation Company. The location for the lighthouse

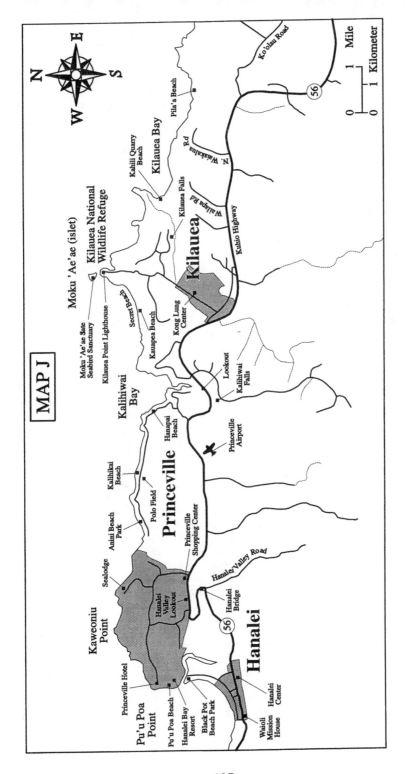

MAP J

N
W — E
S

Ko'olau Road

56

Pila'a Beach

N. Waikalua Rd

Kilauea Bay

Kahili Quarry Beach

Kilauea Rd

Kilauea Falls

Wailapa Rd

Moku 'Ae' ae (islet)

Kilauea National Wildlife Refuge

Kuhio Highway

Moku 'Ae' ae State Seabird Sanctuary

Kilauea Point Lighthouse

Secret Beach

Kauapea Beach

Kilauea

Kong Lung Center

Kalihiwai Bay

Lookout

Kalihiwai Falls

Hanapai Beach

Kalihikai Beach

Princeville Airport

Polo Field

Princeville

Anini Beach Park

Sealodge

Princeville Shopping Center

Kaweoniu Point

Hanalei Valley Lookout

Hanalei Valley Road

Pu'u Poa Point

Princeville Hotel

Hanalei Bridge

56

Pu'u Poa Beach

Hanalei Bay Resort

Black Pot Beach Park

Hanalei

Hanalei Center

Waioli Mission House

0   1   Mile
0   1   Kilometer

was perfectly suited as this grass-covered bluff was surrounded by pounding surf on three sides. Winter swells of twenty feet or more were not uncommon. (We hope you have packed that pair of binoculars!) Work began on the lighthouse in 1912 and was completed in May, 1913, with a light shining to ships 21 nautical miles away. The lighthouse is today on the National Register of Historic Places. The visitor center adjacent to the lighthouse has displays explaining the seabirds and their sanctuaries.

The *Kilauea Point National Wildlife Refuge* was established in 1974 and is recognized as Hawai'i's largest seabird sanctuary, a place that is home to more than 5,000 seabirds. This refuge is a nesting site for the red-footed booby, wedge-tailed shearwater, Laysan albatross, and many other species of Hawaiian seabirds. The acquisition of land has continued ever since with this sanctuary now encompassing 203 acres. The refuge was struck hard by the '92 hurricane. Not only was there much damage to the birdlife and vegetation, but the famous lighthouse was also seriously affected. At Kilauea Point, they reported that about 80% of the native plants suffered damage. On Crater Hill, at least 25% were lost and an additional 50% damaged. Mokolea Point vegetation suffered little damage. Kilauea Point lost the most birds and suffered the worst damage to the habitat. The Kaua'i Natural Wildlife Refuge complex lost several buildings and had general extensive damage. But all is pretty much back to normal and it is an inspiring and peaceful place to visit.

When the lighthouse and support facilities were transferred from the U.S. Coast Guard on February 15, 1985, Kilauea Point became the 425th National Wildlife Refuge. The adjacent Kilauea Point Humpback Whale National Marine Sanctuary was established in 1994. Over 250,000 visitors enjoy the Kilauea Point National Wildlife Refuge visitor center and wildlife viewing areas each year. As many as 1,000 visitors per day may tour the facility over the Christmas holiday. A two-hour guided Crater Hill hike is offered daily, free with the cost of admission to the Refuge. Early reservations are recommended. (Call 828-0168, or sign up at the visitor center.) There is an on-going habitat management program that includes water development, native plant propagation, volunteer conservation group and service club, and nursery activities. Over 200 volunteers donate hours to varied refuge projects. Of the 203 acres, 183 acres are owned, and another 20 acres are conservation easement. *Kilauea Point*, PO Box 87, Kilauea, Kaua'i, HI 96754, is open to the public daily from 10 am-4 pm, closed some federal holidays. (808) 828-1413. Admission is $2 by donation.Drive back to the Kuhio Highway #56 through Kilauea town in order to head on north toward Princeville. At the highway on the left, just past mile marker 23, the turn into Kuawa Road on the *mauka* side of the highway leads to the local guava plantation.

There are 480 acres of guava orchards under commercial cultivation at the *Guava Kai Plantation* in Kilauea, which is considered the "Guava Capital" of the world. Visit the plantation's visitor center and discover how guava is grown and processed into a variety of treats. Guava has fewer calories and more vitamin C than oranges, and it is also a good source of vitamin A, potassium, and phosphorus. Guava is actually not a citrus, but a berry with a fleshy seed cavity and a thick skin.

The guava can survive in dry or very tropical conditions. The Kilauea orchards receive 100 inches of rainfall each year with temperate 65-80 degree weather that is very agreeable to this crop. During dry months each tree receives up to 75 gallons of water per day. The seedlings were planted in this orchard in 1977 and began producing fruit in 1979. The first commercial yield was in January of 1980 with 2,000 pounds per acre harvested. Today the yield is 5,000 pounds per acre or about 400 pounds of fruit per tree per harvest cycle. The fruit at this plantation is hand-picked and harvested year round on a full-scale crop cycling system.

The fruit meat can vary from white or yellow to orange or pink. The variety grown at the Guava Kai Plantation is a hybrid developed by the University of Hawai'i's College of Tropical Agriculture and has a bright pink flesh and an edible rind. The color in your glass of juice is all natural.

The guava was a native of South America and introduced to the islands in 1791 by the Spaniard Don Francisco de Paula Marin, who was an advisor to Kamehameha I. The guava flourished and many now grow wild in Hawaii.

There is a self-guided tour that includes a view of the orchard and of the processing plants as well as an informative eight minute video. There is a man-made fish pond and an assortment of native Hawaiian plants. The snack bar sells ice cream, juice, breads, bakery items, and desserts that are made with guava as well as a variety of other snacks. There are free samples of guava juice, jams, jellies, and coffee. Since they are owned by Mauna Loa, they also sell their products at slightly lower rates than retail outlets. Guava Kai Plantation is open daily 9 am-5 pm. (808) 828-6121.

Back on the highway and continuing north toward Princeville, you'll pass *Banana Joe's*, just outside Kilauea on the *mauka* (mountain) side of the road. A landmark you will definitely want to visit if you have a thirst for a fruit smoothie! Better yet, try a "frostie" - a tropical blend of fresh fruit and nothing but fruit, pureed to the consistency of soft serve ice cream. Or try your papaya, banana, pineapple, or mango yet another way - dried in a dehydrator by Joe's father, "Banana" Tom!

At mile marker 25 is a scenic lookout for *Kalihiwai Falls*. The valley is visible on the makai side of the road and it is a cautious vacationer who must venture down the bridge and over to the other side to view the falls. During the 1957 tsunami, the original bridge was literally lifted up off the foundation and moved 50 - 100 feet up stream. The Kalihiwai Falls is actually two falls, accessible by hike, kayak, or horseback.

You'll want to skip the first sign that says Kalihiwai Road; it no longer goes through. Two miles past the Kilauea Shell Station and between mile markers 25 and 26, take the second turn off to Kalihiwai Road down to *'Anini Beach*.

'Anini Beach is a popular windsurfing location and can be good for snorkeling during calm surf. This is one of the best beachcombing locations you'll find on the island. The kids will love sifting through the amber sand to find shell treasures!

199

This quiet beachfront community might be an ideal location for a vacation home rental. While the real estate values in this area are sky high, there are some good vacation values available. Sylvester Stallone recently sold his beachfront home here and the oceanfront property that was used in the filming of *Honeymoon in Las Vegas* was also quickly snapped up when it was placed on the real estate market. Both reportedly sold for $1-2 million. The beach park here is nicely maintained, with covered pavilions, ideal for a picnic lunch. Across the road from the beach they have polo matches each Sunday beginning in late April and running through the early fall. There is another birthstone located here.

Back to Kuhio Highway and just before mile marker 26 you will pass the airport on your left (*mauka*) and the Princeville Golf Club will be on your right (*makai*). The breathtaking golf course vistas offered by the Princeville course may tempt even the non-golfer. Even if you aren't a golfer, you might be interested in their health club or restaurant. Suddenly the entrance to Princeville appears on your right and access to all the hotels and condominiums is off of this road. The Princeville Center is located at this intersection as well.

The Princeville Library is located adjacent to the Princeville Center. This beautiful new facility became the 50th library in the state system. The attractive new building blends with the Princeville architecture, but has a sleek, modern interior with state-of-the-art computer services and technology systems. Hours: Tues, Thurs, Fri & Sat 9-5, Wed 12-8, closed Sun-Mon. (808) 826-1545.

PRINCEVILLE

The Hanalei area, ringed with gorgeous bays and beaches, has long been a place of beauty and power. In times past, the surrounding area were *kula* lands - land available to the *maka'ainana* or common person for cultivation and fishing. History provided by the Princeville resort tells us that, "overlooking Hanalei Bay was the plateau which is now known as Princeville - a place of spiritual power or mana. From the Princeville Hotel's present site to Po'oku, just beyond the highway, there is said to have been one of the largest *hala* (pandanus) groves in all of Hawai'i. The grove was celebrated in many chants and stories, as the *hala* was very important to the Hawaiians. The presence of the tree indicated that there were abundant water sources, and the long leaves provided weaving materials for mats and other household items. Further up O'oku was one of Kaua'i's largest *heiau* or temples of worship.

"The site of the hotel was known as *'pu'upoa'* or *'pu'u pa'oa'* -- *pu'u* meaning mountain and *pa'oa* meaning the staff of the fire goddess, Pele who, when searching for a new home would strike her staff in the earth to create a new crater. Directly below the hotel is a marshy area known as *kamo'omaika'i*, the site of a large fishpond. The Hawaiians were quite adept at raising fish in ponds next to the ocean. There they also built fishing shrines and altars to pay homage to the gods of the reef and the sea. This area, where ancient rockwalls are still visible, is being restored and preserved."

It was in late January of 1815 that the *Behring* went aground at Waimea Bay. The *Behring*, owned by the Russian-American Company, was headed toward Sitka with a load of seal skins when Kaua'i's king, Kaumuali'i, confiscated the cargo. In 1816 a German named Georg (that's right, no "e") Anton Scheffer was selected by the manager of the Russian-American Company, Alexander Andreievich Baranov, to head to Kaua'i to claim their load of pelts. He arrived in Hawai'i in November of 1815 and arrived on Kaua'i in May of 1816. While Georg and his forces were prepared to take back their cargo by force, the king returned the cargo as a show of good faith. The King had hopes of an alliance with the Russian Empire. Schaffer had ideas that were slightly different, his plans were to take over the entire island chain for the Russian Empire. He constructed a fort at Waimea Bay in September of that year and named it after the Russian Empress Elizabeth and ordered two additional forts to be built, one at Hanalei and another in Princeville. His fort on top of Pu'u Poa in Princeville was named Fort Alexander for Tsar Alexander I. After King Kamehameha learned of his plans to overthrow the government, Georg was ordered to depart from the islands. Georg made his stand at Pu'u Poa, but failed in his attempt and shortly thereafter he sailed to Honolulu and then fled the islands. The grassy area just outside of the porte cochere for the Princeville Hotel has only a few rocky outcroppings, for little remained of a fort made of dirt and clay. A kiosk with an interpretive center sits beyond the plateau and also offers a panoramic view of the Pacific Ocean.

A Scottish physician, Robert Crichton Wyllie, came to Kaua'i in 1844 after making a fortune as a merchant in South America. He had not planned on staying in the islands but was persuaded to accept an appointment by King Kamehameha III as minister of foreign affairs, a post he held for 20 years. He desired a manor with the opulence and elegance as those found in his homeland in Scotland and selected Hanalei as the site. In early days, taro was raised here. When Wyllie purchased the property it was a coffee plantation which he converted to a cattle ranch. Later, rice was grown in the area and now it has returned to taro cultivation. In fact, fifty percent of all of Hawai'i's poi comes from the taro root grown here.

The name *Princeville* was given in the 1860's when Kamehameha IV and his wife, Queen Emma, visited Wyllie's home and plantation along with their young son, Prince Ka Haku o Hawai'i. Upon his death in 1865, Wyllie bequeathed the estate to a nephew. However the estate was deeply in debt and the young fellow was so overwhelmed that he committed suicide. In 1867 the lands were auctioned off. The area later became a cattle ranch and was then sold in 1968 for resort development. Today the Princeville Resort Community occupies 9,000 acres and is a mix of private homes, several vacation rental condominiums, golf courses, and the flagship *Princeville Resort Hotel*.

In 1969, the first major development of the Princeville Resort area began with the State of Hawai'i reclassifying 995 acres from agricultural to urban. There were 532 acres zoned for single and multi-family housing and hotel development, and the remaining 463 acres would become the Makai Golf Club. The 27 hole golf course opened in July 1971 and by 1973, Golf Digest had already selected this course as one of "America's greatest 100 courses." In 1976 the Princeville Airstrip was completed and provided service until 1997. By 1983 the Princeville Shopping Center had expanded to 66,000 square feet and construction began that same year on the *Princeville Resort Hotel.*

The resort opened in September 1985. In 1987 the first nine holes of the *Prince Golf Course* officially opened and by July 1990, the full 18-holes of the course were complete. Between 1989 and 1993 various renovations and improvements were made to the Princeville Resort Hotel.

The Princeville Resort Hotel is worth stopping by to stroll through the lobby and public areas. With a European flare, this outstanding resort is located on a picture perfect location in Princeville. There are gorgeous views across Hanalei Bay and the North Shore area and the surrounding interior mountain peaks. Enjoy afternoon tea in their lobby lounge or plan on splurging for Sunday brunch or the Friday evening seafood buffet at their Cafe Hanalei restaurant. See the review of this property under the accommodations section which follows. It is a very elegant and beautiful hotel with most attractive lobby and public areas.

Just past the entrance to Princeville Resort area is the *Princeville Center*. This small but busy resort shopping center features *Chuck's Steak House*, *Foodland* grocery, a medical center, and assorted shops make for interesting strolling. Foodland has a very good deli with hearty sandwiches to take along on your picnic lunch. *Hale O'Java* serves up a great espresso along with pizza, pasta and sandwiches in their outdoor dining area. The owner has *Paradise Grill & Bar* here as well. There's also a *Lappert's Hawaii Ice Cream Shop* next to the Foodland grocery store. Back on the highway and just past the shopping center

PRINCEVILLE HOTEL

on the left is the scenic lookout for the Hanalei Valley and Hanalei Wildlife Refuge. Be sure to pull off here to admire the beautiful panorama and take some photos of the Hanalei Valley and the checkerboard pattern of taro patches filling the valley floor.

HANALEI

The **Hanalei Wildlife Refuge** was established on 917 acres in 1972 and is located in the Hanalei Valley. Unique to many refuges, taro is allowed to be commercially farmed on a portion of the property and one permit is granted for cattle grazing. Administered by the U.S. Fish and Wildlife Service as a unit of the National Wildlife Refuge System, they actively manage the habitat to provide wetlands for endangered Hawaiian waterbirds. There are 49 species of birds, including the endangered Hawaiian black-necked stilt, gallinule, coot, and duck that make their home here. Of the 49 species, 18 are introduced. There are no native mammals, reptiles, or amphibians, except possibly the Hawaiian bat. Historic farming (taro) and grazing practices are compatible with the refuge's objectives and thus are permitted to a limited degree.The refuge is not open to the public, but this interpretive overlook on the state highway allows an excellent photo opportunity.

About one-half mile past the Wildlife Refuge lookout is another unmarked pull-off area along side the road. It's worth a stop to get a glimpse of this beautiful valley. At the base of the hill you'll cross the rustic, circa 1912, one-lane bridge into the Hanalei Valley. (The bridge is periodically closed for hours or even days when heavy rains cause the river to rise and partially submerge the bridge.) You can imagine why Peter, Paul, and Mary chose this magical place for their enchanted dragon, Puff, although they distorted the name slightly -- no doubt for better lyrical flow. Look off to the mountains for the many small waterfalls which glisten down the cliffs. The Hanalei River is a popular location for kayaking.

Many notable personalities have homes in quiet Hanalei. Sylvester Stallone, Michael Crichton, and Graham Nash (of Crosby, Stills, Nash & Young) among others.

At the first stop in Hanalei town are a couple of shops which merge with the *Hanalei Dolphin*, one of the area's more popular restaurants. *Kai Kane* offers some interesting selections of aloha wear for gentlemen and ladies. Upstairs you'll find surf equipment for sale. The adjoining *Ola's* has glassware and other unusual gift items. *Postcards Cafe* is located in what was once a small museum. This is a small, very attractive restaurant with dining on the veranda or indoors. *Hanalei Town Farmers Market* is a mobile farmers market located on the lot across the street from Postcards and in front of *Kayak Kaua'i*. Michael O'Reilly Rowan offers an array of locally grown, organic fruits and vegetables and is open Tuesday-Sunday from 7 am to 7 pm. His mobile *Hanalei Juice Co.* is "parked" next door. A short hop down the road and you'll find the hub of activity in Hanalei. *Tahiti Nui* is a restaurant that also presents a weekly luau. The *Hanalei Wake Up Cafe* is a little hole-in-the-wall eatery, but offers what may be the best

French toast in Hawai'i. The Wake Up is currently open only for breakfast and lunch. *Zelo's* is on this corner of Hanalei and this intersection is now a happening spot. Their sister restaurant, *Sushi Blues & Grill* (just steps away at the Ching Young Center) now competes with Zelo's with their own live entertainment. Hanalei is really developing into something of an eclectic dining hotspot.

Hanalei means "lei shaped." *The Hanalei Pier* is a scenic location, and one you'll no doubt remember if you saw the movie *South Pacific*. The wooden pier was constructed in 1892 and then 30 years later was reinforced with concrete. It was used by the local farmers for shipping their rice until it was closed in 1933. In 1979, the pier joined other landmarks in the National Register of Historic Places. The pier was recently reconstructed and reinforced. To actually reach the Hanalei Pier and the parking areas along Hanalei Bay turn right on Aku Road or on Malalo Road. Both take you down to Weke Road which runs parallel to the bay.

In 1996, Smithsonian archaeologists began surveying and excavating a wreck in Hanalei Bay at the mouth of the Wai'oli Stream. *Cleopatra's Barge*, a ship which sank April 5, 1824, was once a royal vessel as well as the first ocean-going passenger ship constructed in the U.S. The Crowinshiled family had the 100 foot ship built in New England in 1816 at a cost of $50,000. In 1820 the ship was sold to Liholiho (King Kamehameha II) in trade for $80,000 worth of sandalwood and was renamed *Ha'aheo o Hawai'i*, or the Pride of Hawai'i. Four years after the purchase, the royal yacht ran aground on a reef and sank (reportedly the captain and crew were drunk when the ship broke free from its moorings). The team was ready to terminate the search when a massive hull timber was located. Further excavation will continue. The current research is supported by the Kaua'i Historical Society and the Princeville Resort Hotel.

Continuing through the town of Hanalei is an assortment of restaurants and shops to meet most of the visitors needs. One shop, *on the road to Hanalei* offers browseable gifts and other items and *Evolve Love Artists Gallery* next door continues where the former Hawaiian Artists Guild left off.

At the *Ching Young Center* you'll find a variety store, natural foods store, pizza restaurant, and a Big Save Market which has a Subway inside. *Hanalei Mixed Plate* has become a mainstay in downtown Hanalei offering hearty portions of local style plate lunches affordably priced. *Sushi Blues & Grill* is located upstairs. Check out *Paradise Adventures*, operated by Byron and Dot Fears. They are former activity operators and now operate a gift shop and book island activities as well as B&Bs and vacation rentals (over 75 guest lodgings); (808) 826-9999 or toll free 1-888-886-4969, fax (808) 826-9998, Email: whales@aloha.net or website <www.paradise-adventures.com>

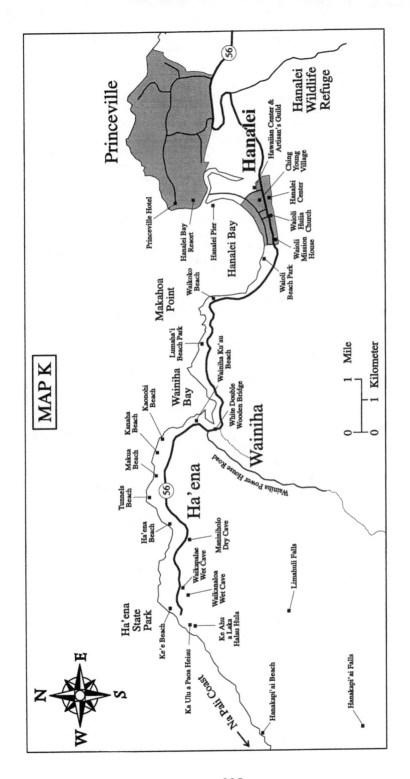

MAP K

Princeville

Hanalei

Hanalei Wildlife Refuge

Princeville Hotel

Hanalei Bay Resort

Hanalei Pier

Hanalei Bay

Waikoko Beach

Makahoa Point

Lumaha'i Beach Park

Waikoko Beach

Hawaiian Center & Artisan's Guild

Ching Young Village

Hanalei Center

Waioli Huiia Church

Waioli Mission House

Waioli Beach Park

Wainiha Bay

Kaonohi Beach

Kanaha Beach

Makua Beach

Wainiha Ku'au Beach

White Double Wooden Bridge

Wainiha

Tunnels Beach

Ha'ena Beach

Ha'ena

Maniniholo Dry Cave

Waikapalae Wet Cave

Waikanaloa Wet Cave

Limahuli Falls

Wainiha Power House Road

Ha'ena State Park

Ke'e Beach

Ke Ahu a Laka Halau Hula

Ka Ulu a Paoa Heiau

Hanakapi'ai Beach

Na Pali Coast

Hanakapi'ai Falls

N E S W

0   1   Mile
0   1   Kilometer

Across the street, the old Hanalei school has been converted to art and clothing shops and the *Hanalei Gourmet Cafe & Deli*. The school, built in 1926, is listed in the National Register of Historic Places. Adjoining is the Hanalei Center where you'll find *Bambo Bamboo* and *Neide's Salsa & Samba*, a small Mexican-/Brazilian eatery. Fronting the complex is the old *Hanalei Coffee Company*, *Shave Ice Paradise*, and *Bubba's Burgers*. Perhaps the most interesting shop is *Yellowfin Trading*. It is tucked in the back, a little harder to find, but worth the hunt. They have Hawaiiana collectibles and antiques along with some unusual gift items.

Following the road through town, you will pass the green Wai'oli Church and the Wai'oli Mission House. **Wai'oli Mission House** is open to the public Tuesdays, Thursdays and Saturdays. Listed in the National Register of Historic Places, the home is open between 9 am and 2:45 pm. The original coral church was built in 1837 with Reverend William Alexander the first clergyman on the North Shore. In 1846, Abner and Lucy Wilcox arrived here as missionaries and while the church was founded in 1834, the present green and white **Wai'oli Church** was not built until 1921. The Wilcox family established themselves on the North Shore and it was Abner and Lucy's three granddaughters that initiated the restoration of the church in 1921. The one-hour guided tour is taken on a walk-in basis with donations welcomed at the end of the visit. Sunday services performed in English and Hawaiian are fascinating. To tour the property for groups of twelve or more, please write or call in advance. Grove Farm in Lihu'e operates the tours here. Call them at (808) 245-3202 for more information and reservations; Grove Farm, PO Box 1631, Lihu'e, HI 96766.

The *Hanalei Farmers Market* is held each Saturday morning at the Hanalei Community Center next to the soccer playing fields next to Wai'oli Church, Kuhio Highway at Malolo Street. There are various local farmers and backyard gardeners from the area with fresh fruits, veggies, and various other produce for sale. It's a good place to pick up fresh bananas, papaya, and whatever else might be in season. Free parking available.

A new landmark in Hanalei is poised along the side of the Kuhio Highway, at the former Hawaiian Tel switching station. An enormous poi pounder, which began as a 1,500 pound boulder, now graces the front yard of the new **Hanalei Poi Company**. Partners Beno Fitzgerald and Hobey Beck plan to produce enough poi to saturate the Kaua'i market. They will begin by processing 2,000-4,000 pounds of taro each week and increase as demand improves! (Not open to the public.) Check the local grocery stores and markets for fresh Hanalei Poi. Once you try it, you'll never eat the stuff in the plastic bags again. It's that good. In fact, the company how markets the poi statewide via supermarkets and other outlets.

The next few miles are dotted with one lane bridges, but just before mile marker 5 is the lookout to *Lumaha'i Beach*. The east end of Lumaha'i Beach, Kahalahala (which means pandanus trees), is where Mitzi Gaynor filmed her famous "wash that man right out of my hair" scene. At mile marker 5 there is a very small pullout along the road that offers an unbeatable photo opportunity. The state recently (2001) acquired the land immediately behind the beach so public access and improvements may be in store but don't look for changes real soon.

The *Lumaha'i Valley* was once populated with Hawaiians. But it was the Japanese who farmed the first taro. Later immigrants cultivated rice. The 23 square mile area is now used for cattle grazing.

Wainiha Beach is a known shark breeding ground and not recommended for swimming or water activities. Pass the Wainiha "Last Chance" store and pick up a cold drink or sandwich. It was in this valley in the 19th century that 65 persons reported their ethnicity as "menehune." A few miles beyond Wainiha Beach is Powerhouse Road: just before mile marker 7, you'll see the road (and road sign) turn off to climb inland through the valley. The road travels through some beautiful, not-to-be-missed scenery and ends at the Powerhouse. Built in 1906, it served to provide irrigation for the McBryde Sugar Company.

HA'ENA

Here is the last vestige of civilization. The *Hanalei Colony Resort* is a quiet getaway.

Now you are entering the Ha'ena area of Kaua'i. *Camp Naue*, a four-acre camp operated by the YMCA, is located between the 7 and 8 mile markers. More information on accommodations will follow under rental information.

Mile marker 8 indicates you have reached *Makua Beach*. You will probably see cars parked alongside the main road and on a short sandy side road. Makua is one of the most popular beaches on the North Shore and is commonly referred to as Tunnels Beach. You can also park down at Ha'ena Beach Park and walk down to Tunnels. While this is among the safest beaches on the North Shore and offers fair snorkeling, there can be strong rip currents even during small surf.

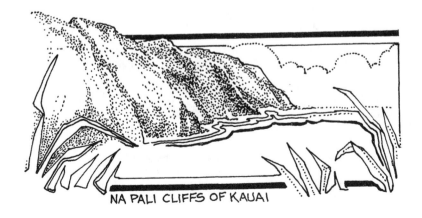

NA PALI CLIFFS OF KAUAI

To cite an example: some years ago, on a boat trip on a day when the surf was fairly calm, a young, muscular male member from our boat tour was caught up in the rip current and while struggling with a face mask which had a broken strap, had to be pulled into shore by one of the crew. Always use caution on Kaua'i's many beautiful beaches. Beauty can be deceptive and we don't want any of our readers to become a statistic! In the past many tour boats that departed from Hanalei would travel up here for a snorkeling trip. (Now new regulations prohibit the departures from Hanalei Bay, so boats coming out of Port Allen don't venture up this far.)

Throughout the North Shore area, you will notice many of the houses are up on concrete stilts. This area has been struck hard by the tsunamis of 1946 and 1957. The stilts makes it a long walk up to carry the groceries and anything else, but gives the homeowners the added benefits of obtaining limited home owners insurance. Whether this precaution will serve its purpose should another tsunami strike the area, will hopefully never be tested. *Ha'ena Beach Park* is a five-acre park maintained by the County of Kaua'i. The foreshore here is steep and therefore the dangerous shorebreak makes it inadvisable for swimming or bodysurfing. Although you may see some bodysurfing done here, it is not for the novice.

Across the road from Ha'ena Beach Park is *Maninolo Dry Cave*. This lava tube was a sea cave in earlier centuries when the sea was higher. You can travel several hundred yards and emerge at the other end. We were told that the cave was larger before it was filled in with sand by the tsunami that hit the island in 1957. Maninolo Dry Cave, according to one legend, was created by the mene-hune who had caught a great quantity of fish. There were too many fish to take them all home in one trip, so they carried as much as they could to their home in the mountain planning to return later for the rest of their catch. When they returned they discovered the remaining fish had been stolen. The menehune noticed a small hole in the mountain which was a clue to the path that the fish thieves had taken. The menehune proceeded to dig out the thieves and the result was this dry cave. Another legend credits the goddess Pele who traveled along the Napali coast searching for fire in the earth. She fell in love with Lohiau, the high chief of Kaua'i, but the couple could not be together until Pele found fire beneath Kaua'i, so she began to dig in search of it. She was unsuccessful and left Lohiau to go to the island of Hawai'i. The "caves" were the result of her efforts. The inner room was used as a meeting chamber by chieftains.

Limahuli Gardens is one of three gardens on Kaua'i which are a part of the National Tropical Botanical Garden and is open to the public. It is located 7/10 of a mile from Ha'ena Park and is well marked with a sign and a HVB marker. This magnificent site, surrounded by towering mountains and breathtaking natural beauty, receives an annual rainfall of 80 to more than 200 inches. Within Limahuli Valley are two important ecosystems -- the lowland rain forest and the mixed mesophytic forest. Together these two ecosystems are the natural habitat of over 70% of Kaua'i's (59% of Hawai'i's) endangered plant species. Thus, Limahuli Garden is vitally important as a botanical and horticultural resource.

The Garden emphasizes rare and endangered plants of Hawai'i, as well as plants of ethno-botanical value. Limahuli Gardens is also a part of an archaeologically significant site known as the Limahuli complex. The entire area has a rich history, and a series of ancient stone terraces, believed to be well over 700 years old, are visible at the garden. The oldest taro patches in Hawai'i are also located here. Limahuli Gardens encompasses 17 acres, and was gifted to the NTBG by Juliet Rice Wichman in the mid-1970's. An additional 990 acres behind the garden are set aside as a natural preserve. In 1994 the gardens were opened up to tours on a limited basis. In the future there is the possibility that they may open up a trail to the 800-foot Limahuli Falls. Guided tours are currently available only by reservation for $15. Self-guided tours include a descriptive booklet and the cost is $10 per person. It's well worth the admission. It's a very scenic, serene park, the tropical plants are beautiful and well-managed, and surrounding mountain scenery is inspiring. Currently open Tuesday-Friday and Sundays from 9:30 am-4 pm. They have recently added a gift shop which features books, posters, and shirts. Parking area and restroom facilities are available. Picnic lunches are prohibited. (808) 826-1053.

Just beyond Limahuli Steam are the *Waikapala'e Wet Caves,* accessible by a short hike up and behind the gravel parking area. One of the caves has a fresh water pool and is a unique phenomenon. The Waikapala'e (the name is commonly thought to mean water of the lace fern) Wet Cave has a cool shady cave known as the blue room. It requires a venture into the chilly waters and, depending on the water height, possibly an underwater swim through a submerged tunnel. This is one adventure we have yet to try, but we are told it is an inspiring experience. (Be cautious, however, many drownings or near-drownings have occurred here.) Apparently the reflection of the light through the tunnel causes the incredible blue effect on the cavern walls. The second wet cave, the *Waikanaloa Cave*, is located roadside. This cave is salt water and not suitable for swimming.

Keʻe Beach is the end of your scenic drive (mile marker 10) and beyond is the Napali Coast, 11 miles of which are accessible by foot along the *Kalalau Trail*. (Note: Correct spelling is Napali, not Na Pali, as verified by Hawaiian linguist and historian Mary Kawena Pukui.) See the recreation chapter for a brief description of this scenic trail. Charges of $10 per person per day for use of campgrounds along the Kalalau Trail. See camping section for details.

While some have remarked that this is the most beautiful trail in the world, be forewarned that the Sierra Club rates the 11 mile hike to the Kalalau Valley as a "ten" on their scale of difficulty. The shorter hike to Hanakapiʻai is a partial day hike and more suited to the recreational hiker.

Keʻe Beach currently has no lifeguard service and dangerous water conditions. Swimming and snorkeling are only recommended during very calm conditions and then using common sense.

Above the beach, a walk of about 5 or 10 minutes will take you to remnants of ancient Hawaiian villages and the *Kaulu o Laka Heiau*. This sacred altar is set among the cliffs of Napali and was built for Laka, the goddess of hula. It is one of the dramatic sites on the island with views of the cliffs and ocean.

The people of Nuʻalolo Kai also left remnants of their shelters. The sandstone slabs were probably used as foundations for a pole and thatch house. The people that lived in this area were agricultural. There is a low boggy area that may have grown taro. The reef fringing the area provide plenty of fish and shellfish for the inhabitants. The Bishop Museum conducted excavations in the area for five years beginning in 1959. They determined that this area had been continuously inhabited from 1380 until 1919. The *heiau* is still used today by hula halaus. Keʻe Beach is the end of your road, but a great place to begin an evening sunset!

BEST BETS

Princeville Resort - elegantly wonderful, what an ideal way to enjoy Paradise! *Sealodge* - affordable with an incredible view of the Kilauea lighthouse. *Hanalei Bay Resort* - Multiple amenities with views of Bali Hai and a lagoon swimming pool. *Hanalei Colony Resort* - a very pleasant resort with a fantastic location near the end of the North Shore road, great beaches, great mountain views, great peace and quiet, superb location.

PRIVATE VACATION HOMES & COTTAGES

The North Shore has a plethora of homes to meet most any need or group size and there are almost as many rental agents to assist you. Following are a few homes and cottages that proved of special interest.

ALOHA CONDOS
78-261 Manukai Street, #203, Kailua-Kona, HI 96740. Toll free 1-877-782-5642, (503) 285-2127, Fax (503) 438-8272; Email: Jim@AlohaCondos.com; Web: <www.alohacondos.com> This condo booking service has fully equipped deluxe condos at Hanalei Bay Resort on the North Shore; available at reduced rates directly from the owners.
Rates: $90-150 nightly

ALOHA SUNRISE INN
4899A Waiakalua Street, PO Box 79, Kilauea, HI 96754. Toll free 1-888-828-1008, (808) 828-1100/828-6170, Fax (808) 828-2199; Email: atp@hawaiian.net; Web: <www.kauaisunrise.com> This is a quiet and romantic 1-bedroom/1-bath cottage on a lush ten-acre estate on the stunning North Shore of the Garden Island, near the town of Kilauea. The enchanted setting is sure to please honeymooners and those seeking seclusion and privacy.
Rates: $85-115 nightly

AN ANGEL ABODE ★
4064 Ka'ahumanu Place, PO Box 3597, Princeville, HI 96722. Tel/fax (360) 456-4040; Email: gail@travelkauai.com; <www.travelkauai.com> This is a private custom-designed modern vacation rental home with three large bedrooms, each with private bath. Rooms have large picture windows and French doors opening onto a lanai providing distant ocean and mountain views. Located in the prestigious activity-oriented Princeville Resort, convenient to golf, tennis, ocean activities, hiking and exploring the North Shore area.
Rates: $95-150 per night; $325 per night for whole house

ANCHORAGE POINT
Located in Ha'ena. RENTAL AGENT: Na Pali Properties 1-800-715-7273. This 2 BR 2 BTH home is elevated with a spacious living/kitchen/dining room offering a panoramic ocean view. It resembles a large cabin with simple furnishings. One of the bedrooms has an adjoining shower large enough to hold a small party. The location of this is a plus and the ocean view couldn't get much better. There is some need for a bit of updating, but the price is a plus.
Rates: $1,050-1,250 per week for two, $300 deposit, $85 cleaning fee.

ANINI BEACH COTTAGES
PO Box 837, Hanalei, HI 96714. Toll free 1-800-323-4450, (808) 828-0068, Fax (808) 828-2067; Email: cottage@aloha.net; Web: <www.aloha.net/~cottage> This north shore accommodation offers four separate guest cottage accommodations: Plumeria is fully equipped and sleeps 6 people; Orchid Guest Cottage sleeps 3 people; The Lily Pad and Mango Cottage each sleep 2 people. All amenities provided for a relaxing vacation; located in the Kaua'i's famed North Shore area. Minimum stay 4 nights.
Rates: $125-175 nightly; inquire on weekly or monthly rates

211

ANINI BEACH HALE

PO Box 419, Kilauea, HI 96754. Toll free 1-877-COCONUT (262-6688), (808) 828-6808; Email: aloha@yourbeach.com; Web: <www.yourbeach.com> This is a modern well-equipped 2-bedroom/2-bath vacation home located just 100 paces from Anini Beach. This non-smoking home is set amidst the exclusive enclave of vacation homes at Anini Beach. It sleeps four in two king beds. Fully and comfortably furnished with kitchen, living room, laundry, dishwasher, and all the amenities. Enjoy one of Kaua'i's best beaches and calm lagoon waters for swimming, snorkeling, kayaking, fishing or just lounging on the sandy shores. *Rates: $1200 weekly (1 week minimum stay)*

ANNE'S CONDOS & STUDIOS AT PRINCEVILLE RESORT

4890 Ka Haku Road, Princeville, HI 96722. Toll free 1-800-481-4991 or (760) 753-2763; Web: <www.choice1.com/Princeville_Golf_Condo.htm> Email: annkauai@gte.net; These nicely furnished condo units and studios are conveniently located right on the Princeville Resort Golf Course. Golf nuts will enjoy the easy access to the links. It's also close to beaches, scenic look-outs, waterfalls, botanical gardens, hiking trails, adventure activities, area dining and shopping. *Rates: Studio $60 and up nightly, $400 and up weekly; Condo unit $85 and up nightly, $550 and up weekly*

CONDOS KAUA'I

3880 Wyllie Road, Princeville, HI 96722; mailing address 6313 O'Bannon Drive, Las Vegas, NV 89146. Toll free 1-877-528-2411, Fax (702) 248-4345; Email: manager@condoskauai.com; Web: <www.condoskauai.com> This is a privately owned two-bedroom/two-bath non-smoking luxury condo unit with all amenities. There are panoramic views just minutes away from a secluded beach and easy access to golf course, area attractions, shopping, dining, etc. Unit sleeps 6 adults. *Rates: $150-200 nightly*

KILAUEA LIGHTHOUSE

DEVAKI'S VACATION RENTAL
PO Box 622, Hanalei, HI 96714. (808) 826-6735; Email: kevdev@poi.net; Web: < www.devaki-kauai.com/hanalei-vacation-rental > This is a spacious one-bedroom beach house located directly across from Hanalei Bay with a backdrop of mountains and waterfalls. The unit has a large two-person outdoor shower plus large indoor bathroom also with a two-person shower as well as fully equipped kitchen. Amenities include king bed, comfortable sofa and loveseat, laundry, TV/VCR, private lanai and BBQ and much more. There is also a separate studio offering privacy for one or two people. Lots of natural lighting and air circulation. Carpeted room has sliding glass doors that open to a small private lanai. There is a fold out futon mattress, small refridge, microwave and bathroom with shower. Host is a personal fitness trainer who can provide healing massage and traditional Hawaiian Lomi Lomi massage.
Rates: Beach House $750 weekly; Studio $60 nightly

GLO MANOR HOUSE ★
PO Box 221, Kilauea, HI 96754. (808) 828-6684; Email: glomanor@hawaiian.net; Web: < www.hawaiian.net/ ~ glomanor > This is a private seaside 8,000 sq.ft. manor house located at the end of Anini Beach on Kaua'i's picturesque north shore. The beach and lagoon, with a resemblance to those of Tahiti, is protected by a large outer reef making for safe swimming, snorkeling and great beach-combing. There are two separate guest studios and an 1,800 sq. ft. 2-bedroom apartment, all fully furnished and equipped. The King's Place is a 2 bedroom/2 bath apartment unit. The Garden Studio has a king bed, kitchen and bath. The Crow's Nest studio has a queen bed and private bath.
Rates: King's Place $115 nightly; Garden Studio $75 nightly; Crow's Nest $65 nightly

HALE HONU TOWNHOUSES
4800 Hanalei Plantation Road, PO Box 223414, Princeville, HI 96722. Toll free 1-888-686-1084, (808) 826-1084, Fax (603) 754-7027; Email: coral-c@aloha.net; Web: < www.aloha.net/ ~ coral-c > There are two well-kept and attractive 3-bedroom, 2-bath vacadion condo units in the Princeville Resort on the Makai Golf Course. Great location for golfers or anyone wanting a convenient North Shore locaton. It's a short walk to the beach from these fully equipped units with kitchens, dining rooms, lanai, laundry facilities, etc.. The two townhouses can accommodate a group of up to 15 people. Great for families.
Rates: $92 nightly (max. 4), $650 weekly; inquire about large group rates

HALE STEWARD ★
5150 Kahiliholo Road, Kilauea, HI 96754, mailing address: PO Box 722, Cardiff by the Sea, CA 92007. (760) 402-0104, Fax (760) 436-6500; Email: hilarystew@aol.com; Web: < www.atlas-iap.es/halesteward > This is a luxurious 3-bedroom, 3-bath country plantation-style home on 5 acres. It overlooks the Kalihiwai River with panoramic views of the ocean and surrounding mountains of north Kaua'i. Sleeps 6-8 people.
Rates: From $1,000 weekly; call/contact for availability and rates

HAMAGUCHI HALE ★

5283 Malolo Place, PO Box 1647, Hanalei, HI 96714. Toll free 1-800-487-9833, (808) 826-7288; Email: rentals@aloha.net; Web: <www.hanalei-vacations.com/hamaguchi> This country home has three separate vacation rental units located close to the water's edge on Hanalei Bay and within walking distance of Hanalei town attractions. Great tropical views in peaceful surroundings of Hanalei. The three Asian-Hawaiian units are fully equipped for comfort. The Hale Makai is a studio with queen bed, private bath and casual kitchen. The Hale Makua is a master suite with king bed, whirlpool bath and gourmet kitchen. Moana Hale is a 3-bedroom unit with full size beds, 2 baths, and a casual kitchen.

Rates: Hale Makai $135 nightly, $800 weekly; Hale Makua $150 nightly, $900 weekly; Moana Hale $150 nightly, $900 weekly; entire Hamaguchi Hale (5 bedrooms) $400 nightly, $2,600 weekly

HANALEI PROPERTIES ★

PO Box 748, Hanalei, HI 96714. (808) 826-6111; Email: HanaleiBay@aol.com This agency has three distinctive vacation rental homes available in historic Hanalei town. The Plantation Guest House is an upscale, ocean view home. The Bed, Breakfast & Beach Home is a moderately priced home just 125-yards from beautiful Hanalei Beach. Tutu's (Grandma's) Cottage is a private two bedroom, one bath home that sleeps four people.

Rates: Plantation Guest House $130 per night; Bed, Breakfast & Beach House $75-125 per night; Tutu's Cottage is $850 per week for two people

HARDY'S HAPPY HULA HUT

PO Box 3400, Princeville, HI 96722. (808) 826-7168 or (510) 444-2913; Web: <www.planet-hawaii.com/hula_hut> Email: hardy@aloha.net, or hardyic@aol.com; This is a comfortable one bedroom condo unit with a fantastic cliffside oceanview. It's located in the resort community of Sealodge at Princeville. Next door to the complex pool and there is a secluded beach down the path. The unit is fully equipped with kitchen, laundry, TV/VCR, king bed, etc. Easy access to all area activities, golf, tennis, hiking on North Shore, shopping, dining, etc.

Rates: $90 nightly, weekly rates available (3 night minimum stay)

JUNGLE CABANA & JUNGLE BUNGALOW ★

Paradise Adventures, the Kaua'i Adventure Company. PO Box 1379, Hanalei, HI 96714. Toll free 1-888-886-4969 or (808) 826-9999, FAX (808) 826-9998. Email: whales@aloha.net; Web: <www.junglebungalow.com> or <www.junglecabana.com> *Wir sprechen Deutsch!* The Jungle Bungalow & Jungle Cabana are privately situated on 2.25 acres of lushly landscaped jungle alongside a rushing mountain stream with Wainiha Valley as a backdrop. Located a few minutes drive to beaches, 10 minutes to Hanalei or the Napali Coast.

The Jungle Bungalow is a secluded modern structure with charm of a different style. If you seek the "tropical style" and like to kick back in a hammock, listen to birds sing and the sound of the rushing river and think that relaxing in a claw foot tub located outside in a beautiful garden is bliss, then this is the place for you. This two story accommodation sleeps up to five guests. There is a complete kitchen with quality cookware. It provides total privacy for those needing a bit of quiet romance. Mountain views and private gardens compliment the tropical atmosphere. *Rates: $125 per night dbl, $800 per week; extra nights $115; extra guests $10 each/$50 week; (4 night minimum stay)*

Jungle Cabana is a cozy first class studio-style lodging with about 350 square feet of interior space which is paneled primarily in woven bamboo, trimmed with bamboo accents. It opens up to soothing views of the rushing mountain stream and spectacular Wainiha Pali (cliffs). The tropical Zen-type decor is enhanced with bamboo sofa and furniture. There is a complete kitchen that also offers that rushing jungle stream as a view! The main living space is the "nature that surrounds." Bathing is in a private riverside garden setting with claw foot tub and shower. Here you can surely transcend reality and enjoy a private and romantic setting! *Rates: $95 per night; $625 per week; extra nights $90; (4 night minimum stay)*

KAI MANA COTTAGE ★
Mailing address: PO Box 612, Kilauea, HI 96754, Toll free reservations 1-800-837-1782, or (808) 828-1280; Email: scash@aloha.net; Web: < www.kai-mana.com >. Kai Mana is a private 1BR/1BTH cottage available as a vacation rental with a 5 night minimum stay. Located near the end of a quiet cul-de-sac in rural Kilauea just west of Kilauea Lighthouse, the wildlife refuge and above Secret or Kauapea Beach. This is the personal retreat of author Shakti Gawain who has written some of her books here. The unique circular-designed cottage has full kitchen, living room, deck, hot tub, shower, TV/VCR, etc. Hammock on the lanai plus lounges, chairs, table, beach gear and BBQ. Overlooks a secluded beach with a private trail (steep but well developed staircase) leading down to the beach. Great for private sunning, beachcombing, super sunsets. Very private with tasteful Hawaiian decor. *Rates: $250 nightly, $1500 weekly, plus $105 cleaning fee and refundable $250 security deposit fee*

KAUAI KONDO
PO Box 974, Kapa'a, HI 96746. (708) 366-5023, or tel/fax (808) 826-0130; Email: krautwright@juno.com; < www.kauaikondo.com > This is a 2-bedroom, 1.5 bath condo unit located in Princeville Resort and near all the attractions and activities of the North Shore. Minutes away from beaches, hiking, botanical gardens, golf, tennis, shopping and dining and much more. Complex has pool, hot tub, sauna and BBQ grills. Units are fully equipped, kitchen, laundry, etc. *Rates: $65 nightly, $420 weekly.*

KAUIKEOLANI ESTATE AND HANALEI PLANTATION COTTAGES ★
PO Box 81, Hanalei, HI 96714. Toll free 1-888-900-1454, (808) 826-1454, FAX (808) 826-6363; Email: halelea@aloha.net; Web: < www.hanaleiland.com >. Kauikeolani, the historic beachside plantation home of Albert Spencer Wilcox, has stood for over one hundred years. Wilcox was a successful turn-of-the-century sugar planter and the fourth son of missionaries Abner and Lucy Wilcox. The estate is bounded by the Hanalei River and guests can look out upon a lovely

and expansive lawn to the beautiful wide beach fronting Hanalei Bay. Mountains of the surrounding Hanalei Valley provide additional panoramic views. The estate has been restored with great attention to detail and the historic era of the 1890's when it was built. The name Kauikeolani means "vision that come in the early morning mist" and the home was named after Albert's wife, Emma Kauikeolani Napoleon Mahelona. The estate includes the main Kauikeolani 7-bedroom home, plus four other 2BR and 3BR cottages: Palaka, Umetsu, Paniolo and Nalu. These cottages were the housing provided for the plantation worker families in the early days of the estate. The main home and all cottages are strictly non-smoking. - Special day rates are available for banquets, incentive groups, and weddings. 3 night minimum for all cottages plus cleaning charges apply on all rentals. This is a very special and historic place. *Rates: Kauikeolani Main Home, 7BR (max 12), $1,200 night, $7,000 week, $25,000 month*
Umetsu Cottage 2BR, (max 4), $250 night, $1,600 week, $5,000 month
Palaka Cottage 2 BR, (max 5), $200 night, $1,200 week,$4,000 month
Paniolo Cottage 3 BR (max 6), $400 night, $2,500 week, $8,000 month
Nalu Cottage 3 BR (max 6), $400, $2,500 week, $8,000 month

LANI AINA BEACH HALE ★
Located beachfront at Ha'ena. RENTAL AGENT: Na Pali Properties 1-800-715-7273. Unlike several other homes we toured, this 2 BR 2 BTH beach cottage was very welcoming. The bathrooms are contemporary and the new bed covers have brightened up the place making the bedrooms more cheery. A large yard offers plenty of room for active youths and roomy front porch and spacious glass doors provide an opportunity to sit and simply enjoy the oceanfront location. *$1,200-1,500 per week. $500 deposit, $100 outclean, sleeps 6.*

LOVE NEST COTTAGE
PO Box 167, Anahola, HI 96703. Toll free 1-877-828-1700; Email: thestars@gte.net; Web: < www.heavenlycreations.org/lovenest.htm > This secluded studio hideaway appeals to the romantically inclined. Beautiful interior decor, spacious and roomy, fully equipped kitchen, hammock for two, dining either indoor or outdoors. There is a queen canopy bed and extra sleeper sofa. Located on a tropical fruit and flower farm and within minutes to sparkling northeast coast beaches. Private jungle area for casual exploration. There is TV/VCR, a jacuzzi hot tub and full breakfast served each morning. Quiet and peaceful location for those intimate privacy-needed times.
Rates: $115 nightly; $690 weekly

NOHO KAI AT ANINI
3617 Anini Beach Road, Kilauea, HI 96754. Toll free 1-800-769-3285 access #00, (808) 828-2815; Email: jill@napanet.net; Web: < www.nohokai.com > This is a modern 3-bedroom/2 ½ bath home that can accommodate up to 6 people. It's just 75 steps from well known Anini Beach on Kaua'i's northeast shore. The two master suites have king beds, private bathrooms and open to the front lanai. The smaller bedroom has twin beds and a private lanai and a half-bath across the hall. The living room and kitchen are very spacious and open with high ceilings, fans and doors to the front lanai. Fully equipped with all the features, comforts and amenities for a pleasant relaxing stay.
Rates: $1450 weekly for 2 people; $125 extra person (1 week minimum stay)

OM ORCHARD RETREAT
4420 Kahili Makai, PO Box 1190, Kilauea, HI 96754. (808) 828-0111, Fax (808) 828-6758; Email: OM@aloha.net; Web: <www.omorchard.com> This is a comfortable and well-kept cottage featuring large glass windows with a nice nature view. The bedroom loft is a roomy 560 sq.ft. and the cottage is furnished in comfortable island-style decor and furniture. There is a large bathroom and a unique private outdoor lava rock shower surrounded by banana trees. Take your shower *a la natural!* There is also a fully furnished kitchenette with all amenities. *Rates: $150 nightly, $1600 per month (September to March); 3 night minimum stay*

PLANTATION MANAGERS HOME ★
Located on Hanalei Bay. RENTAL AGENT: Na Pali Properties 1-800-715-7273. We love it, we love it, we love it. This magical home was built at the turn of the century. Back then it was a ranch house with cattle roaming along the sweeping beachfront on Hanalei Bay. This elegant historic plantation home is furnished with koa wood pieces that are museum quality. With a huge front lawn stretching out to beautiful Hanalei you couldn't ask for more. The living area is roomy with a big screen television. The kitchen has been updated with new appliances, yet not so renovated as to destroy the classic style of this old plantation home. A bedroom and bathroom are located off the downstairs foyer and upstairs are a small bedroom and bathroom along with a master suite. The master bedroom offers large patio doors which open onto a small deck with a panoramic Pacific vistas. The master bath is spacious with a huge contemporary footed tub.

Story has it that when a tsunami struck some fifty years ago, it pushed the home several hundred yards farther from the beach. The '92 hurricane caused serious damage to surrounding homes, but amazingly this lovely home was spared all but slight water damage through the oceanfront doors. This sprawling plantation home, located on an oceanfront acre, may not be in your budget, but if it is, the *$3,500 per week* with $200 cleaning fee is worth it!

RIVER ESTATE
5-6691 Kuhio Highway, PO Box 169, Hanalei, HI 96714. Toll free 1-800-484-6030, security code 2468, or (808) 826-5118. Email: info@riverestate.com; Web: <www.riverestate.com> River Estate is a two acre riverfront botanical garden one block from a secluded beach on the famed North Shore of Kaua'i. This property specializes in private group retreats, honeymoons, weddings, family vacations, private gatherings, etc. The Guest House has two bedrooms, two baths; The Treehouse has three bedrooms, two baths. Units comes with full furnishings and are fully equipped for guest comfort and enjoyment. *Rates: $145 nightly and up*

SECRET BEACH ESTATE COTTAGES
2884 Kauapea Road, Kilauea, HI 96754. Toll free 1-800-820-2862, tel/fax (808) 828-2862; Email: mhughes@rof.net; Web: <www.secretbeachkauai.com> This country estate has three very modern, fully furnished luxury cottages for couples seeking privacy, romance or just place peace, quiet and tranquility. Each 1 BR cottage sleeps two and is well-appointed with contemporary furnishings and Hawaiian island-style decor accents. There is Hale Ke Aloha (Home of Love),

Hale Nanea (Home of Joy and Tranquility), and Hale Lani (Heavenly Home). The cottages are separated for full privacy. Each has a large lanai with outdoor furniture, outdoor jacuzzi, ceiling to floor sliding glass doors, fantastic ocean views, full kitchen, laundry, queen bed, BBQ, and coded gate entry. Very elegant fixtures and furnishings, great location on the hills just above the coast. *Rates: $395 nightly plus out-cleaning fee*

WAIOLI VACATION RENTAL
5539 Weke Road, PO Box 1261, Hanalei, HI 96714. (808) 826-6405; Email: amadeus@aloha.net; Web: < www.hawaiian.net/ ~ mahalo/hanalei > This is a nicely kept private 1 bedroom garden apartment unit for two people right in Hanalei just 150 yards from the beach at Hanalei Bay. It's ideal for honeymooners or those seeking seclusion and quiet. It has 800 sq. ft. of room, full kitchen, bath, master bedroom, laundry, TV/VCR, etc. All the amenities for a relaxing vacation are included. Hostess speaks English; *Wir sprechen Deutsch; On parle Francais. Rates: $107 nightly; $750 weekly*

BED & BREAKFAST

The following are some of the Bed & Breakfast options offered on the North Shore. See the end of this chapter under Rental Agents for companies that offer a wide range of B & B units around the island.

ALOHA AINA BED & BREAKFAST
PO Box 1232, Hanalei, HI 96714. (808) 828-1155; Email: iam@aloha.net This B&B is located on a secluded 3-acre estate in beautiful Kilauea with open mountain and ocean views. There are tropical fruit and flower gardens, a tranquil valley for walking, full kitchen, kingsize bed, Jacuzzi, stone lanai and all the expected comforts. *Rates: $80 nightly*

ALOHA PLANTATION ★
4481 Malulani Street, Kilauea, HI 96754, mailing address is PO Box 683, Hanalei, HI 96714. Toll free 1-877-658-6977 or (808) 828-1693; Email: alohaplantation@hawaiian.net; Web: < www.garden-isle.com/aloha > This is a vintage 1920-era plantation manager's home on the North Shore of Kaua'i. There are two guest rooms. One room has a double bed and shared shower. The second room has two double beds and a private bath. The home is decorated with old Hawaiian antiques including comfortable wrought iron beds with whispering ceiling fans overhead. There is a screened porch overlooking a tropical courtyard. *Rates: $50 nightly, room with shared shower; $60 nightly, room with private bath*

HALE 'AHA ★
3375 Kamehameha, PO Box 3370, Princeville, HI 96722. Toll free 1-800-826-6733 or (808) 826-6733, FAX (808) 826-9052. Email: kauai@pixi.com This is the only B & B overlooking the Prince Golf Course, located along 480 ft. of fairway. There is a nearby trail leading to a secluded beach. The upstairs house is reserved for guests; the living room is pretty and pastel with a cozy fireplace and dining area set up for breakfast. Rooms are cushy and comfy, everything is

very homey, especially the hospitality of your hostess, Ruth Bockelman. Breakfast is at 8:00, but she puts the coffee on at 7 for early risers who might want it with a muffin or cereal, on the run. But if you wait, you'll be treated to a full spread that includes hot homemade bread (with guava butter), muffins, fresh fruit, granola or cereal as well as a tropical smoothie, and even steamed brown rice with brown sugar, crushed almonds, raisins, and fruit plus a baked apple with whipped cream! Rooms have TV's, mini refrigerators, bathroom amenities and extra towels, and pillow. Guests are entitled to substantial golf discounts at the course. They take Visa and MC, but sorry, they don't take children. They provide a brochure that is very detailed and informative. The penthouse suite is the top floor of the property with 1,000 square feet of room, separate living area, large whirlpool tub and washer and dryer. Three night minimum stay.
Rates: $110-275 per night

HALE HO'O MAHA ★
2883 Kalihiwai Road, PO Box 422, Kilauea, HI 96754. Toll free 1-800-851-0291 or (808) 828-1341, Fax (808) 828-2046. E-mail: hoomaha@aloha.net; Web: < www.pixi.com/ ~ kauai > Located in a country farm-like setting (in fact a bull lives just down the road), surrounded by ponds and streams with the ocean and bay just a bit further. The decor is whimsical and eclectic with lots of wood and wood artifacts and an aquarium in the living room. Each room has a personality of its own: the Pineapple Room has a round bed with pineapple bedspread, rugs and knick-knacks, and the romantic guava room has a canopy bed with sheer, wispy draping. Breakfast includes Anahola Granola (made just a few miles away), muffins, and a plate of fresh fruit that not only offers papaya, pineapple, bananas and grapes, but winter seasonal rambutans, too! (They are like lichees with spikes!) Located on 5 acres, this home is within walking distance of two beaches. $20 per night charged for additional person. A 50% deposit is required to confirm your reservation for each room. Visa or Mastercard accepted. Your hosts are Toby & Kirby. *Rates: Four varied accommodations from $60-$85 per night, double or single occupancy.*

HALE LII ★
4620 B Kuawa Road, PO Box 545, Kuawa Orchard Estates, Kilauea, HI 96754. Tel/fax (808) 828-1064; Email: lynch@aloha.net; Web: < www.aloha.net/ ~ lynch > This is a private 3-acre farm surrounded by quiet flourishing tropical gardens. Nice views accent the cozy studio cottage. It offers complete privacy and the peace and quiet of Kaua'i's rural countryside. Convenient to Kilauea town dining and near to area shopping, attractions, activities.
Rates: $75-85 nightly

HALELUIA BY THE RIVER
PO Box 302, Kilauea, HI 96754. (808) 828-6813. Email: river@aloha.net. Owner Joy Finch provides three studios for vacation rentals. Her focus is Healing Hawaiian Vacations for couples or singles. Here you can stay in one of the river edge rentals, receive massages and go on hikes and island tours.
Rates are $50 for minimal view, $70 with private lana'i overlooking the river. $90 for a 1 BR with view and full amenities.

HALE MANU BED & BREAKFAST ★

Kokea Farm, Kilauea, mailing address PO Box 3500, Princeville, HI 96722. Toll free 1-888-828-6641 or (808) 828-6641; Web: <www.bnbweb.com/HaleManu.html> Hale Manu is on Kaua'i's spectacular North Shore in the middle of a 3-acre tropical gardener's paradise. All types of tropical plants, orchids, flowers, palms and more make Hale Manu a botanical garden and working flower farm. Lots of birds inhabit the area as well. There is a spacious one-bedroom guest apartment, nicely furnished with all the expected amenities and comforts.

Rates: $95 nightly

THE HISTORIC BED & BREAKFAST

PO Box 1662, Hanalei, HI 96714. (808) 826-4622. Email: jbshepd@alolha.ne> Built in 1901, this home is included in the National and State Historic Registry as the oldest Buddhist mission on Kaua'i. Following years of neglect, the building was scheduled for demolition. In 1985, a few local businessmen banded together and the building was moved across the island and converted into a residence. Over 95% of the original building was able to be saved. Rooms are furnished with antique bedding and *shoji* Japanese screen sliding doors that open onto the long hallway of polished wood. Located next to Postcards Cafe. Walking distance to the beach. Island style breakfasts.

Rates $59-68, 2 night minimum.

NORTH COUNTRY FARMS

PO Box 723, Kilauea, HI 96754, (808) 828-1513. FAX (808) 828-0805. E-mail: ncfarms@aloha.net; Web: <www.skyfamily.com/northcountryfarms>

North Country Farms is a four-acre organic vegetable, fruit, and flower farm surrounded by horse farms. The 1BR redwood guest cottage includes a full-service kitchenette for snacks and meals. Cottage has a covered lanai, queen bedroom, two futon/couches in living room, stereo CD, lots of games, books, puzzles, etc. Your host, Lee Roversi, adds that they are a family of five and love to open their farm to other families. The cottage and farm are completely child-friendly. Guests are invited to pick their own fruit and veggies; Aloha breakfast fixings provided each day of stay. As the guest house is a separate accommodation, it lends itself very well to a traveling family.

Rates: $95 per night

PAVILIONS AT SEACLIFF

Contact: Estate Manager, PO Box 3500-302, Princeville, HI 96722. (808) 828-1185, FAX (808) 828-1208. RENTAL AGENTS: 'Anini Beach Vacation Rentals 1-800-448-6333 or (808) 826-4000. Homes & Villas in Paradise 1-800-282-2736, (808) 262-4663. Prosser Realty 1-800-767-4707. The property is bordered by the Kilauea Point Wildlife Bird Refuge and Kilauea Lighthouse. The house offers 3 ocean view master suites and 3 1/2 baths. A lap pool with jacuzzi. Washer/dryer, fax machine, plus a complete workout room. Minimum 3 night stay. Rates are for up to 6 guests. 10% monthly discount. $1,000 deposit required.

Rates: $700/600 nightly

INEXPENSIVE

HALE MOI COTTAGES ★
5300 Ka Haku Rd., PO Box 899, Princeville, HI 96714. (808) 826-9602. RENTAL AGENTS: Marc Resorts 1-800-535-0085. Na Pali Properties 1-800-715-7273. Forty units in two story buildings. Hotel rooms, studio suites with kitchens, 1 1/2 bedroom suites with kitchens. Mountain and garden views. Full kitchens and washer/dryer, except in hotel units.

All have remodeled kitchens and bathrooms. The studios are spacious -- one very large room with a nice, full kitchen. The hotel units are actually mini suites with a small bedroom and living area. A tiny alcove provides some basic kitchen-type amenities: mini-fridge, coffee maker, microwave, eating utensils, glasses, cups, and dishes. The units are an interesting cross between a hotel room, condo unit, private cottage, and small apt.! They are just big "enough" with a charming cottage look, both inside and out. Located next door to Winds of Beamreach Restaurant. Check in at Pali Ke Kua office across the street.
Marc Resort Year Round Rates: Hotel Room Mt.V. $119 (2); Studio Suite Mt.V. w/ kitchen $149; One 1/2 Bedroom, 2 BTH Suite Mt.V. $169

HANALEI INN ★
5468 Kuhio Hwy., PO Box 1373, Hanalei, HI 96714. (808) 826-9333 or 826-1506. Owners are Michelle & Parnell Kaiser. Full kitchen, queen beds (3rd person or child okay on futon). Small, rustic apartments, clean and well-kept. Outdoor phone for free local calls. This place is strictly for the backpackers, nature freaks, adventurists, kayakers, hikers, surfers, etc. who require just a barebones roof over their heads, a sack and a shower. Just the basics, not for the fussy. *Rates: $65 per night; Unit without full kitchen $55*

GINGER

PANIOLO
Located in Princeville. RENTAL AGENT: Hanalei Vacations 1-800-487-9833. Cottages (2BR/2BTH), Studios and 1 BR/2 BTH condo units. Swimming pool. Short walk to shopping and beach.
Rates: Cottages (2BR/2BTH), Studio and 1 BR condo units $70-110 nightly

SANDPIPER VILLAGE
Located in Princeville. RENTAL AGENTS: Hanalei Vacations 1-800-487-9833; Oceanfront Realty 1-800-222-5541. This property offers hotel rooms, 1, 2, or 3 bedroom units. Pool and hot tub. Some 2 bedrooms have loft, and some units have washer/dryer. Not all rooms have phones.
Rates: Garden view studio units $75 nightly/$525 weekly; 2 BR plus loft $140 nightly plus outclean fee charged.

SEALODGE ★
Located in Princeville. RENTAL AGENTS: Carol Goodwin rents her J-7 unit with a fabulous view of the Kilauea Lighthouse (plus other units at Sealodge) Write: 3615 Kingridge Drive, San Mateo, CA 94403 or call (650) 573-0636. Oceanfront Realty 1-800-222-5541. Maui & All Island 1-800-663-6962. Hanalei Vacations 1-800-487-9833. Prosser 1-800-767-4707. Ocean view units located along the bluff at Princeville. The exterior is cedar shake which is reminiscent of accommodations on the Oregon beachfront. While each unit has a different view, those on the farther eastern end have a spectacular view of the Kilauea lighthouse and Pacific coastline. Watch the waves come in over the extensive reef, enjoy the seabirds frolicking in the air currents, or during the winter, enjoy this outstanding viewpoint from which to watch whales. Just make sure you pack your binoculars! The trail down to the beach is marked by a "use at your own risk" sign and is steep and very slippery when muddy and recommended only for the hale and hearty. The trail ends on a rocky shore and you will need to clamor over the rocks to your left to reach the crescent shaped stretch of white sand beach that is the length of a football field. Because of the enormous 'Anini reef, this piece of coastline is fairly well protected all year from high ocean swell and surf. With all the comforts of home, an outstanding vista, and value priced, you could hardly do better on the North Shore.
Rates: 1BR 1BTH $99 nightly/$693 weekly; 2BR 2BTH $125 nightly (Cleaning fee charged for stays of less than five nights).

MODERATE

ALII KAI I
3830 Edward Road, Princeville, HI 96722. RENTAL AGENTS: Kaua'i Paradise Vacations 1-800-826-7782. Hanalei Vacations 1-800-487-9833. Hanalei North Shore Properties 1-800-488-3336. Oceanfront Realty 1-800-222-5541. Two bedroom, two bath units, some ocean front. Depending on the owners, units furnished with two double beds, one queen, or one king. Most units have sleeper sofas. Some units have full-size washer/dryer. Pool.
Rates: 2 BR 2 BTH Deluxe $120-135 nightly/$840-945 weekly

ALII KAI II

3830 Edward Road, Princeville, HI 96722. On property management 1-800-648-9988. RENTAL AGENT: Kaua'i Paradise Vacations 1-800-826-7782. Hanalei Vacations 1-800-487-9833. Hanalei North Shore Properties 1-800-488-3336. Oceanfront Realty 1-800-222-5541. Some units with view of the ocean, others offer mountain vistas. Activity desk. Most units 1100 sq. ft. and have been recently redecorated. Most include microwave, TV, many with VCR and washer/dryer. Pool and hot tub.

Rates: 1 BR studio $85 nightly/$595 weekly; 2 BR 2 BTH $125/$110

(THE) CLIFFS AT PRINCEVILLE

Located at 3811 Edward Rd., Princeville. Managed by Premier Resorts. RENTAL AGENTS: Premier Resorts 1-800-367-7052. Kaua'i Paradise Vacations 1-800-826-7782. Maui & All 1-800-663-6962. Hanalei Vacations 1-800-487-9833. Hanalei North Shore Properties 1-800-488-3336. Kaua'i Vacation Rentals 1-800-367-5025. Oceanfront Realty 1-800-222-5541. Prosser Realty 1-800-767-4707. There are two hundred and two vacation studios, 1 BR 2 BTH, 2 BR 2 BTH, and even 4 BR 4 BTH units available through some rental agents. There is an onsite activity director with a variety of classes, hula-aerobics, and even a weekly local farmers market. Attend a free movie night or try out your talents at karaoke! Amenities include pool, 4 tennis courts, two jacuzzis, sauna, BBQ area, and a recreation pavilion. Units have ceiling fans, lanais, full kitchens. Daily maid service. Beach nearby.

Prosser Rates: Oceanfront 4 BR/4 BTH $175
Premier Resorts Rates: start at $155 for a one-bedroom g.v. with two night minimum required.
Oceanfront Realty Rates: 1 BR $120 nightly/$840 weekly; 2 BR $150 nightly/$1050 weekly; 2 BR deluxe $175 nightly/$1225 weekly

EMMALANI COURT

Located in Princeville. RENTAL AGENT: Pacific Paradise Properties 1-800-800-3637, Kaua'i Vacation Rentals 1-800-367-5025. Two bedroom, two bath unit with ocean and golf course views.

Nightly $175, weekly rate $1050/1200, cleaning fee $75 per stay.

HANALEI BAY VILLAS

5300 Ka Haku Road, Princeville, HI 96714. RENTAL AGENTS: Oceanfront Realty 1-800-222-5541, (808) 826-6585, Fax (808) 826-6478; Email: kauai@oceanfrontrealty.com; Web: <www.oceanfrontrealty.com> Marc Resorts 1-800-535-0085. Na Pali Properties 1-800-715-7273. These condominium units are actually single structures, with views of the golf course, mountains, and Hanalei Bay in the distance. The condos are 2 BR 2 BTH with the upper level providing living area kitchen, dining room and half bath. On the downstairs level are two bedrooms and two bathrooms. Beautifully furnished in pastel hues, lots of extras including lanais off both the top and lower levels. Located across from Pali Ke Kua Condo and Winds of Beamreach Restaurant.

Oceanfront Relaty Rates: 2BR $120-195; 3 BR $120-250
Marc Resort Rates:
2 BR Dlx 2 1/2 BTH suite w/kitchen m.v. $199, or bay view $231, maximum 6.

HANALEI COLONY RESORT ★

5-7130 Kuhio Highway, mailing address PO Box 206, Hanalei, HI 96714. (808) 826-6235, FAX (808) 826-9893, 1-800-628-3004 U.S. & Canada. Email: hcr@aloha.net; Web: <www.hcr.com> RENTAL AGENT: Prosser 1-800-767-4707. Hanalei Colony Resort is located on 4.5 acres of beach front, this village of condominiums (13 two-story buildings, each with four condominiums) offers very comfortable accommodations with 2 bedrooms. Situated just prior to the end of the road at Haena near the beginning of the famed Napali Coast, this is the last vestige of civilization on the North Shore. The rooms are decorated island-style and they are open and airy with fabulous large picture window coastal and mountain views and the beach in your front yard. Other condos and resorts are more luxurious perhaps and have more upscale furnishings and amenities, etc. but you'll get the feel of the South Pacific here with its remoteness and sense of being close to nature. It's reminiscent somewhat of places like Moorea and Bora Bora in French Polynesia with the beautiful beaches, jagged mountain peaks and lush green environment. This is truly a place to get away from it all because they don't have TV's, stereos, or phones (although there is a telephone by the pool where guests can make complimentary local phone calls). Units closer to the beach have nicer views (i.e. #G3). It's a short walk from any unit to the parking lot, very convenient. They do offer a weekly complimentary poolside breakfast with tea, coffee, and juice and a selection of fresh fruits and freshly baked pastries. Guest amenities also include pool and jacuzzi. Twice weekly maid service. Car and condo packages available. Weekly discounts. And if you are planning a wedding on Kaua'i, they also have a wedding coordination service and special wedding packages available. Check with them for details. If you're looking for one place on all of Kaua'i to really get away from it all, then you need look no further. This is it.
Rates: 2 BR g.v. $170/145; o.v. $195/175; o.f. $230/205,
premium ocean $265/240.
Prosser rents a corner 1BR 1BTH $145

KAMAHANA

Located in Princeville. RENTAL AGENTS: Oceanfront Realty 1-800-222-5541. Prosser Realty 1-800-767-4707. Pacific Paradise Properties 1-800-800-3637. One and two story condominiums overlooking the golf course. Rooms have high slanted ceilings with ceiling fans which offer lots of sun during the day, though stay cooler at night.Spacious, airy, modern kitchens are well equipped with all the necessities. The picture windows and sliding glass doors are all around and offer plenty of vistas. Room extras include things such as a closet full of books and cards, beach chairs, golf balls and even a boogie board. Since each is privately owned this will vary between units. Small, uncrowded pool area with "rec room" for gatherings. Located next to Sealodge.
Rates: 2 BR 2BTH o.v. $99 nightly/$693 weekly;
Deluxe $135-150 nightly/$945-1050 weekly

PALI KE KUA ★

5300 Ka Haku Rd., PO Box 899, Princeville, HI 96714. (808) 826-9066. RENTAL AGENTS: Marc Resorts Hawai'i 1-800-535-0085, toll free FAX 1-800-633-5085, local (808) 922-9700. Hanalei Vacations 1-800-487-9833. Kaua'i Paradise Vacations 1-800-826-7782. Kaua'i Vacation Rentals 1-800-367-5025. Pacific Paradise Properties 1-800-800-3637. Oceanfront Realty 1-800-222-5541. Maui & All 1-800-663-663-6962. Hanalei North Shore Properties 1-800-488-3336. Located on the cliffs at Princeville, adjacent to the Princeville Golf Courses. Ninety eight units in two story wooden buildings with Hawaiian-style roofing. 1 BR units are 763 sq. ft., 2 BR are 1,135 sq. ft. Each unit is like a small, private apartment with a well-equipped kitchen and washer/dryer (with a starter box of detergent). The furniture is light bamboo with fabrics in rich colors and patterns. The units are fresh and particularly clean and well maintained. There are a number of nice appointments such as eyelet edge lace on the sheets and large counter space in both the kitchen and bathroom. Outdoor amenities include pool and jacuzzi. A short walk to a small beach. Winds of Beamreach Restaurant located on property.
Marc Resorts Year Round Rates:
1 BR dlx mt.v. or g.v. $167; o.v. $183; o.f. $207;
2 BR dlx mt.v. or g.v. $207; o.v. $223; o.f. $263

PALI ULI

Ka Haku Road, Princeville Resort, HI 96714. RENTAL AGENTS: Hanalei Vacations 1-800-487-9833; Oceanfront Realty 1-800-222-5541; Prosser Realty 1-800-767-4707. This is a very private, small complex of individual cottage-style units but very well-appointed and fully equipped for vacation comfort, kitchen, dining area, living room, etc. Each 2BR/2bath unit has a unique soaking tub on a very private lanai. Gerat ocean views, privacy, quiet and all of Princeville Resort's amenities nearby.
Rates: 2BR/2BTH $75-95 nightly, $525-750 weekly

PUAMANA

Located on golf course in Princeville. (808) 826-9768. RENTAL AGENTS: Oceanfront Realty 1-800-222-5541. Prosser Realty 1-800-767-4707. Two bedroom, two bath units, many with ocean views. Swimming pool.
Rates: 1BR 2 BTH $85-99 nightly/$595-693 weekly; Deluxe $120-150 nightly/$840-1050 weekly; Premium $175 nightly/$1225 weekly

EXPENSIVE

HANALEI BAY RESORT ★

5380 Honoiki Road, Princeville, HI 96722. Aston Hotels & Resorts 1-800-922-7866; Email: info@aston-hotels.com; Web: <www.aston-hotels.com>. RENTAL AGENTS: Quintus Resorts 1-800-827-4427. Maui & All 1-800-663-6962. Pleasant Hawaiian Holidays 1-800-242-9244. Hanalei Vacations 1-800-487-9833. Oceanfront Realty 1-800-222-5541. Kaua'i Paradise Vacations 1-800-826-7782. The Hanalei Bay Resort offers three floors with a 153 rooms in one building plus another 75 one, two, and three bedroom suites in separate complexes. No elevators. Suites are equipped with a complete kitchen offering a full-size refrigerator, stove/oven, microwave, dishwasher, and coffee maker.

Units are spacious and nicely furnished, the suites have both a homey and a luxuriant feel. The high-beamed ceilings have tropical fans. Telephones in both living room and bedroom. The upholstered chaise lounge is romantic, elegant, and comfortable. One bedroom suites are 1,091 square feet with two televisions. Two bedroom suites are 1,622 square feet with two bathrooms and three televisions. Three bedroom suites are 2,085 sq. ft with three bathrooms, four televisions, and service for eight guests. Pay per view television on command is available for all! The suites units are a bit of a walk from the lobby and some walkways are steep climbs especially if you are carrying luggage.

There are a lot of free activities for guests: slide presentations, scuba lessons, and a tennis clinic. The on-site Bali Hai restaurant has a spectacular view. Sunday afternoon there is Jazz in the Happy Talk Lounge. The pool and jacuzzi are built in a natural lagoon setting surrounded by waterfalls with an island in the middle. It almost looks like it was there before and the hotel was built around it. The bathrooms are unusually decorated with a Victorian look: green tile and floral decor make it more homey and a lot less sterile than most hotel bathrooms. Resort amenities include the over-sized lagoon swimming pool and eight complimentary tennis courts (some lighted for night play) on the property. Rooms feature balcony, air-conditioning, telephones, and daily maid service. Non-smoking rooms available on request. Hotel rooms are 521 sq. ft. and studios are 570 sq. ft. The Princeville Makai and Prince Golf Courses are adjacent to the property (a total of 45 holes) with golf shuttle service. Conference facilities available.
Rates: Hotel m.v. $180; Studio m.v. $195; Hotel g.v. $200; Studio g.v. $215; Hotel o.v. $260; Studio o.v. $275; 1 BR m.v. $335; 1 BR o.v. $375; 2 BR m.v. $420; 2 BR o.v. $550; 3 BR o.v. $725. Inquire with Aston on available special promotional packages, senior discounts or Island Hopper specials.

PRINCEVILLE RESORT ★
552- Ka Haku Road, PO Box 3069, Princeville, HI 96722. 1-800-826-4400 from the US & Canada, locally (808) 826-9644, FAX (808) 826-1166; also toll free 1-800-325-3535; Email: info@princeville.com; Web: < www.princeville.com > Booking also through Pleasant Hawaiian Holidays 1-800-242-9244. The handsome 252-room Princeville Resort opened in 1985. The resort has won wide acclaim in the media over the years, being ranked as one of the world's top resorts by readers of prestigious magazines like *Conde Nast Traveler, Golf Magazine,* and others.

The Princeville Resort is a stunning property set gracefully on 23 acres on Pu'u Poa Ridge above Hanalei Bay, with Bali Hai mountain forming a majestic backdrop. From the moment you enter the spacious lobby you will feel worlds away. While not traditionally Hawaiian, this hotel is classic elegance with a European flair. The use of water throughout the lobby, above the restaurant, and in the foyer creates reflecting pools that glimmer and glisten. With a lobby so enormous and opulent, it is surprisingly simple to find a quiet corner. Off to one side is the library lounge, a popular spot for taking afternoon tea, reading a good book, or watching the sun slowly sink from either the veranda or a cozy sofa indoors.

The resort comprises three separate buildings that terrace down Pu'u Poa Ridge, reaching from the top plateau of Princeville to the Beach of Hanalei Bay. The lobby and entrance are located on the 9th floor, the pool and beach are on the first floor. A total of six rooms are available for the physically impaired. There is a freshwater swimming pool and three whirlpool spas plus an exercise room and an in-house cinema showing movies daily. A thoughtful addition in the guest rooms is a Do Not Disturb light that you can switch on from next to the bed that glows out in the hallway. The bathrooms are divine, filled with oversize bathtubs, marble double vanities, telephones, and music speakers. In each bathroom there is a "magic" window which electronically changes to allow for view or opaqueness. It is right up there with the Halekulani on O'ahu, a shower with a view! Tasteful additions, such as the fresh orchids in the vase in the bathroom, add that pampered feeling. The view is one of the primary amenities here and from every possible angle of the hotel, they've incorporated that picture perfect setting. The resort is beautiful during the day, but perhaps even more spectacular at night. The Living Room Lounge has a very comfortable and homey feel and you can enjoy afternoon tea while you again get an opportunity to appreciate the view. Inquire about the Princeville Golf Club passes which offer multiple rounds for multiple days at discounts. Resort packages are also available including the Prince Package (which offers golf discounts and Breakfast), Luxury Romance Package, Luxury Taste Package, Luxury Holiday Package.

Cafe Hanalei is much more spectacular than its name seems to indicate. In fact, it doesn't have much at all in common with a "cafe." The bay of Hanalei below and the cliffs best known as Bali Hai create a lovely and romantic dining environment for breakfast, lunch, dinner, or Sunday brunch. Don't miss splurging on dinner here, or better yet, the Friday seafood buffet. The menu is a blend of American, Oriental, Hawaiian and a touch of Italian for good measure. La Cascata offers Mediterranean cuisine seven nights each week. The Beach Restaurant and Bar serves lunch and snacks daily. The resort also has available a very nice selection of meeting and banquet facilities.

Activities include their Hawaiian Cultural program of Hula and Hawaiian implement demonstrations, Hawaiian story telling, and lau hala weaving. Should you feel the need for extra pampering, the Prince Health Club and Spa is located at the Prince Golf and Country Club. Short term membership rates are $12 per person per day, weekly fee $45, two week fee $65, monthly fee $95. All users must be at least 16 years of age. See Spas section in the Recreation chapter for more information.

The Princeville Hotel's Keiki Aloha program is available for children 5-12 years of age and designed with play in mind. Qualified youth counselors plan a full schedule of activities including Hawaiian crafts, sand castle building, beach and pool games, evening movies. There is a charge of $50 per day for the first child and $40 additional child per family. Keiki meals are available and the lunch is charged to the parent's room based on consumption. Daytime program runs 9 am - 3 pm and evening programs run 3pm - 9 pm. Summer program runs June 1 - August 31. For children under age 5, babysitting is available. Current rate is $10 per hour per child plus tax. For children in the same family, an additional cost of $1 per child, maximum 3 children per sitter.

Even if you are not fortunate enough to have the opportunity to stay at this resort, be sure to stop and visit and you are sure to make plans for a stay during another vacation to Kaua'i.

Mountain/Garden $380; partial o.v. $430; o.v. $535; Prince Junior Suites $625, Executive Suites $1100; Presidential Suites $2,800; and Royal Suite $3,600. Third adult person additional $60 per night.

PU'U PO'A ★
5300 Ka Haku Rd., PO Box 899, Princeville, HI 96714. (808) 826-9602. RENT-AL AGENTS: Marc Resorts Hawai'i 1-800-535-0085, toll free FAX 1-800-633-5085, local (808) 922-9700. Hanalei Vacations 1-800-487-9833. Kaua'i Vacation Rentals 1-800-367-5025. Kaua'i Paradise Vacations 1-800-826-7782. Oceanfront Realty 1-800-222-5541. Maui & All 1-800-663-6962. Hanalei North Shore Properties 1-800-488-3336. Pacific Paradise Properties 1-800-800-3637.
Fifty-six units in four-story buildings with ultra-modern exterior. Pool and tennis court. Units have washer/dryer, ceiling fans, full kitchens, and daily maid service. 2 night minimum stay.
Rates: 2 BR dlx o.v. $223; 2 BR luxury o.v. $263; 2 BR o.f. $195-214/$1365-1500 weekly; (max 6)

PRIVATE VACATION HOMES
RENTAL AGENTS

'ANINI BEACH VACATION RENTALS
PO Box 1220, Hanalei Bay, HI 96714. 1-800-448-6333, (808) 826-4000, FAX (808) 826-9636. E-mail: anini@aloha.net; Web: < www.anini.com >

They offer a variety of two, three, and four bedroom rental cottages, beachfront and executive homes on the North Shore. *Rates: Cottages $100 and up nightly; Beachfront homes $200 and up nightly; Executive homes $600 and up nightly*

BALI HAI REALTY, INC.
5-5088 Kuhio Highway, Hanalei Bay, HI 96714. Toll free 1-800-404-5200, (808) 826-7244; Email: info@balihai.com; Web: < www.balihai.com > This realty management company has a large inventory of beachfront vacation homes and condo rental units specializing in the North Shore area and Princeville. Check their latest rates on their website.

GRANTHAM RESORTS
3176 Po'ipu Road, Suite 1, Koloa, HI 96756. 1-800-325-5701 and 1-800-742-1412, (808) 742-7200, Fax (808) 742-9093. Email: info@grantham-resorts.com; Web: < www.grantham-resorts.com > Grantham Resorts offers 100 Po'ipu Beach rental properties at ten different beach resorts in Po'ipu ranging from bungalows to oceanfront condominiums.

HANALEI NORTH SHORE PROPERTIES
PO Box 607, Hanalei, HI 96714. (808) 826-9622, 1-800-488-3336. E-mail: hnsp@aloha.net; Web: < www.planet-hawaii.com/visit-kauai >Condominium rentals, plus many outstanding cottages and celebrity homes. Charo's own beachfront villa is available for vacation rental. It is situated on three oceanfront acres, complete with 4 master suites and 6 baths. Located on Tunnels Beach. Or how about "Club Nash" the premier beachfront estate of Graham and Susan Nash. 4 bedrooms, 3 1/2 baths on Hanalei Bay. This "old Hawaiian" style home was completed in 1992 and runs $4,200-5,000 per week. Other homes from $750-$5,600 per week. Condos from $500 per week.

HARRINGTON'S PARADISE PROPERTIES
PO Box 1345, 5-5408 Kuhio Highway, Hanalei, HI 96714. Toll free 1-888-826-9655, (808) 826-9655, FAX (808) 826-7330; Email: hpprop@aloha.net; Web: < www.oceanfrontkauai.com > A varied selection of homes and cottages in many price ranges, primarily on the North Shore. Five night minimum stay most of the year, with the exception of summer (one week minimum) and Christmas (two week minimum).

INCREDIBLE JOURNEY
Mailing address, PO Box 563, Applegate, CA 95703. Toll free 1-888-729-6899, (530) 878-4988, Fax (530) 878-8515; Email: jc@incrediblejourney.net; Web: < www.incrediblejourney.net > This booking service offers several unique B&Bs, condos, cottages and private homes around Kaua'i. Accommodations range from moderate to deluxe. Rates from $55 and up nightly.

MAUI & ALL ISLANDS CONDOMINIUMS & CARS ★
PO Box 947, Lynden, Washington 98264. Phone 1-800-663-6962. TOLL FREE FAX 1-888-654-MAUI. Website: < www.mauiallislands.com > Rental homes on the North Shore and around Kaua'i as well as a large selection of condominiums.

NA PALI PROPERTIES ★
PO Box 475, Hanalei, HI 96714. 1-800-715-7273, (808) 826-7272, FAX (808) 826-7665. Email:kauai-1@aloha.net;Web: < www.napaliprop.com > Specializes in rental homes on the North Shore. They earn a star for having a wide range of selection and prices. They offer quaint cottages, five bedroom homes or even an outstanding historic 3 bedroom home on Hanalei Bay, built in 1904. Prices begin at $450 per week and go up to $2,000.

PRINCEVILLE REAL ESTATE
3651 Albert Road, Princeville, HI 96722. (808) 826-4492, Fax (808)826-7475; Email: info@kauaigolfproperties; Web: < www.kauaigolfproperties.com > This realtor carries a large inventory of vacation rental homes and condominiums at all price ranges in the Princeville Resort and North Shore areas. They specialize in golf vacation home/condo rentals for the Princeville Resort golf courses.

PROSSER REALTY ★
4379 Rice St., PO Box 367, Lihu'e HI 96766. (808) 245-4711. 1-800-767-4707. FAX (808) 245-8115. E-mail: realty@aloha.net; Web: < www.prosser-realty.com > Prosser Realty gets special mention for having a very interesting selection of rental homes, they also rent condominiums from a wide inventory of properties around Kaua'i. They promise to find you the best possible vacation accommodations for the lowest possible price.

SUMMERS REALTY
1310 Inia Street, Kapa'a, HI 96746, (808) 822-5876, Fax (808) 822-6933; Email: summerre@gte.net; Web: < www.summers-realty-kauai.com > This realtor has a number of vacation rental homes and condos available island-wide, all price ranges.

TROPICAL PROPERTIES
4489 Aku Road, PO Box 826, Hanalei, HI 96714; Toll free 1-888-826-3211, (808) 826-1616, Fax (808) 826-1089; Email: kody@aloha.net; Web: < www.kauaitropicalproperties.com > This realty company has a number of vacation rentals, homes, cottages, condos available on the North Shore. All price ranges available, check for the latest rates.

RETREATS/LARGE GROUPS/REUNIONS

ISLAND ENCHANTMENT
PO Box 821, Anahola, HI 96703 (808) 823-0705, toll free 1-888-281-8292; Email enchant@aloha.net;< www.aloha.net/ ~ enchant/KauaiNatureSites.html > Humberto Blanco runs this accommodation in addition to offering Adventure Tours $75 per person per day. Accommodations are combined with a 6-8 day tour. Their outdoor adventures offer an opportunity to learn and practice the elements of yoga, body/mind techniques, meditation and massage plus swim beneath secluded waterfalls. You can also arrange for a one day custom tour $75. Simply furnished rooms with private or shared bath facilities.
Rates: Single/double w/private bath $70-90 nightly, $450-575 weekly; single-/double w/shared bath $50-70 nightly, $370-450 weekly

KAHILI MOUNTAIN PARK
4035 Kaumuali'i Highway, PO Box 298, Koloa, HI 96756. (808) 742-9921, Fax (808) 245-3100; Email: aua@hawaiian.net; Website: < www.sdamall.com/kahilipark > Owned and operated by the Seventh Day Adventist Church. The camp is 20 minutes from Lihu'e airport and 7 miles from Po'ipu Beach. There are 43 cabins located on 197 acres of beautiful garden park in an area of natural beauty. It's a rustic getaway located in the rolling foothills of Kahili Mountain. Cabins and cabinettes accommodate up to 6 persons each. Cabinettes offer 5 twin beds, 2 that can be made into kings, a kitchenette with a two burner stove and shared bathrooms and showers. $40 double occupancy. Cabins have two twin beds and one double and sleep up to 4 people. (Two cabins sleep up to 6 persons).

Each has 1/2 bath inside and an outdoor private shower. The kitchen includes a two burner stove and small refrigerator. The new cabins have two twin beds and one queen bed, a kitchen with two burner stove. Full indoor bath and shower and screened porch. Laundry on premises. They provide linens (including bedding and towels) dishes, dish soap, cookware.
Rates: Cabinettes $40; Cabins $60; extra person $6

KAUIKEOLANI ESTATE AND HANALEI PLANTATION COTTAGES ★
PO Box 81, Hanalei, HI 96714. Toll free 1-888-900-1454, (808) 826-1454, FAX (808) 826-6363; Email: halelea@aloha.net; Web: < www.hanaleiland.com >. Kauikeolani, the historic beachside plantation home of Albert Spencer Wilcox, has stood for over one hundred years. Wilcox was a successful turn-of-the-century sugar planter and the fourth son of missionaries Abner and Lucy Wilcox. The estate is bounded by the Hanalei River and guests can look out upon an expansive lawn to the beautiful wide beach fronting Hanalei Bay. Mountains of the surrounding Hanalei Valley provide additional panoramic views. The estate has been restored with great attention to detail and the historic era of the 1890's when it was built. The name Kauikeolani means "vision that come in the early morning mist" and the home was named after Albert's wife, Emma Kauikeolani Napoleon Mahelona. The estate includes the main Kauikeolani 7-bedroom home, plus four other 2BR and 3BR cottages: Palaka, Umetsu, Paniolo and Nalu. These cottages were the housing provided for the plantation worker families in the early days of the estate. The main home and all cottages are strictly non-smoking. Special day rates are available for banquets, incentive groups, and weddings. 3 night minimum for all cottages plus cleaning charges apply on all rentals. This is a very special and historic place.
Rates: Kauikeolani Main Home, 7BR (max 12), $1,200 night, $7,000 week, $25,000 month
Umetsu Cottage 2BR, (max 4), $250 night, $1,600 week, $5,000 month
Palaka Cottage 2 BR, (max 5), $200 night, $1,200 week,$4,000 month
Paniolo Cottage 3 BR (max 6), $400 night, $2,500 week, $8,000 month
Nalu Cottage 3 BR (max 6), $400, $2,500 week, $8,000 month

KEAPANA CENTER
5620 Keapana Rd., Kapa'a, HI 96746. (808) 822-7968, 1-800-822-7968. Email: keapana@aloha.net Website: < www.planet-hawaii.com/keapana/ > Located on six acres, the emphasis here is on a nurturing, healthful environment. They have a jacuzzi, steam bath, massage available. Five minutes to Kapaa town and the beach. Continental breakfast included, island fruits and fresh-baked bread. Rooms have shared bath facilities.
Rates: Single, $40-55; Double, $55-70

YMCA CAMP NAUE
c/o YMCA, PO Box 1786, Lihu'e, HI 96766, Office (808) 246-9090, Fax (808) 246-4411, Camp: (808) 826-6419. *Camp Naue* is located on four beachfront acres between the 7 and 8 mile markers on the state highway past Ha'ena on Kaua'i's North Shore. They offer two co-ed bunk houses that will sleep up to 50 people and a bath house with hot/cold showers and restroom facilities. The kitchen seats 60 people. They also have a 2 bedroom/1 bath beach cabin which sleeps up to 6 people.

The beach cabin may be rented as part of a group reservation or for individual use. The beach cabin must be rented in order to receive exclusive use of Camp Naue. Because of the capacity of the camp, they only accept reservations for groups of 15 or more except for the cabin which requires no minimum but a maximum of 6 people.

Camp Naue Rates: Bunk Houses -- Kaua'i resident $11 per person/non-resident $12 per person. Tent use -- one person with tent $10. Each additional person in the same tent $7 per person. Cabin (renter furnishes bedding) with group $40 per day, individual rental $50 per day. Kitchen use: $25 per day and is non-refundable.

YWCA CAMP SLOGGETT

YWCA of Kaua'i, 3094 Elua Street, Lihu'e, HI 96766. (808) 245-5959, FAX (808) 245-5961, camp phone (808) 335-6060; Email: kauaiyw@pixi.net; Web <www.pixi.com/~kauaiyw>.

The YWCA hostel and campground, *Camp Sloggett,* is located in the heart of Koke'e State Park on the island's west side above the Waimea Canyon. The grounds offer 2 acres of open field space, covered fire pit for camp fires, barbecue area, volleyball and badminton nets. Sports and recreation equipment are available.

Henry and Etta Sloggett built the lodge in 1925 as a mountain retreat for their friends and family. Following Henry's death, the Sloggett children generously donated the house and grounds to the Kaua'i YWCA and in 1938 YWCA Camp Sloggett was established.

They offer accommodations in Sloggett Lodge which sleeps 10 in 2 bedrooms (3 people in each) and 4 in the main room. The kitchen facilities offer commercial double ovens and 6 burner stove, 2 refrigerators, cookware, and table settings for 58 people. A covered lanai space of 800 sq. ft. is suitable for dining, meetings, or recreational use. The Weinberg Bunkhouse sleeps 40 people with mixed single and bunk style beds. Two staff rooms sleep 4 each and two common rooms offer space for 16 each. Baths/kitchens available. Camp rates are $15 per person per night for Kaua'i residents. $18 per person per night for Hawai'i residents. Non-residents are charged $20 per person per night. Children age 5 and under are free. A minimum of 5 people weekdays and 8 people weekends. They require 10 people minimum on weekends during peak season May through September. Tent camping is available to Kaua'i residents for $5 per person per night. Hawai'i Residents $7 per person per night. Non-residents $10 per person per night. A 2 night minimum on weekends and 3 night minimum over holidays is required. Kitchenette facilities available. Hostel accommodations are in the Weinberg Bunkhouse and tent sites only and include use of bath and recreational facilities. Barbecue, microwave, and refrigerator are available on the lanai. No reservations. Individuals accommodated on a space available basis.

CRUISE LINES

Before the advent of modern jet airliner travel, most visitors to Hawai'i traveled by elegant ocean liner. Today, it is still possible to arrive via cruise ship. Several cruise ships call in regularly at Honolulu and other Hawaiian ports-of-call on their trans-Pacific and around-the-world cruises. Some have regularly scheduled roundtrip cruises to Hawai'i from various embarkation points. Foreign flag ships are prohibited by law from boarding passengers on the U.S. mainland and discharging them in Hawai'i and vice versa. Thus, many cruise ships have stops in Hawai'i ports while arriving from ports in Canada, Mexico, Tahiti or other Pacific ports. Schedules vary as do itineraries. For details, it is recommended that you check with a travel agent or cruise tour reservation specialist. For the adventurous sailor-types, some freighters also carry small numbers of passengers from west coast ports to Hawai'i and beyond. Check with your travel agent for details.

Among the ships that have made various port calls in Hawai'i, including Kaua'i, on regular sailings recently from North America and other points are: Princess Cruises ships' Island Princess, Sea Princess and Golden Princess; Royal Viking Line's Sagafjord and Royal Viking Sun; Holland America Lines' Statendam, Rotterdam and Maasdam; Cunard Lines' Queen Elizabeth II; Royal Caribbean Lines' Legend of the Seas; Carnival Cruise Lines' MS Tropicale and others. According to visitor industry officials, more cruise ships are planning Hawai'i port calls during Pacific cruises in the near future.

Within the Hawaiian Islands, American Classic Voyages under its American Hawai'i Cruises division offers exclusive inter-island cruises aboard the SS Independence which is home-ported at Kahului, Maui. There is a standard seven-day cruise itinerary departing every Saturday from Maui with the ship making port calls at Nawiliwili on Kaua'i, Honolulu on Oahu, and Hilo and Kona on the Big Island of Hawaii. There are shore excursions and various tours available from dockside at each port. For complete details and information, contact your travel agent or American Hawai'i Cruises, toll free 1-800-513-5022; Email: ahcres@amcvnola.com; Web: <www.cruisehawaii.com> American Classic Voyages under its United States Lines division also offers similar seven-day inter-island cruises departing out of Honolulu. The cruises are aboard the newly refurbished MS Patriot. The 704-ft., 1,212 passenger MS Patriot provides nine passenger decks, five lounges, two restaurants, a fully equipped spa and fitness center, two outdoor pools and a 230-seat theater. It sails a similar itinerary as the SS Independence making port calls at Kaua'i, Maui, Hilo and Kona on the Big Island and Honolulu. For complete details and information, contact your travel agent or United States Lines, toll free 1-877-330-6871; Email: uslres@amcvnola.com; Web: <www.unitedstateslines.com>

United States Lines is looking to expand its Hawai'i cruise offerings in the near future. They are currently building two new 1,900 passenger, 72,000 ton cruise ships in Pascagoula, Mississippi, at Litton Industries Ingalls Shipbuilding unit. The ships are scheduled to enter Hawai'i service in 2003 and 2004 and will significantly expand cruise ship offerings throughout the Hawaiian Islands. On board either the Independence or the MS Patriot, you'll enjoy some outstanding Hawaiiana programs. Hawaiian costumes, hands-on Hawaiian museum exhibits, traditional Hawaiian church services, menus filled with Hawaiian specialties, and tropical flowers in every room are among the changes which bring the essence of Hawai'i on board. American Hawai'i Cruises has *kumu* (Hawaiian teachers) and *kupuna* (Hawaiian seniors) on board to instruct passengers about the culture, history and heritage of Hawai'i. Both ships offer fully handicap-accessible suites. The Independence departs out of Maui while the MS Patriot departs out of Honolulu. The boats cruise a seven day route with stops in Nawiliwili, Kaua'i; Kahului, Maui; sailing past Molokai to Hilo and Kona on Hawai'i Island and Honolulu. They also do a number of "Theme Cruises" which range from Big Band cruises to one which combines with Hawai'i's Aloha Festivals. The ship comes into port at each of the major islands for a day (or in some cases two) for passengers to take tours and excursions, go shopping, dine at local restaurants and participate in other arranged activities. Passengers can even rent cars and follow their own port intinerary for the day. The idea of a cruise is to give you a taste of each of the islands without the time and inconvenience of traveling by plane in-between islands. In fact, it would be impossible to see all the islands in a week in any other fashion.

Newlyweds and honeymooners can also fit an inter-island cruise into their Hawai'i trip plans. "Beautiful Seas" wedding packages are available for couples who choose marriage aboard ship in Hawaii. It includes the services of an official to perform the ceremony, a small wedding cake, live Hawaiian music, a flower lei and floral headpiece for the bride and a lei or boutonniere for the groom, champagne and keepsake flutes, photography service and a 24 5X7 photos in a souvenir album. The wedding package price is $750 plus cruise fares. See Weddings & Honeymoons in this chapter for information on tests and licenses. For honeymooners that marry on the Mainland on a Saturday, they don't have to "miss the boat" to enjoy a Hawaiian Islands honeymoon cruise. While the normal departures are on Saturday from Honolulu, the "Sea and Shore" honeymoon enables couples to board the ship in Nawiliwili, Kaua'i. After six days on board ship, the honeymooners will enjoy a seventh night at a Waikiki Hotel. For more information, contact American Hawai'i Cruises 1-800-513-5022 or Fax (504) 585-0630. Norwegian Cruise Line will begin seven-day inter-island cruises in late 2001, departing Sundays from Honolulu. They will be using the ultra-modern 76,800-ton Norwegian Star (former SuperStar Leo) which was refurbished and entered into Hawai'i service. The Norwegian Star is huge, 884-ft. long, thirteen decks high, 980 cabins and suites, eight sit-down restaurants, and an enormous children's facility plus all the usual entertainment and activity amenities. The Norwegian Star will follow an inter-island itinerary with stops at Kaua'i, Maui, Hawai'i and Oahu plus a stop at exotic Fanning Island in Micronesia, south of Hawai'i. In addition, other Norwegian Cruise Line ships will do occasional Hawai'i sailings as well. For complete information on Norwegian Cruise Line's Hawai'i sailings, call your travel agent or contact NCL: Toll free 1-800-327-7030; Web: < www.ncl.com >

There are other cruise lines that visit the Hawaiian Islands on an infrequent basis and it may be helpful to check all the cruise options out with your travel agent. As more and more cruise lines enter the rapidly growing Hawai'i cruise market, more ships will be plying Hawai'i's waters regularly or on a seasonal basis.

RENTAL AGENTS:

BED & BREAKFAST

AFFORDABLE PARADISE BED & BREAKFAST, HAWAII
332 Kuukama Street, Kailua, HI 96734
(808) 261-1693; Fax (808) 261-7315
Email: barbara@affordable-paradise.com
Web: < www.affordable-paradise.com >

ALL ISLANDS BED & BREAKFAST
463 Iliwahi Loop, Kailua, HI 96734
Toll free 1-800-542-0344; (808) 263-2342; Fax (808) 263-0308
Email: cac@hawaii.rr.com
Web: < www.home.hawaii.rr/com/allislands >

BED & BREAKFAST HONOLULU (STATEWIDE)
3242 Kaohinani Drive, Honolulu, HI 96817
1-800-288-4666; (808) 595-7533; Fax (808) 595-2030
Email: rainbow@hawaiibnb.com
Web: < www.hawaiibnb.com >

BED & BREAKFAST KAUA'I
4170 Kalani Place, Princeville, HI 96722
Contact: Liz Hey
(808) 822-1177; Fax (808) 826-9292; 1-800-822-1176
Email: heyliz@bnbkauai.com
Web: < www. bnbkauai.com >

BED & BREAKFAST HAWAI'I
PO Box 449, Kapa'a, HI 96746
(808) 822-7771; 1-800-733-1632; FAX (808) 822-2723
Email: reservations@bandb-hawaii.com
Web: < www.bandb-hawaii.com >

GO NATIVE
4408 Deer Valley Road, Rescue, CA 95672
Email: sales@go-native.com
Web: < www.go-native.com/Hawaii/HI.shtml
This is an online guide to B&B Inns of Hawaii with listings by town/city.

HAWAIIAN ISLANDS B&B
572 Kailua Road, Suite 201, Kailua, HI 96734
(808) 261-7895; Toll free 1-800-258-7895; Fax (808) 262-2181
Email: hi4rent@aloha.net
Web: < www.lanikaibb.com >

235

HAWAI'I'S BEST BED & BREAKFASTS
PO Box 563, Kamuela, HI 96743
Toll free 1-800-262-9912; (808) 885-4550; Fax (808) 885-0559
Email: bestbnb@aloha.net
Web: <www.bestbnb.com>

B&Bs on all islands with several on Kaua'i.

CONDOMINIUM RENTAL AGENTS

ASTON HOTELS & RESORTS
2155 Kalakaua #500, Honolulu, 96815
1-800-922-7866
From Hawai'i 1-800-321-2558
(808) 931-1400
FAX (808) 922-8785
Email: info@aston-hotels.com
Web: <www.aston-hotels.com>

Aston Kaua'i Beach Villas
Aston Kaua'i Coast (Beachboy)
Aston at Po'ipu Kai
Hanalei Bay Resort
Islander on the Beach
Kaha Lani
Waimea Plantation Cottages

BREADFRUIT

CAPTAIN COOK RESORTS
1024 Kapahulu Avenue, Honolulu, HI 96816
(808) 738-5507
Toll free 1-800-854-8843
Fax (808) 737-8733
Email: info@captaincookresorts.com
Web: <www.CaptainCookResorts.com>

They have a wide selection of vacation rental units, homes, condos all around Kaua'i.

CASTLE RESORTS & HOTELS
1150 South King Street, Honolulu, HI 96813
(808) 591-2235
1-800-367-5004 US & Canada
FAX toll free 1-800-477-2329
Email: info@castleresorts.com
Web: <www.castleresorts.com>

Kiahuna Plantation
Beach Bungalows at Kiahuna
Lanikai Resort
Makahuena
Po'ipu Shores Condominiums

GARDEN ISLAND RENTALS
PO Box 57, Koloa, HI 96756
(808) 742-9537
1-800-247-5599
FAX (808) 742-9540
Email: gir@kauairentals.com
Web: <www.kauairentals.com>

Kuhio Shores
Manualoha
Nihi Kai
Po'ipu Sands at Po'ipu Kai
Whalers Cove
Also many rental homes
including Stone House

GRANTHAM RESORTS
3176 Po'ipu Rd., Suite 1, Koloa, HI 96756
1-800-325-5701, (808) 742-7200
Fax (808) 742-9093
Email:info@grantham-resorts.com
Web: <www.grantham-resorts.com>

Kiahuna
Lawa'i Beach Resort
Makahuena
Nihi Kai Villas
Po'ipu Crater Resort
Po'ipu Kai
Po'ipu Makai
Waikomo Stream Villas
Also rental homes and cottages

HANALEI NORTH SHORE PROPERTIES
PO Box 607, Hanalei, HI 96714
(808) 826-9622
1-800-488-3336
FAX (808) 826-1188
Email: hnsp@aloha.net
Web: <www.kauai-vacation-rentals.com>

Alii Kai
The Cliffs
Pali Ke Kua
Pu'u Poa
Sealodge
Vacation rental cottages, homes, condos from beachfront to estates.

HANALEI VACATIONS
PO Box 1109, Hanalei, HI 96714
(808) 826-7288; 1-800-487-9833
Email: rentals@aloha.net
Web: <www.hanalei-vacations.com>

Alii Kai
(The) Cliffs
Hanalei Bay Resort
Kamahana
Pali Ke Kua
Pali Uli
Paniolo
Puamana
Pu'u Po'a
Sandpiper Village
Sealodge
Plus oceanfront cottages

HARRINGTON'S PARADISE
5-5408 Kuhio Hwy.
PO Box 1345, Hanalei, HI 96714
(808) 826-9655
Toll free 1-888-826-9655
FAX (808) 826-7330
Email: hpprop@aloha.net
Web: < www.oceanfrontkauai.com >

Rental homes and cottages
Specializes in 2-3 bedroom condos at Po'ipu Kai resort.

KAUAI PARADISE VACATIONS
5161 Kuhio Hwy. #205
PO Box 1708, Hanalei, HI 96714
1-800-826-7782
(808) 826-7444
FAX (808) 826-7673
Email: kpv1@aloha.net
Web: > www.planet-hawaii.com/paradise >

Alii Kai I & II
(The) Cliffs
Hanalei Bay Resort
Pali Ke Kua
Pu'u Poa

KAUAI VACATION RENTALS
3-3311 Kuhio Highway, Lihu'e, HI 96746
1-800-367-5025
(808) 245-8841
Email: aloha@kvrre.
Web: < www.kauaivacationrentals.com >

(The) Cliffs
Emmalani Court
Garden Island Sunset
Hale Awapuhi
Kapa'a Shore
Lae Nani
Lanikai
Pali Kai
Pali Ke Kua
Po'ipu Makai
Pono Kai
Prince Kuhio
Wailua Bay View

MARC RESORTS HAWAI'I
2155 Kalakaua Ave., 7th floor, Honolulu, HI 96815
Hawai'i (808) 922-9700
1-800-535-0085 US/Canada
Toll free FAX 1-800-663-5085
E-mail: marc@aloha.net
Web: < www.marcresorts.com >

Embassy Vacation Resort
Hale Moi
Hanalei Bay Villas
Pali Ke Kua
Pu'u Po'a
Pono Kai Resort

MAUI & ALL ISLANDS
CONDOMINIUMS & CARS
US Mail only: PO Box 947, Lynden, WA 98264
Canadian Mail only: PO Box 1089, Aldergrove, BC V4W 2V1
Toll free FAX 1-888-654-MAUI
Local FAX (604) 856-4187
1-800-663-6962 US & Canada
Email: paul@mauiallislands.com
Web: < www.mauiallislands.com >

Banyan Harbor
(The) Cliffs
Embassy Vacation Resort
Hale Awapuhi
Hanalei Bay Resort
Kaha Lani
(Aston) Kaua'i Beach Villas
(Aston) Kaua'i
    Coast Resort (Beachboy)
Kiahuna Plantation
Lae nani
Lanikai
Lawa'i Beach Resort
Makahuena
Nihi Kai Villas
Pali Ke Kua
Plantation Hale
Po'ipu Crater
(Aston) Po'ipu Kai
Po'ipu Makai
Po'ipu Palms
Po'ipu Shores
Pono Kai

MAUI AND ALL ISLAND (CONTINUED)
Prince Kuhio
Pu'u Po'a
Sunset Kahili
Waikomo Stream Villas
Wailua Bay View
Waimea Plantation Cottages
Whalers Cove
Also private home rentals

NA PALI PROPERTIES
PO Box 475, Hanalei, HI 96714
1-800-715-7273; (808) 826-7272
FAX (808) 826-7665
Email: nal@aloha.net
Web: < napaliprop.com >

Specializes in exclusive North Shore
home, cottage, condo vacation rentals- $500-$2000 weekly

OCEANFRONT REALTY
PO Box 3570, Princeville, HI 96722
1-800-222-5541; FAX (808) 826-6578
Princeville office (808) 826-6585
Email: kauai@oceanfrontrealty.com
Web: < www.oceanfrontrealty.com >

Alii Kai I & II
(The) Cliffs
Hanalei Bay Resort
Hanalei Bay Villas
Kamahana
Pali Ke Kua
Pali Uli
Puamana
Pu'u Po'a
Sandpiper
Sealodge

OUTRIGGER HOTELS & RESORTS
2375 Kuhio Avenue, Honolulu, HI 96815
1-800-688-7444 US & Canada; Toll free Fax 1-800-622-4852
(808) 921-6600
Email: reservations@outrigger.com
Web: < www.outrigger.com >

Lae Nani
Outrigger Kiahuna Plantation

PLEASANT HAWAIIAN HOLIDAYS
2404 Townsgate Road, Westlake Village, CA 91361
1-800-2-HAWAII (429244)
(818) 991-3390
Fax: (805) 495-4972
Web: <www.pleasantholidays.com>

(Aston) Kaua'i Beach Villas
Po'ipu Kai
Embassy Vacation Resort
Hanalei Bay Resort
Hyatt Regency Kaua'i
Islander on the Beach
Kaua'i Coconut Beach Resort
Kaua'i Marriott Resort
Kiahuna Plantation
Plantation Hale
Princeville Resort
Radisson Kaua'i Beach
Whalers Cove

PO'IPU CONNECTION
PO Box 1022, Koloa, HI 96756
(808) 742-2233
FAX (808) 742-7382
Reservations 1-800-742-2260
E-mail: poipu@hawaiian.net
Web: <www.poipuconnection.com>

Alihi Lani
Kuhio Shores
Makahuena
Po'ipu Crater
Po'ipu Makai
Po'ipu Palms
Prince Kuhio

PREMIER RESORTS
PO Box 4800,
Park City, UT 84060
1-800-367-7052
Email: stay@premier-resorts.com
Web: <www.premier-resorts.com>

Kaua'i Beach Villas
Lae Nani
(The) Cliffs at Princeville
Whalers Cove

PROSSER REALTY
4379 Rice St. or PO Box 367, Lihu'e, HI 96766
(808) 245-4711
1-800-767-4707
FAX (808) 245-8115
Email: realty@aloha.net
Web: < www.prosser-realty.com >

Banyan Harbor
(The) Cliffs
Hanalei Colony Resort
Kaha Lani
Kamahana
Kuhio Shores
Nihi Kai Villas
Pali Uli
Po'ipu Kai
Po'ipu Makai
Prince Kuhio
Puamana
Sea Lodge
Waikomo Stream Villas
Wailua Bay View
Also homes and cottages

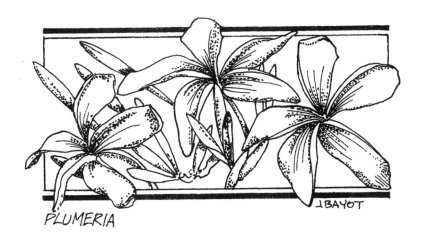

PLUMERIA

REMAX KAUAI VACATION RENTALS
PO Box 223609, Princeville, HI 96722-3609
(808) 826-9675
Toll free 1-877-838-8149
Fax (808) 826-1229
Email: rek@aloha.net
Web: < www.real-estate-kauai.com/rek/rentals

Wide selection of fine vacation rentals all over Kauai.

R&R
Realty & Rentals
1661 Pe'e Road, Po'ipu, HI 96756
(808) 742-7555
1-800-367-8022
FAX (808) 742-1559
Web: < rnr-realty-rental.com >
E-mail: < randr@aloha.net >

Kuhio Shores
Makahuena
Nihi Kai Villas
Po'ipu Crater
Po'ipu Kai Resort
Po'ipu Palms
Prince Kuhio
Also rental homes

SUITE PARADISE
1941 Po'ipu Rd., Po'ipu, HI 96756
1-800-367-8020;
(808) 742-7400
FAX (808) 742-9121
E-mail: < mail@suite-paradise.com >
Web: www: < suite-paradise.com >

Kiahuna Plantation
Lawa'i Beach Resort
Nihi Kai Villas
Po'ipu Crater
Po'ipu Kai
Po'ipu Shores
Whalers Cove

RESTAURANTS

RESTAURANT INTRODUCTION

The cultural diversity of the Hawaiian islands provides many benefits to visitors and residents alike. Over the past 150-years or so, immigrants arrived from various places, many to labor on the once vast sugar and pineapple plantations which were the backbone of Hawaii's agri-based economy for so long. These immigrants from such diverse places as Japan, China, Korea, the Philippines, Puerto Rico, Portugal, and more recently, southeast Asia, brought with them the many varied foods, culinary traditions, flavorings and cookery styles from their native lands. As the story goes, the plantation workers shared their meals thus introducing each other to the flavors and tastes of their respective homelands. This gave rise to modern Hawaii's diverse mix of culinary influences which has resulted in a happy blend of exotic food and flavors. There is probably no other state in the USA which can claim the diversity and range of ethnic cuisines which Hawaii has. The blending of Hawaii's ethnic foods has given rise to Hawaiian Regional Cuisine, recognized as a special cuisine approach utilizing the distinct cookery methods, foods, local produce, flavorings and innovative blending and fusion of Asia/Pacific tastes into a unique Hawaiian cuisine.

Visitors to Kaua'i will find dining out to be an exciting adventure. There is the opportunity to experience quality fine dining at many of Kaua'i's best restaurants and dining rooms. Or, diners can happily dive into a simple Hawaiian plate lunch from a local lunch counter or drive-in. In addition, diners can savor an authentic Hawaiian luau complete with traditional imu (underground oven) roast pig, laulau, poi and a variety of authentic Hawaiian foods plus a Hawaiian music and hula show. The range of cuisine and dining options is quite extraordinary for a small island like Kaua'i. So, come along and explore the many food and dining discoveries awaiting you on Kaua'i. You'll soon learn why it's called "The Garden Island." Bon appetit!

For such a small place, Kaua'i is fortunate to have a wide variety of restaurants, cafes, coffee shops, upscale dining rooms and island-style eateries. There's something for just about everyone, but like most things in life, not everyone agrees on what and where is the best. There are friendly disagreements and differences of opinion about dining out on Kaua'i, as there are just about everywhere else. When it comes to eating, everybody has his/her own personal favorites.

In addition to the dining experiences of this book's author, a great effort has been made to gather the opinions and experiences on dining out on Kaua'i of many other people, readers included. And while its doubtful if anyone can attest to having dined in every restaurant on The Garden Island, it is hoped that this section will provide insight into the variety of restaurants and cuisines that are available.

The restaurants in this section are divided into the same three sections of the island as the accommodations. Hopefully this will simplify locating that special place for breakfast, lunch, or dinner depending on wherever you find yourself. The restaurant listings are first indexed alphabetically and then also by food type. The restaurants description/listings are then divided by geographical area, separated by price range, and listed alphabetically in those price ranges.

245

These ranges are: "INEXPENSIVE" under $10 per person; "MODERATE" $10-25 per person; and "EXPENSIVE" $25 and up per person. The price ranges were decided by comparing an average dinner meal, exclusive of tax, alcoholic beverages and desserts. Due to changes in menus, management, supplies or other factors, restaurant prices are obviously subject to change at any time. If you are a senior citizen, be sure to ask about a "Senior Citizen Discount" as more restaurants are extending such a courtesy.

For simplicity, the restaurant listings in this section do not include fast food outlets like McDonalds, Burger King, Kentucky Fried Chicken, Pizza Hut, 7-Eleven Food Stores and other such outlets and convenience stores located around the Garden Island. Most folks are aware of the type of food to be had in such fast food operations and they do not merit a separate listing in this book. Suffice it to say that if you hanker for that sort of comfort food, you'll have no trouble finding it on Kaua'i.

This book uses a one-star rating system in recommending restaurants instead of multiple-star designations. It seemed a simple solution to the problem of trying to compare restaurants of different stature and caliber which happen to have equally good food, service, decor, etc. i.e. sort of like comparing "apples and oranges." It's like comparing the excellent Hanalei Mixed Plate in Hanalei with the superb A Pacific Cafe in Kapa'a. Each was wonderful for what it was, but did Hanalei Mixed Plate deserve only one or two stars just because it is a lunch counter, has very limited seating and a very different ambiance? Likewise, did A Pacific Cafe deserve four or five stars because it is a fine dining room, has great service, tasteful decor and equally tasty creative Hawaiian Regional Cuisine? The answer lies in the fact that both types of places are great places to eat for different people, at different times and for different reasons. Thus they deserve to be treated equally. They both get a star!

These are our "favored" restaurants or eateries based on their individuality. In their own way, Hanalei Mixed Plate and A Pacific Cafe meet particular needs. They both provide very good food for the vacation dollar. So as you read through the restaurant chapter, we've highlighted these special restaurants with our mark of excellence -- a single ★ !

These restaurants marked with a ★ indicate an exceptional value in quality of food and service, decor and ambiance, or unique and unusual cuisine and dining experience or a combination of these factors and not just cost alone. A real effort has been made to ensure that those restaurants so marked as an exceptional value have in fact earned the accolade. This has been done through personal visit and evaluation of a meal by or by close and careful consultation with reliable patrons, reader reviews and others. In spite of this, restaurants, like everything else, can and do change over time. What may have been an enjoyable dining experience last week or last month, may well be a complete disaster the next time around. The consistency factor of good food and service for the level of dining carries much weight in the evaluation and consideration. Those restaurants marked as an exceptional value have proven themselves consistent on these last points noted.

Readers are encouraged to check ahead with restaurants and call them for specific hours and days of service. One thing for which restaurants are noted is rapid and frequent change of days and hours open plus meal service provided. Several restaurants seem to change their hours seasonally and from time-to-time based on a variety of factors. Some restaurants may offer lunch and dinner hours one week, and then be open for dinner only the next, and then change back to both lunch and dinner hours the following week, things of that sort. So, it is advised to check with a given restaurant before traveling any distance to be sure they are open when you expect them to be and to avoid disappointment. The same thing applies to menu selections and prices. It is reasonable to expect that menus and prices at even the best restaurants will fluctuate from time to time, seasonally and/or with a change in chefs, owners, etc. This book cannot guarantee that changes will not occur in restaurants, menus, service, etc. The only thing guaranteed is that changes probably will occur.

The restaurants have been divided into Central/Eastside which will offer dining options for Lihu'e, Kapa'a, Nawiliwili, and Wailua. The Southern and Western portion of the island includes Po'ipu-Koloa-Lawa'i-Port Allen-Hanapepe-Waimea-Kekaha-Koke'e. Lastly the section on dining on the North Shore features restaurants in the towns of Anahola, Princeville, and Hanalei.

As with our Accommodations section, we've also added additional codes for those who prefer to surf for their Surf & Turf: <WWW> for restaurants with a website; <E> for those with E-mail. A few restaurants have their own websites and email contacts. These web and email addresses have been added to the restaurant listings where possible.

Finally, as you travel around the Garden Island, you may come across a restaurant or dining place not listed in this book. The reason is either that the specific restaurant opened after this book went to press or, for whatever reason, the author deemed the establishment unworthy to be included in this book.

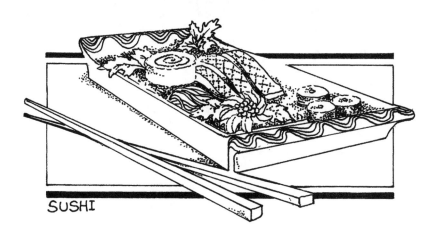

SUSHI

ETHNIC FOODS

A little background on some ethnic foods may tempt you to try a few new foods as a part of your dining adventure on Kaua'i. You're sure to find many of these foods on the various restaurant menus you come across. So, let you imagination flow and sensibilities go and embark on a new culinary and taste adventure! Grab all the gusto you can!

CHINESE FOODS
Char Siu: roasted pork with spices
Egg/Spring/Summer Roll: deep-fried pastry roll with various veggie, meat or shrimp fillings
Won Ton: crispy deep-fried dumpling with meat or veggie fillings; also soft-style cooked in soups or noodle dishes
Pot Stickers: semi-soft pan-fried filled dumplings
Peking Duck: char-broiled duck with char siu flavoring
Kung Pao Chicken: deep-fried chicken pieces
Szechuan Sauce: hot chili flavored sauce used extensively in beef, chicken, pork, seafood dishes
Bean threads: thin, clear noodles made from mung beans
Sweet & Sour Sauce: sugar and vinegar based sauce with tomato sauce, salt, and garlic flavorings
Chow mein noodles: thin noodles prepared with veggies and meat entrees in various combinations, also cake noodles style
Mongolian beef: thin sliced char-broiled beefsteak

FILIPINO FOODS
Adobo: chicken or pork cooked with vinegar and spices
Cascaron: a donut made with rice flour and rolled in sugar
Halo Halo: a tropical fruit sundae that is a blend of milk, sugar, fruits and ice
Lumpia: fried pastry filled with vegetables and meats
Pancit: noodles with vegetables or meat
Sari Sari: soup entree of pork, veggies and flavorings
Dinadaraan: blend of prepared pork blood and meats
Pinacbet: stir-fry of bitter melon, okra, pork and various seasonings
Port and Peas: traditional entree of pork, peas, flavorings in a tomato paste base
Chicken Papaya: chicken soup with green papaya and seasonings

HAWAIIAN FOODS
Haupia: a sweet custard made of coconut milk
Kalua Pig: roast pig cooked in an underground imu oven, very flavorful
Kulolo: a steamed pudding using coconut milk and grated taro root
Lau Lau: pieces of kalua pig, chicken or fish flavored with coconut milk and mixed with taro leaves, then steamed inside of ti leaves
Lomi Lomi Salmon: diced and salted salmon with tomatoes and green onions
Long Rice: clear noodles cooked with squid or chicken broth.
Opihi: these salt water limpets are eaten raw and considered a delicacy
Poke: raw fish that has been spiced. A variety of types of fish are used and are often mixed with seaweed; for example, tako poke is raw octopus

JAPANESE FOODS
Kamaboko: fish cake of white fish and starch steamed together
Miso Soup: soup of fermented soy beans
Sushi: white rice rolls or cakes with various seafood, seaweed and veggie fillings
Sashimi: very fresh firm raw fish, usually yellow-fin tuna (ahi), sliced thin and dipped in mustard-soy sauce; it's especially popular during the New Year's celebrations and commands prices at times in excess of $20 per lb.
Wasabi: very spicy green horseradish root used to dip sushi into
Tempura: deep-fried shrimp, fish, seafood and veggies dipped in a light flour batter
Teriyaki: flavorful, savory soy sauce and ginger marinade for beef, chicken, pork and seafood
Sukiyaki: thin sliced beef with veggies, noodles and tofu in sukiyaki sauce
Shabu Shabu: thin sliced beef with veggies, noodles and ponzu sauce
Tonkatsu: pork cutlet grilled golden brown, served with tonkatsu sauce
Chicken katsu: deep-fried chicken pieces served with katsu sauce
Donburi: chicken, pork or fish entree with veggies and special soy sauce served over steaming rice
Udon/saimin: fat/thin noodles served with soup broth, green onions, fish cake slices, optional meat
Soba/somen: thin noodles usually served cold with/without broth; somen served as salad with veggies

KOREAN FOODS
Kim Chee: spicy pickled cabbage flavored with ginger and garlic
Meat or Fish Jun: teriyaki flavored fried or broiled beef or fish
Spicy BBQ Beef, Chicken or Pork: broiled soy sauce flavored beef, chicken or pork laced with spicy hot chili
Kal Bi Ribs: flavored similarly to teriyaki, but with chile pepper, sesame oil and green onions
Mandoo: fried dumplings with meat and vegetable fillings
Mandoo Kook, Bi Bim Kook, Yook Kae Jang: soups served with mandoo dumplings, noodles, veggies, variety of meats

LOCAL FAVORITES
Plate lunches: a traditional favorite might include teriyaki beef or chicken, hamburger with gravy, roast pork, fried fish or any of several other entrees and always served with two scoops of rice and a scoop of macaroni salad
Loco Moco: a combination of hamburger patty atop a bowl of rice with fried egg and gravy
Bento: a box lunch might include tempura shimp, veggies, scoop of noodles, sushi roll or rice
Saimin: noodles, noodles, noodles!
Shave Ice: ground ice--mainlanders know it as snowcones--topped with a variety of flavored syrups such as strawberry, pineapple, guava, vanilla, mango, rootbeer, lilikoi, etc. and available with a scoop of ice cream under the "snow"

THAI/VIETNAMESE

Pho noodle soup: noodle soup with beefsteak, meatball, chicken or combination with veggies

Rice noodle soup: rice stick noodles with shrimp, pork, fishcake, squid or other seafood

Vermicelli cold noodles: thin, clear noodles combined with meat or seafood entree and veggies

Fried noodles/fried rice: crispy/soft fried noodles with meat entree and veggies-/soft rice with meat and veggies

Mein noodles: egg noodle soup with shrimp, seafood or other entree

Satay sticks: broiled chicken, pork or beef on skewer sticks, served as a side dish

Pad Thai: Thai-style noodles pan fried with choice of meat entree or veggies garnished with sprouts

Red curry: choice of meat entree with bamboo shoots in coconut milk and sweet basil

Green curry: choice of meat entree with peas, string beans, coconut milk and sweet basil

Yellow curry: chicken with coconut milk and potatoes

Massamun curry: curry with onion, peanuts, carrots, and potatoes in coconut milk

A FEW WORDS ABOUT ISLAND FISH

Whether cooking fish at your condominium or eating out, the names of the island fish can be confusing. While local shore fishermen catch shallow water fish such as goatfish or papio for their dinner table, commercial fishermen angle for two types. The steakfish are caught by trolling in deep waters and include Ahi, Ono, and Mahi. The more delicate bottom fish include Opakapaka and Onaga which are caught with lines dropped as deep as 1,500 feet to shelves off the island coast lines. Here is some background on what you might find on your dinner plate.

A'U - The broadbill swordfish, averaging 250 lbs. in Hawaiian waters, is a "steakfish." Hard to locate, difficult to hook, and a challenge to land.

AHI - The yellow fin (Allison tuna) is caught in deep waters off Kaua'i and weighs 60-280 lbs. Pinkish red meat is firm yet flaky and popular for sashimi.

ALBACORE - This smaller version of the Ahi averages 40 - 50 pounds and is lighter in both texture and color.

AKU - This is the blue fin tuna.

EHU - Orange snapper

HAPU - Hawaiian sea bass

KAMAKAMAKA - Island catfish, very tasty, but a little difficult to find.

LEHI - The silver mouth is a member of the snapper family with a stronger flavor than Onaga or Opakapaka and a texture resembling Mahi.

MAHIMAHI - Although called the dolphin fish, this is no relation to Flipper or his friends. Caught while trolling and weighing 10-65 lbs., this is a seasonal fish which causes it to command a high price when fresh. *Beware*, while excellent fresh, it is often served in restaurants having arrived from the Philippines frozen and is far less pleasing. A clue as to whether fresh or frozen may be the price tag. If it runs less than $10-15 it is probably the frozen variety. Fresh Mahi will run more! This fish has excellent white meat that is moist and light. It is very good sauteed.

ONAGA (ULA) - Caught in holes that are 1,000 feet or deeper, this red snapper has an attractive hot pink exterior with tender, juicy, white meat inside.

ONO - Also known as Wahoo. ONO means "very good" in Hawaiian. A member of the Barracuda family, its white meat is firm and more steaklike. It is caught at depths of 25-100 fathoms while trolling and weighs 15 to 65 pounds.

'OPAE - Shrimp

OPAKAPAKA - Otherwise known as pink snapper and one of our favorites. The meat is very light and flaky with a delicate flavor.

PAPIO - A baby Ulua caught in shallow waters -- weighs 5-25 lbs.

UKU - The meat of this grey snapper is light, firm and white with a texture that varies with size. It is very popular with local residents. This fish is caught off Kaua'i, usually in the deep Paka Holes.

ULUA - Also known as Pompano, this fish is firm and flaky with steaklike, textured white meat. It is caught by trolling, bottom fishing, or speared by divers and weighs between 15 and 110 pounds.

DINING BEST BETS

It's difficult to identify the best places to eat that will please everyone. And that's because everyone has different likes and dislikes and tastes. Without a doubt, there will be disagreements. Understandably so. This "Dining Best Bets" section attempts to identify what this writer has found to be pleasant, exceptional, enjoyable or otherwise good places to eat or to have a satisfying dining experience. It is hoped that readers will concur with these suggestions or confirm that they are wrong and perhaps offer other suggestions. So, for better or worse, here is this book's list of "Dining Best Bets" on Kaua'i.

BEST SMOOTHIES: Fruit smoothies at Banana Joe's Fruit Stand or Mango Mama's in Kilauea, and the People's Market in Puhi, near Lihu'e. (Or try the "fruit, the whole fruit, and nothing but the fruit" frosties at Banana Joe's or Hanalei Juice Co.)

BEST BREAKFAST: Kountry Kitchen, Kalaheo Coffee Co. & Cafe, Ono Family Restaurant, and the Po'ipu Bay Resort Grill and Bar.

BEST FRENCH TOAST: Hanalei Wake Up Cafe.

BEST BREAKFAST VALUE: Ma's in Lihu'e.

BEST FINE DINING IN A CASUAL ATMOSPHERE: Roy's, Gaylord's, and A Pacific Cafe.

BEST DINING VALUE: Dani's in Lihu'e

BEST FAMILY DINING: Ono Family Restaurant

BEST VIEW: Al & Don's has a wonderful view, try it for breakfast. Other views can be enjoyed at the Beach House Restaurant (right on the beach!), Bali Hai with a view of Hamolokama Mountain and Waterfall, and JJ's Broiler overlooking Kalapaki Bay. If you can afford it, Cafe Hanalei at the Princeville Resort wins hands down!

BEST SEAFOOD: Generally, fresh fish and seafood are expertly prepared at these favorite Kaua'i restaurants: Gaylord's, Roy's, House of Seafood, Keoki's Paradise, and A Pacific Cafe

BEST SUSHI: We like the variety at Tokyo Lobby and the new creative choices at Sushi Blues. Readers have also recommended Steve's Mini Mart in Kalaheo and Pono Market in Kapa'a.

BEST APPETIZER/PUPU: Keoki's or Duke's (especially the calamari!), "The Kiss" at Casa di Amici Po'ipu, Postcards in Hanalei for their innovative vegetarian selections, and Waimea Brewing Co. for their creative sauces and condiments.

BEST DINNER BUFFET: Hanalei Cafe at the Princeville Resort, the Ilima Terrace at the Hyatt, Japanese cuisine buffet at Hanama'ulu Restaurant on Sunday nights.

BEST ORIENTAL: Hanama'ulu Restaurant has good local-style Oriental and Japanese food and pleasant ambiance as does Restaurant Kintaro. Tokyo Lobby has good Japanese cuisine and is a bit more upscale in atmosphere. Sukhothai and Pattaya Asian Cafe for Thai; Hong Kong Cafe for Chinese.

BEST BREAKFAST BUFFET: The Hyatt Regency Kaua'i

BEST SALAD BAR: There are very few, but Duke's could hold its own - even with a lot of competition!

BEST ISLAND-STYLE AMBIANCE: Keoki's Paradise

BEST SALADS: Warm ahi salad at A Pacific Cafe; the Oriental chicken salad at Princeville Restaurant;Sushi Blues' garlic sauteed mushrooms on lettuce bed

BEST SANDWICH: The lean turkey Reuben at Joe's (either one), the chicken salad sandwich at Lizard Lounge & Deli, the kalua pork at Hanalei Mixed Plate and the healthy, fresh, and colorful veggie sandwich at Mango Mamas.

BEST PLATE LUNCHES: Hanalei Mixed Plate--their shoyu ginger chicken and kalua pork and cabbage are tops.

BEST PIZZA: Brick Oven pizza, a long time favorite. Pau Hana Pizza gets points for its variety of unusual toppings!

BEST MEXICAN: Riccardo's Mexican Food, Tropical Taco or tiny Taqueria Nortenos; there are also good reports about the authentic Mexican fare at Maria's.

GOOD AND CHEAP: Hamura Saimin, Sueoka's, Barbecue Inn, and Waipouli Restaurant.

BEST HAWAIIAN/"LOCAL STYLE": K.C.L. Barbecue Drive Inn, Lawai Restaurant, and Ma's

BEST BAKERY: Kilauea Bakery, Roadrunner in Kilauea or the Bread Box in Kalaheo.

MOST OUTRAGEOUS DESSERTS: Roy's Chocolate Souffle, Keoki's Hula Pie, and the pies at Green Garden. The spumoni ice cream cake at Pomodoro was "ono" and the Toasted Hawaiian "sculpture" at A Pacific Cafe. Camp House Grill has a chewy chocolate chip macadamia nut pie or pineapple cream cheese pie that are both worthy of the calories!

BEST HAMBURGERS: Duane's Ono Burgers-no contest!

BEST SHAVE ICE: Halo Halo Shave Ice in Lihu'e or Kamaka's small roadside stand in Anahola.

BEST VEGETARIAN: Papaya's has good casual fare, but Hanapepe Cafe & Espresso and Postcards in Hanalei both offer wonderful gourmet vegetarian dinners; Caffe Coco also has good veggie fare.

CATERING SERVICES

If you've got guests coming, have a group to feed, or are simply planning a party or celebration and don't want to do all the prep work involved, call one of the many island catering services that can prepare, serve and clean up afterwards, leaving you to simply enjoy the event. You'll find that most hotels and resorts have a catering service, as do many local restaurants. There are several private catering companies on Kaua'i offering custom catering and a personal chef for all occasions. Just give your favorite hotel or restaurant a call. Or you can try one of the following catering services.

Contemporary Flavors, 1610 Haleukana Street, Lihu'e, HI 96766, (808) 245-2522, fax (808) 245-2744; Email: conflvr@gte.net; Web: < www.gtesupersite.com/contemflavor >

Gaylord's at Kilohana, 3-2087 Kaumualii Highway, Lihu'e, HI 96766, (808) 245-9333; Web: < www.gaylordskauai.com >

Green Garden Restaurant, Highway 50, Hanapepe, HI 96716, (808) 335-5422, 335-5528

Heavenly Creations, PO Box 167, Anahola, HI 96703, toll free 1-877-828-1700, (808) 828-1700

Koloa Fish Market, 5482 Koloa Road, Koloa, HI 96756, (808) 742-6199

Lemm's Luau & Catering Service in Anahola, (808) 822-4854

Puhi Fish and Catering, 4495 Puhi Road, Lihu'e, HI 96766, (808) 246-6925

Terrace Restaurant at Kaua'i Lagoons, 3351 Hoolaulea, Lihu'e, HI 96766, (808) 241-6010

RESTAURANT INDEX

A Pacific Cafe 298
Al & Don's 265
Aloha Diner 265
Aloha Kaua'i Pizza 267
Amelia's 321
Ara's Sakana-Ya Fish House 265
Aupaka Terrace 265
Bali Hai Restaurant 331
Bamboo Bamboo 326
Barbecue Inn 284
(The) Beach 327
Beach House Restaurant 315
Beezers 266
Borders Cafe Espresso 266
Brennecke's 307
Brick Oven Pizza 307
Bubba's 266, 321
Bull Shed 284
Buzz's Steak & Lobster 267, 285
Cafe Espresso 266
Cafe Hanalei 332
Cafe Portofino 285
Caffe Coco 285
Camp House Grill-Kapa'a 286
Camp House Grill-Kalaheo 308
Casa di Amici Po'ipu 315
Chuck's Steak House 333
Coconut MarketPlace - restaurants 267
Da Imu Hut 301
Dairy Maid 268
DaKine Dogs 268
Dali Deli & Cafe Cara 301
Dani's 268
Deli & Bread Connection 269, 276
(The) Dock 301
Dondero's 316
Dori's Garden Cafe 269
Driftwood Sand Bar & Grill 269
Duane's Ono Burgers 322
Duke's Canoe Club 287
Eggbert's 267, 269
Emerson's Seafood Restaurant 299
Endless Summer 270
(The) Fish Express 270

(The) Fish Hut 267
(The) Flying Lobster 287
Garden Island BBQ 270
Gaylord's Restaurant 299
Green Garden 308
Grinds Espresso 301
Hale 'O Java 322
Hamura Saimin 271
Hanalei Dolphin 327
Hanalei Gourmet 327
Hanalei Juice Co. 322
Hanalei Mixed Plate 323
Hanalei Wake Up Cafe 324
Hanama'ulu Restaurant 287
Hanapepe Cafe & Espresso 309
Harley's Ribs -n- Chicken 267
Hawaiian Classic Desserts 288
Higashi 271
Hiroka's Okazuya 271
Hong Kong Cafe 271
Ho's Chinese Kitchen 276
House of Seafood 316
Ilima Terrace 317
Island Teriyaki 302
JJ's Broiler 288
JR's Plantation Restaurant 289
Joe's Courtside Cafe 302
Joe's on the Green 309
John's Place 302
Jolly Roger 284
Joni Hana 276
KCL Barbecue Drive Inn 274
Kahanu Snack Bar 272
Kalaheo Coffee Co. & Cafe 303
Kalaheo Steak House 317
Kalapaki Beach Hut 272
Kalapaki Grill 272
Kalena Fish Market 273
Kapa'a Fish & Chowder House 289
Kaua'i Bakery 276
Kaua'i Brew & Burrito 273
Kaua'i Chop Suey 273
Kaua'i Community College (Queen Victoria's Room) 273
Kaua'i Kitchens 274, 303
Kaua'i Mix Plate & Deli 274
Kawayan 274
Keoki's Paradise 317
(Restaurant) Kiibo 281

Kilauea Bakery
   & Pau Hana Pizza 328
Kilauea Farmers Market 324
Kim Chee #9 Restaurant 275
King & I 290
King's Steakhouse and Tropical Bar 310
(Restaurant) Kintaro 293
Koke'e Lodge 304
Koloa Country Store & Internet Cafe 304
Koloa Fish Market 304
Korean BBQ 275
Kountry Kitchen 275
Kukui Grove Shopping Center-restaurants 275
Kukui's Restaurant and Bar 300
Kun Ja's 276
Kupono Cafe at ANARA Spa 310
La Bamba 290
La Cascata 333
La Playita Azul 276
Lawa'i Restaurant 310
Lemongrass Grill & Seafood 290
Lighthouse Bistro 329
Lihu'e Bakery & Coffee Shop 277
Lihu'e Cafe 277
Linda's Restaurant 304
(The) Living Room 333
Lizard Lounge & Deli 277
L&L Drive Inn/Chopsticks Express 277
LUAUS 337
Ma's 278
Mango Mamas Cafe 324
Margaritas, A Mexican Restaurant 291
Maria's 278
Mark's Place 278
Mermaids Cafe 279
Mi Casita 304
Myron's 276
Naniwa 318
Naupaka Terrace Steak House 291
Nawiliwili Tavern & Grille 279
Neide's Salsa & Samba 329
Norberto's El Cafe 291
Oasis Bar & Grill 305
Okazu Hale 279
Oki Diner & Bakery 279
Old Hanalei Coffee Company 325
Olympic Cafe 292

Ono Family Restaurant 280
Pacific Pizza and Deli 310
Palm Tree Terrace 267
Pancho and Lefty's Cantina & Restaurante 292
Panda Garden 293
Papaya's Natural Foods 280
Paradise Bar & Grill 329
Paradise Seafood & Grill 293
Pattaya Asian Cafe 311
Plantation Gardens Restaurant 318
Pizza Hanalei 330
Pizzetta 311
Po'ipu Bay Grill & Bar 311
Polynesian Hide-a-way
    & Haw'n Bar-BQ 325
Pomodoro Italian Restaurant 312
Poolside Grill & Bar 305
Poor Boy's Pizza 293
Po's Chinese Kitchen 281
Postcards Cafe 334
Princeville Restaurant & Bar 330
Puakea Bar & Grill 281
Pualani's Farmer's Market 305
Riccardo's Mexican Food 268
Roadrunner Bakery & Cafe 325
Rob's Good Times Grill 281
Rocco's 294
Roy's Po'ipu Bar & Grill 319
Sampaguita's 281
Shells 320
Shipwreck Subs & Ice Cream 305
Shutters Lounge 282
Sri's Cafe 282
Sueoka's 306
Sukhothai 294
Sushi Blues & Grill 335
Sushi Katsu 294
Tahiti Nui 331
Taqueria Nortenos 306
TC's Island Grill 268
Terrace Restaurant at Kaua'i Lagoons 282
Thai-Thai Cuisine 295
The Dock 301
The Palms Restaurant 295
The Point 306
Tidepools 320

Tip Top Cafe 282
Toi's Thai Kitchen 312
Tokyo Lobby 295
TomKats Grille and Bar 313
Tropical Taco 326
Tropix Island Bar & Grill 283
Village Snack and Bake Shop 326
Voyage Room 296
Wah Kung Chop Suey 283
Wailua Family Restaurant 296
Wailua Marina Restaurant 297
Waimea Brewing Co. 313
Waimea Canyon Snack Shop 307
Wasabi's 297
Waipouli Deli & Restaurant 283
Whalers Brewpub 297
Winds of Beamreach 331
Wong's Restaurant 314
Wrangler's Steak House 315
Zababaz One World Cafe 326
Zack's Famous Yogurt 276, 283
Zelo's Beach House 335

FOOD TYPE INDEX

AMERICAN

Al & Don's 265
Camp House Grill-Kapa'a 286
Camp House Grill-Kalaheo 308
DaKine Dogs 268
Eggbert's 267, 269
Jolly Roger 284
Koke'e Lodge 304
Kountry Kitchen 275
Po'ipu Bay Grill & Bar 311
Princeville Restaurant & Bar 330
Rob's Good Times Grill 281
TomKats Grille & Bar 313
Wailua Marina 297
Winds of Beamreach 331
Whaler's Brewpub 297

BAKERIES

Kilauea Bakery 328
Lihu'e Bakery & Coffee Shop 277
Roadrunner Bakery & Cafe 325

BREAKFAST
Hanalei Wake Up Cafe 324
Kountry Kitchen 275
Ono Family Restaurant 280
Po'ipu Bay Bar & Grill 311

BUFFETS/BRUNCH
Cafe Hanalei 332
Ilima Terrace 317
Kukui's Restaurant & Bar 300
Voyage Room 286

CHINESE-VIETNAMESE-THAI-KOREAN-FILIPINO
Garden Island BBQ 270
Hong Kong Cafe 271
Ho's Kitchen 276
Kaua'i Chop Suey 273
Kim Chee #9 Restaurant 275
King & I 290
Korean BBQ 270
Kun Ja's 276
Lawa'i Restaurant 310
Lemongrass Grill & Seafood 290
Panda Garden 293
Pattaya Asian Cafe 311
Po's Kitchen 281
Sukhothai 294
Thai-Thai Cuisine 295
Toi's Thai Kitchen 312
Wah Kung Chop Suey 283
Waipouli Deli & Restaurant 283
Wong's 314

COFFEE/ESPRESSO, SANDWICHES & SNACKS
Amelia's 321
Bubba's 266, 321
Dairy Maid 268
Deli & Bread Connection 268, 276
Driftwood Sand Bar & Grill 269
Duane's Ono Burgers 322
Hale 'O Java 322
Hanalei Gourmet 327
Hanalei Juice Company 322
Joe's Courtside Cafe 302
Joe's on the Green 309
John's Place 302
Kahanu Snack Bar 272
Kalaheo Coffee Co. & Cafe 303

COFFEE/ESPRESSO, SANDWICHES & SNACKS (CONTINUED)
Kalapaki Beach Hut ... 272
Koloa Country Store & Internet Cafe ... 304
Lizard Lounge & Deli ... 277
Mango Mamas Cafe ... 324
Mark's Place ... 278
Oasis Bar & Grill ... 305
Old Hanalei Coffee Company ... 325
Po'ipu Bay Bar & Grill ... 311
Shipwreck Subs ... 305
Shutters Lounge ... 282
The Beach ... 327
The Dock ... 301
Village Snack Shop ... 326
Waimea Canyon Snack Shop ... 307
Zack's ... 276, 283

CONTINENTAL/INTERNATIONAL
Hanalei Gourmet ... 327
Ilima Terrace ... 317
Tahiti Nui ... 331
Terrace Restaurant at Kauai Lagoons ... 282
Waimea Brewing Co. ... 313
Zelo's Beach House ... 335

FAMILY DINING
Al & Don's ... 265
Barbecue Inn ... 284
Dani's ... 268
Eggbert's ... 267, 269
Green Garden ... 308
Jolly Roger ... 284
Keoki's Paradise ... 317
Ma's ... 278
Ono Family Restaurant ... 280
Wailua Family Restaurant ... 296
Wailua Marina ... 297

HAWAIIAN/LOCAL STYLE
Aloha Diner ... 265
Dairy Maid ... 268
Dani's ... 268
Hamura Saimin ... 271
Hanalei Mixed Plate ... 323
Hanalei Wake Up Cafe ... 324
Island Teriyaki ... 302
Joni Hana ... 276

HAWAIIAN/LOCAL STYLE (CONTINUED)
Kaua'i Mix Plate & Deli 274
KCL Barbecue Drive Inn 274
Lawai Restaurant 310
Lihu'e Cafe 277
Ma's 278
Pualani's Farmer's Market 305
Tidepools 320
Tip Top Cafe 282
Waipouli Deli & Restaurant 283

HAWAIIAN REGIONAL/ PACIFIC RIM CUISINE
A Pacific Cafe 298
Bali Hai Restaurant 331
Bamboo Bamboo 326
Beach House Restaurant 315
Cafe Hanalei 332
Gaylord's 299
Po'ipu Bay Bar & Grill 311
Plantation Gardens Restaurant 318
Roy's Po'ipu Bar & Grill 319
Sushi Blues & Grill 335
The Palms Restaurant 395

HEALTH FOOD
Caffe Coco 285
Kupono Cafe at ANARA Spa 310
Mango Mamas Cafe 324
Mermaids Cafe 279
Papaya's Natural Foods 280

ITALIAN/PIZZA
Aloha Kaua'i Pizza 267
Brick Oven Pizza 307
Cafe Portofino 285
Dali Deli & Cafe Cara 301
Dondero's 316
Hale O'Java 322
La Cascata 333
Pizza Hanalei 330
Pizzetta 311
Pomodoro 312
Rocco's 294

JAPANESE
Barbecue Inn 284
Hanama'ulu Restaurant & Tea House 287
Naniwa 318
Restaurant Kiibo 281
Restaurant Kintaro 293
Tokyo Lobby 295
Wasabi's 297

LUAUS
Gaylord's 337
Hyatt Regency 337
Kaua'i Coconut Beach 338
Princeville Resort 338
Radisson Kaua'i Beach Resort 339
Smith's Tropical Paradise 339
Tahiti Nui 340

MEXICAN
Hanalei Wake Up Cafe 324
La Bamba 290
La Playita Azul 276
Margaritas 291
Maria's 278
Mi Casita 304
Norberto's El Cafe 291
Pancho and Lefty's Cantina & Restaurante 292
Riccardo's Mexican Food 268
Roadrunner Bakery & Cafe 325
Taqueria Nortenos 306
Tropical Taco 326

SALAD BAR
Brennecke's 307
Bull Shed 284
Chuck's Steak House 333
Duke's Canoe Club 287
Flying Lobster 287
Green Garden 308
Wailua Family Restaurant 296

STEAK & SEAFOOD

A Pacific Cafe 298
Brennecke's 307
Bull Shed 284
Buzz's Steak & Lobster 267, 285
Chuck's Steak House 333
Duke's Canoe Club 287
Emerson's Seafood Restaurant 294
Flying Lobster 287
Gaylord's 299
Hanalei Dolphin 327
House of Seafood 316
JJ's Broiler 288
Kalaheo Steak House 303
Kapa'a Fish and Chowder House 289
Keoki's Paradise 317
King's Steakhouse and Tropical Bar 310
Naupaka Terrace Steak House 291
Tidepools 220
Winds of Beamreach 331
Wrangler's Steak House 315

VEGETARIAN

Caffe Coco 285
Hanapepe Cafe & Espresso 309
JJ's Broiler 288
Kalaheo Coffee Co. & Cafe 303
Kupono Cafe at ANARA Spa 310
Old Hanalei Coffee Company 325
Papaya's Natural Foods 280
Postcards Cafe 334
Tidepools 320
Zababaz One World Cafe 326

CENTRAL/EASTSIDE

INEXPENSIVE

AL & DON'S *American*
420 Papaloa Road, Kaua'i Sands Hotel, Kapa'a (822-4221) HOURS: Breakfast 7-9:15 am, Dinner 6-8 pm. No lunch. SAMPLING: Large selection of hot cakes (with a variety of tropical fruit toppings and special coconut syrup), waffles or waffle sandwich, French toast, omelettes, and egg dishes ($4-6). Dinners include French bread, choice of pasta or whipped potatoes and vegetable. There is spaghetti, roast turkey (or hot turkey sandwich), leg of lamb, chicken stir-fry, mahi mahi, lasagna, pineapple baked ham, or ham & turkey combination dinner ($7-10). Senior specials nightly. Chocolate dream cake, strawberry shortcake, cream pies, cheesecake, hula pie, or sundae. COMMENTS: They serve old-fashioned food at old-fashioned prices. Children's menu at half price. Breakfasts are the best bet, but any time before sunset buys you a great beachfront view. Karaoke on weekends.

ALOHA DINER *Local*
971-F Kuhio Hwy, Kapa'a, in the Waipouli Complex (822-3851) HOURS: Lunch Mon-Sat 10:30 am-2:30 pm; Dinner Tues-Sat 5:30-9 pm. Closed Sunday; lunch only on Monday SAMPLING: Local plates for lunch and a few more expensive ones for dinner: Kalua pig or lau lau with lomi salmon and rice or poi; with chicken luau, haupia or kulolo and tea or coffee for dinner ($6-9). Other lunches include tripe or beef stew and various combinations ($6-8). Dinner with additional items as above and in combination ($9-11). All specials items available a la carte along with won ton and saimin. COMMENTS: You can try luau food without the show - or the expense!

ARA'S SAKANA-YA FISH HOUSE *Seafood deli/plate lunches*
4301 Kuhio Hwy., Hanama'ulu (245-1707) HOURS: 8 am-7 pm; Sundays till 5. SAMPLING: Sushi, poke, boiled peanuts or soy beans, kim chee, shrimp, and scallop salad. Plate lunches include rice, potato salad, and kim chee ($5-7). COMMENTS: Eat in or take out.

AUPAKA TERRACE AND SUSHI BAR *Breakfast/evening pupus & sushi bar*
Kaua'i Marriott, poolside (245-5050) HOURS: Continental breakfast 6-10:30 am; Appetizers & sushi bar 5-10 pm. SAMPLING: Pastries, bagels, fruit, yogurt, Anahola granola. In the evening, try the Hawaiian nachos, cheese quesadilla, fish fingers, Volcano wings, shrimp cocktail, jalapeno poppers, burger, teri chicken sandwich, or Caesar salad ($6-10). The sushi bar offers a variety of sushi & sashimi and maki sushi rolls ($5-16). COMMENTS: An attractive restaurant resembling a large gazebo in a park. Choose from a dozen liqueur coffee drinks and specialty martinis. Cigars and board games available upon request.

BEEZERS ★ *Family Dining*

1378 Kuhio Hwy., Kapaʻa (822-4411) HOURS: 9 am-11 pm daily, (dinner from 4 pm - 9 pm), sandwiches and desserts till 11. SAMPLING: Breakfast served all day: scrambled eggs, omelettes, Scramble (eggs, mushrooms, onions, peppers, potato with cheese and Picante Sauce), and loco moco ($4-8); or order from a "serious" selection of burgers ("Cheezer," Boca veggie, chili, egg, char-grilled chicken breast or fresh fish, patty melt) plus turkey club, BLT, cold pastrami, grilled veggie, "Stacker" (ham, roast beef, or fresh-roasted turkey breast), tuna melt, fried egg, grilled ham & cheese, hot dog, peanut butter with jelly, banana, or bacon, and homemade Sloppy Joe or meatloaf sandwiches ($5-9). Homemade soup and chili; salads like the Beezers' Ceezer (with grilled chicken or fish), chef's, turkey, or tuna with homemade dressings. Dinner entrees and Blue Plate Specials feature chicken-fried steak, fried chicken, fish & chips, fresh fish, meatloaf, open-faced turkey sandwich, fresh fish, and grilled veggie platter ($11-19). They're served with sides of mashed potatoes, country gravy, and vegetables and if you clean your (real) blue plate, you can have dessert! Quench your thirst with a flavored coke, ice cream soda, egg cream, or black cow then get into the thick of it with a malt shake or smoothie. And there are all sorts of ice cream desserts, pies, fudge brownies, cakes, cookies, etc. COMMENTS: A Beezer is somebody who loves ice cream and this old-fashioned ice cream parlor is the kind of the place that only a Beezer can love. The decor is "malt shop chic," from the booths in the back to the soda fountain in front. Order at the shiney counter and enjoy the photos from the 50's and the collection of labels and logos - and linoleum! - from long ago.

BORDERS CAFE ESPRESSO *Coffee/Espresso, Sandwiches & Snacks*

Inside Borders Books at 4303 Nawiliwili Road, Lihuʻe (246-0862) HOURS: Monday-Thursday 7:30 am-9:30 pm; Friday-Saturday till 10:30; Sunday 8 am-7:30 pm. SAMPLING: Sandwiches, soups, salads (and combinations), vegetarian chili, eggrolls ($4-6). Flavored slushies and smoothies. Italian sodas, coffee and tea drinks. Chocolate crumb cake, baklava, brownies, cookies. COMMENTS: Small cafe with separate entrance or through Borders. Coffee bar or tables and chairs. Light meals and/or beverages served with plenty of reading material including out-of-town newspapers.

BUBBA'S *Burgers*

1421 Kuhio Hwy., Kapaʻa (823-0069) HOURS: 10:30 am-6 pm. SAMPLING: Bubbas, double bubbas, hubba bubbas plus hot dogs, corn dogs, and Budweiser beer chili. "Alternative" burgers include fish, chicken, tempeh, and Italian sausage or fresh fish sandwich with pineapple lemongrass salsa ($2-6). Side orders of Caesar salad, french fries, onion rings, frings (fries and rings), or chili fries ($2-4). COMMENTS: With a name like Bubba's, you were expecting maybe escargot? They're fun and funny and serve good, old-fashioned burgers to anyone named Bubba. (That means you!) They used to "cheat tourists and drunks", but had to "cease and desist" after receiving a letter from a San Francisco attorney. So now they also cheat attorneys! Not quite as funky as their original location across the street, but still fun at twice the size with an old-fashioned counter and stools, murals and memorabilia on the walls and ocean-view seating on the veranda. They've got another hamburger joint in Hanalei;

both locations have take-out and T-Shirts. Buy a hat or shirt and if you wear it when you order your burger, you'll get a free drink! Email: obubba@aloha.net Web: < www.bubbaburger.com >

CAFE ESPRESSO   *Coffee/Espresso, Sandwiches & Snacks*
1384 Kuhio Hwy., Kapa'a (822-9421) HOURS: Mon-Fri 8 am-2 pm; Saturday till noon; closed Sunday. Light breakfasts: Banana Belgian waffle, quiche, pancakes, breakfast burrito, cinnamon roll, bagels ($3-6); Hawaiian French toast on fresh-baked sweet bread with coffee or tea; turkey, tofu, or chicken salad; tuna or PB&J sandwiches on freshly baked honey-molasses wheat bread ($4-6) plus cakes, pies, pastries, juices, smoothies, and coffee drinks. They also have almond poppyseed, strawberry almond bread and other unique baked goods for sale.

COCONUT MARKETPLACE:
(484 Kuhio Highway, Kapa'a) Lappert's ice cream, Tradewinds Bar, and several small restaurants (Inexpensive for the most part) make this shopping center into a kind of extended food court. Some of the larger restaurants and/or those having something particular to recommend them are also listed individually and alphabetically.

ALOHA KAUA'I PIZZA (822-4511) Variety of pizza ($5-23) and their signature pizza is "Artichoke Eddie" with fresh garlic butter with marinated artichoke hearts, sweet red onions, tangy green olives, fume bueno cheese and tomatoes ($7-23); calzone ($5-7), lasagna ($7), Italian sandwiches ($6), salads ($4-7). Fresh ingredients, turkey meatballs, sausage and sauces from a 120-year-old family recipe have made this an *Entertainment Book* winner several years running.

BUZZ'S STEAK & LOBSTER (822-0041) See individual listing.

EGGBERT'S (822-3787) See individual listing.

(THE) FISH HUT (822-2505) Fish-n-chips plus ahi, ono, mahimahi, charbroiled fish, fried seafood (shrimp, scallops, oysters) in combinations with french fries & homemade cole slaw.

HARLEY'S RIBS-N-CHICKEN (822-2505) No surprise, they serve ribs and BBQ chicken!

PALM TREE TERRACE (823-1040) Sandwiches include grilled garlic chicken, pastrami, crab, mahimahi, etc.; appetizers range from calamari rings, mozzarella sticks, jalapeno poppers to lumpia; salads include grilled chicken salad, tuna, and crab; dinner entrees include choices like beef or chicken kabobs, pork chops, or NY steak; there are several pastas such as chicken Alfredo, chicken Sienna, shrimp Alfredo and seafood linguini; seafood choices include mahi mahi, fish and chips, and shrimp ($5-17) Lunch 11am-2pm, dinner 5-9pm.

RICCARDO'S MEXICAN FOOD ★ (822-2221) If you're hungry for Mexican food, this is a good option. They offer several choices including taco ($3.25), taco plate ($8), burritos ($8-12), enchilada plate ($8), quesadilla ($5-6), taco salad ($8-9), nachos ($7-10), combo plates ($8-10) and more. Open daily 11am-7pm.

TC'S ISLAND GRILL (823-9181) Local-style breakfasts plus hot dogs, hamburgers, salads, sandwiches, chili, and teriyaki beef or fried chicken platters.

DAIRY MAID ★ *Local*
4302 Rice St., Lihu'e (245-2141) HOURS: Mon-Thurs 7 am-9:30 pm, Fri-Sat till 10, Sun 7:30 am-3:30 pm. (Breakfast till 11 am, Dinner after 5 pm.) SAMPLING: Hot cakes, omelettes, waffles, French toast, and egg breakfasts ($4-6). Sandwiches include hot turkey, BLT, pastrami, club, tuna, and hot dogs; burgers with cheese, bacon, mushrooms, teriyaki, and BBQ or you can get your "burger" made with fish, chicken, or as a tuna or patty melt on rye ($2-6). Saimin, soup, salads, loco moco and entrees of pork chops, liver and onions, sweet & sour spare ribs, breaded fish, beef stew, chicken and veal cutlets ($2-9). Dinners offer rib steak, mahi mahi, breaded shrimp, steak and scampi ($10-18). For dessert, ice cream treats like cones, shakes, floats, freezes, and a variety of sundaes. COMMENTS: The emphasis here is on reasonably priced, local-style favorites, plate lunches, ice cream desserts and treats; the whole menu is available for take out and they have catering, too.

DAKINE DOGS ★ *American*
4-1378 Kuhio Highway, Kapa'a (821-1668) HOURS: Mon-Sat 11 am - 8 pm, closed Sunday. This upstairs open-air dining room (located above Beezer's Ice Cream Shop) is in the heart of busy Kapa'a town, corner of Kukui Street and Kuhio Highway. SAMPLING: The emphasis here is hot dogs and sausages of all kinds. They feature Vienna beef-brand hot dogs, Polish sausage, Italian beef sausage, bratwrust and more shipped directly from Chicago. The menu is hot dogs, sausages, chili, burgers and more. Standard hot dog is $2.50; Chicago style hot dog 3; chili dogs $3.50-4.50; Italian beef sandwich $5.50; Italian sausage $4.50; jumbo fire dog hot & spicy $4.50; bratwurst $4.50; Hefty Burger $4.50. COMMENTS: Hot dogs and sandwiches come with all the fixings and condiments, some an extra charge like sauerfraut, cheese, peppers or pickels. They don't cook or make anything until it is ordered, ensuring a flavorful tasty meal. It's a grungy, funky sort of a place which may appeal to those who aren't too concerned about visual aesthetics.

DANI'S ★ *Local*
4201 Rice St., Lihu'e (245-4991) HOURS: Breakfast 5-11 am; Lunch 11:30 am-1 pm. Closed Sundays. SAMPLING: Breakfast meats, eggs, and omelettes including kalua pig and Dani's special with fish cake, green onion, and tomato ($5-7). Pineapple, banana, papaya hot cakes and sweet bread French toast ($4-6). Breakfast and lunch specials include combinations of lau lau, kalua pig, beef or tripe stew and lunch entrees offer hamburger steak, pork chops, roast pork, veal, beef or chicken cutlet, fried shrimp, oysters or scallops, plus burgers and sandwiches ($5-9). COMMENTS: This is a very popular coffee shop eatery with the

RESTAURANTS
Central/Eastside

locals. It's a large open dining room with numerous tables. The standard here is good local-style food and pleasant friendly service in a clean, neat atmosphere. Smoking and non-smoking areas available. If you haven't tried some real Hawaiian cuisine, this is the place to do it at reasonable cost. The lau lau and kalua pig combinations are excellent.

DELI & BREAD CONNECTION   *Deli/Sandwiches*
Kukui Grove Shopping Center, 3171 Kuhio Highway, Lihu'e (245-7115) HOURS: 9:30 am (from 10 on Sundays) to 7 pm (till 9 on Fridays, 6 Saturdays, 5 Sundays). SAMPLING: Sandwiches on freshly-baked bread or rolls include roast beef, pastrami, corned beef, smoked ham, liverwurst, chicken salad, and crab meat ($4-6). French Dip, tuna or chicken with avocado, Reuben, BLT, meatloaf, or club, sub or poor boy with choice of ingredients ($5-8). Vegetarian sandwiches and daily homemade soups ($3-6). COMMENTS: We've heard good things about their fresh (and freshly-made) ingredients and generous portions. They also sell gourmet books, kitchen gadgets, and cookware in an old-fashioned general store setting. Bakery breads include rye, wheat, sour dough, French and their signature Oriental sweet bread plus giant muffins and cookies, cinnamon rolls, manju, brownies, and pies. Indoor and outdoor seating.

DORI'S GARDEN CAFE   *Coffee/Espresso, Sandwiches & Snacks*
Roxy Square (part of Sunnyside Market) 1345 Kuhio Hwy., Kapa'a (822-0494) HOURS: 8 am-7 pm SAMPLING: Hot or cold corned beef, pastrami, or salami sandwiches on rye ($6); gourmet sandwiches include sauteed eggplant, smoked turkey, hummus, and sugar cured ham ($5). Homemade soups like vegetable chili, beef stew, chicken noodle, and clam chowder; garden, tuna, or cobb salad ($3-6). Fruit smoothies in assorted combinations of papaya, strawberry, pineapple, banana, and mango. COMMENTS: Small, casual cafe that's a kind of "patio" to the Sunnyside Market next door. The market offers take-home pineapples, mac nuts, and papayas boxed for shipping and also carries snacks, beverages, coffees, candy, and food products along with crafts, gifts, T-shirts, clothes -- even shrunken heads!

DRIFTWOOD SAND BAR & GRILL   *Coffee/Espresso, Sandwiches & Snacks*
Radisson Kaua'i Beach Resort, 4331 Kaua'i Beach Drive, Lihu'e, (245-1955). HOURS: Lunch-snacks continuously, 10 am - 6 pm daily. This resort poolside bar & grill features beverages, cocktails, snacks and light meals, burgers, sandwiches, salads and general light fare.

EGGBERTS FAMILY SPECIALTY RESTAURANT   *American*
Coconut MarketPlace, by the water wheel (822-3787) HOURS: Breakfast 7 am-3 pm; Lunch 11 am-3 pm; Dinner 5-9 pm SAMPLING: Eggs Benedict in five styles (combos of veggie, ham, or turkey) and two sizes or create your own with additional ingredients - all with Eggbert's own Hollandaise made fresh with tangy lemon ($8-11). Omelette varieties include ham, Portuguese sausage, mushrooms, sour cream & chives, tomato & cheese, and Denver or you can choose your fillings ($4-10). Egg plates, pigs-in-a-blanket, French toast (with cinnamon and vanilla), and banana hotcakes round out the breakfast menu ($4-8). Lunch specialties offer turkey or ham club sandwiches, fried rice "crowned" with a crepe-thin

omelette, pork & cabbage, and the definitive brunch dish: Eggbert's Big "O" omelette sandwich with choice of ingredients ($5-8). Dinner entrees include NY steak, fresh catch, stir frys (fish, chicken, beef, or pork) meat loaf, roast pork, and BBQ chicken ($9-16). Senior and children's portions available. COMMENTS: Eggs Benedict, along with keiki favorites like banana pancakes and pigs-in-a-blanket, are among their specialties. Their "water-wheel" corner of the Coconut MarketPlace is open and airy with comfortable space between the tables and a veranda that's perfect for people watching.

ENDLESS SUMMER *Snacks/Farmers Market*
3366 Wa'apa Road, (adjacent to Anchor Cove) Lihu'e (246-8854) HOURS: 9 am-9 pm (Monday 9 am-5 pm) SAMPLING: Hot dogs, chili & rice, smoothies, shakes, Lappert's ice cream ($3-6). COMMENTS: Fresh fruit stand and mini-farmers market in front. Try an Endless Summer smoothie with papaya, banana, pineapple, lilikoi, and coconut juice.

(THE) FISH EXPRESS *Seafood*
3343 Kuhio Hwy., Lihu'e by Wal-Mart (245-9918) HOURS: 10 am-7 pm Mon-Sat., till 5 pm Sun. SAMPLING: Plate lunches, kalua or lau lau plate, seafood lunch ($6-8). Prepared fish with a variety of sauces: Provencal, passion-orange & tarragon, ginger-curry, blackened with guava-basil. COMMENTS: Seafood deli with limited seating.

GARDEN ISLAND BBQ ★ *Chinese/local*
4252 Rice St. in Lihu'e (245-8868) HOURS: Monday-Saturday 10:30 am-9 pm, Closed Sunday. SAMPLING: Chicken, beef, pork & shrimp dishes plus chow mein, BBQ, soups, and combination plates like lemon chicken, beef curry, pork with bitter melon, shrimp with eggplant, loco moco, BBQ short ribs, sweet & sour spare pork, scallop soup, rainbow tofu soup, and House "Chop Suey Chow Mein!" ($4-8); burgers and sandwiches ($2-3). COMMENTS: Good selection of inexpensive local and now Chinese food located next to the thrift store bakery on Rice Street.

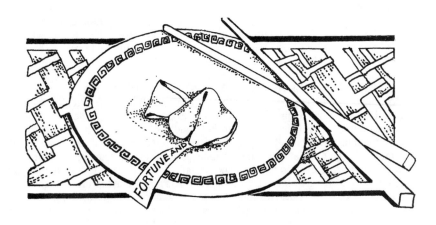

HAMURA SAIMIN ★ *Local*
2956 Kress, Lihu'e, just off Rice Street (245-3271) HOURS: Mon-Thurs 10 am-11 pm; Fri & Sat till 1 am; Sundays till 9:30 pm. SAMPLING: No surprise, they serve saimin - in small, medium, large, and extra large. Also BBQ, udon, fried noodles, and won ton soup. Most expensive item on the menu is the shrimp or special (with lots of meat, veggies, and hard boiled egg) saimin at $5. Fresh lilikoi pie is a specialty. COMMENTS: This is another of Kaua'i's original "hole-in-the-wall" diners. It's a somewhat rundown looking and tacky sort of place with U-shaped formica-covered counters with a variety of unmatched stools. But that's what makes it special. This is a very popular place with the locals or anyone who likes slurping noodles. The menu is on the wall and is limited, so ordering and receiving your food is quite speedy. A good thing too, because during peak meal hours you may have to wait for a vacant stool. You'll find friendly local folks explaining directions to Wailua Falls to a youthful European backpacker and next to them a group with mega numbers of kids sitting with chopsticks in hand eagerly awaiting their steaming bowls of saimin. But don't overlook the chicken and beef sticks. The meat is a good size portion, moist and very flavorful. Order at least one to accompany your noodles! Hamura Saimin is not only popular during regular meals, but since so many of the clubs have closed down, it's actually become a late-night hang out. Oh yes, and heed the warning posted, no sticking gum under the counter! They serve shave ice (as Halo Halo Shave Ice) Monday-Friday from 10 am-4 pm. You may see locals picking up boxes of raw saimin noodles to send home with visiting family and friends. Hamura saimin has something of a cult following throughout the islands among noodle connoisseurs. You may have to hunt for parking on the nearby narrow and crowded streets and lanes but it will be worth a walk to have Humura's saimin.

HIGASHI *Local*
1415 Kuhio Hwy., Kapa'a (822-5982) HOURS: Mon-Fri 6 am-2 pm, Sat 6 am-1 pm. Closed Sunday. SAMPLING: Two eggs, breakfast meat, rice & toast or omelettes. Sandwiches: hamburger (teri or BBQ), egg, tuna, ham, bacon & egg; saimin, oxtail soup, loco moco, chicken moco; beef or curry stew, shoyu chicken, roast pork, mahi, beef or pork cutlet ($3-8).

HIROKO'S OKAZUYA *Local*
3630 Lalo Road across from the school; turn up the hill just past Nawiliwili Harbor. (245-3450) HOURS: Breakfast and lunch 7 am-2 pm. SAMPLING: Breakfast ($5-6); daily plate lunch specials: chicken hekka, pork peas & pimento, fried rice & hot dog, mayo baked chicken, roast beef or pork, sweet & sour meatballs, or mixed plate with two pieces of chicken, two pieces of cooked meat, noodles, luncheon meat, corned beef hash, two scoops rice and one scoop macaroni salad ($5-7). COMMENTS: Sodas and juices. Benches outside with soda machine for after hours.

HONG KONG CAFE ★ *Chinese*
Wailua Shopping Center at 4-361 Kuhio Hwy., Kapa'a (822-3288) HOURS: Open daily except Tuesday closed, 10:30 am-2:30 pm, and 4:30-9:30 pm. SAMPLING: Lunch and dinner plates and combos include rice, macaroni salad and sweet & sour cabbage. House specialties include Kung Pao stir fry chicken, pork or beef, hot & spicy eggplant with meat, stir fry cashew nut or almond with meat, spicy sauteed shrimp and sweet and sour pork ($7-10).

Other menu items include chicken katsu, roast duck, fried shrimp, lemon chicken, BBQ beef stick, fish cutlet, char siu, sweet & sour chicken, and fried stuffed eggplant ($5-8). Sizzling platters offer seafood, fish, or pepper steak ($8-10). Vegan specials include stir fry mushroom with snow peas, stir fry egglant with tofu, Kung Pao tofu and Mongolian broccoli ($6-8) Ala carte dishes range from the traditional to the unusual. You can order your mu shu pork with beef, chicken, or vegetables instead -- either way, the portions are generous with plenty of tasty filling and just enough "crepes" and hoison sauce to make everything come out even! Deep fried crab & cream cheese won tons are just one of the ways to start, but the Chinese chicken salad with shredded walnut and crispy noodle is not to be missed. Roast duck is a specialty as is their spicy eggplant with chicken, minced pork, beef, or shrimp -- both are excellent choices and worthy signature dishes ($5-20). Chow mein, lo mein, saimin, and several vegetarian dishes round out the menu. COMMENTS: The color scheme of aqua & black with green & black marble accents give this inviting Chinese restaurant a sleek art deco look. The ambiance is clean and smoke-free, the attractive chairs have comfortable, cushy seats, and there's a colorful aquarium as a focal point. They use fresh Kaua'i products -- fresh fish and vegetables -- and serve purified, filtered water. Everything we tried was excellent (with friendly, efficient service to match) which makes this a surprising and welcome find!

KAHANU SNACK BAR *Coffee/Espresso, Sandwiches & Snacks*
Holiday Inn Sun Spree Resort, Wailua (823-6000) HOURS: 11 am-6 pm. SAMPLING: Mahi mahi or chicken sandwich, cheeseburger, hot dog on Hawaiian sweet bread bun, garden or fruit salad ($4-8) plus fries, onion rings, corn dog, ice cream and shakes. Traditional tropical drinks like Blue Hawaii, Tropical Itch, Pina Colada or Chi Chi, and Holiday Punch.
COMMENTS: This poolside restaurant also offers an ocean view.

KALAPAKI BEACH HUT ★ *Coffee/Espresso, Sandwiches & Snacks*
Overlooking Kalapaki Bay, 3474 Rice Street, next to Anchor Cove Shopping Center. (246-6330) HOURS: Daily 7 am-7 pm, breakfast till 10:30. SAMPLING: Breakfast egg or pancake sandwich, loco moco, omelettes, mahi & eggs, buffalo & eggs (really!), Branola French Toast ($3-7). Lunches feature their flame-broiled beef or buffalo burgers with a variety of toppings. Caesar salad; fish & chips; mahi, chicken, tuna, or vegetarian sandwiches ($4-6). Try their fresh fruit smoothie with papaya, banana, pineapple, strawberry, and guava - made milk-shake-thick. Keiki menu available. COMMENTS: Cheap eats in a casual outdoor setting or buy your burger or plate lunch to go. Seating available upstairs for a view of the park and bay area or dine at the counter on the lower level.

KALAPAKI GRILL *Snacks/light meals*
Located poolside at the Kaua'i Marriott. (245-5050) HOURS: 11 am-4:30 pm. SAMPLING: Grilled burgers, jumbo hot dog, sandwiches (turkey, tuna, grilled chicken), garden, chicken Caesar, or rotelle pasta salad, shrimp cocktail, jalapeno poppers ($5-10). COMMENTS: Appetizers served in dim sum baskets. Shave ice in 8 flavors, from coconut to lemon-lime. Keiki menu available. Beer, wine & tropical drinks.

KALENA FISH MARKET ★   *Local/Korean*
2985A Kalena St. (next to Lihu'e Fishing Supply), Lihu'e (246-6629) HOURS: Monday-Friday 10 am-7 pm, Saturday till 5, closed Sunday. SAMPLING: Kalua, lau lau, or special Hawaiian plate; Korean plates (BBQ beef, chicken, or short ribs; meat jun, bi bim bap, fried man doo, kim chee soup) with 2 scoops rice & choice of vegetable ($5-8). COMMENTS: Fish or tako poke, opihi, lomi salmon, scallop salad, smoked or dried fish, and other pupus from the deli.

KAUA'I BREW AND BURRITO   *Mexican*
919 Kuhio Hwy., Kapa'a (823-0330) HOURS: Lunch 11 am-4 pm; dinner 4-9 pm. Closed Sun. SAMPLING: Appetizers include nachos, quesadillas, popcorn shrimp or chicken, cheesy potato, hot dog bites with dipping sauce, ahi poke or sashimi, and spicy chicken wings ($5-10). Plate lunches with kalua pork, chicken, steak, veggies, fish, or shrimp with beans & rice, and salad. Burritos, tostados, taquitos, chili & rice, or cheese quesdilla ($4-9). Giant burrito on a 12" tortilla is a special ($10). Dinner specials offer fresh catch, grilled shrimp, teri chicken or beef, grilled veggie plate, fajitas, enchiladas, burritos, tacos, tostado, beef or chicken kabobs, and kalua pork plate ($9-16). COMMENTS: Non-smoking restaurant with good prices and hearty portions. Traditional Mexican favorites and several dishes with a Mexican flair. Their "best" burrito is made with black beans and can be ordered gourmet-style with kalua pork & a ginger cabernet sauce, or try the ocean style ahi or shrimp with white wine & lemon pepper. Beer and wine bar with a good selection of draft beer. Free tokens are given out to children of diners for the video games and on Tuesday nights, kids eat free! (5-9 pm, up to age 12).

KAUA'I CHOP SUEY   *Chinese*
In Harbor Mall, 3501 Rice Street, Nawiliwili (245-8790) HOURS: Lunch Tuesday-Saturday 11 am-2 pm, Dinner Tuesday-Sunday 4:30-9 pm. Closed Monday. SAMPLING: House specials include Kaua'i chop suey with mushrooms ($8) or hon too mein for 4-6 persons ($28). Also chicken, duck, shrimp, scallop, beef, pork, vegetarian, sweet & sour, egg, and noodle dishes ($6-10). Chow mein and noodle soups as well as rice dishes including special fried rice with chicken, pork, mushrooms, beans, shrimp, and more ($4-9). Their sizzling rice platters like beef, chicken, scallop or shrimp with lobster sauce (with 10 pieces of jumbo shrimp) are a specialty ($7-9). COMMENTS: Big Chinese banquet room divided into three areas with round archways and red & gold decor. They don't have a liquor license, so bring your own if you so choose. The food is nicely seasoned and the sizzling platters (which arrive crackling and steaming) are always fun!

KAUA'I COMMUNITY COLLEGE/QUEEN VICTORIA ROOM
Hawaiian/Local Style
3-1901 Kaumualii Highway #50, Lihu'e, inside the Campus Center. (245-8243) HOURS: Wed & Fri at 11:30am - 1:00 pm, when classes are in session during spring and fall semesters. SAMPLING: Three-course continental and Pacific Rim lunches ($9-13) are the fine dining options for spring; fall is more like a "coffee shop" with diner/coffee shop style cooking and casual atmosphere. Salads, sandwiches, and homecooked entrees ($3-8) with paper plates, paper napkins, etc. For the fine dining and tableside-cooked lunches, they bring out the "good" china, silver and linen napkins. COMMENTS: Separate dining room offers lunch

while school is in session as part of the Culinary Arts training program. Students learn all aspects of the restaurant business; they shop, serve, clean, and wait on the tables. The program is only offered during the school year, so be sure and call to check on availability and schedule a reservation.

KAUA'I KITCHENS *Local*
Rice Shopping Center, 4303 Rice Street, Lihu'e (245-4513) HOURS: 7 am-2:30 pm, Saturdays 7:30 am-1:30 pm. Closed Sundays. SAMPLING: Sandwiches, plate lunches, bentos, sushi (maki cone) and daily specials ($2 and up): chicken cutlet, fresh corned beef, breaded crab croquette, baked pork chops, roast turkey with stuffing, lemon chicken, seafood curry, fish filet, pork adobo plus Hawaiian, Filipino, and Oriental plates ($5-7). They also sell Kaua'i Kookies, baked foods and T-shirts retail from the Kaua'i Kookie Kompany. COMMENTS: "Quick Tasty Island Style" that you can eat in or take out. They have another location in Koloa.

KAUA'I MIX PLATE & DELI *Hawaiian/Local Style*
3204 Kuhio Highway, Lihu'e (246-8898) HOURS: Open daily, 7:30 am - 9:30 pm. SAMPLING: This local-style fast food counter serves up a real variety of inexpensive fare. Breakfast items include omelettes ($5-6), steak and eggs ($7), loco moco and eggs ($6), and pancakes ($3-4). For lunch/dinner, choose from burgers ($1-3), stew/chili/curry ($3), oriental chicken salad ($5), different varieties of stir fry noodles ($5-7), plate lunches like lemon chicken, teri beef, mahi mahi, bbq chicken, katsu curry, pork katsu, shrimp, loco moco, beef stew and more ($5-7) with mini-plates ($4-5). COMMENTS: Beach packs and party pans for take out also available. Eat in or take out.

KAWAYAN *Local/Filipino*
1543 Haleukana St., Puhi Industrial Park (245-8823) HOURS: Monday-Saturday 9-9:30 am to 6 pm or later. Closed Sundays. SAMPLING: Pork adobo, pancit guisado, pinkabet, and Thai chicken served daily ($6-7) along with lumpia and spring rolls. Plate lunches have 1, 2, or 3 choices of entrees and are featured as daily specials ($6-8) like curry chicken, pork & peas, chicken papaya (Monday), beef senigang, fish or vegetable curry (Tuesday), chow fun, chicken adobo, Thai fried rice with shrimp & pork (Wednesday), pork tocino, Thai curry (Thursday), mongo beans, beef tocino, fried rice (Friday). COMMENTS: They also have halo-halo, shave ice, and frozen appetizers (lumpia, spring rolls) by the dozen.

K.C.L. BARBECUE & CHINESE RESTAURANT ★ *Local*
3100 Kuhio Hwy., Lihu'e (246-3829) and 4-971 Kuhio Hwy. in the Waipouli Complex, Kapa'a (823-8168) HOURS: Lunch & Dinner, Sun-Thurs 10:30 am-9 pm, Fri-Sat 10:30 am-3:00 am. Breakfast (Kapa'a only) 8-11 am; SAMPLING: Eggs, omelettes, loco moco, French toast, or pancakes for breakfast ($4-6). Burgers, BBQ chicken, shrimp, mahi, or teri beef sandwiches, and hot dogs ($2-4). The menu is an extensive list of 138 items including chicken (lemon, katsu, cutlet, BBQ, ginger), roast duck, char siu, mahi mahi, pork chop, loco moco, teriyaki steak, sweet & sour spare ribs, shrimp curry, and combinations (mixed or BBQ mixed plate, bento box, NY steak & garlic shrimp, seafood or chicken combo, and fried chicken) with macaroni salad and rice ($4-8). Chinese dishes

include chop suey, pot roast, chicken with cashew nuts & vegetables, shrimp with straw mushrooms, beef broccoli, pork with bitter melon, chicken with eggplant, shrimp with black bean sauce and squid with ginger & onion ($6-8). COMMENTS: Hard to find a hamburger for $1.25 - or for that matter, mahi mahi, fried shrimp, and scallops for under $7 - but you can here! The mostly local clientele recommend the BBQ mixed plate and the "great Chinese food." An ideal way to stretch your food budget with a varied menu offering lots of choices. The Lihu'e outlet is across Kuhio Highway from McDonald's.

KIM CHEE #9 RESTAURANT *Korean*
3-2600 Kaumualii Highway, Lihu'e (246-0106). HOURS: Sun-Thurs 10:30 am-8 pm, Fri-Sat 10:30 am-9 pm. SAMPLING: This small restaurant features an all-Korean menu. Choose from entrees like BBQ chicken or beef ($7), Kal Bi Ribs ($15), BBQ pork ($7), meat jun ($7), chicken katsu ($8), shrimp tempura ($10), squid tempura ($9), chicken tofu ($7), steamed man doo ($6), mahi katsu ($8), and chop chae long rice ($8) plus many other selections. COMMENTS: This is probably one of the most unusually named restaurants on Kaua'i. Located next to Long's Drugs on the outside corner near parking lot, Kukui Grove Center.

KOREAN BBQ *Korean*
356 Kuhio Hwy. in the Kinipopo Shopping Center, Wailua (823-6744) HOURS: 10 am-9 pm, Wed-Mon. Open Thurs for dinner only 4:30-9 pm. SAMPLING: Combination plates served with four vegetables, macaroni-potato salad, and two scoops of rice. Kalbi ribs, teri beef, BBQ chicken, fried or rolled mandoo (dumpling), fish jun ($5-8). Single plates: Stir fry squid or long rice (tofu, chicken, or beef), chicken cutlet or katsu, hamburger steak ($6-8); also kim chee, miso, and kooksoo soup.

KOUNTRY KITCHEN ★ *American*
1485 Kuhio Hwy., Kapa'a (822-3511) HOURS: Breakfast 6 am-2 pm, Lunch 11 am-2 pm SAMPLING: Pancakes and waffles (plain, strawberry, or banana), French toast, pork chop and eggs, corned beef hash, loco moco, omelettes with cornbread (Polynesian, Denver, ham & cheese, fresh mushroom, hamburger, tuna, chili, or build-your-own), and vegetable, turkey, or traditional eggs Benedict ($4-10). Lunch fare includes patty melt, BLT, grilled ham & cheese, and tuna sandwiches or create your own burger with your choice of a variety of toppings ($5-7). Lunch plates of hamburger steak, grilled pork chop, mahi mahi, sirloin steak, or fried chicken served with vegetable, rice or fries and cornbread ($7-9). Ice cream, and blueberry or apple crisp. COMMENTS: Looks like an old-fashioned coffee shop of the 50's, but with wood, brick, and copper accents. Family-style restaurant, but they do have beer and wine. (Keiki menu available. Good breakfasts!

KUKUI GROVE SHOPPING CENTER
(3-2600 Kaumualii Highway, Lihu'e) As the draw of most of these small restaurants is their location in the Kukui Grove Shopping Center, we've listed them here with just a capsule review. Most are Inexpensive for the most part. Some of the larger restaurants and/or those having something particular to recommend them are also listed individually.

America Online owner, and formerHawaii resident, Steve Case, recently purchased Grove Farm which owns the shopping center, so be looking for some changes in the near future as plans move forward for upgrading the shopping center.

DELI & BREAD CONNECTION (245-7115) - See individual listing.

HO'S CHINESE KITCHEN ★ (245-5255) Chinese dishes such as lemon chicken, cold ginger chicken, roast duck on rice, beef broccoli chow mein, beef chow fun, pork with Chinese peas, beef tomato, shrimp Canton, mahi mahi black bean, various soup, chop suey, noodle, rice and egg specialties ($5-7). Open Mon-Thurs & Sat 9:30am-6pm; Friday 9:30am-9pm; Sunday 9:30am-5pm.

JONI HANA ★ (245-5213) Menu changes daily and features things like chow mein, teri chicken or beef, lemon shou chicken, chow fun, beef stew, sweet sour spare ribs, chicken broccoli, shrimp tempura, nishime and others; plate lunches, bentos, real "local-style grinds" ($4-8)

KAUA'I BAKERY (246-4765) Donuts, turnovers, cinnamon buns & local pastries: manju, malasadas plus haupia, lilikoi, and guava cakes.

KIM CHEE #9 RESTAURANT (246-0106) See individual listing.

MYRON'S (245-5178) Filipino and local food, plate lunches; menu items such as pork or chicken adobo, tripe stew, chicken papaya, pork & peas, BBQ spare ribs, chicken long rice, lumpia ($5-7).

ZACK'S FAMOUS FROZEN YOGURT & CAFE (246-2415) - See individual listing.

KUN JA'S II   *Korean*
939A Kuhio Hwy., Kapa'a (821-2088) HOURS: Monday-Saturday 10 am-9 pm. Closed Sunday. SAMPLING: Soup and noodles (with beef, vegetables, squid, dumplings, or tofu); Kalbi ribs, BBQ chicken or beef, egg-battered mahi, sauteed squid, kim chee fried rice with beef ($5-7). Popular combination plates with BBQ chicken and beef, mundoo (dumplings), or Kalbi ribs ($7-8). COMMENTS: Entrees served with kim chee, Korean style vegetables, rice, and bowl of soup; nothing but authentic Korean cuisine.

LA PLAYITA AZUL   *Mexican*
831 Kuhio Highway, Kaua'i Shopping Village, Kapa'a (821-2323) HOURS: Lunch 11 am-3 pm, dinner 6-9pm daily, except closed Monday. SAMPLING: Enjoy some authentic and creative Mexican cuisine. This small eatery serves up a big menu of creative and traditional Mexican fare. Chicken mole enchilada ($8), enchiladas verdes ($8), quesadilla ($8), taquitos ($8); try the nachos ($9), chimichanga ($9), Monico's veggie burrito ($9), burrito con carne azada ($9), burrito con pollo or burrito al pastor ($9). Other specials include costilla en chile verde tradicion ($10), taco de pescado ($11), burrito de pescado fresco ($11),

mole poblano de pollo ($12), seafood burrito ($13), camarones al mojo de ajo--garlic shrimp--($15), and camarones a la diabla--shrimp in chipolte sauce ($15). COMMENTS: Eat in or take out. Located just around the corner from Safeway and next to the "Chocolats, Mon Amour" Belgian chocolate shop. Next door to dessert!

LIHU'E BAKERY & COFFEE SHOP *Filipino*
Rice Shopping Center, 4303 Rice St., Lihu'e (245-7520) HOURS: Monday-Friday 5 am-6 pm, Saturday 5 am-4 pm, Sunday 5-10 am. SAMPLING: Unusual Filipino baked goods, also donuts and muffins. Hot Filipino entrees served cafeteria-style from 5 am through lunch ($4-6). COMMENTS: Macaroons, turnovers, and lots of baked goods.

LIHU'E CAFE *Local*
2978 Umi St., Lihu'e (245-6471) HOURS: Lunch only: Tuesday-Friday, 10:30 am-1:30 pm. SAMPLING: Weekly menu specials are chicken hekka, chili dog (Tuesday); roast pork, nishime (Wednesday); pork tofu, chicken curry (Thursday); beef stew, roast turkey, surprise special (Friday). Daily specials vary, but might include chow fun, sweet & sour spare ribs, or fried chicken with rice, kim chee, and salad ($5-7). Teriyaki or chop steak plate; Saimin, won ton mein, bento ($3-6). COMMENTS: Mostly open at night as a bar & lounge, but they serve lunch from a small buffet table for you to pick up and bring to your booth or table.

LIZARD LOUNGE & DELI ★ *Sandwiches/Pizza*
Waipouli Town Center, 771 Kuhio Hwy. (821-2205) HOURS: 10 am-2 am. SAMPLING: Pizza by the slice ($2-3) and a selection of ham, salami, turkey, veggie, tuna, chicken salad, or roast beef sandwiches named after the seven major Hawaiian islands ($5). They're served on a large French roll (fresh and soft) with dill pickles on the side. Chef salad, buffalo wings, or chicken breast sandwich ($7). Smoothies, coffee drinks, and good homemade cole slaw and potato salad. Imported beers and microbrews, modern martinis and tropical drinks like the Po'ipu Passion, Kapa'a Cooler, and a pina colada that they'll put up against any on the island! COMMENTS: This gathering place is bright and inviting with hanging plants and plenty of seating at tables & chairs or the bar/counter. Live entertainment, billiard tables, electric and steel tip dart boards - even playing cards - make this a popular hang-out for workers, singles, families - just about anyone. The shopping center is safe and well-lit so you can take advantage of the 2 am closing.

L&L DRIVE INN ★ *Local*
733 Kuhio Hwy., Kapa'a (821-8880) HOURS: 10 am-10 pm. SAMPLING: At L&L you can get plate lunches including seafood, chicken, pork, beef and vegetarian Oriental dishes, plus burgers, hot dogs, saimin, chili, curry, and stew ($4-6); combinations plates or prime rib ($6-8). Combination plates ($4-7) include up to three entree items. Varied daily entrees from the buffet steam table range from beef with broccoli, orange chicken, vegetable chop suey, black pepper chicken strips, or sweet & sour pork and much more ($5-7). COMMENTS: This is the L&L chain's Kaua'i outlet and they feature local-style plate lunches and favorites at reasonable prices.

MA'S ★ *Local/Homestyle*
4277 Halenani Street, Lihu'e (245-3142) HOURS: Monday-Friday 5 am-1:30 pm, Saturday & Sunday to 11:30 am. SAMPLING: Eggs, Irish omelette, Doctor's omelette (eggwhites only), bacon, Portuguese sausage, pipi kaula, and waffles or pancakes come plain or with pineapple, papaya, or banana ($5). Lunch entrees vary daily but may include things like meat loaf, veal/pork cutlets, fresh ahi or akule fish, Ma's fried noodles with teriyaki meat, beef or tripe stew, curry beef ($4-7). Hawaiian specials include kalua pork and eggs, pipi kaula and eggs, laulau and eggs, lomilomi salmon and eggs, corned beef hash and eggs ($5). Specialty sandwiches such as roast beef and pork plus hamburgers are available ($2-4). COMMENTS: Ma's opened in the mid 1960's and you can still see Ma cooking on the griddle in back - sort of a forerunner to the currently popular open kitchen concept of the trendy fine dining restaurants! The breakfasts are still a bargain. Try a local variety of spam and eggs. Other breakfasts including omelettes, pancakes, or French toast made with Portuguese sweet bread are a real value. This is definitely a hole-in-the-wall, greasy spoon restaurant, but that's what makes it so much fun! It's a real funky sort of place but the service is genuinely warm and sincere, a reflection of Kaua'i itself. Ma herself, a very gracious and grandmotherly lady, will greet you with a smile and plunk down a big thermos of coffee so you can serve yourself. (The coffee is free with meals!) Big portions and great prices make it popular with locals and returning visitors. Turn off Rice Street onto Kress Street and another left onto Halenani. Just around the corner from Hamura Saimin and Barbecue Inn. Limited street parking in front and on nearby narrow streets and lanes. But worth a walk back to try it. This is one of those places that make dining out a real adventure.

MARIA'S ★ *Mexican*
3-3142 Kuhio Hwy., Lihu'e (246-9122) HOURS: Mon-Fri 11 am-8 pm, Sat 5-8 pm, closed Sun. SAMPLING: A la carte nachos, quesadilla, burritos, tostadas, enchiladas, and tacos ($2-5). Combination plates with tacos, enchiladas, chile rellenos, taquitos, and veggie or pork sopes ($6-9). Beer, wine or homemade Sangria available. Dinners to go serve 2 to 6 people ($17-42). COMMENTS: Yes, there really is a Maria and she learned to cook traditional family recipes from her grandmother in Jalisco, Mexico. Located next to Seven-Eleven and across from the Lihu'e McDonald's, this small Mexican restaurant doesn't take credit cards, but not to worry, they're also located next to an ATM!

MARK'S PLACE *Local*
1610 Haleukana Street in the Puhi Industrial Park (245-2722) HOURS: 10 am-7 pm. SAMPLING: Plate lunches with hamburger steak, beef curry or stew, teri or Korean chicken, loco moco, chicken cutlet or katsu in regular or mini sizes ($4-6). Mixed plate with chicken katsu, teri beef, and beef stew ($6). Burgers, and hot teri chicken or beef sandwiches ($2-4). Daily specials might include garlic & herb ahi, 1/2 roasted chicken with mashed potatoes and corn on the cob, or miso pork with eggplant ($6-7). Fresh salads change daily; mini or large bento. Homemade desserts like strawberry Bavarian parfait ($2) or blueberry streusel, haupia bread pudding, and banana nut bread. COMMENTS: This is a real dining discovery, an out-of-the-way place worth searhing for just off Puhi Road and Hanalima Street. They also offer take-out and catering as "Contemporary Flavors, Inc."

MERMAIDS CAFE *Health Food*
1384 Kuhio Highway, Kapaʻa (821-2026) HOURS: Open Mon-Sat 9 am - 9 pm, closed Sunday. SAMPLING: Tofu or Chicken satay plate; tofu or chicken coconut curry plate; stir fry noodle plate; ahi nori wrap; chicken satay wrap; ahi cilantro wrap; organic salad; black bean burrito; foccacia sandwich with ahi tuna or chicken; also breakfast bagels, scones, french toast, eggs, and more; beverages include international teas, coffees, etc. All meals for under $10; sidewalk seating and tables.

NAWILIWILI TAVERN *Italian*
3488 Paena Loop, at Kalapaki Bay near Anchor Cove Shopping Center, Lihuʻe. (245-7079) HOURS: Dinner 4-8 pm, bar open till 2 am. SAMPLING: Spaghetti with marinara, meat, spinach & mushroom, white clam, meatballs, and combination sauces, or chicken parmesean served with green salad and fresh baked sour dough bread ($6-8). Daily specials ($6-8) offer spicy sausage & roasted peppers (Mon); baked lasagna (Tues); braised pork chop pizziola (Wed); eggplant parmesean (Thurs); seafood classic (Fri); chicken catchitori, (Sat); scampi chicken (Sun). Dessert speciality is creamy amaretto tiramisu. COMMENTS: Pool tables, darts, and video games, satellite live sports, plus free email; karaoke every Tuesday. Located in the historic Hotel Kuboyama.

OKAZU HALE *Japanese/Local*
4100 Rice St., Lihuʻe (245-6554) HOURS: Open Monday-Saturday 11 am-2 pm, 5-9 pm. SAMPLING: Spicy chicken & egg plant, shrimp & vegetable tempura, teri beef or chicken, pork chops, and chicken cutlet served with rice and tossed salad ($6-9). Donburi (rice bowl) with chicken, beef, stir fry, or tempura ($6-8). Saimin and sushi as well. COMMENTS: Daily specials include ahi & stuffed cabbage, oxtail soup, stuffed chicken, pot roast, and meat loaf ($6-8); Saturday night sushi and tempura dinner ($16).

OKI DINER and BAKERY ★ *Local/Homecooking*
3125 Kuhio Hwy., Lihuʻe (245-5899) HOURS: Breakfast from midnight to 11 am, the rest of the menu served anytime. SAMPLING: For breakfast, they have omelettes, egg dishes, pancake sandwich, fried rice with meat, and blueberry or banana hotcakes ($4-8). The rest of the day (and night), there are burgers, sandwiches, saimin or won ton min, fried noodles, and noodle salad ($3-7) and local favorites like lau lau, kalua pig, pork adobo, loco moco, spaghetti, kalbi ribs, pork chops, tempura, ginger chicken, and oxtail soup - all served with rice and salad ($6-10). Beef stew, and fried chicken are the "Politically Correct" favorites of noted politicians ($6-8). Create your own stir fry from a selection of meats and vegetables. Hearty eater's loco moco or won ton min. Keiki menu available. Pies from their own bakery with fresh cream topping: lilikoi chiffon, banana or chocolate cream, custard, or "PC" (see above) lime. COMMENTS: It's like a fast and friendly bus station for food: there's a separate stand for shave ice with over two dozen flavors; and a full bakery with coconut or apple turnovers, large cookies, butter mochi, manju, brownies, huge, oversized cream puffs with custard filling, apple squares, and their yummy specialty pumpkin crunch. No real fancy atmosphere or furnishings. This is just a busy local-style eatery with quite decent, reasonably priced food. And they're open 24 hours!

ONO FAMILY RESTAURANT ★ *Family Dining*
1292 Kuhio Hwy., Kapa'a (822-1710) HOURS: Breakfast 7am to noon. Lunch 11 am-2 pm. SAMPLING: The breakfast menu offers a variety of egg dishes and omelettes including meat, cheese, and vegetable combinations (like tomatillo & avocado, fried rice with kim chee, and homemade chorizo), Ono burrito, Ono-style Portuguese pork and eggs, as well as pancakes (including banana or tropical) and French toast and other standard breakfast fare ($4-7). The lunch menu offers "Ono" sandwiches like cod, veggie, tuna melt, turkey, a four-twenty special (half turkey and egg salad sandwich with mac salad and soup) and a farmer's sandwich (turkey, ham, jack cheese with french fries and soup) ($4-7.50). There is also a large burger variety including teriyaki, mushroom, bacon, paniolo BBQ, chili, patty melt, and pineapple and several specialty burgerslike mahimahi, bacon avocado, and charbroiled chicken ($6-7). Lunch specials range from fresh island fish, chicken or beef stir-fry, meatloaf, charbroiled beef, fish and chips, saimin, and fried noodles ($6-8). For dessert, try a piece of their - "onolicious" homemade pies; these are genuine homemade, nothing plastic or artificial tasting in the coconut or macadamia nut custard or the coconut vanilla or macadamia nut vanilla cream. Keiki menu available. They also sell Auntie Ono's homemade pineapple-papaya jam, jelly, coconut syrups, and Kona coffee blends. COMMENTS: This is a funky old place right on downtown Kapaa's main street, the Kuhio Highway. It's the sort of place that seems to have been there forever, almost a local institution. It has an antique island-style decor, woven coconut hats on the wall, some artwork and miscellaneous odds and ends for decorative accents with booths and tables. Their service has always been out-standing: friendly, attentive, very sincere small town-style. It's as if they are actually glad to see you and enjoy serving you! Dress casual and be comfortable, the workers do. There are no uniforms and sometimes you can't tell the help from the patrons. It's as if you were in someone's home and the guests just get up to help - and the regulars here probably do! Good local-style comfort food in a wholesome family-style atmosphere.

PAPAYA'S NATURAL FOODS   *Vegetarian*
4-831 Kuhio Hwy. at Kaua'i Village, Kapa'a. (823-0190) HOURS: Open 9 am-7 pm, breakfast until 1 pm. SAMPLING: Rosemary potatoes, steamed eggs & brie, multi-grain pancakes, tofu scramble, granola, tofutos rancheros, or frittata to start you off ($3-7), then a variety of sandwiches and entrees for lunch or dinner: tempeh or tofu burgers, falafel, hummus or Mediterranean salad plate, Thai vegetable stir-fry, baked tofu, fresh fish tacos, veggie pizza, and spinach & herb lasagna ($5-8). Good selection of muffins, scones, breads, cookies and brownies, and serious desserts. COMMENTS: Teas, coffee drinks and smoothies plus a variety of fat free, sugar free, wheat free, and vegan items. This is a health food store, too, one of the few where the patrons actually look fit and healthy! Order at the counter, then bring your selections to the tables outside. The revised menu is still all organic and still a good value for your dining dollar.

PO'S KITCHEN *Local*
4100 Rice Street, Lihu'e (246-8617) HOURS: 6 am-2 pm, Mon-Sat. SAM-PLING: Bento and box lunches in three sizes: small/regular/deluxe ($5-7). Box lunches include fried chicken, teriyaki meat, egg roll, rice ball, potato salad, luncheon meat, hot dog, side dish, and pickled cabbage. Also teriyaki chicken, meat, or short ribs plate lunch and hot entree that changes daily ($5-8). COM-MENTS: Located in the Ace Hardware annex building. Simple and very inexpensive menu. The fried chicken was a wingette, the luncheon meat is a piece of spam. All the portions in the small bento were appetizer-sized. A good place to sample some unusual local dishes with a lot of small sides and snacks items.

PUAKEA BAR & GRILL *American/Local*
Puakea Golf Course at Puakea (4315 Kalepa St.) across from Kukui Grove Shopping Center (245-8756) HOURS: Sat-Tues 9 am-6:30 pm, Wed-Fri until 7:30. SAMPLING: Burgers, hot dogs,sandwiches (turkey, egg or white meat chicken salad, grilled ham & cheese, roast beef, BLT, club, albacore tuna), fish & chips, chicken Caesar, and chicken or beef taco salad ($4-6). Chile & rice, onion rings, spam & cabbage, chicken wings with fries, diced hot dog & onions ($3-4). Beer & wine, sodas, raspberry tea, lemonade, and snacks. COMMENTS: Small cafe across from the pro shop. Ask about monthly discount specials!

RESTAURANT KIIBO *Japanese*
Just off Rice Street at 2991 Umi St. in Lihu'e (245-2650) HOURS: Lunch Monday-Friday 11 am-1:30 pm, Dinner Monday-Saturday 5:30-9 pm. Closed Sunday. SAMPLING: Lunch special with entree, rice, miso soup and salad ($5-7). Teriyaki chicken, beef or pork plus tempura, sushi, sukiyaki, sashimi, nabe, butterfish nitsuke, saba shioyaki, fried salmon or chicken, ramen, chicken or pork tofu, noodles, fresh fish, and special house bentos ($7-18). COMMENTS: The decor and food are authentic and very traditional but nothing really outstanding.

ROB'S GOOD TIMES GRILL *American*
4303 Rice St., Lihu'e (246-0311) HOURS: 11 am-10 pm. SAMPLING: Lots of appetizers/pupus like sauteed mushrooms, chicken sticks, won ton, egg rolls, fresh veggies, fried chicken or zucchini, kalua pork & cabbage, boiled peanuts, chips & homemade salsa ($3-6). Sashimi, grilled steak, seared poke, or mixed pupu basket. Tuna or Oriental chicken salad ($5-6). Pastrami and swiss, mahi, egg salad, tuna, grilled chicken or turkey, BLT, and turkey club sandwiches ($5-7). Burgers include mushroom, bacon, or chili ($5-7). COMMENTS: Pub mirrors and beer signs on the walls with satellite TV and a dart board. Music, entertainment and karaoke. During football season, they open at 7 am for breakfast with loco moco, omelettes, or sweet bread French toast.

SAMPAGUITA'S/BIG WHEEL DONUT SHOP *Local*
Old Hanamaulu Trading Post (245-5322) HOURS: Donuts from 4 am to 11:30 am. Breakfast 5 am to "whenevah." SAMPLING: Plate lunches ($4-6); Breakfast: eggs, bacon, and hot cakes ($4). COMMENTS: These are two different places, but in such a small building that it's almost impossible not to list them together. Big Wheel also serves coffee, makes their donuts fresh, and frequently has a "Sorry out of Donuts" sign in front. Not surprising, since they start serving them at 4 in the morning!

SHUTTERS LOUNGE   *Sandwiches/pupus*
Radisson Kaua'i Beach lobby (245-1955) HOURS: Open 11am-8 pm. SAMPLING: Cheeseburger; hot dog; turkey, ham & bacon club; smoked ham & swiss sandwiches ($7-9). Crab or pork won tons; spicy chicken wings; potato skins; jumbo onion rings; nachos; and grilled Portuguese sausage on sauteed Kaua'i onions ($5-9). Tea, espressos, and coffee drinks. Smoothies with or without rum. COMMENTS: Cocktail lounge with nightly Hawaiian entertainment.

SRI'S CAFE   *Local*
Rice Shopping Center, 4303 Rice St., Lihu'e (246-3910) HOURS: Breakfast 6-9 am, Lunch 11 am-3 pm. Closed Sunday. SAMPLING: Oxtail soup, pork tofu, chicken or beef stew ($4-7). Weekly specials offer roast beef (Mon), roast chicken (Tues), roast pork (Wed), roast duck (Thurs), and roast turkey (Fri). COMMENTS: This tiny local cafe also has guri guri, a local style creamy sherbet.

TERRACE RESTAURANT AT KAUA'I LAGOONS RESORT
Continental/International
3351 Ho'olaule'a Way at Kaua'i Lagoons Golf Course, Lihu'e (241-6080) HOURS: Breakfast 8-11 am, Lunch 11 am-1:30 pm. (No dinner). SAMPLING: Fruit, cereal, egg dishes, Spanish or kim chee omelette, Hawaiian sweet bread French toast, banana nut hot cakes, crab cake Benedict, steak & eggs ($3-10). Burgers, sandwiches (curried tuna croissant, BBQ teriyaki sirloin, fresh fish or turkey, ham & cheese); grilled ahi, shrimp, fruit, or chicken Caesar salad ($7-10); Oriental stir fry (veggie, chicken or shrimp), donburi teri beef or chicken, and double garlic linguine ($9-10). Luncheon buffet with soup, salads, hot entrees, sandwich bar, and desserts. COMMENTS: Attractive setting overlooking a gazebo garden. Lunch too strenuous? Take a break after to relax and refresh in the European spa next door!

TIP TOP CAFE   ★   *Local*
3173 Akahi, Lihu'e (245-2333) HOURS: Breakfast daily 6:30-11:30 am, Lunch Tuesday-Sunday 11 am-2 pm. SAMPLING: Macadamia or banana pancakes, sweet bread French toast, loco moco, omelettes, bento ($3-6). Burgers, grilled ham and cheese, BLT, and tuna sandwiches plus beef stew, saimin and oxtail soup, a popular specialty ($3-5). Daily specials: meat loaf, corned beef & cabbage, pork tofu, spaghetti, and chili ($5-7). COMMENTS: Move over Hard Rock Cafe, the Tip Top souvenir shop has t-shirts and hats! The bakery continues to make their signature items like macadamia nut cookies, cream puffs, and eclairs. This is an especially popular stop for breakfast and lunch. The macadamia pancakes are light and fluffy ("addictive" according to one of our readers) and the French toast is very good. All menu items are reasonably priced, you can't go wrong! They've been in business since 1916 and moved to their present location in the early 60's. The cafe is part of the Tip Top Motel. Their sushi bar and Japanese restaurant, Sushi Katsu is part of the Cafe. (See individual listing.)

TROPIX ISLAND BAR & GRILL   *American*
1330 Kuhio Hwy., Kapa'a (822-7330) HOURS: Lunch 12-5 pm, Dinner 5-9:30 pm. SAMPLING: Hawaiian chicken stir fry, sauteed mahi, hamburgers, kalua pork COMMENTS: Tropical drinks, 40 different beers. Big screen TV, video and dart games

WAH KUNG CHOP SUEY   *Chinese*
Kinipopo Shopping Village, 356 Kuhio Hwy. (822-0560) HOURS: Daily 4:30-8:30 pm, Lunch Tuesday-Saturday 11 am-2 pm. SAMPLING: Soups, poultry, chop suey, chow mein, gau gee, won ton, seafood, beef and pork, egg, vegetables, and rice. Lunch specials of three items plus rice, pupu plate with fried chicken & shrimp, won ton, and egg roll ($6-9). Roast duck, beef or pork tofu, lup chong (Chinese sausage), shrimp fu young, sweet & sour pork, scallop soup, pot roast chicken ($6-8). Abalone with black mushrooms, seafood with vegetables ($8-10). COMMENTS: Small take-out place with a few tables and chairs. Combination and dinner plates posted on the wall, so you don't have to read, you can just point. While it looks (and it is) pretty dinky, the food is very good and so are the prices! Food is Cantonese style with a few exotic dishes thrown in and the prices make it a good option for filling up those hungry appetites that always seem to develop after a day at the beach.

WAIPOULI DELI & RESTAURANT   ★   *American/Local/Oriental*
771 Kuhio Hwy., Kapa'a (822-9311) HOURS: Breakfast & lunch 7 am-2 pm, Dinner Mon-Sat 5-9 pm. SAMPLING: Eggs with breakfast meats, pancakes, French toast, and homemade corned beef hash ($3-6). Lunch entrees of shrimp tempura, roast pork, chop suey, chow mein, pork tofu, beef broccoli, fried chicken, pork or chicken cutlet, liver with bacon and onions, beef or chicken hekka, mixed plate ($6-8). Burgers and burger platters, sandwiches, and saimin ($2-6). Dinners include fries or rice, salad, and iced tea or coffee. Beef stew, egg fu yung, BBQ teriyaki steak, beef tomato and most of the lunch entrees ($9-15). COMMENTS: Small local restaurant. Children's half order portions available on lunch and dinner entrees. When a restaurant is always packed, you know they must be doing something right. The service is very friendly, the food is good to great, the prices are reasonable -- an excellent dining value.

ZACK'S FAMOUS FROZEN YOGURT AND CAFE
Coffee/Espresso, Sandwiches & Salads
Kukui Grove Shopping Center, Lihu'e (246-2415), open Mon-Thurs & Sat 11 am-5:30 pm, Sun till 5, Fri till 9. SAMPLING: This dessert and snack shop offers a menu of hot dogs, hamburgers, vegetarian specials, soups, salads (Caesar, chicken sesame, or chicken papaya) plus ham, French dip, roast beef, and chicken sandwiches and beef, ham or veggie wraps, pizza ($3-7). There are also things like chili or stuffed baked potatoes including bleu cheese, chili, hot dog, broccoli, cheese, and bacon bits for toppings ($3-6). Chicken and ham plates come with pineapple-papaya sauce and a fresh papaya slice ($5-6). Rounding out the menu are dessert goodies such as ice cream, yogurt, frosted brownies, mac nut cheesecake bars, lilikoi pie and more. COMMENTS: Lots of homemade touches like soups (Portuguese bean, green papaya chicken), cole slaw and potato salad, and fresh salads with homemade bleu cheese and other dressings -- even homemade croutons!

MODERATE

BARBECUE INN ★ *American/Japanese*
2982 Kress St., Lihu'e (245-2921) HOURS: Breakfast 7:00-10:30 am; Lunch 10:30-1:30 pm, Mon.-Fri. Dinner 5-8:30 Mon.-Thurs. 4:30-8:45 Fri. & Sat. Closed Sunday. SAMPLING: Breakfast meats and eggs dishes, pancakes, and Oriental breakfast of miso soup, teriyaki fish, scrambled egg with green onion, rice, and hot tea ($5-8). Lunch and dinner menus change daily. The lunch menu may feature specials like grilled fresh island fish--ono, ahi or mahimahi, fresh fish laulau, lamb shank, shrimp scampi, pork with squash, beef stew luau, charsiu duck, roast beef, chicken Caesar salad, grilled liver and onions, pork tofu and veggies, chow mein with chicken or ribs, and more ($8-13). Dinner choices may include items like sauteed pork tenderloin medallions, mac nut crusted fresh ono, T-bone or New York steak, sauteed breast of chicken and shrimp pasta, kalua pork and cabbage, chicken cutlet and more ($9-19). Both lunch and dinner also feature daily chef's specials, house sandwiches and Japanese specials like teriyaki, tempura, yakitori. COMMENTS: Lunch specials include soup or fruit, drink & dessert. Their homemade cream pies are a delight. Dinner also comes with salad. All sandwiches come on their freshly baked bread. The Sasaki family has owned the restaurant in the same location since 1940 -- that's 60 years plus. It was named by the grandfather and although there are now a few token BBQ items on the menu, the BBQ in the name referred to a hibachi or small grill which was just the regular way of cooking. The restaurant is now operated by the two granddaughters, Kathy and Donna. Kathy manages the dining room while Donna oversees the kitchen and makes the daily fresh bread and homemade pies. They have added a few more gourmet-style entrees and now serve champagne or wine, but basically, this is still a nice family-style restaurant (Keiki menu for both lunch and dinner) with booths and curtains and a plantation-style look. Recent renovations have given it a more open spacious look with lighter colors. Generous portions, good value, and friendly, attentive, efficient service. A previous reader of this book noted about Barbecue Inn, "If you don't eat here at least once during your stay, you're an idiot!" It's a pretty apt summary. Good food, good prices, good service from friendly, smiling "aunties" who wait the tables. A real Kaua'i kind of place. You'll have to hunt around for parking on the narrow streets nearby but it's worth it even if you have to walk a ways to get there. As the man said, don't be an idiot.

BULL SHED ★ *Steak and Seafood*
796 Kuhio Hwy., Waipouli (822-3791/822-1655) HOURS: Cocktails from 4:30, Dinner nightly 5:30-10 pm. SAMPLING: Their trademark prime rib is $21. Other meaty offerings include garlic tenderloin, beef kabob, teri chicken or top sirloin, Australian lamb rack, garlic chicken, and pork baby back ribs ($14-22). Shrimp, scallops, crab, lobster and fresh island fish ($16-market price); and in combination with steak or chicken ($17-market price). Salad bar (included) offers basic ingredients, but a few unusual items like peas, fresh pineapple and garlic bread. Mud pie for dessert; kids menu of teriyaki chicken or fresh fish. COMMENTS: We expected a dark and dingy steakhouse, but this was light and bright; very open with picture windows and a great ocean view. Arrive early for a view table! The food is consistently good and with rice, bread and salad bar, you get a lot for your money.

BUZZ'S STEAK & LOBSTER *Steak & Seafood*
4-484 Kuhio Hwy., Coconut MarketPlace, Kapa'a (822-0041) HOURS: Lunch 11 am-2:30 pm, Dinner 4:30-10:30 pm. SAMPLING: Lunch offerings include soup or salad, and mahi mahi, grilled cheese, teri chicken, burgers, and French dip sandwiches ($3-7). Dinners start with mozzarella sticks, sauteed mushrooms, or teriyaki beef sticks ($5-7). Dinner, naturally, has steak and lobster, alone or in combinations plus shrimp, seafood plate, fresh fish, baby back ribs, and pastas: Alfredo, primavera, chicken cajun, or shrimp($12-19). Prime rib on Fri-Sat only ($20). Cheesecake or homemade ice cream pie for dessert. COMMENTS: The ambience here follows a South Seas/Hawaiian theme with coconut roof thatching over the booths and nautical decorative accents adorning the walls and ceiling. There's even a canoe hanging from the rafters. Dinner is served with fresh bread and choice of fries, rice, or baked potato. Buzz's salad bar is also included with your entree. Early Bird specials from 4:30-6:30 pm include the salad bar!

CAFE PORTOFINO ★ *Italian*
3501 Rice St., Harbor Mall, Nawiliwili (245-2121) HOURS: Dinner nightly 5-10 pm. SAMPLING: Roasted bell peppers, steamed clams, calamari, mozzarella (fried or with tomato), ahi carpaccio, and prosciutto are offered as antipasti ($8-10). Gaspacio, minestrone, or soup of day ($4). Featured pastas are penne with broccoli & spinach, fettucine with shrimp & mushroom or Alfredo, linguine carbonara, pesto, or with clams, ravioli, canneloni, and lasagna($14-20). Choose veal or chicken parmigiana, marsala, or Portofino style (with shrimp & scallops in lemon sage sauce), or veal piccata, or chicken in wild mushroom sauce, sauteed with artichoke hearts, or a la caccitora ($15-21). Specialties include osso buco, Provencale or lemon wine scampi,and eggplant parmigiana ($16-26). Profiteroles, caramel custard, and tiramisu are some of the homemade desserts. COMMENTS: The restaurant is located in the Harbor Mall which has undergone extensive renovation work recently. Located on the complex's upstairs level, the dining room features paned windows, beamed ceilings and a patio (a lanai where you can dine al fresco overlooking the Kalapaki Beach area). Nice bar and lounge areas with live music (usually jazz) on weekends. The cuisine is authentic Italian with ingredients imported from Italy, then made fresh here. Breads, ice creams, and desserts made on the premises. Good Italian food in comfortable surroundings.

CAFFE COCO ★ *Vegetarian*
4-369 Kuhio Hwy., Wailua Village (822-7990) HOURS: Tuesday-Sunday 11am-9pm. Closed Monday. SAMPLING: Light meals include potstickers, Greek or tofu salad, sandwiches on focaccia bread (BBQ or roast turkey, seared ahi, roast eggplant & cheese) and wraps: tofu & roast veggie, Greek salad or fish ($6-9). Platters with rice & salad offer spiced tofu, seared fresh fish, macadamia sesame encrusted ahi, pasta del giorno ($11-15). Morrocan spiced seared fish or tofu, fish burrito, ahi nori wrap, gumbo & rice, homestyle pot pie, sweet potato cakes, spanikopita, pizza, and Thai pumpkin coconut might be some of the blackboard specials. Pumpkin spice cake, haupia pudding with tropical fruit sauce, banana fruit tart, Mexican chocolate tofu pie (vegan), or black mocha ice cream roll are some of the homemade desserts. Coffee drinks and espresso. COMMENTS: Caffe and art gallery surrounded by cane fields in a restored plantation home.

Eclectic collection of tables and chairs in various corners and cozy nooks in side; garden seating amidst hanging foliage, orchid ferns, and lilikoi shade trees outside. The display case offers savory items like curried vegetable samosa plus homemade pastries and desserts. Not inexpensive, but the restaurant has received good reviews all around. They feature fresh fish and locally grown-produce -- whatever they have in their garden that day! Take the time before or after dinner to browse the Bambulei furniture and gift shop next door.

CAMP HOUSE GRILL & BAR ★ *American*
4-831 Kuhio Highway, in Safeway Shopping Center, Kapa'a (822-2442) HOURS: Breakfast 6:30-11 am, lunch 11 am-9 pm, dinner 5-9 pm. SAMPLING: Breakfast quesadilla, pancakes, omelettes, waffles, French toast, biscuits and gravy, eggs benedict, omelettes and a variety of breakfast sandwiches - Monte Cristo with hash browns, or BLT (& egg), pancake or French toast with bacon & eggs ($4-9). They have early bird specials before 8 am, but as they say on the menu: After 8:01, No Way! Lunch features a variety of burgers, salads, Camp House huli BBQ chickens, BBQ pork ribs, varied chicken breasts, sirloin steak Polynesian, and fresh catch served with soup or salad and choice of side ($6-16). Dinner entrees include pork chops, prime rib, steak of the day, scampi, snow crab legs, or fresh island fish ($12-20). They're known for their homemade pies, so save room for dessert. Or, you can buy a whole pie to take with you. Pies include pineapple cream cheese macadamia pie, chewy chocolate chip macadamia nut, and coconut, banana, or chocolate cream, plus Paradise Pie made with macadamia nut, pineapple and coconut. COMMENTS: Camp House is known for its home cooking and homemade pies. Menehune (children's) menu available for lunch and dinner. This restaurant features the same family-style atmosphere and home-style cooking that have been traditions at the original Camp House Grill for more than a decade.

DUKE'S CANOE CLUB ★ *Steak & Seafood*
Located in front of the Kaua'i Marriott at Kalapaki Beach. (246-9599) HOURS: Lunch and Barefoot Bar menu 11:30 am-11:30 pm. Dinner 5-10 pm. SAMPLING: Pizza, burgers & sandwiches, salads, pupus, and Hawaiian local plates for lunch ($4-12). Stir fry chicken cashew, pork ribs, fish tacos, roast beef & cheddar sandwich, and grilled mahi Caesar are just a few of the option; fresh fish, seafood, steaks, and prime rib are among the most popular dinner offerings ($14-22). All include a very serious salad bar that has a fresh Caesar salad station, fresh greens, and variety of veggies, prepared salads like macaroni, cole slaw, pasta and potato plus warm breads, macadamia lemon muffins, and carrot muffins. The menu includes innovative new dishes like Thai seafood coconut curry; linguine with basil and sun-dried tomatoes, Thai chicken pizza (with a delicious sweet chile sauce and light, homemade pizza crust); and appetizers of mac nut & crab wonton, poke rolls (with Maui onion), and thick sticks of perfectly prepared calamari ($7-20). For desserts, the hula pie is the best, but the Kona coffee cheesecake can hold its own. COMMENTS: Named in honor of Duke Kahanamoku (probably the greatest surfer of all time), the restaurant features an extensive collection of Duke memorabilia including photos, an impressive 40-foot outrigger canoe, and three of his surfboards. The 30-ft. lava rock waterfall is quite dramatic, creating a unique centerpiece as it splashes into a koi pond. There is a spacious and attractive area upstairs and a separate area with a salad bar and wide plantation-like verandas which overlook the ocean. (Part of the beachfront lanai is portioned off for private parties, a great place to celebrate a special-occasion anniversary or birthday in your own little corner of the world!) Strolling musicians in the dining room; entertainment in the Barefoot Bar on weekends.

FLYING LOBSTER *Seafood*
Kaua'i Coconut Beach Resort, Kapa'a (822-3455) HOURS: 5:30-9:30 pm. SAMPLING: Signature lobster dinners plus steak, scampi, herb roasted or honey-macadamia chicken, BBQ ribs, and fresh catch; crab legs ($13-25). All-you-can-eat pasta (with mix and match pastas & sauces) includes a small salad ($9). Combination dinners from chicken & ribs to steak & lobster ($15-27). Limited menu of burgers and sandwiches plus Caesar salad with shrimp and appetizers of calamari rings, crab legs, shrimp, hot crab dip with garlic toast or Clams Casino ($4-8). Dinners include soup or salad bar, starch and vegetable. Desserts include cakes, pies, ice cream and Kaua'i Coconut Beach Sand Pie. COMMENTS: Early Bird specials nightly, 5:30-6:30 pm. Friday-Saturday prime rib & seafood buffet. This is called The Voyage Room at breakfast and lunch; see separate listing.

HANAMA'ULU RESTAURANT, TEA HOUSE & SUSHI BAR ★
Chinese/Japanese
3-4291 Kuhio Hwy. #56 in Hanama'ulu just north of Lihu'e Airport (245-2511) HOURS: Lunch Tuesday-Friday 10 am-1 pm, Dinner Tuesday-Sunday 4:30-9 pm. Closed Monday. SAMPLING: Chinese dishes with noodles, pork, beef, chicken, and seafood plus baked mussels and lobster ($5-10). Japanese salads, soups, beef, chicken, pork, seafood, and vegetarian specials ($7-11). Also soups and appetizers from pot stickers to robatayaki. Complete dinners such as the 9-course Chinese or Japanese dinner for 2 or more are available ($16 per person). Special tempura or seafood platters ($14-16). Chinese, Japanese, or teriyaki plate lunches and also available at dinner ($6-9). Sunday night Oriental buffet from

5:30-8:30 pm features sushi, sashimi, salads, fish, chicken, crab, teri beef, and dessert ($22). COMMENTS: The front room is used for lunch and is decorated in a pleasant Oriental style, but the Japanese Dining Room (where you sit on the floor Japanese-style) towards the back is a fantasy setting that overlooks a beautiful garden with koi carp ponds. Restaurant offers robatayaki cooking grilled in front of you as well as a full sushi bar. The food is reliably good and <u>has</u> been for over 75 years! Hanama'ulu is often overlooked by folks passing through in their haste to head north toward Kapa'a, Princeville and the North Shore. But this is one of the best Oriental restaurants, and most reasonably priced, on Kaua'i. And if it were located at a resort destination, prices would be a lot more! Good option for a family meal.

HAWAIIAN CLASSIC DESSERTS *Bakery/Cafe*
4479 Rice Street, Lihu'e (245-6967) HOURS: Open only for breakfast and lunch daily except Tuesday , 7 am-3 pm. Breakfast 6-11 am; Lunch 11 am-3 pm SAMPLING: French toast or pancakes (with apple smoked chicken sausage), omelettes, loco moco, eggs with lup cheong & green onion fried rice, and homemade corned beef hash ($6-9). Plate lunches; ham hoagie, turkey, Hawaiian-style Philly steak sandwiches (with teri beef), and burgers ($8-9); salads with seared poke, broiled lemon pepper salmon, grilled eggplant, or chicken oriental ($9). COMMENTS: Open kitchens in both the restaurant and behind the dessert bar where you can watch owner and pastry chef Fenton Lee create your "just desserts!" As you'd expect, the sandwiches are all on freshly baked bread and buns.

JJ'S BROILER ★ *Steak & Seafood*
3416 Rice Street in Anchor Cove Shopping Center on Kalapaki Bay, Lihu'e (246-4422) HOURS: Lunch 11 am-5 pm, Dinner 5-10 pm, Cocktails 5-11 pm. SAMPLING: Cheeseburgers come with avocado, bacon, mushrooms, pineapple, or chili ($7-9). Salads include Asian grilled chicken, cobb, Caesar, seafood and spinach, and there's ocean chowder, French onion, or beef & vegetable soup ($5-10). Sandwiches of pastrami & swiss, turkey club, mahi mahi, fried egg & avocado, teri chicken or beef, steak, French dip, Monte Cristo, and Reuben are available ($9-13) as are a surprising number of vegetarian offerings, Kaua'i garden or marinated tofu sandwich and vegetable pizza on a flour tortilla. Before dinner, there are oysters, mussels, escargot, scampi, crab cakes, or Peking chicken tacos ($8-11). Seafood entrees offer sauteed scallops, baked lobster tail, coconut shrimp, tempura platter, and fresh island fish; char-broiled meats include NY steak, filet mignon, roasted macadamia lamb rack, prime rib, barbeque pork ribs, Cornish hen, and JJ's signature Slavonic steak ($17-25). Other specialties include black bean shrimp with Asian polenta, spicy wasabi ribeye steak, ahi & crab Napoleon, beef medallions with lobster saute, sugar cane shrimp, chicken fettucine, seafood linguini, tortellini primavera, and baby lamb chops with penne pasta ($16-28). Entrees include table salad bar and choice of rice. Key lime pie, JJ's sea of chocolate, and double decker ice cream pie are some of the after dinner treats. COMMENTS: Nice outdoor patio and deck for lunch; light cafe menu in the evening. Dinner is served upstairs with a big picture window overlooking the beach. They offer quite a few innovative appetizers and entrees, but their Slavonic steak (filets cooked in wine, butter and garlic) is still the most popular.

JR'S PLANTATION RESTAURANT   *Steak and seafood*
3-4221 Kuhio Hwy. 56 in Hanama'ulu (245-1606) HOURS: Dinner 5-9:30 pm. SAMPLING: Appetizers include their special Asian ginger shrimp, escargot, and Cajun stuffed mushrooms ($6-8); ala carte items offer seafood pasta, jumbo burger, roast beef, Hawaiian luau platter, or salad bar. Entrees include salad bar, rice or potato, and homemade garlic bread: NY steak, prime rib, scampi, lamb chops, fresh catch, Hawaiian luau platter, lobster combo, Cajun teriyaki or garlic chicken breast, fried shrimp or their signature Cajun fish & shrimp with ginger scallion sauce ($13-20). "Little Cowboy" dinners include a trip to the salad bar ($6-8). Homemade desserts are hula pie; strawberry or blueberry cream cheese pie or try JR's strawberry haupia! COMMENTS: Tropical drinks served with or without alcohol.

JOLLY ROGER   *American*
Just behind Coconut Plantation MarketPlace next to The Islander (822-3451) HOURS: Breakfast and Sunday breakfast buffet 6:30 am-noon, Lunch 11-4:30 pm, Dinner 3-10 pm. SAMPLING: Omelettes, eggs Benedict, French toast, steak & eggs plus apple pancakes or waffle with cinnamon apples and macadamia nuts ($4-8). Sunday breakfast buffet has eggs, bacon, sausage, corned beef hash, French toast pancakes, waffles, and fresh fruits ($5-8). Burgers, salads, and sandwiches including a chicken or tuna avocado melt, French dip, turkey, and mahi mahi ($4-8). Specialties include teri steak or chicken, fettucini Alfredo with mushrooms or chicken, spaghetti, and stir-fry for lunch ($8-10), for dinner ($10-15). Other dinners offer fresh or fried fish, seafood platters, chicken Polynesian, fried calamari, scallops, smothered chicken, and create-your-own combinations ($13-16). Then there are sundaes, hot fudge cake, or Mauna Kea crunch -- a chocolate chip cookie with sundae toppings. COMMENTS: Familiar chain with a traditional menu, though there are a few creative surprises. Specials like steak & all-you-can-eat shrimp and a senior menu with a choice of teriyaki steak or chicken, ground beef, mahi mahi, ono, sirloin steak, spaghetti, or hibachi chicken including vegetable, potato or rice, soup or salad, and coffee or tea. Food is nothing exotic, but affordably priced with a broad menu offering something for every family member. The breakfast specials are a good value. Karaoke on weekends.

KAPA'A FISH & CHOWDER HOUSE   ★   *Seafood*
1639 Kuhio Hwy. Kapa'a (822-7488) HOURS: Open daily for lunch 11:30am - 4 pm, Dinner 4 - 9:30 pm, (Early Bird 4-5:30 pm). SAMPLING: Naturally, they offer chowder (with or without sherry) or you can also start with escargot, sauteed mushrooms, clams, calamari, shrimp, or Caesar salad ($4-16). Seafood entrees include sauteed Kaua'i shrimp scampi, seafood linguine, coconut shrimp tempura, calamari "almondine," Alaskan king crab legs, lobster tails, stuffed tiger prawns, Kauaian seafood bouillabaisse, or seafood platter. There are also baby back ribs, pork medallions, stuffed breast of chicken, pasta primavera, certified Angus New York steak, Frenched lamb rack noisette, broiled filet of beef vol-au-vent, bamboo pork chop and more ($16-28). Dinners include salad, starch, and fresh baked bread. Cheesecake (passion fruit or mocha) and mud pie (mint or coffee) for dessert. Tropical and ice cream drinks are a specialty. COMMENTS: The screened Garden Room at the back of the restaurant is airy and full of hanging plants. Hawaiian music Friday and Sunday 7pm; jazz night on Thursdays

8:30/11 pm & Saturdays 7:30/10:30 pm. Children's menu is interesting and more "adult" than most. Early bird specials are a good value: Hawaiian chicken, pork tenderloin, grilled mahi, shrimp Louie, or fish & chips ($12-14)

KING & I THAI CUISINE   *Thai*
Located in the Waipouli Plaza, 4-901 Kuhio Hwy., Kapa'a (822-1642) HOURS: Lunch Mon-Fri 11 am-1:30 pm; dinner nightly 4:30-9:30 pm. SAMPLING: Start with the spring rolls with fresh mint and cucumber, ready to wrap in lettuce and dip, then try the lemon grass or coconut soup, green papaya salad, or King & I Noodles with shrimp, pork, or chicken, or sa the meat skewers, and fried calamari ($7-11). You can choose from red, green, or yellow curry ($8-10) and smell the aroma of jasmine rice, and enjoy the Siam fresh basil, spicy eggplant, ginger fish, garlic shrimp, and other Siam dishes with choice of beef, pork, chicken, shrimp, calamari, tofu, or fish ($8-10). Thai iced tea or coffee are a must and be sure to try the coconut milk and black rice, the natural color of the herbal rice from Thailand. If you don't want to make a decision, they also offer set menus for 2, 3, or 4 persons which include five items with rice, tea, and dessert ($28-50). COMMENTS: The owners/chefs grow their own herbs and spices so when the dish says fresh basil or fresh mint, it really is. Some of the entrees are excellent, a few are mediocre. The green curry is wonderful, perfectly seasoned and an ideal accompaniment with fresh fish. The fried shrimp, however, proved to be too greasy and were all batter and no shrimp. The portions are a little on the small side, but the prices are affordable. Ask your waiter to offer recommendations on entrees!

LA BAMBA MEXICAN RESTAURANT   *Mexican*
4261 Rice St., Lihu'e (245-5972) HOURS: 11 am-10 pm; Sunday 4-9 pm. SAMPLING: Seafood salad on a tortilla or taco salad in a shell plus the usual selection of tacos, burritos, enchiladas and quesadilla ($2-9). The carnitas or carne asada burritos are the house specialties ($7-11). Chile verde, tamales, or chile relleno; fajitas with chicken, steak, or seafood for one or two people ($11-24). COMMENTS: Entradas (entrees) and tortas (sandwiches) come with rice and beans (or steak fries with your sandwich if you prefer.) Take out available, but no liquor license so you are welcome to BYOB.

LEMONGRASS GRILL & SEAFOOD ★   *Pacific Rim/Asian*
4-885 Kuhio Hwy., Kapa'a (821-2888) HOURS: 5-10 pm. SAMPLING: Pacific Rim and Asian cuisine; enjoy such appetizers as fried ahi sushi roll, furikake seared ahi, crispy fried ahi lumpias, Kilauea prawns or ahi poki in Thai rice paper ($6-9)). Salads include Caesar, spinach salad, shrimp and Moloaa papaya, and Kapahi ginger chicken ($6-7); soups include papaya bisque and clam chowder ($5). Dinner entrees include specialties like sutffed calamari with chili garlic sauce, braised short rib Walker Hill, Chinese style steamed fish, braised spicy short rib Jardinere, grilled salmon ginger lemongrass aiolii, lemongrass seafood stew, braised lamb shank, hosin BBQ chicken breast, pork loin with tropical mango pineapple relish and other tempting items ($15-20). COMMENTS This is a small house facing the highway with both inside and outside dining; they also have a sushi bar. Interior decor carries splashly Thai batik accents; dishes are bright, colorful and attractively presented.

The adjacent Lemongrass Gallery (822-1221) which features "Pacific Fine Collectibles" in a separate building located behind the restaurant. Browse through the unique selection of antiques, sculptures, gifts, art, and accessories before or after your dinner!

MARGARITAS, A MEXICAN RESTAURANT AND WATERING HOLE
Mexican
4-733 Kuhio Hwy., Kapa'a (822-1808) HOURS: Daily 4-11 pm, dinner served 5 pm, Happy Hour 4-6. SAMPLING: Nachos el deluxo, Mexican pizzas, quesadillas, flautas, jalapeno poppers, quesadilla, caliente wings ($6-8). Entrees include fish tacos, chicken quesadilla (with chipotle & mango salsa), and hickory smoked ribs from the grill, chicken Vera Cruz, Jose's super burrito ($10-17). There are also salads like taco, chicken taco, or chicken fajita ($12-14). Entrees include shredded beef, chicken, sirloin, vegetarian, or ahi burritos; chimichanga; beef, chicken, or vegetarian quesadilla; beef & chicken enchiladas or Enchilada Ranchera; and fajitas with beef and/or chicken ($10-18). COMMENTS: Food is made fresh daily; specials change every few weeks. Live music on Friday and Saturday nights. Good place to watch the sunset during the winter when it goes down between Sleeping Giant Mountain and the coconut grove next door. Good margaritas. There is better Mexican food elsewhere on the island, but this is passable middle-of-the-road cuisine. The menu is large and varied and if you choose to eat on the back porch, the donkey and horse in the adjoining coconut grove might stroll over and say "howdy."

NAUPAKA TERRACE STEAK HOUSE ★   *Steaks & Seafood*
Radisson Kaua'i Beach (245-1955), 4331 Kaua'i Beach Drive, Lihu'e. HOURS: Breakfast 6:30-11 am, dinner 6-10 pm. SAMPLING: Standard breakfast fare includes omelettes, pancakes, Belgian waffles, sweet bread French toast, tropical fruit platter, plus continental breakfast ($7-10). The dinner menu features appetizers such as fried calamari, stuffed mushrooms, Hanamaulu chicken fritters, Naupaka quesadilla and prawn cocktail canoe ($9-10). Salads range from Caesar chicken, Naupaka peppered ahi salad to a standard salad bar ($11-16). Entrees include filet mignon, New York strip steak, top sirloin, ribeye, prime rib, filet mignon and lobster, Wailua chicken, Kauailoa seafood grill, fresh island fish, chilled prawns, pasta Kaua'i Beach and vegetarian divine ($14-33). COMMENTS: With the recent change in hotel management, this restaurant got a full makeover. The arrangement of terraced private alcoves with tables and booths with pleasing tropical color combinations, accents and furnishings create a pleasant dining atmosphere. The dining room provides courtyard and pool views. Pleasant setting for quiet intimate dinners or family meals.

NORBERTO'S EL CAFE ★   *Mexican*
4-1373 Kuhio Hwy., Kapa'a (822-3362) HOURS: Mon-Sat 5:30-9 pm, closed Sun. SAMPLING: Taquitos, tacos, burritos, quesadillas, nachos, and chimichangas are just some of the items offered ala carte ($3-8). Dinner specialties include rellenos tampico, burrito rancheros, burrito el cafe, fajitas made with Kaua'i steak or chicken, fish specials, enchiladas grande with beef or chicken, and a special homegrown Hawaiian taro leaf enchilada in veggie style or with beef, chicken or fish. ($13-16). All entrees come with soup, vegetables, rice and beans, corn chips and salsa. Their homemade desserts have won awards: sample

chocolate cream pie, hula pie, and rum cake. COMMENTS: Locals drive from the west side of Kaua'i just for the bean soup so with such a loyal following, they should be around for a while to come. They serve Mexican beer and a variety of margarita flavors (Midori, passion fruit, and raspberry) available by the glass or by the pitcher. We tried their unique taro enchilada and it was delicious - the taro was cooked just right with a smooth texture and taste that was not too stringy or bitter. The eggplant enchilada was equally tasty getting its flavor from the food, not the seasonings. If you like a bit more "kick" just spoon on the fresh salsa till it's just right! The chile relleno came highly recommended and it had a nice texture (not greasy or overly-fried) and the perfect proportion of chile to relleno: it didn't taste like a fried jalapeno, but it didn't taste like a chile omelette either. It gets a star for their innovative preparations, friendly service, and kitschy (but not too) cantina atmosphere. It's a fun place that makes for good family dining and they have a kid's menu to prove it.

OLYMPIC CAFE   *American with Mexican & Italian*
1387 Kuhio Hwy., Kapa'a (822-5825) HOURS: Breakfast 6-11 am, Lunch, 11am-5 pm, Dinner 5-9:30 pm. SAMPLING: Breakfast burrito or quesadilla, a variety of omelettes and scrambles, coconut pineapple, or blueberry pancakes, and guava jelly-stuffed toast. Several burger options plus sandwiches including BBQ or blackened chicken, mozzarella & pesto, tuna, BLT, and chicken avocado club. Caesar, Greek, cobb, tuna, or grilled chicken salad plus several Mexican entrees. Most lunch items available for dinner or begin with fried calamari, bruschetta, spinach-artichoke dip, or roasted garlic spread and follow with entrees of coconut curry rice, teri chicken, fresh catch, scampi, and a variety of pastas including Caesar salad-style. COMMENTS: This airy room opens right onto the sidewalk along the main street (Kuhio Highway through town) and has a yellow color scheme with colorful tapa print chairs that blend with the colorful books in the used book library for both "browsers and buyers." And those go very well with the selection of teas, juices, coffee drinks, fresh muffins, and pastries available from the espresso bar. But a recent visit on a Sunday at just past 12 noon proved something of a surprise. This diner stopped for lunch and when ready to order was curtly told by the waitress that "...the cook isn't making lunch, he's still making only breakfast." When it was pointed out that it was past noon, the usual lunch time, the diner was admonished, "...the cook isn't making lunch." Duly chastened, the diner headed for the door and another restaurant. Moral of the story: don't go there expecting lunch because you may not get it.

PANCHO AND LEFTY'S CANTINA & RESTAURANTE   *Mexican*
4-1354 Kuhio Highway, Kapa'a (823-9244) HOURS: Mon-Sat 11 am - 10pm, Sun 12 noon - 10 pm. SAMPLING: They have the usual typical Mexican fare ranging from nachos, to soups and salads, tostadas, enchiladas, burritos, chimichangas, tacos and other Mexican standards. Begin with nachos $8-9 or taco salad $9, seafood salad $11, Caesar salad $9. Entrees include toquitos $9, tostadas $10, enchiladas $9, burritos $11, chimichangas $12 and tacos of many types $8-10. Also try seafood Vera Cruz (market price), enchiladas de Marissas $15, enchiladas rancheros $14, chili relieno $14, carnitas $15, carne asada $16 and several other choices. This is an upstairs location with open air views above Kapa'a town and busy Kuhio Highway, no atmosphere and the same gritty, tasteless decor and ambiance of their other Hawai'i outlets.

PANDA GARDEN *Chinese*
4-831 Kuhio Hwy., Kaua'i Village Shopping Center, Kapa'a (822-0922) HOURS: Lunch 10:30 am-2 pm; Dinner 4-9:30 pm, closed Wednesday. SAMPLING: Over 100 offerings of both Cantonese and Szechuan dishes. Appetizers, soups, chicken & duck, beef and pork, seafood, eggs, sizzling platters, vegetarian, chow mein, and rice ($6-12). Scallop with peppery salt, lobster with black bean sauce or ginger & onions, steamed island fish, pot roast chicken, beef with sesame sauce, pork hash, shrimp with chile garlic sauce, and tenderloin steak with black pepper are just a few of the diverse selections ($7-20). Plate lunch specials offer a choice of eight entrees with soup, won ton, and rice ($6) and set dinners for 2 to 10 people are available ($25 and up). COMMENTS: They offer both the unusual and the traditional, but seafood is a particular specialty. Their hot, spicy dishes are marked with a star. Beer & wine; take out available. Food is fair to good, but the portions are a bit small.

PARADISE SEAFOOD & GRILL *Steak & Seafood*
1850 Kaumualii, Puhi (246-4884) HOURS: 11 am-3 pm, dinner 5-9 pm SAMPLING: A variety of burgers including fish and chicken plus smoked turkey, chicken salad, and club sandwiches ($6-8). Caesar salad, fried chicken, lasagna, fish & chips, and seafood: on a platter, in a salad or linguine ($6-8). Dinner starts with steamed clams, fried mushrooms, crab cakes, oysters, mussels, or calamari ($6-10). Entrees include fresh fish, scampi, baby back pork ribs, crab legs, steak, prime rib, and mushroom or teri chicken ($15-25). Chocolate cappuccino brownie, mud pie, or cheesecake for dessert. Wine, beer & espresso. Keiki menu available. COMMENTS: Take-out or seating outside on the lanai or back patio.

POOR BOY'S PIZZA *Pizza & Sandwiches*
1384 Kuhio Hwy., #104, Kapa'a (822-7985) HOURS: Mon-Sat 10 am-10 pm, Sun from noon. SAMPLING: Pizza in 12, 16 and 29 inch sizes plus individual 7" pizzas ($12-30). Calzones, stromboli, and Italian or ham & cheese sandwiches on fresh baked bread ($7-10) plus breaded zucchini, hot wings, or seasoned fries ($3-6). Strawberry or tropical fruit smoothies too. COMMENTS: Take out or delivery available or just sit in front and people-watch in the heart of Old Kapa'a Town.

RESTAURANT KINTARO ★ *Japanese*
370 Kuhio Hwy., Kapa'a (822-3341) HOURS: 5:30-9:30 pm Monday-Saturday. Closed Sunday. SAMPLING: Tempura, sukiyaki, and yakitori dinners, yosenabe, nabeyaki noodles, broiled steaks, and fish combinations plus complete teppanyaki dinners with appetizer: oysters, chicken or NY steak teriyaki, filet mignon, hibachi shrimp, fish with scallops or lobster tail, and tenderloin steak ($13-30). COMMENTS: Good fish and steaks; also hand-rolled sushi and soft-shell crab. Stylized, attractive Japanese ambiance with a sushi bar and aquarium. There are two serving sections: the less expensive general seating area and a moderately expensive area with teppanyaki tables where you can enjoy your meal cooked before your eyes. While it is a bit more expensive, the teppanyaki room is worth it for the show! The service is excellent on both sides.

ROCCO'S ★ *Italian*
4405 Kukui St. in Pacific House Plaza, Kapa'a (822-4422) HOURS: Dinner nightly 4:30-11 pm. SAMPLING: Sauteed or stuffed mushrooms (firm texture and good mushroom taste with just the right amount of garlicky seasoning), white pizza (topped with mozzarella and a side of red marinara sauce), garlic ricotta cheese bread (with lots of both!), antipasta, scampi, or calamari steak are the starters ($4-10). Caesar salads are a specialty. Made with an exceptionally light tasting olive oil, they are served hot or cold with fresh fish, jumbo shrimp, chicken parmesan, veggies, or Italian meats ($7-13). Rock oven pizzas and pasta offerings of ravioli, manicotti (made with spinach pasta), baked cannelloni or lasagna (with lots of bubbling hot cheese), and linguini marinara or Alfredo ($10-15). Eggplant, chicken, or pork parmesan. Additional entrees include scampi, clams, eggplant marsala, and baked or sauteed fresh fish ($15-20). The fish comes in large portions and the ahi was excellent and surprisingly moist - not an easy thing to do with its tuna texture. Main courses all come with a hot loaf of fresh baked bread and dinner salad. For dessert there's homemade NY style cheesecake or tiramisu. COMMENTS: They now have patio seating and the upper level dining mezzanine has been converted to offer a pool table, video games, and a new bar with (occasional) live entertainment until 2 am. This is an upscale, modern version of the old family style pizza restaurants of the 50's and 60's. It's reflected in the ambiance with hanging plants and vines as well as in the prices. Complete dinners, large portions, and homecooking are their hallmarks. The bread is homemade as are the meatballs. This is a great find -- both a fun "hang-out" and an excellent value family restaurant with or without a family.

SUKHOTHAI *Thai/Chinese*
Kapa'a Shopping Center, 1105 Kuhio Hwy. (821-1224) HOURS: 10:30 am - to closing daily. SAMPLING: Soups (ocean golden, lemongrass shrimp or chicken, long rice, spicy fish, coconut chicken); salads like seafood, papaya, or calamari salads ($8-14). Appetizers of spring roll, chicken crepe, chicken sticks, satay, papaya salad, and fried tofu ($7-12). Thai entrees include cashew chicken, pad eggplant, coconut chicken or seafood, garlic mixed vegetable, pad ben-ja-lung (shrimp & vegetables), and fish prig prow and red, green, yellow, Pa Nang, pineapple, and madsaman curries ($8-16). Chinese dishes include chop suey, egg fu-young, lemon chicken, lo meine, garlic calamari, seafood broccoli, pepper steak, Asian fish, stir-fried long rice, or sweet & sour ($8-15). House specials offer seafood with chile paste, whole snapper with garlic, crispy duck with vegetables, spicy chicken angel and shrimp stuffed with minced chicken in peanut sauce ($14-18). For dessert there is fried ice cream, tapioca pudding with coconut sauce, or rambutan stuffed with pineapple. COMMENTS: They also have Vietnamese and vegetarian dishes. Anything on the menu can also be ordered vegetarian style. Order your meal mild, medium or spicy Thai hot to suit your taste. Same menu served all day. They run the Asian gift shop next door which has a variety of Asian gifts, souvenirs, artworks, etc.

SUSHI KATSU *Sushi/Japanese*
3173 Akahi St., Lihu'e (246-0176) HOURS: Lunch (sushi only) Tuesday-Sunday 11 am-2 pm, Dinner 5:30-9:30 pm. Closed Monday. SAMPLING: Lunch: Chirashi sushi, maki mono roll, tekka ju, regular or BIG California roll, and

sushi combinations ($4-14). Special rolls such as soft shell crab, spicy ahi, fresh salmon, or inari sushi. Sushi combination and sushi and sashimi deluxe assortment; udon and soba noodles ($3-22). Dinners (including soup and rice) feature shrimp tempura, teriyaki beef or chicken, chicken katsu, tempura & sushi, oyako donburi, or catch of the day ($10-14). Green tea ice cream for dessert. COMMENTS: This Japanese restaurant and sushi bar is part of the legendary Tip Top Cafe.

THAI THAI CUISINE   *Thai Cuisine*
1388 Kuhio Highway, Kapa'a (823-8511). HOURS: Dinner only Mon-Sat 6-9 pm. This small Thai eatery features a variety of typically hot and spicy exotic Thai cuisine. SAMPLING: The menu features items like satay chicken ($8), spicy beef salad ($9), soups like Tom Kah chicken/tofu, Poe Tag seafood and Tum Yum chicken ($7-16). There are traditional Thai curries of chicken, duck, seafood, prawns, beef ($9-16). Stir fry dishes include prawns and seafood ($12-15) and chicken or beef ($9). There are noodles dishes like Pad Thai ($9-12), Pad See with chicken, beef or prawns ($9-12) and Pad Kee Mow with chicken, beef, tofu, seafood, prawns or squid ($9-16). COMMENTS: This is a generally nondescript diner in the middle of Kapa'a town, one of the many old wood buildings lining Kuhio Highway that make up central Kapa'a.

THE PALMS RESTAURANT   ★   *Hawaiian   Regional/Pacific   Rim Cuisine*
Holiday Inn Sun Spree Resort, Wailua (823-6000) HOURS: Breakfast buffet 6:30-10:30 am; Dinner daily 5:30-9 pm
SAMPLING: Breakfast buffet offers fresh fruits, breads & pastries, cereals plus hot selections of eggs, potatoes, pancakes, and breakfast meats ($12). Dinners begin with shrimp cocktail, sashimi, calamari rings, steamer clams, chicken Caesar salad, Wailus mesclun salad, spinach and papaya salad or seafood chowder or soup du jour ($3-12). Entrees include Togarashi crusted ahi $19, salmon Kekaha $22, shiitake crusted chicken $18, pulehu strip steak $22, Thai crab and shrimp cakes $19, mango li hing mui chicken $17, plus various pastas $15-17. Lighter fare includes sandwiches, burgers, fried fish, quesadilla and more $7-13. Assorted sweets and ice cream for dessert options. There is live Hawaiian entertainment in the evenings. COMMENTS: This is a large spacy restaurant in the hotel's Kuhio Dining Court which includes a small sundries shop and cocktail lounge. The dining room is made more intimate with the addition of tall wood columns and smaller table groupings. The wood and green accent colors now give it a richer, cozier look and feel. They also offer affordable family dining: kids under 12 eat free per each adult that orders from the main menu.

TOKYO LOBBY   ★   *Japanese/Sushi Bar*
Harbor Mall, 3501 Rice Street, Nawiliwili (245-8989) HOURS: Dinner 4:30-9:30 pm, Lunch Monday-Friday 11 am-2 pm. SAMPLING: Unusual and creative sushi offerings like Nigiri sushi assortment, Futomaki roll, Makimono nori roll, Inari sushi with soy bean, Chirashi sushi ($9-14). Appetizers include teriyaki chicken on skewer, tori karaage ginger chicken, shu-mai pork dumplings, soft shell crab and others ($4-8). Lunch entrees include tempura, katsu, chicken teriyaki, and yaki sakana grilled mackerel ($8-10); donburi, udon noodles ($6-12). Japanese dinners include nabemono soups like seafood yosenabe, sukiyaki, and nabeyaki

udon, plus beef or chicken teriyaki, shrimp or veggie tempura, katsu, curry chicken, lemon herb chicken, calamari steak, una-jyu broiled eel, BBQ salmon, and a special Tokyo Lobby donburi ($10-16). The specialty is the " Tokyo Lobby Love Boat," a choice of three combination dinners ($22 per person) brought to the table in a head-turning artistic Japanese wooden boat. Top off your meal with refreshing ice creams in green tea, coconut pineapple, Kona coffee, or Japanese-made red bean. COMMENTS: The tempura was light, crispy and fresh, not mushy or greasy. The sushi was attractively presented in tasty and unusual combinations prepared by Sushi Chef Keiichi. Their sushi is good enough to attract a number of celebrity regulars such as movie stars and baseball players. The restaurant is attractively decorated in bright, fresh hues of pink and green with red & black accents in the Japanese pictures and wall hangings. They have expanded and added on a garden room. It's very bright and open, like a conservatory surrounded by big windows on all sides. Jack Ho is the owner, but his Mom, Lin Ho, is the manager and sweet, friendly, gracious hostess. "Mom" talks and visits with everyone who comes in and even if the sushi weren't so good, she'd be well worth the star.

VOYAGE ROOM   *Breakfast/Lunch/Sunday Brunch*
Kaua'i Coconut Beach Resort, Wailua (822-3455) HOURS: Breakfast 6:30-10 am, to 9 am Sunday (Brunch 10 am-1:30 pm), lunch 11 am-1:30 pm. SAMPLING: Breakfast buffet with fruit, pastries, breads, cereals, eggs, breakfast meats, and potatoes ($12). Also a la carte omelettes, pancakes, Belgian waffle, or roast beef hash Benedict ($7-10). For lunch, there are sandwiches of turkey, ham, tuna or chicken salad, fresh catch, and burgers plus saimin bowl or ravioli, and fruit, cobb, chef's, Greek, and chicken or shrimp Caesar salads ($6-10). Island style iced tea is available with cane sugar and pineapple and there is a variety of cakes, pies, and ice creams for dessert. COMMENTS: Some of the hotel packages include the breakfast buffet with your room which is a real bonus. The Sunday brunch is a good value offering a carving station of roast meats plus sushi, salads, Belgian waffles, omelette station, hot entrees, selection of pies and cakes, and an ice cream sundae bar. The restaurant stays the same, but the name changes at dinner when it becomes the Flying Lobster (See separate listing.)

WAILUA FAMILY RESTAURANT   ★   *Local/American*
4361 Kuhio Hwy., Wailua Shopping Plaza (822-3325) HOURS: Breakfast 6:30 am-11 am; lunch 11 am-4 pm, dinner weekdays 4-9:30 pm, Fri/Sat 4-10 pm. SAMPLING: Breakfast: eggs, pancakes, French toast, ham & turkey Benedict, loco moco, omelettes ($3-9). Burgers and sandwiches (corned beef, fish, club, patty melt, French dip, BLT, and salads ($6-8); stir fry or combination platters of steak, fish, chicken, or shrimp ($7-8). Dinners offer similar combinations plus dozens more with seafood, ribs, pork, and beef, ribeye, New York, sirloin, T-bone steak, or prime rib plus seafood choices like lobster platter, giant fried shrimp, fried oysters, fried scallops, grilled ahi, mahi or ono, and combo plates ($10-23). All-you-can-eat salad buffet ($4-9) has more than just salads: there's soup, a seafood bar, taco bar plus puddings and cookies. COMMENTS: Senior dinners and children's menu served all day from 10 am. The salad bar is a good value with lots of local favorites among the choices.

WAILUA MARINA RESTAURANT ★ *American*
5971 Kuhio Hwy., Wailua River State, Park Building B, near Smith's Tropical Plantation in Kapaʻa (822-4311) HOURS: Lunch 10:30 am-2 pm, snacks and sandwiches 2-4 pm (summer only), dinner 5-9 pm. Closed Monday. SAMPLING: Chinese chicken, pineapple boat and chef's salads and BLT, tuna, egg, turkey, French dip, ham, pastrami, mahi mahi, club, burger, steak, BBQ or teri chicken, Reuben and Monte Cristo sandwiches ($7-10). Many dinner entrees available for lunch ($7-10). Baked stuffed pork chop (with stuffing) or chicken (with plum sauce), Chinese style steamed mullet, char-broiled calamari, prawns or ahi stuffed with crab meat, prime rib, sauteed seafood, teriyaki steak, scampi, filet mignon, spaghetti, or spare ribs ($10-18). Oxtail soup; shrimp, steak & chicken mixed plate ($9-12). Hot lobster salad is a specialty ($20). Desserts include homestyle cream pie (coconut, macadamia nut, or chocolate), ice cream pies (mud, fudge, brownie, or spumoni) or lilikoi chiffon pie (like key lime, only better!) COMMENTS: The stuffed pork chops are big and thick, but you can cut them without a knife! The fish is always fresh and priced at least a couple of dollars less than it would be anywhere else. With more than three dozen entrees on the dinner menu, you are sure to find something for everyone. There are extra long tables for families or groups, with a separate banquet room and cocktail lounge. Seating on the lanai can be more pleasant, however. Wall murals may amuse the younger kids in your family, one across the back wall has 3-D sea turtles, shells, and fish.

WASABI'S *Japanese/Sushi Bar*
1394 Kuhio Hwy., Kapaʻa (822-2700) HOURS: Tuesday-Sunday only for dinner 5:30-10:30 pm. SAMPLING: They specialize in a variety of sushi. For dinner choose Wasabi's sinners including chicken yakitori, shrimp or fish tempura, or fresh fish of the day ($13-15). Ala carte items include yakitori chicken, grilled veggies, tofu tempura, soft shell crab tempura or grilled squid ($6-13). House Favorites sushi include lava roll-smoked salmon or island fish ($13), black dragon roll-seared maguro ($11), lollipop roll-hamachi, maguro and salmon ($12), pokepine rolls-maguro with ponzu sauce ($12), or wasabi balls-mushrooms stuffed with seafood mix ($12). Special sushi rolls include choices like Rainbow Roll-five types of fish with crab, avocado, and cucumber ($9); Sunrise Roll-hamachi, maguro, tobiko, papaya and cucumber ($8); Kauaʻi Roll-unagi, papaya, avocado and macadamia nuts ($8); Full Moon Roll-shirmp, scallops, crab, and veggies ($9); Green Dream Roll-anago, crab, avocado and aspargus ($8). They also have an assortment of nigiri and maki rolls, and fresh sashimi. COMMENTS: This is a very small sushi counter operation, sort of a hole-in-the-wall type of place, located right on Kuhio Highway in the heart of Kapaʻa town.

WHALERS BREWPUB *American*
3132 Ninini Point, beyond the Marriott at Fashion Landing Shopping Center at Kauaʻi Lagoons, Lihuʻe (245-2000) HOURS: Lunch 11:30 am-2:30 pm; Dinner 5-10 pm; Sunday brunch 10 am-3 pm. SAMPLING: For lunch, try the blackened chicken pasta, Amber ale batter fish & chips, teri chicken, pork ribs, or saimin along with a variety of sandwiches: turkey club, Philly chicken, roast beef, salmon bagel, or specialty spiced mahi ($8-12). Fresh fish or garlic stir fry with tofu, shrimp or chicken ($13-16). Dinner entrees also include fiery shrimp harpoons, lamb chops, NY steak, and Hawaiian mixed grill ($17-25). Their signature "whale of a burger" is a specialty for both lunch and dinner.

Also soups, salads, and pupus that include egg rolls, calamari rings, teri chicken skewers, chicken quesadilla, and nachos ($5-10). COMMENTS: This open air microbrewery is located at the back of Kaua'i Lagoons offering a spectacular view of the ocean with the lighthouse in the background. Casual lana'i seating outside; attractive wood booths inside. There's a 4,000-gal. marine aquarium, a pool room upstairs and they have live music on the weekends. Their trademarked Pacific Rim Beer Cuisine incorporates the flavors of nine (brewed-on-the-premises) ales in a lot of their menu items especially pupus like the beer-batter fish, coconut shrimp bites, and flowering onion. Other seasonings range from Asian to Cajun and when they say they have "One Whale of a Burger" they mean it! This isn't a hamburger, it's a buffet on a bun! The 20 ounces of ground beef is served on a huge, homebaked bun and served on a platter filled with a ton of fries, an assortment of onions, tomato, lettuce and other good, fresh toppings for your burger plus a variety of condiments. The platter is so big it almost hangs off the edge! And the best part is that it feeds two or more. They also have a Beer and Brunch Buffet every Sunday that includes all nine microbrews plus salads, carved prime rib, omelettes, and a variety of hot entrees and desserts.

EXPENSIVE

A PACIFIC CAFE ★ *Pacific Rim/Hawaiian Regional Cuisine*
Kaua'i Village Shopping Center, Kuhio Hwy. in Kapa'a (822-0013) HOURS: Dinner nightly 5:30-10:00 pm. SAMPLING: Menu changes daily, but your "First Taste" might begin with an appetizer like poached scallop ravioli with tobiko pearls (scallop flavor, but with a different texture) and lime ginger sauce, deep fried curried oysters with scallion sauce, firecracker salmon with sweet Thai chile sauce, or their signature tiger eye ahi sushi tempura ($8-11). Soup might be Thai coconut curry with island fish & shrimp or you might opt for a salad of spicy ahi, grilled Indonesian shrimp with mango vinaigrette, or Japanese eggplant with goat cheese fritter ($8-10). Entrees from the wood-burning grill might include fire roasted ono with shrimp risotto and Thai coconut green curry sauce (smokey, but lively and flavored with flare!), Moroccan marinated veal chop with cous cous, NY steak with gorgonzola cabernet sauce, smoked chicken breast with mushrooms, spinach, fontina cheese and white truffle mashed potatoes with black truffle jus, or lacquered ahi with mushroom compote & orange soy caramel sauce. Specialties might feature their signature wok-charred mahi mahi in garlic sesame crust with lime ginger sauce, penne pasta with shrimp, tomatoes, capers with black olive butter, mushroom spinach stuffed chicken breast on garlic mashed potato, Pacific salmon with griddle rice cake and miso ginger vinaigrette, Chinese roast duck with braised baby bok choy, scallion flat bread & carmelized pineapple glaze, or grilled beef tenderloin with feta herb crust, crispy shrimp and roasted potato terrine and cabernet stilton sauce ($23-28). They offer a prix-fixe "tasting menu" where you can select a combination of one of the evening's appetizer, entree, and dessert selections with suggested wines for a set price. Distinctive desserts include hot macadamia nut tart, banana lumpia, chocolate bombe (with macadamia mousse filling), steamed white chocolate layered with haupia, toasted macadamia nut mousse and served over caramel sauce and Tahitian vanilla bean creme anglais, and strawberries in lilikoi mint essence with creme brulee. COMMENTS: Celebrity owner/chef Jean-Marie Josselin is one of the twelve acknowledged Hawaiian Regional Cuisine chefs in Hawai'i and has

garnered more than his share of accolades and awards over the years. They grow their own salad greens, vegetables and fresh herbs on their own organic farm often dedicating a night to a special ingredient (fresh mushrooms, for example) throughout a prix fixe menu. Chef Josselin has not only branched out with other award-winning restaurants in Hawaii, but has also written several cookbooks, has a weekly local television show, and a website at < www.pacific-cafe.com > Everything on the menu is good.

EMERSON'S SEAFOOD RESTAURANT   ★ *Steak & Seafood*
4-831 Kuhio Highway, Kapa'a, in the Kaua'i Village Shopping Center (822-3662) HOURS: Lunch Mon-Fri 11 am - 2 pm; dinner Sun-Sat 5:30 - 9 pm. SAMPLING: This restaurant is all about seafood with just a couple of non-seafood selections. Appetizers and salads include things like Caesar salad with seared ahi $7.50; soft shell crab salad $9; ahi sashimi and ahi poke $9; seared sea scallops $7.50; oysters on the half shell $9. For entrees choose offerings like fire grilled marlin $17; fresh herb ahi $19; mahimahi crusted with crabmeat mango sauce $20; bouillabaisse $20; soft shell crab $24; for non-seafoodies choose the orange barbecue chicken $16; grilled pork chop $19; or filet mignon $24. The lunch menu offers similar smaller selections at less expensive prices. Clean, well-kept dining room with tropical artwork decor on the walls with nautical fishnet decorative accents hanging from the walls and ceiling.

GAYLORD'S RESTAURANT ★ *American*
At Kilohana Plantation just outside of Lihu'e (245-9503) HOURS: Lunch Monday-Saturday 11 am-3 pm, Sunday brunch 9:30 am-3 pm, Dinner nightly from 5 pm. SAMPLING: Menus change daily. Innovative lunch salads might include papaya stuffed with shrimp, Oriental chicken, Greek-style roasted vegetable, Caesar with red peppers and mild goat cheese coated with macadamias, or Salpicon: local greens with bell pepper, onion, tomato, ahi, cactus(!), avocado, and feta cheese ($9-11). Sandwiches come with soup or salad and fries or rice: San Francisco Reuben (on sourdough), turkey and avocado, a variety of burgers, Monte Cristo, and a tasty ground ahi burger with pickled ginger and a special sauce ($8-11). Signature lunch dishes range from baby back ribs to sweet & sour chicken or try the Farmer's Pie (vegetables under a crust of whipped potatoes), grilled Alaskan salmon, honey-dipped chicken, or capellini pomodoro ($9-13). Dinners might feature appetizers of coconut shrimp, spicy crab cakes, pan-seared sashimi, hot crab & artichoke heart dip, and honey-baked or garlic brie ($9-11); and entrees of steak, fresh fish, baby back ribs, rack of lamb, seafood rhapsody, prime rib (regular or blackened), and chicken served Florentine, Greek, or Kaua'i style with papaya,pineapple, and macadamia nut wine sauce ($18-30). Sauteed venison is a specialty and the prime rib & lobster duet remains one the most popular double entrees ($30-38). The dessert list is extensive starting with linzertorte, Kilohana mud pie, passion fruit parfait, and double chocolate mousse. Their chocolate truffles are deep fried in coconut on the outside with melting chocolate inside and the homemade banana cream pie tastes of real banana. A good selection of premium wines are offered by the glass. For Sunday brunch, entrees are accompanied by a plate of fresh fruit and home-baked cinnamon roll and feature eggs Benedict, spinach quiche, strawberry French toast, tropical Belgian waffle, crepes, banana macadamia pancakes, a variety of pastas, and their signature dish sweet potato hash with chunks of purple

sweet potatoes & chicken breast topped with two poached eggs and Maltaise sauce ($12-16). COMMENTS: The atmosphere and recreation of the old plantation living and dining rooms makes this a special place to dine. Unfortunately, the dining area is along the courtyard and on a cool or rainy afternoon or evening they drop the canvas walls with plastic windows. While this helps keep the elements out, it does detract a bit from the ambiance. (Sort of gourmet dining in a tent!) The food is excellent, however, and dining here is certainly worthy of a recommendation, but preferably on a warm and sunny afternoon or early evening to enjoy the full experience of its unique ambiance. Gaylord's has received wide acclaim and awards for excellence from various media sources. Their entrees and salads are highly creative, offering unusual ingredients in wonderful taste combinations. The fresh fish is generally recommended, and it sells out quickly. Except for the fresh fish, most dinner entrees are relatively moderate in price and good portions. Desserts are to die-for; the banana cream pie was a special delight, nothing fancy or exotic, just one of those wonderful comfort foods! Reservations recommended. They also offer a twice-weekly luau; see LUAU section for more information. < www.gaylordskauai.com >

KUKUI'S RESTAURANT & BAR ★ *Pacific Rim/Buffets*
Kaua'i Marriott Resort, Lihu'e (245-5050). HOURS: Breakfast 6:30-11 am, Lunch 11 am-2 pm, Dinner 5:30-10 pm, Pizza Cafe 12-8:30 pm. Sunday brunch 8 am-2 pm. SAMPLING: Unusual breakfast offerings should wake up your taste buds: shrimp & crab Benedict, vegetable frittata, breakfast burrito (with scrambled eggs, Portuguese sausage & island salsa), macadamia nut pancakes, and Hawaiian sweetbread French toast with sun-dried fruits ($5-14). Continental and full breakfast buffet ($14-17). Lunch begins with sausage nachos, crab & shrimp quesadilla, vegetable rice paper roll, Maui onion soup plus a variety of salads including ceviche, Oriental chicken soba, or seafood Caesar ($6-10). Entree selections feature Jawaiian chicken, eggplant, or swordfish sandwich, fish tacos, shrimp & crab cakes, mushroom ravioli, burgers, seafood melt, and tempura batter fish & chips ($7-16). Roasted garlic chicken, brie & asparagus, smoked salmon, and eggplant, artichoke & goat cheese are some of the pizzas($8-16). Dinners include seafood crusted mahi mahi, roasted char siu pork, paniolo steak, lemon rosemary chicken, and pasta with seared tiger prawns or garlicky scallops ($16-29). Chocolate mousse, passion fruit cream tart, chocolate mac nut pie, coconut rice pudding, and Kahlua cheesecake are the desserts. Weekly prix fixe specials with soup or salad, bread with seafood mousse, cheesecake, and coffee. Specialty dinner buffets are featured on the weekend from 5:30-9:30 pm: Friday is prime rib & King crab with Hawaiian music ($30), Saturday, Pacific Rim with a keiki hula show ($30). Their excellent Sunday brunch ($28) offers salads, fresh fruit, cheese, fish and sushi platters, breakfast dishes, hot entrees, an omelette station, Anahola granola and other cereals with a selection of nuts and sweet toppings including an unusual treat of dried tropical fruits. Choose pancakes, French toast or potato pancakes at the griddle station, rotisserie spiced mahi at the Southwest wrap & roll station, prime rib at the carving station or try some of the innovative creations at the sushi bar-like tempura sushi with lightly fried edges and soft sushi middles! COMMENTS:This open-air pavilion-style restaurant is located at the edge of the resort's 26,000 square-foot pool, the largest in the Hawaiian islands.

SOUTH SHORE

INEXPENSIVE

DA IMU HUT CAFE *American/local*
3771 Hanapepe Rd., (335-0200) HOURS: Breakfast 8-10:30 am, Lunch 10:30 am-2 pm, Dinner 5-8:45 pm (Fri till 9:45) Closed Saturday and Sunday. SAMPLING: French toast, omelettes, meat, egg & rice plates ($4-6). Local plates: Hamburger steak, teri beef or chicken, saimin (fried or bowl), kalua or lau lau ($4-7). "Burgas," egg or tuna sandwich ($2-4).

DALI DELI & CAFE CARA ★ *Italian Deli & Cafe*
Old Koloa Town (742-8824) HOURS: Deli hours are 8 am-3 pm Mon-Sat; Cafe Cara dinner hours are 5:30 pm to closing, Tues-Sat only. SAMPLING: Deli menu board features items like German pancakes, French toast, frittata, lox platter, bagelwich, granola, fruit plate, or egg breakfast ($5-9) Create your own sandwich from a choice of deli meats, cheeses, toppings, and condiments on a variety of freshly baked breads ($4-7). Specialty sandwiches include marinated eggplant on focaccia, turkey with cranberry relish, Italian sub, or spinach & smoked turkey wrap plus quiche, and Greek, chef's, or curry chicken salad ($4-7). Breads, flavored bagels, pies, tortes, cookies and other baked goodies from the bakery plus coffee drinks and smoothies. The Cafe Cara is a recent expansion of the deli and includes a full dinner menu of authentic Italian specials. Choose from appetizers like arincini, bruschette, polenta, or antipasto misto ($5-10), soups and pastas like ribolitta ($5), risotto asparagus ($9), risotta di mara ($9), fusilli alla pappone ($9), and salads like rucola ($6), caprisce ($7). Main courses are bright and innovative such as fettuccine alla Toscana ($11), Cannelloni veggie style ($12), salmon ai Capperi ($13), Agnello alla Diavola ($15). Varied desserts and beverages round out the menu. COMMENTS: Everything is baked fresh on the premises. Sandwiches are all served on their home-baked bread using organic vegetables and fresh deli meats. They even roast their own turkey and make their own traditional boiled-in-water bagels! The dinner menu features excellent creative Italian cuisine and very friendly, courteous service. It's a small dining room, no fancy decor but some colorful local tropical-style artwork on the walls and generally pleasant ambiance. No liquor available but BYOB. Minimal glassware charge applies on BYOB.

THE DOCK *Coffee/Espresso, Sandwiches and Snacks*
1571 Po'ipu Rd., at the Hyatt Regency (742-1234) HOURS: 10:30 am-5 pm. SAMPLING: Deli sandwiches, burgers, salads (Caesar, grilled or Oriental chicken, pasta, chef's, tuna and a signature Smoked Seafood Salad with Lilikoi Vinaigrette) plus and grilled specialty sandwiches like BBQ chicken, garden burger, fresh fish, spiced beef on focaccia and a Reuben wrapper ($4-9). Ice cream, frozen yogurt, cookies, fresh fruit ($2-4). COMMENTS: Located poolside. Keiki meals available.

GRINDS ESPRESSO ★ *Coffee/Espresso, Sandwiches and Snacks*
Ele'ele Shopping Center (335-6027) HOURS: Daily 5:30 am-9 pm SAMPLING: Skillet breakfasts with potatoes, green pepper & potatoes or rice with a choice of meat (sausage, salami, pepperoni) plus omelettes, French toast, and burger-steak,

or mahi mahi breakfast and a Not-So-LocoMoco ($4-7). Sandwiches ($5-7) on homemade bread are served hot (chicken club, bacon & pineapple, mahi mahi, pesto cream cheese & salami, chili burger) or cold (Italian, smoked turkey & jack cheese, veggie, ham & cheddar). Salads include regular house green salad, an organic Caesar, chicken & walnut, and chef's ($4-8). Local plate lunches include mahimahi, BBQ, Cajun or sweet shoyu chicken, and shoyu beef patty or chili rice ($5-7). Varied pizzas come in 15" and 18" sizes($12-23). Espresso and coffee drinks, smoothies, Italian sodas ($2-4) COMMENTS: There is patio seating with lattice work and flowers if you don't want to dine inside.

ISLAND TERIYAKI *Hawaiian/Local style*
5330 Old Koloa Road, Koloa Town Center (742-9988) HOURS: Open daily 7:30am - 9pm. SAMPLING: Breakfast includes pancakes, frittatas, burritos, omelettes and other standard items ($3-7). Plate lunches or papaya-teriyaki grilled chicken, beef, or fish are served with rice, macaroni salad, or ginger cole slaw ($7-10). Their signature dishes are served in a bowl on top of rice or mashed potatoes, or in a "wrap" surrounded by a plain, sun-dried, or spinach tortilla. Try American-chicken salad or steak; Asian-fish, veggie stir-fry, chicken or beef with hoisin sauce, or chicken with curry, coconut, or peanut sauce; Latin-grilled shrimp, fish with papaya salsa, Mexicana, or quesadilla-style; Mediterranean-steak & peppers, roasted eggplant, or lemon-dill fish; or Local-kalua pig, saimin, or loco moco ($6-8). Po'ipu kabobs, barbecue sticks, fresh smoothies, and shave ice and much more. COMMENTS: This is an all-day and late night take-out spot for innovative food items that appeal to folks wanting to sample good local-style and more cuisine. Good food at reasonable prices.

JOE'S COURTSIDE CAFE ★ *Espresso/Coffee, Sandwiches and Snacks*
Located at Kiahuna Tennis Club, Po'ipu (742-6363) HOURS: Breakfast 7-11 am, Lunch 11 am-2 pm. SAMPLING: Pastries, breads, and healthy fruits, along with eggs Benedict, loco moco, Huevos Rancheros, French toast, Anahola granola, banana macadamia pancakes and their popular tofu scramble, are the breakfast options or you can create your own omelette from a list of ingredients. For lunch, choose your ingredients for a personalized salad or opt for a Caesar with grilled chicken breast or Portuguese bean soup ($4-8). Sandwiches include turkey club, tuna & jalapeno melt, vegetarian, South Shore steak sandwich (like a Philly), and a great, lean, turkey Reuben or try a burger, hot dog (with Cleveland Stadium mustard!) or tasty chicken avocado with jack cheese hot off the grill ($5-9). Try the chocolate toffee or lilikoi ice cream pie for dessert ($3.50). COMMENTS: "Eat at Joe's" for some great sandwiches in an open air restaurant and bar. The gazebo-style house has a tented roof and overlooks the tennis courts.

JOHN'S PLACE *Espresso/Coffee, Sandwiches and Snacks*
9875 Waimea Road, Waimea (338-0330) HOURS: Breakfast and lunch only; daily from 6-11 am, and from 7am Sat-Sun; Lunch from 11 am-5 pm. SAMPLING: Breakfast burrito, croissant sandwich, omelettes, French toast ($4-7) Bagels, pastries, fruit, and assorted coffee drinks ($2-3). Sandwiches on their own homebaked bread (turkey & avocado, grilled ham or tuna & cheese, roast beef), chicken, tuna, veggies, or fish "wrapped" in a tomato or spinach tortilla, burgers, hot dogs, fried chicken, burritos, soft tacos, fish & chips, and Caesar salads and fresh daily soups ($3-7).

Smoothies, shakes, floats, or Cappuccino Blast ($3-4). COMMENTS: The "in" (and only) place in Waimea for "healthy" foods and more with ice cream parlor seating. Tropical ice cream and smoothie flavors include, guava, mango, and Ling Hing Mui. (Sample a Waimea Sunset smoothie with strawberries, bananas, guava juice and vanilla ice cream.)

KALAHEO COFFEE CO. & CAFE ★ *Coffee/Espresso, Sandwiches & Snacks*
2-2436 Kaumualii Hwy., at the light in Kalaheo (332-5858) HOURS: Monday-Friday 6 am-3 pm, Saturday 6:30 am-3pm and Sunday 6:30 am-2 pm. SAMPLING: Breakfast ($3-7) is served till noon and the menu offers Anahola granola, scrambled egg or veggie sandwich, pancakes, Belgian waffles, breakfast burrito tortilla wrap, special breakfasts like Up-Country, Paniolo or Kahili, and "Bagel Bennys," but you can build-your-own omelettes till 3:30pm. Lunch is served from 10:30 to closing with Kaua'i grown salads (with bulgar wheat, herb chicken, or Oriental veggie), homemade soups, and deli or grilled sandwiches like hot pastrami, tuna melt, Cajun tofu & eggplant, chicken & bulgar salsa wrap, grilled Reuben, turkey burger, or fresh vegetable on focaccia ($5-7). Ice cream shakes and pastries including muffins, scones, cinnamon rolls, cheesecake, apple pie, carrot cake, and chocolate raspberry cake. And of course they have plenty of espressos, coffees and teas. COMMENTS: The fresh salads are excellent and the sandwiches are piled high. This is a great place to stop after a visit to the Waimea Canyon for a late lunch and/or leisurely cup of coffee or to pick up some lunch to eat up at Kukuiolono Park! Email: <java@kalaheo.com> Website: <www.kalaheo.com>

KAUA'I KITCHENS *Local*
5516 Koloa Road (near Big Save), Koloa (742-1712); HOURS: Koloa 7 am-2:30 pm. SAMPLING: Sandwiches, plate lunches, bentos, sushi-maki cone ($1-2 and up); plus daily specials like chicken cutlet, fresh corned beef, breaded crab croquette, baked pork chops, roast turkey with stuffing, lemon chicken, seafood curry, fish filet, pork adobo plus Hawaiian, Filipino, and Oriental plates ($5-7). They also sell Kaua'i Kookies, baked foods, and T-shirts retail from the Kaua'i Kookie Kompany. COMMENTS: "Quick Tasty Island Style" that you can eat in or take out. Also located at Rice Shopping Center in Lihu'e.

KONA COFFEE

J BAYOT

KOKE'E LODGE ★ *American*

3600 Koke'e Road, Waimea (335-6061) HOURS: Daily 9 am-3:30 pm. SAMPLING: Continental and light breakfasts, quiche, cornbread, muffins ($2-6). Varied lunch sandwiches are served on 12-grain bread ($6-7). Pear, Greek, or Moroccan salads ($7). And the Koke'e Lodge offers specialties like chili, Portuguese bean soup and cornbread; desserts include carrot cake and lilikoi or coconut pie ($3-5). Wine and Kaua'i beer. COMMENTS: Rustic atmosphere and good place to stop on the way to Waimea Canyon. Considering you're in what seems to be the middle of Kaua'i's wilderness, the food is remarkably good. Nothing like a bowl of bean soup with a side of cornbread to warm you up on a cool afternoon adventure in upcountry Kaua'i!

KOLOA COUNTRY STORE & INTERNET CAFE
Coffee/Espresso, Sandwiches & Snacks

5356 Koloa Road, Bldg. 9, The Courtyard, Old Koloa Town (742-1255). HOURS: Mon-Sat 8am - 8pm, Sun 9am - 5pm. This small cafe is located in a shopping complex opposite the main intersection of Maluhia and Koloa Roads. It's a combination country store operation and internet cafe. The menu features snacks, baked goodies and pastries, desserts, espresso and varied coffees, tea, soft drinks, etc. ($2-5). Lounge area and local arts & crafts display; they provide access to email and internet, check for latest rates.

KOLOA FISH MARKET ★ *Fresh fish/plate lunches*

5482 Koloa Road, Koloa (742-6199) HOURS: Monday-Friday 10 am-6 pm, Saturday till 5, closed Sunday. SAMPLING: Smoked fish, seared ahi, poke, lomi lomi salmon, scallop salad, and other deli items. Lunch specials change daily and might include fresh island fish, laulau, kalua pork, beef stew, chili and rice, teri chicken, chicken katsu, etc. ($5-7). Sides of macaroni and rice; sushi and sashimi trays ($3-4). COMMENTS: Tiny market at the Koloa Town Center; mostly take-out, but a few tables and chairs outside. Real local-style food, variety of flavors, great eating adventure.

LINDA'S RESTAURANT *Local*

3840 Hanapepe Road, Hanapepe (335-5152) HOURS: Open Mon-Fri 10:30 am-1:30 pm, Tues-Fri, 5:30-8:30 pm. SAMPLING: Continuous menu features a variety of burgers (mushroom with Swiss, teri beef or chicken) plus tuna, egg, or grilled cheese sandwiches ($2-3) as well as miso soup, samin, and won ton min ($3-5). Plate specials served with rice, macaroni salad, and hot vegetable: teri chicken or beef, loco moco, mahi mahi, pork chop, veal cutlet, beef stew, and honey dip chicken ($5-7). There are also entrees such as chicken cutlet, chicken katsu, and breaded teri beef or chicken ($6-7). Daily specials might include roast beef, shoyu chicken, meat loaf, chicken hekka, and baked mahi ($6-7). COMMENTS: Small coffee shop that's been serving up good local-style meals for over 30 years.

MI CASITA *Mexican*

5470 Koloa Road, Old Koloa Town by the post office (742-2323) HOURS: Mon-Sat 11 am-9:30 pm; Sun 4-9 pm SAMPLING: Pork, beef, or chicken burritos, beef or chicken chimichanga ($9-10). Fajitas for 1 or 2 ($13-23) with chicken, steak, seafood or a "Fiesta" combination. Specialties include Enchiladas Rancheras, chile verde, carnitas, chile relleno, enchiladas, tacos, taquitos, and tostadas ($8-12). Taco salad or seafood salad in a shell plus a variety of nachos, quesadillas, potato skins, and buffalo wings appetizers ($6-9) COMMENTS: This sister (hermana) restaurant of La Bamba in Lihu'e doesn't have a liquor license, but invites you to BYOB.

OASIS BAR & GRILL   *Coffee/Espresso, Sandwiches and Snacks*
2440 Ho'onani Road, Sheraton Kaua'i Resort, Po'ipu (742-1661) HOURS: 11:30 am-6 pm SAMPLING: Sandwiches, salads, fresh fruit and ice cream ($2-7). Hot items include fried chicken, jalapeno poppers, nachos, burgers, pizza, hot dog (or turkey dog), fish burger,chicken fingers, buffalo wings, and chicken teriyaki sandwich ($5-10). COMMENTS: This is the hotel's casual poolside restaurant and is close to the beach. (The Garden Terrace -- open only during high season - - also offers snacks and light meals.)

POOLSIDE GRILL & BAR   *Snacks/Light meals*
Located at the Embassy Vacation Resort--Po'ipu Point. (742-1888) HOURS: 10:30 am-8 pm SAMPLING: Home-style burgers (including ahi and chicken), sandwiches (turkey, tuna, PB&J), salads (turkey Caesar, penne pasta, fresh fruit), honey-dipped chicken, fish & chips, nachos, saimin ($4-9) and a variety of pizza ($9-13). Ice cream treats from sundaes to Melona melon bars: a creamy melon popsicle that's become a "serious" local addiction! ($2-6). COMMENTS: A good place to enjoy a light lunch or warm day snacks and cooler treats after a spell in the pool or at the beach.

PUALANI'S FARMER'S MARKET ★   *Hawaiian/Local Style*
9652 Kaumualii Highway, Waimea (338-9722) on the south side of the highway on the west edge of town just before the turn onto the Waimea Canyon Road. HOURS: Daily 9am - 6 pm. This is a combination small farmer's produce stand and snack shop. They promote themselves as "The Home of Southern Hospitality and Hawaiian Aloha." In addition to seasonal fruits and veggies, they have a limited menu of sandwiches like roast turkey, roast pork or beef Alabama style, tuna salad, honey-baked ham, egg salad and veggie ($5-6). Salads include tuna and Nelle's Hawaiian curried chicken salad ($5-6). Smoothies range from mango mambo, to Patrick's pride, Pualani's best, and several others ($3-4). Frosties, frozen fruits eaten with a spoon, include banana and strawberry, pineapple and strawberry, banana and mango, mango and strawberry, pineapple and papaya, and more ($4) plus there are a variety of other homemade snacks, plate lunch specials, bagels, and other goodies. There are a few sidewalk/patio tables or you can take your lunch or snacks away. Don't forget to check the fruit and veggie tables for bargains on bananas, papaya, pineapples, fresh island coffee, tomatoes, and lots of other fresh produce.

SHIPWRECK SUBS & ICE CREAM   ★   *Sandwiches & Ice Cream*
2360 Kiahuna Plantation Drive, Po'ipu Shopping Village, Po'ipu (742-7467) HOURS: 11 am-6 pm. SAMPLING: Create your own 6" or 13" subs on fresh white or wheat bread with turkey, roast beef, ham, pastrami, salami, tuna, or egg plus choice of Swiss, provolone, cheddar, jack or pepper jack cheese and condiments. With 1 meat ($5-6), 2 meats ($6-7), or 3 meats ($6-8). Potato and

pasta salad sides($1-2). Lots of ice cream treats. COMMENTS: They have a kid's special for ages 12 and under, a peanut butter and jelly sandwich with chips and a small soda ($3). We have had good reports from readers who have been particularly pleased with their fresh breads, meats sliced to order, friendly service, and reasonable prices.

SUEOKA'S SNACK SHOP ★ *Local*
Located in Koloa next to Sueoka's Grocery Store (742-1112) HOURS: Monday-Friday 9:30 am-3 pm, Saturday 9:30 am-3 pm, Sunday 11 am-3 pm. SAMPLING: Plate lunches, sandwiches and burgers, local foods. COMMENTS: This is Kaua'i's original "hole-in-the-wall" eatery, because that's almost what it is. It's an unobtrusive little structure attached to the side of Sueoka's grocery store. But they have some incredible bargains on some good sandwiches and great local style plate lunches. This is a chance to sample some local dishes, and they serve a variety of plate lunches with specials that change daily.The specials are listed on papers stuck on the window and as they sell out of that item, they pull the paper off. You'll see plenty of local folks picking up their lunch during their break. Hamburgers, grilled cheese sandwich, fishburger, or saimin ($2 or less). The teriyaki sandwich seemed like a splurge ($2.50). It was not a huge sandwich, but very tender and flavorful, and at this price you could order two! Plate lunches like fried chicken, tripe stew, chili-dog, teriyaki beef, humburger steak, chopped steak, mahimahi and roast pork ($3-5 or less). No place to sit and eat, so we recommend you take your order over to the beach and enjoy a bargain meal with oceanfront dining. Cheap but good eats.

TAQUERIA NORTENOS ★ *Mexican*
2827 Po'ipu Road, located in Po'ipu Plaza (742-7222) HOURS: 11 am-10 pm Monday- Sunday. Closed Wednesday. SAMPLING: Mexican fare, still nothing much over $6 (with add-ons); most items priced $2-4. COMMENTS: Burritos and the works. The usual enchiladas, tacos, tostadas, et al, plus chalupas (crispy corn cups filled with beans and cheese), and bunuelos - dessert chips sprinkled with cinnamon sugar. This is the epitome of a Mexican hole-in-the-wall restaurant. The few tables in a small room behind the walk-up counter resemble a large closet full of jumbled misfits. But don't be misled. This place has really great food! The prices appear average, but wait until you see the portions!! You can fill up and then some for $6 or less. Since the ambiance isn't much, grab some food to go and head to one of Kaua'i's beautiful parks or beaches.

THE POINT *Lounge/Appetizer & Dessert menu*
Sheraton Kaua'i Resort, 2440 Ho'onani Road, Po'ipu (742-1661) HOURS: Open 3 pm-1 am; grill 4-10 pm, late menu 10 pm. SAMPLING: Hot and cold appetizers (suitable for grazing!) include crusted seared ahi, cheese plate, prawns, and sashimi plus nachos, wons tons, chicken wings, burgers, fish or chicken sandwich, and tempura ($5-10) Their drink menu offers some creative choices in liqueur coffee drinks, alcoholic (and non-) tropical, and martinis plus beer & wine, ports, cognacs, and cigars. Try the Banana Paradise with macadamia nut liqueur, banana cream, vodka & Bailey's or the Menehune Magic with mango cream, cranberry juice & Stoli Razberi. COMMENTS: So what is The Point? It's an airy, poolside lounge that offers appetizers (enough for a light meal) and an extensive drinks menu in an upscale Hawaiian atmosphere with live music - jazz,

Hawaiian - and other entertainment. A special cigar room with pool table is located next door. Tall, glass windows surround both The Point lounge and the adjacent Shells restaurant offering the dramatic ocean waves as a panoramic backdrop.

WAIMEA CANYON SNACK SHOP   *Coffee, Espresso, Sandwiches & Snacks*
Waimea Canyon Plaza, foot of Koke'e Road on Highway 552 in Kekeha (337-9227). HOURS: Open daily 9 am - 5pm. SAMPLING: This small food counter offers a short menu of sandwiches like tuna and chicken salad, burgers, dot dogs, and various other snacks plus assorted cold beverages, coffee, etc. It is also a Lappert's Ice Cream Shop so you can indulge in some fine widely acclaimed Kaua'i-made ice cream. COMMENTS: Good place to stop for a refreshing drink or snack on the way to Waimea Canyon and Koke'e Park or on the way back.

MODERATE

BRENNECKE'S *Steak and Seafood*
2100 Ho'one Road, Po'ipu, across from Poi'pu Beach Park (742-7588) Web: <www.brenneckes.com> HOURS: Lunch 10 am - 4 pm, Dinner 4-10 pm, Early Bird Dinner 4-6 pm, Happy Hour 2-5 pm daily. SAMPLING: Burgers, sandwiches, soups, and salad bar served all day till 10 pm ($5-12). Pupus all day, too: ceviche, sashimi, nachos, black and blue ahi, teri chicken sticks, Oriental or local style samplers ($8-14). Eary bird and regular dinner choices include scampi, pasta with vegetables, or clams with pasta, prime rib, NY steak, shrimp skewers, Oriental chicken stir-fry, Hawaiian spiny lobster, BBQ pork ribs, and fresh island fish ($14-30). COMMENTS: Excellent children's menu includes cheese or pepperoni pizza, beach burger, fish sandwich, teriyaki chicken sticks and more ($4-9). Salad bar has some interesting items, like whole red skinned potato salad, baby corn, pasta salad, and a good choice of dressings. Things may appear a bit pricey but all meals come with a salad bar and the great across-the-road view of the beach park. You'd pay more at other places for much less of a beachside atmosphere and view. Brennecke's also has T-shirts and a Beach/Activity Center and Beach Deli downstairs.

BRICK OVEN PIZZA   ★   *Italian*
2555 Kaumualii Hwy., Kalaheo (332-8561) HOURS: 11 am-10 pm Tuesday-Saturday, 3-10 pm Sunday, closed Monday. SAMPLING: Whole wheat or white crust with the usual pizza toppings plus homemade Italian sausage, lean beef & green onions, imported anchovies, smoked ham & pineapple, salami, bay shrimp and more; varied sizes ($10-29). Pizza breads and hot sandwiches with sausage, seafood, meats and vegetables, or "pupu" pizza: pizza dough with garlic & cheese and a side of pizza sauce or dressing for dipping ($4-7); green veggie or chef's salads ($2-7). Desserts include aloha pie or ice cream sundae cups; beer & wine. COMMENTS: Hearth-baked pizzas at this family owned operation which has been pleasing residents and visitors alike since they opened in 1977. Good homemade sausage and excellent pizza crust, soft and doughy, but beautifully browned - like a soft pretzel. The garlic butter on the crust is an added flavor treat.

CAMP HOUSE GRILL ★ *American*
Kaumualii Hwy., Kalaheo (332-9755) HOURS: Breakfast 6:30-10:30 am (to 11 weekends and holidays), Lunch/Dinner 10:30 am-9 pm. SAMPLING: Breakfast quesadilla, pancakes, omelettes, waffles, French toast, biscuits and gravy, eggs Benedict, omelettes and a variety of breakfast sandwiches - Monte Cristo with hash browns, or BLT (& egg), pancake or French toast with bacon & eggs ($4-9). They have early bird specials ($2-3) before 8 am, but as they say on the menu: After 8:01, No Way! Grilled fish, veggie, BLT, or turkey BLT sandwiches; chili ($4-8). Lunch and dinner offerings include a variety of burgers, salads, several grilled chicken entrees, BBQ pork ribs, Camp House huli huli chicken, sirloin steak Polynesian, pork chops, snow crab legs, shrimp scampi and fresh catch served with soup or salad and choice of side ($4-19). COMMENTS: They're known for their homemade pies, so if you don't save room for dessert, you'll just have to buy a whole one from the glass case on your way out. Pineapple cream cheese macadamia or chewy chocolate chip macadamia nut sound good enough to eat (and they are!) and so do the cream pies of coconut, banana, and chocolate or the Paradise Pie made with macadamia nut, coconut,and pineapple. The burgers are good, but the ribs are outrageously good! This looks like a funky neighborhood diner, but it is bright, spacious and naturally, it's comfortable and casual. It's home cooking all the way and home baking as far as the pies are concerned. The children's menu is available for lunch and dinner and it is no secret this is a family place. Nothing real fancy about the Kalaheo outlet right on the highway in the middle of town. It's a casual eatery but clean and decent, the food is good and service is fast. Their other location is Kapa'a.

GREEN GARDEN ★ *Family Dining*
Right on Kaumualii Highway #50 in Hanapepe Town (335-5422/335-5528) HOURS: Breakfast Mon-Fri 8:30-10:30am (from 8 am on Saturday and 7:30 am Sunday), Lunch 10:30 am-2 pm, Dinner 5-9 pm; closed Tuesdays. SAMPLING: Breakfast of eggs, breakfast meats, waffles, hot cakes, and French toast ($4-5). For $5.20 you can have dessert for breakfast: a waffle with ice cream, whipped cream, coconut, and strawberry topping! Lunch sandwiches include salad, fries, and beverage and offer roast pork, mahi melt, burgers, and a variety of clubs ($6-7). Entrees also include vegetables and feature chicken chow mein, shrimp tempura, sweet & sour spare ribs, BBQ ahi, BBQ chicken, shrimp Louie salad and more ($7-9) and specials like seafood curry, breaded liver, or chicken tofu. Dinners are complete with homemade soup, salad, rice or potatoes, vegetables, rolls, and beverage. Appetizers include a choice of escargot stuffed mushrooms, shrimp cocktail, mussels, sashimi, or pupu platter ($4-7). They offer some of the same lunch entrees at only slightly higher prices as well as kiawe broiled pork chops, steaks, kabobs, or chicken peppercorn as well as Chinese, Japanese or Hawaiian plates, ahi a la Arashiro, rack of lamb, and teri chicken. Daily specials might include roast turkey or pork, prime rib, steamed crab legs, fresh fish, chicken cutlet, or their "house special" baked seafood salads ($9-21).They're known for their "mile-high" pies like coconut, macadamia nut, or chocolate cream, and especially the lilikoi chiffon ($3). COMMENTS: This family owned restaurant has been here since 1948 serving an eclectic mix of local, homestyle, and gourmet meals in large portions for small prices. Wine & tropical drinks; their house special is a lilikoi (passionfruit) daiquiri. Good selection of children's

choices. The salad bar, given the inflated prices of fresh produce on Kaua'i, is a real value! ($7 for lunch and dinner, $3 with entree.) Very casual and informal with the spacious garden look of a greenhouse. Long family-style tables, generally pleasant atmosphere and courteous small town-style service. Many folks stop just to try the homemade pies.

HANAPEPE CAFE & ESPRESSO ★ *Gourmet Vegetarian*
Located in old Igawa Drugstore at 3830 Hanapepe Road (335-5011/335-8544) HOURS: Breakfast Tuesday-Saturday 9-11 am, Lunch 11 am-2 pm. Dinner served Friday & Saturday 6-9 pm. SAMPLING: Breakfast naturally begins with espresso and other coffee drinks and there are multi-grain waffles and pancakes, homemade oatmeal, home fries, and baked frittatas ($4-9). Lunch includes soups and salads, healthnut or grilled vegetable sandwich, pasta, and garden burgers with various combinations of pesto, sundried tomatoes, sauteed mushrooms, and artichoke hearts ($5-8). Dinners change monthly and might include an appetizer of stuffed tomatoes, ricotta dumplings, roasted garlic bread and macadamia nut pesto, roasted goat cheese cakes, or seared polenta salad ($7-12). Entrees may include things like vegetable & potato Charlotte, Southwest style lasagna, garbanzo bean flour cakes with eggplant & tomatillo relish, four cheese lasagna, primavera and linguine crepes, quesadilla with pesto & portobello mushrooms, purple sweet potato quiche with raisins, cheese & sauteed mushrooms, puree of onion with fresh spinach and a daily fresh pasta. ($13-19). Desserts include macadamia nut creme brulee, passion fruit bread pudding with raspberry sauce & vanilla ice cream, tiramisu, and chocolate cake with lilikoi glaze ($6-6.50). COMMENTS: Owners/Chef Larry Reisor offers gourmet vegetarian dinners that even meat eaters like. They're made with a French and Italian flair and with such fresh, flavorful vegetables that most don't know anything's "missing." (In fact, 90% of their customers aren't vegetarian!) The dishes are creative and colorful, mixing and matching ingredients for bursts of flavor that are both familiar and exciting. BYOWine. Live music on dinner nights with regular or Hawaiian slack key guitar. Reservations recommended. < www.hanapepe.com >

JOE'S ON THE GREEN ★ *Espresso/Coffee, Sandwiches and Snacks*
Located at the Kiahuna Golf Course in Po'ipu. (742-9696) HOURS: Breakfast 7:30-11:30 am, lunch 11:30 am-2:30 pm. Dinner Thursdays only, 5:30-8:30 pm. Cocktails and pupus till 6 on weekends. SAMPLING: Breakfast specials include Joe's special scramble made with ground beef, eggs, and taro leaf; biscuits-n-gravy; eggs Benedict, huevos rancheros and a variety of tropical fruit pancakes ($5-9). For lunch, try the kalua pork sandwich, beer-battered fish-n-chips, Joe Mama burger, tuna melt, or a classic Caesar salad and more ($7-9). Dinner (and great sunsets!) are offered on Thursday nights. The lively and inventive menu features some surprising combinations that really work: prawns wrapped in phyllo with banana curry sauce; kalua pork and lomi salmon ravioli; and fresh mahi mahi in coffee lime beurre blanc sauce are just a few of the Thursday night specials. ($15-23). COMMENTS: No longer just a snack bar, the wide, open-air bar and pleasant seating area is now enhanced by a "real" restaurant. This is a bright, beautiful, clean and very comfortable dining room. The country club setting overlooks the golf course and offers a great panoramic view. Live Hawaiian music on Thursday nights.

KING'S STEAKHOUSE AND TROPICAL BAR ★ *Steak and Seafood*
1-3959 Kaumualii Highway, Hanapepe (335-3611) HOURS: Open daily for lunch 11 am - 4 pm, diner 5 - 10 pm. SAMPLING: The emphasis here is on prime Black Angus beefsteak, a beefeaters delight. Start with pupus like shrimp lahti $10, wontons $7, spring rolls $8, calamari $8, nacho platter $9, or Pacific crab cakes $9. They feature entrees like kiawe grilled Adam's ribeye steak $20-25, The Emperor's 24 oz. Porterhouse $35, Prince 16 oz. Porterhouse $25, filet mignon $25, sirloin steak $17, Mongolian beef skewer $18, Uncle Tony's baby back ribs $19, or try pork chop $17, chicken cordon bleu $18, chicken marsala $17; combo entrees available. Seafood selections include bbq shrimp $17, lobster tail (market price), fresh catch $19, plus various pasta choices. The lunch menu features various sandwiches, tacos, wrap sandwiches, burgers and more. COMMENTS: Located in Hanapepe Place on west edge of town right on the highway. Very friendly and attentive service. It's doubtful there is a better steak available elsewhere on Kaua'i. Excellent!

KUPONO CAFE AT THE ANARA SPA *Vegetarian*
1571 Po'ipu Rd., at the Hyatt Regency (742-1234) HOURS: 6 am-2 pm. SAMPLING: Fresh fruits, cereals, and tropical muffins along with fresh fruit juices and smoothies ($3-$7). Low-fat lunches include red lentil chili with yogurt & baked corn chips, garden burger, and island-grown salads ($5-8). COMMENTS: Located right at the spa so you can enjoy a healthy breakfast or lunch after indulging in a facial or massage, working out in their fitness room, or swimming laps in their 25 yard lap pool. (Although it sounds like an appropriately ethereal and Oriental name, ANARA is actually an acronym for A New Age Restorative Approach.)

LAWA'I RESTAURANT ★ *Local/Oriental*
2-3687 Kaumualii Hwy., Lawa'i (332-9550) HOURS: Mon-Fri 10 am-9 pm, Sat-Sun from 9. SAMPLING: Extensive menu (about 300 items!) of local and Oriental dishes: soup, pork, beef, poultry, seafood, chop suey, eggs, vegetarian, saimin, cake noodles, salad, sushi roll, Filipino dishes, curries, Japanese dishes plus sandwiches, steaks and seafood. Chinese sausage, crispy duck with plum sauce, ham & egg fu yung, seafood spaghetti, duck noodles with vegetables, chicken papaya, sukiyaki don, shrimp tempura, fish teriyaki, BBQ meatballs ($5-12). Full seafood, Chinese, or steak combo dinners ($10-16). COMMENTS: This small eatery is particularly popular with local residents, so it must be a good dining discovery. Follow the locals and you can't go wrong! There are three pages full of dishes on their printed menu and even more on the blackboard. Try their tasty ginger fried chicken!

PACIFIC PIZZA & DELI *Pizza*
9652 Kaumualii Hwy. (part of and adjacent to Wrangler's Steak House across from Big Save), Waimea (338-1020) HOURS: 11 am-9 pm. SAMPLING: A variety of "international" pizzas in small, medium, large ($9-20) sizes and calzone such as Pacific seafood, Japanese, Portuguese, Mexican, Veggie, Thai, Hapa Haole (pesto with sun-dried tomatoes, mushrooms, zucchini, Canadian bacon and Hawaiian pineapple) Lomi Lomi salmon, and Filipino with homemade langanizsa sausage ($4-6). Deli sandwiches (on choice of bread) or cold wraps

rolled in a tomato-basil tortilla come in turkey, ham pastrami, roast beef, seafood and tuna ($5-6). House salad ($4) plus special deli salads sold by the pound. COMMENTS: Eat in or take out. Good pizza and sandwiches.

PATTAYA ASIAN CAFE ★ *Thai & Chinese*
2360 Kiahuna Plantation Drive, Po'ipu Shopping Village, Po'ipu (742-8818) HOURS: Lunch 11:30 am-2:30 pm Monday-Saturday; Dinner nightly 5-9:30 pm. SAMPLING: Spring or summer rolls, fish cakes, sateh, calamari, mee krob appetizers ($7-11). Lemongrass or Thai ginger coconut soup with chicken or seafood ($8-15); Fresh papaya, shrimp, or beef salad ($6-11). Lemon chicken, stir fried eggplant, broccoli with oyster sauce, pad Thai noodles, Evil Jungle Prince, garlic with coconut, pineapple with curry sauce, stir fried bell pepper,and a variety of curries are the entrees ($8-17). COMMENTS: The emphasis at this shopping center sidewalk restaurant is on authentic and traditional Thai cuisine combining the unique and exotic flavors with southeast Asian cookery style.

PIZZETTA ★ *Italian*
5408 Koloa Road, Koloa Town (742-8881) HOURS: 11 am-10 pm, Happy Hour 3-6pm. SAMPLING: Appetizers include mozzarella sticks, garlic bread sticks, stuffed mushrooms and bruschetta ($6-8). Varied salads include blackened chicken Caesar, veggie chop salad, and Greek salad and there is a soup of the day ($3-10). A wide selection of pastas range from spaghetti marinara, to spaghetti and meatballs, fettucini with clams, fettucini Lucia and penne siciliano ($8-12). Specialities include cheese ravioli, lasagne, chicken parmesan, eggplant parmesan, chicken cacciatore, chicken marsala and a fresh island fish of the day ($12-15). The menu also features a number of pizza pies in medium and large sizes such as BBQ chicken, sun dried tomatoes, Florentine, Puttanesca, Margherita, shrimp pesto, piza bianca, meat lovers and more ($13-24). Calzones include veggie, Hawaiian, Italian sausage, spinach and ricotta, pesto and mushrooms, pepperoni and others ($9); and there are Italian grilled specialty sandwiches like vento blackened chickien, calabrese salami, roma herbal cream cheese, hot meatball sub and chicken parmigiana ($6-8). Delightful desserts like cheesecake, ice cream, chocolate decadence, and a perfectly textured tiramisu complete the menu ($4-6). COMMENTS: Full beverage selection with Italian sodas, tropical iced tea, juices, espressos, and coffee drinks as well as wine and beer. They still feature good family-style Italian cooking and use many homemade ingredients in their recipes.

PO'IPU BAY GRILL & BAR ★ *American*
2250 Ainako, just past the Hyatt Regency on the golf course at Po'ipu Bay (742-1515) HOURS: Breakfast 6:30-10:30 am, Lunch 10:30 am-3 pm. (Sandwiches & pupus Thurs-Fri 3-7 pm, till 11 on Sat.) SAMPLING: Variety of breakfast meats and egg dishes plus loco moco, eggs Benedict, omelettes, corned beef or crab hash with poached eggs, Belgian waffle, cinnamon rolls, and great selection of tropical & fruit pancakes: banana, macadamia, mango, berry, and raisin! ($6-9). Japanese breakfasts ($13-15). Lunch options include salads (Caesar, grilled salmon or eggplant), sandwiches (grilled ahi, Korean BBQ steak, hot dog, club, crab melt), and burgers ($5-10). Korean and Hawaiian plate lunches ($9-10). Buffalo wings, chili, calamari, nachos (regular or criss-cut potato), ahi sashimi, and spicy onion rings are some of the pupus ($5-9). For dessert there's mud pie,

apple pie, and ice cream. ($3-5) COMMENTS: Windows all around with views of the golf course. Looks like an old fashioned hotel or country club dining room. Good reviews on the breakfast for quality and price (especially the eggs Benedict and home fries) and we liked the Asian-style cole slaw and garlicky criss-cut french fries served with their sandwiches. This dining room is operated by the Hyatt Regency and for guest enjoyment they have pool tables, a dart board, video games and plenty of sports-filled televisions as well as live entertainment from 8-11 pm on Saturdays.

POMODORO ★ *Italian*
Rainbow Plaza in Kalaheo (332-5945) HOURS: Dinnery nightly 5:30-10 pm. SAMPLING: Antipasti of calamari fritti, mozzarella marinara, or prosciutto and melon ($6-10), a variety of pastas - spaghetti, ravioli, cannelloni, manicotti, baked penne, and lasagna, the house special ($12-17) and Pomodoro specialties like veal parmigiana, pizzaiola, piccata, or scallopini; eggplant or calamari parmigiana, scampi, chicken cacciatore, and chicken saltimbocca, an unusual change from veal ($16-20). Italian desserts like zabaliogne, tiramisu, and spumoni are featured. COMMENTS: Surprisingly attractive tables and settings for its relatively hidden location on the second level of a shopping/commercial complex. They have a separate cocktail lounge. Their food is fresh and flavorful, everything is made to order. The food excellent, traditional Italian -- the lasagna deserved its designation as house special; it was made with both beef and sausage and just the right amount (lots!) of cheeses. The spaghetti and meat balls were excellent and a very generous portion. The calamari was perfect in texture and preparation, and the spumoni ice cream cake easily became one of our Best Bets! The service was excellent (both personable and efficient) and we appreciated the attention to the "little" things -- like napkins under our water glasses! Entrees are served with pasta, vegetable and homemade garlic focaccia bread. They lay claim to the best espresso in Hawaii and that may well be even if we didn't try it. But their regular coffee is just fine. Generally moderate prices on most menu items and there are things for the children to enjoy as well.

TOI'S THAI KITCHEN *Thai*
Ele'ele Shopping Center, near Hanapepe (335-3111) Hours: Lunch 10:30 am-2:30 pm, Dinner 5:30-9 pm. Closed for lunch on Sunday. SAMPLING: Soups (such as tom yum, long rice, tofu, and saimin) are served with rice, papaya salad, and dessert ($6-15). Appetizers include spring rolls, mee krob, and deep fried tofu plus salads with beef, pork or chicken; shrimp, mahi mahi or calamari, and beef, chicken or pork laab ($8-10). Pad Thai, Thai fried rice, lad na, and fried noodle with broccoli are offered with pork, beef, chicken, shrimp, mahi, calamari, tofu, or vegetables ($9-12). Dinner entrees include green papaya salad and choice of jasmine, brown, or sticky rice: jub chai, buttered garlic nua, satay, ginger sauce nua, nua krob, cashew chicken, or shrimp, panang chicken and red, green, yellow, or Matsaman curry ($11-16). Toi's Temptation (choice of meat simmered in coconut milk and chile paste with lots of lemon grass) is a specialty as is Pinky in the Blanket: deep fried shrimp marinated in white wine and wrapped in rice paper with satay peanut sauce ($11-16). American plates (chicken, pork, mahi, or shrimp with fries, salad, and dessert) are available for the non-adventurous types ($9-11). Lunch menu features the same items as dinner, most at $1-3 less.

COMMENTS: Attractive contemporary/Asian decor accents; bright flower pots on each table and individual lace curtains on the windows. The bar is on one side with an open dining area on the other. Karaoke at 9:30 with late night pupus till 1 am, including saimin, pork won ton, calamari, or onion rings, wing dings, poppers, fried mushrooms ($5); sashimi Friday & Saturday ($8)

TOMKATS GRILLE AND BAR ★ *American*
5402 Koloa Road, Old Koloa Town Center (752-8887) HOURS: 11 am-10 pm, Happy Hour 4-6 pm. SAMPLING: Nibblers like fried onion rings, mushrooms, mozzarella sticks, or zucchini plus chicken fingers, calamari rings, jalapeno poppers, and buffalo wings ($5-8). Chef, chicken and seafood salads ($6-9). Good choice of burgers and sandwich traditions like a patty melt, Really Reuben, French dip, New York steak, mahi, turkey "Klub" or veggie burger ($7-9). Hawaiian, Italian, paniolo, or teri chicken sandwiches ($6-7). Homemade chili ($3-4). Also seafood or steak ka-bobs and rotisserie chicken plus nightly dinner specials (from 5 pm) like barbecue pork ribs, New York steak or steak kabobs, rotisserie chicken, chicken marinara, or seafood linguine or kabobs, fresh "Katch" or prime rib ($9-17). Wash it all down with a White Tiger, Banana Cow, or a Mai Tai made with passion fruit and guava juice. COMMENTS: The name of the restaurant was derived from the first names of owners, Tom and Kathy Podlashes, and Katnip is behind the bar. Casual outdoor seating on wood decks in a rustic garden setting. Very good desserts and Tom makes the carrot cake himself! Menu for Kittens 12 and under.

WAIMEA BREWING CO. ★ *Continental-International*
9400 Kaumalii Hwy. at Waimea Plantation Cottages (338-9733) HOURS: 11 am-9 pm, bar & brewery till 11. SAMPLING: This is a restaurant and brew pub combination. Start with such innovative appetizers as Caribbean jerk seared ahi "sashimi" with fire roasted corn salsa, Kalua duck lumpia with black bean hoison sauce, taro leaf goat cheese dip, fiery chicken wings with blue cheese papaya dipping sauce, Gado Gado chicken skewers with peanut sauce, or the "twisted" Caesar salad with grilled lettuce and their own non-traditional dressing ($5-7). Burgers topped with everything from bleu cheese to fried egg plus grilled fish, chicken or portobello mushroom sandwiches ($7-9). "Big Plates" of baby back ribs, fresh catch, kalua pork, or Mediterranean roasted chicken ($13-16), and keikis can order a PB&J, grilled cheese, hot dog, or popcorn chicken off the Short Pants Club menu ($3-4). Nightly dinner specials might offer appetizers of lemongrass crusted ahi satay or smoked marlin lasagna ($9-11) with entrees like "quill" pasta with Kekaha shrimp (served with tomato, lime & Hawaiian chile pepper sauce and cilantro mac nut pesto), herbed mahi with spicy passion fruit sauce, or grilled ono with green curry-lime leaf beurre blanc ($16-21). Roasted banana cheesecake, lilikoi poundcake, and "Chocolate is my Master" are the desserts ($3-5). COMMENTS: This restaurant location has finally found its niche with a plantation-style ambiance that is attractive, but not too upscale and food that has just the right balance of familiarity and creative innovation. There are petroglyph designs throughout and the bar is made from red dirt (cemented and polished) with a view of the gleaming brew tanks. The patio deck has old-fashioned "park bench" chairs. The hardwood floors are smooth and polished and so are the gold faucets and fixtures in the bathrooms! Chef Todd Oldham makes his own condiments and spices so you'll find your burger served with guava chile

or roasted pepper ketchup, your fresh fish with wasabi aioli sauce or your sandwich with jalapeno & beer mustard or wasabi pickled ginger mayo. And there's also their "Damn Good Fries" with hand-harvested Hawaiian salt, bok choy cabbage or Java slaw, and "beginners" kim chee! You can wash it down with a tart, fresh lilikoi margarita, but you'll probably opt for one of the handcrafted brews from their brew pub like the Pakala Porter, Alakai Stout, West Side Wheat or Napali Pale Ale. They also have brew label t-shirts and some really cool mugs with their petroglyph logo designs.

WONG'S RESTAURANT & OMOIDE BAKERY *Chinese*
Hanapepe (335-5066) HOURS: Deli open 8 am-9 pm; Wong's dinner service 5-9 pm. Closed Monday. SAMPLING: In the deli: breakfasts of eggs, pancakes, and omelettes ($3-7), appetizers of spring roll, won ton, gau chee, loco moco, fried shrimp ($7-7), sandwiches, burgers, spam ($3-4), saimin ($7), lunch & dinner plates like spare ribs, oyster chicken, or beef broccoli ($5-7) and dinner specials like roast pork and NY, chop, or pepper steak ($8-13). Char siu pork or roast duck from $7.25 lb. Wong's has an extensive Chinese dinner menu with chicken, duck, beef, pork, egg, seafood, vegetarian, and noodle dishes. Crispy skin chicken, "duck-in-the-nest," Mongolian beef, pork with eggplant, shrimp fu young, steamed sea bass with ginger & onions, Szechwan tofu, and roast pork saimin are just a few examples ($6-9). "Gringo" steak and shrimp entrees ($10-24). The bakery has pies (lilikoi or chocolate chiffon, mac nut cream custard, pumpkin) cakes (haupia, guava, chantilly, "chocolate dream"), plus cheesecake (raspberry, fudge, "turtle pecan"), and almond float. COMMENTS: The restaurant is a banquet room that also does a lot of parties and catering. They're famous for their lilikoi chiffon pie.

WRANGLER'S STEAKHOUSE   *Steak and Seafood*
9852 Kaumualii Hwy. (across from Big Save), Waimea (338-1218) HOURS:
Mon-Fri Lunch 11 am-5 pm; Dinner Mon-Sat 5-8:30 pm. Closed Sunday.
SAMPLING: Burgers, sandwiches, fresh fish ($7-11) or the "Kau Kau Tin"
lunch: Oriental shrimp tempura, teriyaki chicken and Japanese pickled vegetables
served in a plantation workers tin ($8). Dinners offer scampi, crab legs, chicken
cordon bleu, pork chops, BBQ ribs, and seafood platter ($15-20). Mexican
entrees include enchiladas and burritos ($11-12) and a variety of steaks are served
broiled, pan-fried, sizzling (their house specialty), or in seafood combinations
($16-20). Keiki menu ($5-7). COMMENTS: This steak house serves meals in a
large open beam ceiling room and is attached to their nextdoor operation, Pacific
Pizza & Deli in the same building.

EXPENSIVE

BEACH HOUSE RESTAURANT ★ *Pacific Rim*
5022 Lawa'i Beach Road, Poipu, on the way to Spouting Horn (742-1424)
HOURS: Dinner nightly, 5:30-10 pm. SAMPLING: The Beach House has a
reputation for creative and innovative dishes in a recently refurbished atmosphere.
The menu offers exotic appetizers such as sea scallops on green papaya salad with
white truffle vinaigrette and cranberry essence, grilled artichoke, shrimp "pulehu," crab cakes, and a "taster" of ahi prepared as sushi, in a taco, and in a hash
spring roll. Seafood minestrone or Kaua'i asparagus salad are also some of the
possible starters ($6-12). Entrees range from Asian duck breast, to crispy sesame
chicken, lemongrass crusted sea scallops, "local" paella with shrimp, scallops,
seared crusted macadamia nut mahimahi with citrus miso sauce, and seared pork
chops with lehua honey & whole-grain mustard glaze. There are also kiawe-
grilled coriander marinated lamb chops, grilled ahi with black bean chili sauce,
fire-roasted eggplant cannelloni, NY steak with truffles, grilled ono with caper
pesto, or Kaua'i shrimp with spinach & mushrooms ($18-30). Dessert options
($6-8), might be Kahlua poi cheese cake, molten chocolate desire, warm choco-
late tart with white chocolate gelato, coconut butter mochi "sundae," fruit quiche,
sorbetto martini, or apple banana "Foster." COMMENTS: The Beach House has
been voted *"#1 Restaurant on Kaua'i"* by the Zagat 2000 survey. It's also been
lauded by Travel & Leisure and called *"...one of the most romantic restaurants
in the world."* That says something of the wide acclaim garnered by the restaurant. Great oceanfront views along the Poipu Coast.

CASA DI AMICI PO'IPU ★ *Continental/International*
2301 Nalo Road, Po'ipu (742-1555) HOURS: Dinner nightly 6-9:30 pm. SAM-
PLING: Appetizers include such tempting exotics as bandolini filled with
prosciutto, asiago and sage in pancetta, tomato and sage sauce, shrimp and ahi
Thai sticks with wasabi aioli, or rissotto with kalua pork and cabbage ($8-10).
Salads include a Caesar, insalata di Pomodoro, mista, Greek salade mesclun or
Asian salade mesclun ($6-8). Entree specials might include rosemary-garlic-olive
oil lamb loin with cassis-mint sauce, sauteed duck breast with Jamaican spiced
sauce, fennel crusted lamb with orange-hoison-ginger sauce, salmon & shrimp in
Thai coconut lobster sauce, black tiger prawns with ravioli of lobster thermidor
in paella sauce, porcini-crusted chicken breast in cherry port wine, tournedos
rossini in Madeira-shallot sauce with Asian spice pate, or Japanese mahogany-

glazed salmon with jalapeno tequila aioli and black bean chinitos ($18-28). There's also a full page of pastas and sauces to mix and match ($19-23; light portions from $14) plus lasagna, fettucine putanesca, and linguine primavera ($20-23). Chicken or veal prepared marsala, picatta or gorgonzola style ($18-23). Creative desserts include bananas Foster, frozen mango mousse and delicate tiramisu ($6-8) COMMENTS: This restaurant is tucked away in a quiet neighborhood in the Poipu resort area and is surrounded by homes and condos. Turn left above the curve just past Po'ipu Beach Park (as you're heading east). Chef/owner Randall Yates relocated the very popular Casa di Amici to Poipu from Kilauea just a couple of years ago. The cuisine is a blend of Italian-Mediterranean and has been rated #1 on Kaua'i and #5 in the state for their international eclectic cuisine by Zagat's Survey and have received wide acclaim from other media outlets. The fusion of flavors and cross-cultural melding of cooking styles has made Casa di Amici a unique Kaua'i dining experience. The open air alfresco dining and grand piano music makes for a most romantic dining atmosphere and experience.

DONDERO'S ★ *Italian*
1571 Poi'pu Road, Hyatt Regency Kaua'i, Po'ipu (742-6260) HOURS: 6-10 pm. SAMPLING: Antipasti consists of porcini mushroom crepes; beef carpaccio; bruschetta; fresh triangle pasta with shrimp, asparagus & mushrooms, speidini of prawns & artichokes; minestrone soup; artichoke with crab fondue, and several salads including portabella mushroom & goat cheese ($6-13). Pastas include ricotta cannelloni with walnuts; veal rigatoni; seafood spaghettini; fettucine with roasted chicken, porcini mushroom, prosciutto & parmesan cream sauce and risotto with grilled vegetables ($17-27). Savory entrees include veal scallopini with lobster; osso buco; chicken stuffed with spinach, mushroom & fontina cheese; filet medallions with marsala sauce; risotto-crusted fresh fish with lobster & shrimp cannelloni; and cioppino ($24-29). Desserts ($5-6) include tiramisu, gelato, flourless chocolate cake, fresh fruit torte, amaretto cheesecake souffle, or Zuppa Inglaise (translation: "English Soup"), the Italian version of English trifle. COMMENTS: Extensive wine list. The dining room is beautifully decorated with marble flooring, patterned tile accents and colorful Franciscan murals which lend the feel of an Italian bistro and make for an intimate dinner setting. The food is classical Italian with a difference that should appeal to purists as well as the more adventurous Italian food lover. While dining is casual on the Garden Isle, they do request men wear shirts with collars. Reservations suggested.

HOUSE OF SEAFOOD ★ *Steak and Seafood*
1941 Po'ipu Road at Po'ipu Kai Resort (742-6433) HOURS: Dinner nightly from 5:30pm to closing. SAMPLING: Steamed clams, shrimp cocktail, Oysters Rockefeller, and crab stuffed potato are a few of the regular appetizers but they have nightly specials that might include avocado tempura with lobster, crab stuffed mushrooms, or bacon wrapped scallops ($9-10). You can warm up with French onion soup or Wailua clam chowder ($4-6) or try a salad like Casesar or tossed Kawailoa ($5-8). Entrees feature fresh fish as well as Scallops Po'ipu, lobster & shrimp curry, seafood pasta, prawns luau, abalone, paella, cioppino, and bouillabaisse ($22-45). Meat lovers aren't left out, several steaks are offered like filet mignon and New York steak alone or in seafood combinations ($25-36).

The keiki menu offers grilled fish, scampi, shrimp or scallops, New York steak, filet mignon, and burgers ($7-13). COMMENTS: The long-room dining area has beautiful wood floors and large open windows which allow the evening breezes to come in. They do offer quite an extensive seafood menu so chances are they will have something on the menu that you haven't ever tried before. They claim to have Kaua'i's largest seafood selection and that's pretty hard to dispute. They also have prices to match in most cases. You'll get a good seafood meal here with whatever you order from the menu. Reservations recommended.

ILIMA TERRACE   *Buffets/Brunch-Continental/International*
Hyatt Regency Kaua'i, Po'ipu (742-6260) HOURS: Breakfast 6-11 am (buffet till 10), Sunday Brunch 10:30 am-2 pm, Lunch 11 am-2:30 pm, Dinner 6-9 pm. SAMPLING: Assorted cereals, fruits, pancakes, Belgian waffles, banana French toast, smoked salmon plate, omelettes (4-13) and a daily breakfast buffet ($17) or Sunday Champagne Brunch ($30). Lunch starts with a sashimi sampler, smoked chicken quesadilla with sweet chile cream, buffalo wings, Thai summer rolls, or a variety of salads: cobb, pasta, fruit, Caesar, or sesame shrimp & seafood ($6-16). Burgers, pizza, pasta, or entree specialties like Korean chicken, seared ahi loin steak, prawn noodles, or red hot chicken spaghetti along with healthy offerings such as red lentil chili, grilled salmon salad, or whole wheat tortilla chicken sandwich ($6-17). Limited dinner menu with pizza, sandwiches and salads ($6-12) or a nightly theme buffet ($30) that includes salad bar, breads, fruits and cheeses, pastries, and varied buffet food depending on the night. Call to confirm the evening's selection of Italian Night, Hawaiian Seafood Night, Prime Rib Night or Surf & Turf Night as the buffet themes change nightly. COMMENTS: The Ilima Terrace features lush tropical gardens and lagoons filled with koi carp surrounding the open-air dining area. Warm air and sunshine make this a very relaxing dining spot and a great place to people watch while soaking up the ambiance of this fine resort. Reservations suggested.

KALAHEO STEAK HOUSE   *Steak/Seafood*
4444 Papalina Road, Kalaheo (332-9780) HOURS: Dinner nightly 6-10 pm. SAMPLING: Clams by the pound, artichokes, sauteed Parmesan mushrooms, shrimp cocktail , or teriyaki steak stix will start you off ($5-10). The dinner menu features choice midwestern steaks like top sirloin, New York cut, filet mignon and prime rib, plus pork terderloin, baby-back ribs, or chicken breast and Cornish game hen, in addition to seafood specials like Kalaheo shrimp, teriyaki shrimp, Alaska king crab legs, or fresh island fish ($15-25). There are also various combination platters($18-22). All meals come with all-you-can-eat salad, - fresh rolls plus baked potato or rice. For dessert, there's rum cake, ice cream or a daily special cheesecake ($2-4). COMMENTS: Nice wood decor with hanging plants. Located in a quiet, residential neighborhood. The portions are ample and a good value; their Portuguese soup with a house salad makes a satisfying light supper.

KEOKI'S PARADISE ★   *Steak & Seafood*
2360 Kiahuna Plantation Drive, Po'ipu Shopping Village, Po'ipu (742-7534) HOURS: Lunch daily 11am-2pm, dinner nightly 5:30-10 pm; cafe menu for lunch; also seafood and taco bar 11 am-11:30 pm. SAMPLING: Sashimi, fisherman's chowder, and Thai shrimp sticks with guava cocktail sauce to start

($4-9) and entrees of fresh fish (with several preparations), pesto shrimp macadamia, Pacific Rim rigatoni (with seafood), steaks, Koloa pork ribs, Balinese chicken (in garlic and lemon grass), and vegetarian lasagna ($12-21). Ice cream, triple chocolate cake, and "The Original Hula Pie" from Kimo's--and still the best!--($3-5). The Cafe menu has burgers and sandwiches (chicken, steak, roast beef, Reuben); fish tacos, nachos, chicken quesadillas, and a selection of pupus from the dinner menu as well as their superb calamari strips ($4-10); also Hawaiian plates--pork, fish, and chicken--($10). COMMENTS: This is one of the popular TS restaurant chain that also owns Duke's Canoe Club here on Kaua'i and in Waikiki as well as Kimos's and Hula Grill on Maui. The food is good and of a good value, but is not really "fine dining" style cuisine. Dinners come with salad, a basket of hot rolls, carrot muffins, and herbed rice. Appetizers are worth the extra few dollars, especially the calamari: the thick strips are about perfect in taste and texture. The atmosphere at Keoki's is creative with plenty of family appeal. The lagoons with koi, waterfalls, and plenty of lush greenery in this open air, multi-level restaurant create a setting reminiscent of Disney's Jungle Land (albeit without any mechanical elephants or alligators.) The kids will love eating in the tropics! Get there before 6 pm for early bird specials. Reservations are always a good idea even though they may not be quite as busy during low season.

NANIWA *Japanese*
2440 Ho'onani Road, Sheraton Kaua'i Resort, Po'ipu (742-1661) HOURS: Dinner 5:30-9:30 pm. Closed Monday & Friday. SAMPLING: Start with ahi carpaccio, sliced beef with citrus ponzu sauce, smoked salmon with fresh fruit/prosciutto ham with asparagus, chilled tofu, tempura, seafood lau lau, and a variety of sushi including Hawaiian roll poke style ($7-10). Assorted sashimi or sushi ($19-23). Glass noodle, seafood, or Manoa leaf & papaya salad ($7-9). Dinner entrees of beef striploin steak, broiled chicken, butter fish, assorted tempura or sushi, buckwheat noodles with tempura plus fresh fish or lobster & crab ($17-23). Complete dinners with salad, miso soup, rice and pickled vegetables ($23-30). East-West desserts range from ujikintoki (ice cream, shaved ice & red azuki beans) to cappuccino grasse (coffee gelatin with ice cream and Kahlua); mitsumame (fruit, gelatin, ice cream & azuki beans) to haupia with fresh fruit ($4-6). Beer, wine & sake. Saturday night Japanese buffet features sushi, sashimi, salads, entrees, cold seafood, tempura station, and desserts ($32). COMMENTS: Naniwa blends Hawaiian ambiance into a Japanese inn setting surrounding by koi ponds and lagoon gardens. The food reflects the same blend of Japanese with Hawaiian (and European) touches. Like the other restaurants at the resort, the ambiance is upscale, but not intimidating.

PLANTATION GARDENS RESTAURANT ★ *Pacific Mediterranean*
2253 Po'ipu Road, Kiahuna Plantation in Po'ipu (742-2216) HOURS: Dinner nightly 5:30-9:30 pm; pupus and drinks from 4:30 pm at the bar. The former Piatti has changed its name back to its original Plantation Gardens Restaurant. But that's about the only thing that's changed. The cuisine is still Pacific-inspired with Mediterranean accents. This lovely airy dining room is set in the historic 1930's-era Moir House, the old plantation home. The room has an elegant homey atmosphere with rich Brazilian cherrywood floors, koa wood trim, rattan seating and a large verandah for alfresco dining which overlooks the well-kept manicured botanical gardens. The dining room has earned numerous awards and wide acclaim

over the years including top honors in the Zagat Restaurant Survey including a much-deserved star-rating by this book. Pupus (appetizers) include daily plantation home made soup, fresh island ahi sashimi, Hawaiian baked oysters, Kekaha shrimp and fish won tons, Koloa asparagus and pancetta, wok seared scallops, pork ribs, crab stuffed shiitake mushrooms and a Pacific platter ($6-11). Salads range from plantation Caesar (optional fresh fish, lava spiced grilled or seasame seed crusted), to Big Island palm salad, tempura soft shell crab, grilled chicken, plus pears and caramelized onions($7-21). The younger set may enjoy fresh pizzas from the wood-burning ovens including sausage and peppers, Hawaiian imu chicken, veggie, and Puna goat cheese and pesto ($14-21). Entrees are as follows: fresh island fish of the day, veal and chanterelle stew, Hawaiian bouillabaisse, Parker Ranch black angus New York steak, macadamia nut lamb chops, seafood laulau, rotisserie chicken, center cut pork chop, grilled veggies and tofu; pasta and risotto choices include island-style paella risotto, fresh fish and green curry risotto, jumbo scallops, Kekaha prawns and black coral fettuccini and shrimp wasabi ravioli ($18-29). Scrumptous tropical desserts round out the menu. Attentive, courteous service; reservations suggested.

ROY'S PO'IPU BAR & GRILL ★ *Hawaiian Regional/Pacific Rim Cuisine*
2360 Kiahuna Plantation Drive, Po'ipu Shopping Village, Po'ipu (742-5000) HOURS: Dinner nightly 5:30-9:30 pm. SAMPLING: Dim sum and appetizers include potstickers, crispy coconut shrimp sticks, escargot cassoulet, and spring rolls with curry mango sauce ($6-9). Lemongrass grilled chicken, green apple & bleu cheese,and grilled portabella mushroom & roasted eggplant are a few of the salads ($5-7). Kiawe wood oven baked pizzas include Mongolian short rib, Cajun shrimp, eggplant & tomato, pesto summer squash and others($6-8). Roy's entrees feature Chinese duck with lilikoi mango sauce, parmesan crusted lamb shank, imu roasted pork pot roast, garlic mustard grilled short ribs, and lemongrass crusted shrimp with Thai peanut curry sauce ($17-20). There are also nightly specials in every category and may include appetizers like wine steamed clams, shrimp & fish cakes with spicy sesame chile butter sauce, or blackened tomato soup with avocado mousse ($5-9). Special entrees may include wood roasted rack of lamb with five spice Kona coffee sauce, sesame crusted ono with wakame miso shrimp sauce & soba noodles, and kiawe-grilled filet mignon with black bean chile sauce ($20-25). Their nightly "mixed plates" offer a chance to try two entrees as one ($26-30). Roy's signature dessert is the dark chocolate souffle, literally swimming in rich chocolate plus there's apple and macadamia nut strudel, blueberry cheesecake, lilikoi custard tart, key lime brulee, or chocolate mousse toffee bars ($6-7). COMMENTS: Roy's Po'ipu location is one of over a dozen restaurants owned by trendsetter and chef Roy Yamaguchi who first gained accolades and the attention of food critics as one of the founders of Hawaiian Regional Cuisine. - They have enclosed the kitchen behind huge glass windows: you can still enjoy watching the chefs as they prepare your meal, without having to be overwhelmed by the noise, which has been an undesirable element of dining at Roy's. A rust and green theme is carried throughout and when the weather allows, the side panels are opened up to make it a bit more open air. They have also added courtyard seating across the way with seating around the bar that alleviates some of the overcrowding and offers a small bistro feel in an engaging social atmosphere. No view in either section, the food being the main attraction. The "wild

mushroom spinach cream cheese raviolis" ($6) sound like a mouthful, but they are fresh and light -- satisfying without being too filling. By the time we ordered the lemongrass crusted hamachi with roasted banana curry & mango chutney ($24), they had to substitute opah for the hamachi, but we were impressed that they were able to replace one of the more unusual Hawaiian fish with yet another. With the lemongrass and curry to cut the banana and mango, the taste was subtle -- balanced and not too sweet. This was one of the daily specials which are all designed around the best and freshest ingredients each day. The lilikoi tart was tangy and fresh and the toffee bars (with chocolate mousse &, peanut butter toffee layered between a chocolate torte and glazed with ganache) were a delicious mix of flavors and textures. Past visits noted the tendency for the wait help to be a tad over-zealous, perhaps too friendly and attentive, in continuously checking and inquiring "...if everything is all right..." etc. It's hoped that the wait help have toned down their act a bit in order to allow diners to savor and enjoy the great food and experience that is usually associated with Roy's.

SHELLS *International*
Sheraton Kaua'i Resort, 2440 Ho'onani Road, Po'ipu (742-1661) HOURS: Breakfast 6:30-11 am; Sunday Brunch 10 am-2 pm; Dinner 5:30-9:30 pm. SAMPLING: Ala carte breakfast omelettes, egg dishes, corned beef hash, French toast, pancakes, Belgian waffles, fresh fruit, cereals, and "heart healthy" selections ($4-14); continental breakfast ($11); full buffet ($16). Dinners begin with appetizers like crab & prawn cake, ahi carpaccio, oysters Rockefeller, tropical fruit cocktail, shrimp with poha sauce, and gazpacho or Maui onion soup ($3-8). Salad bar ($10) or with ala carte entree ($5). Choice of complete dinners with salad, dessert, and beverage ($15-28) or a la carte ($24-33). Dinner entrees include choices like prime rib, grilled lamb chops, roasted pork loin (with hoison citrus sauce), filet mignon, macadamia-crusted chicken breast, or fresh fish plus pasta primavera, cannelloni, seafood fettucine, prawn scampi, or Oriental pasta with tofu. They also offer a Friday Night Seafood Buffet (5:30-9:30pm) with sushi, salads, and cold seafood plus hot fish and seafood entrees, a shrimp tempura station, beverages, and desserts including hot chocolate souffle with a variety of sauces and toppings ($35). Keiki menu ($3-8). COMMENTS: This is a luxury resort that really is suited for families: the restaurants are attractive, but not upscale and intimidating. The focal point of both Shells and The Point lounge is not the interior decoration, but the tall, glass windows that offer the ocean as a full-wall natural mural. You can dress up, but you can also bring the family!

TIDEPOOLS ★ *Seafood & Steak*
1571 Po'ipu Road, Hyatt Regency Kaua'i, Po'ipu (742-6260) HOURS: Dinner nightly 6-10 pm. SAMPLING: The menu changes frequently, but you might start with almond shrimp cakes, fried oysters, ahi sashimi, grilled sweet chile shrimp & ahi, "Kauaian" ribs, or mussels & clams ($7-10). Follow up with Kaua'i onion soup or clam chowder and Caesar (with crisp onions and Puna goat cheese); Kaua'i onion and tomato, fresh fruit, or green salad ($5-8). Then enjoy a wide selection of entrees: there's pan-fried somen noodles with grilled tofu & vegetables or a "cupboard" of potato, vegetable, and noodle dishes for the vegetarian ($18-20) and filet mignon, prime rib, pork chops, or roast chicken from the grill ($23-28). Specialties of the house include charred ahi sashimi, shrimp & crab

strudel, skewered shrimp scampi, seafood mixed grill, Tidepools' signature macadamia nut crusted ahi, ($25-29), and live Maine lobster (market price). Fresh Hawaiian fish is prepared several ways and a variety of meat & seafood combination plates are available. Desserts range from skillet baked apple pie to mud pie, ginger creme brulee, and white chocolate cheesecake ($5-7). COMMENTS: They offer contemporary Hawaiian cuisine featuring Kaua'i grown products like onions and sweet corn plus vegetables and herbs from an Omao farm, Chinese noodles from Kaua'i Noodle Factory, island-grown fruit, and Hawaiian fish. The choice of entree combinations is a great way to taste and sample - a diverse selection of menu items can really make dining an experience! (If they're available, try some of the more unusual fish offerings like hebi, ehu, or monchong.) Selected entrees are available for the kids in your family at half price, making this rather expensive dining choice a more affordable one. While the children in your traveling party will enjoy the Robinson Crusoe atmosphere, the adults will enjoy fine dining in a romantic setting. The restaurant is built like a series of open-air pili grass-thatched Polynesian hale over a tranquil lagoon - it definitely puts you in the mood for seafood! Reservations recommended; appropriate resort attire suggested.

NORTH SHORE

INEXPENSIVE

AMELIA'S   *Coffee/Espresso, Sandwiches & Snacks*
At Princeville Airport, 3541 Kuhio Hwy. (826-9561) HOURS: 12 noon-8 pm; Music and dancing till 2 am Fri-Sun. SAMPLING: Turkey, ham, tuna, BBQ beef, roast beef, or French dip sandwich ($6-7), hot dogs, chili, nachos ($4-5). COMMENTS: Like a neighborhood roadhouse with more character than most bars enhanced by interesting Amelia Earhart decor and great view. TV with satellite sports.

BUBBA'S   *Coffee/Espresso, Sandwiches and Snacks*
Hanalei Center on Kuhio Hwy. in Hanalei town (826-7839) HOURS: 10:30 am-6 pm, till 8 pm in the summer. SAMPLING: Everything here is burgers, mostly! Bubbas, double bubbas, hubba bubbas plus hot dogs, corn dogs and Budweiser beer chili. "Alternative" burgers include fish, chicken, tempeh, and Italian sausage ($2-6) or fresh fish sandwich with pineapple lemongrass salsa ($2-6). Side orders of Caesar salad, french fries, onion rings, frings (fries and rings), or chili fries ($2-4). COMMENTS: With a name like Bubba's, you were expecting maybe escargot? They're fun and funny and serve good, old-fashioned burgers to anyone named Bubba. (That means you!) Their ads state, tongue-in-cheek, "We cheat tourists, drunks, and attorneys." Perhaps not necessarily in that order however. They also call themselves "an old-fashioned burger joint." No argument on that point. It's a small building just off the street and in front of the Hanalei Center complex. They have a counter to place and pick up your order and a large wall menu. Seating is a couple of benchs and stools at the veranda counters. Good place to have a burger and people watch at the same time. They do have take-outs and T-Shirts. Buy a hat or shirt and if you wear it when you order your

burger, you'll get a free drink! Some folks rave about Bubba's, but others think the drive back to Anahola is worth it for a better burger at Duane's. <www.bubbaburger.com> Email: obubba@aloha.net>

DUANE'S ONO BURGERS ★ *Coffee/Espresso, Sandwiches & Snacks*
On the highway in Anahola (822-9181) HOURS: Monday-Saturday 10 am-6 pm, from 11 am on Sunday. SAMPLING: The teriyaki burger is the biggest seller here, but there are lots to choose from: BBQ, blue cheese, avocado, mushroom, and combos like "Duane's Special" with 1,000 island, grilled onions, pickles, sprouts, cheddar & Swiss, or the "Local Girl" comes with teriyaki, Swiss cheese, and pineapple ($4-6). There are other sandwiches, too, such as fish, chicken, patty melt, tuna, grilled cheese, and a new veggie burger ($3-7). Side orders of fries, onion rings, or salad ($2-3). They have keiki burgers and sandwiches, beverages, ice cream treats as well as some great shakes including marionberry, a yummy combination of boysenberry and blackberry ($3)). COMMENTS: The burgers are still piled high with lots of "stuff," like a Dagwood burger. Try the fries with the special seasoning they have on the counter - ono! The outdoor tables also have a great mountain view. These burgers are worth a stop especially if you are a burger fan. The teriyaki isn't strong and salty, just right! You'll know you are in Anahola when you see the line outside the little red building. After you've sampled one of these burgers, you'll come to understand the meaning of "ono."

HALE O'JAVA *Coffee/Espresso, Sandwiches and Snacks*
4280 Kuhio Hwy., Princeville Shopping Center, Princeville (826-7255) HOURS: Breakfast 6:30-10:30 am, Lunch 10:30 am-2:30 pm, pizza served from 11 am. SAMPLING: Breakfast options include Belgian waffles, French Toast (made from their homemade egg bread), cereals, and omelettes ($4-7); pastries and muffins from ($2 or less). Sandwiches (panini) on focaccia bread in combinations of roast beef, turkey, Black Forest ham, meatballs, artichoke hearts, tomatoes, roasted peppers and provolone, fontina or fresh mozzarella cheese ($5-7); salmon, capers, red onion, and cream cheese on light rye ($8). Also enjoy soup and/or salad bar ($3-4); various pizzas and toppings ($14-20). Gelato, cakes, pastries, and homemade fruit pies ($3-5). Smoothies and gelato milk shakes ($4-5) The usual hot coffee drinks (as well as Italian coffee) plus wine and beer. COMMENTS: Generally good food, but a bit expensive for what you get. Table service or you can order at the counter and serve yourself. The espresso is served in huge Italian style cups and it is perfectly wonderful sitting in the courtyard with a steaming mug and one of their tasty paninis. Panini is simply the Italian word for sandwich which explains why you'll see so many varieties: regular, fried, on focaccia bread all called "panini," like in France where croissant just means "toast." Live jazz every Wednesday (6:30-9 pm); flamenco guitar Tues. & Thurs. (4-6pm).

HANALEI JUICE COMPANY *Coffee/Espresso, Sandwiches and Snacks*
Kuhio Highway #56, east edge of Hanalei town, across Postcards Restaurant and Historic B&B and in front of Kayak Kaua'i. HOURS: Tues-Sun 7 am-7 pm (summer), from 9 am in the winter. SAMPLING: Fresh "squeezed" juices (carrot, apple, beet, celery, banana, guava, pineapple, lilikoi) and 100% fresh fruit smoothies and "frosties" ($3-4) Food offered summer only (June-Sept.).

Salads with seven different combinations of greens and all organic produce plus sandwiches of smoked turkey, provolone, or tuna made fresh to order on homemade bread ($3-5). Muffins, carrot cake, white chocolate macadamia cookies ($2 or less). COMMENTS: This is a nondescript walk-up juice and snack trailer wagon parked next to the highway.

HANALEI MIXED PLATE ★ *Hawaiian/Local Style*
On Kuhio Hwy. at Ching Young Village, Hanalei, PO Box 326, Hanalei, HI 96714, Email: kauaimp@aloha.net (826-7888) HOURS: Mon-Sat, 10:30 am-8:30 pm. Closed Sunday. SAMPLING: Standard mixed plate entree choices are Kalua pork & cabbage, shoyu ginger chicken, and vegetable stir fry or chow mein (all with white or brown rice) are just some of the mixed plates ($5 for one choice; $6 for two, $8 for three). Vegetarian Thai coconut curry, ahi ginger stir-fry, grilled Cajun ahi, or grilled sesame chicken, mahimahi enchilada, and roasted red bell pepper pesto and creamy garlic basil mahimahi are some of the specials ($7). Sauteed mahi mahi, Kalua pork, grilled ahi, and teri or shoyu chicken sandwiches ($7-11); Chicken or mahi mahi Caesar and garden salads ($4-10). Corn dog, chili dog, or hot dog; cheeseburger, tempeh, garden, or buffalo burger ($5-7). Baskets with fish, chicken, shrimp or spring rolls, with chips ($4-9, or any two combo for $11.) COMMENTS: Mostly take-out with a small patio area and open-air tables for eating here. This is one of a very few places left that has Bison-on-a-bun! It's a little coarser and meatier, but not at all tough or chewy. Mixed plates are a good value; the vegetables are fresh and colorful - it's hard to decide when they all look so appetizing! Fresh ahi and mahi mahi dishes and sandwiches are served all summer. Owners Rudy & Shanda Bosma also operate Two Frogs Hugging, an unusual import gift shop in Kapa'a which is where they got their new teak furniture when they remodeled this small, but pleasant outlet. Nothing fancy about this place and it's located right on the highway. Watch the cars and strollers pass by while you dine. They promote their shoyu ginger chicken by saying "...melts in your mouth!" and it practically does. It's that good! Great local-style food for reasonable prices. Definitely worth a stop. Parking in Ching Young Village shopping center parking lot next door.

HANALEI WAKE UP CAFE ★ *Hawaiian/Mexican*
Aku Road (826-5551) HOURS: Breakfast daily 6-11:30 am, Lunch Mon-Sat 11:30 am-2:30 pm. SAMPLING: For breakfast, there's homemade granola, pancakes, French toast, veggie tofu, a scrambled egg quesadilla, and build-your-own omelettes ($4-7). Or try the custard French toast made with Portuguese sweet bread and topped with pineapple, coconut, and whipped cream ($5). For lunch, there is veggie, tofu, chicken, or ahi stir fry ($6-8), or plate lunches with chile pepper ahi or chicken, hamburger steak, teri chicken, chicken cutlets, or charbroiled ahi ($6-8). Chinese chicken, Caesar and garden salads, or sandwich choices of BLT, ham & cheese, tuna melt, beef or veggie burgers, and ahi ($5-7). Mexican entrees offer taco or enchilada plates with choice of chicken or ahi ($7-8). COMMENTS: Small coffee shop-type restaurant, family-owned and operated. The custard French toast called "Over The Falls" is to die for, and while it appears to be a small portion, it is plenty filling, really more custard than toast. The breakfast quesadillas are good-sized portions that should appease those hearty morning appetites. The Mexican meals are flavorful, not too heavily spiced, and served in ample sized portions. The motif here is "surf" from the photos and trophies to the video playing on the television. The atmosphere is strictly casual and most folks that come in look like they just came from the beach, which is probably about right. This is Hanalei afterall and not downtown Honolulu.

KILAUEA FARMERS MARKET *Sandwiches & salads*
Next to Kong Lung Center in the Kilauea Theatre Building, Keneke Street, Kilauea (828-1512) HOURS: Lunch counter 10 am-3 pm; Store & take-out deli hours 8:30 am-8:30 pm SAMPLING: Sandwiches served on freshly-baked Kilauea Bakery bread: turkey, roast beef, ham & cheese, fresh fish, pastrami, peanut butter, chicken salad, or subs. Hummus, tabouli, pasta, pesto, 3-bean, tofu, and garden salads. Homemade soups with garlic toast (fish, minestrone, chicken noodle, and chowder with corn fresh off the cob). Daily specials might feature quiche, stir fry, chicken fajita, stuffed baked potato, or curry made with authentic Indian spices. Desserts include tofu pie, banana delight, mousse, mango cheesecake, organic fruit crisps (apple, apricot, nectarine peach), and a variety of dessert breads like banana, pumpkin, ginger-carrot, poppyseed, and coffee cake. Menu prices range from $3-7. COMMENTS: This small lunch counter and kitchen is located inside a gourmet grocery store which offers everything from organic coffees, Thai cooking ingredients, microbrew beers & organic wines, and local organic produce. Special orders daily for take-out.

MANGO MAMAS CAFE *American*
4460 Hoʻokui, just off Kuhio Hwy. #56 at Kilauea (828-1020) HOURS: 7:30 am-6 pm. SAMPLING: Fresh fruit and vegetable juices & smoothies (just juice & fruit -- no additives) in tropical combinations of mango, banana, pineapple, coconut, guava, and passion fruit. ($3-6). They also have sandwiches like avocado, hummus, rice or soy cheese, PB&J, ham, turkey, tuna, wraps, vegetarian tamales, veggie or tempeh burgers ($3-5) plus fresh fruit, salads, and soup. Sprouted wheat and spelt (wheatless) bagels with various toppings, organic granola, Suzi's pastries ($4 or less); for beverages, choose from flavored coffees, coffee drinks, tea and chai-extra spicy with ginger ($4 or less). COMMENTS: This former smoothie and juice stop is now a cafe. The friendly staff is young, and enthusiastic and if we had a category for "prettiest sandwich" this would be

it: Light green avocado, with orange carrot shreds, red tomato, and dark green lettuce piled up on "basic beige" bread in a bright yellow wrapper! Fresh, colorful, filling -- and delicious!

OLD HANALEI COFFEE COMPANY
Coffee/Espresso, Sandwiches and Snacks
5183 Kuhio Hwy. in the Hanalei Center, Hanalei (826-6717) HOURS: 7 am-6 pm (summers till 8). SAMPLING: In addition to flavored coffees, they offer espresso, lattes, cappuccinos, frosted or hot mochas, teas ($2-4) with free refills on most of the "basic" beverages), smoothies ($3-4) waffles ($5 and up) and bagels plus muffins, mac nut brownies, cookies, pies, and cakes, all baked fresh daily. Lemon bars and "aloha bars" (macadamia nut crust with chocolate chips and toasted coconut) are popular, quick snacks. COMMENTS: Waffles served 7:30-11:30 am. Start with a plain waffle and add toppings like papaya, banana, kiwi, mango, raspberries, blueberries, strawberries, coconut, mac nuts, chocolate chips, and whipped cream or try a Kaua'i waffle with papaya, banana, mac nuts, and whipped cream. The menu offerings are very limited, but what they have is good. Casual and pleasant atmosphere -- homey with curtains and a small selection of gifts. They also offer mail order coffees from their Island Java Roasting Co. (888-4 KAUAI 4).

POLYNESIAN HIDE-A-WAY & HAW'N BAR-B-Q CHICKEN *Hawaiian*
4404 Kuhio Hwy., Anahola (821-8033) HOURS: Sun-Mon 11 am-4 pm; Tues-Sat 10 am-5 pm. SAMPLING: Huli-Huli chicken, teri beef, Bar B-Q pork, fish, and grilled cheese sandwiches ($4-5), burgers ($5-7), and "island favorites" including pork or chicken lau lau, kalua pig, loco moco, smoked meat, and hamburger steak ($6-7). COMMENTS: Dine in or take-out at this roadside stand that now offers plate lunches and sandwiches along with fresh roasted macadamia nuts! They're flown in daily from the Big Island and roasted fresh on the premises. Priced per bag: $4 (1/4 lb.), $7 (1/2 lb.), $12 (1 lb.)

ROADRUNNER BAKERY & CAFE *Mexican*
2430 Oka Street, Kilauea (828-8226) HOURS: Breakfast 8-11 am, Lunch 11 am-5 pm, Dinner 5-8 pm. SAMPLING: Huevos Rancheros, omelettes, breakfast burra, pancake sandwich, French toast, special cheese hash browns (with onion & tomato or salsa & guacamole), chile relleno & eggs ($5-10); handmade bagels and breakfast pastries ($2-3) and espresso bar. Start lunch (or dinner) with taquitos, nachos, chicken flauta, ahi salad, or jicama, almond & chile salad ($7-10) followed by chicken, pork, beef, fish, veggie, or tofu tacos and burras; ($7-8). Black Dog burra with pork & grilled taro ($7). Fish, tempeh, or beef burgers are served on freshly-baked taro buns ($6-8). A variety of sopes, tostadas, fajitas, enchiladas, or combination plates are available for lunch or dinner($7-17). Enchiladas Mole Poblano (chicken, cheese, or eggplant made with traditional mole sauce or chile relleno & Hawaiian fish taco with pineapple salsa are among the entrees. Kids' menu available ($3-6). COMMENTS: This large high-ceiling room features Mexican courtyard decor along with hand-painted murals on the walls. Step around the corner to their adjoining bakery counter for taro, rye-molasses, and multi-grain bread as well as Danish, coffee cakes, and a variety of oversized cookies from coconut macaroon to chocolate-chile (spicy like choco-latey gingerbread -- wait for the kick!)

TROPICAL TACO ★ *Mexican*
5088 Kuhio Highway #56, Hanalei (827-TACO/827-8226) HOURS: Mon-Sat 11 am-8 pm, closed Sun. SAMPLING: Tacos, tostadas, and burritos made fresh daily. The menu is rather limted but they offer some great Mexican food. Choose from a tropical taco with beans, meat, lettuce, salsa, cheese and sour cream; the tropical fish taco is fresh fish deep fried in beer batter; the regular taco comes with the works; the tostada is a flat taco with the works; fat jack has cheese, meat, beans and is deep fried and topped with the works; the chili burrito has beans, meat and the works; the veggie burrito has everything but the meat; the fresh fish burrito has fish and the works; and the baby burrito has cheese and beans only ($4-8); ice cold lemonade to quench that thirst. COMMENTS: This popular North Shore eatery used to operate out of a dark green mobile taco van, which had been retired. Located in the new Halele'a Building at the east edge of Hanalei town right on the highway. Tables to eat here or take out.

VILLAGE SNACK & BAKE SHOP *Deli/Bakery/Coffee Shop*
Ching Young Village, Kuhio Highway in Hanalei (826-6841) HOURS: Breakfast 6-11 am, Lunch 11 am-4 pm (Sundays till 3 pm.) SAMPLING: Breakfast sandwiches, eggs, pancakes, rice, spam. loco moco ($3-6). Tuna melt, teri beef or chicken, BLT, sandwich; burgers, hot dogs ($2-5). Side orders ($1 and up); plate meals (fried or chile pepper chicken, hamburger steak, teri beef) or fish & chips ($5-7). Beach or picnic lunch to go includes sandwich, soda, fruit, or salad ($5-7). COMMENTS: The bakery offers coconut, macadamia or banana cream pies plus their signature lilikoi chiffon pie. Carrot cake, apple cobbler, brownies, cookies and other baked goodies.

ZABABAZ ONE WORLD CAFE *Vegetarian*
Ching Young Village, Kuhio Highway in Hanalei (826-1999) HOURS: 9 am-7 pm. SAMPLING: Organic vegetarian dishes like lasagna, enchiladas, quiche, veggie burgers, potato or green salad, hummus wrap, and several Thai items. Fresh bakery goodies include their popular brownies and oatmeal chocolate chip cookies. The cornbread and banana walnut bread are made with maple syrup instead of sugar. They also have Lappert's ice cream as well as smoothies, juices, and espresso drinks. Prices average $3-6. COMMENTS: Small style vegetarian cafe and juice bar located in the old (original) Ching Young Store. Limited seating at picnic tables with benches.

MODERATE

BAMBOO BAMBOO *Hawaiian Regional/Pacific Rim Cuisine*
Hanalei Center (826-1177) HOURS: Daily lunch at 11:30 am-3 pm and dinner 5:30-9:30 pm, reservations suggested. This is a reincarnation of the previous restaurant (Cafe Luna) at this location. The pleasant open-air dining room is located in one of Hanalei's busy shopping/dining complexes. The main room has a contempory feel and look with lots of warm woodwork accents and there is an adjoining patio or courtyard area for alfresco dining. However, this patio dining area also shares space with the outside dining area of the restaurant nextdoor (Neide's Salsa & Samba) so there can be some additional traffic and noise from

that side. But it can be a good vantage point for people watching. The menu is a somewhat eclectic collection of Italian dishes like pasta and pizza ($9-20) plus Hawaiian Regional and Pacific Rim entrees like fresh island fish, potato crusted mahi mahi, Bamboo salad with fresh ahi, Creole Haena, filet mignon and herb roasted chicken on garlic mashed potatoes ($17-24). Appetizers include crispy ahi spring rolls, veggie summer rolls, ahi sashimi, fresh clams, wonton and smoked salmon bruschette plus soup of the day and house salad ($5-10). The service was, on a recent visit, only marginally efficient and attentive. The night's special entree of chicken alfredo was ordered but when served it was the menu listed herb roasted chicken, which the diner ate simply because it was late and he was hungry. The dish was good but nothing exceptional.

(THE) BEACH   *Coffee/Espresso, Sandwiches and Snacks*
Princeville Resort (826-2763) HOURS: 11 am-5:30 pm. SAMPLING: Turkey club, NY steak, fresh fish, tuna in pita, wrapped Caesar chicken sandwich, or Black Angus burger ($13-15). Cobb, Caesar, grilled chicken (with avocado, papaya & fresh berries), or taco salad ($12-17). Spring rolls, buffalo wings, nachos, crabmeat quesadilla, or ahi trio plate ($10-17) COMMENTS: Wine & beer and a good selection of tropical drinks. Keiki menu ($4-8); desserts ($4-6).

HANALEI DOLPHIN ★ *Steak and Seafood*
Kuhio Highway, on the east edge of Hanalei town (826-6113) HOURS: Lunch 11 am-3:30 pm, Dinner 5:30-10 pm. Pupus served all day: 11 am-10 pm. SAMPLING: Lunch sandwiches such as teri chicken, chilled fish salad, fresh fish, calamari, or tempeh veggie burger on sesame seed roll or Dolphin squaw bread ($7-8). Dolphin salads include two kinds of lettuce, Chinese cabbage, bean sprouts and tomatoes and are topped with calamari, chicken, grilled fish, or fish salad ($6-9). Appetizers include ceviche, seafood chowder, artichoke, sashimi, artichoke, and stuffed mushrooms ($5-7 or market price). Seafood entrees of fresh island fish, calamari, scallops, shrimp, and Alaska king crab plus Haole or Hawaiian chicken, filet mignon steak, New York steak, and steak and seafood combinations ($12-28). Homemade dessert selections change daily, but they always have Dolphin ice cream pie ($5) with banana, mac nut & coconut ice cream in an Oreo cookie crust. COMMENTS: Quite a few of the entrees are under $20 and all come with salad, steak fries, penne pasta or rice, and hot homemade bread. They also offer menehune (kid) portions ($12-18) or light dinners: broccoli casserole, seafood chowder or salad & bread ($9-16). Pretty reliable seafood and good steaks, but nothing real exotic or Pacific Rim! They don't take reservations and unless you arrive early, you will probably have a wait. Put in your name and spend your time browsing through the adjoining gift and clothing stores. The food is hearty, some of the sauces are a bit on the heavy side, but the salads are a very pleasant surprise. Served family style in a bowl, the mixed greens are accompanied by homemade garlic croutons and an assortment of dressings you can add yourself. They have a fish market, too, open from 11 am-8 pm.

HANALEI GOURMET ★ *Continental/International*
5161 Kuhio Hwy. Old School Building at Hanalei Center, Hanalei (826-2524) HOURS: Breakfast 8-11 am; Lunch 10:30 am-4:30 pm, pupus & grilled sandwiches until 5:30, dinner 5:30-9:30. SAMPLING: Pupus include Asian crab cakes

as well as ahi nachos, crab-stuffed mushrooms, sauteed mussels, deep fried artichoke and artichoke toast -- broiled with their unusual and flavorful artichoke dip and lots of gooey cheese ($6-10); boiled shrimp ($9 for 1/4 lb., $24 for a full lb.) Salads include chicken in papaya or avocado boat, Hanalei Waldorf with mango vinaigrette, Oriental ahi pasta, Waioli salad veggies with Sonoma goat cheese vinaigrette, roasted garlic Caesar and good 'ole green salad ($6-9). Pastas include eggplant or seafood marinara, Greek, or gorgonzola chicken. Basic sandwiches like grilled chicken breast, charbroiled island fish, turkey, roast beef, corned beef, chicken salad, and tuna ($5-9) on fresh baked bread with "the works." More gourmet varieties ($7-8) include Oregon bay shrimp (open-faced with melted jack cheese and remoulade sauce), ahi with dill mayo, ginger chicken, and roasted eggplant & red pepper with provolone cheese, a sour cream-lime-cilantro sauce and sweet red onions. Gourmet burgers with gorgonzola or avocado with bacon ($7-9). Dinner entrees include specialty pastas like pasta du jour, Greek pasta with New Zealand mussels, shrimp scampi linguini, gorgonzola chicken and gourmet stir fry with veggies and udon noodles ($11-20). Other entrees include fresh island fish, sauteed scallops meuniere, pan fried crab cakes, mac nut fried chicken and charbroiled pork chops ($16-20 or market price). Breakfast offerings include Huevos Santa Cruz, muesli, bacon & egg sandwich ($5-8) or fruit, bagels, and pastries ($2 or less). COMMENTS: The roasted eggplant sandwich was excellent - fresh, innovative, and full of flavor -- and the gorgonzola chicken had a tasty grilled flavor that went well with the cheesy Alfredo sauce. The place is generally busy, from first thing in the morning with people at the bar by 9 am with others enjoying piping hot coffee and pastries at the lana'i tables. Specials are written on the blackboard left over from when it was a schoolroom. Thursday night is Fish Taco Night: tempura beer batter fish taco with lots of rice and black beans ($9.50). Early bird specials offer $2 off all major entree selections from 5:30-6:30 pm. "Big Tim" is still the personable and proud owner and they still have live entertainment nightly.

KILAUEA BAKERY & PAU HANA PIZZA ★ *Bakery/Pizzeria*
Kong Lung Center on Kilauea Road at Keneke Street on the way to the Lighthouse, Kilauea (828-2020) HOURS: Open daily, 6:30 am-9 pm, pizza served from 11 am to 9 pm. SAMPLING: Croissants, cinnamon buns, scones, and other freshly-baked pastries plus unusual breads like limu sourdough with sea algae, sun-dried tomato and fresh basil, poi bread, feta cheese and sweet red bell pepper, Hawaiian sourdough (fermented from a guava starter), and Na Pali brown bread made with fennel, caraway, orange rind, and cocoa. Pizzas are just as innovative with a lot of unusual toppings and combinations: the "Barbequed Chicken" has BBQ chicken, roasted onions and red peppers, mushroom, and mozzarella cheese, the "Classic Scampi" has tiger prawns, tomato, roasted garlic, capers, asiago and mozzarella cheeses, and the "Billie Holiday" has smoked ono, swiss chard, roasted onions, gorgonzola rosemary, sauce and mozzarella cheese ($11/17/24). Regular pizzas are priced by size and toppings ($7-28); or try their Abrezone, an open-faced vegetable calzone baked in French bread dough! They have a tasty selection of cream cheese spreads with everything from mango-pineapple to red pepper & garlic to tapenade or hummus to put on your bagel. They also have coffee drinks and espressos ($1-4). Pizza/salad lunch specials ($6). COMMENTS: Pastries and breads baked daily. Pizza crust is extra crispy and the staff are extra nice. Owners Tom and Katie Pickett started the bakery in

their home, expanded, then added pizza. If you don't have a big appetite or a family, you can order pizza by the slice. Or try their flavored breadsticks in chile pepper, garlic butter, or sesame & alae (red) salt: they make a great made-on Kaua'i gift to take home! Their signature bakery items include the sourdough and Na Pali brown breads and tropical fruit layer cakes with whipped cream icing. In addition to the bakery operation, they have a full service espresso bar with limited cafe seating inside and a courtyard with a few umbrella tables outdoors. This is a very popular stop for lunch, pizza or a quick snack.

LIGHTHOUSE BISTRO *Continental/International*
Kong Lung Center, Kilauea Road at Keneke Street on the way to the Lighthouse, Kilauea (828-0480) HOURS: Lunch 11 am-2 pm; Dinner 5:30-9:30 pm. SAMPLING: Soups, salads, hamburgers, sandwiches, and tacos for lunch. For dinner, there are appetizers, soups & salads, pastas, seafood and varied entrees. Lunch offerings include fish tacos, falafel taco, hummus wrap, chicken Caesar wrap and pasta marinara ($7-9); sandwiches include fresh fish burger, cheese burger, teri chicken, garden burger, Italian sausage and French dip ($7-9). For dinner, start with appetizers like tossed antipasto (served on wild greens), Jawaiian seared scallops, artichoke picatta, or chicken sateh with peanut sauce ($10-12). There are salads like Caesar (with fish or chicken), mesclun, or garden Romaine lettuce salad ($6-9). Soups include seafood bisque and soup of the day ($6). Feast on pastas like fettucini Alfredo, tri-colored tortellini (with sun-dried tomato pesto), or pasta marinara ($11-13). Varied entrees (served with soup or salad) include stuffed shrimp in phyllo, filet au poivre (in peppercorn brandy sauce), mango cherry chicken breast, seafood linguini, rib eye steak, chicken pesto, veal picatta, cannelloni quatro formaggio, or Cajun BBQ shrimp ($17-25). Seafood selections include fresh island fish offered in four styles: broiled (and served with tropical salsa), blackened, sauteed, or pan-seared with mango sesame sauce ($24 or market price). COMMENTS: The dining room is clean, bright and airy with an old plantation-style look and feel (this is the former Casa de Amici). They feature premium bar drinks and an extensive wine list, featuring a different selection each night. Live entertainment Thursday-Saturday.

NEIDE'S SALSA & SAMBA *Mexican/Brazilian*
5161 Kuhio Hwy., in the Hanalei Center, Hanalei (826-1851) HOURS: 11 am-9 pm. SAMPLING: Quesadillas, burritos, enchiladas, tostadas and chimichangas plus Huevos Rancheros, carne asada, steak ranchero, and fish tacos ($7-12). Brazilian dishes ($7-14) include vegetarian (pumpkin stuffing) or chicken *panqueca* (crepe), *muqueca* (fresh catch with coconut sauce, shrimp and cilantro), *ensopado* (baked chicken and vegetables, *bife acebolado* (steak and onions) or *bife a cavalo* (steak with an egg on top). COMMENTS: The courtyard dining area is shared with nextdoor Bamboo Bamboo Restaurant so it does get a bit busy with some people traffic and noise.

PARADISE BAR & GRILL *American*
4280 Kuhio Hwy., Princeville Shopping Center, Princeville (826-1775) HOURS: Lunch and dinner daily, 11 am-11 pm. SAMPLING: Start with peel & eat shrimp, spring rolls, teri chicken skewers, jalapeno poppers, potato skins, soup, or salad ($4-8). Fish or shrimp & chips, chicken strips, or crab cake "nuggets" plus steak, fish, teri chicken sandwiches, and burgers ($6-9).

Dinner entrees (served from 5 pm) include rice and baked potato and two steamed vegetables: Fresh fish, rib-eye steak, teri chicken, garlic shrimp, sauteed beef tips, crab legs, vegetable platter ($13-16) or combine any two ($18). COMMENTS: Beer & wine, fruit smoothies, and the basic tropicals plus a featured micro brew draft of the month. There's also a keiki menu ($3-4).

PIZZA HANALEI   *Pizza*
Ching Young Village, Kuhio Hwy., Hanalei (826-9494) HOURS: Daily 11 am-9 pm. SAMPLING: The name says it all. This place is all about pizza. Choose your toppings or combine them from pepperoni, homemade sausage, Canadian bacon, pineapple, bell pepper, meatless sausage, onion, mushroom, jalapeno, fresh garlic, zucchini, pesto, and more. Small ($10-14), medium ($13-15), or large ($20-28). They also feature special pizzas like veggie, Lizzy special, and BBQ chicken special. Slices (served all day - only cheese at night) or side of garlic bread ($3 or less). Spinach lasagna, pizzarito (pizza ingredients rolled up in a pizza shell like a burrito), Caesar or garden salad ($4-7). COMMENTS: Pizza Hanalei has been around for a long time and have sustained their popularity. Their pizzas are all hand made to order. Sauce is homemade as are the crusts: whole wheat with sesame seeds or white. Well, it sounds good doesn't it? It even looks good. However, we tried the pesto pizza and could have sworn there was fish on it. The sesame coated crust looked wonderful, but it was dry as a board. One bite was enough! Others report they have enjoyed the pizza here, but we'd suggest you hop in the car and head back to Kilauea for Pau Hana pizza.

PRINCEVILLE RESTAURANT & BAR ★ *American/Oriental*
3900 Kuhio Highway, just before Princeville at the Princeville Golf Club (826-5050). HOURS: Breakfast 8-11 am, Lunch 11 am-3 pm. SAMPLING: Breakfast sandwich, loco moco, omelettes, Belgian waffle, French toast, or banana pancakes topped with macadamia nuts or blueberries ($5-8). For lunch they have burgers, sandwiches (French dip, Reuben, teri chicken, or grilled ahi), local style plates, and variety of Chef's Specials ($5-10). Salads are excellent: The Oriental chicken is fresh and crisp, so big it covers the entire plate and the wasabi sesame dressing is fantastic! The seared ahi is served on fresh greens and goes great with their papaya seed dressing. All the portions are really big. They have also added a number of heart-healthy selections for spa-goers (yogurt, granola, veggie burgers) along with mineral & oxygen enhanced water! On Monday nights they offer a special menu of Japanese cuisine and sushi from 5:30-8:30 pm (Dinners $15-18). On "Pau Hana Fridays" there is a limited pupu and sushi menu with draft beers and karaoke from 6 pm. The Sunday Sports Brunch Buffet (9:30 am-2 pm) has eggs Benedict, breakfast meats, an omelette station, green salad, chicken and beef entrees, sushi, cheese blintzes, potatoes, rice, fruit, cereal, assorted Danish, and desserts with beverage/beer included ($19, children $9). COMMENTS: The restaurant is downstairs in a cool atrium with palm trees, ceiling fans, and garden furniture in pink and green, yet the elegant building looks like a mini version of the Princeville Resort with a gorgeous view of the golf course. It's like fun food in a fine atmosphere. So what's a casual restaurant doing in a marble and glass palace like this?

TAHITI NUI   *Continental/International*
Kuhio Hwy., Hanalei (826-6277) HOURS: Breakfast 7-11am, lunch 11 am-2 pm, dinner 5:30-10pm daily; luau on Wednesday at 6 pm (separate entrance and admission). This nondescript eatery is located in an older wood-frame building right alongside the Kuhio Highway #56 and close to the east edge of town. It still has the old-fashioned (50's style) Polynesian Bar with the South Seas style bamboo walls and ceiling fans and the lana'i out front facing the highway is still a great place to people watch, which seems to be a national pastime with North Shore locals! And while Tahiti Nui has been in place for over 35 years now, the menu has gone through various recent reincarnations, trying to find its place among the mix of restaurants now found in Hanalei. At present, the menu is a general combination of continental and mixed international cuisine. Appetizers include stuffed mushrooms, wonton and chicken wings. Dinner entree selections include New York steak, calamari Provencale, chicken teriyaki, pasta primavera, fresh island fish and varied daily specials ($15-20). For information on their luau, see section on Luaus at the end of this restaurant chapter.

WINDS OF BEAMREACH   *American*
5300 Ka Haku Road, Pali Ke Kua Resort, Princeville (826-6143) HOURS: Dinner nightly 5:30-9:30 pm. SAMPLING: Appetizers include sashimi, poke, steamed clams, gulf shrimp cocktail, and chicken teriyaki ($8 - market price). Entrees are served with soup or salad & fresh baked rolls: smoked Hawaiian pork tenderloin, macadamia nut or garlic herb chicken, pasta marinara, pineapple shrimp, beef or chicken stir-fry, fresh island fish, seafood medley, New York steak, filet mignon ($16-24). For dessert, there's Tahitian lime pie, macadamia nut custard pie, chocolate or rum caramel sundae, hula pie and lava flow ($3-7). Early bird specials (5:30-6:30) offer fresh fish kabob, chicken teriyaki, beef or chicken stir-fry, hamburger steak, or linguini Alfredo ($11 and up). COMMENTS: Fresh fish steamed Hawaiian style with fresh ginger, garlic & green onion is a specialty. The teriyaki steak is also popular. The desserts, salad dressings, and soups are all homemade in this family-owned and operated eatery. No ocean view here, but they do overlook the pool so at least there's water as well as a nice view of the mountains.

EXPENSIVE

BALI HAI RESTAURANT   ★ *Hawaiian Regional/Pacific Rim Cuisine*
Located at the Hanalei Bay Resort, 5380 Honoiki Road (826-6522) HOURS: Breakfast 7-11 am, Lunch 11:30 am-2 pm, Dinner 5:30-9:30 pm. SAMPLING: Unusual island-style items for breakfast like sliced bananas with coconut cream, macadamia nut waffles, or the Taro Patch Breakfast with two eggs, Portuguese sausage, poi pancakes, and taro hash browns ($4-13). Lunch offers Kaua'i onion soup, smoked tofu salad, quiche, island papillotte (fresh fish steamed in a banana leaf), chicken Hanalei (breaded with peanuts and panko), and a good selection of sandwiches: Reuben, seafood salad, turkey club, and burgers ($4-13). Save your decision-making energy for later and start your dinner with a pupu platter of pork ribs, chicken skewers & prawns katsu or shrimp cocktail, diced ahi "fiesta," blackened seared ahi, Bali Hai crab cakes or fresh island sashimi ($12-14). Follow with a Caesar or vegetable salad with chicken or shrimp ($7-11) or go

straight to one of the special fresh fish preparations: Bali Hai Sunset, pan seared over a crispy crab cake with sweet potatoes; Tropical Breeze, sauteed with papaya & pineapple salsa; Rock Jumping Fisherman, broiled with coconut milk, sweet chile & peanut sauce; Black Pot Pulehu, broiled and glazed with sweet lime oriental sauce; or Kaua'i Rich Forest, pan seared and served over veggie medley with shiitake mushroom sauce ($25). Other menu entrees include steak Olowalu, home-style lamb chops, breast of chicken linguini, pan seared shrimp & scallops, chicken stir fry or beef steak Makawao ($16-32). Children-sized portions on selected items. If you want to end with a dessert, banana lumpia, passion fruit mousse cake, coconut macadamia tartlett, fresh berries & Grand Marnier cheesecake, tropical fruits in a pastry shell, or creme brulee are the choices ($6-10). COMMENTS: Whatever you order, it comes with a stunning, panoramic view of the Bay and Hamolokama (Bali Hai) Mountain and waterfall. They now bake all their own breads and in addition to the above, the pastry chef offers a different dessert each night. Their special flambe desserts are also available for special occasions. Reservations suggested.

CAFE HANALEI ★ *Pacific Rim with Japanese specialties*
Princeville Resort (826-2760) HOURS: Breakfast 6:30-11 am, Lunch 11 am-2:30 pm, Dinner 5:30-9:30 pm; Breakfast Buffet to 10:30 am (9:30 Sundays), Sunday Brunch 10 am-2 pm. (Sushi bar menu: Tues-Wed & Sat-Sun, 5-9:30 pm) SAMPLING: Order an a la carte breakfast ($5-13) or sample their buffet featuring crepes, pastries, fruits, omelettes, pancakes, and breakfast meats ($20-.95). For lunch there are salads like stir fry chicken, cobb, soba & somen noodle, and fresh tropical fruit, burgers and sandwiches such as a club with avocado, grilled chicken on focaccia, fresh albacore, or vegetarian wrap ($12-17); Japanese entrees ($15-19). Dinner appetizers include Thai curry & coconut soup, crab cakes, spinach salad wrap, salmon tartar, ahi trio plate, coconut prawns, and California rolls ($6-16). Entrees feature seafood curry, steak & prawns, hoison barbecue lamb chops, Hawaiian bouillabaisse, grilled chicken breast, fresh fish or Japanese unaiu: fresh water eel with miso soup, pickled vegetable, and green salad. ($20-34). They also offer a set three-course dinner with your choice of appetizer, entree, dessert, and beverage ($45). For dessert try a duo of Kona coffee & ginger creme brulees, chocolate torte, Thai tapioca with jellied berries, or lilikoi cheesecake ($5-8). Sunday Brunch offers an elegant buffet for $31.95; $38.50 with champagne. There are salads, fresh seafood, sushi, pastas, hot entrees, carved roast beef, an omelette bar, fruit crepe bar, waffle bar, and plenty of desserts. Keiki menuavailable ($3-6). COMMENTS: Nestled deep down below the opulent lobby at the foot of two elegant staircases, this restaurant has the perfect view of Hanalei Bay with the perfect full-length picture windows to gaze and glory in it unencumbered. The Friday night Seafood Buffet (5:30-9:30 pm) is a pricey but worth the splurge ($45). An entire buffet of hot seafood dishes range from shrimp lasagna to crab & lobster sausage, seafood paella to bouilla-baisse, salmon en croute to escargot with curry butter. There are at least a dozen choices before moving to the cold seafood display filled with sushi, sashimi, fresh Dungeness crab, shrimp, and mussels and seafood salad selections from spicy calamari to bay shrimp with cilantro and avocado. Save room for the barbecue, where a chef will cook your fresh fish to order. We had a selection of fresh ono or salmon or a skewer of scallops and prawns. Did we mention the heavily laden dessert table?

CHUCK'S STEAK HOUSE ★ *Steak and Seafood*
4280 Kuhio Hwy., Princeville Shopping Center, Princeville (826-6211) HOURS: Lunch 11:30 am-2:30 pm Monday-Friday, Dinner nightly 6-10 pm. SAMPLING: Lunch offers a good selection of burgers and salads (including shrimp and/or crab Louie) plus several hot and cold sandwiches (turkey Swiss, teri beef or chicken, BBQ prime rib, tuna melt, or shrimp, crab & bacon;) plus fries, skins, or rings ($4-13). Start your dinner with mushrooms saute, steamed artichoke, or shrimp cocktail ($5-9). Dinners include salad bar, bread, and rice. Entrees include fresh island fish, shrimp Hanalei, Alaska king crab, and Hawaiian spiney lobster plus prime rib, top sirloin, New York cut or Kansas City cut Black Angus sirloin, barbequed pork ribs, New Zealand rack of lamb, and several steak and seafood combinations ($18-29); crab or lobster at market price. There's always mud pie for dessert ($4) or a choice of daily specials. COMMENTS: Even though it's called Chuck's Steak House, they also have a nice selection of seafood entrees too. They feature choice midwest corn-fed Black Angus beef and fresh Kaua'i caught seafod and Kaua'i grown produce. In addition, there is a children's & seniors' menu with slightly smaller portions of teri chicken, BBQ ribs, hamburger, or shrimp Hanalei including salad bar ($9-14). Casual, rustic look with a lot of woodwork trim. Live Hawaiian music on the weekends (Thursday-Saturday).

LA CASCATA ★ *Italian*
Princeville Resort, 5520 Ka Haku Road, Princeville (826-2761) HOURS: 6-10 pm. SAMPLING: Antipasto beginnings include kobocha squash soup with pistachios, beef carpaccio, crispy calamari, seared ahi Nicoise salad, potato-crusted crab cakes, arugula salad with pear, gorgonzola cheese & walnut vinaigrette, espresso-lacquered lamb chop, or tomato & eggplant Napoleon ($7-14). Seafood linguini, smoked chicken ravioli, rack of lamb, stuffed chicken breast, veal picatta, grilled ahi with mushroom risotto, swordfish with cous cous, and snapper with spinach gnocchi are the entrees prepared with an Italian accent ($23-33). The desserts are varied: mango cheesecake, cappuccino creme brulee, Tia Maria parfait, tiramisu, chocolate cake with lilikoi puree, or macadamia nut pie ($6-8). COMMENTS: Dinners begin with focaccia bread squares and olive oil or tomato and garlic tochu sauce to dip them in. A complete three course dinner is available with your choice of appetizer, main entree, dessert, and coffee beverage ($45). They have an extensive selection of wines, by the glass and by the bottle. Keiki menu available ($3-6). The food is good, but you'll pay the price -- slightly more forgivable with its extraordinary panoramic view of Hanalei Bay.

(THE) LIVING ROOM ★ *Afternoon Tea/Hors d'oeuvres/Desserts*
5520 Ka Haku Road, Princeville Resort, Princeville (826-2760) HOURS: Afternoon Tea 3-5 pm, Hors d'oeuvres 5-9:30 pm (Sushi bar Tues-Wed & Sat-Sun) Desserts 5-10:30 pm). SAMPLING: An exquisite Afternoon Tea offers tea sandwiches, scones with Devonshire cream and strawberry preserves, English tea bread, miniature pastries, fresh fruit tarts and, of course, a lovely, hot "cuppa" ($18). Prawn cocktail, California rolls, crab cakes, vegetable crudite, ahi trio plate, spring rolls, Caesar salad, cheese plate, or even a cheeseburger or grilled sirloin are offered as hors d'oeuvres or a light supper ($9-20). Maki and nigiri sushi ($4-10), sashimi ($9-13). Desserts are from the hotel's Hanalei Cafe: a duo

of Kona coffee & ginger creme brulees, chocolate torte, Thai tapioca with jellied berries, lilikoi cheesecake ($6-8). COMMENTS: Wine & beer, tropical cocktails, brandies & cognacs, and a selection of cigars are also available to enjoy with nightly entertainment from 7-11 pm. This is such a charming and elegant room where you can take delight in the view across Hanalei Bay to the mountains beyond from the comfortable, intimate groupings of couches and chairs. It does look and feel like a living room, but one belonging to someone a whole lot richer than anyone <u>we</u> know! Some folks do the afternoon tea just for the experience.

POSTCARDS ★ *Seafood/Gourmet Vegetarian*
5075A Kuhio Hwy., on the east edge of Hanalei (826-1191) HOURS: Breakfast 8-11 am (Sundays till noon or later); Dinner 6-9 pm. No lunch. SAMPLING: Design your own omelette; try the tofu scramble, breakfast burrito, homemade granola, or 7-grain hot cakes; or have a "Bowl of Potatoes" (red roasted with onions, garlic and cheese) or their signature 7-grain English muffin topped with tempeh strips, sauteed greens, and Hollandaise over red roasted potatoes ($5-10). Dinners begin with taro fritters, grilled prawns with teriyaki plum sauce, seared ahi, Thai summer rolls, or "rocket-shaped" salmon strips with sweet chili, ($9-11). Caesar (with eggless dressing) or Kaua'i-grown salads ($5-8) can be ordered with crostinis or prawns. Entrees feature Thai coconut curry, primavera Postcards, seafood Sorrento, and Taj Triangles -- peas, carrots & potatoes with Indian spices in phyllo pastry, ($15-22) and fresh island fish ($market price). Desserts include ginger-spice cheesecake, pineapple upsidedown cake, chocolate raspberry torte, lilikoi mousse, and mac nut pie ($6) as well as some delectable non-dairy offerings. COMMENTS: The taro fritters were delicious! Served with a mound of papaya salsa, they looked a bit like crab cakes, but with a dark brown crust dusted with cornmeal. The "Salmon Rockets" (strips rolled in layers of nori and lumpia) were cut to offer a nice chunk of texture, each a tasty flavor bite inside the crispy crust. The Taj Triangles were a perfect combination of textures and flavors: the flaky pastry with vegetable filling and exotic curry flavor was light

JANORA BAYOT

yet satisfying. (Think of a gourmet comfort food with the most basic of vegetables made exoticly Indian inside a trio of mini-Cornish pasties - and you'd still come up short!) The Hawaiian sea bass special was just that: a special artistic presentation of blackened fish served with papaya cream sauce, colorful tropical salsa (made with big chunks of papaya, tomatoes & pineapple), garlic string beans, and macadamia nut rice. The sea bass had a subtle blackened crust and the flavorful rice had bits of real nuts! Even the mashed potatoes were a cut above, flavored with garlic & herbs with chunks of potato and skin left in. The desserts were unbelievable - literally! Who could believe that the macadamia nut pie could be thick with nuts yet taste so light or that the vegan French chocolate silk pie had neither eggs nor milk? The restaurant was charming (it once housed the old Hanalei Museum); the food was innovative and expertly prepared.

SUSHI BLUES & GRILL *Hawaiian Regional/Pacific Rim Cuisine*
Ching Young Village, Kuhio Highway in Hanalei (826-9701) HOURS: Dinner 6-9:30 pm (Closed Monday) SAMPLING: Naturally, appetizers include sashimi ($ market price); sushi rolls ($8-13) such as tempura shrimp roll, asparagus roll and tuna, rainbow roll with assorted fish layers, veggie roll, caterpillar roll with avocado and eel, grasshopper roll with eel, shrimp and mac nuts and more. Appetizers (pupus) include crab cakes, shrimp & vegetable tempura, and garlic sake sauteed mushrooms, sesame shoyu poke, seared ahi Caesar, gingered crab tiki salad and others ($5-18). Oriental, Caesar, spicy tuna, salmon skin, and tempura shrimp salad ($5-12). Entrees come with miso soup, sauteed veggies, 3-piece California roll, wasabi mashed potatoes or rice. Entrees include fresh island fish in several styles, sizzling seafood stirfry, coconut shrimp with Thai chili plum sauce, kiwi teriyaki chicken, linguini & scallops, hibachi shrimp scampi, sweet & sour pork ribs, and rib eye steak with shiitake musroom au jus ($19-22, fish at market price). Fresh fish is served grilled with garlic sake cream, wok-charred with mango BBQ glaze, or sesame crusted with coconut passion fruit buerre blanc. Desserts include green tea or mango ice cream, chocolate mousse cake, or mud pie ($4-5). COMMENTS: This eatery is the latest of the popular sushi "plus" restaurants. You can have your sushi and eat dinner, too, or mix and match to have just one -- or the other! The sushi is innovative, tasty, and offered in beautifully artistic presentations with swirls of color and design in each sushi piece. The signature Crunchy Roll is made with tempura shrimp, chili sauce & tobiko eggs and rolled in tempura flake roll; the Grasshopper Roll has BBQ eel & mac nuts in a seaweed flake roll; the Sushi Cake is spicy shrimp wrapped in raw ahi, kind of a cross between sushi and sashimi. There's a full page of sakes (that's rice wine to the uninitiated, and samplers are available), several specialty martinis, international beers plus wines and tropicals. There is live music several nights a week ranging from blues to jazz to Hawaiian and swing band dance music. (Call for current days and times.) <www.sushiandblues.com>

ZELO'S BEACH HOUSE ★ *Continental/International*
5156 Kuhio Highway, Ching Young Village Shopping Center, Hanalei (826-9700)
HOURS: Lunch 11 am-3:30 pm, Dinner 5:30-10 pm, Happy Hour 3:30-5:30 pm
with limited lunch & pupu menu SAMPLING: Stuffed baked potato, lunch omelette, fish & chips, fish tacos, or all-you-can-eat spaghetti ($8-12); entree-sized
chicken or fish Caesar, Mediterranean, or Chinese chicken salad ($9-17). Philly
steak, turkey club, or French dip sandwiches; tuna, hummus, Cajun chicken, or
seafood quesadilla wraps ($7-10) plus an extensive variety of beef, chicken, or
fish burgers ($6-9). Dinner entrees feature crab stuffed fresh fish, Hawaiian
chicken, coconut shrimp, prime rib, slow-cooked baby back pork ribs, fresh
island fish, seafood fajitas, fish tacos, beer battered fish & chips, and mushroom-
smothered chicken ($14-30, fish is market price). There are a variety of pastas:
smoked salmon linguini, sun-dried tomato rigatoni, fettucini Alfredo (or with
Cajun chicken, fresh fish, or seafood artichoke picatta), cheese raviolis, chicken
pesto tortellini, linguini with clams and toasted pine nuts, or all-you-can-eat
spaghetti ($10-22). The fresh fish is prepared several ways: char broiled with
pineapple-papaya salsa, cajun pan blackened with garlic aioli sauce, sauteed in
lemon picatta sauce, or done with a Thai sateh peanut sauce over crisp rice
noodles. No room for dessert? Put the rest in a doggie bag and order carrot cake,
macadamia nut cream pie, chocolate suicide cake, or grasshopper pie ($4-5)
COMMENTS: Their logo is the Greek symbol for "exuberance" - and it shows!
The food was surprisingly good with unexpected touches like warm bread with
herb garlic butter, baked potato included with dinner, and more than ample
portions. There is veranda table seating outside or inside the open-beamed main
dining room which has a traditional South Seas-style decor and ambiance with a
typical bar and nautical theme decor. It's a funky beach house-style open-air
dining room right on Kuhio Highway in the heart of Hanalei town. Perhaps a bit
pricey but good food and fun. < www.zelosbeachhouse.com >

GINGER &
ANTHURIUMS

LUAUS

GAYLORD'S AT KILOHANA PLANTATION ("REFLECTIONS OF PARADISE") ★

2087 Kaumualii Highway, Kilohana Plantation, Lihu'e (808) 245-9593; Email: info@gaylordskauai.com; Web: <www.gaylordskauai.com> Luau guests gather outside on the Kilohana Estate grounds and pick up their mai tais as they enter the historic Carriage House for the luau dinner and show. After dinner, a cloud of mist draws your attention to the stage as your MC, Mikela, introduces the opening number: a medley of 1940s Hapa Haole songs accompanied by hula dancers in colorful cellophane skirts. A group of talented musicians guides you through a travelogue of Polynesian, Hawaiian, Tahitian, and Maori dances culminating in a Samoan Fire Knife Dance. The best and most unusual numbers in the show also centered around fire -- literally! In one intriguing bit of choreography, bowls of fire were featured as intimately as dancing partners. Then in the poi ball number (an already mesmerizing display of talent and skill), the excitement was enhanced with twirling poi balls on fire! The costumes were attractive and well-designed especially the skirts made from a provocative collection of leaves and bark with color and texture that certainly made for a unique fashion statement. The buffet consisted of kalua pig, mahi mahi, teriyaki beef, pineapple chicken, fried rice, imu baked sweet potato, fresh vegetables, poi rolls, sweet bread, and a variety of salads and fresh fruit. The macaroni-potato salad was actually quite good, with chunky bits of potato and a well-textured dressing and the strawberry papaya was particularly sweet and tasty. The fried rice was spicy and tasted like it might have had Portuguese sausage in it. The teri beef was good and tender, but the chicken was big pieces on the bone and was a bit messy to eat. The pig was good with poi in tiny little white cups and the taro rolls were a nice touch. Tropical fruit filled cakes, and a potentially interesting imu-baked rice pudding were the desserts. After the show, the dancers and Chief Manu, the fire dancer, greet the guests and pose for photos. The luau is offered Tuesdays and Thursdays at 6:30 pm. Rates: adults $50; senior discount for 55 and over, $45. Children 6-14 are $20; children 5 and under are free. They also do group and wedding luaus as well as special luaus with turkey for holidays.

HYATT REGENCY KAUA'I ("DRUMS OF PARADISE")

1571 Po'ipu Road, Po'ipu (808) 742-1234; <www.hyatt.com>
The luau program includes Hawaiian crafts and displays and a cocktail social along with the Hawaiian buffet and Polynesian show of music and dance. The buffet begins with fresh sliced tropical fruits; Garden Isle greens with cucumber, tomatoes and carrots topped with croutons and grated cheese with papaya seed dressing; lomi lomi salmon; spinach, pipikaula and macadamia nut salad; and poi. Entrees of hulu huli chicken; fresh island fish with macadamia nut butter; kalua pig, and teriyaki steaks are offered with stir fry vegetables; Hawaiian sweet potatoes; steamed island rice; rolls and butter. Pineapple cake, bread pudding, and haupia (coconut pudding) are the desserts. The luau is held outside in the Grand Gardens every Sunday and Thursday at 6 pm. Adults $60, Juniors (13-20 years) $40, Children (6-12 years) $30 and children under 5 are free.

KAUA'I COCONUT BEACH RESORT LUAU ★

Coconut Plantation, Kapa'a (808) 822-3455 extension 651. <www.kcb.com>
This luau has received the "Kahili" Award from the Hawai'i Visitors Bureau for
its "Keep it Hawai'i" program. It features the dances, legends, and lore of
Kaua'i, and includes a show of *kahiko* hula, the traditional ancient style of
Hawaiian dance. The show is choreographed by Kumu hula (master) Kawaikapuokalani Hewett. The dancers are beautifully dressed and make some very speedy
costume changes. They put the pig in the imu at 10:45 in the morning, so if it
works out with your schedule, stop by the Luau Halau Pavilion and see how it
is done. The luau begins at 6 pm with the blowing of the conch shell, torch-
lighting ceremony, and a shell lei greeting. Seating is family style, however, and
it does get a bit crowded around the tables. Haupia and fresh pineapple are on the
table when you arrive. The buffet is a pleasant mix with fried rice, mahi, kalua
pork, baked taro, teriyaki beef, and tropical chicken combined with fresh fruits
and assorted salads. The kalua pork was wonderful and the teriyaki beef was
surprisingly moist and flavorful. Dessert options were coconut cake, haupia, and
a pasty, flavorless rice pudding. Arrive early and wait in line for the better seats.
Open bar throughout the evening. They do have smoking and non-smoking
sections. Luau rates: $55 for adults, $50 seniors (55 years), $33 for teens 12 to
17 and $23 for children 3 to 11. Family Night (currently offered every Monday,
Tuesday, Friday, and Saturday) allows one child to be admitted free when
accompanied by an adult paying full price. Additional children charged at the
regular child rate. Luau held nightly; advance reservations required.

PRINCEVILLE RESORT BEACHSIDE LUAU
("PA'INA 'O HANALEI") ★

5520 Ka Haku Road, Princeville (808) 826-9644; <www.princeville.com>
Held poolside under a pavilion (and partial tent) with Hanalei Bay as the backdrop, this luau begins with the blowing of the conch shell and participation in a
traditional luau ceremony. The food is better than most with a buffet of kalua pig,
chicken lau lau, grilled marinated chicken with macadamia nut sauce (tender
strips of chicken breast in a tasty sauce), mahi mahi with lemon seaweed sauce,
soba noodles with vegetables, and ginger & lemongrass marinated beef. There
was also rice and Hawaiian (purple) sweet potatoes. Two excellent salads were
featured: cold roasted vegetables and a salmon combination that was part grilled
and part lomi lomi style - a delicious blend of textures, flavors - and colors!
Other Hawaiian-style salads included tako with kim chee, cucumber and seaweed,
bean sprout & watercress, as well as Garden Isle salad greens and fruits. The
dessert table featured pineapple upside down cake, haupia, imu-baked rice
pudding, large cookies, and slices of banana bread attractively dusted with
powdered sugar. Beer, wine, and mai tais. The entertainment features *Ho'ike
Nani 'O Ke Kai* (A Show of Splendor by the Sea) in a program that offers kahiko
hula along with a paniolo number, *The Hawaiian War Chant*, and ultimately, two
fire knife dancers, one of whom creates (with slight-of-hand dexterity) a sudden
"line of fire" at his feet - very impressive! The luau is priced at $60 for adults,
$30 for children 6 to 12, and a discounted rate of $48 for seniors (65 years).
Held Monday, Wednesday, & Thursday at 6 pm.

RADISSON KAUA'I BEACH RESORT
4331 Kaua'i Beach Drive, Lihu'e, HI 96766 (808) 245-1955 or (808) 246-0111
The Radisson hosts its "Old Style Island Luau" every Monday evening beginning at 5:30 pm. Guests are greeted with a shell lei upon entering the luau site next to the pool and receive a complimentary mai tai cocktail. Watch the torchlighting ceremony followed by the presentation of the traditional roast pig. Guests then indulge in an all-you-can-eat feast of traditional luau fare including roast pig, huli-huli chicken, beef stir fry, grilled mahimahi and a long list of salads, veggies, and exotic desserts. Then sit back, relax, and enjoy a full Polynesian Revue by Na Punua O Kaua'i featuring Keiki Hula (children), Tahitian and Hawaiian dance numbers plus a thrilling Samoan fire knife dance. Adults $55, seniors $52, children ages 6-13 are $28, age 5 and under are free. For show only, adults & seniors $25, children $15.

SMITH'S TROPICAL PARADISE ★
174 Wailua Rd., Kapa'a (808) 821-6895
Smith's luau grounds are located on their 30-acre botanical and cultural garden. The luau begins with a traditional imu ceremony at 6 pm, but the gates open an hour early for touring of the grounds, either on your own or with an optional guided tram tour. They have an open bar with live music which opens at 6:15 and closes at 7:30, serving beer, wine, and mai tais. Dinner is served at 6:30; an all-you-can-eat buffet of Garden Isle greens, poi, jello, three-bean, nimasu, and macaroni salads, Oriental fried rice, lomi salmon, fresh fruits, kalua pig, teriyaki beef, adobo chicken, sweet & sour mahi mahi, hot vegetables, snowflake and sweet potatoes, hot vegetables, and haupia, coconut cake, and rice pudding for dessert. At 8:00, Madame Pele introduces the luau show with a fiery welcome in the garden's covered lagoon amphitheater. The "Golden People of Hawaii" is an International Pageant depicting dances and songs from the South Pacific. Featured are Tahiti, China, Japan, the Philippines, New Zealand, and Samoa, in addition to Hawaii. The luau is held Monday, Wednesday, and Friday at a cost of $54 for adults, $29 for ages 3-12 years, and $20 for children 3-6 years. International Pageant luau show alone $16 Adult/$9 Child. Reservations required.

TAHITI NUI LUAU

Kuhio Hwy., Hanalei (808) 826-6277

This North Shore luau is offered twice a week on Wednesdays and Sundays at 6 pm. Held indoors in the back of the Tahiti Nui restaurant, it is a narrow room with long tables and a stage at the end. This is a family-style luau and there are always lots of kids. The food is authentic - no glitz or glamour - casually displayed in serving trays and Tupperware-like dishes; it's as if you went to someone's home for a luau dinner and the guests took turns getting up to perform. This is a small luau room (as luaus go) with the advantage that you have a good view of the stage from most any table and they are not so packed together that it is difficult to get in and out of your seat. (Important when you want to hit that buffet line!) A more intimate and local luau with a friendly atmosphere. They cook the pig in an imu out in back, not a very attractive pit, but then it *is* authentic imu cooking. The menu is an all-you-can-eat Tahitian and Hawaiian buffet with mai tais. Buffet items feature kalua pig, fresh fish, teriyaki chicken, Poisson Cru, chicken with coconut milk, fish or chicken lau lau, sweet potatoes, poi, lomi salmon, green salad, potato/macaroni salad, fresh fruit slices, garlic bread, haupia, and chocolate cake. Luau rates now include free mai tai cocktails: $54 adults; $32 teens (12-17), $22 children (3-11) with one child admitted free when accompanied by a full paying adult.

NIGHTLIFE

Bar and lounge hours and live entertainment and music offerings noted in the following section are subject to change at any time without notice.

Hap's Hideaway on Rice Street in Lihu'e is a sports bar.

The bar at Keoki's Paradise seems to be a popular hang out for locals and visitors. Live contemporary Hawaiian music Thursday-Saturday.

Jazz in the Happy Talk Lounge at Hanalei Bay Resort is a Sunday afternoon tradition from 3-7 pm; another tradition is the Aloha Friday "happy hour" from 4-6:30 pm with special pupus and drinks. Also live entertainment Mon-Sat from 6:30-9:30 pm.

Live Hawaiian music on the weekends (Thurs.-Sat.) at Chuck's Steak House.

Hanalei Gourmet has nightly entertainment - recommended by our readers for great musicians and singers.

Karaoke at Rob's Good Times Grill in Lihu'e; JR's in Hanama'ulu; and Jolly Roger in Kapa'a.

Stevenson's Library at the Hyatt is a quiet retreat with a large aquarium, chess tables, and bookcases. Read, browse, or just relax and soak up the atmosphere! The library is open from 6 pm to 1 am with jazz nightly from 8 to 11.

Live entertainment, electric and steel tip dart boards and other games at the Lizard Lounge and Deli at Waipouli Town Center.

Enjoy Hawaiian music and other nightly entertainment in the Living Room Lounge of the North Shore's Princeville Hotel.

Sushi Blues in Hanalei has entertainment several evenings a week usually jazz on Wednesday, blues on Friday & Saturday, and Hawaiian swing music on Sunday.

Live Hawaiian music at Joe's on the Green during their Thursday night dinners from 5:30-8:30.

Jazz at Hale O'Java, Wednesday nights 6:30-9 pm. (Flamenco guitar Tuesdays & Thursdays, 4-6 pm.)

Live music (8-11 pm) Friday & Saturday at Margaritas Mexican Restaurant & Watering Hole in Kapa'a.

Po'ipu Bay Bar & Grill is open Thursday-Saturday evenings with live music (and a pupu menu) from 8 pm.

Live entertainment Thursday-Saturday at the Lighthouse Bistro in Kilauea.

Duke's Canoe Club hosts Tropical Friday every week from 4-6 pm with live music and tropical drink & food specials. Live music in the bar Thursday-Sunday night from 9-11:30.

Amelia's at the Princeville Airport has TV with satellite sports plus music and dancing Friday-Sunday till 2 am

JJ's Broiler has live music Thursday-Sunday at their Anchor Cove location.

Lihu'e Cafe Lounge has dancing on Friday & Saturday, Karaoke on Tuesday & Thursday, and free pool on Monday & Wednesday.

Listen to guitar music on the weekends at Hanapepe Cafe & Espresso and the Royal Coconut Grove lounge at Kaua'i Coconut Beach Resort.

Whalers Brewpub offers a variety of live music: reggae, rock and more from both local and mainland bands.

NA NAI'A HULAHULA

The Dancing Dolphins

Ne'e papa like lākou,
me ta maita'i.
Nā Nai'a hulahula
i lila i Hā'ena

Nā pua 'o ta moana tai,
'oia nā ānela ki'ai,
Nā Nai'a hulahula
i lila i Kē'ē

Ha'aheo e Nāpali,
i ta holo titī,
Na Nai'a hulahula,
i lila i Hanakāpī'ai

He mele teīa nou
nā Nai'a hulahula,
Ha'aheo e Nāpali,
na pua 'o ta moana tai

Their graceful moves,
all in unison.
The dancing Dolphins,
there at Ha'ena

Flowers of the sea,
the guardian angels.
The dancing Dolphins,
there at Ke'e

Pride of Napali,
swiftly moving.
The dancing Dolphins,
there at Hanakapi'ai.
Tell the story,
the dancing Dolphins.
Pride of Napali,
flowers of the sea.

Used with the permission of Chucky Boy Chock

BEACHES

INTRODUCTION

Kaua'i, being the oldest of the major Hawaiian islands, has beaches that have been worn with time. Because of this, you will not find exotic dark sand beaches, but rather those of golden sand that has been gently polished over millions of years. If you are the active beach-goer who likes to snorkel or swim or the type that prefers to find a quiet shady beachfront spot, Kaua'i offers a diverse selection.

Not every beach on Kaua'i has a full description but this section focuses on those that are either the most popular or most beautiful or offered the best activities or a combination of these. Wherever possible, the true Hawaiian names for the beaches have been used, while including the local names as an aside. For more information on Kaua'i's beaches, the ultimate book is *Beaches of Kaua'i and Ni'ihau* by John R.K. Clark, published by University of Hawai'i Press. This reference will provide you with everything you want to know and perhaps a little bit more!

"It has been calculated that 44% of its coastline is fringed by fine white sand beaches, double the percentage of any other Hawaiian Island." (Excerpt from *Ten Years, 250 Islands* by Ron Hall.) With ratings of average, outstanding, and world class, Ron Hall has rated Kaua'i as world class in sandy beaches, coastal spectacle, and island scenery. Most are accessible by foot, three are accessible by water only, and six are by water or by trail. Fifteen of the beaches have public facilities. Kaua'i has more linear miles of sandy shore line than any of the other major islands, approximately 113 miles.

And interestingly, Po'ipu Beach on the South Shore was named as the #1 beach in the entire U.S. for 2001 by the "Dr. Beach National Beach Ratings," conducted by Dr. Stephen Leatherman of Florida International University. The annual beach survey rankings rate the nation's beaches on a variety of quality characteristics. Po'ipu Beach won this year's top recognition, the first ever for a Kaua'i beach.

Following is a two page map of Kaua'i which depicts the location of the most popular beaches around the island. For further directions, refer to the enlarged area maps located in the Where to Stay - What to See section of this guide.

As with all of the Hawaiian islands, the beaches of Kaua'i are publicly owned and most have right-of-way access; however, the access is sometimes tricky to find and parking may be a problem! Please note public access to some Kaua'i beaches is on or through private property and the state of Hawai'i exempts landowners from liability. In other words, you may use their land, but they are NOT responsible - YOU are! Parking areas are provided at most developed beaches, but they are often small. Some have lifeguards on duty.

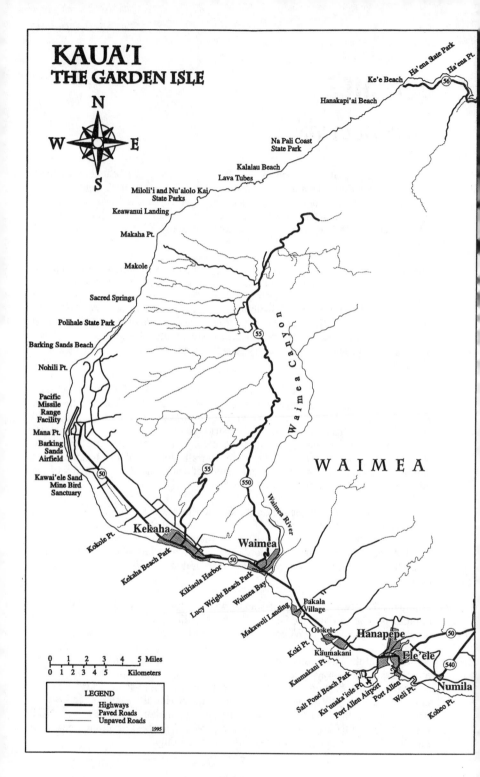

KAUA'I
THE GARDEN ISLE

N W E S

Ke'e Beach
Ha'ena State Park
Ha'ena Pt.
56

Hanakapi'ai Beach

Na Pali Coast
State Park

Kalalau Beach
Lava Tubes

Miloli'i and Nu'alolo Kai
State Parks

Keawanui Landing

Makaha Pt.

Makole

Sacred Springs

Polihale State Park

Barking Sands Beach

Nohili Pt.

Pacific
Missile
Range
Facility

Mana Pt.

Barking
Sands
Airfield

Kawai'ele Sand
Mine Bird
Sanctuary

55

55

550

Waimea Canyon

Waimea River

WAIMEA

50

Kekaha

Waimea

Kokole Pt.

Kekaha Beach Park

Kikiaola Harbor

Lucy Wright Beach Park

Waimea Bay

Makaweli Landing

Pakala
Village

Olokele

Koki Pt.

Kaumakani

Kaumakani Pt.

Salt Pond Beach Park

Ku'unaka'iole Pt.

Port Allen Airport

Port Allen

Weli Pt.

Hanapepe

Ele'ele

50

540

Numila

Koheo Pt.

```
0  1  2  3  4  5  Miles
0  1  2  3  4  5  Kilometers
```

LEGEND
— Highways
— Paved Roads
---- Unpaved Roads

1995

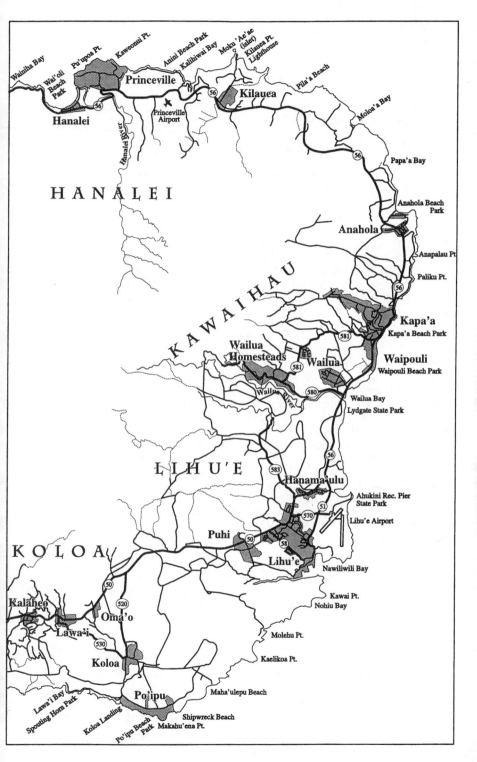

In any parking lot (but even to a greater degree in the undeveloped areas where you will have to wedge your vehicle along the roadside), it is vital that you leave nothing of importance in your car as the occurrence of theft, especially at some of the more remote locations, is high.

At the larger, developed beaches, a variety of facilities are provided. Many have convenient rinse-off showers, drinking water, restrooms, and picnic areas. A few have children's play or swim areas. The beaches near the major resorts often have rental equipment available for snorkeling, sailing, and boogie boarding, and some even rent underwater cameras. These beaches are generally clean and well maintained. (See CAMPING for information about beach facilities.)

Kaua'i's most gentle beaches in the winter are found on the Southern coastline. While the Princeville/Hanalei region receives the brunt of most of the tropical weather, storms can affect the condition of the beaches all around the island. Seasonally, there is also a great change in the island's beaches. While any beach you visit may be calm and idyllic in the summer, there may be high and treacherous surf during the winter months. Unlike Maui, whose southern and western beaches form part of a protected area sheltered by the islands of Kahoolawe and Lana'i, Kaua'i has beaches which are more exposed.

The North Shore of Kaua'i has higher surf during the months of October through May. On the east coast, high surf from the east and north is also more frequent during the same months. The south shore also receives high surf from the west and east and heavier rain during the winter months of October through May, and high surf from the south can occur April through September. High surf from the north and west will affect the west shore beaches October through May and the summer southern swell will affect the west side April through September. Even on a very calm day, there can be an unexpected wave surge. Lydgate and Salt Pond Beaches have two sea pools which are protected from the surf and ideal for young children. You'll find lifeguards on duty at Lydgate Park, Po'ipu Beach, Salt Pond, Ke'e, Kekaha, and Hanalei Pavilion. Other beaches may be manned with life guards during the busier summer months or on busy weekends. Seasonal conditions can also affect the beach itself. Sand is eroded away from some beaches during winter to be re-deposited during the spring and summer.

Here are some basic water safety tips and terms. Most of the north and west shore beaches of Kaua'i do not have the coral reefs or other barriers which are found on the south and eastern shores. These wide expansive beaches pose greater risks for swimmers with strong currents and dangerous shorebreaks. You may see swimmers or surfers at some of the beaches where we recommend that you enjoy the view and stay out of the water. Keep in mind that just because there is someone else in the water, it doesn't mean it is safe. Some of these surfers are experts in Hawaiian surf, and we advise that you do not take undue risks. Others might be visitors just like you, but not as well informed!

A *shorebreak* is the place where the waves break directly on the shore, or very near to it. Smaller shorebreaks may not be a problem, but waves that are more than a foot or two high may create hazardous conditions.

Most drownings on Kaua'i happen at the shorebreak. Conditions are generally worse in the winter months. Even venturing too close to a shorebreak could be hazardous, as standing on the beachfront you may encounter a stronger, higher wave that could catch you off guard and sweep you into the water.

A *rip current* can often be seen from the shore. They are fast moving river-like currents that sometimes can be seen carrying sand or sediment. A rip current can pull an unsuspecting swimmer quickly out to sea and swimming against a strong rip current may be impossible. Unfortunately, these currents are another leading cause of drownings in Kaua'i.

Undertows happen when a rip current runs into incoming surf. This accounts for the feeling that you are being pulled. They are more common on beaches which have steep slopes.

We don't want to be alarmists, but we'd prefer to report the beaches conservatively. Always, always use good judgment.

Kona winds generated by southern hemisphere storms cause southerly swells that affect Po'ipu and the southern coastline. This usually happens in the summer and will last for several days. This condition can cause unusually high summer surf.

Northerly swells caused by winter storms northeast of the island are not common, but can cause large surf, particularly on the northern beaches at 'Anini Beach Park, Kauapea Beach, Kaka'anui Beach, and the beaches at Princeville and Hanalei.

Based on drowning records from 1970 through 1988, according to *The Kaua'i Guide* to Beaches by Pat Durkin, the five most dangerous beaches, listed in order of drownings are Hanakapi'ai, Lumaha'i, Wailua, Hanalei, and Waipouli. Other beaches with high incidents of drownings are Polihale, 'Anini, Kalalau, and Kealia. Pat Durkin notes that "drowning statistics are also a reflection of a beach's popularity. For instance, if Wainiha and First Ditch [Kekaha] were as popular as Lumaha'i or Polihale, they would probably have higher drowning rates, as conditions are similar." *Kaua'i Guide to Beaches* is published by Magic Fishes Press, PO Box 3243, Lihu'e, HI 96766.)

Kaua'i's ocean playgrounds are among the most benign in the world. There are only a few ocean creatures that you should be aware of. We will attempt to include some basic first aid tips should you encounter one of these. Since some people might have a resulting allergic reaction, we suggest you contact a local physician or medical center should you have an unplanned encounter with one of them.

Portuguese Man-of-War is a sea animal seen only rarely but caution is in order. It's one of those ocean critters to be avoided. These very small creatures are related to the jellyfish and drift in the ocean via the currents and the wind. These unique sea creatures are sometimes blown to shorelines by unusual winds and can cover the beach with their glistening crystal orbs filled with deep blue filament. If they are on the beach, treat them as if they were still in the water and stay away. On rare occasions they will be seen drifting in the ocean during a snorkeling cruise or sea excursion and the cruise boat staff may change snorkeling destinations if this is the case. The animal has long stinging filaments which can cause painful stings. If you are stung you can use vinegar to help neutralize the venom. Diluted ammonia or baking soda is said to provide a similar effect, or try out the local remedy which is urine. You'll no doubt find lots of friends willing to oblige with that last remedy!

In the water, avoid touching sea urchins: the pricking of one of the spines can be painful. You will need to check carefully to be sure all of the spine has been removed.

Coral is made up of many tiny living organisms. Coral cuts require thorough disinfecting and can take a long time to heal.

Cone shells look harmless enough, they are conical and in colors of brown or black. The snails which inhabit these shells have a defense which they use to protect themselves and also to kill their prey. Their stinger does have venom and it is suggested that you just enjoy looking at them. Cleaning the wound and soaking it in hot water for 30-90 minutes will provide relief.

Eels live among the coral and are generally not aggressive. You may have heard of divers who have "trained" an eel to come out, greet them and then take some food from their hands. We don't recommend you try to make an eel your pal. While usually non aggressive, their jaws are extremely powerful and their teeth are sharp. And as divers know, sea animals could mistake any approach or movement as an aggressive or provoking act. Just keep a comfortable distance, for you and the eel. Also, should you poke around with your hands in the coral, they might inadvertently think your finger is some food. This is one of the many reasons you should not handle the coral. Eels are generally not out of their home during the day, but a close examination of the coral might reveal a head of one of these fellows sticking out and watching you! At night, during low tide, at beaches with a protective reef, you might try taking a flashlight and scanning the water. A chance look at one of these enormous creatures out searching for its dinner is most impressive.

Sharks? Yes, there are many varied types of sharks. However, there are more shark attacks off the Oregon coastline than in Hawai'i. In the many years of snorkeling and diving, we have only seen one small reef shark, and it was happy to get out of our way. If you should see one, don't move quickly, but rather swim slowly away while you keep an eye on it! If there is any area of murky water, such as the mouth of any river, you should avoid swimming in that area. For a good resource see *Hawai'i Guide to Sharks and Rays*, by Jennifer Crites and Gerald Crow.

Always exercise good judgment and reasonable caution when at the beach. Unfortunately, it is a too common occurrence when a person stretches their limits, or forgets their common sense that the Kaua'i papers must report yet another drowning victim. Even a calm sea might have strong currents.

Here are some additional *beach safety tips*:

1. "Never turn your back to the sea" is an old Hawaiian saying. Don't be caught off guard, waves come in sets with spells of calm in between.

2. Use the buddy system, never swim or snorkel alone.

3. If you are unsure of your abilities, use floatation devices attached to your body, such as a life vest or inflatable vest. Never rely on an air mattress or similar device from which you may become separated.

4. Study the ocean before you enter; look for rocks, shorebreak, and rip current.

5. Duck or dive beneath breaking waves before they reach you.

6. Never swim against a strong current, swim across it.

7. Know your limits.

8. Small children should be allowed to play near or in the surf ONLY with close supervision and should wear flotation devices. And even then, only under extremely calm conditions. The protected pools at Lydgate and Salt Pond are safer alternatives.

9. When exploring tidal pools or reefs, always wear protective footwear and keep an eye on the ocean. Also, protect your hands.

10. When swimming around coral, be careful where you put your hands and feet. Urchin stings can be painful and coral cuts can be dangerous and you can also damage or injure the coral. Yes! Coral is living!!

11. Respect the yellow and red flag warnings when placed on the developed beaches. They are there to advise you of unsafe conditions.

12. Avoid swimming in the mouth of rivers or streams or in other areas of murky water.

NOTE!: Paradise Publications and the author of this guide have endeavored to provide current and accurate information on Kaua'i's beautiful beaches. However, remember that nature is unpredictable and weather, beach, and current conditions can change. Enjoy your day at the beach, but utilize good judgment. Paradise Publications and the author cannot be held responsible for accidents or injuries incurred.

Surface water temperature varies little with a mean temperature of 73.0 degrees Fahrenheit in January and 80.2 degrees in August. Minimum and maximum range from 68 to 84 degrees. This is an almost ideal temperature (refreshing, but not cold) for swimming and you will find most resort pools cooler than the ocean.

BEST BETS

The following is are some of Kaua'i's best beaches. But beach-goers should keep in mind that daily and seasonal climate, weather and ocean conditions affect the quality of the beach conditions and the water. Also, it may be useful to keep in mind that in general, the South Shore has better beach conditions in the winter and the North Shore has better conditions in the summer. That said, here are some of Kaua'i's best beaches:

BEST SNORKELING:
Beginners -
SOUTH SHORE: Po'ipu Beach
NORTH SHORE: 'Anini during calm surf
Intermediate/advanced - Makua Beach (Tunnels)

BEST WINDSURFING:
Beginners - 'Anini
Intermediate - Makua Beach (Tunnels) or Maha'ulepu

BEST FOR CHILDREN:
Lydgate Beach Park and Salt Ponds

BEST FOR SWIMMING:
Po'ipu and Salt Ponds

BEST FOR SUNSETS:
Ke'e Beach, Pakala Beach

BEST FOR SUNRISES:
Lydgate or Maha'ulepu

BEST FOR TIDEPOOLS:
Kealia Beach

BEST FOR BEACHCOMBING:
Wainiha, Nukole, Ka'aka'aniu, Waialkalua Iki, Kauapea, 'Anini, Kealia

The following beach index refers to a variety of beaches and beach parks. Some of them are not true beaches. For example, Spouting Horn is a beautiful beach location, but only for viewing and not for any aquatic activities. Be sure to read all the descriptions of the beaches, even those with which have no recreational activities, yet are accessible and beautiful Kaua'i destinations.

The stars ★ indicate beaches which are recommended for family activities. They are more protected and some have lifeguards on duty.

BEACH INDEX

'ALIOMANU BEACH 364
ANAHOLA BEACH 364
'ANINI BEACH PARK ★ 366
BARKING SANDS BEACH 353
BEACH HOUSE PARK 356
BLACK POT BEACH 368
BRENNECKE BEACH 358
DONKEY BEACH 363
HA'ENA BEACH PARK 371
HA'ENA STATE PARK 372
HANAKAPI'AI BEACH 373
HANALEI BAY 367
HANALEI PAVILION BEACH PARK 368
HANAMA'ULU BEACH 361
HANAPEPE BEACH PARK 356
HONOPU BEACH 374
KA'AKA'ANIU BEACH 364
KALALAU BEACH 374
KALAPAKI BEACH 360
KALIHIWAI BEACH 366
KAPA'A BEACH PARK 362
KAUAPEA BEACH (Secret Beach) 365
KAWEONUI BEACH 367
KEALIA BEACH 363
KE'E BEACH 372
KEKAHA BEACH PARK 354
KENOMENE BEACH 367
KEONELOA BEACH (Shipwreck Beach) 359
KEPUHI BEACH 370
KILAUEA POINT NATIONAL
    WILDLIFE REFUGE 365
KOLOA LANDING 357
LARSEN'S BEACH
    (See Ka'aka'aniu)
LUCY WRIGHT
    BEACH PARK 345
LUMAHA'I BEACH 368
LYDGATE BEACH ★ 361
MAHA'ULEPU BEACH 359
MAKUA BEACH (Tunnels) 370
MOLA'A BAY 364
NAPALI COAST STATE PARK 372
NININI BEACH 360

NUALOLO KAI BEACH 374
NUKOLE BEACH 361
NUKOLII
   (See Nukole)
PAKALA BEACH 355
PO'IPU BEACH ★ 357
PO'IPU BEACH PARK 357
POLIHALE BEACH 353
PORT ALLEN 356
PRINCE KUHIO PARK 357
PRINCEVILLE 367
PU'U POA BEACH
   (Hideaways). 367
RUSSIAN FORT ELIZABETH HISTORIAL PARK 355
SALT POND BEACH ★ 355
SHIPWRECK BEACH
   (See Keoneula)
SPOUTING HORN 356
WAIALKALUA IKI BEACH 364
WAIKOKO 368
WAILUA BEACH 362
WAINIHA BEACH PARK 370
WAI'OHAI BEACH 358
WAIPOULI BEACH 362

WESTERN SHORE

Waimea, Kekaha, and Polihale

POLIHALE BEACH / BARKING SANDS BEACH

The Polihale State Park extends for five miles along the eastern shore and encompasses 140 acres. Large dunes are formed along the back of the beach that can reach up to 100 feet high. You'll know you have arrived at Barking Sands when you see the military installation. The Pacific Missile Range is operated by the Navy, but there are no state signs posted.

The Polihale State Park marks the southern end of the Napali. Dangerous surf conditions preclude swimming, etc. And be sure to bring shade with you, because you won't find much here!

More than 100 years ago, the sand from this area was studied at the California Academy of Sciences and it was discovered that it had small holes or "blind cavities." The resulting vibration of these unusual sand grains causes a sound that is said to be that of barking or singing when rubbed between the hands. Hence the name for this beach area.

Does the sand really bark? Well, you'll have to try it yourself and see. Some seem to think so. Others are unconvinced. A similar anomaly occurs on one beach on O'ahu and another on Ni'ihau. A few other places in the world have sand with this remarkable skill. After you've tried making the sand bark, you might try searching the shoreline for the extremely small shells used in making the necklaces of Ni'ihau. The same currents that bring them ashore on Ni'ihau, also bring some to this stretch of coastline.

In the middle of the beach park, about 3.5 miles along the cane road, is an area cleared of coral. Named the Queen's Pond or the Queen's Bath it is reportedly named for Leilani, the queen of Kaua'i who bathed here. The legend has it that when a chief from O'ahu asked for her hand, a battle ensued between the O'ahu chief and the chief of Kaua'i. After the battle, Leilani was so distraught that she poisoned herself and turned into a seabird. They say you can still hear the groans of pain from this battle in the sand.

While you may see locals driving along the beach, this is not advisable. Not only will the rental car companies not be pleased should you become stuck, but there is also a plant unique to this area that is threatened by beach driving. The Ohai is an endangered beach plant found only in Hawai'i. On Kaua'i, the only place these 30 foot shrubs grow is at Polihale and officials fear that the damage caused by beach traffic is further endangering the survival of this species.

The *Polihale Heiau* is a four terraced temple found on the slopes above the beach, almost indistinguishable after the centuries of erosion. This *heiau* was sacred to Miru, the God of Po. It was said that the oceans below Polihale was the land of the dead. You can see the sculptured cliffs at the end of the beach.

In the early days, the Hawaiians living on this side of the island constructed small houses made of grass. There was one large living room and two doors on opposite sides. Eric Knudsen, an early pioneer on Kaua'i, recalled that his father was curious as to why all the houses were built with their gable-ends east and west and doors facing toward the mountains and towards the sea. The obvious reason might be for tradewinds to create cool breezes through the home, or perhaps for those wonderful ocean and mountain visits. However, when he questioned a fellow he was told, "Why, you know that Po, the abode of the dead, lies under the ocean just outside Polihale, where the cliffs and the ocean meet and the spirits of the dead must go there. As the spirits wander along on their way to Po, they will go around the gable-end of a house but if the house stood facing the other way, the spirits would walk straight through and it would be very disagreeable to have a spirit walk past you as you were eating your meal. In fact we can always tell when a battle has been fought by the number of spirits passing at the same time." And be sure to bring some shade with you, because you won't find much here!

Recommended for: An opportunity to experience the vast barking sands, picnics, a glimpse at the south end of the Napali, and a nice long drive!
Facilities: Picnic pavilions, showers, restrooms
Access: The access road is a miserable 5-mile long badly rutted and pot-holed old cane haul road, now more of an offroad 4WD vehicle trail. Your rental car agency frowns on taking cars on the road and your rental agreement probably stipulates that it is a violation. So, you're on your own if you choose to go there! Follow the Kaumuali'i Highway at Mana to the end and then follow signs along the cane roads approximately five miles. There are no state signs posted, but some smaller, difficult to read signs might be noted along the way. It's a well-rutted, well-used road as you'll see.
Camping: Camping is allowed, but permits from the state are required.

KEKAHA BEACH
This is a 15 mile stretch of coastline reaching from Kekaha to Polihale located on the western end of the town of Kekaha and along the Kaumuali'i Highway. Along the roadside the beachpark is attractive and includes facilities nearby. Several decades ago, this shoreline had severe erosion problems. In 1980 a seawall was constructed along the roadway. Strong rip currents are generated here during high surf that is particularly dangerous during winter and spring months. Surfers occasionally enjoy the surf at a couple of locations along this beachfront. If the wind is blowing up at Polihale, chances are you might find you can enjoy your picnic lunch with less sand in your sandwich here at Kekaha. Shorebreak and rip currents all year make this a dangerous beach for water activities. However, it is an excellent beach for sunsets or a picnic lunch.

Recommended for: Picnics, beach play, and sunsets
Facilities: Picnic pavilions, showers, restrooms
Access: Follow the Kaumuali'i Highway past Kekaha
Camping: No camping

LUCY WRIGHT BEACH PARK
Lucy Kapahu Aukai Wright was born August 20, 1873 in Anahola. She was a well-loved school teacher in Waimea for thirty five years until her death in 1931. This beach is dedicated to her memory. An earlier very notable visitor arrived at this beach site. Captain James Cook landed here on his arrival to the Sandwich Islands in January 1778. Because of the location of this beach on the west side near the mouth of the Waimea River, the beach collects assorted debris and the water is murky. It is not popular for sunbathers or swimmers, but you might see surfers offshore.

Facilities: Restrooms, showers, parking area, picnic tables at Waimea Pier
Access: On the Waimea side of the bridge over Waimea River, turn mauka on Lawa'i Rd. off Kaumuali'i Hwy. and follow to the park
Camping: By county permit on grassy area

RUSSIAN FORT ELIZABETH HISTORICAL PARK
On the east bank of the Waimea River is another of the Russian Forts built by Georg Anton Scheffer during the years of Russian trading on Kaua'i. Georg had his sights set on conquering the islands of Hawai'i in the name of Russia, but when the Kamehameha learned of this he was quickly expelled in 1817. This 17 acre site is now the Russian Fort Elizabeth State Historical Park.
Facilities: Restrooms and a pavilion with historical information

PAKALA BEACH
Great offshore waves make this a popular summer surfing spot. You might enjoy watching the surfers demonstrate their skills. A wonderful location to enjoy a Hawaiian sunset.

SALT POND BEACH PARK
The natural flats along this beach have been used by Hawaiians for generations. Today, this site continues to be used for traditional salt making. In late spring the wells or puna are cleaned and the salt making process runs through the summer months. Mother Nature has been kind enough to create a ridge of rock between the two rocky points at Salt Pond Beach, resulting in a large lagoon area that is fairly well protected, except during times of high surf. Popular for surfing and windsurfing as well. And, because of its protected swimming area, this is an ideal spot for families and children. A lifeguard is generally on duty.

Recommended for: Swimming and snorkeling most of the year, except during high surf. Popular for surfing and windsurfing as well
Access: From the Hwy. turn onto Lele Road, past the cemetery, turn right onto Lokokai St. From the Hwy. Lele Rd is marked Hwy. 543. You can also follow the signs to the animal shelter, which will get you almost to the beach.
Facilities: Picnic areas, BBQs, restrooms, rinse off showers, lifeguard
Parking: Paved parking area
Camping: With county permit

HANAPEPE BEACH PARK
The Hanapepe Beach Park has a picnic area, restrooms, showers, and parking, but is not recommended for beach activities.

PORT ALLEN
Port Allen has restroom facilities and boat launching. Hanapepe Bay is the second largest port on Kaua'i. Port Allen has little to offer in the way of a beach or beach activities. However you might enjoy stopping in at the Red Dirt Shirt Factory near the harbor. Also in the harbor are Target Drones warning that all stay away. (These are boats used for bombing practice!)

Access: In Ele'ele turn mauka off Kaumuali'i Hwy on Waialo Rd., follow it to the parking area at the boat launch

SOUTHERN SHORE

Po'ipu, Koloa, Lawa'i and Kalaheo

SPOUTING HORN
There are a number of places around the Hawaiian islands that have the perfect conditions to form a blow hole. The best displays at Spouting Horn are during high surf when the water and air rushing together make a fine display. The geyser can reach heights of 60 feet. As you'll note by the many cars, tour buses, and vendors booths, this is a popular visitor destination. There is no access to the ocean. "Do Not Enter" signs post the danger of being on the rocks should you attempt to descend down. The obvious danger is that you could be hit by a wave and pulled down. There is a legend about a sea monster which once lived in the area. Listening to the groaning sounds made by the water as it courses underneath the rocky ledge, you can imagine that there truly must be a dragon or other mythical creature sighing and moaning. The sound effect happens even without the hole blowing. Many years ago it was noted that the salt spray was damaging to the crops. So during one night, according to the story, an unscrupulous fellow was sent to blow up the hole, widening it so that the force of the spray would be lessened.

Recommended for: Enjoying one of nature's wonders, a blow hole!
Facilities: Restrooms, vendors selling their wares
Access: Enter from Hwy 520, the road forks into Po'ipu Road on one side, Lawa'i Road on the other. From Lawa'i Road (also known as Spouting Horn Road) it is two miles and located along the roadside
Parking: Large paved parking area

BEACH HOUSE PARK
Located along side the road, this narrow beach is primarily usable only during low tide. Swimming and snorkeling can be good during low surf. The reef makes good snorkeling even for the beginner. This is a very, very small beachfront located right off the road, tucked between hotels and the restaurant with plenty of traffic going past. Not a very scenic or picturesque beach location.

Recommended for: Swimming and snorkeling during calm surf
Facilities: Restrooms, showers, and paved parking area across the road from the beach.
Access: Enter from Hwy. 520, the road forks into Po'ipu Road on one side and Lawa'i Road on the other (also known as Spouting Horn Road). It is not as far down as Spouting Horn and is located across from the Lawa'i Beach Resort

PRINCE KUHIO PARK

This beach park is dedicated to Prince Jonah Kuhio Kalaniana'ole. He was born in 1871 and in 1902 was elected to be a delegate to Congress, where he served until his death on January 7, 1922. He was known as the "People's Prince" because of his achievements for his Hawaiian people. You can see the foundation of Kuhio's parent's home, the royal fishpond, and *Hoai Heiau*, where the *kahuna* (priests) meditated and lived, and a sitting bench that faced the grounds.

Prince Kuhio Park is located on Lawa'i Beach Road. Prince Kuhio was the youngest son of Kaua'i's chief David Kahalepouli Piikoli and the grandson of Kaumuali'i, the last King of Kaua'i. His aunt was Kapiolani and Prince Kuhio was adopted by Queen Kapiolani and grew up in the royal household in Honolulu. The monument at this park marks his birth site.

Recommended for: Swimming, snorkeling and sunning during low tide and calm seas. During high tide, it becomes just a park, with no beach!
Facilities: Public restrooms
Parking: Paved parking area

KOLOA LANDING

In the height of the early plantation days, Koloa Landing was the departure and arriving port for passenger and cargo vessels as well as whaling ships. Today Koloa Landing is a remnant of history, this old boat launch is now used as a departure for beach scuba dives. No facilities.

PO'IPU BEACH ★

The Po'ipu Beach Resort area's main attraction is, of course, Po'ipu Beach. The beach is fronted by the popular Po'ipu Beach Park and a few resorts. The beach is actually is series of smaller golden sand crescents strung together where beachgoers will find snorkeling, swimming, sunning, wading, strolling, surfing and wind-surfing. Palm trees are scattered along the coastline here and the park has expansive grassy lawns. The surf spots are just offshore where a reef creates perfect wave-breaks for beginner, intermediate and advanced surfers. Closer in to shore, swimmers can enjoy the relatively calm waters and snorkel some interesting rocky points where fish and marinelife congregate. There is also a natural and safe kiddy wading pool at Po'ipu Beach Park, perfect for toddlers and young swimmers. Po'ipu Beach was named the nation's #1 beach by the "Dr. Beach Top Beaches Survey for 2001," as conducted by Dr. Stephen Leatherman, Florida International University. The survey annually rates beaches across the country on several quality characteristics and criteria. This is the first time a Kaua'i beach has been so honored with the #1 ranking. Po'ipu Beach Park is a four-acre stretch of land fronting the eastern section of Po'ipu Beach as well as Brennecke's Beach.

The beach park has pavilions, comfort stations, picnic tables, sidewalks and showers plus a convenience store and restaurant right across the road. This park has been the center-piece of the Po'ipu Beach resort area for decades. It is popular with families of young children and novice swimmers and the kiddy wading pool gets good use. The offshore reef provides substantial protection to the shoreline. There is also a lifeguard on duty seven days a week. This site is also popular with surfers, swimmers and snorkelers. Snorkeling around the right side of Nukumoi Point is very good. The beach is protected by Nukumoi Point and a shorebreak on the east. Bodyboarders are attracted to the waves offshore. High surf can occur April through September.

Here you will find another one of Hawai'i's eight tombolos. Without knowing it was something special, you probably wouldn't have noticed it at all. This is a strip of sand which connects one island to another or to the mainland. There are only eight tombolos in all of Hawai'i. On the rocky volcanic shore to the east be on the lookout for green sea turtles frolicking in the waves. This is a great area for swimming and snorkeling during calm seas. From Po'ipu Road, turn south onto Ho'owili Road and drive one block straight south to Ho'one Road and the beach park. There are designated parking areas nearby.

Po'ipu Beach - The sand is fine and great for sunning, sitting, strolling, and watching others. The beach has good snorkeling as a result of the offshore reef. Boogie boarding is popular here and you might see surfers riding the waves farther out. Windsurfers enjoy this site as well. Dangerous water conditions during high surf however. Snorkeling and swimming is good during calm seas but stay inside the reef area. Located at the east end of Ho'onani Road.

Brennecke's Beach - At this beach on Ho'one Road, the shorebreak on the rocks with a small beachfront can be hazardous to the boogie boarder. At one time this beach had what many considered the best body surfing on Kaua'i. In an effort to give Mother Nature a little hand in the restoration of this beach, Kaua'i residents have obtained a county permit to dump sand on the beach above the high water mark. It is hoped that this will help the beach to begin the slow restoration process from hurricane damage a bit more quickly. Resort and community groups have begun donating funds toward the purchase of sand. Brennecke's Beach Center across the street rents beach equipment.

Wai'ohai Beach - This is actually a part of Po'ipu Beach but known as Wai'ohai Beach. It was the original site of the old Knudsen home before resort development began in this area in the early 1960's. Vlademar Knudsen was the son of the premier of Norway, who first went to California and made a fortune in the gold rush before relocating to Kaua'i and making a second fortune as founder of Kekaha Sugar Company. Anne Sinclair was the daughter of Elizabeth Sinclair, the lady who purchased the island of Ni'ihau in 1864. Anne Sinclair and Vlademar Knudsen married in later years and it was this site at Wai'ohai that Anne Knudsen chose for her beach house. This sandy beach is good for surfing, swimming, and snorkeling during calm seas. High surf generates dangerous conditions. It can be reached from the adjoining beach on Ho'one Road. There is parking available in the gravel/dirt parking lot next to Brennecke's.

KEONELOA BEACH (SHIPWRECK BEACH)

This sandy shore fronts the Hyatt Regency. Keoneloa and Maha'ulepu are a part of the same beach. It is commonly referred to as Shipwreck Beach for the long-gone ship that ran aground years ago. Most of the ship has long since washed away, but the motor may still be occasionally visible. A good spot to watch surfers and windsurfers, but swimming, even during calm seas, may not be advised. The Hyatt does erect flags to indicate the condition of the surf, but still use your own good judgment.

Recommended for: Sunning, watching the windsurfers and surfers
Access: A road runs between the Po'ipu Bay Resort Golf Course and the Hyatt
Facilities: Public restrooms, shower facilities for Hyatt guests
Parking: Paved parking area at bottom

MAHA'ULEPU BEACH

It was here that King Kamehameha I made his attempt to conquer the island of Kaua'i in 1796. Unfortunately, a storm forced a retreat, but the advance forces of Kamehameha's troops arrived on the island unaware of the order to retreat and were quickly killed. This is also the beach site where George C. Scott portrayed Ernest Hemingway in the movie *Islands in the Stream*. Maha'ulepu Beach is actually a collection of smaller beaches. They offer a diverse assortment of aquatic activities including fishing, surfing, bodyboarding, body surfing, kayaking, windsurfing, snorkeling, and swimming. The three areas along this beachfront are Gillin's Beach, Kawailoa Bay, and Ha'ula Beach. Gillin's was named for the supervisor of Grove Farm Company, Elbert Gillin, who arrived in the islands in 1912. He relocated to Kaua'i in 1925 and built his home at this beach. He was the supervisor of the Ha'upu Range Tunnel. Following two hurricanes, all that remained was Gillin's chimney, but the house has since been rebuilt. Several feet below this beach are the Rainbow Petroglyphs. Discovered in 1980 when a severe storm took out as much as six feet of beachfront, the petrogylphs were suddenly exposed. Working in reverse, the sea soon chose to cover them up once again. Currents at Kawailoa Bay make it unsafe for swimming or snorkeling. To reach Ha'ula Beach you may park on the east side of Pa'o'o Point and travel to the shore by trail. This area is the south shore's most dangerous beach.

Recommended for: The first beach, Gillin's, on occasion may be good for the experienced snorkeler during calm surf. Ha'ula Beach, is on private land and tends to be less crowded. If you would like information getting permission to fish, phone the Grove Farm Office at (808) 245-3678.
Access: Daylight hours only, sunrise to sunset. The gate is located at night. No overnight camping is permitted. This is private property owned by the Grove Farm Company which allows public day time use. Since access could be denied at any time, it is requested that you take all your litter with you and be respectful of the right to use these gorgeous beaches of Kaua'i. Take the dirt road at the end of Po'ipu Road and turn right onto the cane road.
Facilities: None
Parking: On the side of the road

EASTERN SHORE

Nawiliwili, Lihu'e, Wailua, Kapa'a

KALAPAKI BEACH

This site is of historic significance in surfing history as the location where ancient Hawaiians practiced the skill of bodysurfing. The wave conditions continue to attract surfers and body surfers and the gentle off-shore slope makes it a good option for swimmers during calm seas. During periods of high surf, surfers come out in droves. However, we advise that you leave the high surf to the experienced surfers.

William Harrison Rice and Mary Sophia Rice, arrived on Kaua'i as missionaries in 1841. Their son William Hyde Rice purchased the land around this beach from Princess Ruth Ke'elikolani and here he built his home. Later, the Kaua'i Surf Hotel was built on this wonderful beachfront. In 1987, the old Kaua'i Surf was redesigned and refurbished. The resulting Westin Kaua'i Resort had an elaborate architectural style of gradniose size that some found outrageous, but most thought was garish. In 1992, Hurricane Iniki perhaps performed a great favor by virtually destroying the resort and it sat empty for more than two years. Marriott picked up the option and in 1994 began renovating the property into a blend of hotel and timeshare condominiums. With the town of Lihu'e nearby and the close proximity to the Marriott Resort, you are likely to find this beach more populated than most. This beach is better protected than some, except during east swells, but caution is advised at all times.

Recommended for: Swimming, windsurfing, and bodyboarding during low surf conditions
Access: Beach access is at the left side of the bay or through the Nawiliwili Park public access on the right.
Parking: Public parking area at the west end next to the stream which enters this bay
Facilities: BBQ grills, restrooms, rinse-off showers.

NININI BEACH

There are two beaches located here. Both can be affected by high surf and Kona storms. Snorkeling at the larger sandy stretch can be good when the ocean is calm. During high surf enjoy the bodysurfers. Sometimes it is referred to as Running Waters Beach because of the irrigation runoff that once occurred here. Nearby you'll see the Nawiliwili Light Station located at the point. This area is popular with shore fishermen catching reef fish.

Recommended for: Snorkeling on calm days (only for the experienced)
Access: Turn at Ahukini Rd. follow the dirt road 2.6 miles to Ninini Point
Parking: No parking

HANAMA'ULU BEACH PARK

A lovely picnic location, however, the bay waters are murky. The *Beaches of Kaua'i* by John Clark notes that, "Hanama'ulu Stream crosses the southern end of the beach, discharging its silt-laden waters into the bay." He also adds that "mullet and sharks, particularly juvenile hammerheads, are also found in the bay." Facilities include tables, toilets, pavilion, barbecue, and showers in this 6.5 acre park. Camping is permitted at this county park under the trees in self-contained mobile campers or tents. A lovely location for a daytime picnic, this isn't a safe park to visit after dark.

Recommended for: Picnics
Access: Located 1/2 mile from Hanama'ulu Town.
Parking: Plenty available

NUKOLE

Nukole means "beach of the kole fish," and is the proper Hawaiian name. This beach stretches from Hanama'ulu Bay to Lydgate Park for approximately two miles. It is often referred to as Nukoli'i, after a dairy that once had cattle grazing in the area. Archeological events suggest that prior to that there was a Hawaiian settlement. The Radisson Kaua'i Beach, located on this beachfront, maintains the public beach park pavilion and adjoining bathrooms. You may see local residents trying their hand at fishing, surfing and even diving on this beachfront. Swimming and snorkeling are not recommended at any time of the year.

Recommended for: Sunbathing, beachcombing, and sunrises
Access: Turn mauka on Kaua'i Beach Drive, which leads to the Radisson Hotel to reach the southern portion of the beach
Parking: Parking area for about five cars
Facilities: A county park with the pavilion, rinse off showers and restrooms are maintained by the Radisson Hotel

LYDGATE BEACH ★

This forty-acre state park is dedicated to Reverend John Lydgate, who, more than a century ago founded the Lihu'e Union Church and was a force in the establishment of public parks and historic sites on Kaua'i. Wailua was once the home of the island's royalty. The banks of the Wailua River were a sacred area in ancient Hawai'i and a favored dwelling place reserved for the kings and high chiefs of Kaua'i. Near the mouth of the river in Lydgate Park are the remains of *Hikina-'akala Heiau* which was a place of refuge for those who had broken a taboo. Two large pieces of smooth stone (where women of royal blood or high chiefly rank gave birth) are located on the river's North Shore. Nearby is *Holoholoku Heiau*, believed to be the oldest *heiau* on Kaua'i. About 25 years ago the breakwater was added which created two protected pools, ideal for swimming. The pools have a sandy bottom. Plan on bringing along some bread to feed the fish. Generally there is a lifeguard on duty. You may see windsurfers at this beach during south or Kona winds.
Recommended for: Swimming for adults and children within the protected pools. Not advised beyond the pools. Good location for beginning snorkelers to try out their skills.

Access: South of the Wailua River turn mauka on Leho Drive, then continue mauka on Nalu Rd. If you are heading North, the turn off is easy to spot, heading south there is no marked entrance. Heading north it is just past the Wailua Golf Course, heading south, if you get to the golf course, you've missed it!

Parking: Large parking area

Facilities: Restrooms, rinse off showers, BBQs, picnic pavilions, wonderful playground for kids! Lifeguard may be on duty.

Camping: Permits for camping available from the county

WAILUA BEACH
This is a nice half-mile crescent stretch of beach on the northside of Wailua River. At the north end of the beach are Kapa'a Sands, Wailua Bayview, Lae Nani, Lanikai, and Kaua'i Sands condos/hotels. *The Beaches of Kaua'i* by John R.K. Clark explains that the surfers shorebreak is called Horners, named after Albert Horner, a pineapple industry pioneer. His mansion was built on this beachfront in 1929 and was later moved by new owners Mel and Pauline Venture to an inland location in Wailua. Dangerous currents much of the year make this beach advisable only for walking and sunning. There are lots of resorts located along here and Al & Don's Restaurant in the Kaua'i Sands has a nice oceanview location. There is one small protected pool at Alakukui Point, which during calm surf is safe for wading. Also at Alakukui Point are some remnants of an old *heiau*.

Recommended for: Beachcombing, walking, sunning

Access: All along from Lydgate to River to Kapa'a

Parking: Parking area near Wailua Bridge and limited parking on Papaloa Rd.

Facilities: Phones

WAIPOULI BEACH
This narrow strip of beach runs from the Coconut Plantation Resort to the Waika'ea Canal in Kapa'a. The Kaua'i Coconut Beach Resort is located on this beachfront. While the pedestrian trail among the ironwood trees above the shoreline is popular for joggers or walkers, the beachfront is covered by beach-rock and very strong offshore currents make it unsafe for swimming year round. Some marginal swimming might be pursued at the southern end of the beach, but even then, only under very calm surf conditions. A popular fishing location.

Recommended for: Swimming is marginal in the summer months

Facilities: Only for hotel guests

KAPA'A BEACH PARK
With its location nearer to civilization and the adjoining canal used as a boat launch, you are likely to find this beach more populated. Kapa'a Beach has encountered severe shoreline erosion over the last 30 years. You'll note that some human measures have been made to stop the erosion, such as jetties at the mouth of the canal. In the evening you might want to stroll down the beach (on a moonlit night) and perhaps you'll be lucky enough to see fishermen practicing *lamalama* (torch fishing).

Recommended for: A few areas of the beach offer adequate swimming when the surf is calm, but not especially recommended. Shore fishing is popular here. Great sunrises!
Access: Turn toward the ocean off Kuhio Hwy. at Niu Street, near Kapaʻa ballpark
Parking: Parking area
Facilities: Restrooms, rinse off showers, public swimming pool

KEALIA BEACH
Once the town of Kealia was a thriving plantation town, complete with a train depot, and at the nearby landing an inter-island steamer would stop for passengers. Today it is not much more than a stretch along the highway. The word Kealia means "salt encrusted." (Interesting to note that almost every island in Hawaiʻi has a beach named Kealia!)

Recommended for: Tidepools during low tide, strong rip currents make it unsafe for water activities, particularly dangerous during high surf.
Access: Hwy. 56 at mile marker 10
Parking: Parking along the roadside
Facilities: None

DONKEY BEACH
This is one of the few beaches for which we could find no Hawaiian name. Apparently before the advent of machinery, mules were used to haul cane seed to the fields. Some say that there were only mules and no donkeys at all, but whichever the case, the name Donkey Beach stuck. Located 1 1/2 miles from Kealia Beach, it is a very pastoral setting. Here you will find a popular body and board surfing location, however high surf in winter and spring months can create dangerous rip currents and shorebreaks. There is no public access to this beach, but beachgoers, oblivious to the "No Trespassing" sign continue to find this beach. Its inaccessibility has made this beach the site for nude sunbathing. Nude sunbathing is not legal in Hawaiʻi and periodic arrests are made. At various times, local residents have hired "security guards" to dissuade nude sunbathing.

Recommended for: Fishing
Access: There is no public access
Parking: Only along the road at mile marker 11
Facilities: None

ANAHOLA BEACH and ʻALIOMANU BEACH
This is a popular park during the summer for local residents. There is a reef and pockets of sand that create pools that are pleasant for the kids. Anahola Stream is found at the north end of the beach. ʻAliomanu Beach is at the north side of Anahola Beach. Both are located on Anahola Bay. It is widely used by fishermen and *limu kohu*, a popular seaweed is harvested here.

Recommended for: Fishing, picnics, swimming (watch for currents)
Access: Hwy. 56, look for Anahola Road
Parking: parking lot
Facilities: Picnic tables, rest rooms, rinse off showers, camping

NORTHERN SHORE

Hanalei, Kilauea, and Princeville

MOLOA'A

This is as pristine a bay as you may find on Kaua'i. If you happened to catch the lone airing of the pilot episode of *Gilligan's Island* a few years back on Fox television, you might recognize this bay. (If you want to see this episode, we recommend taking the Hawai'i Movie Tour!) This was also the filming location for *Castaway Cowboys* with James Garner. While this bay can be especially dangerous during winter and spring surf, anytime there is high surf dangerous ocean conditions and powerful rip currents can occur. During periods of calm, you can enjoy swimming, snorkeling, and diving here. There is a hiking trail along the cliff to the left of the bay.

Recommended for: Snorkeling and swimming only during periods of calm
Access: Just past mike marker 16 on Kuhio Highway as you head toward Princeville. Turn right on Ko'olau Road, then turn right again onto Moloa'a Road. At the fork in the road, keep to the left following along the road in front of private residences to the public access trail. Parking is limited in front of these homes, so please respect their privacy and "No Trespassing."

KA'AKA'ANIU BEACH (LARSEN'S BEACH)

L. David Larsen, a Swedish born plant pathologist, arrived in Hawai'i in 1908 and later managed the Kilauea Sugar Plantation. This beach was named for the site upon which he built his home. Dangerous rip currents and a shallow rocky shore make this unappealing for swimmers. The offshore reef is a popular location for the harvesting of *limu kohu*, a type of seaweed. During times of low tide you may see the harvesters at work or net throwers catching fish. The county access, purchased in 1979, was sold with the condition that the access not continue all the way to the beach. This was done in hopes of making the beach less attractive and therefore less populated, so it will take a little bit of effort to reach this sandy crescent. Once you reach the head of the path, it will take you less than 10 minutes to walk down to the beachfront.

Recommended for: Beachcombing, watching seaweed being harvested, fishing
Access: 1.2 miles from the north intersection of Ko'olau Rd and Kuhio Hwy. there is a public access. A 5-10 minute hike to reach the shoreline.

WAIALKALUA IKI BEACH

Dangerous rip currents at Waialkalua Iki make it a lovely spot to visit, and a popular fishing location, but inadvisable for water activities. In 1911 on the hill overlooking the ocean, a *heiau* was discovered. There is a trail from the valley up to this archeological site. The twin beach, Waiakalua Nui is just slightly east and is covered with beach rock.

Recommended for: Beachcombing
Access: Near the end of North Waiakalua Rd. is a public access to the shoreline down a steep trail that requires a 5-10 minute walk
Facilities: This is a private beach so there are no facilities and no public parking

KILAUEA POINT NATIONAL WILDLIFE REFUGE

The Kilauea Point National Wildlife Refuge was established in 1974. The acquisition of land has continued ever since and this sanctuary now encompasses 203 acres. The refuge was struck hard by Hurricane Iniki. Not only was there much damage to the birdlife and vegetation, but the famous lighthouse was also seriously affected. At Kilauea Point, they reported that about 80% of the native plants suffered damage. On Crater Hill, at least 25% were lost and an additional 50% damaged. Mokolea Point vegetation suffered little damage. Kilauea Point lost the most birds and suffered the worst damage to the habitat. The Kaua'i Natural Wildlife Refuge complex lost 12 of their 20 buildings. There was also damage to the lighthouse visitor center and bookstore, storage buildings, fences, and the water delivery system. There are only eight tombolos within the Hawaiian Islands and one example may be found here at Kilauea Point. A tombolo is a sand or gravel bar connecting an island with the mainland or another island. You can view it at the base of Makapili Rock where it connects the rock to the shoreline. Construction began on the 52 foot lighthouse in 1912 and it was not until 1976 that it was put out of commission. Admission is $2 by donation. KPNHA (Kilauea Point Natural History Association) is a non-profit corporation dedicated to environmental interpretation, education, protection, and enhancement. Membership information can be obtained by writing: KPNHA, PO Box 87, Kilauea, HI 96754. (808) 828-1413. Open 10 am-4 pm. closed some Federal Holidays.

Access: Turn off Kuhio Hwy. where the large sign indicates Kilauea Lighthouse
Facilities: Bookstore, restrooms, visitor center, charge for admission
Parking: Large paved parking area

KAUAPEA BEACH (SECRET BEACH)

This 3,000 foot long beach lies between Kalihiwai Bay and Kilauea Point. It's access is a little tricky given that you cannot see the beach from the highway and the access is not clearly marked. The beautiful people of the 1960's referred to it as Secret Beach, and it is still called this today. Dangerous water conditions due to winter and spring high surf make water activities during these times ill advised. During calmer summer months, you may find a wide variety of beach activities including surfing, bodysurfing, and bodyboarding. There is a fresh water stream and you can sometimes see whales in the winter; dolphins in the summer. Again, possibly because of inaccessibility, you should be advised that nude sunbathing does occur at this beach site. Remember that nude sunbathing is not legal in Hawai'i and periodic arrests are made. From this beach you can see Moku'ale'ale Island, a bird sanctuary and part of the Kilauea Refuge.

Recommended for: Beachcombing, bodysurfing, or bodyboarding during summer periods of low surf.
Access: One-half mile west of Kilaueau, from the Kuhio Hwy., turn onto Kalihiwai Road which dog legs to the left. Off to the right is a dirt road with an embankment on either side. Travel down the road and there is a parking lot. Then take the trail leading to the beach. The trail down to the beach requires a 10 minute hike.
Facilities: None
Parking: Parking area along the roadside.

KALIHIWAI BEACH
This crescent of white sand is fringed with ironwood trees. You'll see board-surfing in the summer. Dangerous during the winter, so stay out of the water and just watch the surfers. Stay away from the mouth of the river, where rip currents may occur. Kayaking up the river can be done except during heavy rains or flooding.

Recommended for: Body surfing, swimming, and snorkeling only on calm summer days, fishing
Access: Take the Kalihiwai Road (eastern exit)
Facilities: Picnic tables
Parking: At the beach under the ironwood trees

'ANINI BEACH PARK
Apparently this beach was called Wanini, but sometime during the years, it was abbreviated. (One story tells that the "W" just fell off the sign, so they changed the name of the beach rather than repairing the beach sign.) With a two mile offshore reef, this beach is popular for varied types of fishing (pole, spear, throw-net) and also seaweed harvesting. Snorkeling, windsurfing, beachcombing, reef walking, and boating are also to be found here. Water conditions are very dangerous during high surf which causes strong rip currents. Many drownings and near drownings have occurred here over the years. This beachfront was the location for several scenes in *Honeymoon in Vegas*.

Recommended for: Windsurfing, swimming only during very calm summer surf. Stay away from the west end of the beach where there is a channel. Snorkeling can be good here during the summer. Stay inside the reef, same with swimming.
Access: Follow Kuhio Highway to Kalihiwai Road and take Anini Road to the beach
Facilities: Picnic facilities, showers, restrooms
Parking: Long stretch of grass for parking with an open area next to it for boats and trailers
Camping: With county permit

PRINCEVILLE

Princeville is a 2,000 acre tract of land lying between Hanalei Bay and 'Anini Beach. The resort development began in 1968 and is composed of condominiums, private homes, and several hotels. Most of the development sits along the bluffs with only four small beaches. One is located below the Sealodge condominiums, another below the Pali Ke Kua condominiums, and a third below Pu'u Poa which is sometimes called Hideaways (actually just a separate section of this same beach, but located on the other side of a cliff). The fourth is at the base of the Princeville Resort. There are several accesses to the Princeville shoreline. Seven accesses are available through the Hanalei Bay Resort. None of these beaches are safe for winter time water activities. The Princeville Hotel Resort is located on the hill called Pu'u Poa. Below is the Pu'u Poa Beach which stretches about 1,200 ft. between the resort and the mouth of the Hanalei River. Only during calm summer surf will you find an opportunity to snorkel amid the reef. Pu'u Poa is the best of the three Princeville beaches. Kayaks can be rented at the Beach Activities Center at the Princeville Hotel Resort to explore the river. Public access to some beaches on Kaua'i is via private property. You can use the access, but you are responsible for any liability.

Access to Pu'u Poa Beach: Below the Princeville Hotel. Swimming and snorkeling only during calm summer months at Pu'u Poa Beach. Limited swimming and snorkeling at Kenomene and Kaweonui Beaches during calm surf in summer months. Some parking for beach guests at the Princeville Hotel.

Access to Kaweonui Beach (at Sealodge condominiums): The trail starts at the west end of the Sealodge parking lot. A hike of 10-15 minutes down a very steep goat-like trail is required to reach the shoreline. Please be aware that this trail is very dangerous and slippery and it remains muddy even when it is not raining. Use it strictly at your own risk. No facilities.

Access to Kenomene Beach (at Pali Ke Kua condominiums): Just before the gate at the Princeville Hotel there is a path down to the beach. This beach is also know as Hideaways. It will take a 5-10 minute walk down the stairs and trail to reach this beach. Guests of Pali Ke Kua have a private trail to another (separate) part of Kenomene Beach. No facilities.

HANALEI BAY

The Hanalei Bay begins its two mile sandy stretch at Pu'u Poa and ends at the Makahoa Point toward the west. A small number of beaches and beach parks line this area, including Black Pot Beach, Hanalei Beach Park, Waikoko Beach, and Wai'oli Beach Park. There are three parking areas. The Pier located here has been rebuilt in the last few years.

Access: Turn right on Aku road and another right turn on Weke Road
Facilities: Picnic tables, restrooms, showers
Parking: Parking lot fronting the beach/park area

BLACK POT BEACH
One of the few Kaua'i beaches with no true Hawaiian name, this site was dubbed "Black Pot" for the huge cooking pot that was shared by fishermen. Black Pot Beach Park is located where the Hanalei River meets the ocean on the eastern end of the bay. This is a popular site for local residents to gather for swimming and other water sports.

Recommended for: Swimming, bodyboarding, surfing, windsurfing, and kayaking during calm summer surf
Parking: Parking only along the bay on Weke Road
Facilities: Restrooms, showers, lifeguard on duty seasonally
Camping: With county permits

HANALEI PAVILION BEACH PARK
Hanalei means "lei shaped." The Hanalei Pier, is a scenic location, and one you'll no doubt remember if you saw the movie *South Pacific*. The wooden pier was constructed in 1892 and then 30 years later was reinforced with concrete. It was used by the local farmers for shipping their rice crops to market until it was closed in 1933. In 1979 the pier joined other landmarks in the National Register of Historic Places. A lifeguard is sometimes on duty at Hanalei Beach Park during busy weekends. The beach can be calm and serene during low summer surf, but extremely treacherous during winter and spring high surf.

Recommended for: Picnics anytime, summertime swimming
Access: Turn right on Aku Road, and a second right onto Weke Road
Facilities: Picnic tables and restrooms. Lifeguard at the Hanalei Bay Beach.
Parking: Areas of compacted sand are located for parking at various intervals along the beach

WAIKOKO
Waikiko, which means "blood waters," is the last of the beaches along Hanalei Bay. It offers an offshore reef, making this narrow beach a good place for children to swim. The offshore water is very shallow, in fact, too shallow for most adults.

Recommended for: Snorkeling during calm seas and good swimming for children in the shallow, reef protected ocean. During times of high surf you can enjoy watching surfers on the outer edge of the Waikoko Reef.
Access: Located along Highway 56, a half mile past mile marker 4
Facilities: None
Parking: Along side the road

LUMAHA'I BEACH
In 2001, the state acquired by purchase from the Wilcox Family Estate, the several acres of land behind the beach area. That land is mostly a *lauhala* or pandanus tree forest. This is the plant widely used for woven mats, baskets, and other utility items. It is unknown at present as to whether the state will provide more public access and facilities at this popular beach. The beach is tucked beneath some lush cliffs and became famous for a well known scene in the 1957 film *South Pacific*. Actually, it was the eastern end of this beach, which has a

separate name, Kahalahala (which means pandanus trees), where Mitzi Gaynor filmed her famous "wash that man right out of my hair" scene. A more scenic stretch of beach is hard to imagine. Unfortunately, this is one particularly dangerous stretch of coastline. The width of Lumaha'i Beach is said to vary as much as 360 feet with the seasonal movement of the sand from one end to the other. With the steep shore comes the danger of high surf, dangerous shorebreak and strong currents. There is no protective reef, so the ocean drops off very quickly. The nearby Lumaha'i River may rise dramatically as a result of flash floods. This, in combination with the danger of rough waves, makes even wading along the shore not advisable. You may see body or boardsurfers enjoying this beach, but when the surf becomes even slightly rough, you'll see that even the experts stay out of the waters. With the danger of rogue waves, most common during high surf, again, even wading is not recommended.

You may have heard of *o'opu*, a unique freshwater fish which spends its first few months in the sea before returning to the freshwater stream. They have adapted well to their surroundings by using their lower front fins as a suction cup to hold onto rocks, even those extremely steep rock walls which form waterfalls. Using its tail to propel themselves, the *o'opu* travels slowly upstream. The adults come down the Lumaha'i stream (and others on Kaua'i) in late summer and fall, spawn and then the young head for the ocean. The young (larvae) mature into juveniles called *hinana* and return to their freshwater origins and migrate upstream. These interesting marine creatures are found nowhere beyond Hawai'i and are highly valued as a table fish.

Recommended for: Enjoying the view, and an outstanding photo opportunity at the 5 mile marker post or at several other small pullouts along the road. Swimming is safe at Kahalahala only on the VERY calmest of summer days.
Access: Along the Highway at 4 mile marker before the bridge and parking along the 6 mile marker nearer the river
Facilities: None
Parking: Very limited along the roadside

KILAUEA LIGHTHOUSE

WAINIHA BEACH PARK
The term Wainiha means "unfriendly." This wide beach has no reef, so it is completely unprotected from the open ocean. High surf, therefore, creates very dangerous conditions as a result of rip currents and shorebreaks. Numerous drownings and near-drownings have been reported here. The water is murky as a result of the Wainiha stream and not recommended for any water activities. The stream cuts back into the valley reaching the Wai'ale'ale Crater. Given the heavy rainfall that comes down from the crater, unexpected flash floods can and do occur in the stream. Hence, swimming here is not advisable. Since there is no protecting reef, beachcombing on the dry sandy shore can be good! A few miles beyond is Powerhouse Road, the turn-off to climb inland through the valley. The road travels through some beautiful, not-to-be missed scenery and ends at the Powerhouse. Built in 1906 it served to provide irrigation for the McBryde Sugar Company. Where the road ends, the trail begins: a hiking trail known as the Powerhouse Trail.

Recommended for: Beachcombing
Facilities: No facilities
Parking: Off road parking only, near mile marker 7

KEPUHI BEACH
You may, perhaps, be thinking that you are seeing double. Yes, there is also a Kepuhi Beach on the south shore. This North Shore stretch of beach is actually three beaches: *Wainiha Ku'au Beach*, *Kaonohi Beach*, and *Kanaha Beach*. There is a series of reefs which make this area popular for throw netting. The beach point at Kaonohi is the location of the YMCA Camp Naue. These beaches frequently have strong currents that are especially dangerous during high surf. Not recommended for water activities except on very calm days. Again, the high surf and dangerous currents have caused many drownings and near-drownings over the years.

Recommended for: Summertime swimming on days of calm surf
Access: Along highway 56 there is access on Alamo'o Road and Alealea Road, just before mile marker 8
Facilities: None
Parking: Parking off road among the ironwood trees

MAKUA BEACH (TUNNELS BEACH)
You are not likely to find most people referring to this stretch of beach by its Hawaiian name. This popular beach is better known as "Tunnels Beach" and named for the underwater caves here. Located on Ha'ena Point, it is one of the more popular beach sites on the northern shore of Kaua'i. While the shoreline has much beachrock (making it less attractive to swimmers) the offshore reef offers good snorkeling during calm surf. During the spring and winter time high surf, there are very strong rip currents at Makua Beach. Even during low surf, the current offshore can be treacherous. During high surf this beach is a popular surfing spot, but only for the expert. The surf break on the outer reef is often referred to as Tunnels. You may also see fishermen using spears or nets along the reef. You may recognize this beach as the major location for the television mini-series *The Thorn Birds*.

Recommended for: Watching windsurfing and boardsurfing, swimming and snorkeling during periods of low and calm sea, and beachcombing during high seas. Very dangerous during winter months.
Access: Two public accesses, one at the east side of Ha'ena Point, the other to the west. You'll find the first at .3 miles past mile marker 8 on Hwy. 560 and the second 1/2 mile past the same marker.
Facilities: None
Parking: Limited parking off Kuhio Hwy.

HA'ENA BEACH PARK

This is a five acre park maintained by the County of Kaua'i. In past times, this beach (then called Maniniolo which means "traveling manini fish") was a *hukilau* site where fishermen would come and throw their nets out into the sea and pull their catch onto shore. This is different from net fishing which you might see done by a single fisherman. (Today the *hukilau* style of fishing is never done - except at local luaus! You are probably familiar with the *Hukilau* song and hula that are often performed.) The foreshore here is steep. The resulting shorebreak is dangerous and makes it unsafe for swimming or bodysurfing. Although you may see some bodysurfing done here, it is not for the novice.

Across the road from Ha'ena Beach Park is *Maninolo Dry Cave*. This lava tube was a sea cave in earlier centuries when the sea was higher. You can follow the tube several hundred yards and emerge at the other end. Information has it that the cave was larger before it was filled in with sand by the tsunami that hit the island in 1957. Following another 2/10 of a mile past Ha'ena State Park and just beyond Limahuli Steam are the *Waikapala'e Wet Caves,* accessible by a short hike up and behind the gravel parking area. One of the caves has a fresh water pool which is a unique phenomenon. The Waikapala'e (the modern translation means water of the lace fern) Wet Cave has a cool shady cave known as the blue room. In the past it required a venture into the chilly waters and and a swim through a submerged tunnel. This area, however, is posted as no swimming due to the dangers of this. Apparently the reflection of the light through the tunnel causes the incredible blue effect on the cavern walls. Besides being posted as no swimming, it is also posted that the freshwater, as is the case in all freshwater pools, can be contaminated. Leptospirosis is a viral disease spread by the urine of infected wild animals passed through the soil and into the water system. Symptoms can be severe and include fever, headache, chills, body aches and may not reveal themselves for several weeks after being infected with the virus.

Recommended for: Swimming and snorkeling in the summer with calm surf, particularly dangerous during winter months.
Access: Located on the Wainiha side of Ha'ena
Facilities: Restrooms, showers, picnic pavilions
Camping: Permits available from the county
Parking: Parking along the roadside

HA'ENA STATE PARK and KE'E BEACH

Highway 56 goes as far as this beach before it ends. This is the beginning of the Napali Coast and Napali Coast State Park, which is only accessible by boat or by hiking trail. Swimming here is only advisable during very calm conditions. The 230 acres of Ha'ena State Park include a number of ancient archeological sites. Remnants of ancient Hawaiian villages and the *Kaulu o Laka Heiau* can be found here. This sacred altar is set along a series of tiers on the cliffs of Napali and was built for Laka, the goddess of hula. It is one of the dramatic sites on the island with views of the cliffs and ocean. The *heiau* is still used today by hula halaus.

John Clark's guide to the beaches of Kaua'i tells the story of the Taylor Camp, which was populated by over 100 flower children during the 1960's and 1970's. Howard Taylor, who happens to be the brother of Elizabeth Taylor, offered refuge at his seven acre property for their "hippie" community when they were evicted from a public beach park and threatened with jail time. (Apparently the commune members shared a communal shower and one open air toilet.) If you're over 40 years old, you may remember the *puka* shell fad. It began when these hippies gathered shells, made holes in the center (*puka* means hole) and strung them to make necklaces. Elizabeth Taylor, donning one of these necklaces (a gift from her brother), created a craze which virtually wiped out all of the shells on all the beaches in Hawaii. Great story, eh! Comb the beach for your own shells and you'll have a little piece of this legend. Now back to the hippies who continued to run free and naked, pile trash (to the point of seriously polluting the ocean), and then turned to the cultivation of marijuana for their income -- well, it was a happy ending for the beach. Howard Taylor left, turning the land deed over to the state in 1974 and after several years, the hippies were finally evicted and the state took over the park in 1977. At the very end of the beach park is Ke'e Beach and is best visited during the week when the crowds aren't as large. There can be good swimming and snorkeling, but again (are you tired of hearing this?) only if the surf conditions are calm. Stay inside the lagoon as the area beyond the reef can have strong currents. If the parking lot is full (and it often is on weekends) follow the dirt road that veers to the right. There has been a lifeguard on duty here in the past, but that may have changed due to lifeguard budget cutbacks. If you don't see one around, ask others about whether lifeguards are on duty or not. Ke'e may look familiar to you for it is where the final scene of *Body Heat* was filmed starring Kathleen Turner.

Recommended for: Good swimming and snorkeling at Ke'e in the summer with very calm surf, great sunsets
Facilities: Restrooms, showers
Access: Located at the trail head to the Napali Coast
Parking: Parking areas near the end of Kuhio Highway. If the lot at Ke'e is full, continue on the dirt road and there is more parking beyond the restrooms.

NAPALI COAST STATE PARK

"Napali" means "the cliffs." You will often see it written as "Na Pali" but *Hawaiian Place Names*, written by authoritative historian Mary Kawena Kukui, spells it as one. Thus, this book follows her spelling. Remember in using this term, don't say "The Napali Cliffs," for that would mean "The cliffs cliffs." This 6,500 acre state park is composed of dramatic cliffs, dense rainforests, and lush coastal valleys. There are 15 miles of shoreline between Ke'e Beach and Polihale Beach on Kaua'i's eastern shore. There are a total of five major beaches within this state park: Hanakapi'ai, Kalalau, Honopu, Nu'alolo Kai and Miloli'i. The Hanakapi'ai Beach can be reached in a day's hike. It is a distance of two miles from Ke'e and may take from 30 minutes to two hours to reach. Remember to pack plenty of drinking water, and include sunscreen lotion and a hat, along with comfortable shoes. It might be recommended to also include a small first aid kit with an ace support bandage. You may find remnants of a fishing village and a farming community which once resided here. Due to the remoteness of this coastline, beach lovers need to use extra caution. Sadly, it is perhaps at the Kalalau Beach that more drownings occur, **per visitor**, than anywhere else on the island of Kaua'i. As mentioned before, this is a remote wilderness area and help would be a long time in reaching you should you become ill or injured. As with other North Shore beaches, surf and currents are extremely hazardous. A hike to this beach is recommended for summer when the trail has had time to dry out from spring rains and the ocean is calmer. Another trail which travels two miles inland from the beach and will take you to the Hanakapi'ai waterfall. The falls flow down for about 300 feet to the pool below. Avoid swimming beneath the falls, and resist the urge to drink the water (all fresh water in Hawai'i should be purified before drinking). It is also advisable that you bring along some mosquito repellent! There is an 11-mile trek along the steep cliffs of the Kalalau Trail to Kalalau Beach. Due to the rugged terrain and steep elevations, it may well take an entire day to reach the beach. The Kalalau Valley was called the Valley of Healing Light by the ancient Hawaiians. Remember to treat any *heiaus* and village ruins with respect. Again, the summer months are most advisable. The area was inhabited until 1919. In the late 1960's and early 1970's the area was repopulated, this time by hippies. With serious sanitation problems the state implemented a program which limited access to the area by restricting the number of camping permits. Boat and helicopter landings also came under restrictions. Camping is allowed only at the shoreline at Kalalau and water is available for cooking and drinking following purification, i.e. boiling. With no fronting reef and strong currents, it is dangerous to swim here at any time of the year. The remaining three of Napali's beaches are only accessible by boat. Camping is permitted in areas of the state park. Permits are not required for day hikes.

HANAKAPI'AI

We recommend you simply stay out of the ocean here. This North Shore beach is particularly dangerous, and the #1 beach for drownings between 1970 and 1988. This, combined with the remoteness of this shoreline, means that beach lovers need to use extra caution. As mentioned before, this is a remote wilderness area and help would be a long time in reaching you should you become ill or injured. The Hanakapi'ai Stream flows into the ocean at this sandy beachfront. The rivermouth has dangerous rip currents. Summer trades can cause the current to be especially hazardous. Conditions are even more dangerous during winter months. Even the Department of Land and Natural Resources recommends you avoid the ocean. There are some ponds along the stream for a quick dip, but keep an eye out above the valley as rain in the uplands can result in flash flooding of the streams. A reminder, as with any freshwater on the island, it needs to be boiled or otherwise treated before drinking. Also see the recreation section of this book under camping for more information on this beach area.

BEACHES

Northern Shore

Recommended for: Scenic beauty only
Facilities: Toilets
Access: A two mile trek from the trail head at Ke'e Beach, at the NW end of Kuhio Hwy. It is not recommended that you park and leave your car overnight. Several companies can arrange to drop you off and pick you up.
Camping: By permit with the state

KALALAU BEACH

The trail from the Hanakapi'ai Valley to the Kalalau Valley is a difficult one and should not be attempted as a day trip. An 11 mile hike from the trail head at Ke'e Beach, it traverses along scenic ocean cliffs with significant elevation changes (meaning a lot of ups and downs!). The beach is long and narrow during the summer, but with close shorebreak, it is unsafe at all times of the year. During the winter, the beach disappears. No water activities can be recommended for this location. This is one of Kaua'i's five most dangerous beaches, based on incidents of drowning. As with other valley beaches, the Kalalau Stream mouth area is subject to rip currents which are very hazardous. Also, be alert to the possibility of flash floods during rainfall in the upper region. This is the last beach accessible by foot along the Napali Coast. The remaining beaches are accessible only by boat. See the Recreation and Tours section of this book under *Camping* for more information on this beach area.

Recommended for: Scenic beauty only
Facilities: Toilets
Access: Eleven strenuous miles on foot along the Napali Coastline from the trail head at Ke'e Beach at the NW end of Kuhio Hwy. It is not recommended that you park and leave your car overnight. Several companies can arrange to drop you off and pick you up.

HONOPU and NUALOLO KAI BEACHES

Accessible only by boat, Honopu has no facilities and camping is not allowed. Nualolo is a popular summer destination for the charter/cruise boats - even more well used now since the charter/cruise companies are departing from Port Allen rather than Hanalei. Several companies have state permission to land at this beach, others must anchor offshore. Snorkelers need to stay clear of the shallow reefs due to the danger of surges.

Recommended for: Snorkeling at Nualolo Kai during calm summer months
Facilities: Toilets and picnic tables
Access: Charter/cruise boats during the summer months, especially Nualolo Kai

RECREATION AND TOURS

INTRODUCTION

Kaua'i-The Garden Isle, has much to interest the outdoor-oriented visitor. Whether it is the land, the air, or the ocean that beckons, there are a variety of activities to tempt even the die-hard lounge chair athlete. This chapter lists activities in alphabetical order.

There are a number of activity booking agencies on Kaua'i that can assist you with booking the recreational activity of your choice. Pick up a free copy of the *Beach & Activity Guide Kaua'i*. They list companies which give 5%, 10% or 15% discounts if you book directly.

It is also highly advisable that prior to your arrival on Kaua'i, you check out the online/Internet websites and addresses of related tour operators, vendors, activity booking agencies, etc. listed in this chapter and inquire into current and latest discount rates, special Internet rates, direct booking rates, etc. that may be available. You can often save a considerable amount on related tours and activities by booking online or directly with the operators and/or vendors. Also, keep in mind that prices for various tours and activities can and do change without notice. Prices quoted in this book are the most current that could be determined with the respective vendors or operators prior to publication but may well have changed by the time you read this.

(Author's note: "Napali," as in "Napali Coast" means "the cliffs." You will often see it written as "Na Pali" in the travel literature and advertising of cruise boat and helicopter tour companies. But *Hawaiian Place Names*, written by authoritative historian Mary Kawena Pukui, spells it as one word, thus her spelling is followed in this book.)

BEST BETS

For great snorkeling try Lydgate or Po'ipu Beach on the South Shore or Makua Beach (also known as Tunnels) on the North Shore.

Take a helicopter tour and get a spectacular view of Kaua'i's lush interior mountains and spectacular Napali Coast.

The golf aficionado will delight in the Prince Course at Princeville. Rated as the Number One course by Golf Digest, it is well deserved. Excellent play and outstanding scenery! The same can be said for the Po'ipu Bay Golf Course, a spectacular layout along the Po'ipu Coast, challenging and beautiful. Home of the annual PGA Grand Slam event.

If the whales are in residence during the winter months, take advantage of a whale watching excursion to view these beautiful mammals a bit more closely.

For an underwater thrill consider an introductory scuba adventure, no experience necessary.

For an eye-popping, spectacular aquatic adventure, take a snorkel cruise/tour of the Napali Coast.

For hikers, any of the trail systems in Koke'e Park/Waimea Canyon, but the moderately difficult Awa'awapuhi Trail to the North Shore is one of the better ones; the Waipo'o Falls trek is also a great moderately challenging adventure hike.

Take a tour up the Wailua River by kayak to the Fern Grotto and hike to a secluded waterfalls.

View the Waimea Canyon, one of the most spectacular of Mother Nature's creations; one great way to do it is via one of the Downhill Canyon Bike Rides, offered by various tour operators, a relaxing and fun way to cruise the canyon.

Hike the Kalalau Trail, an 11-mile trek along the rugged Napali coastline not for the novice hiker.

The Grove Farm tour is one of Kaua'i's best cultural and historical experiences. Reserve your space long before your arrival, as they take very small groups.

Enjoy a hiking excursion in the summer months with an interpretative guide from the Koke'e Natural History Museum.

Spend a day, or part of one, at the ANARA Health Spa at the Hyatt Regency Kaua'i.

Take a bottle of something bubbly and watch a romantic sunset at Ke'e Beach or Pakala Beach.

Take advantage of an incredible golfing value on a picturesque course, the 9-hole Kukuiolono Golf Course. Start your play about 3pm, miss the crowds, and if you don't finish you won't feel bad: green fees are a bargain at only $7! The horticulturist or amateur gardener will not want to miss visiting one or all of the island's lovely botanical gardens.

The following is a list of just some of the activities that might be enjoyed on the island of Kaua'i, along with the price per person you might expect to pay for a typical excursion, outing, rental period, etc. Remember to always check the local brochures for coupons, and don't be afraid to ask if they are running a special offer! And also check outfitter/vendor websites where available for unadvertised specials and discounts available only by booking online.

Helicopter tour (55-60 minutes) from $150
Napali Coast ocean excursion from $75
Sunset sail along the Napali Coast from $85
½ day Adventure Hike-Bike Trek from $85
Deep sea fishing (1/2 day trip) from $95
Fresh water fishing (1/2 day trip) from $105
River kayak (1/2 day guided) from $60
River kayak self-guided rental from $26
Scuba diving (2-tank w/equipment) from $100
Hawaiian luau from $50
Downhill Waimea Canyon Bike Ride from $72
Horseback riding (3 hour) from $90
Land tours (island guided bus tours) from $65
Motorcycle day rental from $185
Moped day rental from $50
Golf (nine holes-public course) from $7
Golf (eighteen holes-public course) from $32-44
Golf (nine holes-private) from $50-65
Golf (eighteen holes-private/resort) from $75-170

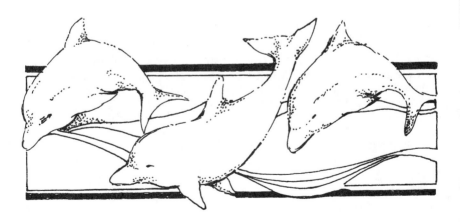

ACTIVITY BOOKING SERVICES

There are several activity booking services on Kaua'i that can provide tour and activity reservations with many of the leading air, water and land tour operators, vendors and outfitters. And they can often do it at discounted rates because they are tour wholesalers. For whatever tour, excursion or activity you have in mind, it might be good to check and compare with any of these booking services to inquire into the current special rates, discounts, etc. that are being offered. Depending on season and demand, it might be a better deal booking with one of these services rather than with the tour operator directly. But be sure to always compare and inquire into any current special rates or discounts being offered, senior rates, etc.

Activity Connection, Waimea, 338-1038

Activity Hut, 2253 Po'ipu Road, Koloa, HI 96756, 742-9522

Activities of Kaua'i, 3-3222 Kuhio Highway, Lihu'e, HI 96766, 245-1664

Activities Unlimited Kaua'i, 6281C Hauaala Road, Kapa'a, HI 96746, 821-1313

Activity Warehouse, 4-788 Kuhio Highway, Kapa'a, HI 96746; Kapa'a 245-4600, Po'ipu 742-2300, Princeville 826-4100

Activity Wholesalers, 5077 Kuhio Highway, Hanalei, HI 96714, 826-9983 and in Anchor Cove Shopping Center, 3416 Rice Street, Nawiliwili, Lihu'e, HI 96766, 245-3926; Web: < www.livekauai.com >

Activity World, toll free 1-800-235-7771; or in Lihu'e/Kapa'a 245-3300, Po'ipu/South Shore 742-9800, Princeville/North Shore 826-6500

Cheap Tours, toll free 1-888-822-5935 or 246-0009, 742-7000; Web: < www.cheaptourshawaii.com >

AIRPLANE TOURS - Also see Helicopter Tours

Kumulani Air/Fly Kaua'i, Lihu'e Airport, (808) 246-9123; Web: < www.airnav.com/airport/LIH/KUMULANI > This flightseeing service offers scenic flights over Kaua'i and Ni'ihau Islands and charter tours statewide in their 9 passenger Piper Chieftain. Kaua'i tours from one-hour long. Three-island air tours available. An aerial tour of all Hawaiian Islands including a volcano tour is available, or an air tour which includes a ground tour on Moloka'i. Call for the latest rates; operator did not respond to inquiries.

ALL TERRAIN VEHICLE ADVENTURES

Kaua'i ATV, PO Box 800, Kalaheo, HI 96741; (808) 742-2734, 742-9654; Email: kauaitv@gte.net; Web: <www.kauaiatv.com> Located in old Koloa Town on Weli Weli Road. This outfitter offers two different outdoor all terrain adventures in Kaua'i's lush, tropical landscape, exploring backcountry areas, old cane plantataion roads into the fields, valleys and mountain areas. Beautiful backcountry views of mountains, coastline, and forest areas. Learn from guides about the social, cultural and natural history of the region, wildlife, plants, etc. The Koloa Tour is 3-hours; Waterfall Tour is 4-hours. They even have a 3-passenger amphibious ATV just right for youngsters. Call for the latest rates; operator did not respond to inquiries.

Kipu Ranch Adventures, Kipu Road, Lihu'e, HI 96766; (808) 246-9288, 634-5478; Web: <www.kiputours.com> Take a leisurely ATV ride on a private ranch. Ride through mountain trails, tropical forests, river valleys and rolling pastures on this working cattle ranch. Beautiful panoramic scenes of forest and mountains, wildlife and tropical plants. Standard tour is 3-hours long. Call for the latest rates; operator did not respond to inquiries.

BICYCLING / MOTOR BIKE ADVENTURES

Chris the Fun Lady, 4-746 Kuhio Highway, Kapa'a, HI 96746, (808) 822-7759. This rental equipment operator has all sorts of recreational equipment available and can book tours, cruises, excursions, etc. They rent mountain bikes too.

Gary's Motorcycles of Kaua'i, 4558 Kukui, Kapa'a, HI 96746, (808) 822-4644; Email: customhogs@hotmail.com; Web: <www.realkauai.com/GarysMotorcycles>. They rent a full line of Harley Davidson motorcycles, many models. Daily rates: Road King $185, Sportster $185, Wide Glide $185, Heritage Softail $185, Harley Buell Blast $150, Moped $50. They also have a special custom-built Trike with a Chevy 350 engine, seats 5 people, hardtop, CD/stereo for $225 day.

Hawaiian Riders, 4-776 Kuhio Highway, Kapa'a, HI 96746; (808) 822-5409; also 2320 Po'ipu Road, Po'ipu, (808) 742-9888. They rent mountain bikes ($10-16 day, $7-10 half day). They also rent mopeds ($50 day, hourly rates available), many Harley Davidsons available (begin at $69 day), or exotic automobiles. Rent a Hummer or Pymouth Prowler for only $399/day! How about a Porsche for $119 a day? Located in Kapa'a across from McDonald's.

Kaua'i Adventure Trek ★, 3-2087 Kaumualii Highway, Lihu'e, HI 96766; (808) 245-3440, cell 635--8735; Email: inquiries@kauaiadventuretrek.com; Web: <www.kauaiadventuretrek.com> This outfitter offers a basic half-day adventure trek which includes biking, hiking and optional swimming. The trek involves a bike ride through the fabled estate of Grove Farm Plantation, once a leading sugar cane plantation. The trek follows meandering backcountry cane roads through the scenic grazing lands and mountains of Haiku country between Lihu'e and Koloa. Bikers pass through the long dark tunnel of the old cane road separating the east side of the island from the south side.

The ride continues gradually downhill through rolling hills and fields to the abandoned Koloa Sugar Mill for a stop. The trek continues through fields of coffee, corn and papaya groves to the beach on the Po'ipu coast. A picnic lunch stop on the beach provides time to relax and savor the beautiful beach of the South Shore. Trekkers can swim or explore the beach before heading to the last leg, a short hike over the hilly coastline of Mahaulepu to a lovely secluded beach and cove. Informative guided narration details the history, culture, and heritage of this region of Kaua'i. This is an excellent family-adventure, for young and old alike. Safe mountain bikes included; tandem bikes available. Includes picnic lunch and drinks. Two treks daily at 8:15 a.m. and 10 a.m., leaving from Kilohana Plantation (home of Gaylord's). Rates: $85 per person.

Kaua'i Coasters, PO Box 3038, Lihu'e, HI 96766; (808) 639-2412; Email: coast@aloha.net; Web: < www.aloha.net/ ~ coast > This outfitter offers 12 miles of scenic downhill biking from Waimea Canyon to the coast at Kekaha. Includes bikes, gear, guides, and breakfast at the crater rim. Their motto: "We've been going downhill since we started!" This is a very pleasant, safe ride; narration on culture, natural history, ecology, heritage, etc. and short walk on canyon nature trail. Half-day adventure ride excursion. Rates: $70 per person.

Kaua'i Cycle and Tour, 1379 Kuhio Highway, Kapa'a, HI 96746; (808) 821-2115; Web: < www.bikehawaii.com/kauaicycle > They rent Cannondale and specialized mountain bikes. Rates: $15-35 day; $40-85 for 3-days; $75-150 for week. Open Mon-Fri 9 a.m.-6 p.m., Sat 9a.m.-4 p.m., closed Sun.

Outfitters Kaua'i, ★ 2827A Po'ipu Rd., PO Box 1149, Po'ipu Beach, HI 96756. (808) 742-9667, 1-888-742-9887. FAX (808) 742-9667. Email: info@outfitterskauai.com; Web: < www.outfitterskauai.com > This outfitter offers mountain bike rentals for your own exploration along with car racks, kid's seats, helmets, and plenty of directions. They have a number of biking tours and biking combined with other adventures including hiking and kayaking. Their Bicycle Downhill Canyon to Coast is a guided trip available for sunrise or sunset tours daily; includes light breakfast, snacks, beverages. Downhill Bike Ride rates: Adults $72, children 10-14 years old, $60.

Ray's Motorcycle Rentals, Kapa'a, (808) 822-HOGG, has only Harley Davidsons for rent; various models and rates.

Tropical Trike Rentals, Kapa'a, HI 96766, (808) 822-5700. They have custom-built trike/bikes, seat up to 4 people, available for rental, special events, weddings, etc. Call for latest rates.

BILLIARDS

Garden Island Billiards is an air-conditioned, smoke-free billiard parlor that offers ten full size tables. Open daily 6pm until midnight. Located next to Anchor Cove Shopping Center, 3366 Wa'apa Rd. (808) 245-8900. They now have liquor and offer ice cold beer. A smoking room is available. Another popular place for pool is at the Stevenson Lounge at the Hyatt Regency. Pool also available at the Nawiliwili Tavern and Sheraton Lounge (The Point).

BOAT TRIPS See "Sea Excursions" and "Snorkeling"

BOWLING

Lihu'e Bowling Center - 28 lanes open daily at 4303 Rice St., in the Rice Shopping Center. They are a smoke-free environment!! Snack bar features kid-friendly foods including burgers, pizza, clam chowder, and cinnamon toast; pro shop, video games, billiards, lounge. Open 9am-midnight Mon-Sat, Sundays noon to midnight. (808) 245-5263.

BRIDGE

Everyone has a passion. You know, that hobby or recreational activity which, in your estimation, exceeds all others? Well, if the game of bridge is yours, then you are in luck on Kaua'i! Visitors are invited to stop by any of three bridge clubs around the island. Locations and playing times vary. Contact Mable Haas at (808) 822-5373 or Colleen Lawshe at (808) 332-9738.

CAMPING

When planning your camping vacation on Kaua'i, remember that space is very limited at the most popular campsites, so make arrangements well in advance. Tent camping only is allowed at County of Kaua'i parks. Hawai'i State Parks on Kaua'i allow for tent camping while cabins are available only at Koke'e State Park through concessionaire Koke'e Lodge. There are no national parks on Kaua'i. Self-contained mobile campers are not permitted in state or county park campgrounds except for one county-operated park, Haena County Park on the North Shore. See the section on hiking for more information on related areas.

CAMPING EQUIPMENT: Pedal and Paddle (808) 826-9069, Fax (808) 826-7869, Web: < www.pedalnpaddle.com > and Kayak Kaua'i (808) 826-9844, both in Hanalei on the North Shore. Backpacking, camping and survival gear as well as kayak, canoe, mountain bike and beach equipment rentals.

STATE PARKS

Camping permits are required for state parks and are available by contacting: Hawai'i State Parks, Kaua'i District Office, Department of Land & Natural Resources, 3060 Eiwa Street, Room 306, Lihu'e, HI 96766-1875; telephone (808) 274-3444 during regular business hours; permits are issued only Monday-Friday 8 a.m. - 4 p.m., closed weekends and state holidays. Camping permit cost is $5 per campsite per night for all state campgrounds except for Napali Coast State Park which is $10 per person per night for camping at the beachparks on the Napali Coast. All campgrounds, except the parks along the Napali Coast, are equipped with restrooms, showers, drinking water, fireplaces, and picnic tables. There are restrictions as to the number of nights you are allowed to camp, and permits for the Kalalau Trail/Napali Coast are in high demand and you should make application months in advance. We understand that permits may be obtained through correspondence, however, you may be required to submit photocopies of your identification (passport, driver's license, etc.) for each adult (age 18 or older) and the names and ages of minors in your group.

Note that it is unwise to leave cars at the trail head when hiking into the Napali Coast area for security reasons.

These uninhabited valleys on the northern coastline were once the home for hundreds, if not thousands, of Hawaiians. Residents inhabited some of these valleys until the early 1900's and several archaeological studies have been conducted in this region.

Hanakapi'ai

The road on the Northern Coastline ends at Napali State Park. Here is the launching site for two of Kaua'i's most incredible hikes. Be sure to wear good sturdy hiking boots, or if you wear tennis shoes, bring old ones as the dirt and mud will cause permanent staining to your footwear.

The trip to Hanakapi'ai Beach can be reached in a day. It is a distance of two miles from Ke'e and may take 1 1/2 to 2 hours to get there. You may find remnants of a fishing village and a farming community which once resided here. Due to the remoteness of this coastline, beach lovers need to use extra caution. Sadly, it bears repeating, but Kalalau Beach has more drownings (per visitor) than anywhere else on the island of Kaua'i. As mentioned before, this is a remote wilderness area and help would be a long time in reaching you should you become endangered. As with other North Shore beaches, surf and currents are extremely hazardous. Even the Department of Land and Natural Resources recommends you avoid the ocean. A hike to this beach is better in summer when the ocean is calmer (albeit still very dangerous) and the trail has had time to dry out from spring rains. The trip to the beach will reward the hiker with outstanding coastline vistas. A side trip that you can take is to follow the Hanakoa Valley along an unmaintained trail for another two miles to the Hanakapi'ai waterfall. The falls flow down about 300 feet to the pool below. Avoid swimming beneath the falls, and resist the urge to drink the water (all fresh water in Hawai'i should be purified before drinking). NEVER DRINK DIRECTLY FROM STREAMS OR PONDS! The upper half of this trail is more difficult, with boulders and fallen trees to negotiate and should be hiked only in good weather to avoid the danger of flash floods. It is also advisable that you bring along plenty of mosquito repellent! Primitive tent camping, one night only. See preceding section to contact State Parks Department for required overnight camping permits.

Kalalau

It is an 11-mile trek along the steep cliffs of the Kalalau Trail to Kalalau Beach and the campsite. Due to the rugged terrain and steep elevations, it may well take an entire day to reach the beach. As you leave Hanakapi'ai Valley, the hiking becomes more strenuous, climbing 800 feet in elevation. After passing through the Ho'olulu and Waiahuakua Valleys, you enter the Hanakoa Valley which is home to many native lowland forest plants. Camping is available near the Hanakoa Stream. In the late 1800's there were terraces of coffee plants grown here (and a few stragglers remain). These cleared areas are now campsites. There is an unmarked 1/3 mile trail to Hanakoa Falls, but unmaintained trail has eroded in some places making hiking hazardous. The next five miles of trail travel through a section which offers a little protection from the sun. Crossing the Kalalau Stream near the mouth of the valley will reward the weary hiker with a small waterfall. Camping is allowed only by this sand beach. During the summer, sea caves just beyond the waterfall can be used as shelter, but during winter and high surf, they are filled with water. An easy two-mile trail follows the Kalalau Valley and ends at a pool in the stream. The Kalalau Valley was called the Valley of Healing Light by the ancient Hawaiians. Remember to treat any *heiaus* you find with respect. The area was inhabited until 1919 and taro was grown here. Now the valley is filled with wild Java plum, guava, and a mango tree or two. In the late 1960's and early 1970's the area was again populated, this time by hippies. With serious sanitation problems the state implemented a program which limited access to the area by restricting the number of camping permits. Boat and helicopter landings also came under restrictions. Primitive camping is allowed just behind the beach at Kalalau and stream water only is available for cooking and drinking following purification, i.e. boiling. AGAIN, NEVER DRINK DIRECTLY FROM STREAMS OR PONDS! With no fronting reef and strong currents, it is dangerous to swim here at any time of the year. Hiking and camping is best here during the summer months, but it is also more difficult to obtain a permit. Maximum camping stay at Kalalau is five consecutive nights.

Miloli'i State Park
Located on the northwestern coast of Kaua'i near the Napali Coast State Park. These forty acres are equipped with a restroom and picnic area, and allow primitive tent camping only and small boat access. No drinking water available. Camping restricted to maximum of 3 nights. Accessible by boat only, from May 15 through Labor Day, weather permitting.

Nualolo Kai
No camping allowed and day use permit is required. It is accessible by small boat only, weather permitting. Many tour boat operators use this oceanfront for snorkeling trips as a part of their Napali boat tours. In the late 1950's, Dr. Kenneth Emory working on behalf of the Bishop Museum, began a project to study the Nualolo Kai area. In Hawai'i's early days, the valley contained all the materials to sustain a substantial native Hawaiian population. The bark of the *hau* tree was used for making twine and this very soft wood was well suited for canoe outriggers and fires. The streams offered fresh water shrimp and along the shore were *opiis* (limpets) and *pipipis* (black shellfish). Salt was gathered from the seas and the *kukui* tree was useful for a variety of needs of the early Hawaiian people. For example, canoe hulls could be made from the wood of the *kukui* and the nuts, high in oil, were strung together made an imperfect, but adequate candle. The bark was also used to dye fishing nets. The leaves of the pandanus trees (*lauhala*) were woven into mats. Another tree, the *noni*, has medicinal properties that were valuable for the early Hawaiians. Robert Krauss, during a trip to visit Dr. Emory in the valley while he was excavating wrote in his book, *Here's Hawai'i*, ... the "gnarled tree with the lumpy fruit is the *noni*. It has medicinal properties. The Hawaiians tied *noni* leaves over boils for drawing out infection. The green juice from the crushed pulp of a young *noni* apple, used as a gargle, is good for sore throat. Taken internally it will cure fish poisoning." It is unknown why the Hawaiians left this valley, but Emory speculated their leaving may have been

influenced by the arrival of the early missionaries who preferred to have their congregations more centralized.

Polihale State Park

Where the Napali meets the west side of Kaua'i is where you'll find Polihale. Located at the end of a 5-mile long dirt road off Kaumualii Highway #50 about 7 miles past Kekaha town and just past the Pacific Missile Range Facility at Barking Sands. There are 138-acres of wild coastline here with a wide sandy beach and large sand dunes. It's a scenic setting with great views of the high sea cliffs of the Napali Coast extending northward. It's also a very warm and windy desert-like climate and there are pavilions which offer some shade from the hot rays of sun. No shade trees to speak of. The park provides showers, restrooms, picnic tables, barbecues and drinking water. Shore fishing and beach combing are good activities but swimming is safe only when conditions are favorable (mostly in summer months) due to strong offshore and hazardous currents.

Koke'e State Park

The cooler climate of upcountry Kaua'i will give you a very different camping experience compared to the beachfront facilities. Koke'e State Park encompasses some 4,345-acres with commanding views of the lush Kalalau Valley from the 4,000 ft. Elevation lookout. Many nearby trails throughout the park offer varied daytime excursions to points along the rim of Waimea Canyon. Hikes range from a 1/10 mile walk that leads to an overlook of Waimea Canyon to a 3-1/2 mile trail through forested terrain. Trails into the neighboring forest reserves include Nualolo, Awaawapuhi, Honopu, Pihea, and Alakai Swamp Trails. During June and continuing through September, the Koke'e Natural History Museum offers a series of guided hikes in the scenic uplands of West Kaua'i. Hikes (each Sunday and Wednesday), are led by one of the trained volunteers of the Koke'e Natural History Museum. The hikes vary in length and in difficulty and since space is limited, they ask that you call ahead to reserve your spot. A small donation is requested. Tours include a hike along cliff and canyon trails to Waipo'o Falls, hikes along the fairly strenuous Pihea Trail or a family hike along Berry Flats Trail. Along the way your interpretative guide will explain about the flora and fauna you encounter along your hike.

For information on cabin rentals contact Koke'e Lodge, Koke'e State Park, 3600 Koke'e Road, PO Box 819, Waimea, HI 96796. (808) 335-6061. Cabins should be booked as far in advance as possible, at least 3-4 months, and are $35 and $45 per night per cabin, plus tax. Cabins sleep 3 to 6 people with five-day maximum stay. Cabins are VERY RUSTIC and self-contained with kitchen, refrigerator, cookware and eating utensils, hot shower, bedding, linens, towels provided. These are backpacker-hiker cabins and not first-class tourist lodgings. Information on the trails in Koke'e Park can be obtained from the Division of Forestry and Wildlife, Department of Land and Natural Resources, 3060 Eiwa Street, Lihu'e, HI 96766; (808) 274-3433.

STATE FOREST RESERVES

State Forest Reserves have some limited campsites available for tent camping only. These are hike-in campsites only and no cabins are available. No-fee permits are required. For information, contact: Hawaii State Forestry & Wildlife Division, Kaua'i District Office, Department of Land & Natural Resources, 3060 Eiwa Street, Room 306, Lihu'e, HI 96766; telephone (808) 274-3433 during regular business hours Monday-Friday, 8 a.m. - 4 p.m., closed weekends and state holidays.

Na Pali-Kona Forest Reserve Campsites
Located approximately 4 miles east of Koke'e State Park headquarters on the Camp-10 Road. A four-wheel drive vehicle is required as the road is steep and often muddy. The two campsites available are:

Kawaikoi Campsite is a 3-acre open grass field surrounded by Koke'e plum trees and native koa and ohia forest. The Kawaikoi Stream flows next to the camping area. There are two picnic shelters and a composting toilet. No drinking water available-bring your own or treat stream water. Maximum stay allowed is 3 consecutive nights. Campsite accommodates up to 30 people.

Sugi Grove Campsite is a shady campsite located across Kawaikoi Sream from the Kawaikoi Campsite. The Kawaikoi Stream Trail, which is one of the most scenic streamside trails in Hawaii, runs 1 3/4 miles upstream from the Sugi Grove Campsite. There is a single picnic shelter, a pit toilet and space for several tents. No drinking water-bring your own or treat stream water. Maximum stay allowed is 3 consecutive nights. Campsite accommodates up to 10 people.

Pu'u Ka Pele Forest Reserve Campsites
Running cool mountain streams and sheer vertical valley walls are part of the Waimea Canyon camping experience. Access to this area is via the Kukui Trail which starts approximately 3/4 mile beyond miler marker 8 on Highway 550, the Waimea Canyon Drive. The maximum stay at any of these Waimea Canyon campsites is 4 consecutive nights. The four campsites available are:

Wiliwili Campsite is a small one-shelter campsite with no drinking water.

Kaluahaulu Campsite is a small one-shelter campsite with no drinking water; this campsite should not be accessed during stormy weather due to dangers of flash floods in the canyon.

Hipalau Campsite is a small one-shelter campsite with no drinking water but stream water at this site can be treated or boiled for drinking.

Lonomea Campsite is a small one-shelter campsite with no drinking water but stream water at this site can be treated or boiled for drinking.

COUNTY PARKS

Camping permits are required. Contact: Parks Permit Section, Division of Parks and Recreation, County of Kaua'i, 4444 Rice Street, Moikeha Bldg, Suite 150, Lihu'e, HI 96766; telephone (808) 241-6660 during regular business hours Monday-Friday, 8 a.m. - 4 p.m., closed weekends and state holidays. Non-resident permit fee for tent and vehicle camping is $3 per adult per night, or permits are available at the campgrounds from park rangers at $5 per night for each adult. Youths under age 18 are free. Hawai'i State residents are exempt from camping fees. Campsites are on a first come/first served basis. Permits may be purchased by mail, but require 30 working days in advance to process. Contact the above office for full information. The following are county parks with campsites for tent camping only unless otherwise designated.

Anahola County Park
Located on the northeast coast on Highway 56 north of Kapa'a town. This is a 1 ½ acre beach park with showers, toilets, swimming and tent campsites available.

'Anini Beach Park
Located on the north coast, Highway 56, turn off road is two miles past Kilauea town. Turn right after a big bridge, Kalihikai, and drive for .2 mile, then turn left onto Anini Road to a dead end sign. It's another .2 mile to the campsite. There are two-acres here, pavilion, toilet, showers, picnic tables, BBQ, and swimming. It's got a secluded beach with a large reef-protected swimming area. Very popular with local families.

Ha'ena Beach Park
Located on the North Shore, Highway 56, passing through Haena Village to the end of the road where the hiking trail to Napali Coast begins. Camping is permitted across Ha'ena dry cave, under the trees. The 4.7 acre park has pavilions, toilets, showers, tables, and BBQ grills. Swimming is unsafe due to a strong riptide. The best swimming area is a mile away at the end of the road at Kee Beach. Self-contained mobile campers are permitted at this park.

Hanalei Beach Park
Located at Hanalei on the North Shore. In Hanalei town, turn right after Saint Michael's Church, make another right and keep on the road parallel to the coast passing Hanalei Pavilion on the left. Continue until you reach the parking lot and wharf area. This is a 1 ½ acre park with pavilion, toilets, tables, and BBQ grill. Safe swimming at the beach which is open only on Fridays, Saturdays and holidays. Restaurants, grocery stores, etc. located in town nearby.

Hanama'ulu Beach Park
Located on the southeast coast ½ mile from Hanama'ulu Town. From Highway 56, turn right at Hanamaulu Road across from Hanamaulu Cafe until you come to a fork. Stay on Hanamaulu Road going down a hill until you come to the beach area. Camping is permitted under the trees. The 6 ½ acre park has tables, toilets, pavilion, BBQ, and showers.

Lucy Wright Park
Located at Waimea on the southwest coast. From Highway 50, turn left on Alawai Road just past the bridge as you enter town. Campsites can be seen from the main highway on your left. The 4 ½ acre park has toilets, showers, swimming and surfing.

Salt Pond Beach Park
Located on the southwest coast. From Highway 50, turn left at Lele Road on the west side of Hanapepe town and stay on the road passing a veterans' cemetery. Turn right at Lolo Kai Road and continue for 1/4 mile passing the dry salt pond beds. Park on the left side of the road. This 6-acre park has pavilion, tables, toilets, showers, surfing, swimming and is a popular snorkeling area.

CANOES

Hawaiian Sailing Canoe trips offered ... see Hanalei Watersports listing in Scuba section.

CULTURAL TOURS: See Museums

DANCING

There are two dance groups that are active on the island. USABDA which is a national organization and the Hawaiian Ballroom Dance Association. For information on events contact Janine at her email address: jb@aloha.net

There are also dance opportunities, in limited degrees, at The Point at the Sheraton in Po'ipu, (808) 742-1661.

COMMON 'AMAKIHI

FISHING

FRESHWATER

Kaua'i offers some diverse fishing options. In addition to ocean excursions, you anglers will delight to learn that Kaua'i offers some outstanding freshwater fishing! Area reservoirs are home to several varieties of bass including the peacock bass (otherwise found only in Columbia and Venezuela). Since there is no restocking program, your outfitter will release all fish that are caught. Several areas are stocked with rainbow trout, although trout season is limited to the first 18 days of August and then only on weekends and holidays through September. And did you know that the largest body of fresh water in Hawai'i is found on Kaua'i? The 422 acre manmade reservoir is Lake Waita. With a potential to cover 841 acres, only Halali'i Lake on Ni'ihau would win out as being larger, however, it is not continually full. Check with the Department of Land and Natural Resources, Division of Aquatic Resources at (808) 274-3344 regarding licensing for freshwater fishing. Ask about seasonal (usually August-September) trout fishing at Koke'e!

Cast & Catch Fresh Water Bass Guides- They offer fresh water bass guided trips aboard their 17 ½ ' boat to catch large-mouth bass, peacock bass and small-mouth bass. Beverages and tackle supplied. Hotel and airport pick-up available!! A four hour trip is $115 for the first person, $190 for two, $260 for three or more. Eight hour trips also available. PO Box 1371, Koloa, HI 96756, (808) 332-9707.

JJ's Big Bass Tour - Sample bass fishing at one of the various reservoirs of Kaua'i. They supply tackle and refreshments along with hotel pick-up. The 17-ft. Monarch bass boat accommodates up to three people. A half day trip for one person is $110, full day $190, two persons $190 half day, $300 full day. 4550 Puuwai Road, Kalaheo, HI 96741, (808) 332-9219, pager (808) 654-4153.

OCEAN

On sport fishing charter boats in Hawai'i, the practice is that generally the boat retains the rights to any fish caught. This may come as a surprise to those of you anglers from other parts of the country. However, the captain will often cut enough for you and your family to enjoy for dinner, if you wish. You might wish to check with your boat captain/crew before the trip to determine their policy. Half day shared fishing trips run $75-$150 per person; half-day private charter can be $450 and up. Full day private charters can be $600 and up. Cold beverages and water are usually provided, but guests are expected to bring their own lunch and snacks.

'Anini Fishing Charters - This is a 33 ft. twin diesel sportfisher boat; specialize in sport and bottom fishing charters, Napali Coast tours. Rates are per person, shared boat: 4 hour $90; 6 hour $110; 8 hour $140. Call for latest private charter rates. Bob Kutkowski is the owner/operator of *Sea Breeze V.* (808) 828-1285; Email: kauaifishing@hawaiian.net; Web: < www.kauaifishing.com >

Captain Don's Sport Fishing and Ocean Adventures, Nawiliwili Harbor, Lihu'e, HI 96766, (808) 826-6264, 639-3012. This water adventure operator has a custom 22-ft. power catamaran for exploring Kaua'i's coastal areas for fishing, snorkeling, dolphin and whale watching, etc. Short-term 2-3-4 hour charters available. Call for current rates.

Capt. Harry's Sportfishing, Nawiliwili Harbor, Lihu'e, (808) 246-0399, 639-4351. The "Happy Hunter" is a 35-ft. Bertram Sportfisher fishes the south and east coasts of Kaua'i for all Hawaiian game fish, marlin, mahimahi, yellowfin tuna, ono, ulua, aku, etc. Call for latest rates.

Hana Pa'a Charters - Captain Tim and Julie Hale invite you aboard their 38' Bertram, the "Maka Hou." Exclusive and shared charters, night ahi fishing, trolling and bottom fishing, private sightseeing and whale watching. Departs Nawiliwili Small Boat Harbor, Lihu'e. (808) 823-6031. Call for latest rates.

Kai Bear Sportfishing Charters - Located at Nawiliwili Harbor, Lihu'e, the *Kai Bear* is a 38-foot Bertram Convertible Sportsfisher. It offers two staterooms with a galley at your disposal and adjacent salon with sofas, chairs, dining table, stereo, VCR, and television plus it is air-conditioned. (On their 8-hour charter *only*, fish are guaranteed! You'll receive your choice of a 3-5 lb. portion of the catch, or a $20 gift certificate for a fish dinner at one of Kaua'i's fine restaurants.) This is a professional outfit, with the crew in uniform. Maximum is six passengers. 4 hours $550, 6 hours $750, 8 hours $950 for private. Ask about their special for $149 each for four passengers for four hours. (They also have a 42' Bertram Luxury that departs Port Allen.) PO Box 3544, Princeville, HI 96722; (808) 639-4556, Fax (808) 826-4556; Web: <www.kaibearsportfishing.com>.

Kekaha Fishing Co., PO Box 1289, Kekaha, HI 96752-1289. (808) 337-2700; Email: gofish@hawaiian.net. The "Susan Lee" is a 34-ft. Fiberglass fisher, departs from Kekaha's Kikiaola Harbor in west Kaua'i. Charter fishing tours along west Kaua'i and Napali Coast. Seasonal whale watching too. Call for latest rates.

Lahela Ocean Adventures, Slip 109, Nawiliwili Harbor, Lihu'e, (808) 635-4020; Email:lahela-adventures@aloha.net;Web: <www.lahela-adventures.com> This 34-ft Sportfisher operator offers light tackle, sport or bottom fishing excursions, half or full-day, private or shared-charters. Fish for marlin, tuna, mahimahi, ono, ulua, and more. Snorkeling and whale watching too. Rates: Shared charter fishing, half-day economy $80, deluxe $150; private charter fishing, half-day $475, 3/4 day $550, full day $650.

McReynolds Fishing Charters - Shared and exclusive charters on their 30' Napali style Wilson fishing boat named *Ho'omaika'i*, which means to make good or thanksgiving. Half and full day trips on the North Shore fishing for marlin, ahi, mahimahi, aku, ono, ulua, kahala, kamanu, etc. Anini Beach, (808) 828-1379.

Napali Sportfishing, PO Box 569, Waimea, HI 96796, (808) 635-9424, 335-9909. This fully-equipped Bertram Sportfisher, the "Kai Runner II" does 4-6-8 hour fishing tours; fishing for blue markine, yellowfin tuna, mahimahi, ono, and aku. They take extended trips to Ni'ihau and other known fishing hotspots around Kaua'i. Call for latest rates.

Open Sea Charter Fishing, (808) 332-8213, departs Port Allen Harbor. This is a luxurious 36-ft. Hatteras, the "Carol Ann." Fishing the south and west shores of Kaua'i for marlin, ono, yellowfin tuna, aku, mahimahi, and shark. 4-6-8 hour fishing tours available. Call for latest rates.

Sport Fishing Kaua'i - This outfitter operates a fully-equipped Betram Sportfisher boat. Rates: Private charters for boat, half day $475, 3/4 day $675, full day $875, Ni'ihau tour $1075; share boat rates per person, half-day $95, 3/4 day $135; special rates for children too. PO Box 1195, Po'ipu, HI 96756, (808) 639-0013; Email: info@fishing-kauai-hawaii.com; Web: < www.fishing-kauai-hawaii.com >

Stand Up! Fishing Charters, PO Box 3650, Lihu'e, HI 96766, (808) 635-8862; Email: capt@fishingkauai.com; Web: < www.fishingkauai.com > This sport fishing charter boat departs from Po'ipu on the sunny South Shore. Fishing charter tours for mahimahi, ono, tuna, marlin, bottomfish, sharks, etc. Rates: Shared boat, half-day $110 per person, 6 hour $130 per person; private charter for boat, half-day $425, 6 hour $525, full day $675; night fishing charter, $750 for boat.

True Blue Charters - 55' Delta vessel *Konane Star* equipped with microwave, TV, VCR, hydrophone (whale listening device), hot and cold freshwater showers, restrooms. Half-day share trips (4 hr) $95-175, 3/4 day (6 hr) $125-225 (price reflects number of anglers). Exclusive charters $650-800. Spectators on share trips half price. Departs Nawiliwili Small Boat Harbor Slip #112. They also operate Island Adventures, kayak trips and Rainbow Runner Sailing aboard a 42' trimaran. PO Box 1722, Lihu'e, HI 96766, toll free 1-888-245-1707, (808) 246-6333. FAX (808) 246-9661. Website: < www.kauaifun.com > Email: funkauai@hawaiian.net

Wild Bill's Fishing Charters, PO Box 413, Kapa'a, HI 96746, Nawiliwili Harbor, Lihu'e, (808) 822-5963. This is a 28-ft. Radon Sportfisher; fish the south and east coasts of Kaua'i for marlin, ahi-yellow fin tuna, ono, mahimahi, aku and more. 4-6-8 hour fishing trips available. Call for latest rates.

FISHING SUPPLIES:

Lihu'e Fishing Supply, 2985 Kalena St. If the "big one gets away," you can always go next door to the Kalena Fish Market! (808) 245-4930.

Rainbow Paint & Fishing Supply Inc., Waialo Road, Hanapepe, (808) 335-6412; all you need to catch and land a trophy

GARDEN TOURS -- See Museums

GOLF

Kaua'i offers seven 18-hole golf courses at five different locations, plus one 9-hole course and one 10-hole course! Each course takes advantage of mountain and oceanviews and utilizes the natural elements of the island to add character to each course.

Stand-by Golf is a great option for you golfers interested in some serious savings. They feature discounted rates at public and private courses. They sell unsold tee times beginning about 6pm until 9pm for the next day of play and after 7 am for the same day. They book your game at a guaranteed price and time. Discounts range from 10% on the lowest priced courses up to 33% and more. Prices always include the cart. Definitely worth a phone call. They don't book municipal courses, however. Bookings are handled by telephone and you pay with a credit card. 1-888-645-2665.

GROVE FARM GOLF COURSE AT PUAKEA

4315 Kalepa Street, Lihu'e, HI 96766, 245-8756. This golf course is built on more than 200 acres of historic property which was once a sugar cane field. It is unusual with its massive ravines, lakes, and volcanic cliffs. Definitely more to the course than you might expect for central Kaua'i! Course rating is 76.2 with slope rating of 135. There are four tee boxes. Designed by architect Robin Nelson, the course is adjacent to the lot on which *Jurassic Park: The Lost World* was filmed. Reservations for the 10-hole course (yes that is TEN) can be made 30 days in advance. Lessons available. $65 for 20 holes, $50 after 2 pm; $45 for 10 holes. Website: < www.golfgrovefarm.com >

RECREATION AND TOURS
Golf

KAUA'I LAGOONS GOLF CLUB
3351 Ho'olaulea Way, Lihu'e, HI 96766. (808) 241-6000, or 1-800-634-6400. Facilities include a driving range, pro shop, putting green, restaurant, and bar. Tee times can be made 29 days in advance. Rental clubs and shoes available.

Kiele Course ★
This 18-hole, par 72 course is 7,070 yards and was designed by Jack Nicklaus. The course features deep ravines, ocean cliffs, and a wedding chapel. Each hole is named for an animal and a white marble statue of the animal adorns each tee. Golf Digest rated this course #3 in Hawai'i and #88 in the United States. With the nearby Kaua'i Lagoons Chapel by the Sea, perhaps this is the perfect course for the groom-to-be to combine a few holes of golf before or after the ceremony! General public $170, Kaua'i Marriott guests $120, other Kaua'i hotel guests $130.

Mokihana Course ★
Designed by Jack Nicklaus, this 18-hole course (par 72) has 6,942 yards of play. This course was named in honor of the mokihana, the "official flower" of the island of Kaua'i and undergone some soft renovations with enhancements to the landscaping. This course is less demanding than Kiele, but the Scottish links style course is popular with the recreational golfer. It has a forgiving layout with wide fairways and four tees for all skill levels. Green fees general public $85; Kaua'i Marriott guests $75; after 11 am $65 and $55.

KIAHUNA GOLF CLUB
2545 Kiahuna Plantation Drive, Koloa, HI 96756. (808) 742-9595. Located in Po'ipu. Robert Trent Jones, Jr. designed this 18-hole, par 70 course. Kiahuna features ocean and mountain views, as well as some surprises. Lava rock walls, a huge lava tube, a Blind Eye Spider cave, and other Hawaiian archaeological sites add to the personality of this course as it winds around remnants of an ancient Hawaiian Village. Championship 6,353 yards. Facilities include driving range, pro shop, putting green, snack shop, and bar. Green fees, including cart: $75 morning; after 2:30 pm $45.

KUKUIOLONO GOLF COURSE ★
Located on Papalina Road, Kalaheo, 332-9151. Open 6:30am-6:30pm. no tee-offs after 4:50pm. This public course is situated on top of Kukuiolono Park and the fourth and fifth holes have spectacular views. This course features ample fairways, a Japanese garden, and ancient Hawaiian rock structures. Play is on a first-come basis, no reservations. The 9 holes are a par 36, with 2,981 yards of play. Facilities include a driving range, pro shop, putting green, and snack shop. Golf club rentals available. At $7 for all day play, it is hard to go wrong. This course is usually very crowded. We suggest you tee off about 3pm: you get through a fair part of the course (and see that spectacular view at the 4th and 5th hole) and for the price it doesn't matter if you don't finish. Carts are optional at $6.

PO'IPU BAY RESORT GOLF COURSE ★

2250 Ainako St., Koloa, HI 96756. (808) 742-8711. Po'ipu Bay Resort Golf Course is an 18-hole championship course situated on 210 oceanfront acres adjacent to the Hyatt Regency Kaua'i Resort and Spa. The course is a Scottish links style course with a par 72 designed by Robert Trent Jones, Jr. It boasts some outstanding ocean vistas and seven holes with water hazards. Set between lush mountains and rugged ocean bluffs, the course includes over 35 acres of landscaped tropical plants and flowers. An archeological site that has been incorporated into the course. During winter, golfers can even catch glimpses of the whales as they pass off-shore. And don't be surprised if you see some *nene* geese wandering about. It's an absolutely beautiful course to play and can be subject to strong winds from mid-morning on. Over the years Po'ipu Bay has won numerous awards and has consistently been rated among the top golf courses in the U.S. and Hawai'i. It has been rated the #1 golf course in Hawai'i on the Gold List as chosen by the readers of Conde Nast Traveler. Since 1994 the course has played host to the annual PGA Grand Slam of Golf, hosting golf luminaries like Tiger Woods and company. Greens fees: Hyatt Hotel guest before noon $120, $105 after; others $170 before noon, $115 after; after 3 pm $65. They also feature a half-off Junior Golf Special Rate for kids 17 years and under when accompanied by a paying adult. Inquire about any special hotel guest or other discounted rates; also check their daily clinics and lessons. Facilities include a driving range, pro shop, clubhouse (with restaurant, lounge, and snackbar), putting green, and practice sand bunkers. Golfers can also reserve tee-times through the internet. The online book service is operated through EZLinks Golf, Inc. at < www.ezlinksgolf.com > For more information on the Po'ipu Bay course check out the website at < www.kauai-hyatt.com//golf.html >

PRINCEVILLE GOLF CLUB

Located at the Princeville Resort, 5-3900 Kuhio Highway, Princeville, HI 96722. (808) 826-5000. 1-800-826-4400.

Makai Course ★

4080 Leiopapa Road, Princeville, 826-3580. Designed by Robert Trent Jones, Jr., this is actually three courses rolled into 27 holes: The Lakes, The Ocean, and The Woods are each nine holes, par 36 with the clubhouse at the hub. With waterfalls, beaches, mountains, and the spectacular Mt. Makana (Bali Hai) as backdrops, it's a spectacular setting. Facilities include driving range, pro shop, putting green, and snackbar. The Prince Course has been listed in Golf Digest Top Resort Courses and in America's 100 Greatest Golf Courses for the last 16 years. The Makai Course has hosted the LPGA Women's Kemper Open more than once. $120 regular rate, $105 for Princeville area guests, $100 for Princeville Hotel guests. Twilight rate (after 1:30pm) is $80. Sunset rate (after 4pm) is $45. An additional round is $35. Club rental $35, shoe rental $15, riders fee $25.

Prince Course ★

5-3900 Kuhio Highway, Princeville, 826-5000. This 18-hole layout is a par 72 with 7,309 yards of play. Scenic vistas include the rugged cliffsides and the famous "Bali Hai" location. The course fits snugly along the cliffsides of Kaua'i's North Shore with hole #13 featuring a waterfall backdrop. With a USGA course rating of 75.3, this course is ranked as the most challenging in the state.

However, multiple tees on each hole accommodate the casual golfer as well. Driving range, pro shop, putting greens, restaurant, and bar are available. Golf Digest ranks this course #1 in the state of Hawai'i and in the top 50 in the United States. It is one of eleven courses in the U.S. to have a 5-Star rating. The Prince Course charges $175 standard rate, $145 for Princeville area guests, and $125 for Princeville Hotel guests. Rates after noon are $115 standard rate for all; $55 replay rate.

WAILUA MUNICIPAL GOLF COURSE ★
Located at 3-5351 Kuhio Hwy., Lihu'e, HI 96766 (808) 241-6666, on the eastern shore between Lihu'e and Kapa'a. The course features an 18-hole, 6,981-yard, par 72 layout and is considered by some to be the best municipal course in the state, With shaded ponds, Pacific Ocean views, and fairly low green fees, this is a great option for the budget traveler who really wants to golf but can't afford the much higher fees at the resort courses. The only cheaper course is Kukuiolono at Kalaheo. Facilities include a driving range, pro shop, putting green, restaurant, and bar. $32 weekday, $44 on weekends and holidays. Ask about their afternoon specials. Club rental $15. Charge is $20 per cart (cart is optional). This is a very busy course with many local folks golfing here.

HANG GLIDING

Birds in Paradise is an opportunity to experience hang glider ultralight flying. Tandem instructional tours are offered in these powered ultralights and a wing mounted video of your flight is available. Mini-Intro Lesson 25-30 minute $100; Full Intro Lesson 50-60 minutes $175; Advanced Lesson 80-90 minutes $255; Round-the-Island Lesson 110-120 minutes $330; Microlight Pilot Certification is typically 10-12 hours, inquire on certification. Port Allen Airport, #543 Lele Road, Hanapepe, HI 96716, (808) 822-5309, FAX (808) 822-5309. Email: birdip@birdsinparadise.com; Web: < www.birdsinparadise.com >

HELICOPTERS

A helicopter tour will set you back some bucks, but it may be an experience that is worth every penny. If you do take a flight, it is suggested that you wait until mid-way in your island vacation, even a little longer, before experiencing the island by helicopter. It is much more interesting to see the island's landmarks by air having first had a close hand look at them on land. It is a chance to view some wonderful sights that can be seen only by air. Helicopters fly around Kaua'i in a clockwise direction, so seating on the right side of the craft offers the best viewing. However, the seat assignment is based on weight and yes, they sometimes have you step on a scale to make sure you are honest. Some helicopter companies are owner-operated and brochures often talk about the owner's flying experience. In some cases, this may not be the person piloting your helicopter tour. In other cases, you'll find that it is indeed the owner that operates each and every tour. Flights depart from Lihu'e Airport and Princeville Airport. The State Department of Transportation recently added the Port Allen Airport (also known as Burns Field) near Hanapepe to the list.

Some revisions in regulations regarding kids! Children 1-35 lbs. must have an "infant" life preserver. Children 36-90 lbs. must have a "child" life preserver. Over 90 lbs. are considered an adult and must have an "adult" life preserver. Up to a child's second birthday, they are permitted to sit on the parent's lap. For a single engine flight over water EVERYONE **must** wear a vest. For a twin-engine flight over water, a vest is not required, but must be easily accessible. On Kaua'i, most tours include a scenic pass along the Napali Coast. Due to weather conditions, and just the view vantage point, the flights must be able to fly out over the water. The only company on Kaua'i currently operating a dual rotor helicopter is Heli USA Helicopters. While most young children don't go on helicopter trips, we were told that there are lots of infants that go as "lap riders." So inquire if you are traveling with a babe in arms, or want to take a youngster up!

Air Kaua'i Helicopter Tours - Chuck DiPiazza and staff fly air conditioned AStars with a two way intercom and custom bubble windows providing exceptional visibility. They are also equipped with a compact disc player and a special noise cancelling system. They offer one concise tour, a 1-hr deluxe air experience that includes Waimea Canyon, Napali, and Wai'ale'ala for $195 per person. Inquire on direct bookings for discounts. The ride is seamless, no jerky stops and starts, with just the right music and narration to accompany a comfortable flight. The pilot skillfully flies close to the magnificent Napali, flying in and out between layers and ridges, so close you can almost reach out and touch them. These are canyon views you've never seen! Kaua'i has magnificent scenery, and seeing it by helicopter is definitely an option to be considered during your island vacation. Toll free 1-800-972-4666, (808) 246-4666, FAX (808) 246-3966. Email for reservations: heliop@aloha.net; Email for information: info@airkauai.com; Web: <www.airkauai.com>

Bali Hai Helicopter Tours - On Highway 50, Hanapepe, next to Lappert's Ice Cream Shop on way to Waimea. Departs from Port Allen Airport. Owner-operated by James Lee and his staff. Family discounts. 4 passenger Bell 206B Jet Ranger helicopter. They are close to Waimea Canyon and the Napali Coast, less time in the air just getting there and more time seeing all the scenic magic of Kaua'i. Two basic tours: Bali Hai Grandeur Tour 55-60 minutes $139 per person; Bali Hai Splendor Tour 45-50 minutes $110 per person. PO Box 626, Hanapepe, HI 96716. Toll free 1-800-325-TOUR, (808) 335-3166, Fax (808) 335-5615. Email: blh@aloha.net; Web: <www.balihai-helitour.com>

HeliUSA - Departs Princeville Resort Airport. They fly Astars. Three basic air tours are offered and take in the major scenic highlights of Kaua'i. The 30 minute Bali Hai is $99 per person. The 45 minute Garden Isle Special is $135 per person. The 60 minute Garden Isle Deluxe is $179 per person. Toll free 1-866-936-1234, (808) 826-6591; Web: <www.heliusa.com>

Inter-Island Helicopters - Operates Hughes 500 with two sit-up-front and two-sit-in-back seats, each have their own window. They like to fly with the doors off so photos will come out clear and their two-way intercom allows communication between pilot and other passengers. They fly from Port Allen Airport in Hanapepe. The one-hour tour covers Olokele Canyon, 3 valleys of the Waimea Canyon, then over Koke'e to Napali Coast. They also have a 1 hour-45 minute

Waterfall Adventure tour that includes a stop at their private landing pad and a short walk on the boardwalk to the Pu'u Ka Ele waterfall with time for a picnic lunch and a quick swim in the pond. Waterfall weddings are also available. PO Box 156, Hanapepe, HI 96716, (808) 335-5009, Fax (808) 335-5567.

Island Helicopters - Flies AStar helicopters and also a 6 passenger A-Star. Depart from Lihu'e. They specialize in just one tour, the "Kaua'i Grand" of 55-60 minutes length which takes in all the major scenic attractions of Kaua'i. Per person rate, $200; from Lihu'e Airport. PO Box 831, Lihu'e, HI 96766. Toll free 1-800-829-5999, (808) 245-8588, Fax (808) 245-6258. Email: fly@islandhelicopters.com; Web: <www.islandhelicopters.com>

Jack Harter Helicopters - Flies Bell Jet Ranger, tours depart Lihu'e Airport. Jack originated helicopter tours on Kaua'i in the '60s. They offer two standard air tours and cover all the major scenic attractions of Kaua'i. The 60-65 minute flight runs $165 per person; the 90-95 minute flight is $235 per person. Toll free 1-888-245-2001, (808) 245-3774; Email: jharter@aloha.net; Web: <www.helicopters-kauai.com>

Ni'ihau Helicopters - Flies an Augusta helicopter which departs from Hanapepe. The flight circles Ni'ihau and lands briefly on one of the beaches. They are a little difficult to reach with short office hours and tour offerings are limited to mostly hunting and fishing excursions only. PO Box 370, Makaweli, HI 96769. (808) 335-3500. FAX (808) 338-1463.

Ohana Helicopter Tours - Flies AStar, departures from Lihu'e Airport. Owner-pilot Bogard Kealoha is a "local boy," born and raised on Kaua'i. There are two separate tours offered. The 50-55 minute Mokihana tour is $146 per person; the 60-75 minute Maile tour is $186. Both tour take in all the scenic beauty of Kaua'i major attractions and features. Toll free 1-800-222-6989, (808) 245-3996, Fax (808) 245-5041; Email: info@ohana-helicopters.com; Web: <www.ohana-helicopters.com>

Safari Helicopters - Flies the AStar and departs from Lihu'e Airport. Their three and four camera video/sound system with two-way intercom captures your trip with pilot's narration. They offer one basic Kaua'i air tour, the 55-minute Deluxe Waterfall Safari for $149-189 seasonal rate per person; check out the internet booking special for $139. PO Box 1941, Lihu'e, HI 96766. (808) 246-0136, or toll free 1-800-326-3356. Email: info@safarihelicopters.com; Web: <www.safariair.com>

South Sea Helicopters - Departs Lihu'e Airport, flies Bell Jet Ranger. Seasonal rates available, inquire when booking. Choose the 45-50 minute "Kaua'i Special Flight" air tour at $115-135 per person; or the 55-60 minute "Golden Eagle Flight" air tour at $130-160 per person; or the 70-75 minute "Flight of the Canyon Bird" air tour at $173-198 per person. Tours take in the best of Kaua'i's scenic highlights. Lihu'e Airport, 3901 Mokulele Loop, Box 32, Lihu'e, HI 96766, toll free 1-800-367-2914, (808) 245-2222, Fax (808) 246-9586. Email: 2ssh@gte.net; Web: <www.southseahelicopters.com>

Will Squyres Helicopter Tours - Will Squyres began his company in 1984 with twenty-two years of flying experience. He uses 6 passenger A-Stars. The "Ultimate Kaua'i Adventure" air tour is 60-65 minutes and will visit the Waimea Canyon, the Napali Coastline, Wai'ale'ale Crater and, the famous *Jurassic Park* waterfall, as well as settings used in many other films made on Kaua'i. Per person cost is $159; private charters for 1-6 people available at $950. Tours depart Lihu'e Airport. PO Box 1770, Lihu'e, HI 96766, toll free 1-888-245-4354, (808) 245-8881; Email: squyres@aloha.net; Web: <www.helicopters-hawaii.com>

HIKING

Also see section on *CAMPING* in this chapter for detailed information on several hiking trails.

The Hawai'i State Department of Land and Natural Resources, Division of Forestry & Wildlife has trail maps of Kaua'i available. Maps are free if you go in person. If you are contacting them in advance, you will need to send a self-addressed stamped envelope with your request and probably a small fee for handling. Call or write for requirements to the Department of Land and Natural Resources, Division of Forestry and Wildlife, 3060 Eiwa St., #306, Lihu'e, HI 96766. (808) 274-3433.

Also check the Na Ala Hele Trail and Access System website for full details on hiking trails throughout the Hawaiian Islands along with relevant hiking information. See, web: <www.hawaiitrails.org>

Holistic Nature Walks, (808) 822-0493, with Dawn "Ka'ula Wena" Cantrell. Dawn has lived on Kaua'i since 1987 as a dedicated artisan, tarot reader, empathic healer and all-around fun person. Join her on an excursion to discover the special nature of Kaua'i. Stroll through a magic bamboo forest, bathe in sacred healing waters, see lush serene beauty of Nature, seek your personal "Aumakua" guardian spirit, create your own aloha spirit amulet. Discover Kaua'i, differently.

GREAT FRIGATE BIRD   JBAYOT

Inner Kaua'i, PO Box 441, Kilauea, HI 96754. (808) 826-1963; Email: paulw@lava.net; Web: <www.paulwaters.com> This guide service offers hiking, museum and cultural activities promoting adventure, culture and discovery on Kaua'i. Hikes range from the mountains to the sea, for couples and large groups, easy to difficult, and half or full day. Rates range from $40-85 per person and include backpacks, food, water and hiking sticks. Contact them for full details.

Island Enchantment Adventure Tours - This operator offers accommodations packages combined with a 6-8 day tour. Their outdoor adventures/hikes are combined with an opportunity to learn and practice the elements of yoga, body/mind techniques, meditation, and massage. They have day excursions that visit jungle waterfalls, wade in mountain pools, swim at secluded beaches and explore the coral reefs. You can also arrange for a one-day custom tour at $75 per person. Located in Anahola, Kaua'i, on the northeast coast. 1-888-281-6292. (808) 823-0705. Email: enchant@aloha.net; Web: <www.aloha.net/~enchant/Kauai.html>

Kaua'i Adventure Trek ★, 3-2087 Kaumualii Highway, Lihu'e, HI 96766; (808) 245-3440, cell 635--8735; Email: inquiries@kauaiadventuretrek.com; Web: <www.kauaiadventuretrek.com> This outfitter combines half-day adventure treks with biking, hiking and optional swimming. The trek involves a bike ride through the fabled estate of Grove Farm Plantation, once a leading sugar cane plantation. The trek follows meandering backcountry cane roads through the scenic grazing lands and mountains of Haiku country between Lihu'e and Koloa. Bikers pass through the long dark tunnel of the old cane road separating the east side of the island from the south side. The ride continues gradually downhill through rolling hills and fields to the abandoned Koloa Sugar Mill for a stop. The trek continues through fields of coffee, corn and papaya groves to the beach on the Po'ipu coast. A picnic lunch stop on the beach provides time to relax and savor the beautiful beach of the South Shore. Trekkers can swim or explore the beach before heading to the last leg, a short hike over the hilly coastline of Mahaulepu to a lovely secluded beach and cove. Informative guided narration details the history, culture, and heritage of this region of Kaua'i. This is an excellent family-adventure, for young and old alike. Safe mountain bikes included; tandem bikes available. Picnic lunch and drinks. Two treks daily 8:15 a.m. and 10 a.m., from Kilohana Plantation (Gaylord's). Rates: $85 per person.

Kaua'i Mountain Tours - Mike and Terri Hopkins, under Aloha Kauai Tours, operate a number of hiking excursions into different trails and areas of Kaua'i. They also offer water/kayak and land tours; check the website for details. Hikes range from easy to moderate to difficult, some combine van or 4WD offroad vehicle rides to more remote trailheads. Hikes cover areas like Koloa to Mahaulepu Coast and Kilohana Crater with a beautiful 360 degree island view. There is also a trek to Blue Hole near Mt. Waialeale in the island's interior, plus other hikes through Kaua'i's splendid Koke'e Park, Waimea Canyon trails, koa forests and much more. Rates: Kaua'i Backroads Half Day $50, kids $44; Aloha Kaua'i Tour Full Day $90, kids $63; Blue Hole Half Day $65, kids $50. Aloha Kaua'i Tours, 1702 Haleukaua Street, Lihu'e, HI 96766. Toll free 1-800-452-1113, (808) 245-7224. Email: tours@gte.net; Web: <www.alohakauaitours.com>

Kaua'i Nature Tours offers day trips with short hikes led by experienced local guides. Choose from a number of interpretative tours, including Waimea Canyon Explorer, Na Pali Hiking Adventure, Kaua'i's Mountain Forest, Mahaulepu Coast Hike, and Beaches of Kaua'i Excursion. Tour/hike rates: $82, kids 12 and under $45. These unique day-long tours include transportation, a picnic lunch and refreshments. Hikers should be reasonably fit, have good walking shoes and sun protection. Most of the tours leave from Po'ipu Beach Park at 9am and return by 4pm. Napali Coast Hike includes east and north side pickup and dropoff or Ke'e Beach rendezvous. Also available are week long adventure vacations. PO Box 549, Koloa, HI 96756. 1-808-742-8305, toll free 1-888-233-8365. Email: teok@aloha.net; Web: <www.teok.com>

Keiki Adventures Kaua'i, Nature/Eco-Tours for kids -- Tours include a hike at a moderate pace and distance for keikis, swimming in hidden waterfall pools, guided snorkeling tour including instruction, healthy lunch and snacks, rain gear, day packs. This company specializes in ECO tours for kids with guides explaining Hawaiian history as well as background on the native Hawaiian rain forest, coral reef life and scenic sights such as Waimea Canyon. Japanese interpretation available. 1-800-232-6699 (808) 822-7823.

Olokele Canyon Overlook Tour, Gay & Robinson Tours, Kaumakani Avenue, Kaumakani, HI 96747, (808) 335-2824; Email: toursgnr@aloha.net; Web: <www.gandrtours-kauai.com> This 3 ½ hour excursion combines an offroad vehicle or van ride plus some limited hiking on a tour of sugar plantation fields, a working cattle ranch and the irrigation system at Makaweli on Kaua'i's south side. This tour takes in the Olokele Canyon Overlook and the water intake at Olokele Canyon. Learn about the Gay & Robinson Plantation, Makaweli Ranch, the 1904 Olokele Ditch System, history, culture, flora and fauna of the area.

Princeville Ranch Hiking Adventures - This outfitter/guide offers three different adventures. The Hidden Hanalei Hike is 3 hours, easy to moderate, hiking trails around Hanalei Bay and to Mt. Namolokama, $59 per person. The Waterfall Excursion is 4 hours, a moderate loop trail, through lush ranch uplands with panoramic overlook and plunging 100-ft. Kalihiwai Falls, $74 per person. A new Jungle Waterfall Adventure combines a kayaking excursion up a jungle stream and short hike through the jungle to a waterfall, $89 per person. Kids 12 and under and seniors get a 10 percent discount. They provide daypacks, water bottles, healthy snacks, walking sticks, tabis (special Japanese shoes for walking through water), even rain gear (just in case) plus informative and educational insight into the history, culture, flora and fauna of the area. PO Box 224, Hanalei, HI 96714. Toll free 1-888-955-7669, (808) 826-7669, Fax (808) 826-7210. Email: prha@aloha.net; Web: <www.kauai-hiking.com>

The Sierra Club publishes a quarterly newsletter, *Malama*, available by subscription for $7 per year. A sample of the newsletter can be received by writing them, including a $1 fee and a self-addressed and stamped envelope. Also available is *Hiking Softly in Hawai'i*, a guide to the enjoyment of the Hawaiian wilderness with useful information on how to obtain hiking and camping permits, etc. Available for $4 from the Sierra Club. Sierra Club, Hawai'i Chapter, PO Box 2577, Honolulu, HI 96803.

Visitors can write to the Kaua'i group a couple of months prior to their arrival and request a schedule by sending a self-addressed stamped envelope and a $1 fee. Bob Nishek on Kaua'i (808) 822-9238, has offered to provide our readers with the latest hiking information. Advance registration is necessary for all outings in the event of last minute changes due to inclement weather. They suggest a $3 donation for each person participating in the outings. Several excellent references are available for the interested hiker. See ordering information at the back of this guide. Craig Chisholm is the author of *Kaua'i Hiking Trails, Hawaiian Hiking Trails,* and *Hawai'i: The Big Island Hiking Trails.* His guides provide excellent topographical maps, good directions, and detailed information including the number of calories you can expect to burn, time required to travel the trail round trip, and elevation.

During June and continuing through September, the Koke'e Natural History Museum offers a series of guided hikes in the scenic uplands of West Kaua'i. Hikes are twice weekly and are led by one of the trained volunteers of the Koke'e Natural History Museums. The hikes vary in length and in difficulty and since space is limited, call ahead to reserve your spot. A $2 donation is requested. Tours include a hike along cliff and canyon trails to Waipo'o Falls, hikes along the fairly strenuous Pihea trail or a family hike along Berry Flats Trail. Along the way your interpretative guide will explain about the flora and fauna discovered on your hike. For dates and times of hikes call (808) 335-9975.

Kalalau Trail/Napali Coast

This time-worn trail of eleven miles starts next to Ke'e Beach at the end of Hwy. 56. There you will find parking, bathrooms, and showers. A sign at the beginning of the trail will provide you with all the pertinent information you will need for your hike. (Maps, permits, mileage, restrictions, etc.) The first two miles/one hour to Hanakapi'ai and additional 1.8 miles/45 minutes to Hanakapi'ai Falls is as far as most people go. Though this hike is relatively short, it is strenuous so it is advisable to bring your own drinking water and snacks. The first half of the Kalalau Trail is more lush with many native plants interspersed with wild orchids and ginger along with papaya and mango trees. Ancient terraced rock walls used for taro-growing are visible and in surprisingly good shape. Further along this pristine coast, there are prehistoric valleys of green velvet, cascading waterfalls, ancient Hawaiian *heiaus*, turquoise water, and ominous sea cliffs. During whale season, these magnificent creatures can be spotted from the trail as they breech out of the water. The coastline is beautiful with incredible vistas from many promontories all the way into Kalalau. This final destination has a refreshing waterfall for bathing. Hikers venturing on from Hanakapi'ai will need overnight camping permits which you can get from the State Parks Office.

Koke'e State Park/Waimea Canyon Trails System

There are numerous hiking trails in the Koke'e State Park and adjoining Waimea Canyon. Only a couple of the trails are highlighted here. It is suggested that hikers obtain maps, brochures, and trail guides for details on the hiking trails in these areas.

Upper and Lower Waipo'o Falls
Access this trailhead 1.4 miles below (south) Koke'e Lodge on the Koke'e Road at Halemanu Road. Parking is on both sides of the road. Follow Halemanu Road .8 miles to the trailhead. A marked trail junction indicates the Canyon and Black Pipe Trails. Past this is a second junction, hang left on the Canyon Trail.

The Upper and Lower Waipo'o Falls and Canyon Trail hike is one of the Waimea Canyon's more enjoyable. This is a moderately difficult 3.2 mile round trip of about 2 ½ to 3 hours. The trail passes through the cool montane forest alive with the sounds of birdlife everywhere and winds down deeper into the canyon, crossing a small stream and coming to a bare knoll. There are great views of the surrounding colorful walls and cliffs of Po'omau Canyon. There are also some surprising wind-eroded rock arches high on the cliffsides. Below this bare knoll a short distance is Koke'e Stream with the Upper Falls to the left. To the right, the main trail leads to the Lower Falls.

The Upper Waipo'o Falls has a large pool and is surrounded by boulders, rocky outcroppings and heavy vegetation. It's a great place to relax and stick you feet in the water. The Lower Waipo'o Falls, a short distance down stream, has several smaller pools and spreads out into showering cascades as it tumbles down a sheer drop. Avoid going too close to the edge! Find a rock or grassy patch to sit on and enjoy your picnic lunch while basking in the magnificent canyon views. It's an incredible experience in solitude. Take food, water and sun protection.

Awa'awaphui
The Awaawapuhi Trail, one of twenty-nine trails in *Kaua'i Hiking Trails*, is reprinted here with permission. Author Craig Chisholm comments that this trail takes a bit more effort than some, but "it is well-marked and the view at its end is, in my opinion, the most impressive in Hawai'i." This trail is located in the Koke'e area. It is 2 1/4 hours up and 1 1/2 hours down. Round trip on this is 6.5 miles. The highest point is 4,100 feet and the lowest point is 2,560 feet. While this trail may be a bit rugged for the family travel with younger children, there are many other trails outlined in Chisholm's that are less strenuous and of shorter duration.

Awesome views of the Napali Coast and its isolated, hanging valleys make this trail one of the best for photography in Hawai'i. The trail descends 1,500 feet through native dryland forests to twin viewpoints above the sheer cliffs that drop into the remote Awa'awapuhi and Nualolo Valleys. The floors of these rarely visited valleys are accessible only by water and then only after difficult climbing from the sea. However, the viewpoints provide good vantage points of the valleys and the great fluted walls enclosing them. From the hiking trail, there are numerous beautiful panoramic sights of valleys and forest wilderness.

The various scenic viewpoints afford a good opportunity to watch the sunlight and shadows play on the cliffs and sea. Mornings and afternoons, helicopters flutter like dragonflies in and out of the steep-cliffed valleys below while cruise boats zip along the coast. It's a moderately-difficult hike, about 2-2.5 hours one way. Nice overlook and grassy rest point at trail's end.

401

Take plenty of water and food. Trail is in very good condition most of the way and marked about every quarter to half-mile. It's a 6.5 mile round trip. The Division of Forestry and Wildlife has marked many endemic plants along the route and has published an interpretive guide which is available at the office in Lihu'e or the Koke'e Museum.

Route: From Koke'e State Park Headquarters go 1.6 miles up Highway 550 toward the Kalalau Lookout. The trail-head is on the left, in the Napali-Kona Forest Reserve, across from a dirt road and just before the 17-mile mark on the Highway. At first the broad trail leads north and goes up a little. It then descends (with switchbacks), generally in a northwesterly direction. Along the way there are many numbered and labelled endemic bushes and trees. At approximately 3 miles form the start, the Nualolo Cliff Trail, which is a connector from the Nualolo Trail, leads in from the left (south). Soon after this junction, the Awa'awapuhi Trail ends at the metal-railed viewpoints overlooking the sea, great cliffs, white-tailed tropic birds, and the inevitable 8am helicopters. Do not go close to the rims of the canyons. The small stones covering the hard surfaces on the eroded areas, like ball bearings on concrete, provide treacherous footing. The drop to the valley floor on either side is between 1,500 and 3,000 feet, depending on the bounce. The plants in the native dryland forest are rare and the danger of fires extreme; thus, neither overnight camping nor fires are permitted. Water is unavailable. Take your own food and water.

HORSEBACK RIDING

Horseback trail ride enthusiasts are afforded the opportunity to enjoy some of Kaua'i's most breathtaking scenery. On the North Shore, you can take a four-hour ride to a mountain waterfall. Near Waimea, visitors can enjoy the island's only ocean rides while watching the sun sinking slowly over the island of Ni'ihau. At Po'ipu Beach, a three-hour breakfast trail ride encompasses scenic views of the ocean, beaches, and mountains. These are among a few of the offerings from Kaua'i's horseback trailride outfitters listed below.

CJM Country Stables - Owner Jimmy Miranda and his crew will take you into hidden valley ranch land, past secluded beaches and bays to discover the pictur-esque beauty of the Po'ipu area of Kaua'i on horseback. The Secret Beach Breakfast Ride is a 3 hour ride which includes gourmet cowboy coffee and continental breakfast, three days weekly on Tues-Thurs-Sat, $75 per person. The Hidden Beach Ride is a 2 hour ride through the ancient Mahaulepu are of the south shore's Po'ipu area, twice daily except Sunday, $65 per person. The Beach Swim/Picnic Ride is a 3 ½ hour beach swim and riding excursion with a picnic lunch included, three times weekly Mon-Wed-Fri, $90 per person. Located 1 ½ miles past the Hyatt Regency Kaua'i Hotel at 1731 Kelaukia Street, Koloa, HI 96756, (808) 742-6096, FAX (808) 742-6015; Email: cjm@aloha.net; Web: <www. cjmstables.com>.

Espirit De Corps Riding Academy - The standard 3 hour Fast Half Ride includes trotting and cantering with panoramic ocean and mountain views, $99 per person. The 5 hour WOW!!! Ride passes along ridges of an old lava flow, and exotic beauty of Kaua'i's mountains and meadow uplands, snack included, $250 for minimum of 3 guests/5 maximum. An ALL DAY ADVENTURE Ride is 8 hours and includes a stop at a mountain swimming hole and lunch, $350, for minimum of 2 guests or $300 for minimum of 4 guests. Private "Honeymoon Rides" available. Private rides with longer arena lesson are available for the less experienced rider. Private lessons are also available. PO Box 269, Kapa'a, Kaua'i, HI 96746, or (808) 822-4688. Email: riding@kauaihorses.com; Web: <www.KauaiHorses.com>

Keapana Horsemanship - This outfitter offers specialized and private horseback riding adventures. Ride retired show champions through native Hawaiian old growth forest, with superb scenery and panoramic views, all the scenic vistas and sights of east Kaua'i, learn the history, legends, heritage, culture of the area. Located on the north side of Kapa'a in Keapana Valley. Varied length trail rides: 1 ½ hour Keapana Valley & Bluff Ride, $89 per person, 2 hour Kalalea View Ride, $119 per person, 3 hour Kalalea Exploration Ride, $195 per person; custom rides on state trail system available with advance reservation. (808) 823-9303; Email: lara@aloha.net; Web: <www.keapana.com>

Princeville Ranch Stables / Adventures on Horseback - A family owned business since 1978, Donn and Gale Carswell offer a variety of trail rides. Minimum age is 8 years. All riders must be in good physical condition. Weight limit restrictions, 180 lbs. for women, 220 pounds for men. Long pants recommended, closed shoes are a must. The 3 ½ hour Waterfall Ride involves riding across ranch land and a short, steep hike (without the horse) down to the base of the Kalihiwai Falls (about 10 minutes), includes a picnic lunch and a swim, the trip takes about four hours, $110 per person. The 2 hour Cattle Drive Ride shows you what it's like to be a real Hawaiian paniolo (cowboy), rounding up cattle at sunrise and driving them across ranchlands to a corral, $125 per person. The Anini Bluff & Beach Ride is a 3 hour adventure along a scenic bluff to spectacular Anini Beach, light snack and swimming at beach included, $100 per person. The Panoramic Paniolo Country Ride is a fantastic 1 ½ hour ride across Princeville Ranch taking in all the scenic vistas of the magnificent Hanalei Mountains, Anini Beach and distant Bali Hai, $55 per person. Most rides offered daily except Sunday. PO Box 888, Hanalei, HI 96714, (808) 826-6777, 826-7473, Fax (808) 826-7210; Email: pstable@aloha.net; Web: <www.kauai.net/kwc4>

Princeville Ranch Wagon Rides - Princeville Ranch offers a unique Sunset Barbecue Dinner Ride, a relaxing horse-drawn wagon ride through the ranch lands, along the bluff above beautiful Anini Beach with scenic sunset vistas. Enjoy a hearty ranch steak barbecue at the cookout shelter; includes narration on history and culture, Hawaiian entertainment, and dinner, $85 per person. They also offer a Hapa Laka Lunch Ride, similar to the dinner ride but with ranch hamburgers, $45 per person. And there is a separate 45 minute Ranch Tour by Wagon, $25 per person. PO Box 672, Hanalei, HI 96714. (808) 826-1677; Email: prdraft@aloha.net; Web: <www.princevilleranch.com>

Silver Falls Ranch Trail Rides - This outfitter has various trail rides through the Mount Namahana area near Kilauea in the North Shore region. The 1 ½ hour Greenhorns Trail Ride is for beginners and scaredy cats (gulp!) and focuses on basic riding skills, $69 per person. The 2 hour Hawaiian Discovery Ride takes in beautiful and peaceful country forest settings and great views along Mount Namahana, $78 per person. The 3 hour Silver Falls Ride takes in a natural mountain pool and waterfall combining a great trail ride, swim, and a picnic lunch, $105 per person. Private rides also available. PO Box 692, Kilauea, HI 96754, (808) 828-6718, Fax (808) 828-0131; Email: sfr@hawaiian.net; Web: <www.hawaiian.net/~sfr>

HUNTING/SHOOTING RANGES

There are no commerical hunting guides currently operating on Kaua'i. Those interested in hunting might inquire with the hunting shop listed below. For hunting information on Kaua'i contact the Department of Land & Natural Resources, Wildlife Division. They can help you with enforcement and licensing information as well as hunting guidelines. (808) 274-3433. Public hunting areas allow seasonal hunting for game birds such as ring-necked pheasant, Erckel's Francolin, chukar partridge, Japanese quail, doves and others. Seasonal hunting is also allowed for wild feral goats, wild pig and black-tailed deer.

The Hunting Shop of Kaua'i is a full service fire arms and hunting shop, including archery. Only authorized Matthews dealer. They also do repairs. 3156 Oihana in Lihu'e. (808) 245-3006. Shooter's Paradise is also located here and is an indoor shooting range. Firearm Safety training courses offered. (808) 246-4867.

Ni'ihau Safaris, Ltd. - This outfitter offers exclusive full day hunting safaris for wild boar and feral sheep, plus fishing as well, to the privately owned island of Ni'ihau. The island is owned and operated as a working ranch by the Robinson family. There is a small resident population of native Hawaiians on the island. They also operate Ni'ihau Helicopters as a joint operation. Hunters must have a Hawai'i State hunting license, which Ni'ihau Safaris will assist in acquiring. There are some rigid rules to follow on Ni'ihau such as no alcohol or smoking allowed. Hunting daily rate: $1650 per person, 4 hunters maximum. Observers allowed on trip at $400 per person. Free chase hunts and stalking are the rule. Game is plentiful but it is not an easy hunt. The daily rate includes use of firearm, one ram and one boar, and one guide per hunter, plus dressing crew to handle animals taken, lunch, snacks, cold drinks, etc. Advance reservations and deposits required. Departs from Port Allen Airport. Their office is located at Kaumakani, 18 mile marker on Kaumualii Highway #50 between Hanapepe and Waimea towns. Office hours are 8am-2pm, Monday through Saturday. PO Box 690370, Makaweli, HI 96769. Toll free 1-877-441-3500, (808) 335-3500, FAX (808) 338-1463.

JET SKIING

This water recreational activity is not permitted on Kaua'i.

KAYAKING

With its many navigable rivers and streams, Kaua'i is a jewel for the kayaker. You can choose an adventure on your own on the Wailua, Huleia, Hanalei Rivers or others, take a guided tour, or go on a group expedition. There are various sea kayaking adventures to be enjoyed along the Napali Coast and South Shore areas, but they are recommended for the experienced kayaker or with a guided excursion group.

In your next game of trivial pursuit, if you should have the question, "How many rivers are there on Kaua'i?" you could answer five, six, seven, or nine and probably be correct. After exhaustive research and pure conjecture, it was decided that it depends on the weather and who you ask. The problem seems to be the determination of just what is a stream and what is a river. A river is usually considered larger than a stream, but how much larger? After a heavy rain, a stream may certainly look river-like. The Hawai'i Visitors Bureau, Parks and Recreation Department, and various maps and guidebooks all have their own answer. The Hawai'i Visitors Bureau goes with seven. It seems there are five that can be agreed upon as being "rivers" by most of these sources: Waimea, Hanapepe, Wailua, Hanalei, and Wainiha. The others are more often called streams: Lumaha'i, Huleia, Kalihiwai, and Makaweli. However, the Huleia and Kalihiwai are referred to by some as rivers. In any case, there are several streams/rivers perfect for kayaking: The Waimea, Hanapepe, Huleia, Wailua, Kalihiwai, and Hanalei. Each can be navigated for only about three miles. The Waimea River, Kaua'i's longest, can be accessed in Waimea at the Lucy Wright Park. This is the location where Captain James Cook first set foot in the islands in 1778. Each river has its own personality and differing picturesque scenery. The Huleia River passes the Haupu Ridge with views of the Boar Head mountains, as well as passing by the Menehune Fish Pond and the Huleia National Wildlife Refuge. The Kalihiwai River/Stream, with its mouth at Kalihiwai Bay near Princeville, travels through lowland areas of Kaua'i. The Hanalei River twists through the valley past fields of taro. The Wailua River is accessible from Wailua State Park and you can reach and enjoy Fern Grotto State Park along the banks. Depending on the seasons and surf, sea kayaking locations will vary. In the summer months, the North Shore may often be calm and perfect for various skill levels of kayakers. The Napali coast trip is a 16-mile kayak adventure and can be accomplished in one day or more, depending on weather conditions and camping permit availability. In the winter, the southern shore offers many options. For more information, pick up a copy of *Paddling Hawai'i* by Audrey Sutherland at local bookstores.

KAYAK RENTALS AND GUIDED TOURS

Choose a guided tour, or rent equipment and explore one of Kaua'i's beautiful rivers at your own pace. There are also several outfitter offering various ocean and river kayaking excursions and tours.

Aloha Canoes & Kayaks - This outfitter offers several kayaking excursions. The 3-3 ½ hour Kayak Adventure Tour combines kayaking, hiking and swimming on the Huleia River, $82 with lunch, $70 without. The 3 ½ hour Hawaiian Double Hull Canoe Adventure is a hike, swim and canoe outing, $82 with lunch. The 1 ½ hour Hawaiian Double Hull Canoe Paddle Tour just cruises the Huleia River, $60 per person. There big excursion is the Helicopter-Kayak-Hike-Swim and Canoe Adventure, $199 per person. They also offer an Ocean Kayak Tour, including snorkel and swim, $150 per person. PO Box 3502, Lihu'e, HI 96766, toll free 1-877-473-5446, (808) 246-6804, Fax (808) 245-6912; Email: kayaks@hawaiian.net; Web: <www.hawaiikayaks.com>

Island Adventures - This outfit features a 2 1/2 hour guided kayak excursion on the Hulei'a River, site of the legendary Menehune Fishpond. The Hulei'a River is in the heart of the 241 acre Hulei'a National Wildlife Refuge with four endangered bird species under protection here. The river is famous as a location for scenes from movies including *Raiders of the Lost Ark* and *The Lost World*. Each person is taught kayak control during a safety briefing. Trip includes picnic snack with juice. Departs Nawiliwili Small Boat Harbor twice daily, 8:30 a.m. and 12:30 p.m. $49 adults, children 4-12, $29. They also operate True Blue Charters (fishing) and Rainbow Running (sailing/snorkeling). PO Box 1722, Lihu'e, HI 96766, toll free 1-888-245-1707, (808) 245-9662. FAX (808) 246-9661. Email: info@kauai-by-kayak.com; Web: <www.kauai-by-kayak.com>

Kayak Adventures - This outfitter offers a standard 5 hour River Kayak Tour Waterfall Adventure, four mile round trip paddle, short hike to waterfall, $85 per person, kids 12 and under $65. They also have custom ocean kayak excursions and surf lessons, 2 hours $65, available. (808) 826-9340; Email: kayaking@aloha.net; Web: <www.extreme-hawaii.com/kayak>

Kayak Ecotour - "A True Kayak Experience" - They take small groups (no more than 8) to hidden waterfalls, quiet rivers, lonely beaches, and enchanted ponds. "Please bring your boy/girl scout's attitude, bathing suit, sports or beach footwear, hat, suntan oil, camera and an open mind." The price includes a gourmet sandwich and beverages for the family, kayaks, and all the equipment. All tours are $75 adults. Children under 10 years are $40. River tours range from 2-5 hours and include the Huleia, Wailua, Kapa'a, Kalihiwai or Hanalei Rivers. They also have three special ocean kayak tours: North Shore Beach Discovery, East Side Beach Explorer, and South Shore Beach Adventure. Ocean tours are weather dependent. They also do kayak rentals. PO Box 884, Kapa'a, HI 96746, (808) 822-9078, 639-7718, 652-2665, 652-3833; Email: valentin@hawaiian.net: Web: <www.kauai-kayaking.com>

Kayak Kaua'i Outbound - Their one or multiple day guided tours are available year round. They can be geared for the active adventurer or for the whole family. Full Day Napali Sea Kayak Voyage $160; Secret Falls Paddling & Hiking Adventure to Ho'olalaea Falls, 5 hours, $80; Blue Lagoon Hanalei River, 3 hours, $60; Sea Kayak Po'ipu, full day, $115; River Rental Packages to rent your own kayak and do your own tour, single kayak $26, double kayak $50. Also surfboard rentals, hiking and camping equipment rentals, bicycle rentals. PO Box 508, Hanalei, HI 96714, toll free 1-800-437-3507, (808) 826-9844, Fax (808) 826-7378, Kapa'a shop (808) 822-9179; Email: info@kayakkauai.com; Web: <www.kayakkauai.com>

Kayak Wailua - This outfitter has kayak rentals available, single-$25, double-$55, to explore the Wailua River on your own. They also offer a guided Wailua River Kayak Tour, including hike to Secret Falls, the 125' Ho'olalaea Falls on the upper reaches of the river, $85 per person. (808) 822-3388; Email: info@kayakwailua.com; Web: <www.kayakwailua.com>

Kaua'i Water Ski & Surf - Kayaks are among the variety of equipment available for rent. Single or two-person kayaks rentals, surfboards, bodyboards, snorkel gear, waterskis, mountain bikes, etc. Monday-Saturday 9am-9pm. 4-356 Kuhio Highway, Kinipopo Shopping Village, Kapa'a, HI 96746. Toll free 1-800-344-7915, (808) 822-3574. Email: surfski@aloha.net

Outfitters Kaua'i - This outfitter has a full line of one and two person kayak rentals and tours available. Information and maps on kayaking locations are provided. Tours include: Napali Coast Kayak, full day 16 mile paddle, $145 per person; a 5 hour Jungle Paddle Stream & Waterfall Hike to Ho'olalaea Falls, $84 per person, kids 12 and under $72; the 4 hour Hidden Valley Falls Kayak Adventure on the Huleia River with picnic lunch is $84, kids $72, same tour without lunch $72/60. 2727A Po'ipu Road, PO Box 1149, Po'ipu Plaza, Po'ipu Beach, HI 96756, (808) 742-9667, toll free 1-888-742-9887. FAX (808) 742-8842. Email: info@outfitterskauai.com; Web: <www.outfitterskauai.com>

Paradise Outdoor Adventures - Rental bikes and kayaks. They also feature guided kayak trips including: a 5 hour Wailua Jungle Tour, $85 per person, kids under 11 $60; Sea Kayaking Whale Watch (seasonal), along South Shore to Po'ipu, $99 per person; Napali Coast Full Day Tour, 16 miles, $175. 4-1596 Kuhio Highway, Kapa'a, HI 96746. Toll free 1-877-42-BOATS, (808) 822-1112, Fax (808) 822-4224.

Pedal and Paddle - They offer summertime guided trips of Napali. River trips are self-guided. Daily rentals of single and two-person kayaks available. Located in Hanalei at the Ching Young Village. (808) 826-9069.

Tropical Kayak Co. - They have a full line of kayak rentals, single-$20, double-$40. Rent a kayak and do your own river paddling excursion. They are just 5 minutes south of the Wailua River. Located on Highway 51 north, just 3 minutes from Lihu'e Airport, 1/4 mile past the traffic light on right side (ocean) of highway. (808) 632-0011.

Wailua Kayak Adventures - Kayak rentals $15-30 to do your own river excursion. Guided tours include: 4-5 hour Wailua Secret Falls Tour to Ho'olalaea Falls, $75 per person; 3 hour Wailua Falls Hiking Tour, $50 per person; 3-4 hour Jungle River Safari, $50 per person. Morning and afternoon departures. (808) 822-5795, 639-6332, FAX (808) 822-5795. Email: sacredriver@hawaiian.net; Web: < www.kauaiwailuakayak.com >

Wailua Kayak & Canoe - This outfitter has kayak rentals, single-$25, double-$50. They also do guided river tours. The 3 hour Wailua River Trip takes in the Fern Grotto and Rope Swing, snack included, $60 per person. The 5 hour Secret Falls Trip includes hike to Secret Falls (Ho'olalaea Falls), Rope Swing and lunch, $80 per person. Located right on the Wailua River, north side, at 169 Wailua Road, Kapa'a, HI 96746, (808) 821-1188.

LAND TOURS

There are several tour operators offering various general scenic attraction coach/bus or van tours for sightseeing plus some other more adventurous operators offering more backcountry, offroad specialized tours and excursions. Check with the following land tour operators for details.

Aloha Kaua'i Tours, 1702 Haleukana Street, Lihu'e, HI 96766. Toll free 800-452-1113, (808) 245-8890, 245-7224; Email: tours@gte.net; Web: < www.alohakauaitours.com > This outfitter/operator offers two basic land tour packages that explore various areas of Kaua'i on vans or 4x4 offroad vehicles. They also have some other hiking and water/kayaking adventures as well. Check their website for latest offerings, rates and applicable discounts.

Kaua'i Backroads - This tour departs for a half-day tour twice daily at 8am and 1pm. Travel former cane roads in the comfort of an air-conditioned 4-wheel drive van to remote areas. Learn about Kaua'i's history as you travel scenic backroads up to Kilohana Crater, past reservoirs and old Koloa Town to the rugged coastline of Maha'ulepu, then take the tunnel through the Mount Haupu Range and back to the plantation home. A photographer's dream. Adults $50, kids $44

Kaua'i Mountain Tour - These 4X4 mountain van tours last 6-8 hours and include picnic lunch. $90 adults, $63 children. Tours go beyond the normal land excursions in their twelve passenger air-conditioned 4X4 vans. They place an emphasis on Hawaiian history and culture as they travel back roads in the Pali-Kona Forest reserve and Koke'e State Park. Load up on a 4x4 air-conditioned mountain tour van with eager visitors and set out with a competent guide to discover the backroad beauty of "upcountry" Kaua'i. The guide is well-versed in Hawaiian culture, history and flora-fauna of the region. Explore Koke'e State Park and the Pali-Kona Forest. While you can hike in on many of these roads to the lookouts visited, the four wheel drive vehicle can get you much closer to the lookouts. This is an excellent option especially for those who might be unable to so some strenuous trekking on foot. Nothing was more that a light walk. The van was cool and comfortable, although there was some expected jostling that occurs over the rough back roads. The guide led an informative narration for almost the entire seven hours of the trip. Examining different types of plants and flowers, learning about their uses, and viewing the majestic Waimea Conayon from several different vantage points were some of the highlights. The excursion included a leisurely picnic lunch. While many choose to drive up to the Waimea Canyon and Koke'e Park independently, you'll miss out on leaning much about some of the secret treasures that Kaua'i has to hold.

Kaua'i Paradise Tours - (Wir sprechen Deutsch.) Island sightseeing in six passenger van to Waimea and Kalalau or the North Shore. There are two basic 6-hour tours offered. Tour 1 - Waimea Canyon, Koke'e Park, Kalalau Valley and other west Kaua'i sights, $66 per person. Tour 2 - Kilauea , Hanalei, Haena, Ke'e Beach, and other East Coast/North Shore highlights, $66 per person. Or combine a land tour with helicopter trip for additional $129 or Fern Grotto Boat Cruise for additional $15. Narration available in English or German with owner/tour guide Max Dereyl. Basic tours with add-ons, extra 2 hours, $88. PO Box 3927, Lihu'e, HI 96766. Toll free 1-800-404-3900, (808) 246-3999, cell 639-9833, FAX (808) 245-2499.

Polynesian Adventure Tours - They offer four basic sightseeing tour packages that take in island highlights. Rates depend on pickup origin on Kaua'i. Tour #1 Waimea Canyon/Wailua River covers canyon views and Fern Grotto cruise, $60-73, children under 12 $43-56. Tour #2 Waimea Canyon Experience covers canyon views and west Kaua'i sights, $40-60, children under 12 $30-50. Tour #3 North Shore Excursion covers all the attractions of Hanalei area, $28-43, children under 12 $18-33. Tour #4 Waimea Canyon/North Shore Excursion combines all the attractions of west Kaua'i, North Shore and Hanalei, $60-65, children $54-58. 3113B Oihana, Lihu'e, HI 96766. Toll free 1-800-622-3011, (808) 246-0122; Email: sales@polyad.com; Web: < www.polyad.com >.

Robert's Hawai'i - They offer full and half day tours to major scenic attractions of the island. The Waimea Canyon & Fern Grotto Tour is 8 hours, $59 per person, children under 12 $44; the Waimea Canyon Tour includes west Kaua'i sights, 5 hours, $40 per person, children under 12 $30; Fern Grotto includes Wailua River cruise, 4 hours, $40 per person, children under 12 $30; Hanalei Valley and North Shore Tour, 4 hours, $33 per person, children under 12 $23. All tours by comfortable air-conditioned mini-coach. Book online and save. Toll free 1-800-831-5541, (808) 245-9558, 539-9400. Web: < www.robertshawaii.com >

Trans Hawaiian - Three trips available: #1 Hanalei and Ha'ena Tour visits the Wailua River and its ancient temples, Opaeka'a Falls, Kilauea Lighthouse and Refuge, Lumahai Beach, Hanalei Bay, the wet and dry caves at Ha'ena, and Ke'e Beach. # 2 Waimea Canyon Tour tours Nawiliwili Harbor, the Menehune Fishpond, Russian Fort Elizabeth, Waimea Town, Waimea Canyon, Kalalau Valley Lookout, Koloa, Po'ipu and Spouting Horn. # 3 Waimea Canyon/Wailua River Tour is a full day trip that circles the island from the Eastern shore to the Northern. Prices quoted vary depending on pick-up location. Ask about discounts for children. This company also operates the Coconut Coast Trolley. 1770 Haleukana, Lihu'e, HI 96766. Toll free 1-800-533-8765, (808) 245-5108; Web: < www.transhawaiian.com >

LUAUS See chapter on Restaurants.

MOVIES/MOVIE RENTALS/MOVIE TOURS (Also see Theater)

The Coconut MarketPlace has a twin theater with bargain prices for matinees (before 6 pm). (808) 821-2324.

Kukui Grove Cinemas has four screens in their theater adjoining the Kukui Grove Shopping Center, 4368 Kukui Grove, Lihu'e. Phone (808) 245-5055 to hear an information recording.

The Princeville Hotel has complimentary movies for hotel guests shown four times daily in their small, private cinema. Non-resort guests who come to the hotel to dine can receive complimentary cinema passes for that evening.

Waimea Community Theatre is now fully restored and offers a variety of films and live productions. Phone (808) 338-0282.

If you have a VCR at your accommodation, there are plenty of options for renting movies. If you don't have a machine you can rent one of those as well. Blockbuster videos is the biggest chain on the island. They have their main outlet at 4-771 Kuhio Hwy. at Waipouli Town Center in the mall next to Foodland. They do have drop off boxes at other places around the island. It is about $5 for a three-day rental. (808) 822-7744. Other video stores are scattered around the island. Check the grocery stores, too, Foodland in Princeville has a good selection.

A few other video rental outlets: Borders Books, 4303 Nawilwili Road, Lihu'e, 246-0862; Canyon Video, 9814 Kaumualii Highway, Waimea, 338-1441; Hanalei Video & Music, 5-5190 Kuhio Highway, Hanalei, 826-9633; Hot Flix Video Rentals, 5470 Koloa Road, Koloa, 742-1154; Kauai Video Rentals 4480 Ahukini Road, Lihu'e, 245-7675, or 9905 Waimea Road, Waimea, 338-0303, or 4469 Waialo Road, Hanapepe, 335-3942; Kilauea Video, 4244 Kilauea Road, 828-0128.

KAUA'I MOVIE/FILM TOURS

If you are a movie buff, or even if you're not, you are sure to enjoy one of Kaua'i's most unusual island tours. *Hawai'i Movie Tours* travels around the north and eastern shores of the island with a guided narrated tour of some of Kaua'i's most famous movie locations. Ground tours combined with air and sea tours are also available. They have arranged special permission to visit private estates and other hidden places not open to the public. As you travel around the island, their on-van video equipment shows clips of just a fraction of the movies filmed on Kaua'i. (And commercials, too!) The film snippet provides an ideal introduction to the scenic location you are about to visit. Trust us, it would be impossible to visit many of the filming scenes on your own.

Hawaii Movie Tours - Their 5 hour Standard Tour includes lunch, $95 per person, children under 12 $76. The Deluxe Tour is 12 hours long (offered three days weekly) and includes a comprehensive tour of varied movie sites by helicopter, ground and river boat cruise, and ends with a fantastic luau experience, $265 per person. The 4x4 Offroad Tour half-day plus tour includes lunch, uses a 15-passenger offroad van and takes in numerous sites where famous movie scenes were actually filmed, $105 per person, children under 12 $95. Book early as tours fill up rapidly. Check the website for applicable discounts or special offers. Maximum 10 people per tour. Hotel pickup available. Their office is located behind Beezers in Kapa'a. 4-1384 Kuhio Highway, Kapa'a, HI 96746. (808) 822-1192 or toll free 1-800-628-8432. Email: tourguv@hawaiian.net; Web: < www.hawaiimovietour.com >

Film Flicks Hawaii Historical Adventure Tours - 3412 Rice Street, Lihu'e, HI 96766. Toll free 1-877-632-0066, (808) 632-0066; Email: information@FilmFlicksHawaii.com; Web: < www.filmflickshawaii.com > This tour operator is noted here even though they differ somewhat from the Hawaii Movie Tours operator listed above. Film Flicks Hawaii offers comprehensive island tours taking in the scenic highlights and popular attractions of Kaua'i. The 15 passenger van used is also TV/VCR equipped and on tour shows informational video clips of Kaua'i history, culture, and subjects of interest to visitors. Tour includes visits to favorite places to shop, dine and experience. Explore the island from east to west. Hotel pickups available. Deluxe Tour is 6 hours and includes lunch, $89 per person, children under 12 $69.

MOVIES MADE ON KAUA'I (Courtesy of Hawai'i Movie Tours)

Some of these will be familiar names and as for others, well, there is good reason they never made it big on the big screen!

2001: Jurassic Park 3
1998: Six Days, Seven Nights; Mighty Joe Young
1997: George of the Jungle
1996: The Lost World-Jurassic Park 2
1995: Outbreak
1994: North
1993: Jurassic Park
1992: Honeymoon in Vegas
1991: Hook
1990: Flight of the Intruder, Lord of the Flies
1987: Throw Mama From The Train
1986: Islands of the Alive
1983: The Thorn Birds, Uncommon Valor
1981: Behold Hawaii, Body Heat
1981: Raiders of the Lost Ark
1979: Seven, Last Flight of Noah's Ark
1978: Deathmoon, Acapulco Gold

411

1977: Fantasy Island, Islands in the Stream, King Kong, Waterworld (television)
1974: Man with the Golden Gun, Castaway Cowboy
1970: The Hawaiians
1969: Lost Flight
1968: Yoake No Futare, Lovers at Dawn
1966: Hawaii
1965: Lt. Robinson Crusoe, U.S.N, Operation Attack, None But The Brave
1963: Gilligan's Island (pilot episode), Donovan's Reef
1962: Girls! Girls! Girls! (original title Paradise Hawaiian Style), Diamond Head
1961: Blue Hawai'i, Seven Women From Hell
1960: Wackiest Ship in the Army
1958: South Pacific
1957: Forbidden Island, Jungle Heat, Voodoo Island
1956: Beach Head, Between Heaven and Hell, She Gods of Shark Reef,
      Thunder Over Hawaii
1953: Miss Sadie Thompson
1951: Bird of Paradise
1950: Pagan Love Song
1933: White Heat

MUSEUMS/GARDEN TOURS/CULTURAL TOURS

Kaua'i offers some of the finest garden and cultural tours in the Hawaiian chain. Be sure to find time to take in at least one of the following varied options.

The ***National Tropical Botanical Garden*** ★ is a nationally-chartered, privately funded, non-profit organization. It is the nation's only tropical botanical garden chartered by the U.S. Congress. Headquartered on Kaua'i, its principal mission is research, conservation, and education relating to the world's tropical plants. The NTBG consists of five distinct gardens in the Hawaiian Islands and in Florida. The three Kaua'i gardens are: Lawa'i, Allerton and Limahuli, with another on Maui. Each of the gardens has an individual name, but they are sometimes incorrectly referred to individually as the "National Tropical Botanical Garden."

WILIWILI

The *Lawa'i Garden* ★ (National Tropical Botanical Garden Headquarters) is located on Kaua'i's southern shore in the lush Lawa'i Valley, and was the first garden site to be acquired by the National Tropical Botanical Garden. In discussion of the Lawa'i Garden, we would like to provide a little background on the area. Little is known of early Lawa'i. According to an account by David Forbes in his book, *Queen Emma and Lawa'i*, the early maps and photographs show that the valley was cultivated in taro and later in rice. Queen Emma, the wife of Kamehameha IV, probably first saw Lawa'i during her visit in 1856, but returned for a more lengthy stay during the winter and spring in 1871. On arrival she found the area rather desolate, and compared with the busy life in Honolulu, it must have seemed so. In her correspondence with her family on O'ahu she requested many items to be sent, including plant slips. With these plant starts she began to develop one of the finest gardens in the islands. Queen Emma leased the Lawa'i land to Duncan McBryde for a span of fifteen years in 1876, however, she reserved her house lot and several acres of taro patch land.

According to Forbes, "In 1886, after the Queen's death, Mrs. Elizabeth McBryde bought the entire Ahupuaa for $50,000. The upper lands were planted to sugar cane, and the valley was apparently leased to Chinese rice growers and taro planters." In 1899, Alexander McBryde obtained the land and with a love of plants, he continued to enlarge and cultivate the gardens which had been begun by the queen. Alexander McBryde died in 1935 and the land was sold to Robert Allerton and his son John in 1938. They continued to enlarge the gardens, searching out plants from around South East Asia. Today Lawa'i is a horticulturist's dream, with an outstanding collection of tropical plants.

The NTBG headquarter facilities are located adjacent to the Lawa'i Garden. The headquarters complex includes a scientific laboratory, an herbarium housing nearly 30,000 specimens of tropical plants, an 8,000 volume research library, a computer records center, an educational center, and offices for staff and visiting scientists. *Lawa'i Garden* is a research and educational garden comprising 186 acres. The garden's extensive collections include tropical plants of the world that are of particular significance for research, conservation, or cultural purposes. Special emphasis is given to rare and endangered Hawaiian species and to economic plants of the tropical world.

Of particular interest is the endangered *kanaloa kahoolawensis* (one of only four in the world). This small, woody plant is known only to exist on Kahoolawe. In 1992, two specimens of this plant were discovered on Kahoolawe. This was the first new genus discovered in Hawai'i since 1913. Two *kanaloa kahoolawensis* have since been grown from seeds at the NTBG. There is also a collection of familiar household products - sugar, vanilla, cinnamon - all seen here in their natural plant state. Palm oil, sandalwood (for scent), koa (for wood items including canoes and furniture) and cuari (used to make sodium pentathol) can also be seen in their original form. *Three Springs* is at the interior of the Lawa'i Garden (makai or toward the mountains). This 120-acre area was acquired as a bequest to the Garden and is yet undeveloped. It will eventually be designed as an additional garden section, emphasizing the beautiful natural land and water features.

RECREATION AND TOURS
Museums / Garden Tours / Cultural Tours

The nearby **Allerton Garden** ★ is located oceanfront at Lawa'i Kai, adjacent to the Lawa'i Garden. The new visitor entrance is at Spouting Horn. This was formerly a private 100-acre estate. The beautifully designed garden is managed by the National Tropical Botanical Garden pursuant to an agreement with the Allerton Estate Trust. The gardens, started by Queen Emma, were lovingly developed and expanded over a period of 30 years by Robert Allerton and his son John. The sculpted gardens contain numerous plants of interest, outstanding examples of garden design, and water features, as well as Queen Emma's original summer cottage. The cottage was severely damaged by Hurricane Iniki and plans for restoration are underway. The Moreton Bay fig trees here have giant buttress roots and helped create a prehistoric scene for the filming of *Jurassic Park*. While these trees appear ancient, they were actually planted in 1940. Reservations are required for the separate tours of the Lawa'i and Allerton Gardens. Only guided tours are available and operate Tuesday through Saturday, 9am, 10 am, 1 pm, and 2pm, and are approximately 2 ½ hours each, walking at an easy pace for about one mile. Tour fee is currently $25 for each tour. For information on scheduled tours and reservations, contact: National Tropical Botanical Garden, PO Box 340, Lawa'i, HI 96765, (808) 742-2623; Email: tours@ntbg.org; Web: < www.ntbg.org >

The **Limahuli Gardens** ★ , in Ha'ena, on Kaua'i's North Shore is an area of overwhelming natural beauty. Located one-half mile past the nine-mile marker on Kuhio Highway #56 and a quarter-mile before the end of the road at Ke'e Beach, this is another branch of the National Tropical Botanical Garden. This lush garden offers a walking tour that leads you uphill through a 15-acre garden and forest to a beautiful viewpoint overlooking the ocean. This is a 3/4 mile loop trail, steep in some areas. Comfortable walking shoes necessary; umbrellas provided for occasional showers. You will see ancient taro terraces, many of the plants introduced to Hawai'i by the early Polynesians, as well as plantings of native Hawaiian species and the pristine Limahuli Stream. Their guided tours are 2 - 2 ½ hours long; self-guided tours are about 1 - 1 ½ hours. Advanced reservations are required for guided tours and they request that visitors meet promptly for their tours. If you must cancel your reservation, they request a phone call at least two hours in advance of your scheduled tour. All visitors are met by the National Tropical Botanical Garden staff at the garden's entrance. Parking area and restroom facilities are available. Picnic lunches are not allowed on the grounds. Guided tours are offered Tuesday to Friday, and Sunday at 9:30 am to 4 pm, at a cost of $15 per person. Self-guided tours are $10 per person during the same times. (808) 826-1053 for information. Email: tours@ntbg.org; Web: < www.ntbg.org >

The **Children's Discovery Museum** on Kaua'i has temporary exhibitions and programs at locations all over the island. For information on what and where call them at (808) 823-8222.

Grove Farm Homestead ★ in Lihu'e is an example of the old style of plantation living. This was the plantation home of George N. Wilcox until 1978. A fascinating two and one half hour tour is given. This, in our opinion, is the best cultural tour on the island. Tours by advance reservation only. Admission $5.

Currently tours are offered Monday, Wednesday, and Thursday 10am and 1:10pm. Call to verify schedule. PO Box 1631, Lihu'e, HI 96766. (808) 245-3202.) For additional information see WHERE TO STAY/WHAT TO SEE

Guava Kai Plantation in Kilauea has some 480 acres of guava orchards under commercial cultivation. Guava Kai is considered the Guava Capitol of the world. Visit the plantation's visitor center and discover how guava is grown and processed into a variety of treats. Guava has fewer calories and more vitamin C than oranges, and it is also a good source of vitamin A, potassium, and phosphorus. Guava is actually not a citrus, but a berry with a fleshy seed cavity and thick skin. The guava can survive in dry or very tropical conditions. The Kilauea orchards receive 100 inches of rainfall each year with temperate 65-80 degree weather that is very agreeable to this crop. During dry months each tree receives up to 75 gallons of water per day. The seedlings were planted in this orchard in 1977 and began producing fruit in 1979. The first commercial yield was in January of 1980 with a 2,000 pounds per acre harvested. Today the yield is 5,000 pounds per acre or about 400 pounds of fruit per tree per harvest cycle. The fruit at this plantation is hand-picked and harvested year round on a full-scale crop cycling system. The fruit meat can vary from white or yellow to orange or pink. The variety grown at the Guava Kai Plantation is a hybrid developed by the University of Hawai'i's College of Tropical Agriculture and has bright pink flesh and an edible rind. The color in your glass of juice is all natural. The guava was a native of South America and it was introduced islands in 1791 by the Spaniard Don Francisco de Paula Marin, who was an advisor to Kamehameha I. The guava flourished and many now grow wild in Hawaii. There is a self-guided tour that includes a view of the orchard and the processing plants as well as an informative eight minute video.

There is a man-made fish pond and an assortment of native Hawaiian plants to enjoy as your stroll the grounds. The snack bar, open only in the summer months, sells ice cream, juice, breads, and other bakery items made with guava. There are free samples of guava juice, jams, jellies, and coffee. Since they are owned by Maunaloa, they also sell their products at slightly lower rates than retail outlets. Guava Kai Plantation is open 9am-5pm. Located at Kilauea, just off the Kuhio Highway #56 on Kuawa Road, watch for sign. (808) 828-6121.

West Kaua'i Visitor & Technology Center, 9565 Kaumualii Hwy., Waimea (808) 338-1332. HOURS: Open daily 9am-5pm. This is a unique place to gain an understanding of the Waimea area of Kaua'i. It's a one-of-a-kind educational technology center and museum. Pictorials, graphics, and displays with touch-sensitive screens provide information on all of Kaua'i's activities, not just Waimea. This is a high-tech, state-of-the-art 7500 square foot center facility. Utilizing the theme, "Enduring Engineering," visitors follow cultural and historic photographs showing the development of engineering on Kaua'i from ancient days to modern times. From the Polynesian voyagers to NASA's most sophisticated technology. Enjoy old photographs of Waimea, back to the days of grass shacks! There is even a photo of the first movie filmed on Kaua'i, *White Heat,* by director Louis Weber. (The film has long since been lost or destroyed.) One unusual model is the Pathfinder which is a pilotless aircraft that was flown at an altitude of 80,000 feet over Barking Sands beach. The museum blends the history of the area with information on the nearby Pacific Missile Range Facility. Not an easy task to undertake, but one that seems to work here. In addition to the displays there are several tenants in the facility. Currently they include Oceanit Laboratories, Inc., Solipsys Corporation, Textron Systems and Trex Enterprises.

Kamokila Hawaiian Village ★ , has been around for several years. The quaintness and authenticity of the village gives a glimpse of an early Hawaiian lifestyle. The admission fee of $5 included a guided tour. A guide explains the meanings of each of the various thatched structures and their uses. Experiences include opening a coconut for guests to sample (the young green ones that have soft pudding-like coconut meat), picking flowers for your hair, and even picking a fresh guava off the tree to eat. Dashing between huts to avoid the off and on again rainshowers, the guide played the ukulele and sang as we explored the birthing place, the sleeping huts, and other accounts of early Hawaiian life. It does what the oversized Polynesian Cultural Center on O'ahu can never do, provide a truly personalized and interpretive cross-cultural experience. Guests can buy a lei for $2 or a freshly made pandanus hat for just a little bit more. Located opposite Opaeka'a Falls, the Kaumo'o Road entrance is just past the Wailua Bridge on the Wailua River, Wailua. For information, call (808) 823-0559.

Kaua'i Coffee Company Visitor Center & Museum ★ - Make a stop at this informative and interesting visitors center and museum and learn about the islands' coffee industry. This is Hawai'i's largest coffee estate and you can sample a freshly brewed cup, view exhibits and displays tracing the coffee growing, harvesting and production process of Kaua'i estate-grown premium coffees. A retail gift shop features unique Kaua'i gifts, fresh ground and whole bean coffees, and lots more. Free admission. Located on Highway #540 (870 Kalewili Road) which leads off from Highway #50 near Eleele and Port Allen. PO Box 8, Eleele, HI 96705, toll free 1-800-545-8605, (808) 335-0813, fax (808) 335-3149. Web: < www.kauaicoffee.com >

Kaua'i Sugar Plantation Tours - Hawaii's cultural history can be intimately explored through the heart of the sugar planation. Hawaii's multi-cultural history is due to the need for laborers in the labor-intensive sugar fields of yesterdays. Now you have the opportunity to view field to factory operations at Gay & Robinson. The two-hour bus tour, conducted by Gay & Robinson Tours LLC, is available weekdays and includes the history of the plantation, its operation, processing, the plantation's miles of irrigation systems, and views of the private plantation lands. Harvesting operations are seasonal with the months of April through October the best times to visit Gay & Robinson. Tour routes depend on the day-to-day operations. If you don't have time for the full tour, stop by their office on Kaumakani Avenue and view the historic displays. The office is located in the historic Field Office (circa 1900) on Kaumakani Avenue. From Lihu'e, travel Hwy. 50. Just past mile marker 19, turn left on Kaumakani Avenue with its monkeypod tress and old-fashioned streetlights. It is open 8am-4pm Monday through Friday, with the exception of plantation holidays. Tours are at 9am and 1 pm, Monday through Friday. All visitors on the tour are required to wear safety equipment to enter the factory. They must also wear pants (shorts are okay), low-heeled, closed shoes and they will be provided with safety glasses and hard hats. Tour cost is $40. Reservations at (808) 335-2824, Fax (808) 335-6852.

Email: toursgnr@aloha.net; Web: <www.gandrtours-kauai.com>. For more in-depth information on Waimea, pick up a copy of *Touring Waimea* by Christine Fayé. Available at local bookstores.

Kaua'i Historical Society Museum - This is the official historical documents archive of Kaua'i and is housed in the County of Kaua'i Building in Lihu'e. It holds varied historical collections, documents, records, books, papers, donated memorabilia, etc. on various Kaua'i subjects. It is free and open to the public. 4396 Rice Street, Lihu'e, HI 96766, for information and open hours call (808) 245-3373.

The ***Kaua'i Museum*** - Through murals, artifacts, and artwork, discover how the islands have changed since Captain Cook's arrival at Waimea in 1778. The Museum Shop specializes in Hawaiian Island memorabilia, Hawaiian books, and local crafts. They also have rotating exhibits so there will be something new and different every time you visit. Open weekdays 9am-4:30pm, Saturday 10am-1pm, closed Sunday. The first Saturday of the month is free admission day and it features special family events and activities. Admission $5, senior admission $4, children under 17 are free. Located in downtown Lihu'e, 4428 Rice Stree, PO Box 248, Lihu'e, HI 96766, (808) 245-6931, Fax 245-6864; Email: museum@midpac.net; Web: <www.kauai.qpg.com>.

Kapa'a History Tour - This 90-minute long walking tour is led by interpretive guides familiar with the history and architecture of old Kapa'a Town. Tour begins and ends at the Kapa'a History Shop located in the famous Kawamura Store in the heart of Kapa'a Town. Learn about Kapa'a's history as an agriculture service center for the once bustling sugar cane and pineapple industries. Learn about the colorful multi-ethnic population of the area, culture and heritage. Tours conducted Tuesday, Thursday and Saturday at 10 a.m. Adults $10, children under 12 $5. Kaua'i Historical Society , PO Box 1778, Lihu'e, HI 96766, (808) 821-1778, 245-3373. Web: <www.kauaihistoricalsociety.org>

KILOHANA

Kiahuna Plantation offers free self-guided tours of their **Moir Gardens** (or *Pa'u a Laka Garden*) or *Hawaiian Gardens*. Guided tours are available as well. Phone (808) 742-6411.

Kilohana is reminiscent of the grandeur and elegance of an earlier age. At the time when sugar was king on the island and prosperity reigned, plantation owners would build luxurious homes. One of the grandest on Kaua'i was the home of Gaylord Parke Wilcox and is known as Kilohana. Built in 1935, it was designed by a British architect named Mark Potter. The grounds were carefully landscaped and inside furniture arrived from the exclusive and expensive Gump's in San Francisco. Today, in addition to the gift shops, galleries, and Gaylord's Courtyard Restaurant, you'll find several tour options for this 35 acre estate. The Canefield Tour is a step back into the history of sugar cane on Kaua'i. A horse-drawn wagon helps return you in time to 1835. The Carriage Ride is a romantic excursion around the grounds, with a short narration. The rides are available daily from 11am-6:30pm, cost is $8 adults and $4 children. Horse drawn Sugar Cane Tours are twice daily by advance reservations, cost is $21 adults and $10 children. For information phone (808) 246-9529. Admission to Kilohana and its beautiful grounds is free. Kilohana and the shops open daily at 9:30am. Gaylord's serves brunch Sunday 9:30am-3pm, lunch Monday-Friday 11am-3pm and dinner from 5pm. Located just outside Lihu'e, travel east along Kaumualii Highway, Route 50. Kilohana is on your left just before the town of Lihu'e. If you are arriving from the north or east, travel Kuhio Hwy., Route 56 south and west through Lihu'e. Bear right at the traffic light at the end of Kuhio Hwy. Kilohana will be 1.4 miles down Kaumualii Highway on your right.

Koke'e Natural History Museum contains geographic maps of Kaua'i along with exhibits of native plant and bird species. Admission is free, but donations are accepted. They regularly offer free or inexpensive guided hikes and other interesting annual activities. Check their website for calendar of events, hiking information, canyon and state park information, birds, etc. PO Box 100, Kekaha, HI 96752, (808) 335-9975, Fax 335-6131; Email: kokee@aloha.net; Web: < www.aloha.net/ ~ kokee >

Koloa Heritage Trail - This is essentially a self-guided excursion in the Po'ipu Beach Resort and Koloa area on the south side of Kaua'i. Look for a copy of the "Koloa Heritage Trail" guide/map where visitor information is available. The guide/map lists and details 13 different historic sites and attractions in the Koloa and Po'ipu Beach areas. Included are Spouting Horn Park, Prince Kuhio Birthplace & Park, Koloa Landing, Po'ipu Beach Park, Hapa Road, Koloa Jodo Mission, Sugar Monument, Koloa Missionary Church, Yamamoto Store & Koloa Hotel, and others. These sites give a sense of the history, culture and heritage of the region. A free copy of the guide/map can be obtained by contacting the Po'ipu Beach Resort Association, PO Box 730, Koloa, HI 96756, (808) 742-7444, fax (808) 742-7887; Email: info@poipu-beach.org; Web: < www.poipu-beach.org >

At the Kukui Grove Shopping Center in their **Exhibition Hall** you'll discover a cooperative effort between the Garden Islands Arts Council, the Kaua'i Society of Artists and the shopping center. Their Exhibition Hall regularly features the most creative and energetic efforts of the art community. Kukui Grove Center, 3-2600 Kaumualii Highway, Lihu'e, HI 96766, (808) 245-7784.

Na 'Aina Kai - This is a combination botanical garden, sculpture park and hardwood plantation. There are 12 acres of beautifully landscaped gardens, surrounded by 45 acres of exotic fruit trees and 110 acres of tropical hardwoods. This is a botantist's or gardener's delight. Combining Hawaiiana and Americana botany, Na 'Aina Kai presents a rich tapestry of gardens and forests of tropical diversity. Tours are available Tuesday, Wednesday and Thursday and require advance reservations. Must be 13 or older. The Garden & Plantation Tour is 3 hours, 8:30 a.m. and 1:30 p.m., by motorized cartram, and takes in the various gardens including the Orchid House, Shower Tree Park, Ka'ula Lagoon Garden, Poinciana Maze, International Desert Garden, Carnivorous Plant House, Forest Garden, Hardwood Plantation and Ocean Overlook Gazebo; this tour cost is $35 per person. The Walk on the Wild Side Walking Tour is 4-5 hours, 8 a.m., includes most of the previous stops plus Kuliha'ili Canyon, Koli Ridge Bird Garden, and the Makai Meadow and Marsh; this tour cost is $70 per person and is a three-mile guided walking trek requiring some ascents and descents on pathways and steps. Comfortable walking shoes recommended, with hats, sunscreen, etc. Na 'Aina Kai, 4101 Wailapa Road, PO Box 1134, Kilauea, HI 96754. (808) 828-0525, fax (808) 828-0815; Email: NaAinaKai@msn.com

Ni'ihau Safaris, Ltd. - As detailed in the earlier section on Hunting/Shooting Ranges in this chapter, this outfitter offers exclusive full day hunting safaris for wild boar and feral sheep, plus fishing as well, to the privately owned island of Ni'ihau. However, those interested in doing a cultural tour of the "Forbidden Island" of Ni'ihau can join a hunting party as an "observer" for the helicopter trip over to Ni'ihau. Don't expect any luxuries. There are none. The island is owned and operated as a working ranch by the Robinson family. There is a small resident population of native Hawaiians on the island. They also operate Ni'ihau Helicopters as a joint operation. There are some rigid rules to follow on Ni'ihau such as no alcohol or smoking allowed. You may get a chance to see the main settlement, pristine beaches, towering cliffs and the general countryside of Ni'ihau's stark landscape. Observers are limited on trips and the rate is $400 per observer. Advance reservations and deposits required. Departs from Port Allen Airport. Contact their office for full details. Their office is located at Kaumakani, 18 mile marker on Kaumualii Highway #50 between Hanapepe and Waimea towns. Office hours 8am-2pm, Mon,-Sat. PO Box 690370, Makaweli, HI 96769. Toll free 1-877-441-3500, (808) 335-3500, FAX (808) 338-1463.

Wai'oli Mission House was the home of island missionaries Abner and Lucy Wilcox. This 19th century New England-style home was shipped in pieces from Boston around Cape Horn to Kaua'i. The home features beautiful koa wood furniture and other items from the period. Open to the public Tuesdays, Thursdays, and Saturdays from 9am-2:45pm. Wai'oli Mission House Museum in Hanalei was built of coral limestone blocks in 1837. Guided tours at no charge. Donations appreciated. PO Box 1631, Lihu'e, HI 96766. (808) 245-3202.

Waimea Sugar Mill Camp Museum and Plantation Lifestyles Walking Tour.
Reservations are required for this historical and informative tour which is limited
to 12 people. Volunteers lead a tour which begins at the administration building
of the Waimea Plantation Cottages. The tour is currently offered Tuesdays and
Saturdays at 9am and lasts about one hour. Cost is $6 adults, $5 seniors 65 and
older, and children 12 and under are $4. Kaumualii Highway, PO Box 1178,
Waimea, HI 96796. (808) 335-2824, 337-1005.

POLO

You might not expect to find this recreational option on a Hawaiian island, but
polo season begins in late April and runs through September. Matches are held
each Sunday at the 'Anini Polo Field, 3pm. The field is located across the road
from 'Anini Beach. Access via Kalihiwai Road.

RENTAL EQUIPMENT

Kayak Kaua'i - Camping equipment, kayaks, mountain bikes, beach equipment,
etc. (808) 826-9844.

Outfitters Kaua'i - Biking and kayaking equipment. (808) 742-9667.

Paradise Outdoor Adventures - Rents bikes and kayaks. (808) 822-1112.

Pedal and Paddle in Hanalei - Backpacking, camping gear, kayaks and beach
equipment rentals. (808) 826-9069.

RIVER EXCURSIONS

Also see section on Kayaking.

Smith's Tropical Paradise/Smith's Boats cruise up the Wailua River to the famous
Fern Grotto. Trips operate daily starting at 9am. The last boat departs at 2:30pm
or 3:30pm, depending on the day of the week. Trip duration is 1 hour, 20
minutes. Current scheduled departures are every half hour from 9am-11:30am
and 12:30pm until 3pm. Additional 3:30pm departure on Monday, Wednesday
and Fridays. No reservations needed, just arrive 15 minutes before departure.
They are located near the mouth of the Wailua River on Wailua Road at the
Wailua Marina State Park. Adults $15, children 2-12 $8. Fern Grotto Contact:
Smith's Tropical Paradise, 174 Wailua Road, Kapa'a, HI 96746. Cruise information phone (808) 821-6892 or 821-6893, fax 822-4520. For information on
Smith's Tropical Paradise Botanical Garden tours and Garden Luau, phone (808)
821-6895 or 821-6896. For their Wedding Department phone (808) 821-6887 or
821-6888. Email: smiths@aloha.net

Wai'ale'ale Boat Tours Inc. presents Fern Grotto Cruises. A 1 ½ hour tour up the Wailua River which includes music, hula, historical facts, and legends. Adults $15, children $8, senior discounts. Trips start at 9am and run on the half-hour until 3:00 pm or 3:30 pm, depending on the season. Located at 6455 Makana Road, Kapa'a, HI 96746 in the Wailua State Park Marina,Wailua. (808) 822-4908, fax 823-0822.

RUNNING

Kaua'i has no official running organization. If you'd like to know more about marathons or running events, see the EVENTS section of this guide or try calling the Kaua'i Athletic Club, Foot Locker, or Dan's Sports Shop as they usually have entry forms and information for any current running events. Also check the events calendars for the Hawai'i Visitors & Convention Bureau at www.gohawaii.com and/or Alternative-Hawaii at < www.alternative-hawaii.com >

SCUBA DIVING

Scuba divers can explore the General Store, a 65-80 foot deep reef with a variety of marine life and a 19th century steamship, or the Sheraton Caves which have interesting lava formations and plenty of green sea turtles. At Koloa Landing, divers might discover bottles or fittings from old whaling ships and parts of the train track that once ran between Koloa and the area's sugar mill. On the North Shore there are underwater lava tubes and archways. While on the eastern shore, divers can explore the wreck of the *Lukenbach*, a German freighter that sank 40 years ago. Off Ni'ihau there are 130 foot deep reef walls with abundant marine life, considered by some to be the best diving in Hawai'i.

Popular shore diving beaches include Makua Beach (Tunnels) on the North Shore and on the southern shore, Koloa Landing and Prince Kuhio Park in Po'ipu. If you'd like to do an introductory scuba dive, a boat dive on Kaua'i will run you $75-100. Shore dives are available from several dive companies. Dive Certification usually takes two or more days; some offer PADI while others offer NAUI. The cost of certification on Kaua'i starts at $225. A few dive companies offer prescription masks. Most of them offer a three-tank dive to Ni'ihau ($235-270) a little steep, but quite an adventure to see the reef wall. Some dive shops suggest that visitors with limited time do "PADI" dive preparation on the mainland and they can then be certified on Kaua'i in just two days. Classes are generally no more than six persons. Private lessons, which run slightly more, are also available. Many of the following dive companies also rent gear.

Bubbles Below - Offers scuba charters that specialize in marine biology. Their 35 ft. vessel, *Kaimanu*, takes out only eight divers at a time. They do a variety of dives including a multi-level drift dive. Morning 2 Tank Dive, 4 ½ hours, 7:30am - 12 noon, $100; Afternoon 2 Tank Dive, 4 ½ hours, 12:30-5pm, $100. Snorkelers/riders are $50. They do a Ni'ihau/Lehua Rock Dive Trip, but warn that the rougher channel conditions make this trip only for the hearty and the 20-mile open-ocean crossing usually takes an hour to go across and an hour and a half to come back. The all day trip includes three tanks at three different locations. This trip goes twice weekly. If you are interested in underwater photography, they have a professional camera system for rent. Ni'ihau/Lehua Rock Dive is $235 per person. Night and Twilight dives are two-tank dives for $100. Equipment is available for rent including wetsuits, regulators, and buoyancy compensators. Owners Linda and Ken Bail have years of experience. Linda began her scuba diving experience at age six and has instructed divers since 1977 as a NAUI course director, and PADI master scuba diver trainer. Ken has been a NAUI instructor and PADI master scuba diver trainer since 1982. They share their love for the marine environment and include the marine ecosystem in their briefing. PO Box 157, Eleele, HI 96705, (808) 332-7333, 822-3483. Email: kaimanu@aloha.net; Web: <www.aloha.net/~kaimanu

Dive Kaua'i Scuba Center - Dive tours, boat charters, equipment rentals, introductory dives and PADI certification. Scuba intro tours $98-125, shore dives for certified divers, 2 tanks $78, 2 tank boat dive $95, Night Dive $78, scooter dive $98, PADI certification $225 and up. Equipment rental by day or week. 976 Kuhio Hwy., Kapa'a, HI 96746. Toll free 1-800-828-3483, (808) 822-0452. Email: email@divekauai.com; Web: <www.divekauai.com>

Fathom Five Divers ★ Full service dive store and PADI certification. Introductory dives from one of their two 26' dive boats. They visit more than 20 dive locations ranging from 30 to 90 feet. Some dive sites include Sheraton Caves, General Store, Ice Box, Brennecke's Ledge, Turtle Bluffs, and Zack's Pocket (named after their Hawaiian boat captain who discovered this site). Their dive sites are only 10-15 minutes from the harbor, which makes a two-tank boat dive a half day trip and provides adventures for the experienced and beginning divers. Maximum of six divers. Introductory two-tank boat dive, no experience necessary $135 includes class, dives, and gear. Introductory shore dive with one-tank $95. Their 4 or 5 day course for PADI certification includes lectures, diving each day, and two boat dives on the last day. $369 includes it all. Open water check out dives available $230. 3450 Po'ipu Road, PO Box 907, Koloa, HI 96756, 1-800-972-3078, (808) 742-6991. Web: <www.fathom-five.com>

SCUBA DIVING

Hanalei Water Sports - Offers PADI scuba certification. They have daily guided snorkel and scuba tours as well as rentals. Located on the beach at the Princeville Hotel, they conduct their dives from the shore or offer special dive tours to Tunnels Reef, Koloa Landing, or Ahukini Landing. Guided snorkeling tour (1 hour) includes pool lesson, equipment, and wet suit $35, surf lessons (2 hours) including equipment also available. Outrigger Canoe Tours 1 1/2 hours up the Hanalei Bay and River $55 adults, $45 child or a sunset canoe tour $65. Scuba dives $105-140 for introductory dives, certified divers $75-125. 5570 Ka Haku Road, Princeville Hotel, Princeville, HI 96722, (808) 826-7509, fax (808) 826-1166.

Mana Divers Scuba - This operator is a PADI dive center They choose from several dive sites depending on conditions and offer introductory dives, Eco-informed guided dives, PADI instruction and specialty dives, private tours and specialized dives, and night dives for certified divers. Their Discover scuba diving experience is for mature guests 8 years and older, cost is $35 for 1 1/2 to 2 hours. It is a chance to get a little hands-on dive at a minimal cost. The experience can include a lagoon dive and the fee can later be applied to an ocean dive if desired. Refresher dives ($85). Introductory dives $110/75 based on weather permitting. Offered to mature guests 12 and older. Maximum depth 40 feet, average depth 20 feet. 4310 Waialo Road, Bay 3, Hanapepe, HI 96716, (808) 335-088; Email: manadivers@hawaiian.net; Web: <www.manadivers.com>

Ocean Odyssey - This outfitter offers a variety of dive tours, boat dives, scuba certification courses, intro scuba dives, and more. Check their website or call for latest rates and details. PO Box 957, Lawai, HI 96765, (808) 245-8681. Web: <www.oceanodyssey-kauai.com>

Ocean Quest Watersports - Owners Jeannette and George Thompson specialize in small groups, no more than 4 persons, and offer excursions for beginners or advanced divers. North Shore eco tours are their summer specialty; South Shore tours in the winter. Diving tours are also available for the "Differently Abled." They include dives at Tunnels, Ahukini, and Koloa landing and other advanced sites can be arranged. For certified divers, 1 tank dive $60-75; 2 tank dive $80-95; Night Dive $60-75; Certification Course $450 per person; Intro Discover Scuba Dive $95; Boat Dive 100-125. PO Box 514, Kapa'a, HI 96746, (808) 821-1000; Email: info@trykauai.com; Web: <www.trykauai.com>

Seasport Divers - Excursions depart aboard their 32 ft., 12-passenger boat from the Kukui'ula Boat Harbor. With 26 different dive sites to choose from, they can address all levels of diving enthusiasts. They offer a morning (8am-noon) or afternoon (1pm-5pm) two-location dive or an evening (6pm-9pm) one-tank dive. Underwater videos will be filmed by the divemaster and are available for $39.95. They also offer 35 mm camera rentals. Certified divers 2 tank dives $95-115, One-tank dives $80; Shore dives, 2 tank $85-120, 1 tank $70-95; Intro Boat Dive $135, snorkelers/riders $55; Certification Course starts at $225 per person. - Ni'ihau All Day Dive, $250-270. They also offer Referral dives and Advanced certification. They offer complimentary pool lessons daily. Call for the scheduled lesson nearest to your location. Reservations are suggested. Also available are watersport equipment rentals including snorkel gear, boogie boards, beach chairs, and scuba gear. 2827 Po'ipu Road, PO Box 639, Koloa, HI 96756, (808) 742-9303, (808) 245-2592, 1-800-685-5889. Email: seasport@pixi.com; Web: < www.kauaiscubadiving.com >

Nitrox Tropical Divers and Sunrise Scuba Adventures - No swimming skills are required for this diving experience. They do shore dives and outfit you in shallow water where the scuba gear becomes weightless. They conduct all dives from a calm beach and keep the group size down to six divers. The minimum age for all scuba activities is 12 years, with parental consent. All beginners are required to participate in a FREE scuba orientation in calm shallow water prior to the ocean dive. Prices are $98 for intro dive tour for uncertified divers. $98 for shore or boat dive for certified divers. Underwater Scooter Tour, $98. Kayak Dive Tour $98. Snorkel Tour $48. PADI certification available. They are a PADI 5-STAR enriched air facility. 976 Kuhio Highway, PO Box 1255, Kapa'a, HI 96746. (808) 822-7333; Email: doctrox@aloha.net; Web: < www.sunrisescuba.com >

North Shore Divers - They offer a variety of adventure dives, boat dives, night dives, crack and wall diving, shark dives, turtle dives, lobster fest, etc. Shore dives: 1 tank $98; 2 tanks $128; 2 tank boat dive $175. Dives for certified divers: 1 tank shore dive $78; 2 tank shore dive $108; 2 tank boat dive $135; 1 tank turtle, shark or lobster fest dives $78; Night Dive $78; Scooter Dive $98; Certification Course $350 per person. PO Box 577, Hanalei, HI 96714, toll free 1-877-688-3483, (808) 826-1921 or 828-1223. Email: sacredseas@hotmail.com; Web: < garden-isle.com/nsdivers >

Wet 'n Wonderful - Free introductory scuba lesson, refresher courses, PADI certification, wetsuits (It might be Hawaii, but it gets cold down under!) Shore dives and night dives. Call for latest rates and details. (808) 822-0211.

SEA EXCURSIONS, SAILING, CRUISES-- Also see Snorkeling

Sea excursion options on Kaua'i are more limited than on some of the other islands, but what makes it special on the Garden Island are the intimacies of the trips. Most use small boats, with as few as 6 people with maximums of 25, so that the experience is much more personal. Depending on the time of year, the roughness of the water can vary greatly. If you are concerned about motion sickness, there are several over-the-counter medications that you could discuss with your doctor. Dramamine has been used by millions of people for years, however, many who have used this for motion difficulties have been so significantly affected by the sleepiness (which is a side effect for some individuals) that they can virtually sleep away the entire trip. While this might be an option for avoiding discomfort, they can't be having nearly as much fun as those who remain alert! Bonine is another motion medication that can be purchased over-the-counter that, for some people, has less of a drowsiness effect. Ginger, which can be purchased in capsules at health food stores is recommended as a preventative for motion sickness as well. Check with your physician as to what options might work for you (and with your health conditions and with other medications you may already be taking).

Using simple techniques such as keeping your eye on the land and avoiding a heavy, greasy meal before a boat trip are the only precautions most people need to use! A final note which bears mentioning! Most of these small craft DO NOT have bathroom facilities on-board. In some cases, there might be a "lua" (Hawaiian word for toilet) but it may not be available for public use. The larger boats will have facilities. It is recommended that you ask when booking!

Recent court rulings have impacted on commercial cruise boat operations on Kaua'i and especially in the Hanalei area. A couple of years ago, the State of Hawai'i banned commerical boating operations from Hanalei Bay from where many Napali Coast tours used to originate. In the meantime, many tour boat operators relocated to boat harbors on the south and west sides of Kaua'i. After considerable legal battling, a recent court decision upheld the ban and now most commerical boating operations are relocated to Kukuiula Small Boat Harbor at Lawai in Po'ipu, the Port Allen Harbor on the south side or Kikiaola Harbor at Kekaha on the west side. A few river kayak rental operations and outfitters are about all that remain of commercial boating at Hanalei and one or two operate from area beaches.

And, by the way, "Napali" means "the cliffs." You will often see it written as "Na Pali" but *Hawaiian Place Names*, written by authoritative historian Mary Kawena Kukui, spells it as one word. And thus we follow her advice. Remember in using this term, don't say The Napali Cliffs, for that would mean, "The cliffs cliffs."

Blue Dolphin Charters, Ltd. - Snorkel, sun, fish, eat, try out their water slide, and scuba aboard their 56' sailing trimaran *Tropic Bird*. The 5 hour Deluxe Napali Coast Tour is $99 per person, includes a continental breakfast and sandwiches for lunch. The 7 hour Deluxe Ni'ihau Island Tour is $139 per person. The 3 ½ hour Napali Sunset Cruise is $65 per person. The 2 hour Romantic Po'ipu Sunset Sail is $45 per person. Departs from Port Allen and Kukuiula Harbor at Po'ipu. 4380 Maha Road, PO Box 869, Eleele, HI 96705, toll free 1-877-511-1311, (808) 335-5553; Email: dolphin@aloha.net; Web: < www.kauaiboats.com >

Bluewater Sailing - Their newer 42 ft. all aluminum, Navy reconnaissance hull power boat, the *Northwind* is certified for 32 passengers, but 20 are "invited." Cushioned shaded seating in the open-air cabin or outside deck seating. A swim step and fresh water showers are added conveniences for snorkelers and all gear is provided along with a deli box lunch and soft drinks. Bluewater Express tours on the *Northwind:* The 5 hour Napali Coast Experience is adults $110, kids under 12 $85; the 4 hour Sunset/Napali Coast Tour, adults $90, kids under 12 $65. Private charters for *Northwind:* 5 hour Experience is $2,200; the 4 hour Tour is $1,700. You can also choose their snorkeling trips aboard their 42' Pearsen ketch, *Lady Leanne II*. Summer sail rates: the Half-Day Sail to Makua is adults $105, kids under 12 $85, includes light meal; 2 hour Sunset Sail is adults $60, kids $55; Half-Day Charter is $1,260; Charter Sunset Sail is $720. Winter sail rates: Half-Day Sail is adults $105, kids under 12 $85; Sunset Sail for adults $60, kids $55; Half-Day Charter is $1,260; Sunset Sail is $900. The "Express" departs from Port Allen. The sailing excursions depart from Hanalei in the summer, Port

Allen in the winter. Exclusive charters available for either vessel. PO Box 1318, Hanalei, HI 96714. (808) 828-1142. FAX (808) 828-0508. Email: bluwat@aloha.net; Web: <www.sail-kauai.com> or Web: <www.bluewater-sailing.com>

Captain Andy's Sailing Adventures - Their motto says it all, "Nobody has more fun!" Sail aboard the 55' catamaran *Spirit of Kaua'i*. Seasonal whale watching. This vessel was designed and built for Capt. Andy in the Virgin Islands, then tested out on the 12,000 mile trek to Kaua'i. This operator offers several cruises. The 5 ½ hour Napali Coast Snorkel/BBQ Cruise is adults $109, kids under 12 $79. The 4 hour Napali Dinner Cruise is adults $99, kids under 12 $69. The 5 ½ hour Napali Coast Snorkel/Picnic Sail is adults $109, kids under 12 $79. The 5 hour Napali Snorkel/Sunset Sail is adults $109, kids $79. The 2 hour Po'ipu Cocktail Sail is adults $59, kids under 12 $40. Departs Port Allen and Kukuiula Harbor in Po'ipu.. PO Box 876, Ele'ele, Kaua'i, HI 96705. (808) 335-6833. FAX (808) 335-6838. Email: fun@sailing-hawaii.com; Web: <www.sailing-hawaii.com>

Captain Sundown - The "Ku'uipo" is a 15-passenger sailing catamaran. The operator has a 6-hour Snorkel Sail-Napali Coast daily 9 a.m.-3 p.m. (April-November only) showing you the whole Napali Coast, dolphins, flying fish, with snorkeling and lunch, $135. A 4-hour Whale Watch Sail (December-April only) departs twice daily, 9 a.m. and 2:30 p.m., $75. The 3-hour Bali Hai Sunset Sail goes every evening, 4-7 p.m., $68. The boat is available for private charters, 2-4-6 hours or more, call for rates. Winter whales guaranteed. PO Box 697, Hanalei, HI 96714. (808) 826-5585. E-mail: sundown@aloha.net Website: <www.captainsundown.com>

Catamaran Kahanu - Tours the Napali coastline in their power 36 ft. catamaran. Maximum 18 passengers. Covered area and restroom. There are power engines on this catamaran so you can cruise near the coastline. Whale tours offered seasonally. The 5 hour Napali Coast Morning Tour: adults $105, kids under 12 $75. The 4 hour Napali Coast Sightseeing Tour: adults $85, kids under 12 $65. Departs Port Allen. PO Box 51006, Eleele, HI 96705. (808) 335-3577, fax (808) 828-0935. Email: kahanu@hawaiian.net; <www.catamarankahanu.com>

HoloHolo Charters -- '61 *HoloHolo*, motor vessel/catamaran custom built on Kaua'i. Large trampolines or huge open air cabin. The *HoloHolo* offers a 7 hour Napali-Ni'ihau Supertour, 7am - 2 pm, adults $156, children under 12 $109, includes continental breakfast, lunch, snorkeling. The *HoloHolo* also does a 3 ½ hour Napali Sunset Tour, adults $85, kids under 12 $60, includes champagne for adults and dinner pupus. Aboard their 48 foot sailing catamaran *Leila* you can enjoy their 5 hour Napali Sail, adults $109, kids under 12 $75, twice daily, 7 a.m.-12 noon, 1-6:30 p.m. Seasonal whale watching. Only children ages 6 years and older for excursions, 5 years and older on sunset trips, no "expecting" mothers. Departs from Port Allen Harbor. Located at the Ele'ele Shopping Center, Eleele, HI 96705. Toll free 1-800-848-6130, (808) 335-0815, Fax (808) 335-0916. Email: reservations@holoholocharters.com; Web: <www.holoholocharters.com>

Kaua'i Sea Tours - This cruise operator sails out of Port Allen Harbor. The ride to the Napali Coast from this direction is 1 1/2 hours. They offer various cruise packages with choice of power catamarans or ocean rafts. The 6 hour catamaran Deluxe Nualolo Kai Day Tour is adults $135, children under 12 $105. The 5 hour catamaran Half-Day Nualolo Kai Tour is adults $119, kids under 12 $89. The ocean raft 5 hour Sightseeing Tour is adults $132, kids under 12 $105. The ocean raft Half-Day Tour is adults $108, kids under 12 $78. The seasonal catamaran Napali Sightseeing/Sunset/Whale Watch Tour, 4 hours, is adults $89, kids under 12 $59. The seasonal ocean raft Napali Sightseeing/Sunset/Whale Watch Tour, 4 hours, is adults $89, kids under 12 $59. The 5 hour raft tour includes a beach landing at Nualolo Kai with a narrated hike of the area and time to snorkel. PO Box 51004, Ele'ele, HI 96705. 1-800-733-7997, (808) 826-7254. Email: seatour@aloha.net; Web: < www.seatours.net >

Kaulana Pali Kai Tours -- Group or private charters. Sunset cruises, snorkeling, whale watching aboard this 25' Bayliner Trophy. Freshwater shower and enclosed toilet. Departs Kiki'aola Harbor in Kekaha. Their Napali run costs $96 per person for the 4 1/2 - 5 hour cruise including lunch and refreshments. 4573 Akialoa Road, Kekaha, HI 96752, (808) 337-9309.

Liko Kaua'i Cruises - Departing from Kiki'aola Harbor near Kekaha but check-in at their office in Waimea. Board their 49' power catamaran with bathroom, fresh water shower, and shaded area for a relaxing cruise experience. Their 5 hour Morning or Afternon Napali Coast Snorkel Tour is adults $110, kids under 12 $75. The 2 ½ hour Napali Sunset Cruise is adults $75, kids under 12 $45. Day cruises include lunch/snacks/beveraves. Sunset sightseeing cruise three times each week with snacks and soft drinks. Seasonal whale watching. 9875 Waimea Road, PO Box 18, Waimea, HI 96796. 1-888-SEA-LIKO, (808) 338-0333, fax (808) 337-1544. Email: liko@aloha.net; Web: < www.liko-kauai.com >

Na Pali (Eco) Adventures - ★ They are dedicated to the understanding and protection of our eco system. (Their boats use 100% recycled fuel made from cooking oil!) Their guided trip along the Napali coast is led by a trained naturalist. They use motor-powered, hard-body catamarans (passenger maximums of 26 and 35) that provide a smoother and drier ride than the inflatables or rafts, but there are still provide plenty of thrills! The morning Napali Coast Tour/Onboard Picnic trip is 5 hours with snorkeling and sightseeing and includes a full lunch, $115 adults, $86 kids. The 3 ½ hour Napali Coast Sunset Tour is adults $80, kids $45. The 6 hour Ultimate Napali Coast Tour, Snorkel, Whale Watch and Onboard Picnic Tour is seasonal, adults $115, kids $75. The seasonal 3 ½ hour Napali Coast Sunset/Whale Watch is adults $85, kids $45. The 2 hour seasonal Whale Watch Cruise is adults $59, kids $35. The operators are genuinely concerned with the welfare of whales and other aquatic life and it shows in the way they run their cruise. If the whales are out there, they'll find them. An underwater microphone allows you to hear the whales' musical conversation. In addition to whales (in season), you might also be treated to a pod of dolphins swimming along your boat, green sea turtles floating like huge army helmets upon the water, or if you look quickly, you may spot a flying fish. On a recent excursion, the cruise was greeted by Kaua'i's rarest aquatic animal. On first sighting, the monk seal appeared to be lounging in the water, however, on the return trip he appeared in another bay giving us what appeared to be a smile! Realizing that there are estimated to be only three monk seals living in the waters around Kaua'i, the captain felt that the same seal had been seen twice as they are rarely seen more than a couple times a year. Departs from Port Allen Harbor. Location, 4310 Waialo Road, Hwy 541, Eleele, HI 96705; mailing address PO Box 1017, Hanalei, HI 96714. (808) 826-6804. FAX (808) 826-7073. 1-800-659-6804. Email: reservations@napali.com; Web: < www.napali.com >

Na Pali Explorer - Enjoy a Napali excursion on the comfortable adventure raft *Na Pali Explorer.* This 48' rigid hull inflatable is mounted on Scarab ocean racing hulls and is powered by twin Volvo turbo supercharged diesels which each generate 230 horsepower. Needless to say, the *Na Pali Explorer* gets to where it is going pretty quickly, cruising at 25 knots and the potential to reach 33 knots. This vessel offers a smoother, more comfortable ride than the zodiac-type raft experience. Capacity is 49 passengers, but we're advised they take only 35. There are two tours. The 5 hour Napali Snorkel Expedition coastal tour is adults $118, kids under 12 $70, includes light meal/beverages. The 3 ½ hour Napali Coast Expedition sightseeing/swim cruise is adults $79, kids under 12 $59. The seasonal Whale Watching Expedition is adults $79, kids under 12 $59. There is also a chance to swim and snorkeling (gear provided) on a protected reef with a beach landing at Nualolo Kai, an ancient Hawaiian fishing village (weather permitting). Comfort features include a canopy for shade, and padded seating. Their expert naturalists share little-known facts about marine life and Hawaiian places along the way. Departs Kiliaola Harbor in Kekaha. 9935 Kaumualii Highway, Waimea, HI 96796, 1-877-338-9999, (808) 338-9999, FAX (808) 335-0188. Email: napali@hawaiian.net; Web: < www.napali-explorer.com >

Rainbow Runner Sailing - 42' Kantola designed Trimaran, maximum of 18. Nawiliwili Small Boat Harbor or Kalapaki Beach, weather permitting. A one-hour Kalapaki Fun Sail is one featured cruise, $45 adult/$35 children. High performance speed sailing. Includes soft drinks/juices. Their Nawiliwili Sunset is $59 adults, $39 children and includes champagne and snacks. Other short cruises available. All trips include performance sailing and seasonal whale watching. They operate True Blue Charters for those avid fisherfolks and Island Adventures for kayaking fans. PO Box 1722, Lihu'e, HI 96766. (808) 632-0202, FAX (808) 246-9661. Email: kamal@kauaifun.com; Web: < www.sailingkauai.com >

SNORKELING -- Also refer to Sea Excursions which precedes this section

Since weather and ocean conditions cause very dramatic differences in the snorkeling conditions from day to day, a dive shop is a great place to find the tip for the best spot of the day. The staff is friendly and they are eager to ensure you have a great snorkeling experience. If weather conditions are just right, Tunnels on the North Shore is a wonderful snorkel spot. Po'ipu Beach on the South shore will be of interest to the novice and intermediate snorkeler. You can purchase a disposable underwater camera to capture memories of your underwater adventure. You'll get some interesting souvenir photos, but the quality isn't nearly as good as the real thing. Several areas around the island have fish that are accustomed to being fed. In fact, they almost expect it! They go for bread or try the dried packages of noodles. A number of dive shops (and some grocery stores) carry little packages of smelly fish food pellets. The price tag is a couple of dollars for two tubes of food. You can cut off one end of the plastic tube-bag and slowly shake out the pellets. However, many folks are discouraging feeding the fish at all. It can make them more aggressive and it provides a false habitat, develops dependency and is not their natural food supply. Kids will take to snorkeling with little effort. The only difficulty might be in their excitement when they spot the fish for the first time. They may forget they have a snorkel in their mouth when they try and shout out their glee. For the child who lacks confidence, use water wings for extra buoyancy. A life jacket, of course, is even more security. An adult may find taking a paddle board out and positioning themselves over the top of it (face in the water on one side and feet in the water on the other) a way to get over their initial jitters. Rest assured that snorkeling is much, much easier than swimming. Even easier than walking! All you have to do is float and breathe! Lydgate is a fine beach for the novice child snorkeler. It has a very sheltered area which will inspire confidence. Perhaps the most difficulty for a beginning (child or adult) snorkeler is just getting into the water. Waves make this a more difficult task. Once in the water and enjoying the sights, they'll wonder why they never tried it before. Poʻipu Beach is generally good for beginning snorkelers as well. For intermediate snorkelers Keʻe, Hideaways, or Tunnels can be good during calm summer surf. The dive shops can advise you which locations are best at the time of your visit. Rental equipment is available at a number of locations around the island. With snorkel gear you will get what you pay for. Prices range from $4-5 a day and up. Silicon gear is preferred, but you generally won't find that at the economy prices. If you plan on adding snorkeling to your list of regular recreational activities, you may find it worthwhile to bite the bullet and invest in your own set of gear. You can pick-up an inexpensive set of fins, mask, and snorkel for a child at Long's Drug Store, Costco, Big Kmart, or Walmart. Better yet would be to bring your own gear with you from home. Several cruise operators include snorkeling adventures in their various excursions. Several are listed here but also refer to the previous Sea Excursions section for additional information on snorkeling trips which are available from various departure points around the island. Also listed are some outlets which provide snorkel gear rentals. Also see SCUBA.

Blue Dolphin Charters - Various Napali sailing trimaran and snorkeling adventures. (808) 742-6731

Bluewater Sailing - Combination sightseeing and snorkeling excursions on Napali Coast. (808) 828-1142

Capt. Andy's - Napili snorkel & sightseeing cruises. (808) 335-6833

Capt. Sundown - Daily Napali snorkel sail to North Shore's best spots. (808) 826-5585

Captain Zodiac - This operator used to run ocean raft snorkeling cruises along the Napali Coast from Hanalei. But due to the recent banning of commerical boating from Hanalei, this operator is currently closed. There were plans to try to relocate elsewhere around the island at press time. It's advised to keep checking their website for the latest information: www.planet-hawaii.com/zodiac.

Catamaran Kahanu - Discover snorkeling thrills along the famed Napali Coast. (808) 335-3577

Fathom Five - Half day scuba/snorkel trips available to secluded south side dive sites. (808) 742-6991

Hanalei Sport Fishing & Tours - Sport fishing cruises as well as snorkeling, sightseeing, etc. (808) 826-6114

Hanalei Surf Company - Offers a range of rental equipment: mask, fins, and snorkel, $20 per week; boogie board, $30 per week; wet suits, $4 per day. Optical masks available. Located at 5161 Kuhio Hwy. (808) 826-9000.

Holoholo Charters - Catamaran sailing cruises include snorkeling adventures. (808) 335-0815

Kaua'i Sea Tours - Ocean power raft excursions on Napali Coast include snorkeling. (808) 826-7254

Liko Kaua'i Cruises - Napali Coast power catamaran cruises offer snorkeling adventures. (808) 338-0333

Mana Divers Scuba - They offer shore and boat scuba dives plus snorkeling for non-divers too. (808) 335-0881

Napali Eco Adventures - Various sightseeing and snorkeling cruise adventures available. (808) 826-6804

Pedal and Paddle Hanalei - Basic rentals for regular or optic mask and snorkel set is $5 day/$20 a week (but the good news is their rental week is eight days long!) (808) 826-9069.

Rainbow Runner - Adventure sails and snorkeling on Kaua'i's east and south shores. (808) 632-0202

SeaFun Kaua'i - SeaFun is a shore based, half-day, guided snorkeling tour. Some of the islands best snorkeling is inside protective reefs where boats cannot go. Transportation (from most hotels), including wet suit, instruction from the auctions, snacks and drinks are included. An underwater video of your tour is available for an additional fee. Experienced snorkelers will appreciate learning more about the environment from marine biologist experts. They snorkel off Lawa'i Beach and Prince Kuhio Park. $69 adults (age 13 and up), $53 children (5-12 years). (They also operate Kaua'i Mountain Tours and Kaua'i Backroads Tours, guided four-wheel drive and hiking adventures.) 1702 Haleukana Street, Lihu'e, HI 96766. 1-800-452-1113, (808) 245-6400, FAX (808) 245-4888. < www.alohakauaitours.com > E-mail: < tours@gte.net >

Snorkel Bob's has shops at 4-734 Kuhio Hwy, (808) 823-9433 and Koloa at 3236 Po'ipu Road, (808) 742-2206.

True Blue Charters & Ocean Sports - They do snorkel/dive cruises in addition to charter fishing and fun sails on east and south shore coasts. (808) 245-9662, 246-6333

SNUBA

Snuba Tours of Kaua'i - Snuba, as it sounds, is a blend of snorkeling and scuba. The air source is contained within a floatation raft that follows you as you move beneath the ocean. The guided underwater tour includes personalized instruction, fish food, and equipment, $55 per person. They take small groups, 1-6 divers at a time. Tour length is 1 ½ hours with 35-40 minutes underwater. They dive from Lawa'i Beach in Po'ipu on the South Shore. (808) 823-8912. Email: snuba@aloha.net. Web: < www.hshawaii.com/kvp/snuba >

SPAS & FITNESS CENTERS Also see "Retreats"

Ever considered taking a vacation from your vacation? Well, here's a tip for you! Let's face it, shopping, beaches, terrific dinners, more shopping, fabulous lunches, more shopping...well, you know, it all gets pretty tiring! Indulge yourself in a day at the *ANARA Spa* at the Hyatt Regency. (ANARA is an acronym for "A New Age Restorative Approach"). When you consider the amenities, it is one great value and you deserve it! Select a facial, half-hour or 50-minute massage, or perhaps an herbal wrap. With any of their pampered treatments you'll get a full-day pass to enjoy their spa facilities.

It's recommended getting there in advance of your appointment. There are ladies' and mens' facilities which are private, as well as some co-ed facilities. The co-ed area offers a complete exercise room and a lap pool, or for the less aerobically inclined, enjoy some sun or shade on lounge chairs around the pool, have a light lunch, or relax in a jacuzzi. In both the womens' and mens' facilities you'll find a private jacuzzi tub, 12-jet jacuzzi shower, eucalyptus steam room, sauna, multi-person jacuzzi, lava rock shower garden, and more lounge chairs. Get in that relaxation mode and then enjoy your therapy treatment. When you are finished, there is more time to choose from the aforementioned facilities before freshening up with their specially formulated mango scented shampoos, conditioners, and body soaps. Make it a whole day event! Prices for daily spa membership inclusive with any spa/salon treatment: hotel guests $15/non-guests $20. Massage therapy or skin care treatments runs $55-130. Loofah scrubs, personal training sessions, herbal wraps and other services $35-90. Can't decide? Try a mini-day at ANARA for $215, or the ANARA Sampler for $115 or discover the new you with the 6 hour "Day at ANARA" for $325. Open daily from 6am-8pm. Salon services are also available. Any salon services over $40 includes a comple-mentary ANARA spa membership for that day. (808) 742-1234 for reservations.

Kai Mana - Shakti Gawain, author of books including *Creative Visualization*, and *Living in the Light* offers week-long "intensives" in Kilauea at her Kai Mana estate. The week long programs are $2,000 plus tax per person or $3,500 per couple plus tax per person. Included are group sessions, classes and two massag-es by a licensed practitioner. (415) 388-7140. (The Kai Mana Cottage is available for rental. See North Shore accommodations.)

Kaua'i Athletic Club - They offer aerobics, racquetball, handball, freeweights, and have now added Cybex equipment. Other facilities include a swimming pool, jacuzzi, pro shop, child care, and deli that features low-cal and low-fat options. Hours Monday thru Friday 6am-9pm, Saturday and Sunday 8am-5pm. Single day visit $12. Weekly and monthly unlimited passes also available. 4370 Kukui Grove, Lihu'e, HI 96766. (808) 245-5381.

Princeville Health Club and Spa - Located at the Prince Golf and Country Club on the North Shore in Princeville. Available amenities are massages, facials, seaweed wrap, and aromatherapy treatments along with their complete health and fitness facility. Passes start at $15 per day (for hotel guests only), weekly rates run $45, and monthly passes are $95. The "Spa Experience" includes: use of whirlpool sauna, steam room, 25 meter lap pool, personal locker, robe, unlimited classes, one hour lomi lomi massage for $130 Princeville Hotel Guest, Spa Guest $140. Spa admission is included in regular Prince and Makai Golf Course green fees. Unlimited daily exercise classes including body conditioning, step aerobics, aquacize and yoga are offered. Spa hours are Monday-Saturday from 9am-6:30pm. Sunday 9am-4:30pm. (808) 826-5030.

SURFING

Anini Beach Windsurfing - this operator offers instruction in both surfing and windsurfing; intro and certification lessons; rental equipment, sails, boards, etc. PO Box 1602, Hanalei, HI 96714. (808) 826-9463

Hanalei Surf Company rents fiberglass surfboards for $15 per day, $65 per week. Soft surfboards $12 per day, $50 per week. Boogie boards rent for $5 per day, $20 per week. They are located at 5161 Kuhio Hwy. (808) 826-9000.

Kayak Kaua'i Outbound offers Hawaiian surf boarding lessons, $35 per hour lesson. Kapa'a (808) 822-9179; Hanalei (808) 826-9844, 1-800-437-3507. Email: outbound@aloha.net

Learn to Surf School - this instructional operator offers guaranteed surf lessons that will teach you how to do it. They offer surf lessons daily and daylong. Rates: 1 person/1 hour, $30; 1 person/ 1 ½ hours, $35; 2 persons/1 hour, $50; 2 persons/ 1 ½ hours, $60. Group rates available. Hanalei (808) 826-7612

Margo Oberg's Surfing School - Located between the Kiahuna Plantation and the Sheraton in Po'ipu. Margo won world titles seven times between 1968 and 1981. Her school has been operating now for well over 25 years. Three times daily lessons are offered at $45 per person with 6-7 in a class; 1 hour instruction, half-hour practice time. Private lessons $75. Po'ipu Beach (808) 742-8019, or 639-0708

Mikie's Surf School - Instructor Mike Crowder is a certified Hawaiian Ocean Lifeguard and skilled waterman. He shares his passion for the ocean and surfing with students on Kaua'i's east side. Call for details (808) 635-6664, 823-8681

Pete's Surf School - This instructor operates small classes of 3-4 people, all ages, one hour lessons. Everything included. Emphasis is on being safe and having fun. Call for details (808) 639-4109

Progressive Expressions, Inc. in Koloa since 1974. They manufacture and sell surfboards, bodyboards, and surfing accessories for all ages. 5420 Koloa Road. (808) 742-6041.

Windsurf Kaua'i - Certified Master Instructor Celeste Harvel offers surfing instruction along with windsurfing lessons for beginners and up. Beginner surf lessons are 1 ½ hours long at Hanalei. Rental equipment available. PO Box 323, Hanalei, HI 96714, (808) 828-6838. (See Windsurfing for more information)

TENNIS

Kaua'i County has eight free municipal public tennis courts which are available on an open first-come, first-served basis. Available courts are in Waimea, Kekaha, Koloa, Kalaheo, Lihu'e, Wailua Homesteads, Wailua Houselots, and Kapa'a New Park. Also, many hotels have courts available for both public and guest use. Tennis facilities are located at resorts around Kaua'i. Call them for open hours and rate details:

Hanalei Bay Resort , Princeville (808) 826-6522
Kaua'i Lagoons Racquet Club, Lihu'e (808) 241-6000
Kiahuna Tennis Resort, Po'ipu (808) 742-9533
Po'ipu Kai Tennis Complex (808) 742-1144
Princeville Resort Tennis Complex, Princeville (808) 826-3620
The Tennis Garden, Hyatt Regency Kaua'i (808) 742-1234

THEATER

The Kaua'i Community Players does several productions annually for children and adults. If you're on the island in December, check out their breakfast with Santa! Call (808) 245-7700 for more information on plays and dinner theater productions.

Kaua'i Community College opened its Performing Arts Center/Theater in 1995. The theater complex was almost complete in 1992 when Hurricane Iniki struck and caused extensive damage. The beautiful hall seats 550 persons and adds an exciting dimension to theater possibilities on Kaua'i. They currently offer an annual concert series and special performances throughout the year. It is proving to be an invaluable community cultural resource. For information on upcoming events, call (808) 245-8311, or 245-8270.

The Kaua'i International Theater has been open for a couple of years. The theater features air conditioning and a 62 seat capacity. Artwork of local artists is on display as well. They plan on six shows per season with each show running about 4 weeks. They anticipate guest performers and other entertainment in-between productions so there will be lots happening here. Located at 4-831 Kuhio Highway, Kapa'a, HI 96746 in the Kaua'i Village Center. (808) 821-1588.

The Kaua'i Marriott Resort stages "A Nite of Broadway" Dinner Theater and Musical Revue. Held variously throughout the year, this is a series of favorite Broadway musical performances. Shows begin with a no-host cocktail party at 6pm followed by a dinner buffet. One recent edition of the show included selections from Les Miserables, The Phantom of the Opera and Guys and Dolls. The show changes so audiences can come back and enjoy new songs for continuing family entertainment. The sets and buffet dinner are intertwined to create an entertaining evening of food, drama, music and fun. Call the Marriott (808) 245-5050 or Showtunes (808) 245-8046. Cost is $65 per person inclusive tax and tip.

Waimea Theatre, Waimea, was reopened in 1999 after a period of being closed. The 1938-art deco era influenced theater has 500 seats. The small town rural movie house closed in 1972 and was converted into warehouse and retail space. In 1992, Hurricane Iniki assisted with renovations and destroyed the decorative marquee. Over the course of six years, preservation and patience have saved the landmark structure and restored its vitality. The fully restored theatre now offers a variety of films and live productions. (808) 338-0282, 338-2027.

WATERSKIING

Kaua'i Water Ski & Surf Co. - Rates run $100 per hour, $55 per 1/2 hour, accomodates up to two people. They ski up the Wailua River. Mondays through Fridays 9am-5pm. Surf shop at Kinipopo Shopping Village, 4-356 Kuhio Highway, Kapa'a, HI 96746, toll free 1-800-344-7915, (808) 822-3574.

WHALE WATCHING

Whale watching is seasonal, officially December 15 through May 15, although a few stragglers may linger into May and some anxious for those warm waters of the Hawaiian islands may arrive a bit ahead of schedule. The best vantage points for whale watching are from one of the boats that make excursions out in search of these magnificent mammals. See the previous section on SEA EXCURSIONS, SAILING AND CRUISES. You can also view them from above during a helicopter tour. As for a best bet, we would recommend one of the condos above the bluff at Princeville or the northern most point of the island at the Kilauea lighthouse. A good pair of binoculars would be useful.

WILDLIFE REFUGES

As you pass the Princeville Shopping Center you are at mile marker 28 on Kuhio Highway 56. Opposite the shopping center is an overlook area with a great view of the Hanalei Valley, the taro patches and distant mountains. The road winds on down the Princeville bluff a mile or so to the one-lane iron bridge spanning the Hanalei River. This section of the highway passes through the *Hanalei Wildlife Refuge*. The Hanalei Wildlife Refuge was established on 917 acres in 1972 and is located in the Hanalei Valley. Unique to many refuges, taro is allowed to be commercially farmed on a portion of the property and one permit is granted for cattle grazing. Administered by the U.S. Fish and Wildlife Service as a unit of the National Wildlife Refuge System, they actively manage the habitat to provide wetlands for endangered Hawaiian waterbirds. Historic farming (taro) and grazing practices are compatible with the refuges' objectives and thus permitted to a limited degree. There are 49 species of birds, including the endangered Hawaiian black-necked stilt, gallinule, coot, and duck that make their home here. Of the 49 species, 18 are introduced. There are no native mammals, reptiles, or amphibians, except possibly the Hawaiian bat. The refuge is not open to the public, but an interpretive overlook on the state highway just north of the refuge allows an excellent photo opportunity. Located along the Huleia River in southeast Kaua'i near Lihu'e is the *Huleia National Wildlife Refuge*, which is home to the endangered koloa duck. In 1973, 241 acres were purchased to provide a water bird habitat. The lands, once taro and rice fields, are now breeding and feeding grounds for a variety of waterfowl. The refuge is located in a relatively flat valley along the Huleia River which is bordered by a steep wooded hillside. There are 31 species of migratory birds which inhabit the area and 18 of these species were introduced.

Special permits are issued annually to a commercial kayaking businesses for access through an upland portion of the refuge. The refuge, adjacent to the Menehune Fish Pond, is not open to the public, however, a view of it from the overlook along Nawiliwili Road above the harbor is possible.

The *Kilauea Point National Wildlife Refuge* was established in 1974 and is recognized as Hawai'i's largest seabird sanctuary, a place that is home to more than 5,000 seabirds. This refuge is a nesting site for the red-footed booby, wedge-tailed shearwater, Laysan albatross, and many other species of Hawaiian seabirds. The acquisition of land has continued with this sanctuary now encompassing 203 acres. The refuge was struck hard by Hurricane Iniki. Not only was there much damage to the birdlife and vegetation, but the famous lighthouse was also seriously affected. At Kilauea Point, they reported that about 80% of the native plants suffered damage. On Crater Hill, at least 25% were lost and an additional 50% damaged. Mokolea Point vegetation suffered little damage. Kilauea Point lost the most birds and suffered the worst damage to the habitat. The Kaua'i Natural Wildlife Refuge complex lost 12 of their 20 buildings. There was also damage to the lighthouse visitor center and bookstore, storage buildings, fences, and the water delivery system. Today, the center is fully restored. When the lighthouse and support facilities were transferred from the U.S. Coast Guard on February 15, 1985, Kilauea Point became the 425th National Wildlife Refuge. The adjacent Kilauea Point Humpback Whale National Marine Sanctuary was established in 1994. Over 250,000 visitors enjoy the Kilauea Point National Wildlife Refuge visitor center and wildlife viewing areas each year. As many as a thousand visitors per day may tour the facility during the peak of the holiday seasons. There is an on-going habitat management program that includes water development, native plant propagation, service club, and nursery activities. Over 200 volunteers donate hours to varied refuge projects. Of the 203 acres, 183 acres are owned, and another 20 acres are conservation easement. The refuge is open to the public daily from 10am-4pm, closed some federal holidays. *Kilauea Point*, PO Box 87, Kilauea, Kaua'i, HI 96754. (808) 828-1413. Admission is $2 by donation.

WINDSURFING

Once again, weather conditions will determine where this activity is best suited. 'Anini is the best for beginners. Located near Princeville, it offers a lagoon with protected waters and steadily blowing winds that make it ideal for the beginning or intermediate windsurfer. Advanced windsurfers enjoy Tunnels on the North Shore and Mahaulepu on the South Shore. There are a few windsurfing schools that can provide instructional lessons and equipment rentals.

'Anini Beach Windsurfing - Windsurfing equipment rentals $50 per day. Intro and certification lessons available; three hour windsurfing lessons $65. PO Box 1602, Hanalei, HI 96714, (808) 826-9463.

Windsurf Kaua'i - Located on the North Shore with instruction at the 'Anini lagoon. Celeste Harvel is a master instructor who offers state-of-the-art beginning windsurf boards. These boards are a foot shorter, 11' as opposed to the conventional 12' board, which allows for easier maneuvering. The boards are also just slightly wider. The 'Anini lagoon has a maximum depth of seven feet and 10-20 knot winds year round. Half of the lagoon is designated for windsurfers, the other half for swimming and snorkeling. Lessons for first timers run $75 for a three-hour class with a maximum of 6 people in the class. This phase of instruction includes learning how to steer, sail, and come back to shore. The second level class is the same price and length, but completes certification. This three-hour instruction includes learning how to jibe, beach start, and rig. The equipment makes windsurfing easy for everyone. For the less athletic individual, Celeste utilizes a 15 square foot sail with a 4 1/2 foot boom which is very manageable. She has custom equipment for children and can teach anyone five years and up. She also offers extensive windsurf equipment rental. Rental equipment is $75 all day, $50 half day or $25 per hour. In the winter, spring, and fall Celeste also offers surfing lessons at Hanalei Bay. Windsurfing lessons offered weekdays at 'Anini Beach. She also teaches the physically disabled and challenged. PO Box 323 Hanalei, HI 96714. (808) 828-6838.

RECOMMENDED READING

Bailey, Paul. Those Kings and Queens of Old Hawaii. Tucson, Arizona: Westernlore Press. 1975.

Ball, Stuart M. The Backpackers Guide to Hawai'i. Honolulu: University of Hawaii Press. 1996

Barrere, Dorothy. Pukui, Mary K., Kelly, Marion. Hula, Historical Perspectives. Honolulu: Bishop Museum. 1980.

Beekman, Allan. The Ni'ihau incident: the true story of the Japanese fighter pilot. Honolulu: Heritage Press of Pacific. 1982.

Berger, Andrew J. Bird Life in Hawai'i. Honolulu: Island Heritage. 1993.

Berger, Andrew J. Hawaiian Birdlife. Honolulu: University of Hawaii Press. 1994.

Bird, Isabella. Six Months in the Sandwich Islands. Tokyo: Tuttle. 1988.

Carter, Frances. Hawaii on Foot. Honolulu: The Bess Press. 1990.

Chisholm, Craig. Hawaiian Hiking Trails: The Guide for All Islands. Oregon: Fernglen Press. 1999.

Chisholm, Craig. Kaua'i Hiking Trails. Lake Oswego: Fernglen Press. 1991.

Clark, John R. K. Beaches of Kaua'i and Ni'ihau. Honolulu: University of Hawai'i Press, 1990.

Clay, Horace F. and Hubbard, James C. The Hawaii Garden Tropical Exotics. Honolulu: University of Hawaii Press. 1987.

Cook, Chris. Kauai-The Movie Book. Honolulu: Mutual Publishing Co. 1996.

Crites, Jennifer. and Crow, Gerald L. Guide to Hawai'i's Sharks and Rays. Honolulu: Mutual Publishing Co. 2001.

David, Reginald E. Hawai'i's Birds. Hawai'i Audubon Society. 1996.

Dawrs, Stu. Discover Kauai-The Garden Island. Honolulu: Island Heritage. 1999.

Daws, Gavan. Shoal of Time: A History of the Hawaiian Islands. Honolulu: University of Hawaii Press. 1974.

Daws, Gavan. Hawai'i, the Islands of Life. Honolulu: Signature Hawai'i. 1988.

Day, A.G. and Stroven, Carl. A Hawaiian Reader, Vol. I. Honolulu: Mutual Publishing Co. 1985.

Day, A. Grove. Hawai'i and its People. Honolulu: Mutual Publishing Co. 1993.

Day, A.Grove. Mark Twain in Hawai'i: Roughing It in the Sandwich Islands. Honolulu: Mutual Publishing Co. 1990.

Day, A. Grove. A Hawaiian Reader, Vol. II. Honolulu; Mutual Pubishing Co. 1998.

Elbert, Samuel H. Hawaiian Antiquities and Folk-Lore. Honolulu: University of Hawai'i Press. 1959.

Fielding, Ann. Hawaiian Reefs and Tidepools. Hawai'i: Oriental Pub. Co.

Fielding, Ann and Robinson, Ed. An Underwater Guide to Hawaii. Honolulu: University of Hawaii Press. 1991.

Harrison, Craig Seabirds of Hawai'i: Natural History & Conservation. NY: Comstock Pub. 1990.

Hawai'i Audubon Society. Hawai'i's birds. Honolulu: The Society. 1993.

Hobson, E. and Chave, E. H. Hawaiian Reef Animals. Honolulu: University of Hawaii Press. 1990.

Hoover, John. Hawai'i's Sea Creatures: A Guide to Hawai'i's Marine Invertebrates. Honolulu: Mutual Publishing Co. 1999.

Hoover, John. Hawai'i's Underwater Paradise. Honolulu: Mutual Publishing Co. 1998.

Hoover, John. A Pocket Guide to Hawai'i's Underwater Paradise. Honolulu: Mutual Publishing Co.

Juvik, Sonia P. and Juvik, James O. Atlas of Hawai'i. Honolulu: University of Hawaii Press. 1998.

Knudsen, Eric Alfred. Kanuka of Kaua'i. Tongg. 1944.

Kndusen, Eric. Teller of Tales. Honolulu: Mutual Publishing. 1946.

Koch, Tom. Six Islands on Two Wheels: A Cycling Guide to Hawaii. Bess Press, Honolulu, HI. 1990.

Laudan, Rachel. The Food of Paradise-Exploring Hawaii's Culinary Heritage. Honolulu: University of Hawaii Press. 1996.

London, Jack. Stories of Hawai'i. Honolulu: Mutual Publishing. 1965.

Ludwig, Myles. Kaua'i in the Eye of Iniki. Hanalei Bay, Kaua'i: Inter-Pacific Media. 1992.

McMahon, Richard. Adventuring in Hawai'i: Hawai'i, Maui, Molokai, Lanai, Oahu, Kauai. Sierra Club. 1996.

McMahon, Richard. Camping Hawai'i-A Complete Guide. Honolulu: University of Hawaii Press. 1997.

Merlin, Mark. Hawaiian Coastal Plants. Pacific Guide. 1995.

Merlin, Mark. Hawaiian Forest Plants. Honolulu: University of Hawaii Press. 1996.

Morey, Kathy. Kaua'i Trails: Walks, Strolls, and Treks on the Garden Island. Berkely, CA: Wilderness Press, 1991.

Moriarty, Linda. Ni'ihau Shell Leis. Honolulu: University of Hawai'i Press. 1986.

Pratt, Douglas. A Pocket Guide to Hawai'i's Beautiful Birds. Honolulu: Mutual Publishing Co. 1996.

Pratt, Douglas. Hawai'i's Beautiful Birds. Honolulu: Mutual Publishing Co. 1998.

Pratt, Douglas. Enjoying Birds in Hawai'i. Honolulu: Mutual Publishing. 1993.

Pratt, Douglas. Pocket Guide to Hawai'i's Trees and Shrubs. Honolulu: Mutual Publishing Co. 1999.

Pratt, Douglas. Bruner, P.L. and Berrett, D.G. A Field Guide to the Birds of Hawaii and the Tropical Pacific. Princeton, N.J.: Princeton University Press. 1987.

Pratt, Helen. Hawaiians: An Island People. Vermont: C.E. Tuttle. 1991.

Pukui, Mary and Korn, Alfons. The Echo of Our Song. Honolulu: University of Hawai'i Press. 1973

Pukui, Mary Kawena et al. The New Pocket Hawaiian Dictionary. Honolulu: The University of Hawai'i Press. 1975.

Pukui, Mary Kawena. Tales of the Menehune. Honolulu: Kamehameha Schools Press. 1985.

Rayson, Ann. The Hawaiian Monarchy. Honolulu: The Bess Press. 1983.

Rayson, Ann. Modern Hawaiian History. Honolulu: The Bess Press. 1984.

Rayson, Ann and Bauek, Helen. Hawai'i: The Pacific State. Honolulu: The Bess Press. 1997.

Riznik, Barnes. Waioli Mission House. Kaua'i: Grove Farm Homestead. 1987.

Ronck, Ron. Kauai: A Many Splendored Island. Honolulu: Mutual Publishing Co. 1985.

Russo, Ron. Hawaiian Reefs: A Natural History Guide. Wavecrest Publishing. 1994.

Sanburn, Curt. Kauai Travelogue. Honolulu: Mutual Publishing Co. 1996.

Smith, Robert. Hawai'i's Best Hiking Trails. CA: Hawaiian Outdoor Adventures. 1994.

Smith, Robert. Hiking Kaua'i-The Garden Isle. Long Beach, CA: Hawaiian Outdoor Adventures. 1999.

Soehren, Rick. The Birdwatcher's Guide to Hawai'i. Honolulu: University of Hawai'i Press. 1996.

Sohmer, S.H. and Gustafson, R. Plants and Flowers of Hawaii. Honolulu: U of Hawaii Press. 1987.

Sohmer, S.H. Manual of the Flowering Plants of Hawai'i. Honolulu: U of Hawaii Press. 1990.

Stevenson, Robert Louis. Travels in Hawai'i. Honolulu: University of Hawai'i Press. 1973.

Stone, Robert. Day Hikes on Kauai. Red Lodge, Montana: Day Hike Books Inc. 1997.

Tabrah, Ruth. Kaua'i, The Unconquerable Island. Las Vegas. K.C. Publications. 1988.

Tabrah, Ruth. Ni'ihau, the last Hawaiian Island. Kailua, HI: Press Pacific. 1987.

Tava, Rerioterai. Ni'ihau: the traditions of a Hawaiian island. Honolulu: Mutual Publishing. 1989.

Teilhet, Darwin. Russian Flag Over Kaua'i. Honolulu: Mutual Publishing Co. 1986.

Thrum, Thomas G. Hawaiian Folk Tales. Honolulu: Mutual Publishing Co. 1998.

Titcomb, M. Native Use of Fish in Hawai'i. Honolulu: University of Hawai'i Press. 1952.

Valier, Kathy. On the Na Pali Coast. Honolulu: University of Hawai'i Press. 1988.

Westervelt, William. Myths and Legends of Hawai'i. Vermont: C.E. Tuttle. 1991.

Westervelt, William. Hawaiian Historical Legends. Honolulu: Mutual Publishing Co. 1999.

Westervelt, William. Hawaiian Legends of Ghosts and Ghost Gods. Honolulu: Mutual Pub. Co. 1999.

Wichman, Frederick. Kaua'i Tales. Honolulu: Bamboo Ridge Press. 1985.

Wichman, Frederick. Polihale and Other Kaua'i Legends. Honolulu: Bamboo Ridge Press. 1991.

Wong, Helen and Rayson, Ann. Hawai'i's Royal History. Honolulu: The Bess Press. 1987.

Yau, John. Hawaiian Cowboys. Black Sparrow. 1995.

Zurick, David. Hawaii, Naturally. Berkeley, CA: Wilderness Press. 1990.

INDEX

'ALIOMANU BEACH 363
'Anini Beach 199
'ANINI BEACH PARK 366, 386
Accommodations
        North Shore 192
        South Shore to West Shore 148
AIRLINES 71
AIRPLANE TOURS 378
Allerton Garden 154, 414
American Classic Voyages 70
American Hawaii Cruises 55, 70, 71
ANAHOLA 192
ANAHOLA BEACH 363
Anchor Cove 114
ANNUAL KAUA'I EVENTS 86
Awa'awaphui 401
BABYSITTING 42
BARKING SANDS BEACH 353
BEACH HOUSE PARK 356
BEACH INDEX 351
Beach safety tips 349
BED & BREAKFAST
        North Shore 218
        South Shore 174
        Central and Eastside 129
Bell Stone 119
BEST BETS
        General 13
        Recreation 375
        Restaurants 252
BEST BETS:
        Beaches 350
BICYCLING 379
BILLIARDS 380
BLACK POT BEACH 368
BOWLING 381
BRENNECKE'S BEACH 358
BRIDGE 381
Bufo toad 67
Camp Naue 207, 231
Camp Sloggett 232
CAMPING 381
Captain Cook 162
CHILDCARE PROGRAMS 43
Children 41
Children's Discovery Museum 414
Ching Young Center 204
Coco Palms Resort 122
Coconut Coast 99
Coconut MarketPlace 122
Condominiums 100
CONDOMINIUM RENTAL AGENTS 236

CONDOMINIUM AND HOTEL INDEX 102
COUNTY PARKS
    camping 386
CRUISE LINES 233
CULTURAL TOURS 412
DANCING 387
DINNER CRUISES 427
DONKEY BEACH 363
EAST SHORE - Accommodations 99
Eels 348
Ele'ele 155
EMERGENCY 70
Ethnic Foods 248
Fern Grotto 117
FISHING
    Freshwater 388
    Ocean 388
FISHING SUPPLIES 390
FITNESS CENTERS 431
FOOD TYPE INDEX 259
Fort Elizabeth 160
GARDEN TOURS 412
Gecko 67
GETTING AROUND 80
GETTING THERE 70
GOLF 391
GROCERY SHOPPING 84
Grove Farm Homestead 111, 414
Guava Kai Plantation 198, 415
HA'ENA 207
Ha'ena Beach Park 208, 371, 386
HA'ENA STATE PARK 372
Hamura Saimin 108
HANAKAPI'AI 373, 382
HANALEI 203
    Accommodations 99
HANALEI BAY 367
HANALEI BEACH PARK 368, 386
Hanalei Pier 204
Hanalei Wildlife Refuge 203, 435
Hanama'ulu 117
HANAMA'ULU BEACH PARK 361, 386
Hanapepe 148, 156
HANAPEPE BEACH PARK 356
HANG GLIDING 394
Hauola O' Honaunau (Place of Refuge) 118
Hawai'i Movie Tours 410
HAWAI'I VISITORS BUREAU (See Kaua'i Visitors Bureau)
Heiau 20, 26, 27, 40, 57, 63, 118, 119, 124, 140, 143, 151, 200, 210
HELICOPTERS 394
HELPFUL INFORMATION 61
HIKING 397
Historic Kilauea Theater 195
HONEYMOONS 52

Hongwanji Temple 124
HONOPU 374
HORSEBACK RIDING 402
HOSPITALS 70
Huleia National Wildlife Refuge 115, 435
HUNTING 404
HURRICANES 92
Iliau Nature Trail 168
JET SKIING 405
KA'AKA'ANIU BEACH 364
Kalaheo 155
KALALAU BEACH 374
Kalalau State Park 382
Kalalau Trail 210, 400
KALAPAKI BEACH 360
KALIHIWAI BEACH 366
Kalihiwai Falls 199
Kamokila Hawaiian Village 119, 416
Kapa'a 124
KAPA'A BEACH PARK 362
Kaua'i Historical Society 109
Kaua'i Historical Society Museum 417
KAUA'I LAGOONS GOLF CLUB 392
Kaua'i Museum 109, 417
Kaua'i Village 123
KAUA'I VISITORS BUREAU 60
Kaua'i War Memorial Convention Hall 108
KAUAPEA BEACH 365
KAYAK GUIDED TOURS 406
KAYAK RENTALS 406, 408
KAYAKING 405
Ke'e Beach 210, 212, 214, 216, 218, 220, 222, 224, 372
Keahua Arboretum 120
KEALIA 192
KEALIA BEACH 363
Kekaha 148, 164
KEKAHA BEACH 354
Kekaha Beach Park 164
KEONELOA BEACH 359
KEPUHI BEACH 370
KIAHUNA GOLF CLUB 392
KILAUEA 195
Kilauea Point 196
Kilauea Point National Wildlife Refuge 198, 365, 435
Kilohana 110, 418
Koke'e 148, 168
Koke'e Natural History Museum 168, 418
Koke'e State Park 168, 384
Koloa 148, 149
Koloa Church 150
Koloa Landing 150, 357
Kuilau Ridge Trail 120
Kukui Grove Exhibition Hall 419
Kukui Grove Shopping Center 109, 110, 115

KUKUIOLONO GOLF COURSE 392
Kukuiolono Park 155
LAND TOURS 408
LARSEN'S BEACH 364
Lawa'i 148, 153
Lawa'i Garden 153, 413
Lehua 164
Lighthouse 196
Lihu'e 106, 108
Limahuli Gardens 208, 414
LIMOUSINE 81
LUAUS 337, 410
LUCY WRIGHT BEACH PARK 355, 387
LUMAHA'I BEACH 368
Lumaha'i Valley 207
LYDGATE BEACH 361
Lydgate Park 117
Maha'ulepu 152
Maha'ulepu Beach 151, 359
Makua Beach 207, 370
Maninolo Dry Cave 208, 371
MAP INDEX 95
MEDICAL SERVICES 51
Menehune 32
Menehune Ditches 32, 161
Menehune Fish Pond 114
Miloli'i State Park 383
Moir Gardens 418
MOLOA'A 364
Mongoose 67
MOVIE RENTALS 410
MOVIE THEATERS 46
MUSEUMS 412
NAPALI COAST STATE PARK 372
National Tropical Botanical Garden 153, 412
Nawiliwili 106, 114
Ni'ihau 33
NIGHTLIFE 340
NININI BEACH 360
NORTH SHORE - Accommodations 99
NUALOLO KAI 374, 383
NUKOLE 361
Opaeka'a Falls 119
Pacific Missile Range 164
PAKALA BEACH 355
PERIODICALS 62
PHONE NUMBERS 69, 70
PHYSICALLY IMPAIRED 50
Po'ipu 148, 151
PO'IPU BEACH PARK 357
Po'ipu Shopping Village 151
Poli'ahu Heiau 119
Polihale 164
POLIHALE BEACH 353

Polihale State Park 166, 384
POLO 420
Port Allen 148, 155, 356
Prince Kuhio Park 151, 357
PRINCEVILLE 200, 201, 366
Princeville Center 202
PRINCEVILLE GOLF CLUB 393
PRIVATE HOMES-South Shore 170
Profile of Queen Victoria 110
Pu'u Ka Pele Lookout 166
Queen's Pond 164
RECEPTIONS 59
RECOMMENDED READING 436
Relocation 63
RENTAL AGENTS 235
RENTAL CARS 82
RENTAL EQUIPMENT 420
RESTAURANT INDEX
    Alphabetical 255
    Food Type 259
RESTAURANTS 245
    Best Bets 252
    Catering 254
    Central/Eastside 265
    Ethnic Foods 248
    Luaus 337
    Night Life 340
    North Shore 321
    South Shore 301
Rice Shopping Center 108
RIVER EXCURSIONS 420
RUNNING 421
RUSSIAN FORT ELIZABETH HISTORICAL PARK 355
SALT POND BEACH PARK 355, 387
SCUBA DIVING 421
SEA EXCURSIONS 424
SENIORS 48
Sharks 348
SHIPWRECK BEACH 359
SHOOTING RANGES 404
Sleeping Giant Mountain 120
Smith's Botanical Gardens 118
Smith's Tropical Paradise 420
SNORKELING 428
SNUBA 431
SOUTH SHORE-Accommodations 99
SPAS 431
Spouting Horn 151, 356
St. Raphael Catholic Church 150
St. Sylvester's church 195
STATE PARKS- Camping 381

SUN SAFETY 66
SUNRISE and SUNSET 94

SURFING 432
TELEVISION 61
TENNIS 433
THEATER 433
TIDES 94
TRANSPORTATION 81
TRAVELING WITH CHILDREN 41
TSUNAMI 93
Tunnel of Trees 148
VACATION HOMES
    Central and Eastside 125
    North Shore 210
    Rental Agents 228
    South Shore 170
Wai'oli Church, ... 206
Wai'oli Mission House 206, 419
WAIALKALUA IKI BEACH 364
Waikanaloa Cave 209
Waikapala'e Wet Caves 209
WAIKOKO 368
Wailua 106, 117
WAILUA BEACH 362
Wailua Falls 116
WAILUA MUNICIPAL GOLF COURSE 394
Wailua River 117, 118
Wailua River State Park 119
Waimea 148, 158
Waimea Canyon 166
Waimea Canyon State Park 168
Waimea Foreign Church & Waimea Hawaiian Church 162
Waimea Sugar Mill Camp Museum 420
Waimea Theatre 161
Wainiha Beach 207
WAINIHA BEACH PARK 370
WAIPOULI 120
WAIPOULI BEACH 362
Waipouli Town Center 123
WATERSKIING 434
WEATHER 91
WEBSITES 63
WEDDINGS 52
WEST KAUA'I VISITOR & TECHNOLOGY CENTER 161
WHALE WATCHING 434
WHAT TO PACK 41
WHERE TO SHOP 115, 151
WHERE TO STAY
    General Information 99
WILDLIFE REFUGES 434
WINDSURFING 436
YMCA / YWCA 231, 232

ORDERING INFORMATION

NEWSLETTERS

Quarterly newsletters are published by Paradise Publications for Maui and Kaua'i. They highlight the most current island news and events. Each features late-breaking tips on the newest restaurants, island activities, or special, not-to-be-missed events. Each newsletter is available at the single issue price of $2.50, or a yearly subscription (four issues) is $10 per year, $12 to Canada, International-al is $16 per year. **FREE OFFER!** If you'd like to receive a sample issue of either newsletter, send a self-addressed, stamped envelope and we will be happy to forward you a copy of the most recent edition.

HAWAI'I, THE BIG ISLAND: A Paradise Family Guide by John Penisten
Outstanding for its completeness, this well-organized guide provides useful information for people of every budget and lifestyle. Each chapter features the author's personal recommendations and "best bets." In addition to comprehensive information about island accommodations you will find a full range of water and land activities, plus tours from which to choose. Then enjoy dining at one of the more than 250 restaurants which range from local style drive-ins to fine dining establishments. Sights to see, beaches, and helpful travel tips. 300 pages $16.95, 6th edition. Copyright 2000.

KAUA'I, THE GARDEN ISLAND: A Paradise Family Guide John Penisten
Completely revised and rewritten since Hurricane Iniki, this information-packed guide describes island accommodations, restaurants, seclude beaches plus recreational and tour options. "If you need a "how to do it" book to guide your next trip to Kaua'i, here's the one." Over 400 pages, multi-indexed maps and illustrations. $16.95 Copyright November 2001

MAUI AND LANA'I: A Paradise Family Guide by Christie Stilson.
You're holding this one in your hands, but perhaps you'd like a copy for a friend! Over 500 pages with completely revised, user-friendly island maps! $16.95. Copyright 2001.

REFERENCE

New Pocket Hawaiian Dictionary
This concise dictionary is fun and useful, too! You'll resolve just what all those Hawaiian words mean and how to pronounce them! $4.95

MAPS & MORE MAPS

A great addition to your travels are full-color topographical maps by cartographer James Bier. Maps are available for $3.95 each for the islands of O'ahu, Maui, Kaua'i, Lana'i plus Moloka'i, and the Big Island of Hawai'i.

The *Hawai'i Volcanoes National Park* and *Haleakala*, Earth Press Topographical maps are a must-purchase if you are planning on enjoying these magnificent parks in depth. Water resistant! Each map $3.95

PHOTOGRAPHIC JOURNALISM

KAUA'I THE UNCONQUERABLE or *HALEAKALA* or *HAWAI'I VOLCANOES*
Each of these three fascinating and informative books is filled with vivid full color photographs depicting some of the most incredible scenery in the islands.

VIEWBOOKS
Doug Peebles is quite possibly Hawai'i's best photographer and his finest photography has been showcased in these full-color paperback books. Ideal for the armchair traveler or trip planner, these affordable pictorial guides make wonderful souvenirs and great gifts. Choose from these five: *Hawai'i (The Big Island), Maui, Kaua'i, O'ahu, Volcanoes,* or *Flowers.* Each is paperback, 10x13, 32 pages, $7.95

RECREATION AND EXPLORATION

HAWAIIAN HIKING TRAILS by Craig Chisholm. This attractive and accurate guide details 40 of Hawai'i's best hiking trails. Hikes for every level of ability. Includes photography, topographical maps, and detailed directions. An excellent book for discovering Hawai''s great outdoors. 152 pages. $15.95

ROBERT SMITH HIKING GUIDES, each guide is $10.95
Hiking Kaua'i with over 40 trails. 116 pages.
Hiking Maui, 27 hiking areas, 160 pages.
Hiking Hawai'i: The Big Island, 18 hiking areas, 40 hiking trails, 152 pages

COOKBOOKS

COOKING WITH ALOHA. Discover all the flavors of the Hawaiian Islands in your own kitchen with this easy-to-follow cookbook. Features everything from appetizers to desserts. A great and inexpensive guide to cooking your favorite Hawaiian foods. 9x12 paperback. 184 pages. $9.95.

VIDEO

HAWAIIAN PARADISE. Produced by International Video Network. More than a travel log, this is one of the best of many, many videos we have reviewed. The journey covers all six of the major Hawaiian Islands. The narrative begins with the formation of the islands and deviates from the average video by exploring the culture, legend, lore, and history of the islands. The lover of Hawai'i will learn new and interesting island facts and points of history and the newcomer will thrill to the visual treats. The next best thing to being there. $29.95. 90 minutes.

FLIGHT OF THE CANYONBIRD. An inspired view of the Garden Island of Kaua'i from a bird's eye perspective, an outstanding 30-minute piece of cinematography. The narration explores the geologic and historic beginnings of the island. A lasting memento or a great gift. $19.95

FOREVER HAWAI'I. This 60-minute video portrait features all six major Hawaiian islands. It includes breathtaking views from the snowcapped peaks of Mauna Kea to the bustling city of Waikiki, from the magnificent Waimea Canyon to the spectacular Haleakala Crater. $24.95

FOREVER MAUI. An in-depth visit to Maui with scenic shots and interesting stories about the Valley Isle. An excellent video for the first-timer or the return island visitor. $19.95. 30 minutes.

KUMUHULA: KEEPERS OF A CULTURE. This 85 minute tape was funded by the Hawai'i State Foundation on Culture and Arts. This beautifully filmed work includes hulas from various troupes on different islands, attired in their brilliantly colored costumes. This film explores the unique qualities of hula as well as explaining its history. $29.95

HULA LESSONS: ONE AND TWO. "Lovely Hula Hands" and "Little Brown Gal" are the two featured hulas taught by Carol "Kalola" Lorenzo who explains the basic steps. A fun and entertaining video for the whole family. 30 minutes $29.95.

SHIPPING: In the Continental U.S. (U.S.P.S. First class priority Mail)
For books or videos: 1-2 items $4; 3-4 items $5; 5 or more items $6. Maps are $1 shipping each if purchased separately. If purchased in combination with a book or video, there is no additional charge for shipping. If you'd prefer US Mail bookrate or Federal express, please call for a quote. **Canadian Orders**
Please add $4 for the first book or tape, $1 for each additional book or tape. No additional shipping charge for maps when ordered with book or tape. For maps ordered separately, please add $2 postage. Orders to Canada are shipped U.S. Small Parcel Airmail. We accept check, money order, or Visa/Mastercard. Send your order to:

TITLE   QUANTITY   PRICE

_____   _____   _____

_____   _____   _____

_____   _____   _____

ADD SHIPPING   _____

TOTAL   _____

SHIP TO:

_____

_____

_____

Paradise Publications, 8110 SW Wareham, Portland, Oregon 97223-6992
Phone (503) 246-1555
Email at: < Paradyse@worldnet.att.net >